Real Estate EconomicS

4th Edition

Designed for 2008 Appraisal Requirements for appraisal electives, residential applications, case studies, college real estate courses, and Continuing Education.

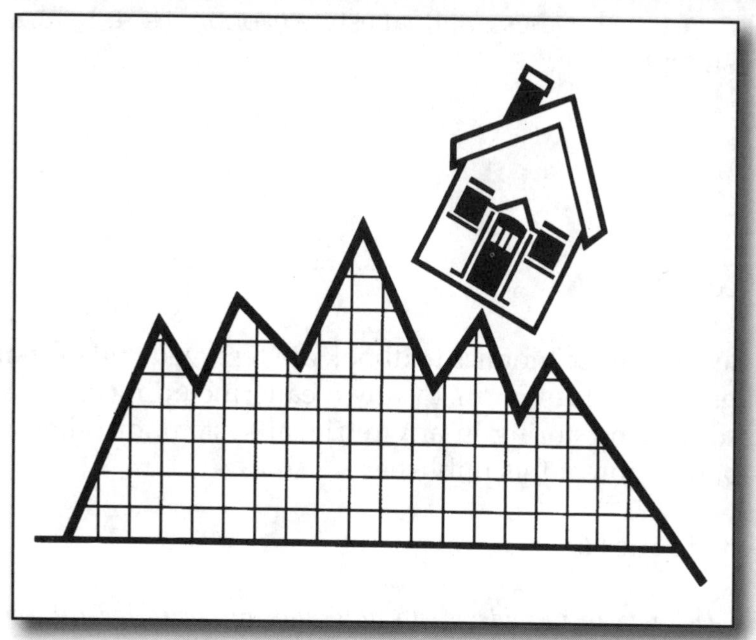

Walt Huber
Glendale College

Levin P. Messick, IFAC
Mt. San Antonio College
President, AC Appraisals, Inc.

William Pivar
Professor Emeritus

Educational Textbook Company, Inc.
P. O. Box 3597
Covina, California 91722
(626)339-7733
(626)332-4744 (Fax)
etctextbooks.com or etcbooks.com

Library of Congress Cataloging-in-Publication Data

Real Estate Economics / Walt Huber, Levin P. Messick, William Pivar

1. Real estate 2. Real estate business 3. Real estate economics 4. Real estate appraisal
5. Real estate investment

HD 1375. M37 2004

ISBN 0-916772-68-3

Printed in the United States of America

This publication is designed to provide up to date and authoritative information in regard to the subject matter covered. ate up to date and authoritative information in regard to the subject matter covered. Numbers and percentages were taken from government, industry, and financial publications as well as their websites. While we believe the material to be accurate, we cannot guarantee accuracy. It is sold with the understanding that the publisher is not engaged in rendering legal or other professional services. If legal or other expert assistance is required, the services of a competent professional person should be sought.

Preface

REAL ESTATE ECONOMICS by Walt Huber, William Pivar, and Levin P. Messick raises the understanding of why some real estate goes up in value and some goes down. All essential real estate concepts are highlighted for special emphasis. We've selected key topics and reinforced them in this way so that they jump off the page and stand out in your mind.

You will enjoy the way that important words and concepts are typeset:

Vocabulary Words are in **bold**

Definitions are in *script*

Economic Concepts are *highlighted*

A special thanks to Glenn Vice, Professor of Real Estate and Economics, Mt. San Antonio College, for his proofreading, and to Fred Martinez, MBA, of City College of San Francisco, for his encouragement to change editions and meet our deadlines.

Walt Huber - Glendale College

Walt Huber is still happily teaching real estate and other business courses.

Real Estate Professor - Over 30 years
Real Estate Broker - 35 years
Real Estate Author - 25 years
Real Estate Books Published - 12+

Levin P. Messick, IFAC - Mt. San Antonio College

Qualifications: Appraises both conforming and non-conforming commercial and residential properties. Instructs both beginning and advanced college classes in appraisal. Author and editor of articles and books on various aspects of appraisal practice.

Independent Fee Appraisal Counselor
Real Estate Professor - 10 years
President, AC Appraisal, Inc. - 11 years
Textbooks Published - 3+

William Pivar - Professor Emeritus

Dr. William Pivar is a retired professor of business. He has taught economics at the undergraduate level as well as the graduate (MBA) level. He has also taught a wide range of real estate courses. *Money* magazine, *Bottom Line* and many major newspapers have quoted Dr. Pivar.

Real Estate Professor - Over 25 years
Real Estate Author - 25 years
Real Estate Books Published - 35+

Special thanks for the valuable assistance given by the people who helped design and produce this book: Philip Dockter, art director; Melinda Winters, cover design; Linda Serra, Andrea Adkins, Colleen Taber, editors; and Rick Lee, pre-press and layout editor.

Acknowledgments

Professor Carol Jensen
Cabrillo College

Professor D. Cogan
Chaffey College

Professor F. Martinez
City College of San Francisco

Professor Steinhart
Columbia College

Professor E.J. Dixon
East Los Angeles College

Professor R.C. Lipscomb
East Los Angeles College

Professor D. Grogan
El Camino College

Professor L. Hoffman
Long Beach City College

Professor B. Monroe
Los Angeles City College

Professor A. Yguado
Los Angeles Mission College

Professor E. Culbertson
MiraCosta College

Professor G. Vice
Mt. San Antonio College

Professor W. Nunally
Sacramento City College

Professor R. Okikawa
Sacramento City College

Professor M. Young
Shasta College

Professor Lenz
Sierra College

Professor A. Purdy
Solano Community College

Professor C. Grover
Victor Valley College

Professor J. Fox
West Los Angeles College

Dr. P. Stubbs
West Valley College

Jim McCloskey RA, CREA
A.J. Educational Services

Jim Lawson
Educator
Technology Consultant

Seth Gakpo, Ph.D.
Eastern Kentucky University
Richmond, KY

Carlton H. Segars, Jr.
President
FYI Seminars, LLC

William J. Cahaney
Associate Professor
Jefferson Community College
Louisville, KY

Terry Zajac Seminars, DREI
Mesa Community College
Mesa, AZ

Table of Contents

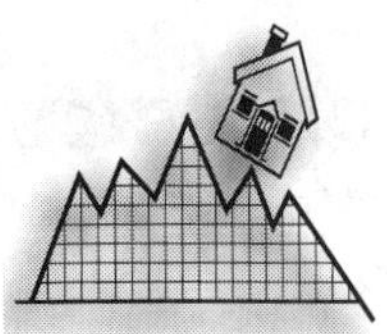

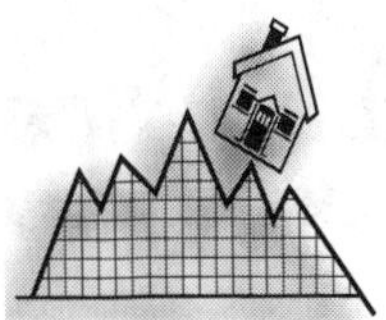

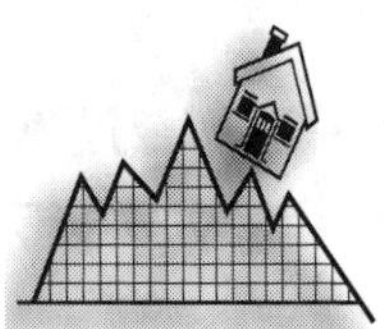

LEARNING OBJECTIVES

This chapter will introduce you to the meaning of real estate economics as well as economic terms and principles that will aid you in understanding the reasons for and effects of changes in the real estate marketplace. You will also gain a basic understanding of economic cycles and how they relate to real estate.

Learning about economic principles and cycles gives us an advantage in that they provide us with the tools to make informed decisions.

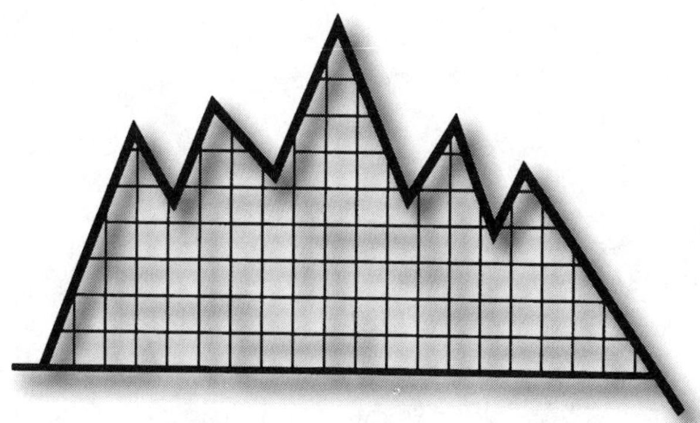

Chapter 1
Economic Cycles and Appraisal Principles

I. Economics

Economics is primarily concerned with the efficient allocation of scarce resources.

In economics we are concerned with:

1. Production,
2. Distribution, and
3. Consumption of goods and services.

A. REAL ESTATE ECONOMICS

Real estate economics is used to analyze national, regional, city and neighborhood trends in an effort to interpret what effect these trends will have on the real estate market.

Our desires for goods and services frequently exceed the supply available, and economics attempts to determine how these limited goods and services can be utilized efficiently without waste. Real estate economics is a field of study that uses economic principles to help solve real estate problems. Like general economics, real estate

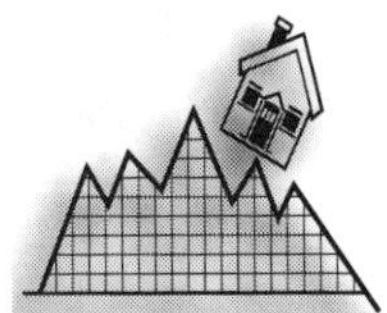

Chapter 1

CHAPTER 1 OUTLINE

economics is concerned with the allocation of scarce resources, but the main focus is on the use of real property.

Real estate economics deals with the mechanisms that society creates to allocate different types of land among individuals.

1. Why Study Real Estate Economics?

In economics, our goal is to determine how the market system prices and distributes goods and services throughout the economy. ***REAL ESTATE ECONOMICS****, simply stated, is the application of economic principles to the real estate marketplace.* It is the study of the divergent forces that determine the use and value of real estate, our nation's most valuable physical asset. Not only is an estimated two-thirds of our national wealth in real estate but also, after the government, more people make their livelihood directly or indirectly through real estate development and marketing than any other American industry. The largest investment the average person ever makes is in real estate: a home. It could take 30 years to pay for making such a decision.

Buildings have a long life, far longer than depreciation periods used for tax purposes. Many structures, if reasonably maintained, could have physical lives of a hundred years. The wrong use, the wrong location, or even the wrong design could have a lasting effect on future owners and users. Therefore, decisions in real estate should be made utilizing the resources that are available.

Every real estate decision has an effect on other decisions. The type of structure built could affect what is built in the area in the future. Even the rent policy will have an influence outside of the structure itself. Every transaction can have a ripple effect on others.

In economics, we study what has happened in the past in order to explain and predict what will happen in the future.

By gaining an understanding of basic real estate economic principles, we have the tools that enable us to make the economic decisions of the future.

Real estate economics has long been treated as a stepchild of economics. Until recently, traditional economists have largely ignored the field of real estate, despite

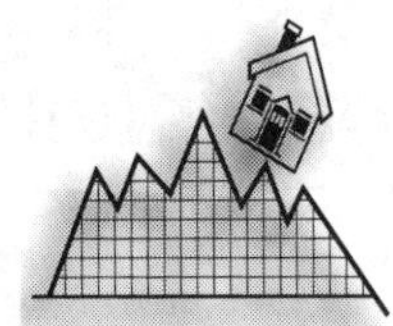

the fact that real property offers true utility value, that real property value far exceeds the value of our supply of gold and greenbacks combined, and that the value of mortgages, trust deeds and land contracts exceeds the value of all stocks and bonds.

Economists avoided applying their principles to real estate, possibly because there were just too many different factors influencing value. External influences and inter-related theories make forecasting difficult, but not impossible. Economic theory in relationship to real estate cannot be studied in a vacuum; hence it is more of an applied science than a pure science.

The real estate marketplace is vibrant with change and interacting factors that influence economic trends. A danger to avoid is oversimplification. Economic change results from many factors, sometimes working together, sometimes in different directions. Every aspect of our economy, from national debt to unemployment changes, can be significant. Even local changes of a new road or a changed use can have a lasting effect on other property.

As a professional, you are expected to advise clients. That advice should be based upon an understanding of economic principles as well as trends and factors influencing value.

Understanding real estate economics will NOT guarantee your success, but it can certainly reduce your chance of failure. Hopefully, you will gain a framework for economic decision making. Will Rogers said, "Who can predict what is going to happen in the future is entitled to the spoils."

B. REAL PROPERTY

There are two types of property: ***REAL PROPERTY*** *(immovable)* and ***PERSONAL PROPERTY*** *(movable)*.

Real property is the land and buildings or improvements attached to land. Real property consists of:

1. Land;
2. Anything permanently attached to the land;
3. Anything incidental or appurtenant to the land; and
4. That which is immovable by law.

By definition, any property that is NOT real property is considered personal property.

C. AMERICA'S ECONOMIC HISTORY

America's early economic growth was fueled by a seemingly unlimited supply of free or low-cost land. Horace Greeley's advice "Go West, Young Man" was based largely on land opportunities. With the advent of the railroad came access to markets as well as an aid to Westward movement. Besides crops, early economic growth was stimulated by what the land could support, including fur, game, and domestic animals, as well as the mineral wealth the land contained.

The industrial revolution resulted in factories for the goods needed by Westward expansion and a growing population. Immigration was encouraged to provide workers for industry as well as consumers for its goods.

Our nation's economic base changed from agricultural, fur, and mineral to manufacturing, and now towards technology and service related industries. However, agriculture, mining and traditional manufacturing industries still play a significant role in our nation's economy.

The days of the wide-open frontier are long gone. The larger the population, the scarcer and more valuable the land becomes. The highest priced land is now concentrated in the most populated areas—urban areas—because that's where the jobs are.

D. NATIONAL AND LOCAL ECONOMIES

You will see that many factors affect our national economy as well as local economies. The local economy could be based upon an industry or even a single employer and the growth or contraction of that industry or employer could affect the local economy and the local real estate marketplace.

A local economy can be far different from the regional or national economy.

The economic base of a community can change. A new plant, a closed plant, government decisions, and new recreational opportunities are just a few factors that could change a community's economic base.

E. REAL ESTATE ECONOMICS (Analysis of Trends)

Real estate economic analysis is inductive in nature. It is a logical process that begins by looking at the neighborhood and the site itself. We start all analysis by looking at the economy on the following four levels:

1. National
2. Regional

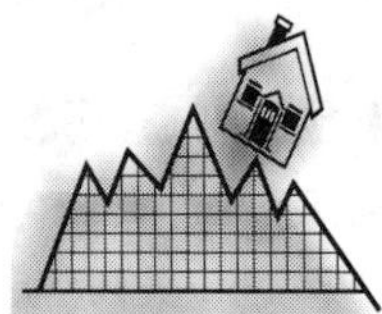

RENO... "THE BIGGEST LITTLE CITY IN THE WORLD"

Reno owed its growth to gambling as well as divorce law. Because of the liberalization of divorce laws in other states, Reno is no longer thought of as the divorce capital of America. Gambling has been on a decline for many years. Hoover Dam construction, military installations and Bugsy Siegel took the gambling spotlight away from Reno. In 1960, Las Vegas surpassed Reno in gambling and thirty years later, Atlantic City pushed Reno into third place. By 1996, Chicago area riverboat gambling knocked Reno down another peg. Investment money for new casinos has been going to areas offering more promise.

Reno contributed to the decline of gambling. City planners, who were afraid of Las Vegas-style growth, put a red line around the downtown area in 1947. They wanted to keep the casinos in a central area. This line was not lifted until the late 1970s, which was too late for Reno to recoup the ground lost. The central city was plagued with vacancies.

Today, Reno has reinvented itself. The city has been diversifying. Reno is hinging its economic hopes on high technology businesses and the warehouse industry. (Nevada does not tax inventory stored there.)

The fact that Nevada is a "right-to-work" state as well as lower real property costs has resulted in many businesses relocating to Reno primarily from California. Reno currently has a growth rate of over 3 times the national growth rate. Forbes-Milken Institute has ranked Reno as one of the top 50 places for business and career advancement.

3. City
4. Neighborhood

II. Supply and Demand

The underlying principle of economics is the law of supply and demand.

A. LAW OF SUPPLY

The amount producers supply increases with price.

It is just common sense for producers to increase production (supply) when prices rise in order to maximize their profits. It is a simple application of the old adage: "Make hay while the sun shines."

However, in a free market, the entry of additional suppliers creates an upward shift in the supply curve. As a result, there will be a greater supply. As supply increases, exceeding demand, prices start to decline. Therefore, profits are lowered and production is reduced. A ***SUPPLY CURVE*** *indicates the number of units that will be available on the market at a given price.*

In response to higher prices in real estate, more owners are willing to place their property on the market for sale, and developers will be encouraged to produce more units.

The supply curve (**Figure 1-1**) indicates how a higher price will increase the quantity supply.

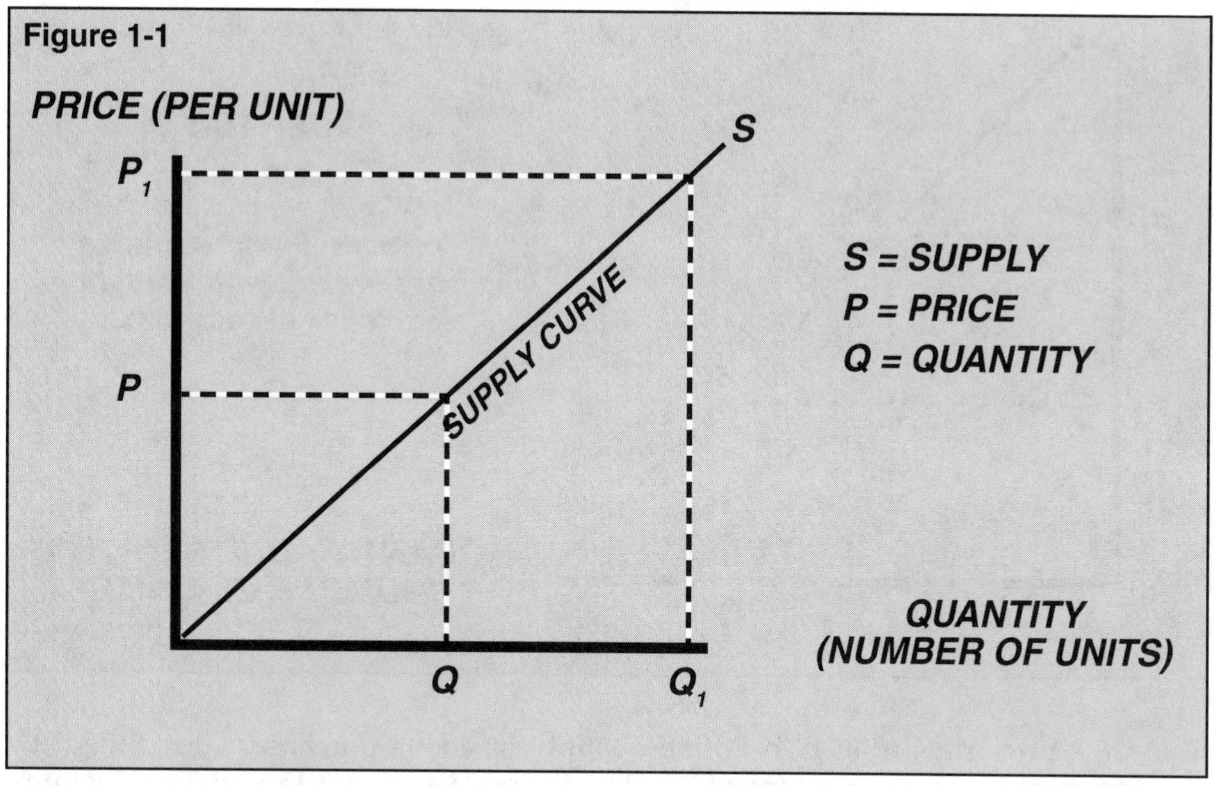

As the price rises from P to P_1, the output increases from Q to Q_1. While the supply curve is depicted as a straight line, it is more likely to be a curve, which would indicate some limiting factor of supply such as labor or material. If there was a limiting factor, at some point an increase in price would fail to increase the supply, in which case the supply curve would be a vertical line.

B. LAW OF DEMAND

The amount consumers purchase varies inversely with price.

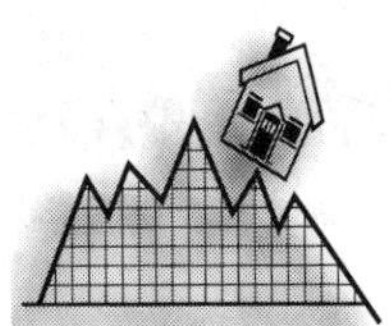

At higher prices consumers will buy less, and at lower prices consumers will buy more. At a higher price, the quantity demanded will be less, but as the price falls, the quantity demanded will increase. You can readily see this principle in action when a department store offers significant price reductions. The lower prices bring in many new buyers. A demand curve slopes downward, to the right. A ***DEMAND CURVE*** *indicates the number of units consumers purchased or are willing to purchase at a given price.* The following demand curve in **Figure 1-2** illustrates this principle.

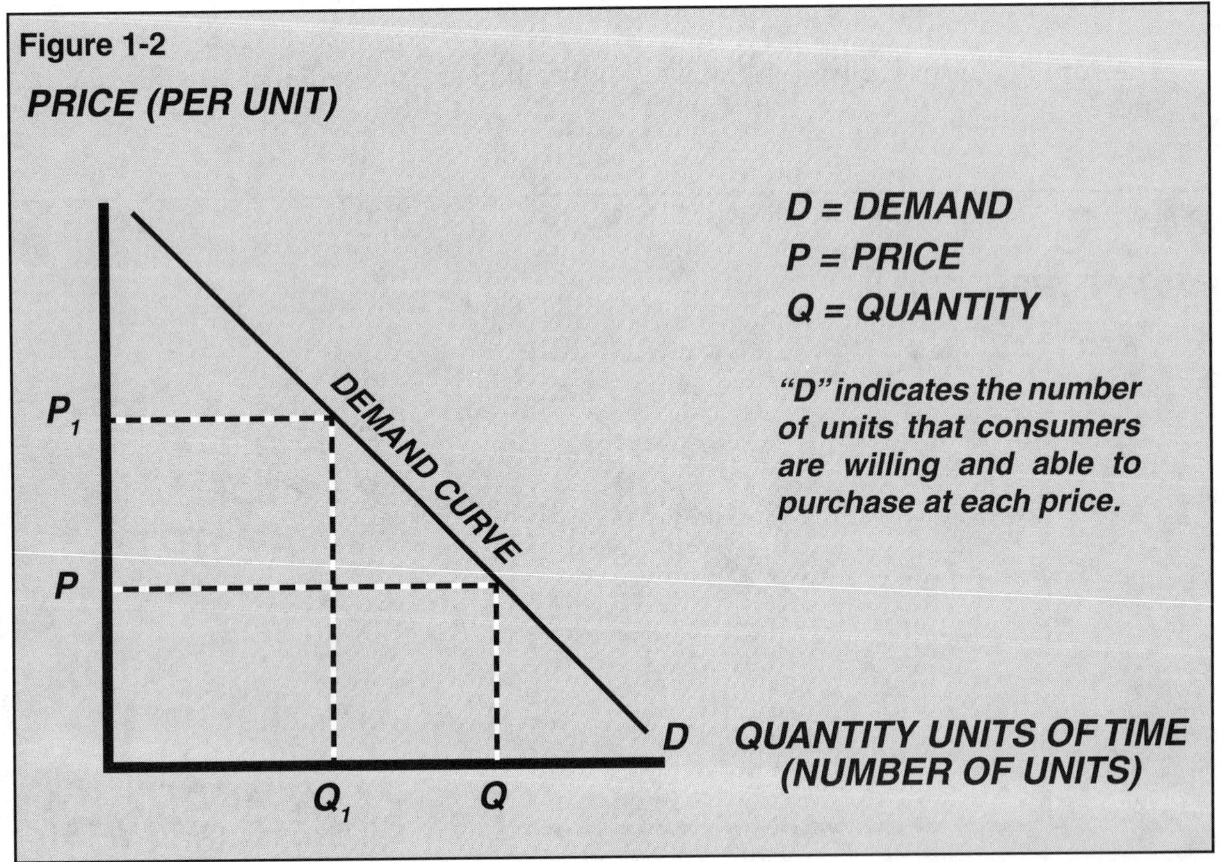

As the price rises from P to P_1, the quantity of goods purchased (demanded) by consumers would decrease from Q to Q_1. If the price decreases from P_1, to P, quantity of goods purchased (demanded) will increase from Q1, to Q.

More purchasers create a shift in the demand curve. Demographers see the world population increasing to 9.4 billion by 2050. The U.S. population, estimated at 296 million, is expected to increase to 420 million by 2050.

Because most real estate purchases are financed, financing costs become an element of price. Lower finance costs effectively lower the price and increase demand while higher financing costs would reduce demand.

C. EQUILIBRIUM (Point and Price)

In a free market, an **EQUILIBRIUM** *will be established at a price which will result in a quantity supplied that will satisfy the demand of buyers at that price.*

Equilibrium, more simply stated, is the point where the demand and supply curves cross, establishing the market price.

At any other price, the quantity demanded and quantity supplied would be different. When the market is at equilibrium, there is no shortage or oversupply at a particular price. Equilibrium is the price obtained when the supply and demand curves intersect by clearing the market of excess goods.

The **price equilibrium (PE)**, illustrated by **Figure 1-3**, shows both the supply and demand curves. Where the curves cross, equilibrium is reached. At that price the demand will be sufficient to consume the supply. There will not be demand pressure causing prices to rise, or excess supply causing prices to drop.

Figure 1-3

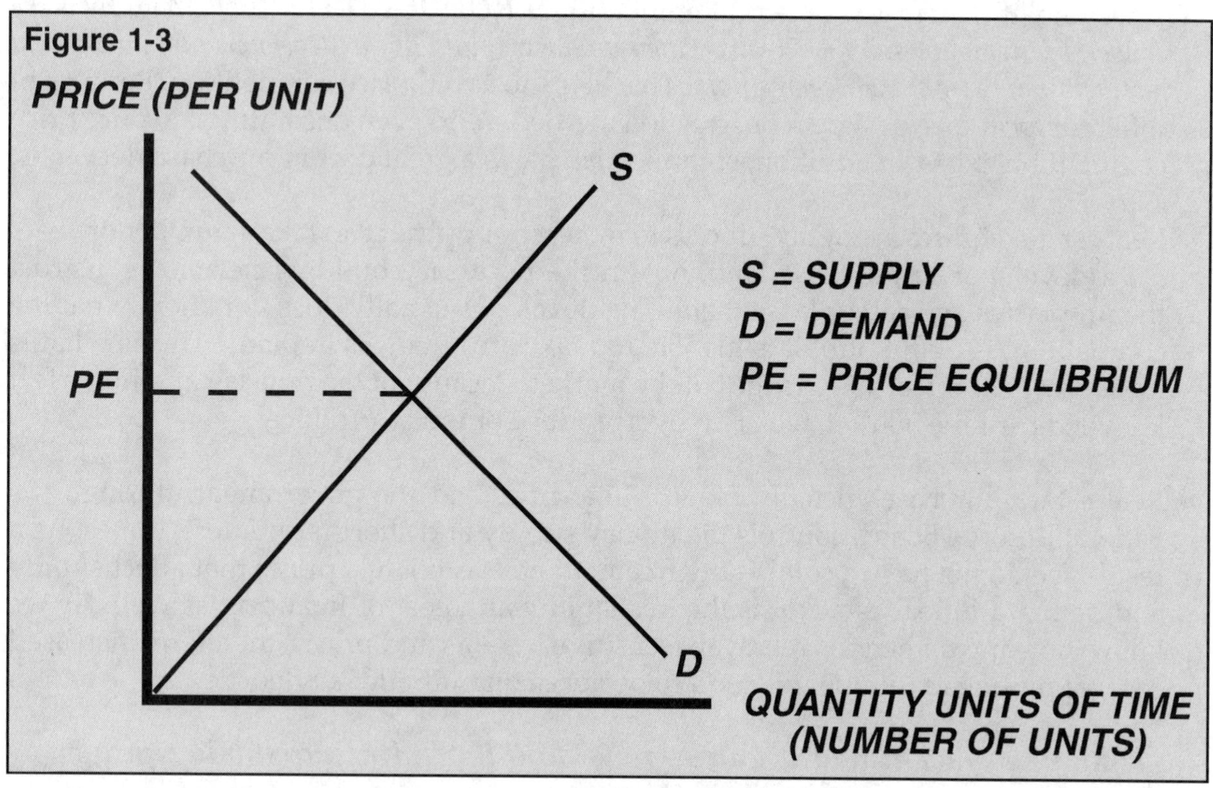

Since the marketplace is constantly changing with new sellers and buyers, the equilibrium point does NOT remain constant.

When supply and demand are not at an equilibrium point (or price), there will be either a shortage or an oversupply. In many markets, the price will react to either of these situations by eventually reaching equilibrium.

To understand the forces leading to equilibrium, you should consider these points:

1. **When supply increases, the price will decrease, which in turn will increase demand**. At a price above the equilibrium price, the quantity supplied would exceed the quantity demanded. Producers will lower the price to deplete unwanted inventory. As the price falls, the quantity demanded will rise, and the quantity supplied will fall. The price will eventually settle at PE, the equilibrium price.
2. **When supply decreases, the price will increase to reduce demand**. At a lower price, the quantity supplied is less than the quantity demanded, creating a shortage. Consumers would bid up the price. As the price increases, producers will supply more. The price would then settle at the equilibrium price, PE.

D. THE REAL ESTATE MARKET IS AN IMPERFECT MARKET

Real estate does NOT lend itself to perfect economic supply and demand models.

To begin with, there is product differentiation. ***PRODUCT DIFFERENTIATION** is the deliberate attempt by suppliers to make their products (buildings or developments) unique and distinct from those of their competitors.* This helps to avoid price competition. Because of different locations, designs, construction methods, and even decorating, no pure price competition exists. In addition, emotion also plays a great part in purchase decisions.

Real estate requires a lengthy process to increase supply. It can take a number of years for a developer to purchase land, obtain the necessary building permits, construct the properties and sell or lease them. The developer usually does not know what the competition is doing until it is too late to make any changes in plans. This is what is meant by "imperfect knowledge" of the market. Because of the time lag and imperfect knowledge of the market, we often overproduce or fail to produce.

Real estate purchases usually require financing, and the government, through the Federal Reserve Board, controls the money supply and short-term interest rates. As a result, we do not have a completely free market. It is not just prices that affect supply and demand in real estate; it is the availability and cost of financing as well. As we know, housing demand is relatively sensitive to rents and prices; therefore, increased costs of renting or buying will tend to decrease quantity demanded.

Demand is meaningless unless it is coupled with purchasing power and/or financing ability.

Demand without the ability to complete a purchase is merely a wish that, by itself, does not affect the marketplace.

Supply and demand forces are so strong that they have resisted government attempts to control prices. During World War II, the Office of Price Administration (OPA) set price controls by rationing goods. The result in many areas of the economy was that products disappeared from the conventional marketplace and a vast black market developed.

In a market system, items will NOT be produced if there is no market. If there is demand, there will be production.

Will Rogers said, "If you want to make money in real estate, find out where the people are going and get there first." What he was talking about was basic supply and demand economics: Increases in demand will increase value.

E. ELASTICITY OF SUPPLY AND DEMAND

ELASTICITY *is the size or magnitude of a reaction to a change in price.* The ***ELASTICITY OF SUPPLY*** *is the measure of the response of the quantity of a good supplied to a change in price.* Demand and supply are each either elastic or inelastic. An ***ELASTIC SUPPLY*** *means that a small change in price will greatly affect the quantity supplied.* An ***INELASTIC SUPPLY*** *means that a change in price will have little effect on the quantity supplied.*

The total supply of land is relatively inelastic.

Although some land can be created (reclaimed) from the sea and swamps that have been drained, we generally regard land as being an asset of fixed dimension. It is difficult to create more land.

The supply of land **for a particular use** is fairly elastic in that higher land prices will make more land available for that use. As an example, an increase in agricultural prices would result in more land being placed in production. Marginal land would be farmed, land would be reclaimed, and desert land would be irrigated. Similarly, higher prices will make more farmland available for sale on the marketplace.

While there is some elasticity in supply of housing in that higher prices will bring more units into the marketplace, to add new units is a lengthy process of land acquisition, approvals, financing and construction. The supply of new units for buyers is therefore relatively inelastic.

The ***ELASTICITY OF DEMAND*** *is the ratio of the percentage change in quantity demanded to the percentage change in price.* An ***ELASTIC DEMAND*** *means that a small change in price will greatly affect the quantity demanded.* An ***INELASTIC DEMAND*** *means that a change in price will have little effect on the quantity demanded.* An example of an item with a relatively inelastic demand is table salt. If the price were cut in half, people would not use more salt as seasoning. Similarly, doubling the price would likely have little effect on demand.

The difference between elastic and inelastic demand is the degree to which a price change affects the quantity purchased. The importance of this measurement cannot be overstated. Without this ability to measure and predict how people are likely to respond to economic changes, all the economic theory in the world would be of little help to us.

The demand for real estate is elastic.

The demand for real estate is elastic because of:

1. Available alternatives. Where two similarly desirable houses are available, the lower priced house will lower the demand of the other. Consumers will substitute lower priced goods for more expensive goods.
2. Relative high price of real estate.
3. Long time dimension of the purchase decision.

Within the housing market there is supply elasticity. Alternatives to buying are renting, commuting from other areas, relocating, or moving in with others.

A demand curve that is straight up and down would indicate a completely inelastic demand. In such a situation, lowering prices would not affect the quantity demanded (see **Figure 1-4**).

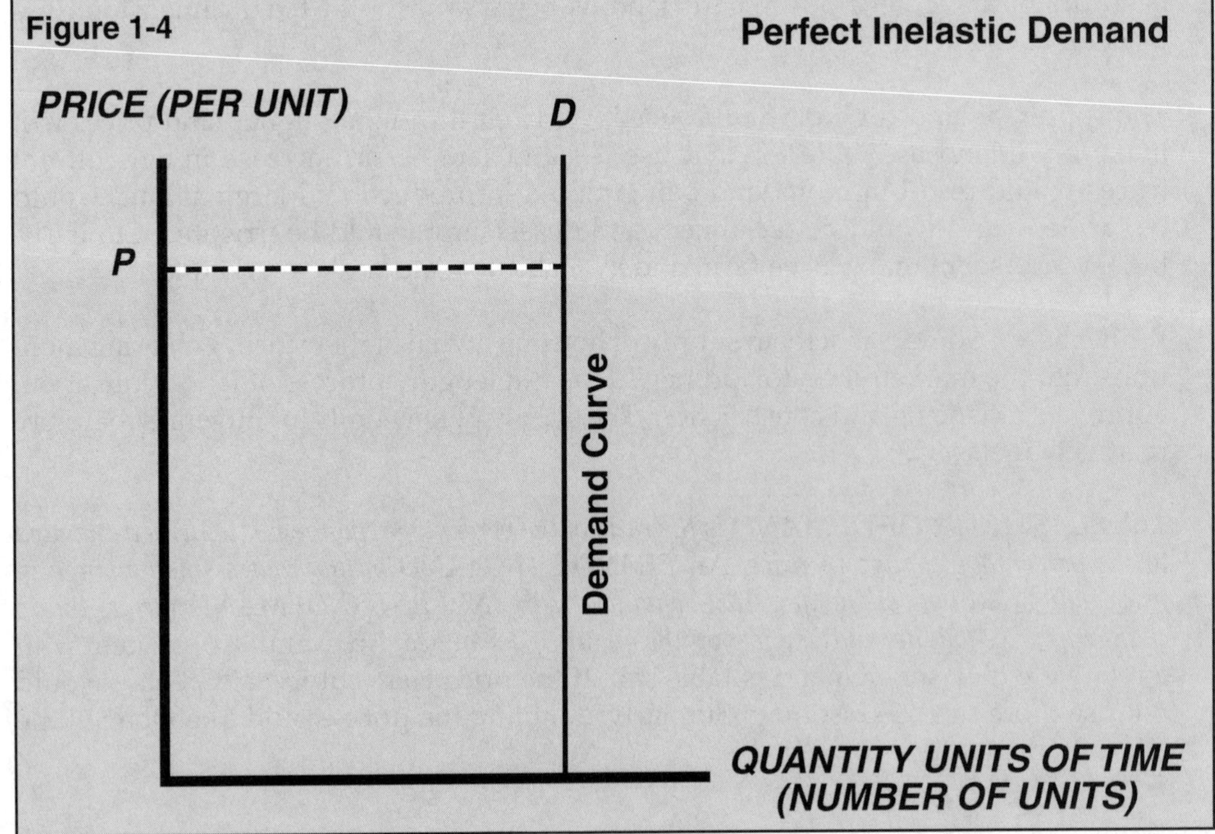

F. REAL ESTATE SUPPLY AND DEMAND IN THE MARKET

Informed sellers and buyers will act upon changes they anticipate in the marketplace.

If sellers believe prices will rise, they will not sell their property or, if they do sell, they will ask for a higher price. As sellers hold back property (decrease supply), prices will rise. Sellers, who believe prices will fall, will list their properties for sale as soon as possible. Because many people place their property on the market at the same time, the oversupply will lead to lower prices. As more properties are put on the market (supplied), prices fall because there are more properties for sale at the time than buyers.

When buyers believe real estate prices will rise, or that there will be a shortage of property for sale, they buy as soon as possible. Many buyers entering the market at the same time tend to bid up property prices. When buyers believe real estate prices will fall, they try to postpone purchases.

The exodus of buyers from the market will cause property prices to fall.

A ***SELLER'S MARKET*** *exists when there are few sellers and many buyers, who keep real estate prices up because less property is available for sale or rent.* In a seller's market, a buyer has few alternatives and must either pay the price required or do without.

A ***BUYER'S MARKET*** *exists when there are many sellers but few buyers, who keep real estate prices down because there is an abundance of property for sale or rent.* In a buyer's market buyers have far more power to negotiate prices and terms. They also have more choice in selecting an ideal location within a neighborhood.

A neighborhood is the basic market unit of supply and demand in real estate.

Both buyer's and seller's markets can exist at the same time within a metropolitan area because there are many neighborhoods within a city.

From an economist's point of view, the real estate is primarily a local market.

In a market economy, the party who will pay the highest price for a property or product determines ownership.

The party who is ready, willing and able to buy property now will obtain it by offering the highest price.

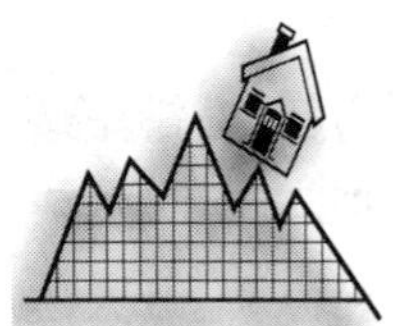

III. Inflation and Deflation

A. DEFLATION AND INFLATION IN REAL ESTATE

In a deflationary period the dollar buys more.

A ***DEFLATIONARY ECONOMY*** *exists when there are more goods than there is purchasing power.*

After World War II, we had some periods of high inflation, but practically no deflation. We also had relatively short-term periods where regional real estate values declined, despite a generally inflationary economy.

Since the late 1980s, inflation has been in check and consumer price increases have been relatively modest. On the other hand, since the early 1990s and into the 2000s, we have seen a dramatic increase in real estate prices.

The dollar buys less in an inflationary period.

Inflation is either pulled by demand or pushed by costs (see **Figure 1-5**). Inflation in real estate aids trustors and mortgagors (borrowers). They benefit by the increase in value of the underlying real estate (security). In addition, borrowers get to pay back their loans with dollars having less purchasing power (inflated, cheaper dollars).

Inflation can be self-perpetuating so that it continues despite other trends in the economy. Workers whose wages are tied to the cost of living get raises during inflationary periods. Pension benefits are often tied to the cost of living. Their increased wages help drive up the price of goods. This, in turn, causes the cost of living to increase so that wages increase further. The only way to break this spiral is to break the psychology of inflation. One way to do this is to impose strict wage and price controls. Former President Nixon attempted to freeze wages, although with very limited success. Inflation statistics are maintained by the Bureau of Labor Statistics (U.S. Department of Labor), **www.bls.gov**.

B. STAGFLATION

STAGFLATION *is the name given to the phenomenon of inflation during a recessionary or no-growth period.* This unusual condition was at its greatest following President Nixon's resignation, during the Ford and Carter Administrations.

During a recession, the increase in unemployment should reduce the purchasing power for goods and stem inflation. This does not always work because the market cannot always quickly adjust to changes in supply and demand. Many costs, such as labor cost, are fixed by contract. Wages cannot be lowered unilaterally to meet market

Figure 1-5

Inflation

Demand Pull or Cost Push?

DEMAND-PULL INFLATION

Demand-pull inflation has nothing to do with cost. It relates simply to the interaction of supply and demand in the marketplace. ***DEMAND PULL INFLATION*** *occurs when the price of goods is bid up due to demand increasing faster than supply increases.*

An increase in unemployment should logically stem inflation, as unemployment will decrease the number of dollars available to purchase goods. Unemployment has a tremendous effect on controlling inflation, both through the reduction in wages and reduction in worker bargaining power.

During much of the 1970s, the purchasing power of the dollar was falling. People were afraid that the value of their savings would be eroded by inflation. This resulted in a tremendous interest in buying assets such as real estate. Real estate was considered a hedge against inflation in that real estate values had generally increased at a rate in excess of inflation.

Coupled with the idea that real estate was a safeguard against inflation, real estate profits were formerly taxed advantageously at a lower capital gains rate. This made real estate a very attractive investment during the '70s. During this era, the price of real estate was driven up to unrealistic levels.

Housing inflation has an effect on the entire economy. As the proportion of income allocated for housing increases, other purchases suffer.

Starting in the late '90s, lower interest rates caused a tremendous increase in demand that fueled price inflation for housing. Because of a stagnant stock market after 2000 and low returns on fixed income investments, many investors and speculators entered the residential marketplace. In some areas of the country, over one-third of residential purchases are now being made by persons who do not intend to occupy the properties.

By 2006, low interest rates and low inflation continued to contribute to the ongoing residential real estate boom.

COST-PUSH INFLATION

COST PUSH INFLATION *occurs when increasing costs push up prices.* Increases in land, material, and labor costs are reflected in the pricing of new units.

When production costs increase, the increase is largely passed on to purchasers in increased costs. In real estate, when costs of new units rise, it generally causes prices of existing units to rise.

conditions. In addition, government unemployment benefits, welfare benefits and employer supplemental unemployment benefits tend to reduce the dampening effect of unemployment on inflation.

IV. Basic Real Estate and Appraisal Principles

The rest of the chapter will be devoted to presenting basic real estate economic principles and theories that will be applied over and over throughout the book.

A. LEVERAGE

LEVERAGE is obtained by using other people's money (borrowed capital) to purchase real property. The advantage of leverage is that, for a relatively low capital outlay, a person can control real estate of high value. In periods of rapid inflation, leverage can make millionaires of those who have placed relatively small amounts of capital at risk in real estate.

It was commonly believed that sophisticated investors should purchase with as low a down payment as possible. While leverage makes economic sense in a rising market, it can be disastrous in a falling or stagnant market. Many highly leveraged real estate syndicates (partnerships) managed by skilled professionals have lost their property to foreclosure when anticipated occupancy rates and increases in revenue were not forthcoming and the properties could not be sold at a profit.

"Real estate values always go up" is not an economic principle or truth. Values do decline. Conservative real estate investors increase the percentage of their down payments so that the borrowed amount and their loan payments will be less, thereby reducing risk.

Investors using leverage are interested in their cash on cash return. If an investor buys a building for $1 million with $100,000 down and realizes an annual cash flow of $50,000 (cash flow is spendable cash after all cash expenses) then the investors have cash on cash return of 50 percent since the investor receives $50,000 cash each year on a $100,000 investment.

If the real estate market is heading into an inflationary period, then risk capital should be highly leveraged in real property, keeping in mind that it is risk capital.

B. MULTIPLIER EFFECTS

A *MULTIPLIER EFFECT measures the outcome of an economic event as a multiple of the amount of the initial change.* A large change in a variable results from only a small initial change in another variable. An initial one-dollar change will result in more than a dollar's change overall.

1. Manufacturing and Service

There is approximately one manufacturing position for every service type position. Therefore, in the United States, for each additional manufacturing position created, an additional service position should also be created.

2. Dollar Multiplier

Dollars spent in a community are generally multiplied in effect by a factor of between two and three. When a dollar is spent, the person receiving it will spend a portion and save a portion. The net effect of a $1,000,000 per year payroll would therefore be between two and three million dollars spent per year. The exact multiplier value could vary based upon the propensity to save or spend.

3. Marginal Propensity to Save

Marginal propensity to save is affected by expectations.

Based on negative expectations for the future, a person might save a larger proportion of the money he or she receives. If the future is expected to be good, savings could be reduced. Increases in the marginal propensity to save would be deflationary, as it would reduce the demand for goods.

Fear of a depression or recession can become a self-fulfilling prophecy because it can cause spending to fall. A large reduction in spending after applying the multiplier effect will result in fewer goods being produced, which will mean layoffs and fewer dollars spent, which will lead to further layoffs, and so on.

In the 1950s, Americans saved roughly 8 percent of their income. In 2004, the rate of savings fell to just 1.3 percent according to the Bureau of Economic Analysis. This lack of savings is coupled with an increase in household debt. After food and housing costs, 20 percent of what income is left goes for debt payment. Credit card debt averaged $7,200 per American household in 2005.

4. Marginal Propensity to Consume

In the same way, the propensity to consume will be greater when there are positive expectations. It will fall when expectations are lower.

Increases in the propensity to consume will mean less money saved and a greater demand for goods. This increase in demand could be inflationary.

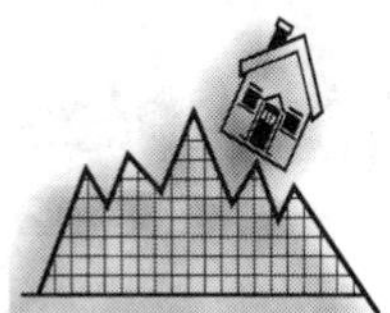

C. THEORY OF FILTERING DOWN

FILTERING DOWN is the principle by which housing tends to be passed on to lower economic groups. With quality new housing available, people tend to "move up," leaving more marginal housing units available for people on a lower economic scale. For example, if a couple sells a $500,000 home and then buys a million-dollar home, their economic status has increased and their former house will be passed on to someone on a lower economic scale who is moving up. As you can see, this principle applies to all socio-economic groups. The least desirable housing should then become vacant and will be demolished. In many areas the less desirable housing units are not demolished because of the demand caused by natural and immigration population growth.

D. ECONOMIES OF SCALE

ECONOMIES OF SCALE are obtained by producing more and spreading fixed costs over a larger number of units, and results in savings to the producer. As production increases, the average cost per unit declines.

As an example, the price per unit to build 100 identical homes would be much less than the price for a single unit. Lower material costs, handling costs and even labor and management savings would be possible. In property management, firms realize that it does not take twice the effort and expense to manage 1,000 units as it does to manage 500.

It is more economical to build a large structure on a large lot than a small structure on a small lot. Doubling the square footage of a structure does not double the length of its exterior walls; nor does it generally double the cost of plumbing, electrical, heating and air conditioning. Therefore, as structures become larger, the price per square foot is reduced.

Similarly, two-story structures are more economical than one-story structures, as they can double the square footage without doubling the foundation and roof costs.

DISECONOMIES OF SCALE occur when increases in production increase the per-unit costs. In other words, large production units are inefficient.

E. LAW OF DIMINISHING RETURNS

The *LAW OF DIMINISHING RETURNS states that at some point, as production is increased, additional units will result in increasing costs, so that as units are added, profits may decrease.*

This law is applicable not only to factory production, but to real estate development and real estate brokerage as well.

The savings possible on structures of three or more stories are somewhat offset by the added costs of elevators. Eventually, the cost for each additional floor increases due to the expense of cranes and elevators to lift workers and materials. Increasing the number of floors eventually leads to a point of diminishing returns.

In advertising, a point will be reached where additional ads provide smaller and smaller benefits; finally, the cost of advertising will exceed the benefits.

In agricultural production, additional labor applied to a fixed area of land will result in diminishing returns and will finally reach a point where labor costs will not be covered by the increased production.

F. ECONOMICS OF SUBDIVIDING

There are more buyers for smaller parcels than there are for larger parcels. The lower prices for smaller parcels make smaller properties affordable for more people. The increased demand and an economy of scale allow a subdivider to make more money on individual, subdivided parcels than on a larger parcel (not subdivided) that was originally sold as one unit.

G. ECONOMICS OF ASSEMBLAGE

ASSEMBLAGE is the concept of assembling a group of smaller lots to form one large lot, which can net a larger profit.

Once an area has been fully developed, it becomes difficult to put together a group of properties under common ownership for a larger development or redevelopment. In many older cities developers will buy two single-family lots, raze the two homes, and build 10 new condominiums.

The shortage of larger parcels within a highly developed area allows an owner or assembler to get a higher price for the group of properties than the total value of each of the individual properties.

As an example, four adjacent small commercial parcels of land might be worth $100,000 each but if they were combined might bring a sale price of $500,000. This increase in value of $100,000 from the assemblage process is known as the plottage increment.

H. ECONOMIC OBSOLESCENCE AND ECONOMIC LIFE

More buildings are torn down than wear out.

ECONOMIC OR EXTERNAL OBSOLESCENCE occurs when the value of a property decreases because of negative factors affecting the neighborhood (rather than the property itself). For example, a slaughterhouse opens for business next to your home; your home then

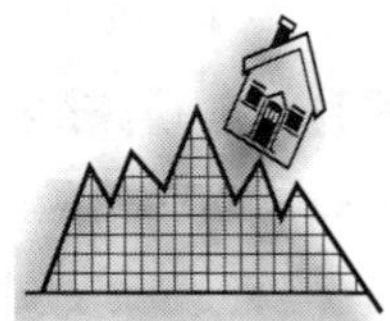

loses its value. Economic obsolescence cannot be cured because it is based on external forces.

The ***ECONOMIC LIFE*** *of a structure is the period in which the structure is worth more than the economic benefit of tearing it down.* When improvements no longer contribute to property value, they have exceeded their economic life and should be replaced with improvements offering a higher use.

As an example, assume there is a hotel with a net income of $3,000,000 per year. Also assume that an appropriate capitalization rate would be 10 percent. By capitalizing the net income you will find the value of the property to be $30,000,000. To capitalize income, we divide the net income by the capitalization rate.

$$\frac{\$3.000.000}{.10} = \$30,000,000$$

Assume also that the value of the land alone to be used for alternative purposes is $50,000,000. In this case, the hotel would have exceeded its economic life because as a hotel the land and building together would justify a price of only $30,000,000. A good economic decision would be to tear the hotel down and put the land to a higher valued use.

Often, fairly new structures are razed (torn down) because the value of the site has so increased that the income attributable to its present use is less than the value of the land alone.

These structures do not represent the highest and best use. The ***HIGHEST AND BEST USE*** *would be that use which provides the greatest net income attributable to the land alone.*

I. PRINCIPLE OF FIRST CHOICE

The ***PRINCIPLE OF FIRST CHOICE*** *states that a business that needs a particular type of location for a specific use will pay the most.* What this means is that uses which are limited, such as a marina, will result in a higher price for a suitable location than uses which are not as limited. There is a competition of uses and the use that will pay the most will prevail. This use will be the highest and best use for the location.

The principle of first choice does not always work. In some harbor areas, residential condominiums are forcing out marine activities, leaving them no place to go. Marine activities simply cannot compete against developers who want the land for multi-million dollar condominiums.

J. PRINCIPLE OF COMPETITION

The ***PRINCIPLE OF COMPETITION*** *states that when extraordinary profits are made in a field, then competition will enter the field and profits will decline.* We saw this principle applied several years ago in the area of nursing homes, and more recently in mini-warehouses. The first mini-warehouses filled immediately to capacity and showed an exceptional cash return to total cost and investment. As additional units were built, however, the vacancy factor increased. Competition also reduced rental rates in many areas.

K. PRINCIPLE OF SUBSTITUTION

This appraisal principle is also a basic economic principle. The ***PRINCIPLE OF SUBSTITUTION*** *affirms that the maximum value of a property tends to be set by the cost of acquiring an equally desirable alternative property*. It really is a corollary of the principle of supply and demand.

L. PRINCIPLE OF CHANGE

Property is NOT static; it is always changing. (Sometimes change is imperceptible, while in other cases it is dramatic and swift.)

The ***PRINCIPLE OF CHANGE*** *states that real estate values do not remain constant but are always in a state of flux*. Outside forces work to increase or decrease value. Short-term changes follow the "business cycle" but the "real estate cycle" is subject to longer-term changes.

M. PRINCIPLE OF REAL ESTATE CYCLES

During the ***DEVELOPMENT STAGE (INTEGRATION)***, *property is going up in value. The property and its surrounding area then generally reach a plateau, or* ***MATURITY (EQUILIBRIUM STAGE)***. ***DECLINE (DISINTEGRATION)*** *happens when the deterioration of the structure or neighborhood reduces the useful life of the property* (see **Figure 1-6**). Occasionally an area is revived or discovered so that the real estate development cycle begins again. In a renewal stage, values will begin to increase.

N. BUSINESS CYCLES

We know that there are recurring patterns or business cycles in the economy (see **Figure 1-7**). Economists don't all agree about the length of these cycles or the means to measure them. Cycles are not precise, but vary in length and intensity, influenced by war, government policy, and often by unknown factors.

Cycles are waves that have a high point or peak. After the peak a recessionary period is entered into as activity decreases. The cycle bottoms out with a trough, and the recovery period then starts. Cycles are not geometrically precise, as there may be undulations within the general wave of the cycle.

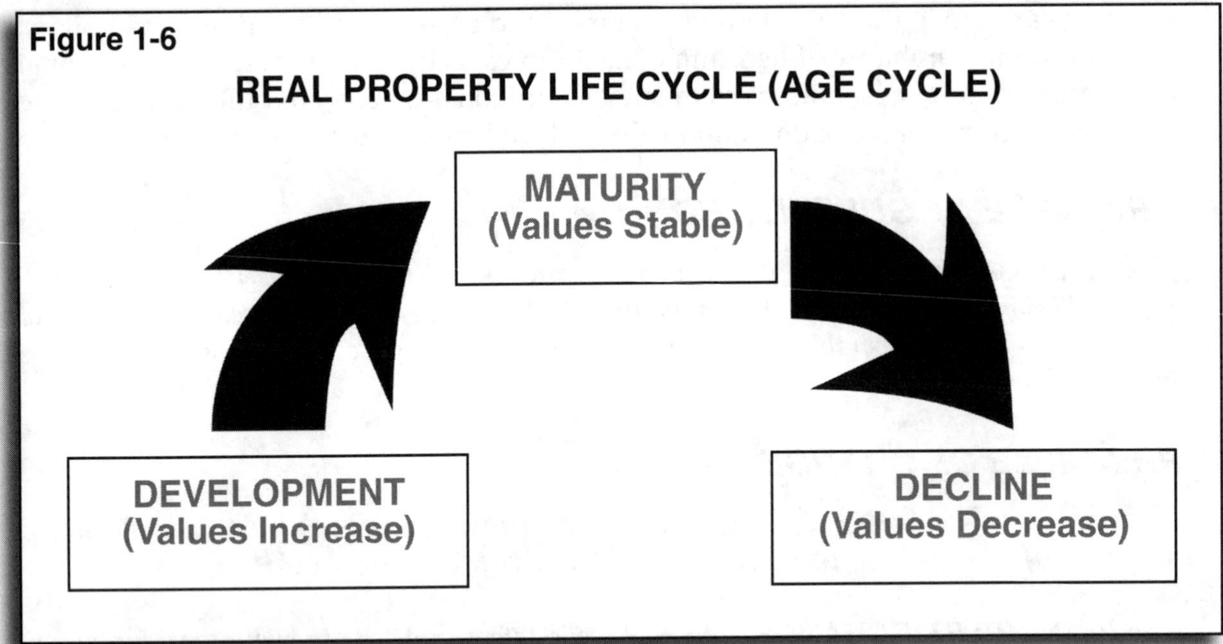

O. FORECASTING REAL ESTATE CYCLES

Kondratieff, a Russian economist, developed a 50- to 60-year long wave theory, which consists of major expansions and contractions in construction, debt, prices and interest rates.

Within Kondratieff's long wave, there are separate business cycles that seem to run from 15 to 20 years.

Within these cycles are even shorter waves or cycles of three to seven years. Each recessionary period of the business cycle gets worse as the long wave contracts. Since no wave is precise, we don't really know where it will bottom out.

The economist Henry Hoyt believed that there were three K waves (18-year cycles) within a long wave 54-year cycle that reflect the real estate market. Our real estate market should have hit a low point in 1988. This did not happen, but two years later it did. While the cycle theory indicates another low point as to real estate values in 2008, we must realize that cycles are not precise.

Lenders can accelerate a downward construction cycle by restricting credit and can stimulate an upswing in the cycle by loosening credit requirements.

Because real estate activity is dependent upon the availability and cost of money (interest), changes in these factors can cause wild swings in activity. In a boom period, the demand for money will drive up interest rates. The Federal Reserve is also likely to raise interest rates further to ward off what they perceive as inflationary trends.

Figure 1-7

Business Cycles

Four Phases of the Business Cycle

The business cycle described here is a generalization of the business cycles we actually experience. No two cycles are quite the same, yet they all have much in common. In real life, actual business cycles will vary, but the characteristic patterns described here (peaks, recession, bottom and recovery) can always be observed. It would be helpful to learn to identify the distinctive aspects of each phase of peaks, recession, bottom and recovery. Each phase is characterized by different economic conditions.

PEAK (TOP)

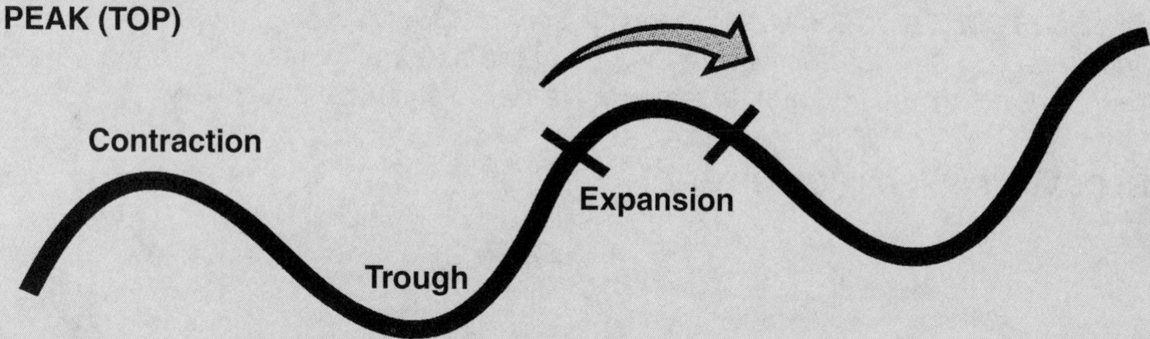

The ***PEAK*** *is the highest point in a new business cycle, and is usually higher than the peak of the previous cycle.* It is the upper or top part of the business cycle. Goods sell briskly and inventory selection is good. Good jobs are available and unemployment is low.

RECESSION (CONTRACTION OR SLUMP)

A ***CONTRACTION OR SLUMP*** *is the period in the business cycle from the peak down to a trough during which output and employment fall.*

Recession follows the peak with a slow downturn in business activity. Interest rates may have increased. People are experiencing job losses as inventories are reduced and production is cut back to reduce operating costs.

As unemployment increases, the demand for goods and services also decreases which can result in even further cutbacks in business.

(continued)

BOTTOM (TROUGH)

The ***BOTTOM (TROUGH)*** *is evidenced by a fall in output and employment followed by an increase in business activity.* At the end of the bottom, interest rates usually have been lowered by the Fed and remain low in order to stimulate a recovery.

RECOVERY (EXPANSION OR BOOM)

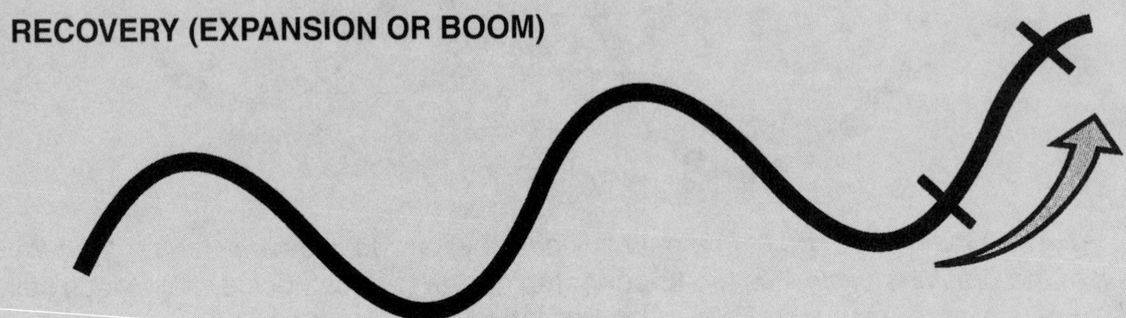

The ***RECOVERY (EXPANSION or BOOM)*** *is the period in the business cycle from the bottom up to a peak during which output and employment rise.*

The recovery is a prosperous period during which the economy is expanding. People are purchasing more from an expanding inventory of consumer goods.

Even political elections follow the business cycle; in a recession, politicians in power often get voted out, while they are more likely to remain in office when the economy is strong.

SEASONAL VARIATIONS AND TRENDS

One must realize that seasonal patterns and long-term trends will disturb the business cycle. Retail sales go up every Christmas and beach area hotels are crowded every summer. Long-term trends, such as the automobile industry trends, must be taken into consideration when evaluating the business cycle. Business conditions never remain static. Prosperity is eventually followed by an economic recession, although, in good times, people tend to expect prosperity to continue unabated.

While a commercial building cycle tends to follow the general business cycle, the residential building cycle declines as commercial building is peaking. Because housing requires longer-term debt, residential buyers appear to be more sensitive to interest rate changes than commercial users. Added interest costs for commercial enterprises might be passed on to consumers.

The downward swing of the real estate cycle tends to lead a general business recession.

During a period of economic contractions, demand of both business and industry for capital decline. The lowered demand for borrowed funds causes interest rates to decline. A recovery is likely to occur when inventories have fallen to the point where manufacturing must increase. Increased business activity coupled with low interest rates will tend to stimulate the real estate market.

With a business recovery, speculators will enter the real estate marketplace with the expectation of profit. Speculator activity will accelerate the real estate recovery.

A real estate recovery tends to lag behind a general business recovery.

There is a shorter real estate cycle that seems to run approximately three and a half years. It is related to interest rates and the low point of real estate activity tends to match the high point in interest rates.

There is a commercial construction cycle of about seven years. According to the Massachusetts Institute of Technology's (MIT) Professor Jay Forrester, "It takes three and a half years to get overbuilt and three and a half years to start building again."

During any cycle there are industries that run counter to the cycle. For example, in a business recession new machinery sales could be slow, but parts and repairs of existing machinery could conceivably be booming.

In snow areas where construction is seasonal, there are annual construction cycles based on climate. The market in lots becomes active in the early spring prior to the building season and declines in the late summer.

Sales of family housing are generally strongest in the spring until September, when the market slows down.

The reason for this slowdown is that family buyers generally want to be settled before school starts in the fall.

There are local cycles as well as national cycles. A strong local economy based on a strong industry can cause that local economy to expand while the national economy

is in a recession. In the same way, a local economy can be in the depths of a depression while the national economy is expanding, as evidenced by the economic situation in aerospace and defense industries in California from 1991 to 1993 (see **Figure 1-8**).

While economists tend to agree on the validity of cycles, they do not always agree on where the economy will go next. As an example, during recessionary periods, some economists will predict an imminent turn-around while others might predict that conditions will get much worse before they get better. With the large number of economic indicators that abound, it is understandable that there will be differences among economists as to the immediate future of the economy.

P. RECESSIONS AND DEPRESSIONS

Many economists define a ***RECESSION*** *as a minimum of two quarters in which the growth of real Gross Domestic Product (GDP) is negative.*

Researchers have agreed to accept the decisions of the National Bureau of Economic Research (NBER) as to when a recession starts (nber.org).

This nonprofit bureau usually has a lag time of about six months in determining and analyzing the various economic indicators. Therefore, by the time they have determined that a recession exists, the economy would be well into the recessionary period.

During a business recession, inventories are depleted and labor is laid off. Profits decline, as does demand for credit, which results in lowered interest rates. A ***DEPRESSION*** *really is nothing more than a severe recession, during which the economy shrinks considerably.*

The recovery period usually takes place after inventories are depleted and production must be increased. Just as the economy can go into a downward spiral, it can also build up with new hiring. More demand for goods means more production and hiring.

Q. GOVERNMENT AND CYCLES

Government fiscal policy affects the business cycle. Fiscal policy is the responsibility of our federal government (President and the Congress) to tax its citizens and wisely spend our money to benefit the nation. Increased government spending and lower taxes would stimulate an economy and could lead the country out of a recession. Likewise, increasing taxes and reducing government spending would act to slow a booming economy. The government, by its fiscal policies, ideally seeks a slow and steady growth, which will not result in excessive inflation.

The Federal Reserve controls the money supply and usually short-term interest rates through monetary policy.

Until recently, Alan Greenspan, the long-time chairperson of the Federal Reserve, used the power of the Federal Reserve to keep inflation in check, thereby avoiding the hard landing of a recession.

Figure 1-8

1990-1993
California's Long, Deep Recession

California's economic downturn (1990-1993) was the longest in the state in over 50 years, whereas the national recession lasted only a year.

California's long, deep recession from 1990 to 1993 was the most severe since the 1979-1982 recession. The national recession was relatively short, from 1990 to 1991. All of California's major economic indicators—jobs, income, spending, construction, and home prices—were worse than the nation's.

Approximately 600,000 jobs were lost in California between July 1990 and December 1993. The national economy recovered, while job losses and recession continued in California.

FOUR REASONS FOR CALIFORNIA'S LONG RECESSION

1. Defense Spending Cutbacks

Since California had more defense contracts than the rest of the nation (over 20 percent of U.S. defense spending and related jobs), defense-spending cutbacks were more severely felt, especially as military bases continued to close.

California's defense industry underwent a structural change.

A ***STRUCTURAL CHANGE*** *is a permanent change in the economic equation.* In California's case, the nation had downsized military bases and continued to trim all types of defense spending.

2. The Decline of Commercial Aerospace Jobs and Exports

A drop in commercial and export aircraft sales caused aerospace jobs in California and the nation to decline sharply. As a result of the global recession, the airline industry placed fewer orders for commercial airplanes. Exports from California fell from $45 billion to $37 billion in 1993.

(continued)

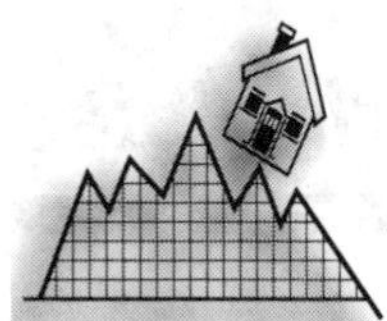

3. The Decline of Residential Construction

California experienced a substantial drop in residential construction after 1989 in response to the increases in home prices and, later, the economic downturn. This contributed to huge losses in construction jobs, and in construction-related jobs in manufacturing, which amounted to an industry unemployment rate of 50 percent.

4. Falling Consumer Confidence Curtails Spending

Spending declined much faster than income in California. The decline in spending relative to income, which was rooted in falling consumer confidence, had a large impact on retail trade and service sector jobs. Retail sales, adjusted for inflation, fell by 10 percent in three years. If spending had kept pace with the state's poor income growth, retail sales would have been $28 billion higher, with a gain of $2 billion in sales tax revenues and parallel gains in retail jobs.

Recent U.S. military activities in the middle east have resulted in an upswing in California's defense and aerospace industries.

V. CHAPTER SUMMARY

Economics deals with how the market prices and distributes goods and services. **Real estate economics** is the application of economic principles to the real estate marketplace.

America's early economic growth was fueled by low cost and free land. Our economic base has moved from traditional manufacturing toward high technology and service industries.

Prices are the result of the interaction of **supply** and **demand**. An increased demand without a corresponding increase in supply will result in higher prices. Similarly, a decrease in demand without a corresponding decrease in supply will result in lower prices. Changes in supply without corresponding changes in demand will also affect prices.

With an **elastic supply**, at a higher price more goods will enter the marketplace and at a lower price there will be fewer goods. The point at which the quantity supplied and the quantity demanded are in balance is known as **equilibrium**.

When individuals believe that the economic future is bright they reduce their propensity to save and increase their propensity to spend, thus increasing production and employment. Conversely, when individuals believe the economic future is bleak they will reduce their propensity to spend and increase their propensity to save. This will result in lower production and unemployment.

A **deflationary period** is one in which prices fall on average. In an **inflationary period** the prices rise on average. Inflation caused by increases in cost is known as **cost-push inflation**, while inflation resulting from a demand increase is known as **demand-pull inflation**. **Stagflation** is an economic situation in which there is reduced growth or a recession, yet prices continue to rise.

Leverage is the use of borrowed capital. During an inflationary period, high leverage investments allow the investor to achieve maximum appreciation as well as have the advantage of paying back borrowed capital with cheaper dollars.

There is an approximate one-to-one relationship between manufacturing and service jobs, with each new manufacturing position serving to create another service position. Dollars also have a **multiplier effect** with each dollar added to the community changing hands and being spent again and again. The effect of each added dollar would be affected by the propensity to save or consume by those receiving the dollars.

There are **recurring cycles** in our economy, which are similar to waves. The **crest** or **peak** would correspond to a prosperous period; the **downward slope** is a recessionary period; and the low point, which is also the turnaround point, is the **trough**, the lowest point of the recession. An upswing would be a **recovery period**.

A real estate recession tends to precede a general business recession although a real estate recovery tends to lag behind a general business recovery.

There appear to be longer-term cycles such as the **Kondratieff wave**, which has a number of smaller cycles within a longer wave. There are cycles for residential construction, commercial construction, real estate activity and values, as well as general business cycles.

VI. GLOSSARY OF KEY TERMS

Assemblage – The process of joining contiguous properties under common ownership so that the sum value is more than the values of the separate properties.

Cash on Cash – The ratio between cash invested and cash received (net spendable).

Cost-Push Inflation – An increase in sale prices caused by an increase in production and distribution costs.

Cycles – Recurring waves of economic activity.

Deflation – An economic period where prices fall on average.

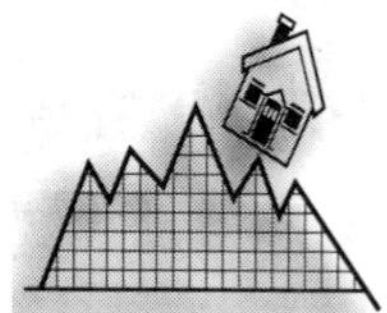

Demand-Pull Inflation – An increase in prices caused by demand exceeding supply.

Demographics – A statistical study of a population with respect to age, sex, education, income, movement, etc.

Disequilibrium – A point in the marketplace where supply and demand are not equal, creating pressure for the price of goods to rise or fall.

Economics – The science that studies how the market system prices and distributes goods and services.

Economic Life – The period over which a property will yield a return on the investment.

Economic Obsolescence – A loss in value from forces extraneous to the property.

Economy of Scale – A decrease in production costs per unit resulting from efficiencies in production or procurement when producing large quantities.

Elasticity – The size or magnitude of a reaction to a percentage change in price.

Equilibrium – The point or price in the marketplace where supply and demand are in balance.

Filtering Down – Housing passing down to lower economic groups.

Highest and Best Use – That use which provides the greatest net income attributable to the land alone.

Hyperinflation – An inflation rate so great that money ceases to have value.

Inelastic – A supply or demand that will not materially change when the price is raised or lowered.

Inflation – An economic period where prices rise on average.

Kondratieff Long Wave – A 50- to 60-year economic cycle.

Law of Diminishing Returns – The principle that as additional units are added to production, a point will be reached where production will start to decrease with each additional unit added.

Leverage – The use of other people's money (borrowed capital) for investment.

Marginal Propensity to Consume – The ratio of consumption to increases in disposable income.

Marginal Propensity to Save – The ratio of savings to increases in disposable income.

Multiplier Effect – The relationship that the increase in one activity has on another. There is approximately a one-to-one relationship between new manufacturing positions and service positions. A dollar spent in a banking community will have the effect of being spent by those receiving it between four and five times before being removed from circulation by savings.

Plottage Increment – Increase in value from assemblage.

Price Elasticity – The size or magnitude of a reaction to a percentage change in price.

Principle of Change – Real estate values do not remain constant; they are always changing.

Principle of Competition – When extraordinary profits are being made, competition will enter the market and profits will decline.

Principle of First Choice – A business that needs a particular type of location for a certain use will pay more for that location than would others.

Principle of Integration, Equilibrium, and Disintegration – Property goes through a development stage (integration), a period of stability (equilibrium) and a decline in use and value (disintegration).

Principle of Substitution – A person will not pay more for a property than he or she would have to pay for another property having equal utility and desirability.

Recession – That portion of an economic cycle in which growth in the Gross Domestic Product and employment are negative.

Recovery – That portion of an economic cycle in which growth in the Gross Domestic Product and employment are increasing.

Stagflation – A period in which the economy is not growing as quickly as before (or is in a recession), but in which consumer prices are increasing.

Supply and Demand (interaction of) – The relationship between the amount of goods supplied and the demand by those consumers who are willing to pay for them. When elastic, supply and demand will react significantly to changes in price.

VII. CLASS DISCUSSION TOPICS

1. Identify the most recent cycles for residential and commercial sales activity in your community. Where are we in these cycles at the present time?
2. Give examples of both buyer and seller markets within your area.
3. Estimate the inflation in residential values in your area for the past five years.
4. Considering your area, where has the supply of real property not quickly responded or adjusted to market conditions?
5. Give reasons why you believe specific buildings in your area have been destroyed (razed).
6. Identify local areas as to present economic stage (integration, equilibrium, or disintegration).

VIII. CHAPTER 1 QUIZ

1. We study real estate economics in order to:

   a. meet state education requirements.
   b. predict what will be happening in the future.
   c. impress clients with our knowledge.
   d. balance our needs with the needs of others.

2. In comparing the national economy with a local economy we should realize that:

   a. a local economy could be different than the national economy.
   b. the local economy tends to lag behind the national economy.
   c. the local economy will closely mimic the national economy.
   d. while the national economy can change the local economy remains constant.

3. If we increase demand and decrease the supply of an item:

   a. prices will fall.
   b. prices and supply or (supplies) will remain in equilibrium.
   c. the demand will increase further.
   d. prices will rise.

4. At the equilibrium point:

   a. quantity supplied would exceed quantity demanded.
   b. quantity demanded would exceed quantity supplied.
   c. quantity demanded would equal quantity supplied.
   d. consumers will not buy and producers will not supply.

5. Which of the following is a true statement regarding demand?
   a. Demand for real estate is inelastic.
   b. Demand is meaningless without purchasing power.
   c. Demand increases with supply increases.
   d. Demand decreases with increases in supply.

6. A totally inelastic demand curve would be depicted as a:
   a. horizontal line.
   b. vertical line.
   c. round circle.
   d. elliptical curve.

7. The real estate marketplace is primarily a:
   a. national market.
   b. market having inelastic demand.
   c. local market.
   d. market regarded as a perfect economic model.

8. Prices of waterfront homes in a developed area have been rising dramatically because of:
   a. demand-pull inflation.
   b. cost-push inflation.
   c. stagflation.
   d. leverage.

9. A sophisticated investor would consider paying with maximum leverage when:
   a. prices were falling.
   b. prices were expected to continue to rise rapidly.
   c. seeking to reduce risk.
   d. interest rates were expected to fall.

10. Kondratieff's long wave refers to:
   a. supply curves.
   b. demand curves.
   c. a long-term business cycle.
   d. changes in the money supply.

ANSWERS: 1. b; 2. a; 3. d; 4. c; 5. b; 6. b; 7. c; 8. a; 9. b; 10. c

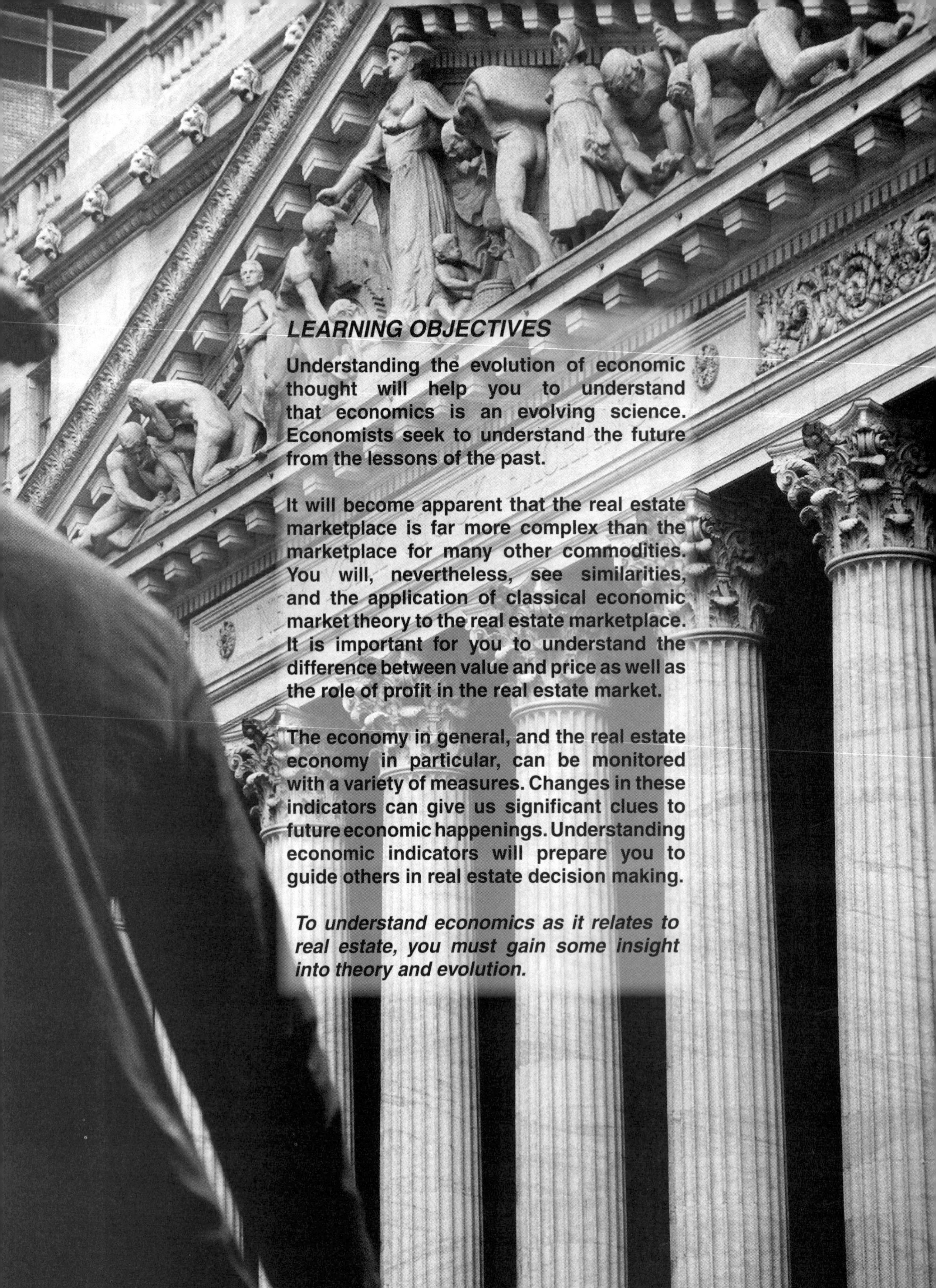

LEARNING OBJECTIVES

Understanding the evolution of economic thought will help you to understand that economics is an evolving science. Economists seek to understand the future from the lessons of the past.

It will become apparent that the real estate marketplace is far more complex than the marketplace for many other commodities. You will, nevertheless, see similarities, and the application of classical economic market theory to the real estate marketplace. It is important for you to understand the difference between value and price as well as the role of profit in the real estate market.

The economy in general, and the real estate economy in particular, can be monitored with a variety of measures. Changes in these indicators can give us significant clues to future economic happenings. Understanding economic indicators will prepare you to guide others in real estate decision making.

To understand economics as it relates to real estate, you must gain some insight into theory and evolution.

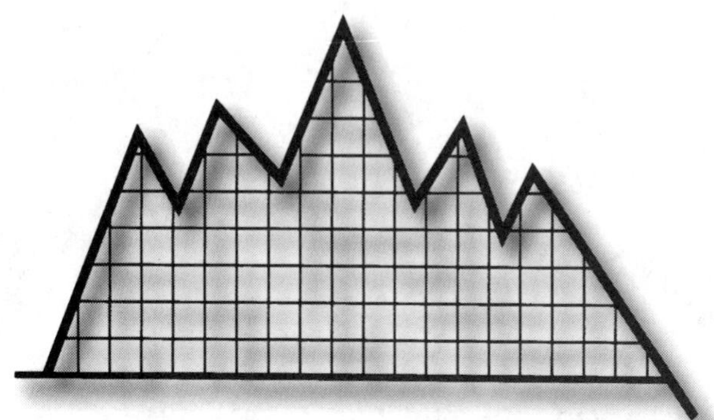

Chapter 2
Economic Theories/ Appraisal Concepts

This chapter presents early economists and their theories, economic systems, and the tools we use to measure economic activities.

I. The Early Economists

Adam Smith founded the concept of economic theory. However, economic thought had been taking shape for centuries before its formal birth with Adam Smith.

A. ADAM SMITH (1723-1790)

Adam Smith is the father of modern capitalist theories.

In 1776, ***ADAM SMITH****, a Scottish professor of economics (University of Glasgow), published "The Wealth of Nations."* He is considered the founder of the Classical School of Economics. Smith believed the concepts of private ownership and free competition with free trade would work for the benefit of all. He also believed that a laissez-faire economy would stimulate production. ***LAISSEZ-FAIRE ("Let people do as they please")*** *is a governmental policy allowing an economy to grow without government interference or direction.*

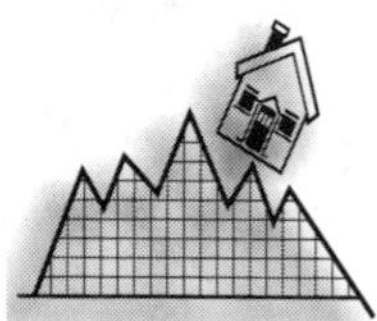

Chapter 2

CHAPTER 2 OUTLINE

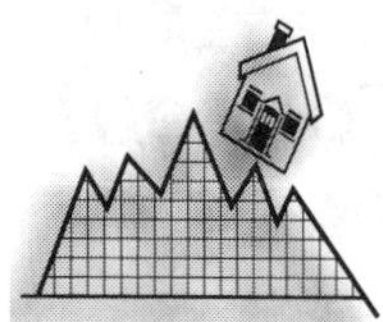

ADAM SMITH

Adam Smith's approach to economics was almost mystical in nature in that he believed the economy moved as if guided by an "invisible hand," which coordinated the actions of individuals through supply and demand in order to maintain equilibrium in the marketplace.

Smith held that if the price of a good was so high that the demand for it was less than the available supply, the "invisible hand" would lower the price so that the demand would increase to equal the supply. In other words, the equilibrium point would be reached. Conversely, if the price were so low that demand exceeded supply, the invisible hand would raise prices to the equilibrium point. According to the Classical School of Economics, supply, demand, and price are all considered flexible.

Smith never proved his doctrine, but he enumerated countless cases of governmental follies. He understood how markets worked and established the foundations of the supply and demand theory.

B. THOMAS MALTHUS (1766-1834)

The Malthusian theory was set forth by Thomas Malthus in *An Essay on the Principle of Population*, published in London in 1798. ***THOMAS MALTHUS** lived in an England that was still primarily an agrarian society.* An ***AGRARIAN ECONOMY** is based on the ownership of agricultural land for agricultural purposes.* Malthus was concerned about the possibility of overpopulation. He believed the only alternative to war and pestilence as a means of keeping the population in check was abstaining from marriage.

Malthus believed population would increase to the limits set by the amount of farming. Malthus held that a population increases geometrically and will continue to double itself in succeeding generations until it reaches its "misery level." He felt that if the ceiling on agricultural production were raised, the population would again rise to the misery level to meet the new ceiling.

Malthus believed that population growth was bound to reduce worker wages. Population increases would mean higher rents and prices, thus resulting in a lower standard of living.

The world's population is growing at a rapid pace. In many developing countries much of the farmland is already in use, while the farming population is very poor. Strict birth control measures in China were instituted to avoid the Malthusian problems of overpopulation. Malthus did not consider that agricultural production would increase as dramatically as it has in the Western world.

Food production has kept ahead of population growth in most areas of the world, so there is an economic problem caused by surpluses, not shortages. Malthus did not consider contraception, sterilization, or abortion as means to control population growth. The world's population has not grown by the geometric rates predicted by Malthus.

In an agrarian society, larger families are an economic benefit.

Farm life requires many people to produce the crops. Mechanization, urbanization, and child labor laws have removed the economic incentives for large families. In fact, they have made large families an economic burden.

Malthusian economics would seem to indicate that the more affluent, who can afford more children, would bear more children. This would appear a corollary to the basic principle of Malthus that the population would increase to the level of subsistence.

However, just the opposite is true. Family size bears an inverse relationship to income, with the more affluent having fewer children, while the less affluent have larger families. The actual need for housing space is therefore greater for the poor than it is for the rich, although the needs of the poor are less likely to be met.

C. JOHN MAYNARD KEYNES (1883-1946)

Keynes believed an economy reaches a balance at less than full employment. Keynesian economics advocated government intervention in the economy to fight unemployment and inflation.

In 1936, ***JOHN MAYNARD KEYNES****, an English economist, wrote "The General Theory of Employment, Interest, and Money."* Keynes did not believe that the economy would automatically adjust itself as did Adam Smith. He was influenced by the Great Depression, and believed in government economic planning and intervention in the economic system. Keynes thought raising consumer demand would reduce unemployment. He believed that to increase demand or total spending in the economy, the government could either increase government spending or reduce taxes. This would provide consumers directly or indirectly with more income, which would lead to increased total spending.

JOHN MAYNARD KEYNES

Keynes held that people would increase their consumption as their incomes increased. Consumption would not increase by the full amount of the change in income, but by a certain percentage known as the "marginal propensity to consume."

Keynes is considered the founder of modern "macroeconomics," which is the study of the entire economic system as a whole, rather than its individual parts.

***MICROECONOMICS** is the study of the individual components making up the economic system.*

II. Economic Systems

Several types of economic systems exist. The major systems used today in the Western world are capitalism and socialism. Capitalism (free market system) prevails in the United States. Therefore, we will concentrate on this economic system.

The United States was founded by capitalists who came here for economic gain.

While some immigration was the result of people looking for refuge from persecution, the majority came to our shores in the hopes of a higher standard of living. There were no class or religious barriers to economic advancement in the United States. The freedom that was sought in America was primarily economic freedom.

Capitalism and socialism are economic systems, not political systems. Terms like democracy, monarchy, and anarchy describe political systems.

Capitalism occurs in a "demand" economy, whereas socialism takes place in a "command" economy.

If the majority of decisions are made by private individuals demanding land, goods, or services in competitive markets, the system is called **CAPITALISM**. *If the government makes the majority of decisions, the system is called a command economy, more commonly known as* **SOCIALISM**. In other words, a capitalist economy is based on consumer demand and how much the consumer is willing to pay. In a socialist economy, the government dictates both production and prices for basic goods and services.

A. CAPITALISM

Capitalist markets answer the questions What?, How?, and For Whom?

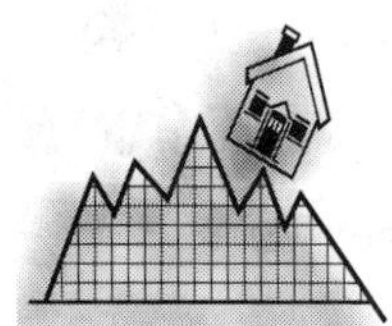

WHAT (what to produce) is determined by what buyers are willing and able to purchase. If an item is not selling, there will be no additional production. If an item sells quickly, more will be produced.

HOW (how to get more of an item or service) is determined by companies, the costs of different manufacturing processes, and choosing the method that produces an item at the lowest cost. Lower production costs mean higher profits, eventually higher wages, and lower consumer prices, which suggests more sales.

FOR WHOM (who will purchase a product or service) is simple to answer under capitalism: goods and services go to those who are willing and able to pay the most.

1. Basic Principles of Pure Capitalism

The basic principles of capitalism form the backbone of America. Although the United States has drifted away from pure capitalism, the basic principles remain central to our way of life.

a. **Private Property** – Individuals have the right to own, dispose of, and control real and personal property.
b. **Private Enterprise** – The majority of businesses are owned and operated by private citizens, not by the government.
c. **Competitive Markets** – Numerous buyers and sellers negotiate for the exchange of goods and services. No one person can manipulate prices.
d. **Profit Motive** – The desire for personal gain is the motivational force that entices people to make investments and to earn a living.
e. **Laissez-Faire ("Let people do as they please")** – The government should not interfere in private economic affairs.

2. Mixed Capitalism

Ours is a "mixed economy," in which both public (government) and private (individual) institutions exercise economic control.

This system evolved as a result of public pressure—to correct what the majority believed were serious faults in a "pure" capitalistic economy. Consequently, the government became active in many areas of the private economy (see **Figure 2-1**).

The United States is basically a free market economy, but the government purchases about 20 percent of everything produced, employs about 17 percent of all workers, and collects taxes worth about 35 percent of all income.

Figure 2-1

U.S. GOVERNMENT POLICIES
(Political and Economic)

INCOME REDISTRIBUTION

1. Taxation
2. Unemployment compensation
3. Medical and retirement benefits, Social Security, Medicare, Medicaid, welfare, food stamps, etc.

GOALS OF NATIONAL PUBLIC POLICY

1. Full employment
2. General economic stability
3. Price stability
4. An acceptable rate of economic growth from year-to-year
5. Suitably acceptable housing for every family

3. How Capitalism Works

A *CAPITALIST SOCIETY exercises private control over production and distribution through individuals working for individual gain.* In such a free enterprise system, goods will not be produced unless there is a market for the goods. Demand must be coupled with purchasing power in order for a market for goods to exist.

Demand is determined by taste, income, and prices of related goods among others. Demand is inversely related to price. This was shown by the typical demand curve in Chapter 1.

At higher prices, fewer goods are demanded, while lower prices increase the quantity demanded.

The sources of production under capitalism are land, labor, capital, and management. We pay for these sources by:

Land = **Rent**
Labor = **Wages**
Capital = **Interest**
Management = **Profit**

The fuel for capitalism is the hope or expectation of profit.

Only for profit will people start businesses and risk their capital. Increased risk must be balanced by the possibility of increased profit.

An **ENTREPRENEUR** *is a risk-taker who combines land, labor, capital, and management to provide a market-desired good or service that can be sold for more than the cost of producing it—hopefully, for a profit.*

In a pure capitalist society, wherever extraordinary profits are being made, other businesses will enter the marketplace and competition will result in lower prices.

Capitalism is the only economic system that gives consumers a say in what is produced.

Capitalism is the system that is most efficient at meeting the needs and wants of its citizens. In a capitalist society, citizens are free to vote for what they want. They vote with their dollars.

In a pure laissez-faire economy, the marketplace would be supreme. There would not be any government control or regulation. Our capitalist system is not pure capitalism because we have governmental controls of many types. As an example, federal, state, and local governments regulate real estate activity.

Federal statutes, which control or regulate the real estate industry, include the following:

1. **Real Estate Settlement Procedures Act**
2. **Truth In Lending Act**
3. **Equal Credit Opportunity Act**
4. **Fair Credit Reporting Act**
5. **Civil Rights Act of 1866**
6. **Civil Rights Act of 1968**
7. **Americans With Disabilities Act**
8. **Interstate Land Sales Act**
9. **Sherman Anti-Trust Act**

Every state regulates the licensing and conduct of real estate brokers and salespersons, as well as appraisers and lenders.

Many states also regulate contractors. States regulate subdivisions and set minimum construction and health and safety standards. Local governments control land use and set their own local health, safety, and construction standards. We have, therefore, what is known as a modified, or mixed, capitalist system.

Progressive state and federal income taxes, inheritance taxes, and social programs all tend to redistribute wealth in our society. One purported purpose is to reduce the danger of our society developing rigid class lines.

B. SOCIALISM (Government Ownership of the Means of Production)

Under ***SOCIALISM****, major industries are owned by the government.*

Karl Marx is the father of socialism.

1. Karl Marx (1818-1883)

KARL MARX *participated in the violent revolutions in Europe in 1848 and is considered the prophet of socialism.* He authored *Das Kapital* and *The Communist Manifesto.* Marx believed dramatic economic change was possible only through revolution.

Marx maintained that the value of goods should be computed simply as the sum total of the wages necessary to produce the goods. He believed there should be no rent for land since land should not be privately owned, no interest for the use of capital, and no profit for either management or risk-takers.

Under socialism, private ownership of the means of production is replaced by state ownership.

Socialists believe private ownership and competition lead to an inefficient use of the means of production and the benefits of such a system go to only a few.

In a socialist state, economic decisions regarding what and how much should be produced, as well as prices, are determined by leaders, not consumers. Under socialism there is no incentive to meet society's needs, nor is there any motive to improve production. Socialism requires a ***COMMAND ECONOMY****, with economic decisions mandated by governmental leaders,* rather than a ***MARKET ECONOMY****, such as exists under capitalism, where the demands of the marketplace determine what is produced.* Russia has realized that pure socialism does not work and they have moved toward a market economy. Even China, which formerly followed rigid rules against private ownership, is now allowing individuals to produce and compete in the marketplace.

In communist countries there is an active "black market" for Western style goods.

This black market illustrates the inability of state decisions to meet market demands. In state-controlled factories operating without competition, there is no incentive to improve quality, design, or efficiency.

In the U.S. we realize that even our government programs, such as welfare, require incentives for individuals to end their dependence on such programs.

Incentives are the key to motivating people in a mixed capitalist society. Socialism does not have a way to motivate efficient economic activity.

III. Land and the Real Estate Market

When mankind was nomadic, land use had no real value.

Land was for all to use. The concept of individual ownership came with an agrarian society. The Native Americans who traded away Manhattan thought they were getting the better deal because they didn't think they were giving up anything. They did not understand the concept of ownership. Our modern concepts of ownership evolved out of the European feudal system, in which a monarch owned the majority of a society's land but gave certain rights to farm the land to his or her lords, who in turn allowed serfs to use the land in return for rents.

Land, by itself, has NO intrinsic value.

The benefits that can be derived from the use of land are what give it value. To obtain and increase these benefits, land is often improved.

The real estate market is in a constant state of flux with different buyers and sellers emerging and the inventory of available property changing.

In a perfect economic model, we would have willing, informed buyers and sellers. We do not have a perfect market in real estate because of a number of imperfections. (Market imperfections are detailed in Figure 2-2.)

A. THE BROKER IN THE MARKETPLACE

Real estate brokers and salespeople do not set the market price but they do influence the real property market in a positive manner. Each broker, in effect, controls a miniature marketplace. By offering numerous properties for sale, brokers representing both buyers and sellers exert a stabilizing influence on the real estate market.

Informed buyers and sellers make for a narrower range of sales prices.

Through multiple listing services, Boards of Realtors® provide greater structure to the marketplace by providing listing and sales price information on a great many available properties over a wide area. A ***MULTIPLE LISTING SERVICE (MLS)*** *is an* *association of real estate agents providing for the pooling of listings, recent sales, and sharing of commissions on a specific basis.* This allows agents to provide price information to both buyers and sellers.

Cooperation in the form of multiple listing services has been generally accepted in the real estate profession for decades. Exposing property to more agents and buyers has helped to increase the likelihood of a sale within a reasonable period of time as well as to bring a degree of price stability to the marketplace.

Most large real estate offices now have their own websites featuring their inventory. Local, regional, state, and national organizations also provide property websites. The wealth of property information available has significantly reduced the likelihood of uninformed buyers and/or sellers.

newyorkmultiplelistingservice.com
New York Multiple Listing Service

Real estate transactions require technical knowledge on how to reach binding agreements that meet the needs of both buyers and sellers, as well as knowledge of how to finance purchases. By providing expertise, real estate agents increase the ease of making a real property purchase and thus help to improve our entire economy.

Real Estate agents stabilize local markets by providing information about current selling prices as part of their service.

The dramatic increase in brokers acting as buyer's agents has resulted in more informed buyers. Buyers represented by an agent are less likely to purchase property at prices that cannot be justified by market data. As such, buyer's brokers have helped stabilize the real estate marketplace.

B. THE INTERNET AND THE REAL ESTATE MARKETPLACE

The Internet is a significant real estate marketing tool and provides for a marketplace with informed buyers and sellers. Where buyers and sellers are cognizant of prices asked for property in specific areas, sellers are less likely to sell below current market value and buyers are less likely to pay more than market value.

Seeing property in other areas encourages both job and retirement relocation decisions.

According to the National Association of Realtors®, in 2003, 71 percent of buyers surveyed used the Internet to shop for a home. In 1995, only 2 percent of the buyers

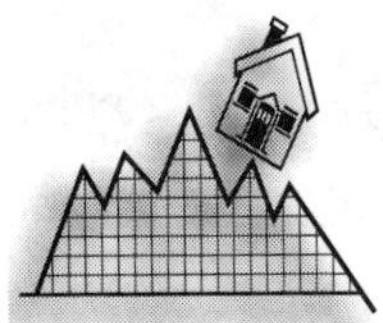

indicated they had used the Internet in their home searches. National sites for homebuyers include:

homescape.com
homestore.com
househunt.com
realestate.com
realtor.com
rent.net
homeseekers.com
homes.com

Homestore.com is the largest website provider for online homebuyer information. They own **homebuilder.com**, **rent.net**, and **homefair.com**. They also control a majority share in **realtor.com**, a hugely successful site that has over two million visitors each month and features over two million available homes.

Keep in mind that website addresses appear and disappear with regularity.

Not all websites cease to exist because of failure. Many successful sites are acquired by other more successful sites.

For example, by 2004, homeadvisor.com became houseandhome.msn.com, a search for springstreet.com would take you to rent.net, and move.com was swallowed up by homestore.com.

Large Real Estate Investment Trusts (REITs), like Avalon Bay Communities, Inc. and Equity Residential (formerly Equity Residential Properties Trust), have created websites for the purpose of handling showings and the actual leasing of their numerous apartment units over the Internet.

1. Seller Internet Services

There are Internet sites that help homeowners in choosing a broker. Some websites allow homeowners to post their property and the form of agency representation they want. Brokers then submit proposals to the owner.

Other online brokers offer so-called "cut-rate" commission plans for sellers. One company, **ziprealty.com**, promises to save 25 percent in commissions to sellers, and offers to share 20 percent of their selling commissions with buyers.

The services offered and the fees charged by "low-fee" or "discount" Internet brokers vary widely.

Some sites charge relatively small fees for posting homes on their site and offer access to virtual tours, but may provide limited services. For example, flyers and yard signs may be provided to a seller, but he or she is then responsible for procuring a buyer. A licensed agent handles the negotiation of the contract and manages the contract through closing, but the property is not placed on an MLS, nor is it available to be shown by brokers.

Other online "discount" brokers charge sellers a low sales commission, say two percent, but also charge a buyer's commission (perhaps three percent). These commission-based plans are more expensive than flat-fee plans, but they often provide better services as well. Advantages may include wider exposure through placement with local multiple listing services, and the benefit of having local agents showing the homes to prospective buyers.

To date, the success of Internet-based firms has been mixed.

According to the National Association of Realtors®, over 7.2 million homes are sold annually, with gross commissions of more than $46.3 billion. It's no wonder that Internet-based brokers have been dramatically increasing.

Unfortunately, as frequently as new low-fee brokers appear on the web, others disappear. Regardless of this high turnover rate, many real estate brokers still wonder if Internet-based programs will eventually supplant traditional home brokerage.

Some of the largest real estate companies in the country are testing lower-priced, limited service Internet-based brokerages in selected markets.

As a greater percentage of Americans begin to rely on the Internet, it is likely that online brokerage firms will handle more transactions. However, the authors express doubt that online brokerage will ever supplant conventional brokerage firms.

Some experts predict that the pressure of lower priced online brokerage will result in traditional brokerage firms lowering rates in a manner similar to that seen in stock market brokerage firms. According to Real Trends, Inc., average broker fees are already on the decline.

IV. Types of Competition

There are two basic types of competition:

1. **Perfect Competition** – many sellers, selling identical items, together with many buyers.

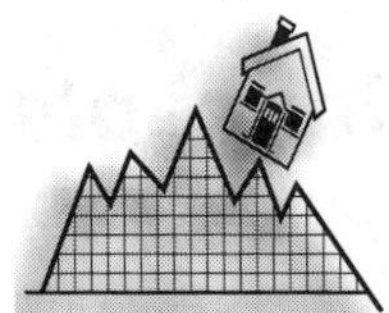

2. **Imperfect Competition** – fewer sellers, possibly different products, possibly fewer buyers.

   a. **Oligopoly** – few sellers
   b. **Monopoly** – one single seller
   c. **Monopsony** – one buyer
   d. **Oligopsony** – few buyers

A. PERFECT COMPETITION

***PERFECT COMPETITION** is an economic situation in which no single seller or buyer can influence prices.* Perfect competition requires the product needed to be nearly homogeneous (identical), for example, oil, wheat, and corn.

Real estate does NOT fit into the perfect competition category because the product is NOT homogeneous and the sale of one property can affect the sale prices of other properties.

B. IMPERFECT COMPETITION

***IMPERFECT COMPETITION** is an economic situation in which many sellers and buyers have some degree of control over prices.* Real estate fits into this category because the sale of only one property can change the sale price of another property. Real property is unique in that each location is different from any other location. Different types of buildings and individual designs create a wide variance in sale prices. Good marketing and persuasive advertising can create sales as well.

Imperfect competition is the arena in which most sales of real estate take place.

With imperfect competition, when the number of sellers becomes smaller, an oligopoly or monopoly situation may occur. **Figure 2-2** explains the different types of imperfections commonly seen in real estate markets.

1. Oligopoly

An ***OLIGOPOLY** is an economic situation in which a market is controlled by a small number of firms such that the production and pricing of one will affect all.* In an oligopoly, smaller firms cannot sell for a price higher than that charged by the dominant firms. A ***DUOPOLY** occurs in a market controlled by two firms.*

While price fixing is a violation of antitrust laws, in an oligopoly each firm realizes that lowering prices will not increase its market share for long since any action by one will be followed by a similar action by others. In an oligopoly, sellers tend to follow a price leader. When the price leader raises prices, the other suppliers follow.

Figure 2-2 **Imperfections in Real Estate Markets**

A. Knowledge – Uninformed sellers result in a fairly wide range of asking prices and uninformed buyers result in a greater range of actual selling prices.

Real estate agents and Internet house-hunting sites help reduce the problem of limited knowledge.

B. "Must Sell" and "Will Sell" Sellers – Sellers who, for various reasons, must sell quickly will often accept a price less than what would be acceptable for a sale not made under pressure. Similarly, a seller who does not need to sell immediately, but who will wait to sell at the right price, is likely to sell only for a premium price.

C. "Must Buy" and "Will Buy" Buyers – Alternatives are often not available. Therefore, a buyer under pressure to buy quickly or to buy a particular property for a particular need might be willing to pay a premium price. However, a buyer who is not particularly motivated to buy would be unlikely to buy unless the price is particularly attractive.

D. Product Differentiation – ***PRODUCT DIFFERENTIATION*** *occurs where an item for sale can be distinguished from other similar items for sale.* Real estate is not a homogeneous product. Every piece of real property is unique. Factors such as age, condition, shape, size, location, and even design and color could affect value. Because of product differentiation, it is not possible to set an exact market value for each parcel.

E. Immobility – Real estate is immobile, and most people work at fixed job sites. This tends to result in real estate marketplaces being localized by commuting capability. The mobility of prospective buyers is also limited by leases or the need to sell other property prior to purchase.

F. Production Time – Because it takes a long period of time to produce additional new inventory of improved property, present prices could exceed the cost of producing new similar property.

G. Financing – Because most real estate sales are financed, the real estate marketplace is directly influenced by the availability of financing and the cost of financing (the interest rate).

H. Discrimination – While great strides have been made in recent years to eliminate discrimination, some de facto discrimination still remains, which limits the access of buyers and renters to the marketplace.

Discrimination is far greater in the rental market than in the sales market. All ethnic and racial discrimination is against the law.

(continued)

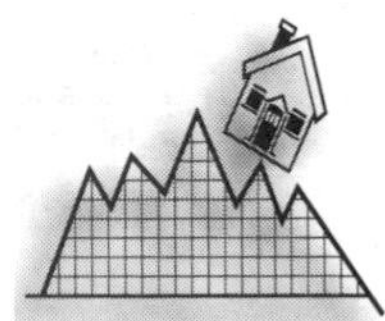

I. Bargaining Skills – A buyer's ability to bargain adroitly will, in many cases, result in a lower sale price. In the same manner, a lack of bargaining skill can result in a buyer paying a higher price.

In reality, market price is determined more by buyers than sellers. What buyers will pay ultimately determines prices.

Buyers and sellers generally have some flexibility as to what they will pay or take for property. Even when limits are expressed, they are often not absolute.

J. Price Setting – Prices of property tend to be set at what others are asking for similar properties, not at the prices other properties are actually selling for. Sellers who do list their properties at prices close to actual selling prices tend to close sales in a shorter time than sellers of property listed at higher prices.

Prices set above market prices create a surplus. If the quantity supplied exceeds the quantity demanded, properties are harder to sell. Prices set below market prices create a shortage, since the quantity demanded then exceeds the quantity supplied and property sells quickly.

When actual selling prices are analyzed for similar properties, the sales prices do not generally appear to be significantly different among properties listed at or above prices paid for comparable properties.

In some areas the real estate marketplace resembles used car sales where sellers often hope to get asking prices, but do not really expect to get them. By asking more, they hope that the final sales price will be greater.

Asking prices for similar properties generally range from the reasonable to the excessive.

In a seller's market, where there are more buyers than sellers, sale prices tend to be closer to offering prices than in a buyer's market, where sellers outnumber buyers.

K. Decision Time – Real estate usually involves a substantial investment. For the average person, a home purchase is the largest purchase and credit obligation he or she will ever make. Buyers, therefore, tend to take more time than purchasers of other goods. They tend to compare and often visit property several times before making a purchase decision.

An oligopoly-like situation might occur in a real estate market where lots are available only from a small group of subdividers.

2. Monopoly

In a monopoly there is NO competition to act as a curb against higher prices and excess profits.

A ***MONOPOLY*** *occurs where there is only one producer in a market*, as compared with an oligopoly, where there are a few producers. Unchecked, capitalism could lead to monopolies or oligopolies. In a monopolistic market, one individual or firm controls the marketplace, whereas in a free market of many buyers and sellers, prices are determined by the forces of supply and demand. On a limited scale we do find monopolistic situations in real estate, where one individual or firm controls all available land within a certain market area. As an example, one firm might control the only industrial sites in an entire area.

The federal government has a monopoly on leasing rights to our natural forestlands.

Our government regulates businesses to prevent monopolies because in a monopolistic market the consumer and the economy will suffer. We can expect any business to raise its prices to maximize profits in the absence of competition.

The National Association of Realtors® (NAR) realized that monopoly and oligopoly situations would work to the detriment of the public. The preamble of the Realtors® Code of Ethics states:

"Under all is the land. Upon its wise utilization and widely allocated ownership depend the survival and growth of free institutions of our civilizations."

3. Monopsony

A ***MONOPSONY*** *is a market situation in which there is only one buyer*. It is similar to a monopoly in that only one person or firm really controls the market. It is unusual to find a true monopsony situation in the real estate marketplace.

The right of governmental agents to acquire property through eminent domain is an example of monopsony.

4. Oligopsony

OLIGOPSONY *is a market situation in which there are only a few buyers.*

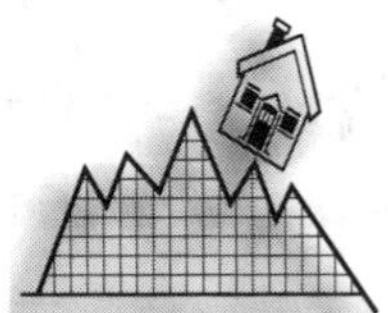

These few buyers tend to have a power similar to that of the sellers in an oligopoly. They realize that offering a higher price for available goods will not work to their benefit. A buyers' market in real estate with many sellers and only a very few buyers is really an oligopsony situation.

V. Economic and Appraisal Definitions of Value

Economists speak of a model person known as the economic person. The ***ECONOMIC PERSON*** *is guided in all decision making solely by economic considerations.* As with any model, it is a model only; no one uses economic reasoning alone.

People are often slow to react to economic changes. We often hesitate to make a change even when that change would be in our best interest. Our individual needs and wants affect our decision-making as well as our failures to make decisions. Our passions, prejudices, preconceived ideas, and even the choices of others, affect our decision-making. In addition, we often have incomplete or erroneous knowledge, so that the proper economic analysis necessary before making a decision is not possible.

A. HIGHEST AND BEST USE

The ***HIGHEST AND BEST USE*** *of land is that use which will provide the greatest net value attributable to the land itself.* As an example, assume a lot has two possible uses; one as a parking lot and the other as space for an office building. Assume the parking lot would require $75,000 in improvements, but when completed, the land and improvements would have a market value of $500,000:

Value of land and improvements	$500,000
Cost of improvements	-75,000
Value attributable to the land alone	$425,000

Assume the improvements for an office building would cost $900,000, but when completed, the land and improvements would have a market value of $1,250,000:

Value of land and improvements	$1,250,000
Cost of improvements	-900,000
Value attributable to the land alone	$350,000

When comparing the above two uses, the highest and best use would be the parking lot, which provides the greatest net value attributable to the land itself.

B. VALUE

"A moment's reflection must convince you of two things: first, that lands are of permanent value, that there is scarcely a possibility of their falling in price but almost a moral certainty

of their rising exceedingly in value and, secondly, that our paper currency is fluctuating; that it has depreciated considerably, and that no human foresight can, with precision, tell how low it may get as the rise or fall of it depends on contingencies which the utmost stretch of human sagacity can neither foresee or prevent." – George Washington

While George Washington felt that the value of land could only go up, you will see in your studies that as with all "truths," there are exceptions.

Values are NOT static.

They are in a constant state of flux moving both up and down due to changes in the use of other properties as well as in the supply and demand forces of the marketplace.

The value of property is its worth measured in benefits.

We normally relate value to exchange benefits, to what goods and services could be obtained in exchange. If the dollars received in a sale will buy more benefits than the dollars paid for the property, then the property has increased in value at a rate greater than the rate of inflation.

Value can also be related to use benefits. Real estate value is often defined as "the present worth of future benefits." The benefits referred to are the economic use benefits of ownership. Cost (what a buyer paid) has no real relationship to value defined in this way, as it reflects neither the benefits of use nor the exchange benefits. Buyers ultimately determine value. What buyers perceive as the future benefits determines value.

For raw land, potential agricultural benefits tend to set the minimum value. The possibility of other higher uses will result in a higher value.

There are four forces influencing value:

1. **Physical** – Size, shape, accessibility, location as to other uses and conveniences, utilities, climate, topography, environmental considerations, transportation, etc.
2. **Social** – Change in population size and attitudes towards education, recreation, etc.
3. **Economic** – Economic trends, employment wage levels, credit availability, etc.
4. **Political** – Building codes, zoning, health and fire ordinances, rent control, environmental legislation, etc.

As a corollary to land having value, you should realize that space has value as well.

There can be a three-dimensional aspect to value. The Merchandise Mart in Chicago was constructed partially over a rail line; skyscrapers use land in a way unimaginable 200 years ago.

C. PRICE

Price is NOT necessarily the same as value.

A ***PRICE*** *is the amount obtained when an item or service is actually sold*. Because of deficiencies in the marketplace, properties will often be sold for more or less than their beneficial use should indicate as a fair value.

In the real estate market, a price is generally directly related to the time available to sell, with a higher price possible when more time is provided and a lower price necessary when a sale must be completed in a short period of time.

The price paid will be based upon the relative advantages for the purchaser that one property has over alternative properties.

Price can be a function of terms. A low down payment and low interest rate can result in a premium price while cash could result in a much lower price.

There is a direct correlation between rents and price. This is understandable since buyers of income property will formulate offers based upon estimates of value obtained by capitalizing the income.

Unlike value, the most important determination of price is not imputed benefits, but the marketplace itself. The market forces of supply and demand will determine what price will have to be paid to effect a purchase. In a depressed market, a purchaser may be able to buy property at a price considerably lower than that the purchaser believes the value to be.

Market forces will clear the market. This means that the price level will adjust to a point where there is no surplus or shortage. *The price that will clear the market is known as the* ***EQUILIBRIUM PRICE***.

D. RENT

RENT *is the economic return from use of land or improvements*. While a higher use can result in a higher rent, tenants will pay what they must based upon supply and demand in the marketplace. The fewer the alternatives available to a user, the more that user will be willing to pay. Rents are not necessarily related to owners' costs, although owners will customarily request rents sufficient to cover their costs and provide a return on their investment. Rents are more directly related to the effects of market competition.

Vacant units do NOT compete against units that are already rented since these units are NOT available to prospective tenants. They compete only with other vacant units.

If there are few alternatives, then demand is relatively inelastic. More alternatives demand more sensitivity to price (elastic). An increase in rent, where there are few alternatives will lead to a relatively slight decrease in the quantity of rental units demanded.

The rental market is not perfect, as some owners lack perfect knowledge as to what other owners are charging for similar space. Tenants, however, are much more likely to have a feel for the current rental market and are unlikely to pay significantly more in rent than the marketplace requires.

For a tenant already in possession, an economic landlord (who is an economic person) will strive for an equilibrium rent, one that will maximize his or her income given the market situation. The rent could be higher than competitive rentals, but not so high that the tenant would relocate. The cost and time of relocating will affect a tenant's decision to relocate and induce him or her to remain if the rent is not too high.

Often rents are not what they seem. Owners are generally reluctant to cut their scheduled rentals but instead will offer tenants concessions. ***TENANT CONCESSIONS*** *are reductions in the effective amount of rent paid*. Tenant concessions can be two months of free rent or paying for the moving, etc.. The owner's reasoning is that prospective buyers or lenders will concentrate on appraisal income (capitalize the income to determine value). While lower rents would reduce the appraisal, rent concessions would be less likely to do so.

Also, owners are reluctant to raise rents since tenants are more likely to remain on a new lease at an existing rent than at a higher level of rent.

Because of leases and the reluctance of some owners to raise rents, rent often will lag behind the value determined by the marketplace.

E. PROFIT

PROFIT *is a return beyond the value of the land, labor, material, and management that goes into a project*. It is a return "on" an investment rather than only the return "of" the investment itself.

Without profit as a motivation, decisions would be based on non-economic considerations.

Profit is directly related to risk. As risk increases, investors demand greater profit. ***UNEARNED INCREMENT or UNEARNED PROFIT*** *is profit which did not result from an owner's efforts*. As an example, a property tax reduction would result in greater profit, as expenses would be reduced.

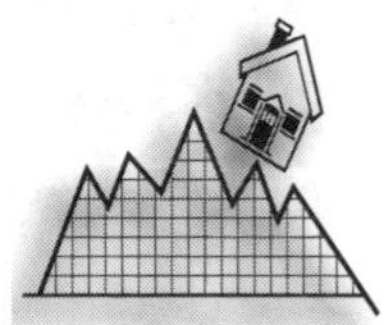

VI. Economic Measurements (Tools)

There are a great many indicators used to measure the health of our economy in general and of our real estate economy in particular. By studying changes in these indicators, economists attempt to predict future economic changes. The most popular measurement tools are discussed below.

A. NATIONAL ECONOMIC MEASURES

A number of government agencies provide information on measures of our national economy.

1. Federal Reserve

The Federal Reserve keeps a number of statistics that are of interest to economists including:

a. Statistics on money and debt
b. Reserve data on depository institutions
c. Assets and liabilities of U.S. commercial banks
d. Selected interest rates

federalreserve.gov
The Federal Reserve

2. Bureau of Economic Analysis

The Bureau of Economic Analysis is responsible for statistics as to:

a. Gross Domestic Product
b. Nonresidential fixed investment
c. Residential investment
d. Personal savings rate
e. Corporate profits
f. Personal consumption expenditure
g. Gross Domestic Purchaser Prices
h. Disposable personal income
i. Per-capita income

bea.doc.gov
Bureau of Economic Analysis

3. Energy Information Administration

The Energy Information Administration keeps statistics as to crude oil prices.

eia.doe.gov/neic/quickstats.html
Energy Information Administration

4. Bureau of Labor Statistics

The Bureau of Labor Statistics keeps a number of statistics as well as indices including:

a. Consumer Price Index
b. Employment Cost Index
c. Employment situations
d. Producer Price Index
e. Productivity and costs
f. Real earnings
g. U.S. import and export
h. Price Indexes
i. Civilian labor force
j. Unemployment
k. Unemployment rate
l. Employees on nonfarm payrolls
m. Average weekly hours
n. Average hourly earnings

bls.gov/blshome.htm
Bureau of Labor Statistics

5. U.S. Census Bureau

The U.S. Census Bureau keeps statistics on:

a. Housing starts
b. Advance reports on durable goods, manufacturers shipments, and orders
c. Industrial productivity
d. Capacity utilization
e. Household income
f. Poverty rate
g. Household wealth

census.gov
U.S. Census Bureau

Economic indicators can be seen on the front page or business section of your local newspaper and in national newspapers such as The *Wall Street Journal* or the *Investor's Business Daily*. National business-oriented magazines such as *Forbes*, *Newsweek*, and *Business Week* will often mention economic indicators as they discuss current issues.

6. Gross Domestic Product (GDP)

The ***GROSS DOMESTIC PRODUCT*** *is the total market value of all final goods and services produced in the country within a year*. It is normally expressed as an annual figure. In a growing economy the gross domestic product should be growing at a rate in excess of the rate of inflation. *The Gross Domestic Product, when adjusted for inflation, is known as the* ***REAL GROSS DOMESTIC PRODUCT***. The rate of growth and any change in the rate of growth are closely watched as indicators of economic change.

7. M_1

This is the nation's money supply, which includes coins, currency, and demand deposits held by the public. Increases in the money supply can be inflationary. A decrease in the money supply would mean fewer available consumer dollars, which could be deflationary.

8. M_2

Another measure of our money supply is M2. It adds to M1 all savings deposits and mutual type funds, which can readily be converted into cash.

9. Prime Rate

The ***PRIME RATE*** *is customarily described as the rate of interest a commercial bank offers to its most favored customers*.

Adjustable loans are sometimes tied to the prime rate. As an example, interest might be set for each period at 2 percent above the prime rate for the lender at a certain date.

Increases in the prime rate indicate a tightening of credit nationally, while a lowered prime rate indicates cheaper credit and can be expected to lower all interest rates, including those on mortgage type instruments. Lower interest rates have a directly positive effect on business activity, while higher rates tend to discourage purchases that must be financed, as well as building up inventory. Because real estate interest rates are based on long-term debt, they are not as responsive to changes in the prime rate as shorter-term loans for consumer credit.

10. Wholesale Price Index

The wholesale price index of various selected items is an excellent indicator of future inflation, as any increase in wholesale prices would be passed on by retailers to consumers if demand were inelastic. With an elastic demand, both retailer and consumer might share the burden of increased wholesale prices.

11. Consumer Price Index (CPI)

The ***CONSUMER PRICE INDEX (CPI)*** *is an inflationary indicator that measures the change in the cost of products and services, including housing, electricity, food, and transportation. Published monthly, the CPI also called* ***COST-OF-LIVING INDEX***. Leases are often tied to the Consumer Price Index so that rents will adjust to give the lessor the same relative purchasing power from rents during a period of inflation.

The CPI is our best inflation indicator.

12. Balance of Trade

A trade surplus, in which the value of exports exceeds the value of imports, means that more money is infused into the economy from foreign sources. Increased money will tend to reduce the interest rate. At the same time, the infusion of more money tends to be inflationary.

A ***NEGATIVE BALANCE OF TRADE*** *means the nation purchases more foreign goods than we export*. Normally, this would lead to a lowering of the exchange rate of the dollar because more dollars are being sold on the international market. This would lead to spending more dollars for the same amount of foreign goods.

With the demand for dollars remaining constant, an increase in the supply of dollars will reduce the exchange rate. As the value of the dollar falls, imports become more expensive, as it takes more dollars to buy the same amount of imports.

The American dollar may remain strong even with a substantially negative balance of trade. Compared to most countries, we have a low rate of inflation coupled with relatively high interest rates. If interest rates are attractive, foreign investors reinvest American dollars, keeping the dollar strong despite the negative balance of trade. When real estate is popular with foreign investors, many areas will experience an inflation in real estate values.

13. Personal Income

A rise in personal income adjusted for inflation means an increase in discretionary income and a growing economy.

14. Savings

Significant increases in personal savings do not necessarily mean a booming economy. It could mean that people are spending less of their discretionary income and saving more. It could be a sign of a weakening economy, as people who are fearful of the future will be buying fewer goods, which translates into lower production and greater unemployment.

When expectations of the future are positive, people tend to save less and make more major purchases such as cars and homes.

15. Consumer Credit

An increase in consumer credit is a sign that people have faith in their future and are spending more. This spending stimulates the economy.

16. Federal Deficit

Increases in the federal deficit means that the government is spending more than it is taking in. Government borrowing to finance the deficit causes interest rates to rise, inflation to occur, and crowds out the private borrower. If we pay down the national debt, we would be borrowing less. The reduction in Treasury bill offerings would result in higher prices because of supply and demand. Higher prices paid for T-bills would mean a lower yield and should lower interest rates for all long-term obligations such as corporate bonds and mortgage loans.

17. Currency Valuation

Changes in the exchange rate for the Mexican peso is a significant economic indicator for a number of California and Texas border communities. When the value of the peso fell, it had a significant effect on the economy of Calexico, a California border town, whose economy was largely based on sales to Mexican citizens. The loss of business increased unemployment and resulted in depressed markets for both residential and commercial property.

When the European Union (EU) launched its new currency, the Euro, on January 1, 1999, it was valued at $1.17 U.S. dollars. By October 2000, the Euro had temporarily fallen to 82.28 cents, resulting in many Americans purchasing second homes in Europe for what they considered discount prices. (By September 2005, the Euro had rebounded, and was worth $1.22 U.S. dollars). Currency valuations were also a significant reason for previous Japanese investments in U.S. property. In the 1970s and 1980s, Japanese investors were able to take advantage of a strong yen to buy U.S. properties at discount prices.

18. Poverty Rate

The U.S. Census Bureau determines the poverty rate in every state and county in the nation. Poverty levels are based on income thresholds that vary by family size and composition.

In 2003, the National Poverty Rate was 12.5 percent. The poverty rate tracks the economy, rising during recessionary periods and falling during a recovery period.

Factors that increase poverty rates include declining unionization, global economic competition, cuts in defense spending, and a trend from an industrial-based economy toward a service-based economy.

19. Standard Metropolitan Statistical Areas (SMSAs)

Each of these units for economic statistical study consists of a core of at least 50,000 people, the county containing the core, plus other counties economically and socially dependent on the core county. There are about 286 SMSAs in the U.S., excluding Alaska and Hawaii.

B. MANUFACTURING-ORIENTED MEASURES

Manufacturers, wholesalers, and retailers are primarily interested in measures of production or inventory.

1. Capital Expenditure

Increases in capital expenditures indicate that business is confident of future growth, while decreases indicate uncertainty or negative feelings toward the future. Changes in planned capital expenditures would tend to be a leading economic indicator in that changes in expenditures would likely precede changes in the economy.

2. Help Wanted Advertising

The volume of help wanted advertising is an expectant economic indicator. The indicator measures classified help wanted ads in 51 of the nation's major newspapers. The index is maintained by the Conference Board (**www.conference-board.org**), a nonprofit economic research organization. Help wanted ad volume tends to reflect present economic conditions. Variations adjusted for normal seasonal differences indicate what is presently occurring in the economy.

For a particular area, many newspapers separately track the volume of their help wanted classified advertising. A local area could run counter to a national economic trend.

3. Unemployment

Unemployment can be measured in a number of ways:

a. Percent of unemployed heads of household;
b. Percent of people 16 or over seeking employment;
c. Total number of persons 16 or over not working but actively seeking employment.

A problem with unemployment statistics is that they do not show discouraged workers who are not looking because they do not feel jobs are available and underemployed workers who want to work more hours.

Increases in unemployment mean fewer dollars spent on merchandise in the marketplace. Fewer dollars mean fewer goods will be produced, which in turn leads to more unemployment and can lead to a vicious downward cycle. This is offset to a great extent by government unemployment benefits as well as union contracts that provide supplemental unemployment benefits.

Increases in production will, of course, reduce unemployment. As a rule of thumb, for every three percent of GDP increase (adjusted for inflation), unemployment will decrease one percent (3-to-1 ratio).

An increase in the labor force can be an inflationary indicator. A lower unemployment rate and upward changes in wages would be inflationary. However, if productivity increased along with wages, the increased dollars available to purchase goods could be absorbed by the increase in goods and would not lead to increased prices.

4. Inventories

Managers who misjudge the strength of future sales can allow their inventories to grow too large. When they realize this problem, they normally attempt to make adjustments as quickly as possible. Adjustments customarily take the form of layoffs to reduce or halt production. Therefore, in the beginning of an economic slump, we see decreasing sales and increasing inventories. Efforts to reduce the inventory build-up tend to speed up the economic downturn.

Inventory fluctuations are cyclical in nature.

Eventually inventory will be reduced to the point where firms will have to increase or resume production. The resumption or increase in production will mean more jobs, which will mean more spending and a favorable economic upturn.

Intended inventory decreases by merchants indicate their concern about a downturn in the economy, while intended increases in inventory are an indication of confidence.

When merchants reduce their orders, the inventories of manufacturers and distributors tend to increase. When merchants increase orders, distributor and manufacturer inventories tend to decrease unless met by increased production. Economists closely watch general changes in inventory as an indicator of a change in our economy.

5. Collection Account Billings

An increase in accounts going to collection is a leading economic indicator of a downturn in the economy. A reduction in collection accounts would indicate a recovery period.

6. Unused Plant Capacity

A decrease in the amount of unused plant capacity could indicate an increase in the rate of new plant expansion, while an increase in unused plant capacity would have the effect of reducing new plant construction. When plants are operating close to capacity, we can expect any demand increase to result in increased prices.

7. Machine Tool Orders

Because of the lag-time between the production of machine tools and the production of consumer goods, an increase in orders for machine tools generally precedes an economic recovery, while a decrease would likely precede an economic downturn.

8. Fiberboard Orders

Most products are shipped in fiberboard (cardboard) containers. When businesses expect to reduce shipments, they curtail or reduce orders for fiberboard. When they anticipate increasing production and shipments, they increase their orders for packaging materials.

Fiberboard orders can be a leading index of what will happen in the economy.

9. Ratio of Corporate Debt to Corporate Inventory

This ratio measures the short-term borrowing of corporations. When corporations believe the economy will expand, they tend to increase short-term borrowing in order to increase production and inventories. When a business expects a bleak period, it usually reduces short-term, high interest debt.

10. National Defense Spending

Changes in national defense spending tends to have significant impact on defense oriented firms and the communities in which they are located.

11. Vendor Performance

This index shows the percentage of companies experiencing a slowdown in deliveries, which is indicative of shortages. Shortages normally indicate that prices will rise and future production will increase.

C. THE POWER OF INDEXES (Also Called Indices)

INDEXES *use a single number to measure the changes in the price or quantity of something from one period to the next.* It is a way of measuring price or quantity changes from month-to-month or year-to-year. For example, if the average purchase price index of a house in San Diego County was 100 in 1977 and today it is 200, it indicates the price of houses has doubled. Indexes can be used to measure the inflation over a period of time.

An index helps people visualize changes over a period of time.

1. Value Indexes

The Office of Federal Housing Enterprise Oversight (OFHEO) prepares a quarterly house price index that indicates value appreciation trends.

ofheo.gov
Office of Federal Housing Enterprise Oversight (OFHEO)

A number of indexes were developed that were designed to indicate changing value of commercial property. Most of these indexes are no longer maintained.

Solomon Brothers, a major investment and research firm, made a proposal to the National Council of Real Estate Investment Fiduciaries to develop a broad-based transaction index, which it claimed would allow an owner to draw conclusions as to specific property value.

It is doubtful that the use of indexes will replace appraisals as the accepted means of estimating market value. However, they can be useful tools to indicate both changes and rates of change in the general real estate market.

2. Housing Affordability Index

The affordability index of the National Association of Realtors® indicates the percentage of required income that the typical entry-level buyer possesses for the purchase of a median-price starter home. As an example, if the affordability index were at 84.6, it would mean that the average income buyer would have only 84.6 percent of the income necessary to buy a home. When the affordability index is rising, more buyers would qualify for home purchases and when it is falling, fewer prospective buyers could become homeowners.

The affordability index rose with low interest rates but higher sales prices have significantly reduced the index.

The California Association of Realtors® maintains a California Housing Affordability Index. In March 2005, only 18 percent of state households could buy the state's median priced home ($485,700). The income required was $113,340 based on a 20 percent down payment and a 5.78 percent mortgage. While these figures would seem to predict a market with few sales, this was not the case. Move-up buyers dominated the higher priced homes while first-time buyers were active in the lower edge of the price range.

Factors that affect the affordability index in a particular market include home prices, interest rates, and area wages.

In September 2005, on a national level, housing affordability was at a 14-year low. Some analysts feel that the low affordability index indicates that housing prices are close to peaking out.

3. Housing Opportunity Index (HOI)

The ***HOUSING OPPORTUNITY INDEX (HOI)*** *is a monthly measurement of the percentage of homes sold that a family earning the median income could afford to buy.* The National Association of Home Builders, in conjuction with Wells Fargo, keeps this index.

In December of 2000, the national median income was $50,200; that yearly income would allow a family to purchase 58.1 percent of the homes sold nationwide that quarter (HOI score of 58.1). The index also covers more than 170 separate metropolitan areas. In the same quarter the highest index was in Springfield, Illinois, where the median income of $59,100 and a median home price of $95,000 allowed a family having the median income to purchase 80 percent of the homes sold (HOI score of 80). The lowest HOI score in the country was in San Francisco with an HOI of only 5.7. The areas median family income of $74,900 was sufficient to purchase just 5.7 percent of the homes sold. The median home price in San Francisco was $505,000. The composite index rose to 70 percent by the end of 2003 largely due to low interest rates.

4. Composite Index

A group of six indicators compiled by the Commerce Department, also known as the Index of Lagging Indicators, includes such diverse items as the volume of commercial and industrial loans and the per-unit labor costs of manufacturing.

The composite index of lagging indicators includes:

a. Average duration of unemployment
b. Ratio of manufacturer and trade inventories to sales
c. Change in labor costs per unit
d. Average prime rate
e. Commercial and industrial loans (in 1987 dollars)
f. Ratio of consumer installment credit to personal income
g. Change in consumer price index

5. Leading Indicators

Leading indicators tend to predict changes in the overall level of economic activity. A composite indicator is made up of leading indicators.

The composite index of leading indicators includes the following components:

a. Average weekly hours (manufacturing)
b. Average weekly claims for unemployment
c. New orders for consumer goods and services (in 1987 dollars)
d. Vendor performance (slow delivery)
e. Contracts and orders for plants and equipment
f. Building permits
g. Change in unfilled orders of durable goods
h. Changes in the price of sensitive materials
i. Stock prices
j. Money supply (M_2)
k. Index of consumer expectations

While the leading indicators can be used to predict changes that will occur in our economy, lagging indicators tell us why changes are occurring or have occurred.

D. REAL ESTATE ORIENTED INDICATORS

Some of the tools listed below are used to measure the local real estate economy in your area. These are just a sample of measures that may be available to you as a member of the local board of Realtors® or multiple listing services. Many of the measures that come from U.S. Census data are broken down by census tracts.

1. Occupancy Rate

The Bureau of the Census measures occupancy by person per room. It considers overcrowding to be more than one person per room. Overcrowding is an indication of either financial need or a housing shortage (gap), which is the difference between current demand and current inventory in housing. There may be a housing gap at only one price level. Often we find overcrowding in low priced housing and vacancies in high priced housing. Overcrowding indicates a need for larger or more housing, but it does not necessarily indicate an effective demand. To be effective, demand must be coupled with purchasing power.

2. Vacancy Rate

The vacancy rate is an indication of available inventory. A vacancy rate of eight percent means that, on average, every unit is vacant for one month each year. A general rule is a vacancy factor must be in excess of eight percent to create meaningful pressure for reduced rents. (The fear of higher vacancy rates can, however, influence owners to reduce rents.) Because of time to prepare vacant units for rent and occupancy dates, property managers consider a vacancy factor of 5 percent or less to be full occupancy.

High vacancy factors can exist with overcrowding, which indicates that the market has NOT been responsive to needs.

Lower interest rates increase the affordability index and many residential renters are able to become homeowners. The residential vacancy factor can actually increase in a strong real estate market if the market is fueled by lower interest rates.

Economic surveys, such as those relating to vacancy rates, often lead to varying conclusions. There are a number of reasons for the difference among surveys. Often geographical areas are defined differently, with one survey concerned with a metropolitan area and another focused on its central city. Different urban economists will view a downtown area differently. The size of structures studied can vary. In addition, when owners and property managers supply information, the data given is often intentionally false. Managers do not like to indicate that they have serious problems. Owners, especially those who are weak financially, also do not like to acknowledge their difficulties. When surveys conducted differently and at different times are compared, the apparent conclusion drawn could be fallacious, simply because it is like comparing apples and oranges. Besides surveying owners and property managers, vacancy factors are sometimes based on figures from utility providers. A problem is that utilities are often left on for renovation, protection and/or rental purposes.

Changes in vacancy rates are extremely important, especially in areas such as office space.

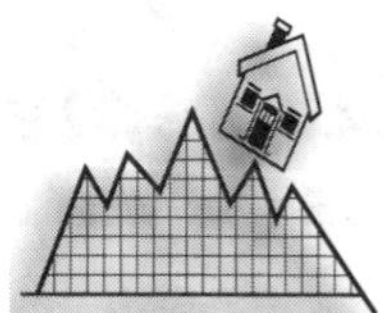

Because it could take years to create new space, even with a high vacancy factor, a dropping trend could result in decisions to start new projects.

3. New Building Permits

Increases and decreases in the number and dollar amount of building permits are good indicators of the health of the local and national economy, because they reflect the health of the construction business. Increases indicate confidence in the future economy. The construction of new retail space tends to lag behind increases in retail spending.

4. Home Resales

Increases or decreases in the number of home resales beyond normal seasonal adjustments are specific indicators of what is happening within a local market.

5. Time to Sell

Changes in the average time it takes to sell an existing home is an excellent indicator of market trends. While a shortened sell time is a positive sign of an improving market, a lengthening of the time would indicate a slowing trend.

As of August 2005, real estate brokers around the country were experiencing significant increases in the time to sell. This is an early indication of a cooling-off of the housing market.

6. Rental Growth Rate

Increase in the number of units rented and square footage rented indicates the absorption of vacant property and future needs for space. A negative growth with more vacancies than new rentals could indicate future falling rents and values.

7. Bankruptcy and Foreclosure

BANKRUPTCY *is a federal discharge of an individual's or organization's debts;* ***DEFAULT*** *is the state of being behind in one's loan payments;* and ***FORECLOSURE*** *refers to losing one's property to a lender.* Bankruptcy rates of businesses and individuals are excellent indicators of trends in the economy. Increased bankruptcies indicate a worsening economic climate.

8. Mortgage Default Rate

Loans in default are different from loans in foreclosure.

An increase in the percentage of loans in default is an indicator of future foreclosure rates.

While foreclosure rate changes are significant economic indicators, lenders in sellers' markets are often reluctant to foreclose. Therefore, foreclosure rates might not reflect the extent of a problem. Many lenders who have made large real estate loans hesitate to foreclose because foreclosure could mean realizing losses that, at best, would result in lower earnings and, at worst, could lead to an insolvency of the lender. Therefore, in many cases, lenders have restructured loans to keep them performing rather than show them as delinquent and foreclosed.

A more advantageous marketplace, where property can be sold more easily, will result in lenders more readily foreclosing. You might find a greater number of residential foreclosures when the real estate economy is in a recovery period than during an economic recession in the real estate marketplace.

According to the Mortgage Bankers Association, in 2004 the delinquency rate for mortgage loans on one-to-four residential units was 4.43 percent. This was actually down .54 percent from a year earlier. The inventory of loans in foreclosure was 1.16 percent, a drop of .19 percent from the prior year. While we have not seen alarming default and/or foreclosure rates, some analysts are predicting a significant increase in 2006 and 2007 because of loan products being aggressively sold that have low initial payments. Buyers are encouraged to buy more expensive homes than they can afford with a normal 30-year amortized loan.

VII. Real Estate Bubble?

A bubble occurs when investors put so much demand on a product that the price is driven up beyond any rational explanation of value. A bubble bursts when a great many owners try to unload the product and realize their gain, only to discover that there are fewer buyers than sellers at the high prices. Some sellers begin to panic and will sell at any price, which threatens the entire market.

1634-1637 Tulip Bulb Mania

In 1593, tulip bulbs were brought from Turkey to Holland. The novelty of the flower and its beauty made it sell at a premium. A virus attacked the tulip creating color variations and these bulbs were quickly sought after. Everyone began to deal in tulip bulbs making their availability scarce. Prices rose due to the scarcity and demand. People invested life savings to buy a single bulb A single bulb rose in value to astronomical value. But the value could not be sustained when many people tried to unload their bulbs at the same time. Prices plummeted. Investor panic led to sales regardless of loss. The value of a bulb fell to the value of an onion.

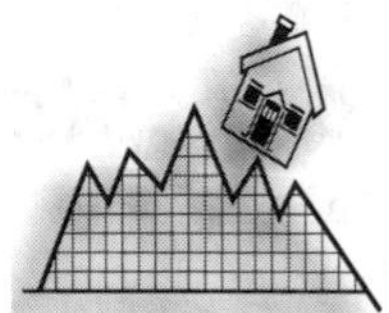

The buildup in price is based on "the bigger fool theory" that no matter what you have to pay for a product someone will pay more.

In 1920, Florida became a popular winter destination. Because demand far exceeded available supply, prices for homes doubled and even tripled within a single year. The news of tremendous value appreciation brought in speculators. Huge amounts of money were poured into Florida real estate. A common expression at the time was "Florida is divided into two groups of people, real estate investors and real estate agents."

The Florida land boom could not be sustained, it became speculators selling to speculators. When the prices reached a point where speculators became unwilling to buy, panic set in and the great Florida real estate bubble burst. Paper millionaires became paupers.

A more recent bubble occurred in high technology stocks. In 1999, of the 457 initial public offering of stocks (IPOS), 117 doubled in value on the first day of trading. Most of these offerings were for Internet-related ventures. Everyone wanted to get on board. A path to wealth was to give a company an Internet-related name and take it public. The price would go up with little regard for the company's likelihood of success.

Values could not be sustained and from March 11, 2000, to October 9, 2002, the NASDAQ composite lost 78 percent of its value, falling from $5,046.86 to $1,114.11. The bubble had burst. By 2001, there were only 76 IPOS of which none doubled in value on the first day of trading.

A great many economists claim that there is a giant real estate bubble, which will burst resulting in dire consequences for our entire economy. Robert Shiller, the Yale economist, says that home prices could fall 50 percent from their peek. These predictions of an imminent crash have been made with increasing frequency since the mid-1990s.

In mid-2005, signs began emerging that the real estate market was in trouble. They included:

1. Increase in low- or no-down payment loans and interest-only loans to encourage buyers.
2. Decrease in the housing affordability index.
3. Lengthening of selling time.
4. Large numbers of speculators entering the market in some areas.
5. Double digit annual increases in housing prices over the past 5 years in many areas.

Since real estate marketplaces are local in nature, the authors do not believe there is any national real estate bubble. There are likely many mini-bubbles in areas where real estate value increases were fueled by speculators. However, in most of the real estate markets, end-user occupants are fueling the market. Job growth, belief in the future and low interest rates coupled with an increase in population and household formation have been the demand forces that have increased values. Over the last 10 years there have been permits issued for an annual average of 1.63 million housing units. Depending on whose figures are used, this is from 10 percent to 19 percent less than the number of new households considering second homes and demolition.

Unlike tulips or stock, real estate has intrinsic value based on use benefits, so instead of a bubble bursting, we are more likely to see market corrections and then only if we see significant increases in interest rates where buyers become priced out of the marketplace.

However, predictions of analysts that the real estate bubble will burst can become a self-fulfilling prophecy if enough people believe it and start to unload property at the same time. In August 2005, with daily articles that the housing market was ready for a fall, the Dow Jones Home Construction Index (an index of homebuilder stocks) fell 11 percent. This was a huge loss for businesses that had been experiencing record growth.

VIII. CHAPTER SUMMARY

A number of economists played a part in the development of modern economic theory.

Adam Smith, the founder of the Classical School of Economics, believed in **pure capitalism**, whereby free enterprise would determine how much and what would be produced. Smith believed the natural forces of the marketplace would work to restore **equilibrium**.

Thomas Malthus believed population would increase geometrically in the absence of war, famine, or pestilence until a misery level of bare survival was reached. He believed increased population would increase demand and prices, and that rents would rise, thereby lowering the standard of living.

John Maynard Keynes believed income and employment levels are directly related to private and public expenditure, and that economic movements can be explained by changes in the money supply.

Karl Marx talked about the "exploitation of the masses" by the owners of capital—the capitalists. He believed the state should own the means of production and distribution.

The real estate market differs from other commodity markets in a number of ways, including the following:

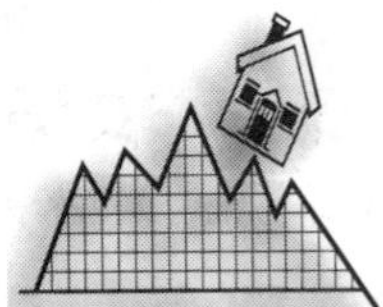

1. Buyers and sellers are constantly changing.
2. Buyers and sellers have incomplete knowledge.
3. The motivation of buyers and sellers affects prices offered and accepted.
4. Product differentiation.
5. Immobility of real estate.
6. Necessity of financing and effects of financing.
7. Market discrimination.
8. Effects of bargaining skills on price.

Real estate brokers help to create uniformity in the market by providing information about prices and offering comparison properties.

The Internet adds stability to the marketplace because it provides current offering and price information to both buyers and sellers.

A **monopolistic market** is one in which one firm or person controls a marketplace. An **oligopoly** is the control of a market by a small number of firms. A **monopsony** occurs in a market that is the opposite of a monopoly, in that a single buyer controls the market. An **oligopsony** is the control of a market by a few buyers.

That use which provides the greatest net income to property is regarded as its **highest and best use**.

The **value** of property is the present worth of future benefits of the property. **Price** is the amount paid for an item in the marketplace.

We have many economic measurements. Some are **leading indicators** because they tell us what the future will likely be. **Lagging indicators** tend to confirm what we probably already know.

In some areas of the country, indications are that speculators have driven up prices to a point where they cannot be sustained. Because real property has local rather than national markets, there may be many mini-bubbles in the marketplace. Because real estate has intrinsic value of benefits to be derived, there may be market corrections but value will not disappear.

There is a worry that we have a real estate bubble with prices driven up by speculators. We saw local bubbles but most markets experienced a gradual economic slowdown.

IX. GLOSSARY OF KEY TERMS

Affordability Index – An index prepared by the National Association of Realtors® which indicates the percentage of families who can afford the median priced house, based on the median sale price, financing, and current income.

Bubble – Demand for a product that drives the price up beyond any rational explanation of value.

Capitalism – An economic system where control over the means of production and distribution is under private control by individuals and firms working for profit.

Command Economy – An economy where economic decisions are made by the government rather than by individuals reacting to the marketplace.

Composite Index – A group of leading and lagging economic indicators compiled by the U.S. Commerce Department.

Consumer Price Index (CPI) – An index of consumer prices used to measure the rate of inflation or deflation.

Demand Economy – An economy where demands of the marketplace, rather than governmental decisions, determine what and how much is produced.

Federal Deficit – The amount spent by the federal government exceeding what it receives in taxes and other revenues. Government bonds are issued to finance the deficit.

Federal Surplus – An excess of federal revenues over federal spending.

Gross Domestic Product (GDP) – The market value of all final goods and services produced in the country during a designated period, always one year.

Highest and Best Use – That use which will lead to the highest net income attributable to a property.

Housing Opportunity Index – Index showing the percentage of homes sold that a family with the median income could afford to buy.

Keynes, John Maynard – An English economist who believed demand could be increased by increasing government spending or reducing taxes. He believed income and employment levels are directly related to private and public expenditures.

Laissez-Faire ("Let people do as they please") – The policy of government not interfering with business.

Lagging Indicators – Economic indicators that show what is happening in the economy after it has happened.

Leading Indicators – Economic indicators that indicate what will be happening in the future as to the economy.

M_1 – The nation's money supply in currency and coins, plus checking account balances and travelers checks.

M_2 – The money supply of the nation that includes, as well as currency and coins, checking accounts, savings accounts, and money market account balances.

Macroeconomics – The study of the entire economic system as a unit rather than of its individual elements.

Malthus, Thomas – An English economist who believed that, in the absence of war or pestilence, the population would increase geometrically, while the food supply increased arithmetically, until it reached a misery level.

Marx, Karl – The prophet of Socialism. Marx believed capitalism was an inefficient means of production that benefited only a few. He believed the means of production and distribution should be in the hands of the state. Marx believed socialism could be accomplished only through revolution.

Microeconomics – The study of the individual components, which together make up our economic system.

Monopoly – A market in which the supply for an item is controlled by a single supplier.

Monopsony – A market where there is only one buyer for goods.

Oligopoly – A market in which there are limited suppliers so that the actions of one would affect the actions of others.

Oligopsony – A market where there are only a few buyers for goods.

Potential Gross National Product – The total of all goods and services, which would be possible if all of our resources were fully utilized.

Price – The amount paid for an item in the marketplace.

Prime Rate – The rate of interest offered by a commercial bank to its most favored customers.

Profit – That portion of the return on an investment or business, which exceeds the cost of the investment or operation.

Real Gross National Product – The gross national product adjusted for inflation.

Smith, Adam – The economist who founded the Classical School of Economics. Adam Smith believed in a capitalist system without government interference or direction. He also believed individual reactions to the economy would work to maintain an equilibrium.

Socialism – An economic system where the means of production and distribution are controlled by the state.

Standard Metropolitan Statistical Area (SMSA) – Population units used in economic study that include a core metropolitan area plus economically dependent adjoining areas.

The Economic Person – A model person used for economic study, whose decisions are based solely on economic considerations.

Value – The present worth of goods based on future benefits that can be derived from them.

X. CLASS DISCUSSION TOPICS

1. Give examples of monopoly and oligopoly in the real estate market in your area.

2. Give examples of land use in your area that is not the highest and best use.

3. Give examples of disparity in sales prices and/or rent, which reflects our imperfect marketplace. Consider the reasons for the disparity.

4. If there were no real estate agents, describe what you think the real estate market would be like.

5. Do you perceive any discrimination in your market area? Explain.

6. In real estate transactions that you have been involved in, describe purchase decisions made other than for economic reasons.

7. Discuss changes in any economic indicators over the past month, as reported in the business section of area newspapers as to what effect they could have on your local real estate economy.

8. Do you feel that there is a real estate bubble in your local marketplace? Why?

XI. CHAPTER 2 QUIZ

1. Adam Smith believed in a:

   a. Laissez-Faire policy.
   b. command economy.
   c. government guidance to influence the economy.
   d. socialistic state.

2. Private property, private enterprise, competitive markets and a profit motive are elements of:

   a. communism.
   b. socialism.
   c. capitalism.
   d. a command economy.

3. A market controlled by a single producer would be a:

   a. oligopsony.
   b. monopsony.
   c. oligopoly.
   d. monopoly.

4. Which of the following would be the best inflation indicator?

   a. Balance of trade
   b. CPI
   c. Federal deficit
   d. Unused plant capacity

5. Which of the following would be a lagging economic indicator?

   a. Vendor performance
   b. Change in Consumer Price Index
   c. Building permits
   d. Index of consumer expectations

6. A developer considering building new office space would be most interested in:

   a. changes in the office vacancy rate.
   b. changes in vendor performance.
   c. changes in the Consumer Price Index.
   d. changes in the housing affordability index.

7. The return beyond the cost of land, labor, material, and management would be:

   a. rent.
   b. M_2.
   c. gross domestic product.
   d. profit.

8. Value would be measured by:
   a. price.
   b. benefits.
   c. profit.
   d. the highest and best use.

9. The term net value attributable to the land would be related to:
   a. price.
   b. highest and best use.
   c. elasticity of demand.
   d. rent.

10. Imperfections in the real estate market are caused by all except:
    a. bargaining skills.
    b. must sell and will sell sellers.
    c. production time.
    d. informed buyers and sellers.

ANSWERS: 1. *a*; 2. *c*; 3. *d*; 4. *b*; 5. *b*; 6. *a*; 7. *d*; 8. *b*; 9. *b*; 10. *d*

LEARNING OBJECTIVES

You will understand the role of money in our economy and the effect changes in its velocity, supply and cost have on our real estate marketplace. You will understand the monetary and fiscal controls available, and the goals that are sought. You will also gain an understanding of our primary and secondary mortgage markets and reasons for the changes in these markets as well as in financing instruments. By gaining a basic economic comprehension of financing, you will better understand the necessity of making informed decisions in a changing economy.

Monetary policy and fiscal policy are government tools used to influence the economy. These tools are necessary in order to understand how real estate financing works.

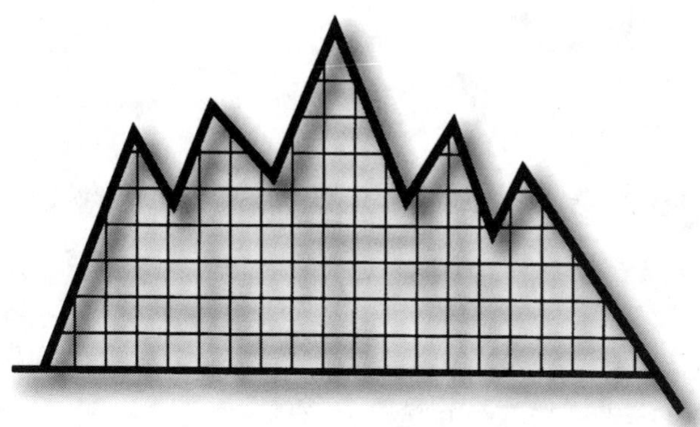

Chapter 3
Money and Financing

Money is a medium of exchange and a convenient way to measure and store value.

I. Money and Monetary Policy

***MONEY** is manufactured under the control of the Treasury Department, but the Federal Reserve System controls its distribution*. In our economy, (physical) money is either in the form of paper currency or metal coinage. Paper money has no intrinsic value. The Federal Reserve will not exchange it for gold or silver. Its value is based wholly upon the faith that others will part with beneficial goods in exchange for money. Money, to be an effective medium of exchange, must be acceptable to others. If people were unwilling to part with property for money, we would be reduced to a barter economy.

The value of money in a supply and demand economy is directly related to the amount of money available to purchase existing goods. *When there are more dollars available than goods to buy, the price of goods will go up and we will have an **INFLATIONARY ECONOMY**. When there are more goods on the market than dollars to buy them, prices will go down and we will have a **DEFLATIONARY ECONOMY**.*

CHAPTER 3 OUTLINE

***CHECKS** are demand deposits that must be paid by the depositor's bank to the payee upon presentation if the bank is holding sufficient funds of the depositor*. The ***MAKER** is the depositor, who writes the check*. The ***PAYEE** is the person receiving the check*. The depositor's bank must pay the check immediately, if there are sufficient funds.

Most people get paid by check and deposit their paycheck into a checking account. They then pay their major obligations by check. The individuals and firms receiving these checks act in similar fashion, depositing the checks received into their checking accounts. This reliance on **checkbook money** greatly reduces the need for currency in our economy. The need for paper is further diminished with the advent of electronic deposits and payments. As of July 2005, the money supply was estimated at $1,356 billion by the Financial Forecast Center (**www.forecast.org/ml.htm**).

A. VELOCITY OF MONEY

The ***VELOCITY OF MONEY** is the number of times money changes hands, on average, to purchase newly produced goods or services during a period of time throughout the entire economy*. In order to determine the annual velocity of money, divide the Gross Domestic Product by the amount of money in circulation. With a greater propensity to spend, there would be a higher velocity, which would result in a higher real Gross Domestic Product. If the economy were at or near full employment, an increase in the propensity to spend would increase the velocity of money and would result in inflation.

B. SAVINGS

We have long regarded saving as a virtue. **However, if everyone would suddenly increase their savings by a substantial amount it would decrease spending, and the short-term effect would be a decrease in the Gross Domestic Product (national growth) and an increase in unemployment**. But by having more funds available for investment, the long-term effect of increased savings would be beneficial.

C. MONETARISM AND MONETARY POLICY

In 1911, the American economist Irving Fisher theorized that doubling a nation's money supply would simply double the price level. This is referred to as the Quantity Theory of Money.

The equation in Fisher's theory is:

MV = PQ
M = Money Supply
V = Velocity of Money
P = General Price Level
Q = Total Production of Goods

Fisher believed that the velocity of money was relatively constant due to the dependability of people's spending habits, and that Q was constant at full employment. (Fisher's theory also assumed that, in the long run, market forces would automatically put the economy at full employment.) Therefore, doubling M would merely double P.

Milton Friedman, a noted economist of today, substantiated Fisher's theory, but concluded that a stable economy required that the money supply be increased steadily in relationship to our ability to produce. Friedman believes the economy has the ability to expand 3-5 percent annually. Increasing the money supply by this amount would allow Q to grow, with P remaining stable. Any growth in M larger than this would cause the price level to rise. Friedman's ideas are known as the "monetarist" view. ***MONETARISM** is the economic school of thought which holds that the entire economy can be controlled by increasing or decreasing the supply of money.* Monetarism has had a major influence on the Federal Reserve's control of our money supply.

Increasing the money supply, while being inflationary, causes firms to expand, more goods to be produced, and employment to increase; decreasing the money supply has the opposite effect.

II. The Federal Reserve System (Fed) Our Independent Central Bank

The ***FEDERAL RESERVE SYSTEM (Fed)** is our central bank, which is administered by an independent governing board.* **Figure 3-1** explains how the Fed affects all Americans.

The job of the Fed is to control the supply of money and credit so that the economy grows steadily at its optimum rate without causing either high inflation or high unemployment.

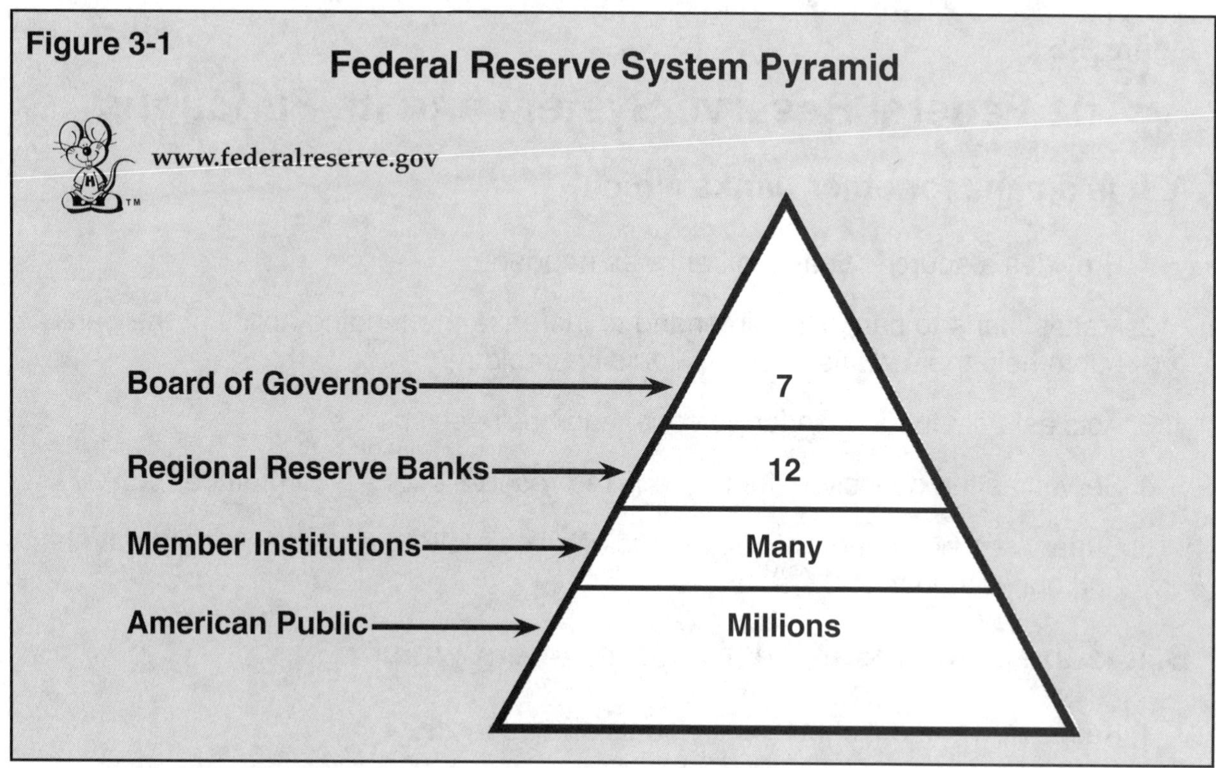

The Federal Reserve Board's seven members are appointed by the President and confirmed by the Senate, and serve for 14 years. The purpose of the long term is to insulate the Board members from political pressure. The Federal Reserve is further protected from outside influence because it operates on its own earnings and not on funds allocated by Congress (see **Figure 3-2**).

The Fed is kept as independent of politics as possible, so that its actions will not depend as much on the administration in office or the time of the next election.

The Federal Reserve Act of 1913 set up 12 regional banks, each with its own Regional Board of Governors. The regional banks carry out the policies of the System's Board of Governors and the Federal Open Market Committee of the Federal Reserve (see **Figure 3-3**).

California is in the 12th District of the Federal Reserve System.

The control of the Federal Reserve is not complete, because banks can hold excess reserves, and there are large foreign holders of dollars and dollar credit. The Federal Reserve can "neutralize" the effect of foreign spending in the U.S. by selling government securities to absorb this extra money. Large divestiture of these dollars could serve to devalue our currency. In addition, there are many dollars held in actual currency form that are not in circulation, as well as dollar credits in various forms of savings accounts. The Federal Reserve has no control over the spending of these dollars.

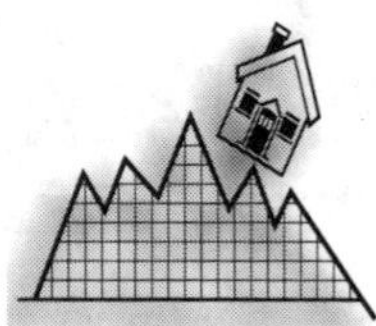

Figure 3-2

The Federal Reserve System and Its Functions

A. It is a bank for other banks which:

1. Provides a source of cash to banks as needed.
2. Makes loans to banks, not intended to increase the lending ability of the banks, but to help them with short-term liquidity problems.
3. Acts as a clearinghouse for personal and business checks.
4. Serves as the depository for the required reserve deposits of member banks.
5. Supervises the reserve requirements of all depository institutions, both member and non-member.

B. It is the bank of our federal government which:

1. Keeps government checking accounts and deposits.
2. Handles the sale of government bonds for government borrowing.

C. It protects consumers in credit transactions by:

1. Drawing up Truth in Lending regulations.
2. Issuing Equal Credit Opportunity regulations.

D. It manages the nation's money supply through:

1. The Discount Rate.
2. Reserve Requirements.
3. Open Market Operations (most effective and most frequently used).
4. Margin Requirement for Security Firms (rarely changes).

While the Federal Reserve System has no control over production of goods and services, it does have a great deal of control over our money supply.

Figure 3-3

Certain interest rates that are controlled by the Fed have a direct effect on the supply of money available for investment.

A. INTEREST RATES

At a low rate of interest, people will not have a great incentive to save money. On the other hand, at a high rate of interest people will be motivated to save. As interest rates increase, people will save rather than hold excess money in the form of currency or checking accounts.

Interest rates strongly affect the demand for money.

The ***DISCOUNT RATE*** *is the rate of interest at which member banks borrow from the Federal Reserve Bank.* By changing the discount rate, **the Federal Reserve affects primarily short-term interest rates, but primarily the short-term rates, and can thus encourage or discourage borrowing and the expansion of our economy**.

Interest rates directly affect the real estate industry. Most homebuyers require loans, and the amount of monthly payments varies according to the interest rate prevalent at the time a loan was obtained. So, in high interest rate periods, the number of home sales will be low, but sales will generally go up when interest rates fall. Higher interest rates also result in higher mortgage payments, meaning fewer people will be able to qualify for the same loan amount they would have when interest rates were low.

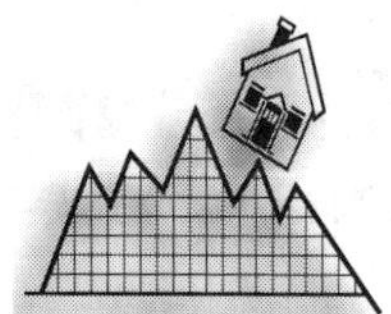

Buyers, therefore, begin purchasing less expensive homes. As interest rates go up, adjusted rate mortgage loan payments also go up, requiring borrowers to make higher payments on the same loan amount. This effect raises monthly payments and makes people less likely to contemplate purchasing real estate.

In an effort to control anticipated and actual inflation, Chairman Alan Greenspan directed the Fed to raise interest rates between 1999 and 2000, and lower them between 2000 and 2004. When interest rates were high, a healthy economy and consumer confidence kept real estate sales and residential construction surprisingly strong. The trend continued, despite a downturn in the economy, due to increasingly lower interest rates and disenchantment with the stock market. In 2004, the Fed reversed course and began raising rates in small increments to ward off inflation.

Historically, the real estate housing market is "interest rate sensitive." Generally, home sales and prices go down when interest rates go up, and up when interest rates fall.

Figure 3-4 shows the circular flow diagram (households, firms, government and world), which the Federal Reserve System controls through its monetary policy.

B. RESERVE REQUIREMENTS

RESERVE REQUIREMENTS *are the percentage of deposit funds (reserves) that a bank must keep and not lend out again.* By changing reserve requirements, the Federal Reserve can limit or expand the lending of funds. Banks must set aside this portion (the percentage set by the Fed) of their checking deposits in reserve; the rest is available for lending. As new deposits come in, a portion of these must also be set aside as reserves. Because banks have most of their money out in the form of loans, they do not have anywhere near enough cash to cover all of their deposits at once.

C. OPEN MARKET OPERATIONS

OPEN MARKET OPERATIONS *consist of the buying and selling of government securities (bonds) by the Federal Reserve's Open Market Committee; it puts money into or takes money out of circulation.*

By its open market operations in buying government securities, the Federal Reserve puts money into circulation. By selling government securities, the Fed takes money out of circulation.

Federally chartered banks must join the Federal Reserve System and carry insurance coverage from the Federal Deposit Insurance Corporation (FDIC). State chartered banks can obtain FDIC coverage even if they are not members of the Fed. Because of the failure of many uninsured state banks, states require their banks to obtain FDIC coverage. There are no longer panic withdrawals by depositors because member banks

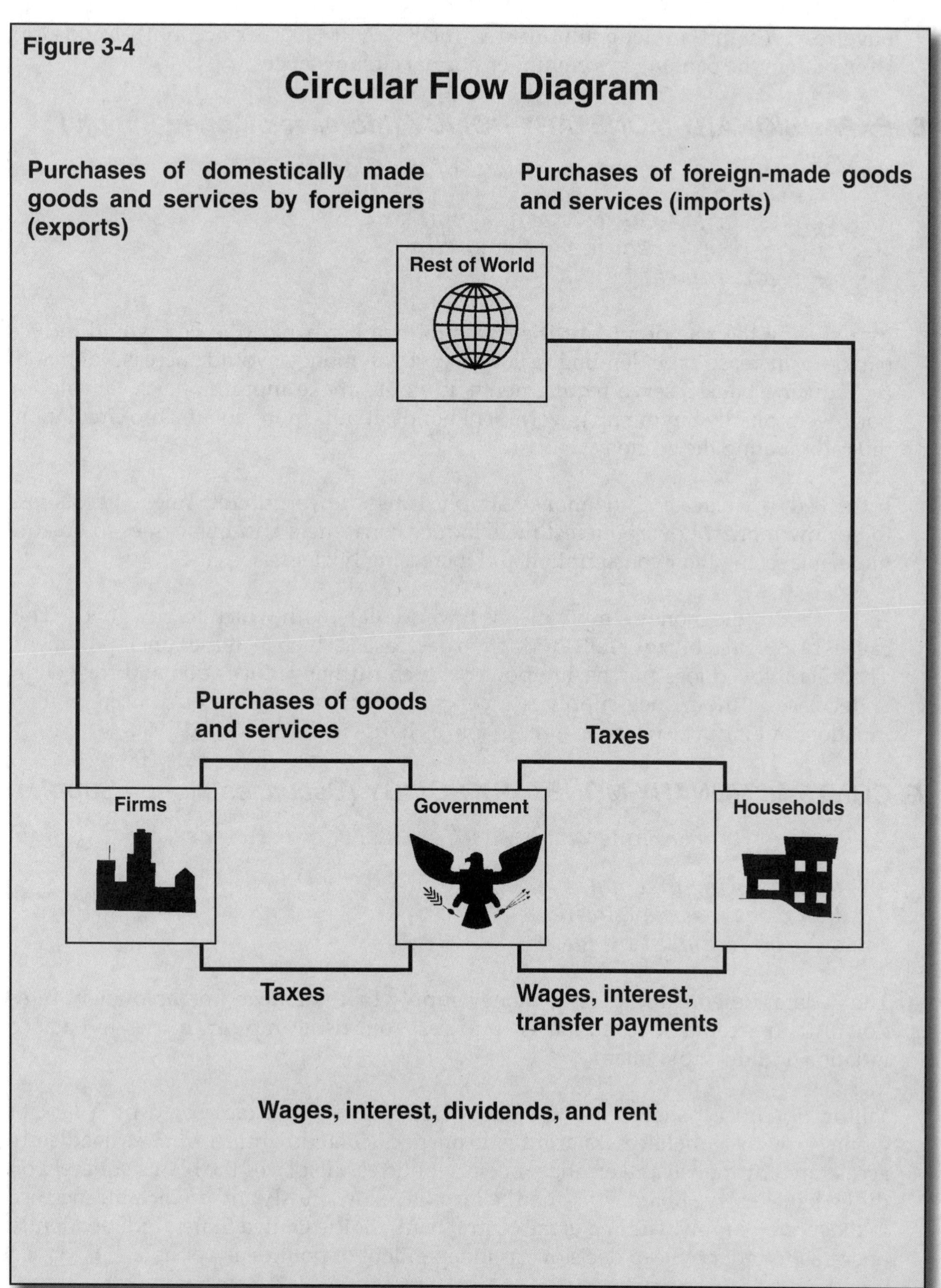
Figure 3-4
Circular Flow Diagram
Purchases of domestically made goods and services by foreigners (exports)
Purchases of foreign-made goods and services (imports)
Rest of World
Purchases of goods and services
Taxes
Firms
Government
Households
Taxes
Wages, interest, transfer payments
Wages, interest, dividends, and rent

have reserves and are federally insured (FDIC - $100,000 per account). Depositors have faith in the banking system under normal circumstances.

D. EXPANSIONARY MONETARY POLICY (Increases Money Supply)

An "expansionary monetary policy" of the Federal Reserve:

1. reduces the federal reserve discount rate,
2. reduces reserve requirements, and/or
3. buys government bonds.

By reducing the rate of interest it charges to member banks, the Fed would induce banks to increase their lending; a lower cost for money would increase demand. By reducing bank reserve requirements, it would make more money available for borrowers; and by buying up government bonds; it puts more dollars into circulation, thus stimulating the economy.

If the Fed, by increasing the money supply, causes lower interest rates, it costs less to borrow money. Lower interest rates induce consumers and businesses to borrow more, increasing their consumption and increasing business activities.

A decrease in the money supply means fewer dollars with which to buy goods. This causes prices to stabilize or fall. Production decreases, which increases unemployment. The unemployed lose purchasing power, which further reduces demand for goods. A decrease in the money supply is a contractionary monetary policy used to fight inflation, but it can also lead to a recession, as happened in 1980 and 1990.

E. CONTRACTIONARY MONETARY POLICY (Deceases Money Supply)

A "contractionary monetary policy" of the Federal Reserve:

1. increases the discount rate,
2. increases reserve requirements,
3. sells government bonds.

The Federal Reserve strives for a money supply that will keep unemployment rates down to an acceptable level, but keep prices from rising rapidly. It tries to balance inflation and unemployment.

Milton Friedman believes that the Great Depression was exacerbated by a lack of money growth. He believes it started as an unspectacular downturn, but was needlessly accelerated by foolish and erratic monetary policies. He places the blame squarely on the Federal Reserve Board. Friedman believes in a slow, steady and predictable increase in the money supply. The Fed is the central bank for the United States, independently operated in order to keep decisions as independent of politics as possible.

Because the Federal Reserve's policies are not the sole factor in determining our money supply, its task is often difficult. In addition, the goals of combating inflation and striving for a high level of employment call for contradictory measures. Increasing the money supply to combat recession is likely to cause inflation, and reducing the money supply to fight inflation is likely to increase unemployment.

According to Edward G. Boehne, the former president of the Federal Reserve Bank of Philadelphia, the two major monetary goals of the Federal Reserve are the following:

1. To keep the economy at, or near, full employment;
2. To reduce the inflation rate until price stability is achieved.

Alan Greenspan attempted to achieve both of these goals by fine-tuning the economy with changes in the discount rate. By raising or lowering the rate, Mr. Greenspan established a policy of peremptory changes to avoid both inflation and recession. This can be a very difficult balancing act.

Economic theory tells us there are two ways to conduct monetary policy:

1. *Target the money supply to achieve the desired rate of growth of the money supply and price stability;*
2. *Target interest rates by setting them at a level, which will produce the desired growth and price stability.*

While this is an oversimplification, these are the general principles the Federal Reserve follows. If the economy is shocked by major changes in demand, however, then the role of the Fed becomes more controversial. While it is relatively easy to agree on goals, it is much harder to agree on specific policies to meet these goals. Economists differ widely as to how, when, and to what degree the Federal Reserve should use the instruments of monetary control at its disposal.

> *"The appeal of a simple rule is obvious. It would simplify our job at the Federal Reserve, make monetary policy easy to understand, and facilitate monitoring of our performance. And, if the rule worked, it would reduce uncertainty... but, unfortunately, I know of no rule that can be relied on with sufficient consistency in our complex and constantly evolving economy."*
>
> – Paul Volcker, Former Chairman of the Board of Governors of the Federal Reserve System.

III. Fiscal Policy (Federal Taxing and Spending)

The Federal Reserve's job of controlling monetary policy includes smoothing out the fiscal policy (taxing and spending) of the Federal government. Remember, our elected officials usually do what is politically best for "them" not necessarily for the economy.

An ***EXPANSIONARY FISCAL POLICY*** *increases government spending and/or decreases taxes.* This would increase the income available to consumers. A ***CONTRACTIONARY FISCAL POLICY*** *decreases government spending and/or increases taxes, which would reduce the income that consumers can spend (disposable income).* While the fiscal policy of the government will change disposable income, it does not necessarily change the money supply unless it is accompanied by the Federal Reserve's monetary policy. (See The Federal Debt Clock: **www.brillig.com/debt_clock**.)

The government's fiscal policy can be either expansionary or contractionary for our economy.

A. THE FEDERAL BUDGET DEFICIT

Too often our federal elected officials (Congress and the President) go for the "quick fix" and spend more money than is collected in income taxes; this produces a "deficit." It takes courage to implement the much harder long-term decisions to cut spending or increase income taxes and create efficient, measurable government programs.

When the federal government spends more than it receives, the money must come from somewhere. It comes from government borrowing. By borrowing money, the government takes away capital that would otherwise be available to finance homes, cars and business investments. This is known as "crowding out" the private sector.

The federal government's spending, like most governmental bodies, is usually inefficient. The private sector (made up of individual companies) is generally efficient because it forces businesses to compete against each other to make a profit. Government agencies do not have the same incentives to cut expenditures or produce more work for the money allocated to them.

Since there is NO efficiency rating system and little oversight of each program, there is no incentive to improve. As a matter of fact, there is a tendency to continue programs long after the need for them has disappeared.

When the government finances a deficit by borrowing money from the private sector, the demand for money increases, causing interest rates to rise. With higher interest rates, there will be less borrowing in the private sector, which discourages capital investment.

The federal government (when taxing and spending) essentially "crowds out" private investment in the economy.

A great many economists recommend tax increases as a means to control the federal deficit. Milton Friedman, however, is not one of them. He does not believe taxes should be raised as a solution to the deficit; he believes increasing taxes will not eliminate the deficit, but will instead only encourage the federal government to increase spending.

The federal government rarely reduces a tax once it is established. The need to borrow huge amounts of funds by the government results in higher interest rates for all sectors. At the present time, the federal government takes one dollar out of every four that is available for investment.

As of July 31, 2005, the national debt was $900,676,048,586.49. The population of the United States on this date was estimated at 296,651,030. Based on these figures, each citizen's share of the national debt is $26,624.14. Since September 30, 2004, the national debt has been increasing at a rate of $1.64 billion per day.

For the fiscal year 2004, the interest expense on our national debt was $321,566,323,971.29. If this amount of money were available in the private sector, it would be enough to finance more than 1.6 million homes with an average loan of $200,000.

As recently as 2000, we had a federal surplus, meaning that more dollars in the form of taxes and other sources were coming into the government than the government was spending. While spending more than received is "expansionary," but not necessarily inflationary, a federal surplus is "contractionary," as it takes dollars out of circulation. If the U.S. had used its surplus to significantly pay down the national debt, then government borrowing would have decreased. Smaller treasury offerings, by the law of supply and demand, would have resulted in lower interest rates, as investors competed for a dwindling supply of treasury bills. This should have resulted in lower interest rates for other long-term debts such as mortgages and corporate and municipal bonds. In addition, paying off the national debt would have reduced our annual interest payments, which could have increased the surplus.

Returning a surplus to taxpayers in the form of lower taxes would be an expansionary policy as more money would be available for goods.

IV. Balance of Trade (Imports Equals Exports)

FREE TRADE *is the concept that trade between countries should be free of restrictions, tariffs, and quotas so that the people of each country benefit economically from it as much as possible.* The ***PRINCIPLE OF COMPARATIVE ADVANTAGE*** *states that if each country specialized in what they do or produce best at the least cost, then all countries would benefit.* From an economic viewpoint, the principle of comparative advantage is just common sense. However, many

countries make economic decisions based on political considerations. They will often want to support local production of a commodity even though they could not compete favorably with a comparable foreign commodity. They can do this by either subsidizing the domestic commodity so it can be sold at a lower price or by restricting imports, which is a ban of free trade.

A ***POSITIVE BALANCE OF TRADE*** *results from a greater value of exports than imports in U.S. international trade and brings foreign dollars into our economy.* A positive balance of trade also tends to increase the value of the dollar in relationship to other currencies based on the supply and demand of our dollars in the international exchange market.

A ***NEGATIVE BALANCE OF TRADE*** *results when the value of our imports exceed the value of our exports.* Generally, this results in a lower dollar value in relationship to other currencies, due to the glut of dollars in the international exchange market. This has not been happening, as the dollar has remained strong despite large trade deficits. The reason for the dollar retaining its relatively high value has been relatively high U.S. interest rates coupled with a low rate of inflation and stability. It thus made dollars very desirable for foreign investment in the United States.

Our over-consuming economy spends more dollars on imports (e.g., Japanese and Korean-made cars, Korean electronics, and products of all categories from China) than our U.S. exports are worth.

> ***Our negative balance of trade was growing through most of the 1980s to the present. It still represents only a small portion of our national output.***

In 2005, our trade deficit was expected to be around $490 billion. As large as this seems, it is relatively small when compared to our over $12 trillion economy. In addition, the trade deficit does not reflect the amount earned by U.S. firms from their foreign investments. Contributing in large part to our trade deficits are unfair practices in a number of countries that restrict U.S. imports.

Negative balance of trade dollars are not totally lost to the U.S. economy. As long as foreign investors hold onto U.S. bonds and real estate or corporate stocks in America, there is no problem. Foreign investment in the U.S. can help to create jobs and keep interest rates down.

Daniel Griswold, the Associate Director of the Center for Trade Policy Studies, feels that the primary cause of our trade deficit is the gap between our savings and investment expenditure. This investment shortfall allows for foreign investment. We, in turn, use the foreign capital to buy foreign goods. On the whole, Mr. Griswold views a trade deficit as a healthy sign. Other experts don't agree with this economist and believe a point will be reached where the value of the dollar will dramatically fall because foreign holders will lose faith in the value of the dollar. This will create high prices for foreign goods that we have come to rely on and lead to a recession.

A. EXCHANGE RATES

EXCHANGE RATES *refer to the value of one country's currency compared to another's.* The changing value of the dollar in relationship to other currencies will affect our economy. When the dollar has a lower value, imports are discouraged, since they become more expensive. A low-valued dollar encourages exports, as it reduces the price of American goods to foreign buyers, who can purchase our goods with less of their currency.

A low-valued dollar encourages exports, whereas a high-valued dollar encourages imports.

A high-valued dollar encourages imports because foreign goods become less expensive to American purchasers. Similarly, a high-valued dollar discourages exports, as American goods become more expensive to foreign purchasers. When the value of the dollar drops too low, the major central banks of the world (US, Japanese and German) dip into their national treasuries to bolster the dollar by buying dollars.

This action by the central banks slows the decline in value of a currency, but generally will not stop its fall. Central bank activities only amount to a small percentage of the total trading volume in a currency (generally less than 10 percent). The forces of the marketplace govern the other 90 percent of trading volume.

B. JAPANESE INVESTMENTS IN U.S. REAL ESTATE

In the 1970s, the Japanese entered the U.S. real estate market with a strong presence. However, by 2000, their presence had materially diminished. When the Japanese economy was booming and the yen had a strong value against the dollar, Japanese companies considered U.S. investments to be very attractive. They were able to obtain low-interest loans from Japanese banks secured by corporate stock or Japanese real estate, which had dramatically increased in value. At one time, the supposed value of Tokyo real estate alone was estimated to be equal or greater than the real property value of all of California.

U.S. real estate investments that would have been negative cash flow situations for U.S. investors offered positive cash flows for Japanese investors who were paying less interest for their money. Japanese firms purchased a variety of properties from homes and ranches to hotels, office buildings, and golf courses. The Japanese firms were especially attracted to "trophy" office buildings; the competition to buy such structures in the Los Angeles area was primarily between various Japanese firms.

A number of factors contributed to a significant exit of Japanese investors from the U.S. market. A stronger dollar reduced the value in yen of the U.S. investments. The

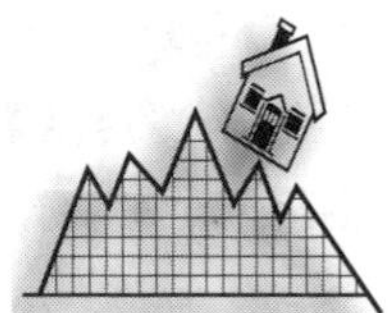

collapse of the Japanese stock market and real estate marketplace left lenders with insufficient security for their loans.

Increases in the interest rates charged by the lenders turned positive cash flows into negative cash flows. The result was lender foreclosures and properties being unloaded in a depressed marketplace.

C. THE STOCK MARKET

While there is no direct relationship between stock market cycles and real estate values in general, there is a relationship in specified areas such as luxury homes and vacation property.

In the late 1990s and early 2000s, the exuberance of the stock market, particularly in technology-related stocks, resulted in many mid-level management people as well as trades people becoming very wealthy based on the paper profits of their shares in personal accounts as well as IRAs. This increased wealth resulted in greater expectations as to life style with many people moving up to homes that they never thought they could afford. It also affected vacation homes sales. Both of these areas experienced unprecedented activity, and because of the economic function of supply and demand, significant increases in market value as the number of families with net worth exceeding $1,000,000 dramatically increased.

V. The Federal Government and Financing

A. NATIONAL HOUSING ACT OF 1934

This National Housing Act of 1934 established the Federal Housing Administration (FHA).

The ***FEDERAL HOUSING ADMINISTRATION (FHA)*** *is operated by the Department of Housing and Urban Development (HUD) and administers the federal loan program which insures mortgages, reducing lenders' risks and making them willing to give longer term residential loans at lower rates.* Because FHA loans allow a high loan-to-value ratio (LTV), the need for secondary financing was eliminated.

At times the interest rates set for FHA loans were unrealistically low. This resulted either in seller points to make the loans competitive, or in the unavailability of money for these loans. Therefore, the FHA went to a floating interest rate rather than a fixed rate. This insures the availability of FHA financing.

The purpose of FHA was to increase home ownership among lower income Americans. However, a recent study of FHA home loans made indicated that only 18 percent of the FHA insured loans made were in census tracts that were designated as low or moderate income.

The delinquency rate is more than double on FHA insured loans than for conventional loans. This is understandable because the lower down payment requirements attract borrowers who have been unable to save the down payment required for conventional loans. Such buyers don't have much of an incentive to sacrifice to prevent foreclosure when times get difficult.

B. VA LOANS

The GI Bill of Rights (U.S.C. Title 38, Chapter 37) established government guaranteed loans for veterans.

The ***DEPARTMENT OF VETERAN'S AFFAIRS (VA)*** *administers loans, which are guaranteed up to a maximum of $60,000.* Approved lenders are willing to make low or no down payment VA loans, since they will only suffer a loss on a defaulted loan if the loss suffered exceeds the VA loan guarantee.

C. FEDERAL NATIONAL MORTGAGE ASSOCIATION "FANNIE MAE"

FEDERAL NATIONAL MORTGAGE ASSOCIATION (FNMA) *is a federally sponsored, privately owned corporation that buys FHA, VA, and conventional mortgages or trust deeds from lenders in order to supply new funds (provides a secondary mortgage market) to mortgage companies and banks.*

FNMA buys loans for its portfolio, repackages loans, and sells them as mortgage-backed securities.

D. FEDERAL HOME LOAN MORTGAGE CORPORATION "FREDDIE MAC"

The ***FEDERAL HOME LOAN MORTGAGE CORPORATION (FHLMC)*** *is also a federally sponsored, privately owned corporation that buys FHA, VA and conventional mortgages or trust deeds from lenders in order to supply new funds (provides a secondary mortgage market) to savings banks, mortgage companies, and banks.*

The FHLMC buys mortgages and generally resells them as mortgage securities.

Fannie Mae and Freddie Mac are the two largest suppliers of mortgage capital. They buy conventional fixed-rate loans and adjustable rate mortgages (ARMs) on single-family homes and condos. They also purchase FHA/VA and multi-family loans. *Loans that meet the purchase requirements of Fannie Mae and Freddie Mac are called* ***CONFORMING LOANS***. ***NONCONFORMING LOANS****, which cannot be sold to Fannie Mae or Freddie Mac, would generally bear a higher rate of interest.* Jumbo loans are nonconforming loans because they exceed the dollar limitation for loan purchases set by Fannie Mae and Freddie Mac. This amount is changed annually. Like other nonconforming loans, jumbo loans bear an interest premium.

Effectively, Fannie Mae and Freddie Mac establish loan standards (guidelines) for most real estate loans in America.

There is current concern about accounting and management problems at Fannie Mae. The Bush administration asked congress for the power to reduce FNMA and FHLMC's portfolios, which now total $1.5 trillion. The Office of Federal Housing Enterprise Oversight stated that Fannie Mae's condition warrants significant supervision. Fannie Mae and Freddie Mac's problems could make it more difficult to obtain housing loans in the future.

E. GOVERNMENT NATIONAL MORTGAGE ASSOCIATION "GINNIE MAE"

The ***GOVERNMENT NATIONAL MORTGAGE ASSOCIATION (GNMA)*** *is a government corporation and an agency of HUD that guarantees assistance loans where other financing is not available.* Unlike Fannie Mae and Freddie Mac which actually "buy" mortgages, Ginnie Mae acts as a guarantor for a pool of FHA and VA loans from approved lenders. By selling government guaranteed certificates, it makes investments in mortgages easy. Ginnie Mae also purchases special assistance mortgages. These are usually low-income housing loans for which financing would not otherwise be available.

VI. The Secondary Mortgage Market

The ***SECONDARY MORTGAGE MARKET*** *is a marketplace that allows lenders to sell their loans to obtain cash to make new loans.* Fannie Mae, Freddie Mac and Ginnie Mae, as well as private firms, allow the mortgage market to generate new funds. This secondary mortgage market allows lenders to recoup loaned funds so that they can make loans again. The national secondary mortgage market results in more uniform mortgage rates with only slight regional differences.

Credit deficit areas benefit from the secondary mortgage market, bringing in investment capital from other areas of the nation and even from other countries.

During a credit crunch, lenders are willing to make long-term housing loans when they know they can liquidate the loans that meet specified requirements in the secondary mortgage market. Mortgage securities generated by the secondary mortgage market attract investors who ordinarily would not invest in mortgages. Government insured mortgage securities offer a safe and rewarding investment.

A. MORTGAGE WAREHOUSING

Mortgage bankers will accumulate inventories of loans that they will sell, in packages, to other lending and investment institutions. *Because of the need for capital, these mortgage originators will borrow on their inventory of loans. Borrowing on this inventory of loans is known as* ***MORTGAGE WAREHOUSING.***

If lenders believe that interest rates will drop they are likely to hold off selling their inventory of loans. If interest rates do drop, then the higher rate loans can be sold on the secondary mortgage market at a premium price. However, if a lender believes interest rates will rise, the lender will try to sell loans made as soon as possible after the loans were made. Otherwise the lender could be forced to sell loans at a discount to their value should interest rates rise.

When interest rates dropped sharply in the mid-'80s, and early 2000, savings and loan institutions found themselves with stacks of mortgages, which had a higher market value than book value. These loans were sold at a premium on the secondary mortgage market. Some firms unloaded their residential mortgage inventory to offset losses suffered in non-performing commercial loans.

B. FOREIGN INVESTMENT IN MORTGAGE-BACKED SECURITIES

European and Asian investment in mortgage-backed securities in 2004 and 2005 served to help the booming real estate market. Because of low returns from other investments and a significantly higher yield than U.S. Treasury notes, foreign cash is pouring into the market. An estimated 80 percent of the current $2.8 trillion in mortgages is expected to end up as mortgage-backed securities.

Strong investor demand has allowed lenders to offer better terms with relaxed qualifying standards. Just about any type of loan can be sold. The statement "Even a bankrupt arsonist can get financing" was attributed to a mortgage bank.

VII. Credit

Credit is essential to our present American economy.

It would be impractical for people to postpone large purchases, such as real property, until they save the cash.

As previously mentioned, if people suddenly decided to save for what they want, the demand for money would drop and interest rates would fall. Production would significantly slow down and we would have massive work layoffs.

During recessionary periods, lenders tend to be in a more liquid position because of the lessening demand for credit. Businesses tend to reduce inventory to eliminate short-term debt and reduce capital expenditures, which means less new, long-term debt as well. During expansionary periods, lenders are in a much less liquid position because of the demand for credit to expand inventories (short-term debt), as well as to expand production with new capital expenditures (long-term debt).

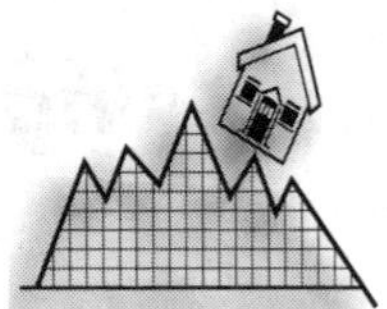

Chapter 3

A. INTEREST

Interest is the rental charge for the use of money.

Interest is expressed as a percentage of the money being used. Loan costs are based on the supply and demand for funds, and on risk. A risk-free loan (such as on government securities) would, therefore, establish a base interest rate. Because loans cost both time and money to service, it would be possible to obtain better terms for one large loan than for many small loans, provided the risk factors were equal.

Since second trust deeds and mortgages present greater risks to lenders, they generally carry a higher rate of interest than would primary financing.

The ***ANNUAL PERCENTAGE RATE (APR)*** *is the effective interest rate that includes all loan charges.* Due to various loan origination fees, points and loan fees, the true or annual percentage rate (APR) could be greater than the rate specified on the note (nominal rate). In comparing loans, the effective rate is, therefore, more important than the nominal rate.

Lenders who require a compensating balance on deposit effectively increase the rate of interest they receive. A ***COMPENSATING BALANCE*** *is a deposit that must be kept with the lender as a condition of making the loan.* For example, assume a lender requires the borrower of a $100,000 loan at 12 percent to keep 25 percent, or $25,000, on deposit at 2 percent interest. The borrower would be paying $12,000 interest per year on $100,000, and receiving 2 percent on $25,000, or $500, making the net cost of the loan to be $11,500. However, the borrower is really getting only $75,000. The borrower is paying $11,500 on a $75,000 loan:

$$\frac{\$11,500}{\$75,000} = 15\ 1/3\%\ \text{Interest}$$

B. POINTS

If a lender wanted an interest rate of 8 percent, the lender would not want to give a loan at 7¾ percent interest unless the loan yielded the equivalent of 8 percent interest. *The lender can obtain this equivalency by charging* ***POINTS****. One point is 1 percent of the loan amount.* Lenders consider each point to be the equivalent of 1/8 percent interest. Therefore, a lender who wanted 8 percent interest could obtain the equivalency of 8 percent by making a 7¾ percent loan and charging 2 points. For tax purposes, points are considered interest for the buyer and are therefore deductible.

If the buyers expected to live in a home for 20 years, they would likely be better off to pay points and obtain a lower rate of interest. However, if they expected to remain in the home for only a few years, they would likely be better off with a higher rate of interest and a lower or no-point loan.

Points are really prepaid interest, in the form of more money down on a loan. Points are sometimes called "loan origination fees."

By being charged points, the borrower really pays a higher rate of interest than the rate stated; the psychological effect of charging points is believed to be less negative than a higher interest rate. Lenders who intend to sell loans want sufficient points to cover any required sales discount, as well as to enhance their profit. Points are generally added to the loan principal.

Besides points and costs associated with a loan, lenders charge fees for their services in making the loan. For example, they might charge appraisal fees, fees for drafting instruments, escrow fees (if they perform the escrow), etc.

Some lenders charge fees that seem unrelated to the cost of services and appear to simply be a means of improving the lender's profit. Such "garbage" fees include:

1. Loan Application Fee
2. Review Fee (a charge to review the escrow settlement figures)
3. Courier Fee (a fee for the movement of documents)
4. Verification Fee (a charge to verify account balances)
5. Warehouse Fee (a fee charged for holding the loan until it becomes part of a large package sold to investors)

C. INTEREST BARRIER

When the demand for loan funds exceeds the funds available, a credit crunch occurs. The demand for funds causes interest rates to rise, bringing more investment funds into the market.

Housing is one of the first areas to feel the effect of tight money. Because of the large amount financed, a change in interest can have a significant effect on the monthly payments. For many years real estate lenders believed that there was an interest barrier of 10 percent. They did not believe that borrowers would pay more than 10 percent for a housing loan. When interest rates soared to 18 percent in the early 1980s, this barrier was crossed and new loan activity ground to a virtual halt. Later, when interest fell to 10 percent range, borrowing was stimulated.

Many real estate analysts hold to an 8 percent or 10 percent barrier. They believe high interest rates of to be the "kiss of death" for home sales. It is a hard barrier for buyers to cross.

When consumer confidence is high, a raise in interest rates below the barrier will not have a significant effect on homebuyers who can still qualify for loans. However, the higher rates will reduce the number of potential buyers who can qualify for a loan.

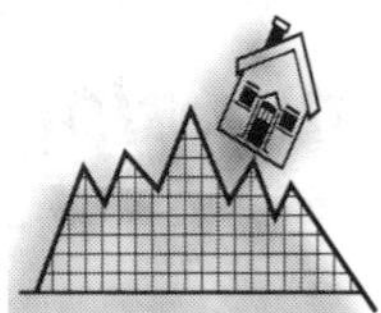

D. EFFECTS OF HIGH INTEREST RATES ON RELOCATION

Owners who have fixed rate loans below current interest rates do not like to give up bargain rates in favor of new loans at market rates. Owners who are economically able to move up to better housing or who desire a smaller home or a different area have less of an incentive to move, since this would mean the loss of an advantageous rate.

VIII. Source of Loan Funds

New development and real estate purchases depend on a flow of funds.

The source of funds for real estate financing comes from either private or business deposits in financial institutions (which make loans), or from investors lending directly to borrowers. Direct loans are generally made through a loan broker or a member of a mortgage syndicate.

Life insurance companies invest their money in stocks, bonds and real estate until they need to pay off a beneficiary of their policies. Life insurance companies are large depositories of funds, which result from the forced savings provisions of many cash value life insurance policies as well as from those of retirement programs.

Savings banks previously invested the majority of their funds in mortgages and trust deeds. Due to deregulation changes, savings banks have increased investment options, making them indistinguishable from commercial banks.

Commercial banks have been increasing their mortgage loans largely because of high interest home equity financing and their ability to profit on loans they originate and sell. Federal regulations actually encourage mortgage loans by banks, as these loans call for the lowest category of reserve requirements.

Pension funds have a great deal of money to invest, but pension directors have a duty to obtain the highest rate of return consistent with safety. Pension funds have been investing both in mortgages as well as mortgage securities. Some pension funds have formed partnerships with Real Estate Investment Trusts to buy or develop real estate for investment purposes. They are going to ownership to increase the return on their investments.

A. REAL ESTATE INVESTMENT TRUSTS (REITs)

These popular publicly owned trusts avoid the double taxation of corporations. They must invest in real estate or real property securities. Some REITs invest solely in mortgages (mortgage REITs) while some invest in both real estate and mortgages (hybrid REITs).

REITs are seldom loan originators. They generally buy their loans on the secondary mortgage market.

B. MORTGAGE BROKERS AND MORTGAGE BANKERS

Mortgage brokers arrange loans between borrowers and lenders.

MORTGAGE BROKERS *do not make loans. They are middle persons who bring together lenders and borrowers.* They often handle sub-prime lending where the borrower's credit is impaired. These loans are at relatively high interest and the borrower usually pays significant loan origination fees (points). Lenders might be individuals or lending institutions. Mortgage brokers generally keep the origination fees. However, mortgage brokers might arrange loans at market interest rates for banks and other lenders, usually at a lesser fee.

Mortgage bankers use their own funds to make loans, which they then sell to lenders.

Lenders may be pension funds, mortgage REITs or lending institutions. They keep all or part of loan origination costs for their efforts.

MORTGAGE BANKERS *(also called mortgage companies) generally service the loans they sell and receive a fee for this service while mortgage brokers seldom service the loans they arrange.*

C. THE ROLE OF THE INTERNET IN LOAN ORIGINATION

In 1999, an estimated 900,000 loans were processed on the Internet. In 2006, the number of loans will likely exceed 2,000,000. The Internet can cut the processing time for the average loan down from over one month to just a few days. A prospective borrower can be qualified for a loan in a matter of hours.

In some cases, Internet loan applications are handled by the sales agent, although many borrowers arrange their own loans. Exposed to many lenders on the Internet, borrowers can become informed as to which lender is offering the loan that best meets their needs.

Eventually, competition should reduce loan costs. Some mortgage bankers and mortgage brokers are afraid that the growing importance of the Internet will reduce their roles in the mortgage market. Other mortgage brokers and mortgage bankers are getting their own Internet lending sites.

Some of the consumer loan sites are:

eloan.com
homeshark.com

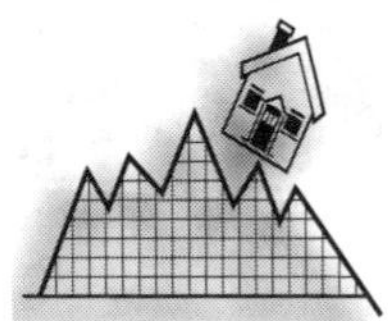

homeadvisor.msn.com
mortgageloan.com
countrywide.com
lendingtree.com
loantek.com
homeowners.com
mtgtech.com
priceline.com
quickenloans.com
mortgageexpo.com
nationalmortgage.com
ditech.com
mortgagecentral.com

In addition, most home marketing sites have links to mortgage lending sites.

D. COMPETITION FOR SAVINGS

There is a competition for savings among banks, savings banks, insurance companies, brokerage firms, etc. The government is also a competitor (by means of offering Treasury CDs, notes, and bonds). By offering high yields, the Treasury attracts a portion of savings, which reduces the amount of funds available for lending purposes. In the process, interest rates may be forced up due to increased competition for the available funds.

E. INTERMEDIATION AND DISINTERMEDIATION

When individuals are uncertain of the future, the propensity to save increases and more money is deposited into savings institutions. *The depositing of funds into savings institutions (banks and savings banks) is known as* **INTERMEDIATION**.

The rapid withdrawal of funds from savings institutions is known as **DISINTERMEDIATION**. It is usually the result of greater returns being available elsewhere, such as from broker money market accounts or bonds. To counter the loss of funds, savings institutions would raise interest rates on their deposits, which would mean a higher interest rate charged to borrowers.

F. ASSUMABILITY OF LOANS (Due on Sale Clause)

Except for FHA, VA loans, and some adjustable rate mortgages, most loans made by institutional, as well as noninstitutional lenders, contain due on sale (or alienation) clauses. A ***DUE ON SALE CLAUSE*** *states that the entire loan becomes due and payable when the property is sold, assigned, or transferred*. This clause prohibits loan assumptions without the lender's consent. Due on sale clauses are enforceable for all loans by federal law as of October 15, 1985. This gives a lender of a long-term loan an opportunity to review the interest rate being charged on a loan. The lender has the option of allowing an assumption at the old interest rate, granting a new loan at a different rate, or requiring that the loan be paid in full.

IX. Lender Crisis

Lenders never anticipated the inflation and high interest rates of the late 1970s.

The typical savings and loan had invested the majority of its funds in low-interest, fixed rate mortgages. As interest rates rose, lenders had to pay higher interest to borrow money. In many cases, the average cost of savings accounts exceeded the average interest rates being received, which resulted in losses that eroded the lenders' capital.

In an attempt to balance the high interest paid on savings and the low interest received on fixed loans, many lenders engaged in a furious expansion program. They opened new branches to bring in new money that they could lend out at higher interest rates, and thus raise their average yield above their costs.

Some lenders who suffered losses tried to recoup these losses through more aggressive lending policies. Regulatory changes allowed savings and loans to invest in other types of real estate. High-risk loans and investments, such as junk bonds, contributed to many savings and loan failures.

Because of the high interest rates paid to depositors, lenders were attracted to the high yields of large foreign investments, as well as to large office and commercial developments in areas such as Texas, where there seemed to be an insatiable demand for capital. Many lenders put too much of their capital into a single investment or a single industry. During the 1980s, the drop in oil prices resulted in Texas lenders holding a great many loans in default.

Lenders were also badly hurt by the huge drop in farmland values in the 1980s, as well as by the overbuilding of office structures.

Lenders, after the savings and loan and bank failures, retreated from aggressive lending policies and adopted a more conservative attitude, including higher down payment requirements.

The ***RESOLUTION TRUST CORPORATION (RTC)*** *was set up by the U. S. Treasury to bail out the failed saving and loan associations.* It was formed to pay off depositors who had insured accounts of up to $100,000 (now FDIC insured). The RTC seized over 800 S&Ls, whose savings accounts were sold to other financial institutions. Their loan portfolios (real estate properties) were also liquidated by auction all across the nation.

A. PROBLEMS OF LOW DOWN PAYMENTS

A disproportionate share of problem loans stem from low down payment loans.

During the 1980 and 1990 recessions, a great many low down payment borrowers defaulted on their loans. Causes included the loss of jobs, as well as a market in which many owners' equity disappeared with lower sales prices as sales declined.

The Federal Home Loan Mortgage Corporation (Freddie Mac) now considers all loans for 90 percent or more of purchase price to be high-risk. Loans from 80 to 89 percent are rated medium-risk, and loans of less than 80 percent are rated low-risk.

Lenders, by requiring higher down payments, not only reduce their own risk, but also make their loans more readily saleable on the secondary mortgage market. Higher down payment requirements adversely affected first-time homebuyers. By 2000, housing loans were again being made with down payments in the 5 percent to 10 percent range because of competition in the marketplace.

In 1994, Fannie Mae's Community Homebuyer's Loans were introduced in order to stimulate the economy. Financial institutions could offer 5 percent down (only 3 percent of which must come from the borrower) loans to qualified low-income, first-time homebuyers. This helped get people out of apartments and into houses.

B. PRIVATE MORTGAGE INSURANCE (PMI)

For many years, private mortgage insurers did little besides make money through insuring low-risk loans.

PRIVATE MORTGAGE INSURANCE *is insurance charged by private companies to cover the top 20 percent of a loan amount if the buyer does not meet the lender's 20 percent down payment requirement.* Private mortgage insurance is paid up front when a loan is obtained or simply added to monthly payments. In an appreciating marketplace their risks were relatively slight. Even in cases of default, high property sale value usually resulted in little or no loss. They allowed many people to become homeowners by insuring mortgages with 10 percent or even less down. Without this insurance, many lenders would have required 20 percent or more as a down payment. General Electric Capital Mortgage Insurance also required prospective borrowers to attend classes on homeowner responsibilities in order to qualify for loans. It was thought that if people understood the importance of credit and prompt monthly payments, the default ratio would be low.

During recessionary periods, there have been wholesale defaults. Instead of homes appreciating, many areas experienced a dramatic decline in value. What had previously been an almost risk-free business became a high-risk business. Several insurers left the mortgage insurance field.

Private mortgage insurance allows people who can afford only a low down payment to own a home.

C. LOAN-TO-VALUE RATIO (LTV)

A lender's ***LOAN-TO-VALUE RATIO (LTV)*** *is the ratio (percentage) of a loan amount to the value of a property, based on risk exposure*. The loan-to-value ratio is much higher for residential property than it is for commercial property that historically has presented greater risk to investors.

It generally takes longer to sell improved, nonresidential property because the market is not as large and is more susceptible to economic fluctuations. Lenders will, therefore, customarily provide lower loan-to-value financing for this type of property. Because industrial property has a thinner market than commercial or office buildings, lenders will generally provide an even lower loan-to-value ratio for industrial property. Unimproved non-agricultural property would likely have the highest loan-to-value ratio.

Lenders are, however, likely to lend more for residential lots than they would for nonresidential building sites.

The ***FEDERAL FINANCIAL INSTITUTIONS REFORM, RECOVERY, AND ENFORCEMENT ACT OF 1989 (FIRREA)*** *set up the Resolution Trust Corporation to deal with failed lenders*. It also included requirements for licensing and certification of appraisers. One of the supposed causes of the failure of many lenders was the fact that loans were made based on appraisals that bore little basis in reality. The appraisers, not the lenders, were considered to be at fault. Every state is required to set minimum appraiser standards, and the Appraisal Standards Board (ASB) of the Appraisal Foundation was given the responsibility for the Uniform Standards of Professional Appraisal Practice (USPAP). Appraisers were required to conform to these standards. FIRREA failed to address the cause of unrealistic appraisals, which was lender pressure to come up with values that reflected sale prices.

Real estate agents want sales to close and mortgage bankers want to make loans. A completed transaction means financial success. An appraisal that does not justify a required loan means a broken transaction and no profit. By 2000, lenders were again putting pressure on appraisers as they did in the 1980s. Instead of pressure from savings and loans, the pressure was coming from mortgage bankers that had replaced S & Ls and banks as the major originators of mortgage loans. Since mortgage bankers do not retain the loans they originate, they do not really bear the risk of default. Their interest is to make and sell loans.

There have been many articles written about the fact that the appraisal process has again become corrupted. Appraisers are regularly receiving information from mortgage bankers and mortgage brokers with terms such as target value or value needed. What the lender is really asking is for the appraiser to justify a set value. In other words, work backwards from a value set by a purchase contract. Appraisers who consistently fail to reach values required for funding a loan risk future business. Apparently, there are many appraisers who will meet the targets set. According to Freddie Mac, 97 percent of home purchase appraisals "hit" the value of the sales contract. Because of these results, Freddie Mac does not require a formal appraisal for mortgages with 20 percent or greater down payment.

While there is no significant problem with "optimistic" appraisals should values continue to rise, a recession could bring catastrophic losses to lenders holding home real estate mortgages as well as to Freddie Mac and Fannie Mae.

D. PREPAYMENT PENALTIES

If a loan specifies payments of a set dollar amount or more, the loan can be prepaid without penalty. Otherwise, if a borrower wished to prepay a loan there could be a significant prepayment penalty. Law limits this penalty in some states, such as to six months' interest. The penalty may also be limited by state law to a set period of time, such as it may only be charged if the loan is paid off within the first 5 years. Generally, adjustable rate loans do not have prepayment penalties. If a purchaser only expected to remain in a house for a few years, the purchaser might be better off with an adjustable rate mortgage rather than a mortgage with a prepayment penalty. In that case, the purchaser would also be able to take advantage of the introductory or teaser interest rate.

X. Other Forms of Loans and Financing

A. HOME EQUITY LOANS

Tax law changes that have phased out the deductibility of interest on consumer loans have made home equity loans more attractive.

While there are some limitations, home loan interest generally remains deductible. These changes have resulted in the increased use of home equity loans. Homeowners are able to use their proceeds to buy goods or to pay off consumer loans with non-deductible interest and still retain the income tax deduction. Interest on a home equity loan up to $100,000 is deductible, providing the total home loan does not exceed the home's fair value. Home equity loans are presently available up to 125 percent of a home's market value. Lenders making such loans demand good credit as well as a premium interest rate.

B. CREATIVE FINANCING

CREATIVE FINANCING is simply seller financing. Seller financing is used when other acceptable financing is unavailable or when there is an interest advantage to the

Changes in Financing

In the late 1970s and early 1980s, lenders who had large inventories of fixed-rate mortgages were in serious financial trouble. They were obtaining a lower rate of return on their loans than they had to pay depositors. Because of this problem period, many lenders indicated that they would never again make long-term, fixed-rate mortgages. For a period of time, some lenders made only adjustable rate mortgages, but competition of the marketplace has resulted in the great majority of mortgages again being long-term loans at fixed rates of interest.

Financing has undergone many changes as to loan types.

Adjustable Rate Mortgages (ARMs). With these mortgages, the interest rate is adjusted to the cost of money. Lenders are protected against paying more for money than they receive.

Adjustable rate loans are not desirable for people on a fixed income. They are also not desirable for commercial and business property, unless rents that the property owners charge are similarly adjustable to the same criteria as the loan. Otherwise, an increase in interest could result in a negative cash flow.

Adjustable rate mortgages generally have an initial (or teaser) rate, which is less than the index rate for the loan plus the margin over the index at which the loan is pegged. The low initial rate is often used for loan qualifying purposes, allowing buyers to qualify for loans having an adjustable rate while unable to qualify for fixed rate loans for the same amount. Interest adjustment periods will vary. There is customarily a cap on any adjustment as well as a cap on the interest rate for the life of the loan.

Renegotiable Rate Mortgage. A Renegotiable Rate Mortgage is a short-term, fixed-rate mortgage that has elements of an adjustable rate mortgage. As an example, a 5-30 mortgage would be written for 30 years. There would be a fixed interest rate for 5 years. At the end of the 5-year period, the borrower could pay off the loan or the lender would rewrite the loan at the then prevailing interest rate. The lender would be protected against rising interest rates, as the greater lender risk would be for a relatively short term.

Fixed Rate Loans have a constant interest rate over the term of the loan.

While lenders originally went to long-term loans to keep payments down, 15-year loans are now gaining popularity among buyers who are concerned about financing costs. Payments on a 15-year loan are not significantly greater than payments on a 30-year loan, but the total interest paid is much larger on the 30-year loan. For example, a $100,000 loan for 15 years at 13 percent would have monthly payments of $1,265.27.

(continued)

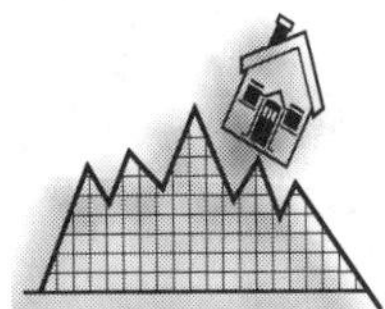

The payments for the same loan for 30 years would be $1,106.21, a difference of only $159.06. However, the total interest paid on the 15-year loan would be $127,748, while the interest on the 30-year loan would amount to $298,235. Lenders like these 15-year loans, since their risk is thereby reduced.

Some lenders offer a one-eighth to one-half percent interest reduction for these shorter-term loans, which means an even lower payment differential between the 15-year and 30-year loans.

Between a 15-year and a 30-year trust deed (mortgage), there is a significant savings in the amount of interest paid.

The advantages of the 15-year loan over the 30-year loan assume that a person making payments on a 30-year loan will not invest the difference in payments. However, if it were invested, it would reduce and could even eliminate the advantage that a 15-year loan appears to have over a 30-year loan. The advantage of 15-year financing further decreases for higher tax brackets because borrowers have less interest to deduct.

The Trustco Mortgage Company of Toronto has changed its monthly mortgage payments to weekly and biweekly. A biweekly payment (one-half of the monthly payment) is paid every two weeks or 26 times a year. Some U.S. lenders have adopted this idea, but require the borrower to maintain a checking account where the payments are deducted automatically. This tends to overcome the objection of most lenders to the added paperwork of additional payments.

An economic advantage of weekly payments of one-fourth of the monthly payment, or biweekly payments of one-half the monthly payment, is that the borrower is paying for the equivalent of 13 months each year. On a $50,000, 13 percent trust deed for 30 years, the interest payment is reduced from $149,113 to $78,171, and the 30-year loan is actually paid in full in 17.8 years.

80-20 Loans. A number of mortgage companies are putting together no down payment loans by using both a 1st and 2nd mortgage. The first mortgage is at 80 percent of value so that mortgage insurance is not required. The second mortgage is a much higher interest rate loan for 20 percent of value. Because the homebuyer does not have any equity invested, the loans are very risky.

Interest-Only Loans. There are a variety of interest-only loans but they all have a day of reckoning when payments must start on the principal or the loan must be paid off. Some of these loans are adjustable loans. In some cases, the payment is fixed but the interest rate can increase meaning negative amortization. The result is that when the interest-only period ends, payment will have to be made on a much larger loan. High housing prices have made these loans quite popular.

(continued)

Option ARM. The option ARM allows the borrower to choose the monthly payment from several choices that could even be less than the interest, which would result in negative amortization. The option payment is for a stated period of time after which there will be some sort of amortized loan or loan payoff.

Sub Prime Loans. Borrowers with credit problems can still obtain home financing. Many lenders specialize in high-interest mortgage loans for borrowers who fail to meet the loan criteria of most major lenders.

Buy Down Loans are common for new construction. The developer pays cash (points) to the lender in return for a below-market interest rate. The below-market rate may be for only a few years or for the life of the loan.

Zero Interest Loans are actually buy-down loans where the buyer pays the interest as part of the price of the property. A typical zero interest loan requires a one-third down payment and the balance to be paid over a short period, such as five years. For example, on a $90,000 condominium the buyer might pay $30,000 down and make 60 monthly payments of $1,000 each.

Graduated Payment Mortgages (GPMs) meet the needs of many younger buyers. The low initial payments fit their current budget and the payments increase in the same manner as the borrower's income normally would. Some of these loans have a negative amortization during the first few years. Loans with negative amortizations generally require a substantial down payment.

purchaser. In times of high interest rates, there is great interest in creative financing. The majority of conventional loans have alienation clauses (due on sale) that prohibit loan assumption. However, if a loan does not include this prohibition, the loan can be assumed by a buyer, and the seller can partially finance the buyer by use of a carry-back second trust deed (or mortgage) or by use of wraparound financing.

A ***WRAPAROUND LOAN*** *is a new loan written for the amount of the existing loan, together with the seller's carry-back financing*. With a wraparound loan, the seller makes the payments on the existing financing, and the buyer pays the seller on the wraparound loan.

Creative financing can benefit both buyers and sellers in that sellers can get higher returns on loans than they can from most investments and still provide buyers with below market financing. However, sellers can also assume considerable risk in this way, since they rely on buyers not defaulting.

Since prices are affected by financing, exceptional financing can result in a higher price. For example, the monthly payments on a $100,000, 20-year loan at 13.5 percent would be $1,207.40, but at 9 percent interest that payment would cover a loan of $134,000.

A disadvantage of seller financing is that the seller's equity remains non liquid (the seller cannot sell the loan). To sell the loan, which is usually a second trust deed at a below-market interest rate, the seller will usually be required to give a significant discount.

Another disadvantage of seller financing is the fact that the seller has the burden of servicing the loan. For a fee, the seller can turn this duty over to a financial institution.

C. THE PRIME RATE

The term ***PRIME RATE*** *has historically referred to the interest rate that a lender offers to its most favored corporate borrower*. This rate is tied to the rate set by the Federal Reserve for short-term loans. Because many loans are tied to the prime rate, an increase in the rate has significant effect on a lender's income. Generally, the stated prime rate of a lender is not necessarily the lowest rate offered to a triple A rated firm. Big businesses are able to negotiate lower loan rates.

A number of borrowers had brought suit against lenders who they alleged had artificially pegged their prime rate above their actual prime rate in order to increase interest charged on loans pegged to the prime rate. Today the prime rate is regarded as that rate declared by the lender to be the prime rate, even though loans may be made at lower rates.

D. MINORITY FINANCING

Lenders are prohibited from discriminating based on race under the Equal Credit Opportunity Act. However, race is a factor in owner financing. Whites appear to be more reluctant to supply owner financing to black purchasers than to white purchasers. Lenders still tend to discriminate, and as a result, minority borrowers are more likely to pay more in fees, points, and interest than would a non-minority borrower. Many lenders have been fined or have paid damages for various discriminatory practices.

E. ARBITRAGE

ARBITRAGE *is the process of taking advantage of a price or interest differential in order to make a profit*. An example would be to borrow at one interest rate and invest at a higher rate. When sellers finance buyers with land contracts or wraparound type loans, they usually get a higher rate of interest than they are paying on prior secured debts.

F. TRADING ON EQUITY

TRADING ON EQUITY *is trading in real estate making use of the concept that sophisticated investors are not concerned with the rate of interest they must pay as long as they can obtain a higher rate for the use of the money*. Sophisticated investors are concerned with their total return, which includes their cash flow and benefits to income sheltered from taxes. In an inflationary market, equity created by inflation can be used to pyramid real estate holdings. By refinancing, or by secondary financing, cash can be pulled out of real property to use as down payments on other property. As long as the total return from the new investment exceeds the loan costs, trading on equity is an economically favorable course of action. However, an economic downturn can lead to disaster.

XI. CHAPTER SUMMARY

Money is our medium of exchange. While **paper money** has no intrinsic value, it is accepted based upon the faith that others will also accept it. **Checkbook money** is money that is transferred in the form of checks.

The **velocity of money** is the average number of times each dollar is used to purchase new goods and services, on average, within a period of time within the entire economy. An increase in the propensity to save would reduce the velocity of money and decrease the Gross Domestic Product.

Irving Fisher theorized that doubling the money supply would double prices. **Milton Friedman** carried Fisher's theory further with the idea that for a stable economy, our money supply should increase in correspondence to our ability to produce. Friedman's views, known as **Monetarism**, have influenced the Federal Reserve System.

The **Federal Reserve System** is our nation's central bank. It is a bank for other banks making loans, and it acts as a clearinghouse for checks. It is also the bank of the federal government. It protects consumers in credit transactions and manages the nation's money supply.

The Federal Reserve, by its **monetary policy**, can have a large effect on our economy. The Federal Reserve can control the money supply by changing the reserve requirements, raising or lowering its discount rate, and through the buying or selling of government securities.

Besides the Federal Reserve's monetary policy, the economy is affected by our government's **fiscal policy**. By increasing or decreasing government spending and taxes, the federal government can affect disposable income. When the federal government finances a deficit by borrowing from the public, it "crowds out" private investment and raises interest rates because of an increased supply of bonds, which lowers bond prices and simultaneously raises interest rates.

Other influences on our financial economy are the **federal deficit** and our **balance of trade**.

By creating a secondary market for existing loans, **Fannie Mae**, **Freddie Mac**, and **Ginnie Mae**, as well as private firms, allow lenders to generate funds for new loans.

The sources of real estate loans are private and business savings. There is a competition for savings, and investments offering higher yields tend to be the users of savings. A variety of loan types are available to meet various situations.

XII. GLOSSARY OF KEY TERMS

80-20 Loans – 100 percent financing using an 80 percent first mortgage and a 20 percent second mortgage.

Adjustable Rate Mortgage (ARM) – A mortgage subject to future interest adjustment based on future changes in an interest rate index.

Arbitrage – Taking advantage of a price or interest differential. In real estate it has come to mean buying a property at one interest rate and selling it at a higher rate.

Balance of Trade – The difference between the value of exports and that of imports.

Checkbook Money – Money transferred in the form of checks rather than currency.

Compensating Balance – A lender requirement that a portion of the loan proceeds be kept on deposit with the lender.

Conforming Loan – A loan that meets Freddie Mac and Fannie Mae purchase requirements.

Creative Financing – Seller carried financing.

Crowding Out – Government borrowing that raises interest rates and thus excludes some private borrowers from the marketplace.

Discount Rate – The interest rate charged by the Federal Reserve for loans to depository institutions.

Disintermediation – The rapid withdrawal of funds from lending institutions because higher interest is being offered elsewhere.

Due On Sale Clause – A clause in a trust deed or mortgage requiring that a loan be paid upon sale (not assumable).

Exchange Rate – The exchange value of the dollar in relationship to other currencies.

Federal Deficit – The spending of more money by the federal government than it receives in taxes and other revenues.

Federal Deposit Insurance Corporation (FDIC) – A federal agency that insures depositor bank accounts to a maximum of $100, 000.

Federal Home Loan Mortgage Corporation (FHLMC, Freddie Mac) – A federal agency created to increase the availability of mortgage credit. It buys approved conventional residential loans and sells them to investors, in addition to selling mortgage participation certificates.

Federal Home Loan Bank – The federal regulatory and credit agency for all federal savings banks.

Federal National Mortgage Association (FNMA, Fannie Mae) – A private corporation that provides a secondary mortgage market.

Federal Reserve – Our nation's central bank that controls our money supply.

Fiscal Policy – The government's policy of increasing or decreasing both spending and taxes to affect the disposable income of consumers.

Fisher, Irving – The economist who theorized that doubling a nation's money supply would merely double prices.

Friedman, Milton – An economist who believes the economy can expand 3-5 percent per year and that increasing the money supply at the rate of growth will allow prices to remain stable. Friedman's views are known as "Monetarism."

Government National Mortgage Association (GNMA, Ginnie Mae) – A government corporation within the Department of Housing and Urban Development (HUD). It attracts financing for residential loans by selling mortgage-backed securities (MBS). It purchases mortgages for low income housing where loans are not otherwise available, and also disposes of federally owned mortgages.

Graduated Payment Mortgage (GPM) – A loan in which the payments increase at agreed times without a change in the interest rate.

Growing Equity Mortgage (GEM) – A graduated payment mortgage designed to materially shorten the payoff period.

Interest – Money charged for the use of money or credit.

Interest Only Loans – A non amortized loan with lower payments (interest only).

Intermediation – The deposit of savings into bank and savings bank accounts.

Jumbo Loan – A loan that exceeds the maximum amount for a home loan to be purchased by Fannie Mae or Freddie Mac.

Loan-To-Value Ratio (LTV) – The ratio or percentage of value that a lender will lend on a property.

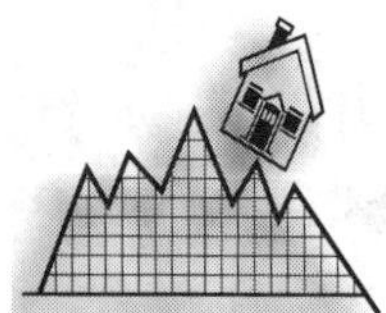

Chapter 3

Monetarism – The views expounded by Milton Friedman that the money supply could grow proportionately to the economy without causing prices to increase.

Monetary Policy – The policy of the Federal Reserve in controlling the money supply.

Money – Our medium of exchange.

National Housing Act of 1934 – The act that established the Federal Housing Administration (FHA).

Nonconforming Loan – A loan that fails to meet Fannie Mae and Freddie Mac purchase requirements.

Open Market Operations – The Fed's ability to buy and sell securities to regulate the money supply.

Option ARM – Loan where borrower at his or her option can make payments of interest only or possibly less.

Points – Percentages added to a loan to make a loan more attractive to a lender.

Prepayment Penalty – Penalty for paying off a loan early.

Prime Rate – The rate of interest offered by a commercial bank to its most favored borrowers.

Private Mortgage Insurance (PMI) – Insurance protecting lender against buyer's default.

Reintermediation – The return of dollars to savings accounts after their previous withdrawal.

Reserve Requirements – The requirement of the Federal Reserve as to the proportion of a bank's deposits that must be kept in reserve.

Secondary Mortgage Market – The purchase and sale of existing mortgages and trust deeds.

Sub Prime Loan – High-interest loan made to person who does not qualify for normal loan.

Trading On Equity – Borrowing on property in order to invest in other property offering a greater return than is being paid in loan interest.

Velocity of Money – The number of times money changes hands on average during a period of time throughout the entire economy.

Warehousing – A lender borrowing on its loan inventory until it can be sold.

XIII. CLASS DISCUSSION TOPICS

1. Why would you favor a tax cut?

2. What rates are currently being paid in your area for daily deposits and one-year deposits? How can these rates affect the mortgage market?

3. What are current down payment requirements of your local lenders?

4. What action might be taken to combat inflation?

5. What action might be taken to combat a recession?

6. Would you advise a 15-year loan to a buyer who could afford the additional payment over a 30-year loan? Why?

7. How can lenders affect the growth and character of your community?

XIV. CHAPTER 3 QUIZ

1. If everyone in the United States began to double his or her rate of savings, the effect would be:

   a. greater unemployment.
   b. an increase in the gross domestic product.
   c. an increase in the velocity of money.
   d. inflation.

2. According to Irving Fisher, doubling the nation's money supply would:

   a. lower prices by one third.
   b. double prices.
   c. increase the velocity of money.
   d. be deflationary.

3. To fight inflation, the Federal Reserve could:

   a. buy government securities.
   b. increase government spending.
   c. lower taxes.
   d. raise interest rates.

4. The following are expansionary monetary policies of the Federal Reserve, except:

   a. reducing the discount rate.
   b. buying government bonds.
   c. raising taxes.
   d. reducing bank reserve requirements.

5. Exports from the U.S. would be encouraged by:

   a. a low valued dollar.
   b. a negative balance of trade.
   c. U.S. deficit.
   d. U.S. inflation.

6. A loan that meets the purchase requirements of Fannie Mae and Freddie Mac would be a:

   a. jumbo loan.
   b. nonconforming loan.
   c. conforming loan.
   d. commercial loan.

7. The following are active in the secondary mortgage market, except:
   a. Ginnie Mae.
   b. FHA.
   c. Freddie Mac.
   d. Fannie Mae.

8. When would a mortgage banker be interested in selling mortgages it originated in quick fashion?
   a. When it believes interest rates will drop.
   b. When it believes interest rates will rise.
   c. When the loans are conforming.
   d. When points are involved.

9. A difference between mortgage bankers and mortgage brokers is:
   a. mortgage brokers require PMI.
   b. mortgage bankers act as middlemen.
   c. mortgage bankers use their own funds.
   d. mortgage brokers service the loans.

10. An economic advantage of taking out a home equity loan to pay off a credit card balance would be:
   a. the shorter repayment period.
   b. credit repair.
   c. points.
   d. the deductibility of interest.

ANSWERS: 1. a; 2. b; 3. d; 4. c; 5. a; 6. c; 7. b; 8. b; 9. c; 10. d

LEARNING OBJECTIVES

By understanding reasons for urban growth, growth patterns, and the economics of cities, you will be prepared to predict future urban development patterns.

City development dates back to the ancient city of Babylon, with hanging gardens, one of the seven wonders of the world.

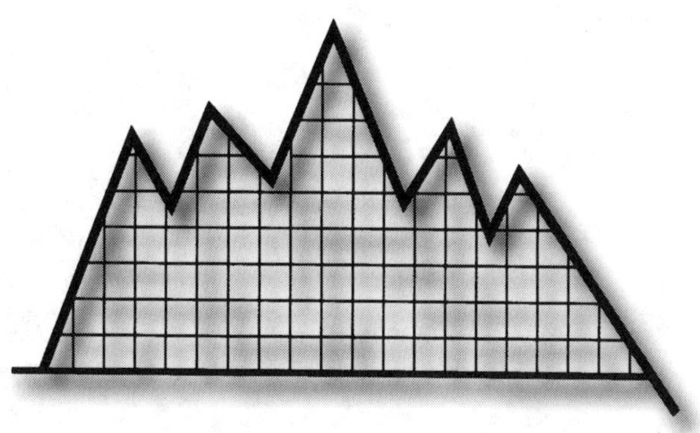

Chapter 4
Cities: Their Origins and Growth

A Latin word for city is "civitas." City dwellers were considered civilized.

I. Cities

CITIES *are simply concentrations of people who live in close proximity for a variety of reasons, such as protection, commerce, religion, education, recreation, etc.*

It was not until 1830 that mankind achieved a world population of one billion. By 1930 our population had doubled to two billion. By 1960, we had three billion people. By the year 2006, the world population should exceed 6.4 billion people.

Approximately 80 percent of Americans live in communities having more than 2,500 people. The U.S. Census Bureau classifies every municipality having more than 2,500 people as "urban." The Census Bureau also classifies an "urban area" as 50,000 or more with a density of 1,000 or more per square mile. (Communities of 2,500 to 50,000 are classified as other urban places.)

Population increases in the U. S. have been primarily urban.

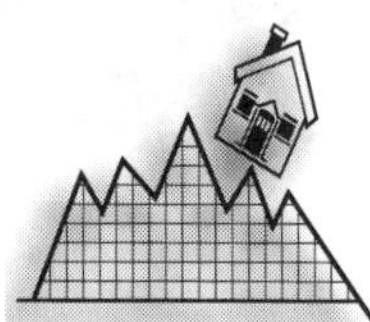

CHAPTER 4 OUTLINE

The 2000 census showed that 141 million people lived in suburban metropolitan areas, 85 million lived in central cities and only 55 million lived in non metropolitan areas.

Not only do most people live in cities, most live in larger cities. As late as 1800, only 3 percent of the world's population lived in cities having more than 100,000 people. By 1995, that number exceeded 45 percent.

Cities offer opportunities of economics, experiences, and education. City life is also associated with freedom.

*A **METROPOLIS** is a core city with suburbs or satellite communities that have physically become one sprawling, metropolitan, urban center.*

Metropolitan areas may encompass a number of cities.

A. HISTORICAL BASIS

It has been hypothesized that people do not need a reason to live together because they are social creatures and have a strong desire to associate with others. This may be so, because cities are a universal phenomena. Every recorded civilization has had cities. The early Greek and Roman cities were actually city-states; they were independent entities.

Primitive humans were hunters, so families or tribes moved (nomadic) with the herds. The development of agricultural skills allowed a fixed habitat and more permanent structures, which set the stage for the development of cities. While homosapiens have existed for at least 40,000 years, cities have existed for less than 10,000 years.

In order for cities to grow, it was necessary to free large numbers of people from agriculture. The early large cities were in areas of moderate climate, with long growing seasons and fertile soil. This allowed greater agricultural productivity. In central Europe, the curved "moldboard" plow (pulled by a horse, it lifts and turns over soil) stimulated rapid growth of cities because it was the first major agricultural breakthrough that increased production. The improvements in agriculture allowed for a greater specialization by occupation, as more people were freed from the land. These improvements are still continuing. They are very evident in less developed countries, where we are seeing a rapid growth of cities.

The size of early cities was limited by transportation.

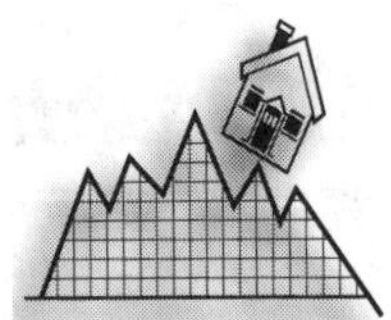

Larger cities required that goods be brought from a larger area. Generally, early roads were not adequate to supply large cities, which explains why most of the early, larger cities were located on waterways in fertile areas.

Also, because of transportation and distribution problems, early large cities had extremely high population densities. Physical size was limited by foot and hoof transportation. At its pinnacle, ancient Rome had an estimated population of 800,000 to 1,000,000 people. Most of these people lived within an area of approximately four square miles. Roman apartment structures were commonly seven to eight stories high.

Following the barbarian invasions of the 4th century, the world's great cities declined. Besides being targets for plunder, the war-ravaged countryside could no longer provide the food to support great concentrations of people. Supply sources and routes were also disrupted. Constantinople was the only European city with a population more than 100,000 people that was able to survive the Dark Ages.

The feudal system evolved during the 7th century. ***FEUDALISM** was a decentralized land system based on loyalties and mutual protection.* It allowed for the reclamation of agricultural land. Strong loyalties and class structure under feudalism discouraged large concentrations of people.

The revival of trade, starting around the 10th century, increased the importance of trade centers and reversed the decline of the cities.

Gunpowder eliminated the small feudal states of Europe and lead to the formation of modern nations, as well as the rebirth of cities.

II. Location of Cities

A number of factors have served to determine locations for cities.

A. MEETING NECESSITIES OF LIFE

Most cities developed in areas with fresh water, good drainage, and were relatively close to productive farmland.

Most large cities are located in coastal areas or on inland waterways.

B. DEFENSE

Locations of early cities were often defensive. Athens was founded around the inaccessible rock of the Acropolis. Rome's seven hills were originally defensive, as they were surrounded by the marshes of the Tiber River. In Europe, craftsmen and merchants gathered around castles for the dual purpose of commerce and protection.

The city of San Juan, Puerto Rico, was developed behind Fort El Morro, which protects the entrance to San Juan Bay. This famous fort came under the possession of several foreign governments, including, of course, the United States. (The people of Puerto Rico are American Citizens.)

Military forts such as Fort Dearborn in Michigan and the Presidio in California were also the nucleus of cities. Artisans and suppliers of services gathered around these forts.

C. COMMERCE AND TRANSPORTATION

Commerce routes have always been logical sites for cities. The best location has been where two or more trade routes intersect. This applies equally to trails, railroads, or rivers. Pittsburgh was founded at the confluence of the Allegheny and Monongahela Rivers. Ports and passes, where goods had to be loaded and unloaded, were also logical economic sites for cities.

Cities established on commerce routes were trade centers for sales and services. They required inns, warehouses, blacksmiths, etc.

Pure economics brought many people together. For example, in earlier times weavers and tailors were economically dependent upon each other. Therefore, they tended to locate in close proximity to each other. We see the same thing today. Support and service industries will tend to cluster around a major industry.

The Transcontinental Railroad realized that rail stations would spawn a city. Therefore, they sited their stations at locations where they had accumulated land beyond their right of way.

D. HARBORS

Large natural harbors, such as those in New York, Boston and San Francisco, became the natural site for cities, as ships could be provisioned, unloaded and loaded in relative safety. Our port cities have developed into areas of the largest concentration of people. Fishing villages also developed in locations with protected harbors.

Approximately one-half of the population of the United States now lives within 50 miles of an ocean or the Great Lakes.

E. MINING AND LUMBER

Mining was the basis for the establishment of many cities. While a number of early mining and lumber cities simply disappeared as the mines became unproductive and the forests were cleared, others continued with a change in the economic base.

Many mining and lumber towns established in the late 1800s and the first part of the 1900s, were company towns. They were often well planned, with housing provided by the mine owners. They had bachelor housing as well as family housing for workers. Supervisory workers had better housing, often on separate streets. There were even retail and service areas.

Where there were a number of mines or logging interests in an area, the cities often grew with little or no planning because no one employer controlled the labor force.

F. INDUSTRY

When a large industry locates outside of a metropolitan area, it acts as a catalyst for growth, attracting support industries, workers' homes, service providers, and merchandisers.

The villages of Kohler, Wisconsin and Hershey, Pennsylvania were company towns. ***COMPANY TOWNS*** *are towns in which all or almost all of the real estate is owned or controlled by a single company*. Many company towns have become regular cities. Other company towns include Lynch, Kentucky (U.S. Steel), Kannopolis, North Carolina (Cannon Mills), and Sugarland, Texas (Spreckles Sugar).

G. RELIGION

Religion was instrumental in the formation of a number of cities. In California, the Mission San Diego de Alcal'a became San Diego, San Gabriel Arcangel became San Gabriel, San Luis Obispo de Tolosa became San Luis Obispo, San Francisco de Asis Dolores became San Francisco, and San Buenaventura became Ventura.

The missions were established where there were the greatest concentrations of Indians.

These locations were in the coastal areas offering water and game. These sites, in many cases, also were excellent economic locations for modern cities.

English clergyman, Roger Williams, founded Providence, Rhode Island after he was banished from Massachusetts. He wanted a place where religion could be practiced freely. Providence was founded as a city free from religious intolerance.

Salt Lake City, Utah was established by a group of Mormons who wanted to practice their religion without persecution.

Rev. John Alexander Dowie, who headed the Christian Catholic Apostolic Church, founded Zion, Illinois. He wanted a utopian religious city endowed with a biblical sense and purpose. Most of the street names were taken from the Bible.

H. RECREATION

Recreational cities were developed because of sports and/or climate. Examples of such cities are Vail, Colorado, and Mammoth, California. Cities such as Palm Springs, Palm Beach, Vail and Miami were largely developed as recreational and retirement communities.

I. RETIREMENT

Prior to World War II, few retirees left their neighborhood. However, after World War II, retirees have been more likely to relocate. This has led to the growth of retirement developments in the Sun Belt. The ***SUN BELT*** *is generally considered to cover states in the South and West, ranging from Florida and Georgia, through the Gulf States and into California.*

The U.S. census estimates that nearly 21 percent of the U.S. population was 55 years of age or older in 1997. The number was estimated at 55.9 million. The U.S. census expects this number to hit 74.7 million in 2010, due to a longer lifespan and an aging boomer bulge.

It is estimated that by the year 2030, close to 70 million Americans will be over the age of 65. This is approximately double the figure for 2005. These figures would seem to indicate a tremendous potential for retirement housing.

Most retirement communities have been established in areas with mild winter temperatures.

By far the largest planned retirement development is Sun City, Arizona, which has a population 46,000 people, mostly aged 55 and older. Many of the residents in Sun City have paid cash for their residences (either as the result of savings or the sale of a residence elsewhere). Residents of retirement communities tend to be financially stable. Arizona banks have over $2 billion in deposits from Sun City residents. One-third of the residents are over 75 years of age. They are considered to be healthier than average. (Possibly this is because it is the more "active" retiree who relocates, as well as the active lifestyle.)

Criticism of large retirement communities has been that their voting strength and insular attitude results in the defeat of bond issues. Sun City, Arizona, actually withdrew from the local school district, refusing to contribute.

Del Webb, the developer of Sun City, Arizona, has also built Sun City developments in California, Nevada, South Carolina, Illinois, and Texas.

delweb.com

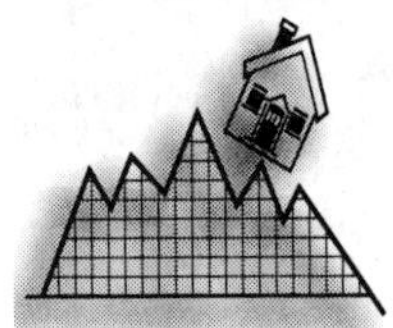

The Illinois Sun City development is the first major retirement community built in the ***SNOW BELT****.* Del Webb indicates that there is a good response as many seniors wish to be close to their children but still maintain a private and active life.

Retirement communities tend to be primarily Caucasian. Sun City, Arizona is 98.44 percent Caucasian. Retirement communities also tend to have a higher median income with very few residents having incomes below the poverty line.

J. AGRICULTURE

In areas of good soil and water, there was a need for agricultural cities to serve the farms. In the Midwest, many small towns developed, each serving a rural area within approximately one day's wagon journey. Before modern transportation, these towns were needed to provide supplies and a market for goods. With the advent of railroads, highways, and trucks, many of these communities lost their economic significance. We have been seeing a steady decline in population in many of these agriculturally based communities. However, others have had a resurgence from people attracted to a small town lifestyle.

K. PROMOTERS

A great many cities were the result of promoters who simply took an area of land, subdivided it into lots and called it a city. California City, near Mohave, is such a promotional city.

Lake Havasu City, Arizona, is an example of a city promoted by its developer to sell lots.

Pahrump, Nevada is now one of the fastest growing communities in the West. However, Pahrump was once a community that existed in land speculators' dreams. There were accusations of land fraud, with thousands of parcels sold with alleged false information. When sold, most of the parcels had no utilities or hope of getting any.

L. POLITICAL DECREE

Some cities, like Brasilia in Brazil, or our own Washington, D.C., were established by government decree. Brasilia's location was chosen as the site for the capital in order to bring people into Brazil's interior and foster the development of a huge wilderness area.

California pueblos at Los Angeles, San Jose, and Santa Cruz were formed by governmental decision to encourage civilians to settle in California. Nine soldiers, settler families, and one vaquero founded San Jose, which is California's oldest continuously inhabited community, as a pueblo on November 29, 1777. It was founded as a farming community at a location that offered water and level farmland, yet was close to ocean transportation.

The logical, economic reasons for site selections helped to insure the success of cities.

III. Growth of Modern Cities

In 1790, the date of the first decennial census (every 10 years), there were only 24 urban areas in the United States having populations of 2,500 or more. By 1970, this number had increased to 7,062. By the year 2000, the U.S. had 10 cities with populations of more than 1,000,000 people. We have changed from a country dominated by agriculture to one dominated by manufacturing, service and trade.

A number of factors have played a role in the growth of our modern cities.

A. AGRICULTURAL REVOLUTION

Before there could be an industrial revolution, people had to be freed from the land. Even with most of the population engaged in agricultural pursuits, agricultural production barely met the demand of the population. Between 1760 and 1830, a number of innovations increased production to allow workers to become free from the land. These factors included:

1. A new system of rotation of nitrogen fixing and cereal crops. This replaced a system where one-third to one-half the land was allowed to lie fallow each year.
2. The seed drill, which allowed a greater portion of the crop to germinate as seeds are set below the surface and thus protected from birds and wind.
3. Introduction of heavy manuring.
4. Systematic stock breeding and cross breeding for quality and quantity.
5. The draining of swamps.
6. Common areas (England) were allowed to be fenced and passed to private ownership.
7. Planting of potatoes, which allowed poor soil to be productive as well as large crops per acre.
8. Introduction of corn, which had a high yield and nutritious value.
9. Planting of fodder crops for animals instead of use of vast acreage for pasture.
10. Individuals accepting market agriculture where excess was planned and was intended for sale or barter.

B. INDUSTRIAL REVOLUTION

The Industrial Revolution, with the steam engine, industrial machines and the railroad, led to the rapid growth of our cities during the 19th century. The prosperity of the cities attracted workers to the factories, causing cities to serve not only as the source of labor to produce goods, but as a market for the goods as well.

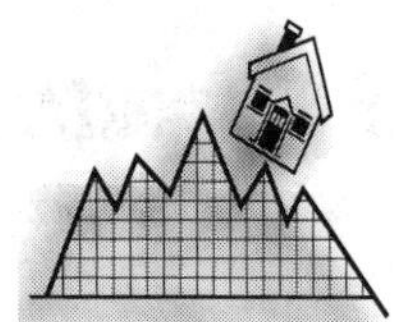

Nevertheless, by 1900, one-third of our population still resided on farms. Farm mechanization of the 20th century, coupled with greater use of fertilizers and more productive hybrids, have now expanded production to the point where less than two percent of our population grows crops.

Less than two percent of the population make their livelihood growing crops or from animal husbandry.

C. TRANSPORTATION IMPROVEMENTS

Greater access to land away from larger cities was afforded by transportation improvements. This resulted in land far from cities attaining greater value. The land could not only provide agricultural products for the city, it could now also be used for housing and industry.

Many private companies built canals in the early 1800s. The canal use was relatively short lived because steam power made railroads possible and steamships expanded the use of waterways.

The development of cheap electricity resulted in the electric trolley, which made commuting fast and inexpensive, opening up vast areas for development.

Automobiles, roads, and railways allowed people to travel longer distances to work and purchase or market goods.

Developments in transportation have made it possible for industries normally linked together to be geographically separated. As an example, the small city of Chippewa Falls, Wisconsin was originally the home of Cray Research, Inc. (Cray Research, Inc. manufactured the Cray X1 and X3, the world's most powerful computers.) It was chosen simply because it is the home of its founder, Seymour Cray. Cray Research, now owned by SGI, has moved its executive offices to a Minneapolis suburb.

Cray Research, Inc., (**www.cray.com**) is an exception because most computer firms want to be geographically close to similar firms. We can see this in the Silicon Valley (near San Jose, California), where computer-related firms have congregated. The advantages of being close to similar computer firms include a large labor pool of engineers and technicians, close proximity to service firms, as well as the stimulation that close contact fosters. The Silicon Valley developed because of its close proximity to professors and graduates of Stanford University, who specialize in computer technology.

D. PLANNING

Planning is playing an increasingly important role in the growth of our modern cities.

While many cities have developed without any central plan, we have had planned cities since early times. In the Indus Valley (modern Pakistan), Mohenjo Daro and Harrapa, dating from the 3rd Century B.C., had a well-planned rectangular street pattern. Mohenjo Daro also had an elaborate sewer system.

Rome, which was a well-planned and organized city, was able to support nearly one million people 1,800 years before London reached that population level.

In Colonial America, French, Dutch, Spanish and English colonizers drew up formal town and city plans prior to settlement. The Dutch trading company that founded New Amsterdam (New York) sent detailed plans for the city with the first colonizers. However, later development was in a haphazard fashion until the middle of the 18th Century.

Philadelphia was ordered thoroughly planned by its developer, William Penn. He stated, "Our purpose is...to erect and build one principal town, which by reason of situation must in all probability be the most considerable for merchandize, trade and fishery in those parts."

Other planned towns were:

Jamestown 1607
New Haven 1638
Charleston 1680
Annapolis 1695
Williamsburg 1699
Mobile 1711
New Orleans 1722
Savannah 1733
St. Louis 1762-1764
Louisville 1779

When the Great Fire of 1666 devastated much of London, Christopher Wren saw it as an opportunity to design a beautiful and functional city.

While Wren's plans were NOT used, they strongly influenced Charles L' Enfant, who is credited with the design of Washington, D.C.

L' Enfant's architectural design, with its open and spacious park-like malls, was well suited for numerous monuments and has added grandeur to our nation's capital. L' Enfant's home was Paris, a city with a rich history of grandeur.

Washington, D.C. was the only significant exception to the gridiron plan where the area was marked off in rectangular parcels and blocks. L' Enfant overlaid a basic gridiron with broad tree lined, diagonal avenues and 15 major public squares.

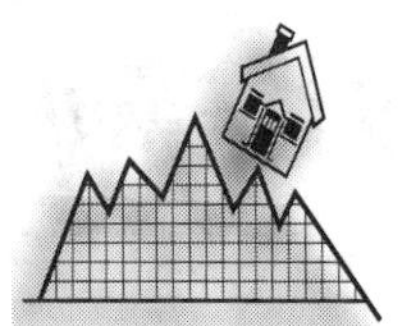

PIERRE CHARLES L'ENFANT.

SKETCH
OF
WASHINGTON IN EMBRYO,
VIZ:
Survey by Major L'ENFANT.

PLAN
of the City of Washington
in the Territory of Columbia.
ceded by the States of
VIRGINIA and MARYLAND
to the United States of America
and by them established as the
SEAT of their GOVERNMENT,
after the Year
MDCCC.

GEORGE TOWN.

Rock Creek.

Tiber Creek

Lat. Capitol. 38.53. N.
Long. 0. 0.

President's House

Capitol

PART OF VIRGINIA WITHIN THE TERRITORY OF COLUMBIA.

POTOMAK RIVER.

EASTERN BRANCH.

PART OF MARYLAND WITHIN THE TERRITORY OF COLUMBIA.

Observations
explanatory of the Plan.

I. THE positions for the different Edifices, and for the several Squares or Areas of different shapes, as they are laid down, were first determined on the most advantageous ground, commanding the most extensive prospects, and the better susceptible of such improvements as either use or ornament may hereafter call for.

II. LINES or Avenues of direct communication have been devised, to connect the separate and most distant objects with the principal, and to preserve through the whole a reciprocity of sight at the same time. Attention has been paid to the passing of those leading Avenues over the most favorable ground for prospect and convenience.

III. NORTH and South lines, intersected by others running due East and West, make the distribution of the City into Streets, Squares, &c. and those lines have been so combined as to meet at certain given points with those divergent Avenues, so as to form on the spaces "first determined" the different Squares or Areas.

SCALE OF POLES.

Breadth of the Streets.

THE grand Avenues, and such Streets as lead immediately to public places, are from 130 to 160 feet wide, and may be conveniently divided into foot ways, walks of trees, and a carriage way. The other Streets are from 90 to 110 feet wide.

IN order to execute this plan, Mr. ELLICOTT drew a true Meridional line by celestial Observation, which passes through the Area intended for the Capitol: this line he crossed by another due East and West, which passes through the same Area. These lines were accurately measured, and made the basis on which the whole plan was executed. He ran all the lines by a Transit Instrument, and determined the acute Angles by actual Measurement, and left nothing to the uncertainty of the Compass.

New York City had an expansion plan in 1811 that expanded Manhattan growth northward in a gridiron that ignored topography. According to the lead surveyor, the justification for the plan was to aid the buying and selling of land. It made for neat parcels.

Sir Thomas More described the ideal city in his book, Utopia (1516). His ideal cities would be carbon copies of each other. For many travelers who come into commercial areas of large cities today, the sameness envisioned by Sir Thomas More seems to have been met.

IV. Growth Patterns of Cities

There are a number of theories or patterns on how cities grow. While no city strictly follows any one model, review of these theories will help in understanding city growth.

A. CONCENTRIC CIRCLE THEORY

Johann Heinrich Von Thunen, in *Der Isolierte Staat* ("The Isolated State"), first developed the theory of concentric circle growth in 1826:

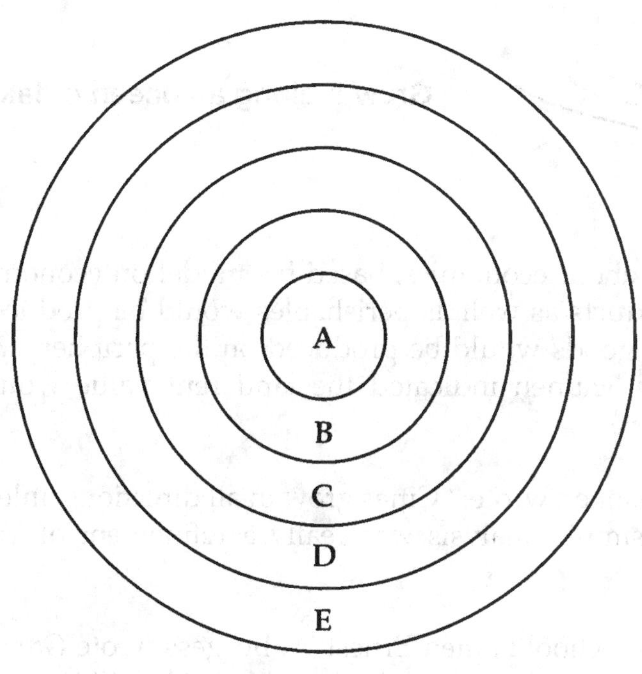

A - The central city (commerce and housing)
B - Gardens and poultry
C - Forests
D - Cropland
E - Grazing

Von Thunen assumed a concentric growth from the core (intense area) of the city to less intensive uses.

His model demonstrated the spreading out from the core of the city to less intensive land uses, based on an agrarian economy. At that time, forests were closer to the city core than cropland because cities required huge amounts of wood for fuel. It was, therefore, more economical for forests to be closer to the city core than primary food sources. Von Thunen's 1826 concentric circle growth was based on an isolated city and assumed a uniform topography and equally desirable soil without navigable waterways and bounded by wilderness. He also did not consider any cross-influences from other cities.

Because cities are frequently built along waterways and highways, the circular growth pattern would be modified. As an example:

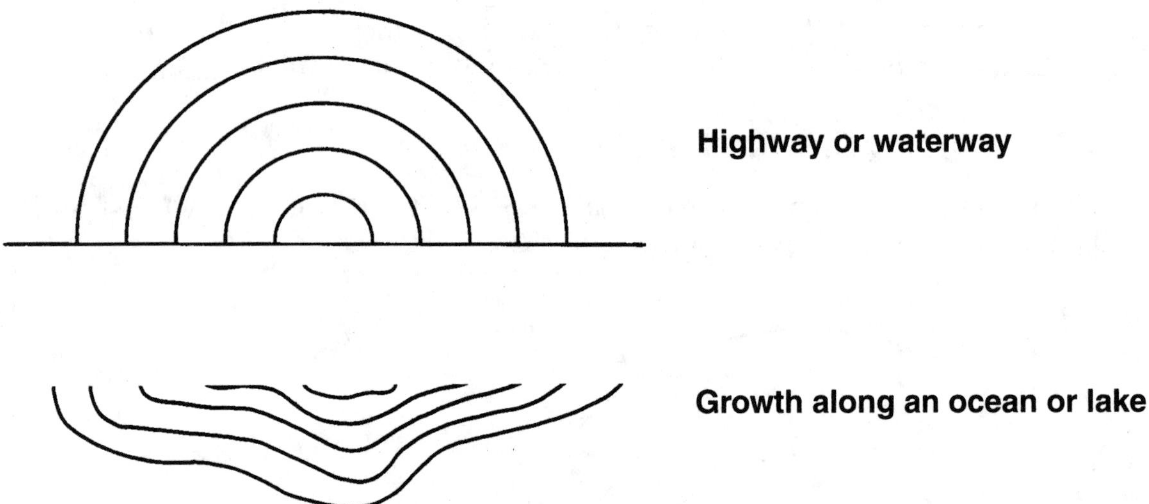

Von Thunen, who had also written about economics, based his model on economic costs. Considering costs, heavy products as well as perishables would be produced close to home. Lighter and durable goods would be produced on the periphery. As transportation costs increased, Von Thunen indicated the land rent value would decrease until land value reached zero.

In 1903, Richard Hurd, a mortgage banker, wrote: "Cities grow in all directions unless hindered by topography." Hurd's simple analysis was really a refinement of Von Thunen's theory of growth.

In 1925, an economist of the Chicago School named Ernest W. Burgess wrote *Growth of the City*. He expanded upon Von Thunen's concentric circle idea using Chicago as a model. According to Burgess, commercial office and civic areas are in the center. Around the central business district are low-cost homes.

According to Burgess, higher cost homes would grow outward from the central area in all directions.

Burgess believed that the rings melded into one another and were not distinct. An example of the circular growth as Burgess envisioned it would be:

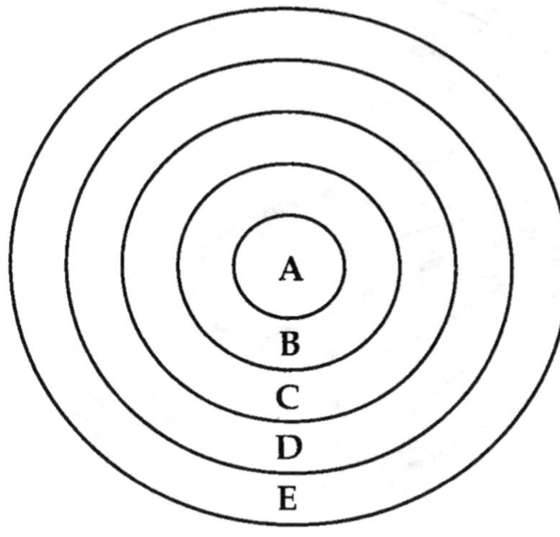

A - Central business zone
B - Transition zone, commercial and warehouse area, and light manufacturing
C - Worker's homes
D - Middle class housing
E - Suburban area. Middle and upper income residents (commuter zone)

Burgess believed that each inner zone tends to push outward toward the next zone. Burgess called this the **PROCESS OF SUCCESSION**. Burgess believed that rapid urban growth would result in crime, vice and disorder.

In actuality, most cities are NOT circular because of their location along waterways or topography.

Even when the topography would allow circular growth, parks, forest preserves, cemeteries, etc. frequently upset the pattern, which cause the growth to go in another direction.

B. AXIAL THEORY OF GROWTH

F. M. Babcock developed the axial theory in 1932.

Babcock believed that cities developed along axis routes to their center based on the time/cost relationship of transport.

Axis routes would be along major roads, railroads, and waterways. The growth pattern resembles a star. An example of axial growth is shown at the top of the next page.

As the areas between the arms of the star became accessible because of transpiration, the area would fill in by development.

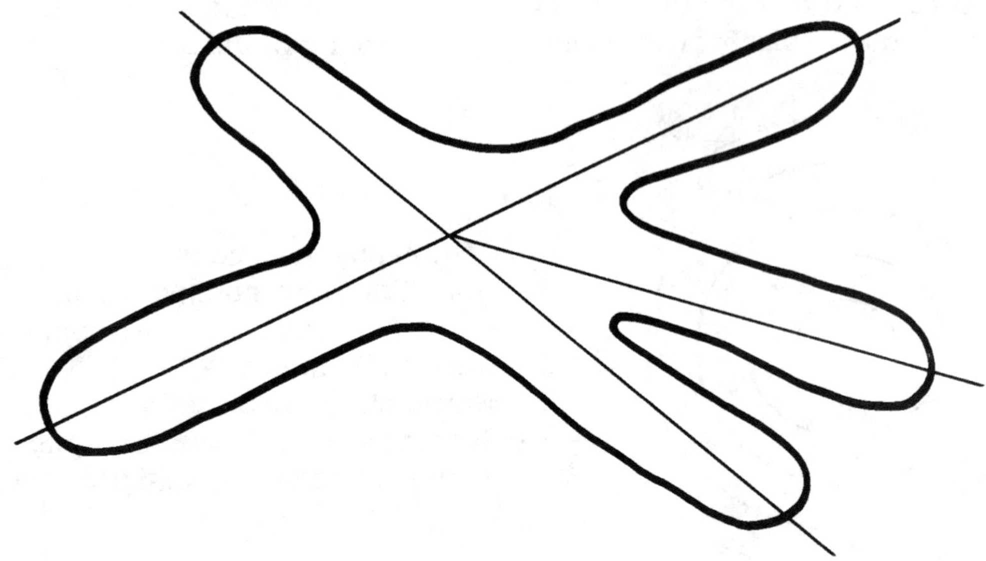

C. SECTOR THEORY OF GROWTH

In 1939, Homer Hoyt wrote *The Structure and Growth of Residential Neighborhoods in American Cities.*

Hoyt was critical of the concentric circle theory of growth. Hoyt's theory was that spatial relationship is not the only determinant of city growth. Other factors such as a prestigious location, social kinship, and affinity played a role in growth. While prestigious locations move outward from the city, like concentric circle growth, Hoyt believed that growth was along a sector.

Hoyt stated that new increases in growth would continue in the same direction as the old type of growth.

Better housing moves further out in the same area toward high ground. Lower income housing also follows a pie-shaped growth pattern. High-rent apartments extend outward from the city center, usually along traffic arteries or rivers. The homes of the wealthy have lined streets leading out from the city. Wealth has sought seclusion of the suburbs. Rarely is this outward movement reversed. An exception is redevelopment. The wealthy do not move into previously occupied homes. However, as they move outward, lower income persons tend to follow as people move outward as their income allows.

Homer Hoyt believed that persons living on the outer reaches of the residential sectors had great economic control and political influence of the city.

As newer structures are built, those closer to the city center are passed down to other users (filtering down).

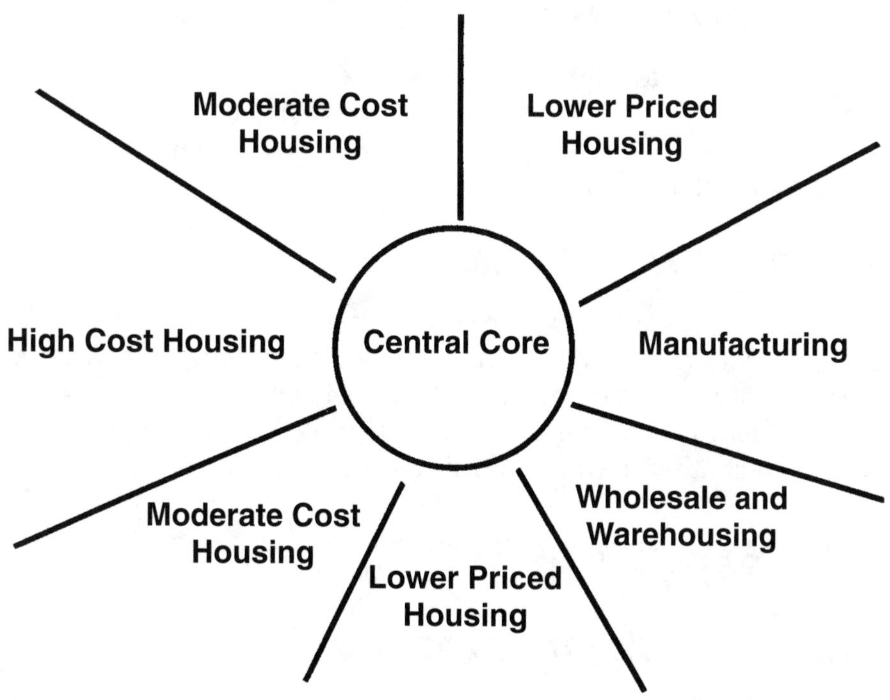

D. MULTIPLE NUCLEI THEORY OF GROWTH

Multiple Nuclei theory is the development of cities from separate, independent points.

In *The Nature of Cities* (1945), Chauncy Harris and Edward Ullman proposed the idea that cities grow from a number of separate nuclei which are individual cores. The centers may simply be a number of similar activities grouped together. San Jose, California, is often cited as an example of a city that grew together from many separate points.

Each center of growth has its own retail, industrial, and housing support areas. These separate areas expand to form one larger city.

The multiple nuclei theory also appears valid for greater Los Angeles, with its many centers of activity. Chicago, with its central loop, would appear closer to Von Thunen's model.

E. STRIP DEVELOPMENTS

Many small towns in the West follow a highway for miles but are less than 1,000 feet wide. These cities generally developed along major travel routes and the economy of the city is based on travel along the highway. Principal businesses are likely to be motels, restaurants, and service stations.

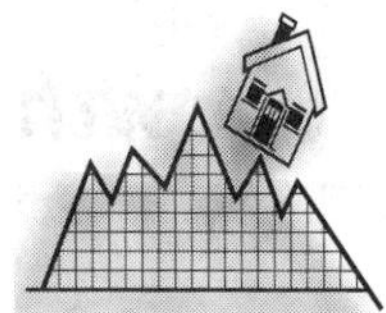

F. CLUSTER DEVELOPMENTS

Around exits on interstate highways as well as where highways intersect, there are often small developments which are not part of any incorporated city. These developments might consist of several service stations, motels, and restaurants. They might not include residential housing.

G. CHANGE IN GROWTH PATTERNS

Besides physical barriers affecting growth patterns, one development can change growth and use patterns. A decision as to a school site will attract residential construction to the area. A development of low-cost or subsidized housing could result in the exclusion of luxury housing from an area, while a development of luxury homes could serve to attract other luxury and middle-income housing and businesses.

V. How Cities Continue to Grow

A. PERIPHERAL GROWTH (ANNEXATION)

PERIPHERAL GROWTH is accomplished by extending the boundaries of the city. Annexing areas to cities is not necessarily orderly. *ANNEXING is the legal process, through a vote, by which an area becomes incorporated into a city.* It is often based on political and private interests. Speculators like annexation, as it offers great profit potential when outlying land is joined to the city and becomes eligible for city services.

The growth by extending the city tends to be land use intensive. As an example, from 1950 to 1990, Chicago had a population growth of 38 percent but a land growth of 124 percent. During the same period, Cleveland had a population growth of 21 percent but land growth of 112 percent.

B. UP GROWTH (Additional Stories)

In ancient Rome, as the city became more populated, buildings became taller, often seven to eight stories high. The slow transportation system required vertical growth. The tallest buildings in a city are generally built where land is most expensive and therefore must be efficiently utilized. As use in a city intensifies, smaller parcels will be joined together to provide sites for high-rise structures.

otis.com
Otis Elevators

The modern elevator developed by Elisha Otis in 1853, coupled with structural steel construction, made possible the skyscrapers of today.

C. FILLING IN (Small Lot Development)

After a city has reached peak development, the development of remaining small lots is referred to as **FILL-IN PROJECTS** *or "infill."* As a city increases in population, vacant parcels will be developed and underdeveloped parcels will be redeveloped.

D. AIR SPACE (Over and Under Structures)

As land becomes more valuable, it becomes feasible to use the space over other uses. In downtown Chicago, the Merchandise Mart is built partially over railroad tracks and the Post Office is built over a highway. In Japan, where space is at an even greater premium, there have been many developments over roadways. In many of our cities, an estimated 25 percent of the land is devoted to roads. This offers interesting opportunities for growth. The amount of land devoted to streets can be reduced with longer blocks as well as one-way streets, which reduces the need for greater width.

Caltrans, which maintains California's highway system, will allow the leasing of space over, around, or under freeways. (Caltrans is paid a commission for this service.)

E. LEAP FROG DEVELOPMENT

Cities generally do not expand in an orderly pattern of development block by block, with vacant lots developed prior to further expansion. Developments leap frog each other.

LEAPFROGGING *is directional development in an inconsistent pattern, where there are many vacant, underdeveloped parcels between developed parcels.* Often people just do not want to sell or want too much for their vacant land. Other times, property is prematurely subdivided, so ownership has become so diffused that reasonable development is now impossible. In addition to higher costs closer in, zoning and building codes often encourage developers to build outside the political boundaries of a city. Sometimes these isolated developments become the center of their own growth patterns.

F. PUBLIC USE

About one-third of urban land is publicly owned. This includes streets and alleys, land used for parks, schools, civic, and cultural purposes.

Cemeteries occupy over 2 million acres of land in the United States. While some land use experts have suggested cremation or high-rise mausoleums, the land use for cemeteries does provide green space. Cemeteries were generally built on the outskirts of cities and, with growth, have often become obstructions to logical growth and traffic. It is politically difficult to move cemeteries or dispose of them. In 1901, San Francisco prohibited further burials within San Francisco. In 1937, because land in San Francisco was becoming too valuable for cemeteries, an ordinance was passed that

resulted in 145,000 bodies being exhumed and sent to Colma, a suburb about 10 miles away. The tombstones were used to make a breakwater for a San Francisco yacht harbor. In 1950, Colma's city planning commission limited development to cemeteries and accessory uses. A city of 730 residents, Colma has 13 cemeteries that contain more than 2 million dead.

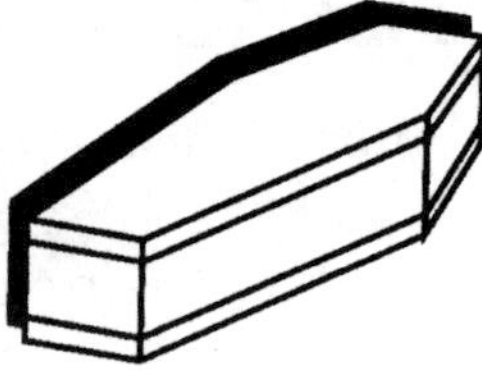

G. CITY POPULATION MIGRATION

The population migrates both to and from cities.

During World War II, America saw a tremendous migration for jobs with high wages in the defense industries. After World War II, the Western cities, particularly in California, had a tremendous influx of people from other areas. People who are most likely to relocate for employment are younger, more productive workers.

Older workers are less likely to voluntarily relocate for work, as opposed to younger workers who will.

At one time, it was common to have three or even four generations of a family living in one house. It was also common to have a large extended family of parents, siblings and cousins living within just a small radius. Today, people are less likely to remain with a single employer during their entire careers. They are more likely to change jobs and relocate. Our population has become very mobile based upon both economic and lifestyle choices.

There has been an increase in the movement of young people toward the centers of cities, especially among singles and childless couples. Restaurants, shopping, and the culture of the city center as well as the closeness to work attract them. While the number of young people is actually quite small, their presence has resulted in a resurgence of entertainment, restaurants, and retailing in central city areas. They have also served to make central city living attractive for others, such as avant-garde businesses and artists who have renovated vacant warehouses and added lofts to old buildings.

The increased interest in downtown area living is primarily by working singles and couples. Travel time has become important for many of these people. While blue collar workers generally do not want to live close to their place of employment, office workers seem to be attracted to high-rise living within walking distance of their employment, restaurants, entertainment, and cultural centers.

The back-to-the-city movement is known as **GENTRIFICATION** *(or* ***regentrification****).* The growth in the number of one and two person households has resulted in the revitalization of many central areas.

Retirees tend to move away from the cities, as do families with children.

There is still a slight movement from farms to the cities, as mechanization and farm surpluses require fewer farmers. This is more than offset by a counter migration to rural areas by city people who desire a rural lifestyle.

In periods of severe winters, the sun belt communities attract retirees as well as the unemployed. The decline of smokestack industries in the Midwest also caused many to migrate to the sun states.

Manufactured housing (often and incorrectly called "mobile home") residents tend to remain longer on the average than conventional homeowners in some states. Manufactured homes are often purchased for retirement and retirees do not relocate for jobs and seldom relocate for economic changes.

H. NEW CITIES

Large developments or industries located outside a city will often become the nucleus of a new city. It may be according to plan or based on economic decisions of individual developers.

New cities tend to be developed within relatively close proximity to major metropolitan areas and are likely to coalesce (blend) into the metropolitan area.

I. MEGALOPOLIS

A ***MEGALOPOLIS*** *is a combination or series of cities that have joined together to form an extremely large urban area.* Jean Gottman, a French geographer, coined the word "megalopolis" in a book by the same name in 1961, for conurbations (urban regions) that are extremely large, densely populated, and joined together.

An excellent example of a megalopolis is the greater Los Angeles area, which spills over into several counties.

It is believed by some planning experts that within a few more years the entire California area from Ventura to the Mexican border will be one huge megalopolis.

These are cities along major transportation routes that have physically merged together. "Boswash" is the name given to the Boston to Washington, D.C., conurbation.

Strip cities are really a type of megalopolis.

J. NEIGHBORHOODS

NEIGHBORHOODS *are areas of social conformity*. They are areas where property is in similar use and residents have similar values. The cohesiveness of the neighborhood may be based on residents having similar backgrounds as to income or social status. Churches, schools, civic and fraternal organizations, the Scouts, and Little League help to maintain a neighborhood's cohesiveness and pride. Neighborhood pride serves as a strong motivator to maintain the neighborhood.

Neighborhoods might have definite physical boundaries, such as a street, railroad, river, or even a school district. Some neighborhoods have less clearly defined or even hazy boundaries. In the Southwest, where many walled subdivisions are built, the subdivision tends to be the neighborhood.

Neighborhoods with a high percentage of owner-occupied homes tend to be well maintained and relatively stable.

Areas where homes are sold with no or very low down payments are less likely to be well maintained, as are areas where homeowners are subsidized by government aid. This is generally true even among people with similar incomes.

The original homeowners in an area were likely to have been of similar backgrounds, income, and values. As neighborhoods age, children grow up and leave, and owner resales increase. The percentage of rental property within the area might also increase.

Newer areas might also induce owners to relocate their families to areas with newer schools and homes with the latest amenities. As other areas develop and people move away, local merchants will often leave, following the socioeconomic groups to the suburbs.

As areas age, greater tax revenue is needed for maintenance and repair of city streets and facilities. While costs tend to increase with aging, the tax base tends to decrease because the value of older homes in deteriorating areas is less than newer homes in newer areas. The result is that the revenue available is less than required for maintenance and repair services in older areas. This accelerates the value difference between older and newer neighborhood properties.

As an area shows signs of deterioration, lenders tend to lower values in order to minimize risks. Values set by lenders for loan purposes tend to be a force in lowering actual market values.

GRESHAM'S LAW *is that bad money drives out good money*. As an example, when paper money was introduced, people hoarded gold money. Gresham's Law as applied to neighborhoods would be: "When a neighborhood is in change, a poorer use will drive out better or more productive uses." New buyers may be dissimilar from the majority of former residents as to age, social background and income. Poor zoning enforcement and failure to enforce restrictive covenants can cause further decline or transition. Large homes may be broken up into several rental units. Zoning variances and rezoning will increase density. Normally, neighborhoods do not change for one reason, but a combination of reasons. The stability of an area can be analyzed by changes in the turnover rate of homes.

Neighborhoods do not have to decline. Many areas in Europe have been well maintained for centuries. Community pride and the reputation of an area can allow the area to compete favorably with newer areas.

Once an area has changed, it can be changed back. Much of Georgetown in Washington, D. C. was revitalized. Areas with Victorian homes and old townhouses have become much in demand. In San Francisco and areas of Los Angeles, we can see a similar revitalization.

The ***PRINCIPLE OF CONFORMITY*** *states that maximum value is obtained when a property is in an area of similar properties.* A home in the center of a neighborhood would, therefore, have greater value than one on the edge of a neighborhood adjoining a less desirable neighborhood.

Neighborhoods are of great significance because location is the most important element of value. How people view it determines market value. Keep in mind that real estate is immobile.

K. CITIES AS ECONOMIC MODELS

Cities require export industries to bring in money from outside.

Money flows out of the city for imported goods and services as well as for investments. This money flowing out must be generated from sources inside or outside the city.

Besides the export of goods and services from the city, money flows into the city in the form of government and private pensions and returns on outside investments and payment for exports. We have retirement cities where no goods are produced and few services are exported. These cities exist from accumulated monies brought in by new residents as well as pensions and the investment income of its residents.

Non-retirement cities that fail to bring in money to match outgoing funds have an imbalance of trade. They do not have funds for expansion. A lack of funds generally results in high unemployment within the city. Communities that fail to provide employment opportunities can expect to suffer an exodus of their young people.

L. ECONOMICS OF USE

Urban property values are based on location. ***LOCATION*** *refers to the relationship between property and other amenities or uses.*

Location, location, location – these are the three most important determinants of property value.

A community leader's home will often act as a magnet in attracting better homes. In the same manner, a nucleus of quality homes will attract other quality homes. Middle class housing tends to cluster around quality housing.

The tallest building in the city will be built where the land is the most expensive. The deluxe apartment high-rise, as well as office structures, will generally be close to the city center.

Sites compete against each other for a use, and uses compete against each other for a site. In the city center, nonresidential uses will generally outbid residential uses for available sites. Central locations are generally of greater importance for commercial-type uses that, due to their importance, will bring more money for the site than a residential use would. *The user who needs a site the most will pay the most for it (**PRINCIPLE OF FIRST CHOICE**).*

There is a linkage of use that makes locations more valuable for particular uses. Examples are warehouse areas close to ports or rail yards, and apartment housing close to universities. Suppliers and service firms like to be close to their customers. Small shops like to be in areas of heavy shopping traffic close to major stores.

Businesses, such as auto dealerships, want to be close to one another because they realize the competition will actually increase traffic, as a number of dealerships will draw from a larger area (Principle of Conformity).

Employers requiring a skilled work force will usually want to locate close to that work force. Similar industries are, therefore, often located in close proximity to one another.

The expansion of existing uses in developed areas will result in uses that are more profitable, squeezing out less profitable uses of those who cannot afford to bid for the locations.

Because of zoning, a use may be excluded from an area where that use would be the highest and most economic utilization of the property.

Industrial use generally follows rail lines, major streets, rivers, as well as airport areas. Better homes tend to locate toward open country and along transportation routes away from the city center. They also tend to seek higher ground.

Modern transportation has allowed the growth of larger cities, as well as greater commuting distances. Transportation has allowed industries to leave central city areas. Planning has also contributed to modern city growth.

Uses within a city are going to be determined by economics. The use that needs or wants a site the most will bring in the highest bid for that site.

VI. CHAPTER SUMMARY

Our earliest recorded civilizations show the existence of cities flourishing until the barbarian invasions of the 4th century. Cities declined under **feudalism**, which was a decentralized system, but saw resurgence with the resumption of trade and the end of the feudal system. The **Industrial Revolution** resulted in a period of rapid urban growth.

Locations for cities have been chosen for a variety of reasons, such as defense, commerce, recreation, mining, fishing, agriculture, religion, recreation and retirement purposes. Locations were also chosen by developers, and even by government decree.

Cities exhibit a number of different patterns of growth, including:

a. **Concentric circle growth** – cities grow out in all directions in the absence of physical obstructions.

b. **Axial growth** – cities grow outward following principle transportation routes.

c. **Sector growth** – industry, commerce and housing all seem to grow outward from central area in wedge-shaped patterns.

d. **Multiple nuclei growth** – cities grow from a number of separate centers and join together to form a single city.

e. **Strip development growth** – cities grow along a central highway artery.

Cities grow by **annexing** new areas; building upward due to **zoning changes** or additional stories; filling in the remaining undeveloped smaller lots; and utilizing air space above, under, or around structures. Developments appear to **leap frog** each other.

Populations **migrate** both in and out of cities. While older workers are less likely to voluntarily relocate for work, many younger workers will. The back-to-the-city movement is known as **gentrification**. California is one of the most mobile states and has more renters than any in the nation. The average homeowner moves every five to seven years.

A **megalopolis** is a large area created by many cities joining together. On the East Coast, Boswash is the megalopolis from Boston to Washington, D.C. In California, a huge megalopolis is forming from Ventura to the Mexican border.

Neighborhoods are areas where there is a high degree of social conformity. Neighborhoods with a high percentage of owner-occupied homes tend to be well maintained and relatively stable. The neighborhood greatly influences the value of a house within its boundaries.

The **value of property** depends on the location, amenities, and uses. Quality homes attract other quality homes. Better homes locate towards open country, on hills, and away from city centers. **Tall buildings** will be built where the land is the most expensive in order to fully utilize the space. **Industrial properties** are located next to rail lines, major streets, rivers, and areas surrounding airports.

VII. GLOSSARY OF KEY TERMS

Axial Growth – Growth outward from the city center following transportation routes.

Babcock, F.M. – The developer of the "axial theory," which states that cities developed along axis routes based on the time/cost relationship of travel.

Burgess, Ernest – An urban economist who expanded upon Von Thunen's concentric circle idea regarding city growth.

Company Town – A town founded by an employer with the real estate owned by the employer.

Concentric Circle Development – The growth of a city in a circular pattern of uses from the city center.

Conurbation – An urban region.

Gentrification – A displacement of older residents by younger, more affluent residents.

Gottman, Jean – The French geographer who coined the word "megalopolis."

Gridiron Plan – City plan based on rectangular blocks.

Harris, Chauncy – With Edward Ullman, he developed the "multiple nuclei theory" of city growth.

Hoyt, Homer – Developed the "sector theory" of city growth.

Megalopolis – A vast urban sprawl of cities that have grown together.

Metropolis – A large urban center that can include more than one city.

Multiple Nuclei Development – A city that has developed from a number of separate centers.

Neighborhood – An area of social conformity.

Other Urban Places – A Census Bureau classification for communities having populations from 2,500 to 50,000.

Principle of Conformity – Maximum values will be obtained when a property is in an area of similar properties.

Sector Growth – City growth outward from the city center, with uses expanding in pie-shaped areas.

Strip Development – Development in a relatively narrow band along a major transportation route.

Ullman, Edward – A co-developer (with Chauncey Harris) of the "multiple nuclei theory" of city growth.

Urban – A classification by the U.S. Census Bureau of a community having 2,500 or more people.

Urban Area – A classification of the Census Bureau for communities having 50,000 or more population with a density of 1,000 or more per square mile.

Von Thunen, Johann Heinrich – The developer of the "concentric circle growth theory."

VIII. CLASS DISCUSSION TOPICS

1. What economic factors were responsible for the formation of your city (neighboring cities)?

2. How would you describe the growth pattern of your city (neighboring cities)? Why?

3. What economic factors influenced the growth of your city (neighboring cities)?

4. Give examples of cities that seem to follow a(n):

   a. Concentric circle growth
   b. Axial growth
   c. Sector growth
   d. Strip development growth
   e. Multiple nuclei growth

5. Give examples of particular developments that have affected the growth pattern of your city.

6. Give examples of recent developments that are likely to affect the future growth of your city.

7. What areas are available for the future growth of your city (neighboring cities)?

8. Identify specific neighborhoods within your community.

9. Identify the highly desirable housing areas within your community and their relationship to other housing.

10. Give a local example of land use linkage in your area.

11. What effect have cemeteries and parks had upon land use and growth patterns within your community?

IX. CHAPTER 4 QUIZ

1. A city that was developed by promoters to sell lots was:
    a. Fort Dearborn, Michigan.
    b. Pittsburgh.
    c. San Francisco.
    d. Lake Havasu, Arizona.

2. Which city growth pattern is Von Thunen associated with?
    a. Concentric circle theory
    b. Axial theory
    c. Sector theory
    d. Multiple nuclei theory

3. Which city growth pattern is Homer Hoyt associated with?
    a. Concentric circle theory
    b. Axial theory
    c. Sector theory
    d. Multiple nuclei theory

4. Skyscrapers were made possible because of:
    a. greater use of masonry construction.
    b. the development of the Internet.
    c. structural steel and the electric elevator.
    d. cluster development.

5. The term gentrification refers to a(n):
   a. more docile environment.
   b. male dominated society.
   c. aging population.
   d. back-to-the-city movement of young people.

6. An area where cities have merged together to form a vast urban sprawl is known as a:
   a. cluster.
   b. megalopolis.
   c. commercial zone.
   d. gentrification.

7. The most important determinant of real estate value is:
   a. taxes.
   b. location.
   c. age.
   d. distance from a city's center.

8. A neighborhood most likely to be relatively stable with well maintained properties would have:
   a. a high percentage of renters.
   b. commercial and industrial property mixed among residential uses.
   c. a high percentage of owner-occupancy.
   d. a high percentage of subsidized housing.

9. According to the principle of conformity, the property in a neighborhood of maximum value would be:
   a. the nicest property among deteriorating structures.
   b. in the center of an area of similar properties.
   c. a single-family home surrounded by boarding houses.
   d. the largest property in the neighborhood.

10. The principle that the user who wants a site the most will pay the most for it is known as the principle of:
   a. competition.
   b. supply and demand.
   c. first choice.
   d. change.

ANSWERS: 1. *d;* 2. *a;* 3. *c;* 4. *c;* 5. *d;* 6. *b;* 7. *b;* 8. *c;* 9. *b;* 10. *c*

LEARNING OBJECTIVES

By understanding the challenges to our cities from an economic viewpoint, you will gain an insight into their future. This will also lay the groundwork for you to visualize the future of real property development.

This chapter will introduce you to the challenges facing cities today and how they relate to the economy and real estate. Our wish is to enable you to understand and predict future real estate values.

> ***Cities have a dynamic past based on economic growth. We are seeing numerous problems arising in the cities, while in many instances the suburbs are doing quite well.***

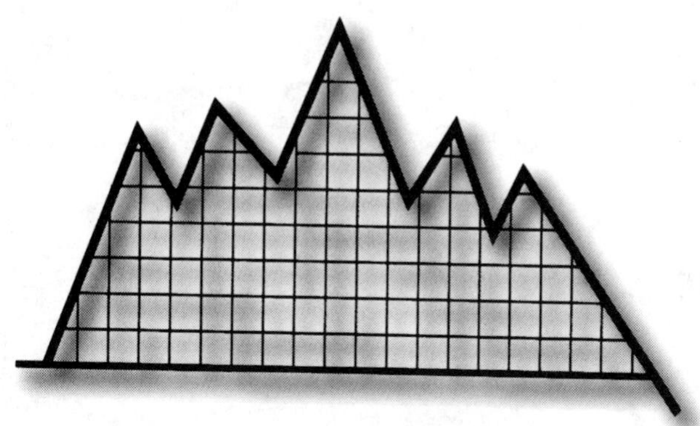

Chapter 5
Problems of the Cities

I. Cities

Over 70 percent of Americans live in cities and their surruonding suburbs.

There are numerous problems arising in many cities while the suburbs (surrounding areas) may be flourishing. Rings of incorporated suburbs that effectively block city growth have surrounded older cities. In many cities, growth has been limited to filling in undeveloped areas or redeveloping property to a higher and better use.

As cities age, the principle of "filtering down" comes into play. *Housing passing down to lower economic groups is the principle of* **FILTERING DOWN**. As persons with higher incomes move outward from the city center, lower income persons tend to move into their former homes. The percentage of low-income persons in the central city tends to increase as the suburbs grow. Many cities have become predominantly minority cities surrounded by primarily middle class suburbs.

A. WHITE FLIGHT

In many urban areas we have seen blocks and whole areas change from almost entirely Caucasian residents to almost entirely other ethnic/racial residents within very short periods of time. The reason whites flee areas is fear. The fear is economic, physical, and social.

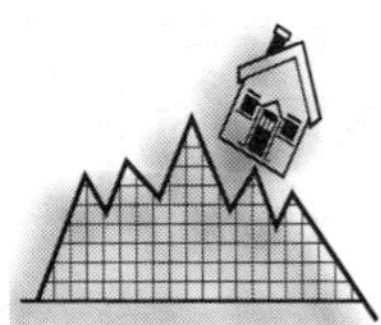

CHAPTER 5 OUTLINE

Economic fear is based on the belief that values will decline if the area is regarded as an African American or other minority neighborhood. In the 1950s and 1960s, this fear was so prevalent that in many cities when an African American family moved into a neighborhood, "For Sale" signs would be at neighboring homes within a matter of days. While the first sales to minorities in a neighborhood would normally be at or above market value, panic-stricken owners would now sell for less than they had previously valued their homes in order to move out quickly. Buyers were often other minority group members. As the neighborhood changed, other owners became even more desperate and would sell at even lower prices. Basically, there was a market with sellers who felt that they had to sell. Market forces reduced prices and the result was a self-fulfilling prophecy with lower values. As homeowners became desperate, properties would be purchased by investors who would rent out the properties to non-whites. Investors would often let their property deteriorate. Uncared-for property would further accelerate the exodus of remaining whites and would negatively affect neighboring values. The displaced whites tended to move as far away from the city centers as they could afford to.

Physical fear was based on the fear of harm to the body and/or property if their neighborhood became a minority area. Whites often associate minorities with gangs and crime.

Social fear is fear of the unknown in that many whites had limited social contact with minorities and did not feel that they could relate in a comfortable manner.

Coupled with those fears, many whites had deep-rooted prejudices in that they simply did not want to live near non-white groups.

"White flight" has been more prevalent in lower-income neighborhoods that adjoin minority-dominated neighborhoods than in higher-income neighborhoods.

Cities that have been hurt by white flight include Detroit, Michigan and St. Louis, Missouri, which lost nearly half their peak populations by outward movement of residents. Detroit is now 80 percent African American while its suburbs are predominantly white. In many cases, the only whites that remained in neighborhoods were very low-income families and seniors who didn't want to upset their lives and/or couldn't afford to relocate.

White flight was aided by FHA and VA programs, which made it easy to buy in the suburbs. In addition, Federal money for highways made it easier for people to commute from suburban locations.

With the passage and enforcement of fair housing legislation, we now have minority group members in almost every residential area of our cities. Whites will generally

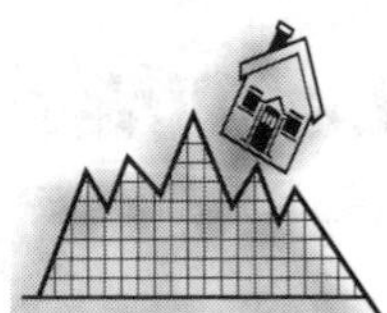

remain in a neighborhood when non-whites enter the area. Unless they believe that the area will become a non-white neighborhood, they no longer respond with immediate white flight. However, there appears to be a **"tipping point"** where whites will exodus an area. If non-whites entry to an area is slow, the tipping point would require a higher percentage of non-whites than if the entry was over a shorter period of time.

It isn't just African Americans entering an area that results in white flight. Hispanics, Asians, Middle Eastern and even Russians entering a neighborhood can result in U.S.-born white Americans leaving the neighborhood.

White flight can also occur in a neighborhood because of the entrance of non-whites in the schools. When it appears that minorities will dominate a public school, some whites will move so that their children can attend schools in another district. Desegregation of the schools as well as school busing programs pushed many white families further from the central city.

White flight is not just a U.S. phenomenon. Many cities in Great Britain have experienced white flight when Indians, Pakistanis or Black West Indians moved into a neighborhood.

What we call "white flight" isn't all white. As a neighborhood starts to decline, non-white residents who are able to relocate will often join whites in their move toward the suburbs.

The flight of whites to the suburbs coupled with the flight of businesses reduces the employment opportunities for those remaining in the central city. Businesses relocate for a number of reasons, which include:

1. To be closer to the residences of management and employees.
2. Difficulties in hiring skilled new employees for central city locations.
3. Availability of newer facilities in suburban areas offering greater amenities and/or cost savings.
4. To follow their customers to the suburbs.

White flight is continuing, but not all is racially motivated. City crime, educational problems, and loss of higher paying jobs are significant factors in the movement of families from the cities. Between 1990 and 2000, the number of whites declined in 120 U.S. metropolitan areas according to census figures. Only nine cities suffered a loss in African American population and no U.S. city suffered a decline in its Hispanic population.

White flight is not confined to the central cities. Suburbs have also experienced white flight. While Chicago lost 14 percent of its population during the 1990s, its southern suburbs also experienced white exodus and a doubling and tripling of minority populations.

The Village of South Holland, south of Chicago, tried to reverse white flight. To keep their white residents, they touted their low crime rate and rising property values. They enacted ordinances against racial steering. They even offered lower assessments for taxes to residents who agreed not to move for five years. Despite these efforts, South Holland lost half of its non-Hispanic white population during the 1990s. However, South Holland seems to have stabilized as a racially mixed community.

Historically, statistics show that African Americans and Hispanics have been the last to be hired and the first to be laid-off. Minorities generally make up the bulk of unskilled workers. Minorities have an extremely high unemployment rate. They also tend to have larger than average families.

This change in our cities creates an increasingly hard economic burden on the city for schools, social services, and health care.

B. SPRAWL

***SPRAWL** is outward growth of a metropolitan area.* As population increases, developers seek large parcels of reasonably priced land on the outskirts of the area. Sprawl crosses political boundaries. In many cases, sprawl will result in huge metropolitan areas that cross city, county, and even state lines.

White flight has played a significant role in urban sprawl. The ten fastest growing communities in the Detroit metropolitan area during the 1990s were all more than 80 percent white. The ten communities that have been projected to grow most rapidly during the first quarter of this century are all more than 95 percent white.

Since state and federal funds go to communities based on population, the communities that are growing are rewarded and the central cities are penalized. Less money for services encourages continued exodus from the central cities.

Urban sprawl takes land out of agricultural production. This is usually our best agricultural land, as cities are often located in fertile areas close to oceans, lakes, or rivers. Thousands of acres are lost daily to sprawl. California's central valley, a major agricultural area, has been losing 10,000 acres per year to new housing.

As an area grows geographically larger, people tend to commute longer distances to work, which results in traffic problems and greater air pollution.

Sprawl tends to foster poor land utilization. Suburban growth is usually lower density than central city areas with significantly more land per resident. Sprawl results in the need for more police, increased fire protection costs, greater road costs, transportation difficulties, and greater pollution. A website devoted to problems of urban sprawl is **www.sprawlcity.org**.

C. PROBLEMS OF THE POOR

There appears to be a direct relationship between the size of the city and the percentage of its residents who live at, or below, the poverty level. Larger cities must spend proportionately more on services for their poor.

The poor in central city areas place greater reliance than others on public transportation.

In many cities, it is extremely difficult to commute to jobs far removed from central city neighborhoods because of cumbersome public transportation systems.

Middle class people are much more likely to move when it is to their economic advantage to do so. Mobility seems directly related to financial status. The poor, however, are relatively immobile. As industries leave the central areas, unemployment increases and the unemployed poor remain behind.

D. IMMIGRATION

Net legal immigration to the United States is approximately one million people.

The Immigration and Naturalization Service (INS) estimates that 80 percent of legal immigrants to the U.S. are low skilled with 40 percent having less than a high school or equivalent education. The majority of legal immigrants locate in cities as do a great portion of illegal immigrants.

The number of illegal aliens in the U.S. is unknown, as is the number of new illegals who come to the U.S. each year. As late as 1995, the Immigration and Naturalization Service was using 3.2 million as the number of undocumented persons living in the U.S. Bear Sterns puts the 2005 estimate at 20 million illegals while the Census Bureau places the number at between 10 and 12 million.

The number of new illegals each year is believed to be a half million, although this figure may be low. Estimates of illegal immigrants vary depending on who is doing the estimating. Besides illegal border crossings, many individuals with tourist and student visas who legally entered the U.S. have chosen to remain in an illegal status.

Illegal immigrants are most heavily employed in the agriculture, gardening, hotel, restaurant, meat packing, and garment industries. In many cases they fill jobs that legal citizens would not take. In the absence of these generally low-skilled workers, many businesses would be adversely affected.

Despite efforts to halt illegal immigration, government action has actually encouraged it. By our past amnesty programs and giving green cards to persons who come here illegally, we foster a hope for future amnesty.

Local law enforcement agencies seldom cooperate with the INS in removing illegal immigrants.

The Federal Personal Responsibility and Work Opportunity Act denies public benefits to illegal immigrants. However, many benefits, such as schools, are still generally available.

Landlords often take advantage of illegal immigrants by failing to make repairs to housing and by charging high rents even where there are rent controls.

Illegals are unlikely to go to public authorities to complain about health and safety problems or rents in excess of rent ceilings.

Any time there are dramatic economic differences between two nations, we can expect those who have less to immigrate to the country that has more.

Besides the pressures on cities from legal and illegal immigration, we also have pressure from natural growth and migration from other areas.

Legal and illegal immigrants create pressure for housing needs at the bottom of the economic scale. Because immigrants, especially illegals, are often willing to accept substandard housing, few units are demolished due to deterioration. This demand pressure on available housing keeps rents up, even in substandard housing.

E. THE HOMELESS

Homeless "street people" were largely ignored until relatively recently. Today, however, increasing homelessness has become a social and economic issue.

While many of the homeless are alcoholics, drug addicts, or people with mental problems, some are just not able to afford minimum shelter. Some are people unable to get employment and others are underemployed, with income insufficient to afford housing costs. Other causes of homelessness are runaways and family breakups. The homeless include entire families, often living in cars. The homeless are not a homogeneous group. Street people are a problem in every major city. The small resort city of Santa Barbara has a problem with homeless people attracted by its fine parks. Many church and civic groups have arranged temporary housing. In most cities, the cost to house the homeless has been met by charities. To date, the government has not taken a major role in housing the homeless.

The presence of street people can have a negative effect on property values.

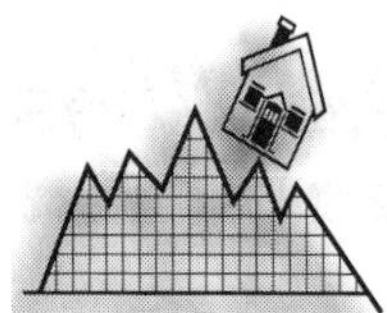

Panhandling street people in the central city areas intimidate shoppers. Developers are not willing to construct new high-cost buildings in an area where people are likely to sleep in the entry ways.

In 1981, a court order required New York City to provide shelter for the homeless. New York's shelter population has increased by 72 percent from 1998 to 2005. The shelters give the homeless a place to sleep but they are on the street during the day. In addition, many homeless refuse to go to shelters except in periods of extreme cold.

Chicago has 6,000 shelter beds, but a homeless population estimated at 15,000 to 20,000. Many of Chicago's homeless sleep in cars or abandoned buildings.

New York City is spending over $1,500 per month to house each homeless welfare family in hotels because of the lack of apartments. In order to entice owners to rent to these families and reduce costs, New York was offering landlords a bonus of $6,000 to house a family of four for $270 per month for two years. New York has been able to move 400 of the 3,400 families housed in hotels into apartments through the use of the bonus. It has since increased the bonus to $9,700. New York City believes that a side effect of the bonus is that it will enable landlords to bring structures up to code standards.

Los Angeles had a program of taking away the mattresses and "cardboard condos" of street people to reduce crime and solve problems. The net effect to date has been solely to make the homeless more uncomfortable.

Some cities, like Santa Monica, have set aside areas for the homeless, where they have relative safety and are not harassed by authorities.

While this offers protection to the homeless, it does not solve any problems.

II. Other Negative Factors Facing Cities

A. AGING

As cities age, city maintenance costs increase dramatically. There is the need for repair or replacement of roads, bridges, sewer and water systems, public transportation, etc. There are cities with sewer lines over 100 years old that leak like sieves, unsafe bridges, and roads full of potholes. There have been outbreaks of dysentery from drinking public water. Many cities have problems that we associate with those of third world countries.

The American Society of Civil Engineers gave the U.S. infrastructure a rating of "D" in 1998. In 2001, they increased the rating to "D+."

With lower tax revenue and insufficient federal monies, no improvements for the problems can be seen for the near future.

B. LOSS OF TAX BASE

Coupled with the increasing needs of aging, older cities have been suffering a reduction in their property tax base as well as a decline in sales tax revenue. Not only have more affluent residents left cities for the suburbs, businesses have followed as well.

The decline in property values have been offset by higher tax rates. Higher city tax rates encourage more residents to leave. People vote with their feet and will move to low tax areas.

Besides commercial businesses, cities have also been losing industry. Many of our industries have been adversely affected by foreign competition. These include labor-intensive industries such as steel, automobile, machine tool, textile, heavy equipment, etc. The cities in deepest trouble are those that have relied heavily on industries that have experienced a rapid decline. When an industry shrinks or disappears, skilled workers leave, unless another industry can take its place. Those remaining are usually the unskilled poor who have the most difficulty relocating. They are likely to be minorities.

The demand for services has not declined with the declining tax revenue. The cost for basic services per person is far greater for the poor than it is for more affluent residents.

Chicago is typical of older cities with problems. While Chicago has had tremendous growth and revitalization in its Loop and Gold Coast areas, much of the city has suffered. Manufacturers have left the city for other areas, and it has been steadily losing jobs. The problems of Chicago are similar to the problems in other older cities—high property taxes, increased crime, and numerous other factors have driven small employers elsewhere.

Pittsburgh had an almost total collapse of its economic base: steel. Forty thousand steelworkers lost their jobs over a five-year period. Today, Pittsburgh is a developer of robots, medical technology, and computer software. Over 40,000 new jobs were created in new industries. Pittsburgh is one of only a few older cities able to attract high tech industries. Pittsburgh's revival, which is still in progress, has been the result of cooperation between the city, the state, and the universities to supply support to the new industries.

Older cities unable to attract new industry to replace what has been lost have been described as "donut cities," an economic void surrounded by healthy suburbs.

C. RENT CONTROL

***RENT CONTROL** is any action by a city government to regulate and control the amount of rent and any future increases charged by a landlord.*

This is an emotional issue. However, in economic terms, rent control does not make sense, because it: 1) reduces the supply of new housing, and 2) usually benefits only the original people (renters) who initiated it.

States may permit cities to enact rent control.

In rent control's usual form, the government restricts, by percentage, annual increases in rental payments. Such restrictions may be applied at the city, county, and even the state level. Commercial, industrial, and luxury rentals are generally exempt from this control.

Rent control takes a social burden of helping low-income people and places this burden on the owners of rental property. Actually, it is not just low-income persons who benefit by rent control. Many tenants of rent-controlled units in New York are wealthy and even own weekend homes while they enjoy landlord-subsidized rent in their city residences.

Rent control has been called "a welfare program for the rich." A weekly television show hosted by Sam Donaldson pointed out that Alistair Cooke, Ed Koch, Mia Farrow, and many other celebrities live in rent-controlled units. In many cases, affluent residents are paying less than one-fifth of what their unit would rent for on a free market.

In the opinion of many informed real estate analysts, rent control is a form of economic suicide. It discourages new construction by removing economic incentives for developers. This results in a limited supply of new units available to renters.

A rent ceiling increases the likelihood of lower maintenance, as there is a profit incentive to spend the bare minimum on maintenance expenses. Improvements that will not contribute to the net income will not contribute to the value and are therefore economically unsound. In 2005, it was estimated that 29 percent of rent controlled property was classified as "deteriorated," requiring major remedial work. Only 8 percent of uncontrolled units were classified in such a state of disrepair.

Landlords, who feel victimized by this profit squeeze, are often forced to convert their apartments into condominiums. This further reduces the number of units available in the open market.

New York City enacted the ***WAR EMERGENCY TENANT PROTECTION ACT** during World War II to protect tenants from rent gouging by landlords*. The end of the war did not end rent control. In a city with more renters than property owners, politicians were subject to pressure to leave the controls in place. The political decision to do nothing has served to reduce the supply of housing in the face of an ever-increasing demand.

Rent control is more prevalent for mobilehome parks than for apartments. California has 13 communities with rent control over apartments but over 100 local rent control areas. The reason why mobilehome parks are more likely to be subject to rent control is that mobilehomes (manufactured homes) are not truly mobile. While an apartment resident can easily relocate if the rent becomes too high, a space renter in a mobilehome park cannot readily relocate the mobilehome. The costs to do so make most moves impractical and, even when economically possible, few parks will accept an old mobilehome. Rent control for mobilehome parks resulted from a few park owners raising rents to an unconscionable level.

In the authors' opinion, the real solution to the rental crunch will not involve more government regulation. **The answer lies in the government providing more incentives and increased profits to developers, thereby increasing availability of rental units and allowing rents to settle at their natural level on the open market.**

Rent control is a discriminatory price control that affects more than the owners of buildings. Rent control, generally enacted for the purpose of helping current residents, has worked to the detriment of many cities. Rent control keeps the value of rent-controlled property down. Lower values are reflected in lower property tax assessments. The net effect of rent control to a city is fewer property tax dollars available for city services.

There has been a movement away from rent control. Boston and Cambridge have ended rent control while some cities have placed limitations on their rent control ordinances to cover only existing and/or poorer tenants.

D. POPULATION LOSS

According to the U.S. Census Bureau, the population of 284 of our nation's largest cities declined an average of 0.6 percent between 1980 and 1990. Many cities suffered substantial losses. New York City lost 11 percent of its population during this period, but the suburban population grew by 17.4 percent.

Despite arguments to the contrary, cities apparently lost population during the 1970s as well as the 1980s. During the 1990s, 30 percent or more of high poverty rate areas suffered a population loss of 5 percent while more affluent areas had population increases.

Some cities, like Cincinnati, had large population losses in the 1990s. Cincinnati's loss was 9 percent of its population. It apparently will exceed this rate in this decade.

While many central cities have experienced population losses, the number of households has generally increased. This is due to the growth of households headed by a single person.

The 2000 census reveals that a single person heads over 40 percent of American households.

Many cities have challenged the accuracy of census figures. They claim they are being short-changed by census counts that show significantly fewer people than the city estimates.

Poor and illegal immigrants in the central city who often have more than one family per housing unit, are less likely to admit the presence of others.

The poor, as well as illegal immigrants are often apprehensive when dealing with authority. They are less likely to admit the presence of others to census takers. Census statistics show that many minorities and illegals are likely to be omitted from official counts. From past experience, census errors in the central cities are likely to be an underestimation of population.

E. CRIME

The birth rate is higher for minority groups than it is for the white population. Most crimes are committed by young males. Economic conditions in central cities make crime seem more attractive than in more affluent areas. It can therefore be understood why poor minority areas also are likely to be high-crime areas. These are usually in the central cities.

High crime rates have caused individuals, businesses and industry to leave cities. Besides loss directly related to crimes, crime results in increased insurance costs, and a fear mentality that makes it difficult to attract customers as well as skilled workers. Several of the factors that contribute to high crime rates within many of our central cities include:

1. **Congestion:** Many law enforcement officers believe congestion is conducive to crime.
2. **Unemployment:** Especially among the unskilled young, there seems to be a direct relationship between unemployment and crime. Recently we have seen a decrease in crime in many of our cities while unemployment also decreased.
3. **Drugs and Alcohol:** There is generally a readily available supply of drugs and a heavy rate of addiction in the cities. Addicts often steal to feed their habits.

4. **Breakdown of Family Influence:** Peer pressure has replaced the family influences in many cases.
5. **Increase in Gangs:** Membership in gangs provides a sense of identity for many. The presence of gang activity scares people away from a neighborhood. There is a strong peer pressure to belong to gangs. Large gangs like the Bloods and Crips are believed to be responsible for a great deal of urban crime. In Los Angeles, some 600 active Hispanic gangs exist as well as a growing number of Asian gangs
6. **Hopelessness:** A feeling that there is no future.
7. **Racial Animosity:** This justifies crimes against others.

F. BROWNFIELDS

BROWNFIELDS *refer to real property where the expansion, development, or re-use may be complicated by the presence of hazardous substances, pollutants, or contaminants.* The presence in the soil of toxic substances presents real danger to residents of an area. The dangers can be translated to potential liability. In some cases, the contamination was caused by owners' tenants or even occupants of neighboring property as long as 100 years ago when dangers were not known. Developers are afraid of such sites because of possible liability for problems, as well as the cost of cleaning the site. Lenders are often afraid to loan for either purchase or development of these sites because of possible cleanup liability of the owners.

Many states have toxic waste acts, whereby the government can clean up a site if the owner fails to do so. A judgment against the owner can then be obtained, which becomes a lien on the property.

Vermont, Maine, and New Hampshire have super lien acts. Under these acts, if the state has to clean up a private land site, the state obtains a ***SUPER LIEN*** *that applies to all of the owner's property and takes precedence over all other liens, including purchase money loans secured by the property.* The effect of these lien laws is to make a present owner liable for what prior owners, tenants and even trespassers might have done on the site. There has been proposed federal legislation that would establish federal super liens for toxic waste cleanup.

To protect themselves against super liens, lenders are likely to require extensive soil tests. Because so many substances formerly used have been found to be unsafe, a soil test might not reveal a particularly dangerous substance. The onerous liability of a general lien will affect the number of buyers for sites where toxic substances have been used. The threat of possible liability can depress the market for older industrial sites that have had many previous uses.

The National Bank of Fredericksburg, Virginia, decided not to foreclose on a $200,000 loan secured by real property after discovering the land was contaminated with creosote and cleanup costs could reach $2.5 million. While the bank was not the polluter, it feared that if they foreclosed it could, as the legal owner, be held liable for cleanup.

Possible liability, as well as cleanup costs, are factors that work against redevelopment of old industrial sites for new industries.

G. TRAFFIC CONGESTION AND PARKING PROBLEMS

Highway congestion causes traffic backups on city streets. *This can result in seemingly hopeless traffic jams known as* ***GRIDLOCK***. Recurring traffic problems have motivated many businesses to relocate.

Driver frustration is believed to be, in large part, responsible for the phenomenon known as "road rage." In Los Angeles, road rage has resulted in numerous incidents of freeway violence. These include motorists shooting other motorists, and the case of a man who was sentenced to three years in jail for tossing a dog to its death following a minor traffic accident with the dog's owner. The average Los Angeles commuter spends more than 93 hours stalled in traffic.

The average cross-town traffic speed in the borough of Manhattan is 5.2 miles per hour. Ambulances in New York City take twice as long to respond to an emergency than in any other city in the country.

Paul Dempsey, a transportation professor at the University of Denver believes that transportation bottlenecks cost more than $100 billion per year. Our transportation system is simply overloaded and infrastructure projects such as airports are not adequately linked to the transportation networks. The problem has been only getting worse as more workers move to suburban locations further clogging the roads.

The Texas Transportation Institute estimates that in our 85 largest cities, 3.5 billion hours are lost per year because of traffic problems. Traffic problems have caused many industries and individuals to relocate to smaller communities far from central cities.

The solution until recently has been to build more and bigger freeways and more one-way streets within cities. Building new highways seems to be only a temporary measure as better transportation routes usually bring in more motorists and the new or widened routes become clogged. There is no room to widen major streets in mature cities.

The quote "If you build it, they will come," from the film *Field of Dreams*, apparently had it right when it comes to transportation. Better routes attract motorists until the advantage of the routes disappear.

Because of the massive costs of expanded highways, few new major highways are being built.

The ***SOUTHERN CALIFORNIA ASSOCIATION OF GOVERNMENTS (SCAG)*** *is a voluntary association of cities that regularly meets to discuss any problems or items of mutual interest.* SCAG projects that delays due to traffic congestion will account for half the travel time by 2010. A side effect of daily driving trips, which will double in time as well as number, will create added air pollution. On the Hollywood Freeway, overcrowding results in average 20 mph traffic 14 hours per day. SCAG predicted that unless commuting habits changed, the 10-lane Hollywood Freeway would need 11 lanes each way. Traffic habits did not change and needed lanes were not added. Traffic has worsened.

According to Caltrans, a state agency, there is a hidden demand (disguised need) for space on the freeways, and adding lanes will only add former street users to the new roads.

A study by SCAG indicates that more than $42 billion will be needed in Southern California to maintain the status quo of freeway speeds by the year 2010. Further, if planners cannot alter where population growth and new jobs will occur, the cost could exceed $110 billion. By 2010, SCAG estimates traffic congestion will play havoc with California's economy.

If changes do NOT occur, SCAG predicts that the average commuting speed of 31 miles per hour will decrease to 11 miles per hour, with half the commuting time spent in traffic snarls.

Traffic problems will increase with population increases. New residents will move into areas with adequate and more reasonable housing and will commute greater distances to work.

In the District of Columbia, many homes and apartments were built before the automobile, or before its use was as prevalent as it is today. They have inadequate parking. It is not unusual for a person returning home late to find all the parking spaces filled and forced to park six to eight blocks from his or her residence.

In downtown Miami there are approximately 5 drivers seeking every 4 parking spaces. Slow drivers looking for spaces and waiting until others pull out create traffic congestion. New office construction in Miami creates a greater need for the available spaces. Miami's problems are not much different from those encountered in many cities.

Double parking for loading and unloading creates significant traffic blockage on city streets. Traffic and parking has continued to grow worse each year.

While more central city parking spaces will solve some traffic problems, it will create others by encouraging more people to drive.

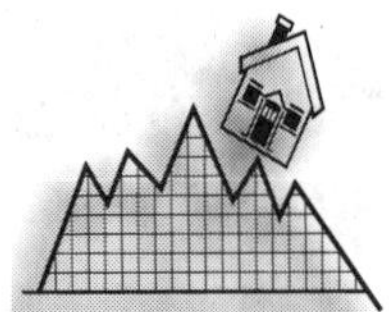

H. RAIL LINES

While some planners believe we need greater reliance on rail, America's railroads are not considering expansion. In fact, railroads have been tearing up under utilized lines and postponing investments so that even railroads now have bottlenecks.

The profitability of railroads has been in freight, not passenger service. Use of containers and computer tracking to get maximum utilization of rail cars has helped the railroads. Because passenger traffic has not been profitable, the passenger traffic expansion has been left to Amtrak.

The federal government had hoped that rail transportation would alleviate highway problems. Between 1971 and 2000, Amtrak received $23 billion in federal operating subsidies yet the effect of Amtrak on transportation problems has been negligible.

Congress has ordered Amtrak to be financially self-sufficient. While many experts believe this goal will not be met, Amtrak had high hopes that 20 new high-speed trains capable of 150 M.P.H. would bring profitability. The first of these trains, which seats 304 passengers went into service in December 2000 with approximately one-third of the seats occupied on its maiden run. The financial success of these new trains has not been realized.

Amtrak failed to meet the statutory mandate of becoming self sufficient by 2003. The future of AMTRAK hinges on the willingness of the federal government to fund financial shortfalls each year. It is doubtful that private interests will be willing to take over AMTRAK services without federal guarantees against losses.

I. URBAN BLIGHT

URBAN BLIGHT *results from failure by owners, tenants, and the city to maintain the property and area.* While primarily a problem of the cities, blight can also affect small towns and suburban areas.

Blighted properties and blighted areas place a financial burden on local government because a decline in value results in a decrease in the tax roll. While crime and the need for social services tend to increase with blight, the funds to fulfill these needs are diminished.

A decline in tax revenue is likely to result in a decline in municipal services.

Industries tend to leave areas as blight sets in and new industries tend to avoid such areas because of concern with possible brownfields, as well as the perceived difficulty in attracting skilled workers to the area.

Urban blight is more likely to be seen in areas where neighborhood cohesiveness has weakened with a high percentage of renters. Absentee owners who allow property to deteriorate affects the attitude of all owners.

Owner neglect can be caused by increased fixed costs, such as taxes or utilities, which the owner is unable to pass on to the tenants. More often than not, failure to maintain is due to the fact that the landlord does not have to maintain.

If tenants will accept the premises as they are, there is no need to maintain or repair. This is often the case with illegal immigrants.

There also appears to be a correlation between landlords' attitudes toward maintenance and tenants' neglect.

Where an owner anticipates demolition or abandonment, the owner is likely to attempt to milk the property, that is, obtain the highest possible cash flow without regard to maintaining value. The owner is planning for the short term only.

The difficulty in obtaining loans for rehabilitation in declining areas also accelerates the blight.

In order to maximize income, owners will overcrowd units. Greater occupancy results in greater wear and tear on the unit, infestation of rodents and insects, and a greater likelihood of fire.

Abandoned cars on the street reflect what has been happening to real property. Philadelphia appears to be the graveyard of many of the automobiles Detroit has produced. In 2004, there were 61,686 abandoned vehicles towed off the streets of Philadelphia, one every 8.5 minutes. The reason is usually a cheap unregistered car with a costly problem. In areas of New York and other cities, abandoned cars sit for months and even years because of lack of funds for removal.

High population density generally means children, gangs, and graffiti.

The presence of graffiti, as well as congregating teenagers, will tend to intimidate people, and shoppers with alternatives will go elsewhere. The remaining businesses are generally based on local trade.

Taggers are not necessarily gang members. They like to leave symbols to enhance their importance, but many members of the public view tagger and gang-related graffiti in the same negative light.

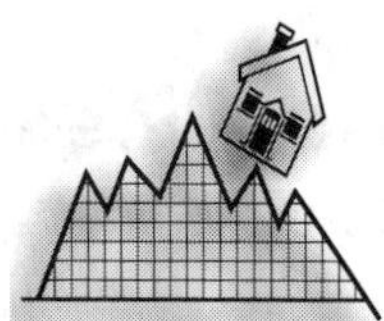

J. ABANDONMENT

In New York, enough buildings were abandoned in a three-year period to house 250,000 people.

Cleveland, Detroit, Chicago, Philadelphia, Washington, D.C., and New Orleans also experienced abandonment. In California, abandonment of buildings has not been common because of the influx of illegal immigrants, who will accept substandard housing, as well as the moderate climate, which makes even dwellings lacking proper heating habitable year-round.

For a variety of reasons, landlords said; "We quit." They ceased to provide water and heat. Tenants are being forced to leave. Many structurally sound buildings have been abandoned.

Increased energy costs coupled with poorly insulated structures and inefficient boilers resulted in owners not being able to operate many structures economically. Negative cash flows that cannot be offset by depreciation benefits often lead to abandonment.

In some cases, health and safety code enforcement have encouraged abandonment when the costs offset the benefits of ownership. In New York, some owners have deeded their property to nonexistent grantees or derelicts in an attempt to escape liability arising from health and safety code violations and to avoid being forced to bear the difficulty in collecting rents as well as aggravation connected with owning substandard housing. This, in effect, is abandonment.

Other times, landlords have a debt service that does not make sense. In some cases fraud was involved in borrowing on properties the owner intended to walk away from.

When a unit in a multi-unit structure has been destroyed by fire or vandalism, the costs of rehabilitating the unit could exceed its economic value so it will be left vacant.

The abandoned unit becomes home to gangs or derelicts, such as the infamous "Hotel Hell" in Hollywood. Other tenants are intimidated and leave, and their units are vandalized. The entire building is soon abandoned. Once a building has been vacated, vandals frequently take over.

The likelihood of residential buildings being abandoned has decreased as property values have increased. However, many large commercial and industrial facilities have been closed and are now idle and deteriorating.

When a building becomes abandoned, the tax roll is decreased which means less money for services. Even when the building is boarded up, people get in. Abandoned buildings become the centers of crime including drugs and prostitution. For legal reasons, police are reluctant to enter abandoned properties without a warrant for a specific purpose.

III. What's Happening?

Physical problems of deterioration can be addressed in three ways: conservation, correction, and clearance.

CONSERVATION *deals with keeping the structures and areas maintained;* ***CORRECTION*** *is the reversal of the deterioration process by physical improvement;* and ***CLEARANCE*** *is the removal of what is viewed as the problem.*

A. CLEANUP CAMPAIGNS

Most cities with blighted areas have seen numerous community cleanup campaigns where trash and abandoned vehicles are removed and graffiti is painted over. These types of programs are often the result of church or civic groups and city cooperation. For example, the mayor of Philadelphia asked that religious leaders mobilize to fight urban blight.

Cleanup campaigns show immediate, but too often, temporary improvements. It is fairly easy to bring out people for a one-time community cleanup, but it is difficult to maintain a continuing effort.

Capitalism will foster long-term commitment, but altruism is usually short-lived.

B. REHABILITATION

Deteriorating housing is just one of the problems facing cities.

Rehabilitation interrelates with problems of drugs, violent crime, school dropouts, and unemployment. Solving all of these problems requires education and jobs. New housing alone is not the answer, but areas can be rehabilitated. It is estimated that the cost to renovate substandard housing is less than half the cost to build replacement housing of similar quality.

A new development, standing alone in the midst of a ghetto, is going to have some impact on the neighborhood. For proper rehabilitation of an area, the building, safety, fire and health codes must be vigorously enforced. Owners must not be given the option to continue as they are, or to allow further decline.

For rehabilitation to be meaningful, we need more than just new or rehabilitated structures. There must be neighborhood involvement and pride.

Otherwise, all the problems that existed in a deteriorating neighborhood will still be there. Rehabilitation of a neighborhood must include the economics of the neighborhood. Decisions of employers to locate in a particular area are economic decisions based upon alternative choices. Ways to attract new employers include tax moratoriums, low interest loans, etc. Businesses must have economic incentives to locate in problem areas.

Redevelopment can have benefits. Besides providing employment, redevelopment adds to the property tax base and can provide significant sales tax revenues.

The 1986 Tax Reform Act made all real estate investing less attractive to investors. The fantastic tax benefits of rapid depreciation were eliminated. This tax reform served as a disincentive to redevelopment. This has had a negative effect on private investment in our blighted inner city areas.

C. SLUM CLEARANCE

Simply clearing an area of old housing does not solve any problems. Slum clearance causes other problems. Those displaced are going to seek other substandard housing to conserve their resources. A problem with redevelopment has been destruction of residential neighborhoods without providing replacement housing. When replacement housing is provided, it is often not affordable to the lower income people whose housing was replaced. New skyscrapers have displaced poor residents in demolished residential hotels. This displacement causes further pressure on the lower end of the housing market because there are fewer apartments available. This tends to keep up demand and rents, because there is increased competition for the remaining apartments, as well as serving as a disincentive for owners of marginal properties to improve their properties.

There is a reluctance of cities to demolish properties as was formerly common because of awareness of hazards from lead paint, asbestos, and possible chemical contaminants.

D. GENTRIFICATION

Housing formerly available to the poor and middle-class is being taken over by middle and upper income young urban professionals. *This movement of young professionals to the central city is known as* ***GENTRIFICATION***. When both lower- and higher-income families desire housing units, those with higher incomes will take the units.

Many of the new central city residents are singles and unmarried couples that want to be where they believe the action is. They want to be close to restaurants, theatres, and artistic events. They also want to avoid long commutes.

Gentrification results in neighborhoods with fewer minorities, generally an increase in property values and tax dollars, greater commercial property, and a reduction in family size.

The new residents tend to have more political influence and the infrastructure of the areas can be expected to improve.

Not only has the demand by higher-income groups increased values, it has also resulted in the exodus of poor white, African American, and Latino populations. San Francisco is one of the few cities in the nation to show a decline in the African American and Latino populations between 1970 and 1980 (about 10 percent). The Asian population in San Francisco is, however, on the rise and currently is about one-third of the population.

The loss of that portion of the population that generally has the largest families is expected to reduce the total population of San Francisco. The California Finance Department projects that San Francisco will be the only California metropolitan area to show a decrease in population by the year 2020. It projects a population of 684,200 in 2020, compared with an estimated 744,000 in 2004.

Many residents feel that San Francisco will lose much of its charm if new high-rises are built. The increased business density is causing extreme traffic congestion on both the freeways and city streets. In addition, parking space is at a premium. After New York City, San Francisco has the highest population density of any U.S. city.

While gentrification means higher values and property taxes, it does present a problem.

The problem with gentrification is: Where does the replaced population go?

The refugees forced out of an area by gentrification must seek housing elsewhere which places pressure on other areas of low-cost housing.

The West Adams area of Los Angeles is just northwest of the University of Southern California (USC). The area was home to the rich and famous in the early 1900s. The homes are large and the architecture is very distinctive with Victorian, California Craftsman and Colonial Revival styles. The area was all white until 1947, when the first African American family moved into the neighborhood. In the 1950s middle and upper-income African Americans moved into the area, causing a white flight.

Since 1981, middle-income whites, largely professionals, have started to move into the area. They were drawn by both bargain prices and distinctive homes. A great many homes have been restored and affluent whites are replacing poorer African Americans. Homes in the area are being sold to preservationists who wish to restore and live in the area. Because of the white influx, area prices have risen from an average of $81,500 in 1981 to an average sale price of $122,500 by 1985 and to $250,000 by 2005.

Currently, completely renovated homes in the West Adams area are selling for anywhere between $450,000 and one million dollars, depending on size and architectural style.

Some African American residents regard the white influx as reverse "blockbusting."

With higher prices, sales in the area are now mainly to whites. This has led to some neighborhood animosity toward the new residents. It is anticipated that market forces will result in the future exodus of more African Americans from the area.

E. CENTRAL AREA RENAISSANCE

Many cities have seen remarkable revitalization of their central areas with offices, shops, restaurants and expensive housing. However, these showcase developments often fail to solve the basic problems of the cities. The need for unskilled workers decreases, as cities become more office and entertainment-oriented. In our older, Eastern cities, we are seeing what appears to be a healthy core area with new civic centers, hotels, offices, restaurants, etc., but the core is deceiving, as the cities have great economic and social problems.

F. CHOICE OF SOLUTIONS

The economic solutions available to cities are:

1. Unincorporate and place the burden on the county.
2. Attract more intensive uses that will increase tax revenues.
3. Increase taxes.
4. Reduce expenses (the cities in the worst trouble have already reduced services to a dangerous level).
5. Create much larger municipal units that include suburbs.

Of the courses available to cities, the second seems to be the most logical long-term solution. The more trouble a city is in financially, the more desirable less attractive uses become. For example, economically depressed Blythe, California, vigorously lobbied for a prison in their area while other communities made it clear they did not want a prison. The prison in Blythe has created many local jobs.

Some communities have even sought dump sites. To most people an environmental concern is not as great a concern as having a decent income.

Problems of cities are often interrelated. A cure in one area could have an adverse effect on another problem area.

It is likely that many challenges faced by cities will not be actively addressed until they reach a point where people will no longer tolerate anything but a solution.

Cities provide a challenge for the future.

G. THE FUTURE

Economist Richard Nathan of Princeton University predicts that our large cities will decline in all aspects in the 21st century. He does not believe that troubled cities like Detroit can be revived. With the decline of the central cities there will be a growth of large suburban centers, called "Satellite Downtowns."

George Sternlieb, an urbanologist at Rutgers University, predicts that the residential portions of our central cities will become "...more of a repository for those who have fallen off the train." He also believes that cities will still be the center for entertainment, but not for industry.

Sternlieb predicts that we will have an enclave of well-to-do residents close to the city center and a great number of poor, making up the majority of residents, surrounded by decay.

Other planners believe cities will be revitalized and will be very attractive in the future. However, to make this a reality, many problems must first be overcome. In the following chapter, you will see how some of these problems are being met.

Gambling and Entertainment Cities (2006)

By 2006, most heavily populated cities will have gambling or casinos within twenty miles of them. The biggest casino states* by casino revenue are:

Nevada	$10.6 Billion
New Jersey	$4.8 Billion
Mississippi	$2.8 Billion
Indiana	$2.4 Billion
Louisiana	$2.2 Billion

*Source: American Gaming Association

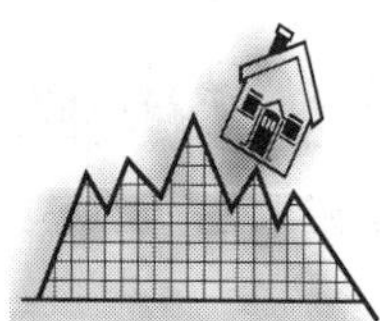

IV. CHAPTER SUMMARY

Over 70 percent of Americans live in cities and suburbs. While in many cases suburbs are flourishing, many cities have serious problems.

Cities have become blocked from expansion by rings of incorporated suburbs. **Urban sprawl** increases traffic problems. In many cases, cities have become **minority centers** with whites fleeing to the suburbs. The percentage of poor seems directly related to the size of cities. The poor create a greater demand on public transportation and social services. As cities age, maintenance costs increase for roads and systems. In addition, loss of business and industry has resulted in a reduction of the tax base of many cities. Many cities have also suffered a reduction in population, which has reduced federal revenue sharing.

Additional problems of cities include **high crime rates**, which further drive business and industry away, traffic congestion on street systems not designed for the automobile as the principal means of transportation and lack of **adequate parking**. Cities also are experiencing a migration of both legal and illegal immigrants. **Homelessness** (street people) is a problem in every major city.

There are many reasons why property is not maintained and **urban blight** results. Because of pressure for housing from the poor and the mild climate, fewer units are demolished in California cities than in many other areas of the nation.

While the central areas have seen some rejuvenation, most of our older cities have a vibrant core surrounded by blighted areas, with high unemployment rates. Some planners, however, believe that cities will be rejuvenated and become attractive in the future.

V. GLOSSARY OF KEY TERMS

Abandonment – Owners walking away from property because continued ownership is not economically viable.

Brownfields – Areas having contaminated soil.

Donut Cities – Central cities that have serious economic difficulties but are surrounded by a ring of healthy suburbs.

Gentrification – The movement of young professionals to the central city.

Gridlock – Traffic blockage on city streets backing up from overcrowded freeway exits.

Light Rail Transportation – Railed trolley cars, usually electric.

Redevelopment – The clearance and development of an area. Generally areas are redeveloped for uses other than previous uses.

Redlining – The unlawful refusal of lenders to make loans within particular areas.

Rehabilitation – The repair of existing structures.

Sprawl – Uncontrolled outward growth of metropolitan areas.

Street People – Homeless people.

Super Liens – Priority liens against owners of toxic waste sites that the state has to clean up. The liens apply to all the property of the owner.

Tipping Point – The point at which white residents will panic and desert an area. It is based upon the number and speed of minorities entering an area.

Urban Blight – Deterioration caused by failure to maintain by landlords and/or tenants as well as by vandalism.

White Flight – The exodus of Caucasians from an area. It is generally based on fear that minorities will dominate the area.

VI. CLASS DISCUSSION TOPICS

1. What are ways cities could encourage new business, industry, and private redevelopment?

2. What are the traffic problems of your area? What are possible solutions?

3. Analyze current migration to and from your area. Who are the migrants and why are they arriving or leaving?

4. What would be the economic effect, if any, on your local economy if all illegal immigration were to cease and all those with illegal status left?

5. Identify areas in your city where gentrification is taking place. What are the positive and negative effects?

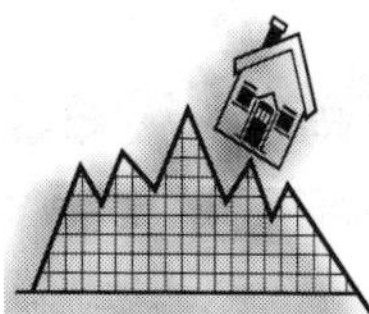

VII. CHAPTER 5 QUIZ

1. Tipping point refers to:
   a. zoning change.
   b. white flight.
   c. immigration.
   d. transportation.

2. Growth outward from the city is known as:
   a. sprawl.
   b. white flight.
   c. in-fill development.
   d. gentrification.

3. Effects of rent control include all, except:
   a. encouraging apartment conversion to condominiums.
   b. increasing likelihood of lower maintenance.
   c. placing a social burden on landlords.
   d. encouraging new apartment structures.

4. Which group of people is most likely to be omitted from census statistics?
   a. Wealthy
   b. Families with children
   c. Working families
   d. Illegal immigrants

5. "Brownfields" refer to:
   a. areas without city water.
   b. desert land.
   c. areas with contaminated soil.
   d. minority areas.

6. Results of urban blight include all, except:
   a. a decline in tax revenue.
   b. greater need for social services.
   c. attraction to industry because of lower cost land and labor.
   d. increase in crime as an area deteriorates.

7. All of the following contribute to urban crime, with the exception of:
   a. gentrification.
   b. high unemployment.
   c. congestion.
   d. peer pressure.

8. A problem associated with gentrification is:
   a. the increased tax base.
   b. industries being attracted back to the city.
   c. new jobs.
   d. where do displaced residents go?

9. Properties where the landlord lacks an incentive to maintain the premises would be rented to:
   a. families with children.
   b. single professionals.
   c. illegal immigrants.
   d. tenants on signed leases.

10. The government has encouraged illegal immigration by:
   a. past amnesty.
   b. denial of welfare benefits to noncitizens.
   c. subsidized housing.
   d. controlling inflation.

ANSWERS: 1. *b*; 2. *a*; 3. *d*; 4. *d*; 5. *c*; 6. *c*; 7. *a*; 8. *d*; 9. *c*; 10. *a*

LEARNING OBJECTIVES

Saving many cities was once viewed as a herculean task because of the multitude of problems that resulted in deteriorating structures and infrastructures, loss of jobs, transportation gridlock and crime.

> ***This chapter will help you understand how private and government action coupled with free market forces have overcome many problems of cities and are working to make cities desirable for living and economically viable.***

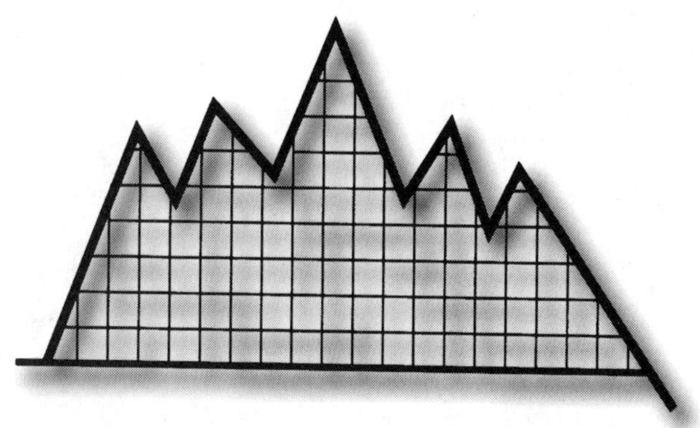

Chapter 6
Overcoming Problems of the Cities

I. Overcoming Problems of the Cities

Thirty years ago the problems of the cities seemed insurmountable. With abandoned structures, rubble, trash, high crime rates, declining tax rolls, and public services, transportation gridlock, and a deteriorating infrastructure led to a general doom and gloom forecast.

Even with this multitude of problems, many cities have come back with community revitalization, a decline in crime, and a vibrant economy. Urban economists now see opportunities where they formerly saw despair.

Private, as well as governmental action, has worked to revitalize many of our cities.

A. WHITE FLIGHT

While urban planners claim that white flight can be reversed by education and communication, white flight is really emotionally based so presenting facts is unlikely to change it. What will change white flight is the belief that the area not only offers benefits but the area will likely become even more desirable in the future rather than decline.

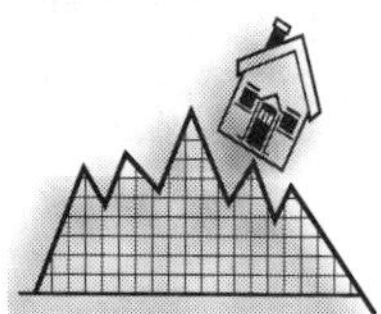

Chapter 6

CHAPTER 6 OUTLINE

Community actions that can help to keep an integrated neighborhood and solve other city problems are new development, the restoration of existing properties, new facilities, rebuilding infrastructures, and strict code enforcements. Better schools and magnet schools that offer special curriculums have made cities more desirable for families.

B. SPRAWL

Some sprawl is inevitable. It is the result of population growth. Between 1970 and 1990, Seattle's developed land grew twice as fast as its population growth. On the other hand, Vancouver B.C. had growth at one-third the rate of Seattle based on population. Vancouver is one of the best cities for pedestrians.

Vancouver reduced sprawl by inward growth consisting of in-fill developments and redevelopment of under utilized sites.

SMART GROWTH is the management direction of growth that minimizes environmental damage and enhances livability. Smart growth involves restoration of central-city areas and provides a balanced mix of land uses, as well as transportation systems that accommodate pedestrians, bicycles, public transit and private vehicles.

Smart-growth advocates claim that the neglect of our central cities and older suburbs foster sprawl and all its problems. With smart growth, a city can enhance its tax base and restore community vitality.

Smart growth can be achieved by:

1. Directing development towards existing communities.
2. Creating neighborhoods friendly to pedestrians—a walkable environment.
3. Mixture of land use so residents are close to employers and commerce.
4. Distinctive communities around the best of existing structures, rather than cookie-cutter designs.
5. Allowing for a range of housing opportunities covering the economic ladder.
6. Providing for a variety of transportation choices.
7. Utilizing compact designs.
8. Presentation of open spaces and consideration of natural beauty.

smartgrowth.org

Maryland's former Governor Parris Glendenning proposed "smart growth." His plan consisted of expanding mass transit, limiting infrastructure expenditures outside of growth zones and subsidizing closing costs of persons who buy a home within walking distance of their place of work.

In many areas, civic and even business groups are opposing new highways, as they are agents of sprawl as well as pollution.

The tendency for jobs to move outward from cities must be reversed. When jobs move outward it not only hurts the cities' tax base but it also makes jobs inaccessible to many of the poor in the inner cities. One way to discourage growth in an area and encourage growth in inner areas is to have high impact fees in some areas and tax incentive in other areas.

The "punishment or reward" approach makes employers act in their economic best interests.

In Greenwich and Stamford, Connecticut wealthy residents are using their wealth to block development. They are fighting sprawl by acquiring hundreds of acres of undeveloped property for conservation trusts. Wealthy communities have also been buying up property to prevent development. (Chapter 13 shows how planning can reduce sprawl.)

C. CRIME REDUCTION

While there have been many programs to reduce crime in inner city neighborhoods, some of these programs have been worthwhile, yet others seem to have been a waste of money.

1. Severe Penalties and Diversion Programs

Increasing penalties for crime, such as longer sentences, resulted in more citizens behind bars and a heavy tax burden for keeping them there. It does not appear to have had a material effect on decreasing crime.

Programs of job training and counseling have been more effective in reducing crime than long-term incarceration. From an economic viewpoint, it can accomplish more at a far lower cost than prison. Crime diversion programs such as these have resulted in a 47 percent reduction in the level of violent crime in San Francisco. While a "get tough on crime" policy works well for elections, it doesn't translate to crime reduction.

2. Police Involvement

Some people feel that more involvement by police in their communities has been successful. Local community programs include:

a. Foot patrols getting the police closer to citizens.
b. Bike patrols.
c. Increasing the number of officers on the street.
d. Police involvement in community programs such as athletic and scout programs.
e. Officer programs at local schools.

While these programs may help reduce crime, the greatest reduction has likely been based on the economy. A strong economy results in higher employment. There is a direct correlation between the availability of jobs and crime.

3. Block Parents

In some communities, schools have worked with parents to designate block parents who have a designation card in their window. It indicates to a child that it is a place to go should there be a problem. The purpose is to provide guidance and reduce crime.

4. Neighborhood Watch

A neighborhood with a watch organization installs signs indicating there is a neighborhood watch. Residents cooperate with police by reporting what they believe to be or will lead to illegal activities. With police cooperation, these community organizations can result in dope dealers, prostitutes, and gang members seeking other areas to ply their trade or hang out in because they can expect to be watched and reported.

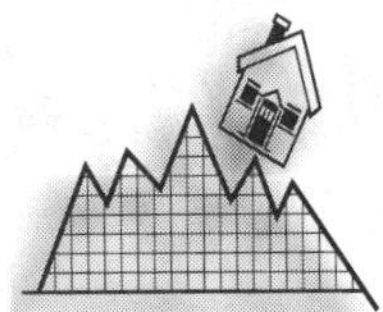

5. School Uniforms

A number of public school districts now require students to wear school uniforms, such as dark blue trousers or skirts and white shirts or blouses. Ties may be required as well as designated shoe styles and colors.

6. Combating Gangs

After decades of dealing with gangs, the best approach appears to be a two-prong attack. First is to target the more violent and criminal active gang members for police actions. Hard-core gang members must be taken off the streets. The second more important approach is to keep children out of gangs. The Federal Bureau of Alcohol, Tobacco, and Firearms developed a school-based gang prevention curriculum. This plan, along with other similar plans, offers alternatives to gang involvement and have shown significant effects in reducing gang enrollments. By providing boys 13-20 years of age with programs that interest them and offer relevance to their lives, the attractiveness of belonging to a gang diminishes.

D. TRAFFIC CONGESTION

Because automobile users pay so little of true highway costs, people tend to live farther from city centers to obtain cheaper land, causing greater highway use.

The problem of alleviating traffic congestion is being addressed in a number of ways.

1. Flextime Workers

Allowing workers to set their own work schedules generally results in workers choosing schedules that will reduce their commuting time.

For the majority of urban workers, flextime is NOT feasible.

2. Off-peak Workweeks

Programs where employees begin work earlier or later to avoid the normal morning traffic rush and finish work earlier or later spreads out the commute period and eases traffic flow. Gridlock was predicted during the 1984 Los Angeles Olympics. It never happened despite an 11 percent increase in daily freeway traffic because employers voluntarily adjusted workdays during the Olympic games.

3. Toll Road Pricing

The technology for a road use pricing system with different fees for different times of the day is available now. Hong Kong experimented with such a system. An electronic license plate device identified vehicles from sensors connected to a central computer. The computer recorded use and billed each owner monthly. While the Hong Kong idea could reduce rush hour traffic by having fees for rush hour use high enough to discourage drivers, the idea of such fees would be politically difficult to sell. Besides public reluctance to pay additional fees, the public monitoring of a person's movements is abhorrent to many.

It has been proposed that toll roads have higher tolls during peak periods to spread out the traffic.

An editorial feature in the Wall Street Journal recommended an economic cure for our traffic problems. It recommends charging automobile users with substantially higher rush hour fees. The article claims that proper pricing of use would result in a dramatic cure. Commuters would stagger their use, and car pools and bus use would increase. The result would be faster traffic, and the public would save by canceling or postponing new highways, and by cutting back subsidies for public transportation. In addition, it would curb urban sprawl.

4. One-Way Streets

One-way streets offer a partial solution for traffic on city streets in that they allow a faster traffic flow. One-way streets generally restrict or prohibit parking to keep the traffic flowing. This also has a negative effect on businesses on these streets.

The buzzword of transportation planners today is "traffic management," which means spreading the traffic out one hour more, and getting people to ride together.

5. Coordinated Traffic Signals

By coordinating traffic signals in the direction that most traffic is flowing, commute time to and from work can be significantly reduced.

6. Car and Van Pools

To encourage carpools, some firms reserve the prime parking spaces for employees who carpool. In several industrial parks, carpools are being set up on a park (industrial complex) basis rather than a company basis to increase the likelihood of meeting employee needs.

In some cities, local legislation mandates that employers achieve by a specified date a stated percentage of employee car pool use.

Car and van pools are encouraged to use express lanes on major highways that are limited to bus and carpool use.

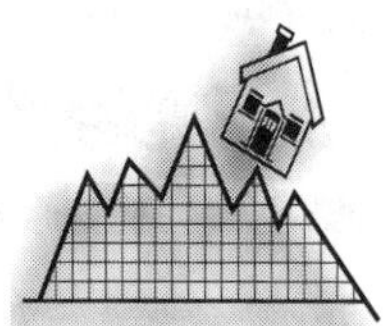

Our income tax laws work against employers' efforts to subsidize transportation for employees.

While free parking is a tax-exempt benefit to employees, free bus or van transportation to work would be a taxable benefit. When the federal government ended the investment tax credit for firms to buy vans, 25 percent of commuter van pool firms dropped their programs. The IRS has also ruled that employer subsidies of van transportation are taxable income to employees, which further hurts van use. However, staggered hours are probably a better solution than vans.

7. Trip Reductions

Trip reduction ordinances require employers to develop and implement measures to limit the number of solo automobile trips to their establishments during peak hours. These ordinances have led to van pools and ride sharing programs. However, the problem with trip reduction ordinances is that they seldom set significant penalties.

8. Paving Technology

Many cities are experimenting with new paving materials such as aggregate made of ground up tires mixed in asphalt. By improving paving materials for longer life use, it reduces a major cause of traffic delay—highway repairs.

9. Home-Based Workers

With modern communication technology, many employees can conduct their jobs from home. Employers who work with telecommuting employees have generally experienced positive results in terms of greater productivity. In addition to employees working in their homes, many service and outside sales people no longer need to report to job sites each day to receive their daily schedules and messages.

10. Gas Prices

Some environmentalists thought that higher gas prices would discourage the use of private automobiles. They even suggested higher taxes for gas when sold for noncommercial use. The higher price of gas will not get people out of their cars. The price of gas may influence the type of vehicle purchased, but the cost of alternative modes of transportation must be considered, and these costs have risen.

11. Police Policy

By implementing a fast-response policy for accidents, traffic can be kept moving. In the same manner, a zero tolerance policy for double parking will reduce traffic bottlenecks.

12. Off-Peak Deliveries

Requiring commercial deliveries during off-peak hours will reduce traffic hold ups.

13. Stop Sign Evolution

Many stop signs have been installed because of political pressure after concerns were raised involving various individuals' safety. By evaluating stop signs for necessity and removal of unneeded stop signs, traffic can be kept flowing.

14. Parking

What will take Americans out of their vehicles is not having places to park them.

Policies of governmental agencies and private employers who provide free employee parking encourages automobile use and exacerbates transportation problems. If employees had to pay market rates for private parking, which in some cities has reached $50 per day, employees would be forced to consider car pools or public transportation. We cannot provide cheap or free parking and expect people to leave their vehicles at home.

While stiff employee resistance would likely prevent the elimination of free parking, many traffic planners are encouraging it. Former President Jimmy Carter suggested ending free parking for federal employees and ran into a stonewall of resistance at every level.

Former Los Angeles Mayor Tom Bradley tried to raise the $5 per month fee city workers pay to park but was unsuccessful. The feeling is if workers were given a sum (such as $150 a month) to either pay back as a parking fee or pocket and use car pools or buses, a great many would find other ways to get to work.

To wean Americans from their vehicles would require either decreased travel time (a quicker way to go) or financial incentives.

In Portland, Oregon, more than 40 percent of downtown workers use public transportation. Car traffic has stabilized while the number of workers in the central area of the city has increased. Portland achieved this result with a moratorium on downtown parking growth and turning a large parking lot into a town square. The "build it and they will come" principle was reversed in that taking parking away cut traffic.

Portland provided an alternative with good public transportation. They use television monitors with current bus schedules, ticket vending machines, wheelchair lifts, bike racks, and bus shelters to encourage the use of their public transportation.

15. Encouraging Bicycles

Many communities are becoming bicycle friendly. Bike racks are now commonplace at public buildings as well as at all types of businesses. Bike racks are attached to many buses so that commuters can bicycle from their homes to the bus stop and from the bus stop to their workplace. The health aspect of the bike-and-bus concept appeals to many people and has increased ridership on public transportation.

Many roadways now have bicycle lanes that provide greater rider safety and encourage bike use.

16. Light Rail Systems

"Light rail" refers to the electric streetcar systems common in American cities up to shortly after World War II. These systems provided clean transportation.

Light rail transport is really different from the old-fashioned type electric streetcar.

Light rail is a far faster service, using stations as stopping points rather than street corners. With far fewer stops, multiple cars like a train, and a greater speed, light rail can carry passengers faster than automobiles. Since most light rail systems travel on their own right of way, higher speeds are possible.

With post World War II prosperity and greater ownership of automobiles, passenger use declined and in most cases, tracks were torn up and the streetcars junked. Exceptions have been elevated systems in cities such as Chicago and subway systems such as New York. Because of their speed, ridership has remained high.

Every modern light rail system in the nation has requested additional federal funding for operating assistance. Operating revenues are insufficient to meet operational expenses, usually because they tend to be under utilized. The percentage of operating costs that must be paid by the taxpayers (not construction costs) are as follows:

Baltimore	75%
Los Angeles	85%
Pittsburgh	72%
Portland	53%
Sacramento	69%
San Diego	31%
San Jose	89%
St. Louis	72%

As of this date, light rail has been one of the most expensive forms of transportation, largely because people have been unwilling to utilize it. Light rail has been an economic failure. Nevertheless, many more cities are planning light rail projects.

Government agencies seem to gravitate toward fixed rail transit as a solution.

According to John Kain, a Harvard economics professor, the interest in light rail is attributable to "boosterism" (appeals to civic pride) and a fondness of politicians for building monuments. Over 190 cities have requested federal funding for light rail systems with many more likely to get on the bandwagon.

Construction cost for light rail is approximately $8,000 per new rider because so few new riders have been attracted to it. In Miami, a new rail system was expected to serve 200,000 riders per day. Instead, it served just 32,000 of which many are elderly and no longer drive. As long as automobile transportation is available as an alternative, it is unlikely that light rail transportation will be the magic bullet to solve our transportation problems.

With the federal government showing unwillingness to fund expensive subway programs, light rail ground-level systems are one of the few alternatives available.

Detroit has developed a Disneyland-style, monorail people mover. The cost for the 2.9-mile project was nearly double its original $137 million dollar estimate. The project was designed to move people between offices, restaurants, and the central business area. Because many large retailers left the area between the planning phase and its completion, the Detroit monorail did not serve the purpose for which it was designed. It has acquired a local nickname, "The Muggers' Express," due to crime on the monorail. The Detroit project was 80 percent funded by the federal government. Projects such as this are likely to be too expensive in the future due to federal budgetary constraints.

Fairfax County, Virginia, spent $40 million on mass transit, which is utilized by less than six percent of the area's workers. The expenditures for road improvements were nowhere near that figure, yet roads transport over 94 percent of the workers. Critics of mass transit question its cost-effectiveness.

An exception is the light rail success in San Diego.

San Diego has a 16-mile line in service running from the downtown area to the Mexican border, as well as an East line, which connects the downtown area with predominantly minority neighborhoods in the southwestern part of the city. These two lines were built for $150 million, which is over $80 million less than Los Angeles spent on just planning its 18-mile Metro rail subway. The San Diego trolley system was built under budget without federal subsidy. Ridership on the South line is almost 20,000 people per day. More than 90 percent of operational costs are met by fares. The economic effects of this rail system are significant. It brings minority area shoppers to central city areas, as well as brings Mexican shoppers from the border.

While the costly metro rail system for Los Angeles was heralded as a cure-all for Los Angeles traffic problems, one nationally known traffic expert said, "Metro rail will do for Los Angeles traffic what Ben-Gay does for cancer."

For light rail to work, stations in outlying areas must have adequate low-cost parking. The rail lines must go to the major employment areas so riders can walk or take a short bus ride to their job site. Most important, riders must realize the advantages of light rail commuting over driving their own vehicles.

17. Buses

A problem with fixed rail solutions, besides the initial start-up costs and operational costs, is inflexibility.

Buses are much more flexible and less costly. Express bus lanes are being used as an incentive for people to use public transportation, but even with subsidized rates, buses have not significantly reduced automobile traffic.

It is doubtful that public transportation will increase significantly beyond population growth during the next decade in the majority of U.S. cities.

E. THE HOMELESS

In Los Angeles, a private nonprofit organization is addressing some of the problems of the homeless. Single Room Occupancy Housing Corporation (SRO) has been purchasing old hotels and renovating them for permanent housing. SRO derives its funds from public and private sources. Rooms are rented at relatively low rates. Renters are singles and couples. Most renters are day laborers, but include those with mental problems and alcoholics. SRO claims to be a tough manager and insists that rooms be kept clean.

In many cities, the homeless have been the burden of charitable organizations that are often economically limited to the number of persons they can assist. City-owned shelters are available in some communities. It has been suggested that government assistance be given to nonprofit organizations that are currently carrying the burden of the homeless.

While some sort of shelter is needed, especially in inclement weather, many people will not go to shelters. Complaints of those who would rather be on the street are:

1. Having to be preached to in order to be fed and given a bed.
2. Thefts in the shelters.
3. Fights in the shelters.
4. Refusal of help if under the influence of alcohol or drugs.
5. Feeling that they are being treated like children.

More costly, single-room occupancy type housing would better meet the needs of the homeless than large dormitory shelters. Instead of being homeless, they would have a private secure space of their own. Counseling should also be available when desired.

The private sector could solve problems of the homeless with the use of economic incentives.

II. Economics and Revitalization

Although we have a great many government programs aimed at revitalization of neighborhoods, economic forces unrelated to government action have resulted in the reclamation of many blighted areas.

Because of the traffic congestion and commuting time associated with getting in and out of the cities, people have looked for alternatives. These have included conversion of factories and warehouses to loft apartments, building new high-rise apartments, and even new homes. The people moving into the city centers earn above-average incomes. The economic success of central city developments has resulted in a great many new residential projects as well as new businesses to serve the upscale residents. These residents are usually either single person households or ***TINKS*** *(two incomes, no kids)*, who have a high disposable income.

Interesting architectural styles are often sought for residences and business. In Portland, Oregon the Pearl District now houses architects, software designers, fancy stores, and upscale restaurants. The artists, who had preceded businesses to the area, have been leaving as rents have shot up in the past few years.

The Bowery in New York was once synonymous with street people and flophouses. It is now becoming upscale. The use that will pay more for the sites has prevailed. One-bedroom apartments in the Bowery are renting for over $2,000 per month. New structures with penthouses are replacing flophouses.

Private development is successful because it is motivated by profit.

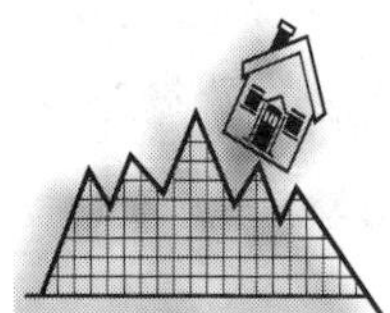

Chapter 6

Private developers are motivated by profit. Besides profit attributed to market forces developers have received various subsidies for redevelopment and development in economically distressed areas. Subsidies have made marginal projects very desirable. Some developers feel they need subsidies because of greater risks encountered in leasing and environmental concerns as to demolition, as well as possible soil contamination.

To encourage private development of housing as well as industry in our cities, it has been suggested that the federal government allow investors rapid depreciation.

Construction would boom by reducing depreciation to 15 years for private housing units as well as some commercial and industrial construction within designated inner city areas.

The costs to the federal government would be negligible and the benefits would be higher property taxes in the community, income tax revenues from the jobs created and a lowering of public assistance benefits.

San Francisco is attempting to solve the minority exodus problem by requiring developers to provide housing for the poor. The developers of a Ramada Inn agreed to spend $3 million for housing the poor, give $200,000 to social agencies and employ local residents.

A. TAX BENEFITS OF OWNER-OCCUPANTS

Some states allow lower tax rates for owner-occupied dwellings than for rental dwellings. Other states give owner occupants a tax credit against their property taxes. What these owner-occupant benefits do is make it less desirable to move out and rent a former residence, as taxes will increase. The greater the tax increase will be, the less desirable renting becomes.

Tax benefits can help retain residents.

As a general rule, rental property owned by absentee landlords is not maintained as well as property owned by owner-occupants, so having fewer homes rented in an area will keep the neighborhood from becoming blighted.

B. INCENTIVES FOR LOW-INCOME HOUSING

The Tax Reform Act of 1986 provides Federal Tax Credits for developing low-income rental housing and tax incentives for developing low-income owner-occupied housing. For rental housing, the developer must conform to rental limitations. Each state administers a fixed allocation.

In exchange for state tax credits or government sponsored financing, many new apartment complexes have included hundreds of units of low-income family housing. As an example, in New York City, Tishman Speyer is renting an agreed number of units at $465 per month to low-income renters where the market would indicate a $2,800 per month rent was possible.

Inclusionary zoning might also require redevelopment as well as development to include a low-income housing element.

C. SUBSIDIES FOR INDUSTRIAL DEVELOPMENT

In Japan, the Japanese Minister of Labor offers significant subsidies to employers who create jobs for local residents in designated communities.

The desire to obtain new industry and resulting jobs in America has created a fierce competition between communities for the same industries.

Many industries are playing city against city to obtain maximum benefits. The result is corporate welfare.

In many cases, significant subsidies have been given to industries that have brought in low-wage jobs and relatively few benefits to the community. Garden City, Kansas had a high unemployment rate and the local economy was very weak. Garden City attracted IBP, the huge meat processor, by offering incentives of $3.5 million in property tax relief and $100 million in industrial bonds to build a new facility.

While IBP caused the population to grow, the income of residents has not shown any significant increase and unemployment actually increased because of the influx of low-income residents. Between 1970 and 1990, income adjusted for inflation, rose only 2 percent in Garden City while Kansas experienced a 12 percent increase. While Garden City placed great hopes on growth, it was not a magic bullet in solving their problems and did not bring prosperity or a better quality of life to the area.

In some cases, the cost of bringing in industry does not appear to make much economic sense. In Kentucky, state officials gave Willamette Industries tax credits totaling $132.3 million for expanding a paper and pulp mill in Hawesville, Kentucky. According to the agreement, Willamette was required to create 15 new jobs. This is a tax credit of $8.8 million per job. It is unlikely that Willamette Industries will pay any state income tax on their Hawesville project for 15 years.

In Minnesota, Good Jobs First Inc. (a labor issue think tank), found 38 Minnesota projects with over $100,000 in subsidies per job created of which 10 were $200,000 or more. These are not isolated instances. It is normal today for industry to ask for subsidies and other benefits. Some footloose industries that can readily move have relocated simply because of the economic benefits offered to them.

In some communities, development agencies will build facilities for industries and provide below-market rent, low interest loans as well as tax incentives.

Chicago has 64 tax financing districts. When a new development results in increased tax revenues in a district, the increase is used to subsidize more private development, not for infrastructure needs.

A business does NOT have to move into an area to gain subsidies. Threatening to move out of an area also works.

The New York Stock Exchange (NYSE) had 1,482 direct employees and between 3,000 and 4,000 other workers sustained by its activities. A retention agreement, where NYSE agreed to remain where it was, resulted in a package of benefits estimated to be worth between $600 and $900 million. That's just for maintaining the status quo.

It should be realized that someone must pay the tax burden when subsidies are given. The burden falls on residents and existing businesses.

D. COMMERCIAL INCENTIVES

When cities think of new jobs, they generally think of new industries. However, commercial developments can bring jobs to a community.

West Palm Beach, Florida was considered the poor sister of the more prestigious Palm Beach. The city wanted an attraction and enticed a developer to build a mall with 60 stores, 10 restaurants and a 20-screen theater on 72 acres reclaimed through slum clearance. A second phase is scheduled to include a convention center.

Besides practically giving away the site, which was valued at $20 million, the city picked up $80 million of the cost of the mall (one-third). The city also built a giant row of parking garages with free parking for mall customers as well as picking up the cost for public areas including a $3 million fountain. While the developer is to pick up interest payments on $55 million of municipal bonds, city and county sales tax revenues will be used as well.

Time will tell as to the extent of the benefits of this project for the city. Owners of existing stores feel the mall will cannibalize other shopping areas. The new mall has had difficulty filling its spaces and two other large malls are currently being planned in neighboring communities.

While incentives for developments to bring in jobs makes sense, it is clear that a city must analyze what it gives away in terms of the long-term economic effects.

E. IN-FILL DEVELOPMENTS

IN-FILL DEVELOPMENTS *describe building in existing urban areas.* A number of cities are providing land for in-fill developments at no cost or very low cost to the developers.

The city benefits by including vacant parcels onto the tax rolls.

Besides vacant urban sites, developers have been redeveloping under utilized urban sites. In many cases, cities have also cooperated by churning out permits in record time.

Developers have found that there is a market for in-fill developments among first-time homebuyers, empty nesters, single buyers and "tinks." Kaufman and Broad, the giant homebuilder, maintains that the profit margin on in-fill developments is higher by 15 percent or more than for new developments.

III. Fighting Blight

A number of private and public programs exist that together have arrested blight and increased the livability of many neighborhoods. Besides fighting blight, many of these programs also created jobs for inner city residents.

A. TAKING LANDLORDS TO COURT

By making code enforcements a priority, communities can force landlords to maintain rental property and keep it habitable.

In some communities, city attorneys have vigorously prosecuted slumlords who milk substandard housing by collecting rents, but fail to keep the property in a habitable condition. In some cases, landlords who failed to comply with court orders as to cleanup have been sentenced to jail for contempt of court.

In California, masonry and improperly reinforced concrete structures posed a serious danger in the event of a significant earthquake. Walls could crumble, resulting in collapsing ceilings. A great many of the buildings constructed prior to 1960 did not meet the new seismic construction codes. The cost to bring many of these structures into compliance in many cases exceeded the value of the structures, making demolition and redevelopment the best economic decision. The seismic construction codes are being enforced, and their enforcement has had a significant effect on redevelopment. Neighboring residents have successfully sued owners for damages where property is being used for drug activity with the owners' knowledge, thus allowing a nuisance to interfere with the use and enjoyment of the neighboring properties.

The government has seized properties where the owners' knew illegal activities were present.

When owners realize that it is not in their best economic interests to fail to maintain their property or by allowing tenants to remain who engage in obvious illegal activities, they will likely act in a manner consistent with their financial interests.

B. BRADY STREET

A little over a decade ago, the Brady Street neighborhood in Milwaukee was described as a war zone. Many storefronts were boarded up, a great many homes were run down and the only booming area of the neighborhood economy seemed to be based on drugs. In addition, the government housed chronic drug users and alcoholics in two subsidized high-rises in the area.

While the situation appeared hopeless to many, the problems became a focal point to bring residents and merchants together. They jointly applied pressure on the city to enforce codes so that housing units would be cleaned up as well as to police the area to kick out menaces. A business improvement district brought in holiday lights, new sidewalks, and re-routed a cross-town trolley into the area. The merchants and residents worked together to decide what liquor licenses should or should not be approved as well as to have billboards removed. The groups also sponsored community events to help form a sense of community. A strong parent group applied pressure on the school administration to improve the quality of area schools.

The result has been positive. Besides improving the quality of life and having a safer neighborhood, property values doubled between 1993 and 2000.

C. CHRISTMAS IN ACTION (Formerly Christmas in April)

CHRISTMAS IN ACTION is a nonprofit Christian organization involved in the rehabilitation of homes for low-income persons, primarily elderly, handicapped, and families with children. The organization's new name is based on their principal of putting Christian values in action. Using volunteer labor and private donations, the organization has completed $500 million in renovations involving around 40,000 properties. While Christmas in Action does not increase the stock of housing, they help maintain it. In the year 2000, the organization rehabilitated over 7,100 homes using 231,000 volunteers (**www.christmasinaction.org**).

D. COMMUNITY DEVELOPMENT CORPORATIONS (CDCs)

Approximately 2,000 community development corporations exist in the United States. *COMMUNITY DEVELOPMENT CORPORATIONS (CDCs) are nonprofit organizations formed to revitalize economically distressed areas.* Primarily, they construct, as well as rehabilitate, low and moderate-income housing, but also encourage job creation.

While some funds for CDCs come from bank loans as well as private foundations, CDCs also rely on government support (HUD) in the form of grants and block grants.

E. COMMUNITY DEVELOPMENT BLOCK GRANTS (CDBGs)

This multi-billion dollar program provides entitlement communities that are eligible metropolitan cities and urban counties with annual direct grants that can be used to revitalize neighborhoods. The projects chosen by the recipients must benefit low and moderate-income persons, prevent slums or blight, or meet other community development needs. About 1,000 communities are recipients of these block grants.

Activities covered by the block grants include, but are not limited to:

1. Acquiring real property for public purposes such as redevelopment.
2. Reconstruction or rehabilitation of property.
3. Building public facilities (streets, sidewalks, sewers, etc.)
4. Helping train people for employment.
5. Assisting for-profit businesses development.
6. Providing services for youths, seniors and/or the disabled.
7. Crime reduction programs.
8. Assisting low-income homebuyers through down payment assistance.
9. Enforcing codes.
10. Planning.

F. EMPOWERMENT ZONES (EZs)

Some cities have obtained empowerment zone (EZ) designations from HUD. The HUD program was designed to afford communities the opportunity for growth and revitalization. The plan supports local plans that coordinate economic, physical, environmental, community and human development. As part of the plan, the federal government will waive regulations wherever feasible and provide special preference to other government programs. There are a number of benefits for businesses to locate or expand in empowerment zones.

The Internal Revenue Service will allow the total cost of some improvements to be written off in the year they were made rather than spread out the recovery period using depreciation.

Employee wage credits are available for new hires of residents of the zone. Wage tax credits to employers are up to 20 percent of the first $15,000 of salary or training expenses.

Empowerment zones are eligible for federal grants that can be spent at the discretion of the zone. Plans for national rebuilding after Hurricanes Katrina and Rita were fostered by empowerment zones.

G. ENTERPRISE ZONES

Some states provide for state designations of communities as enterprise zones. States may give tax credits and benefits to firms that locate in their designated zones. In Kentucky, vehicles used in the zone may be exempt from sales tax and motor vehicle use tax and 10 percent of wages paid employees in the zone can be a credit against state taxes.

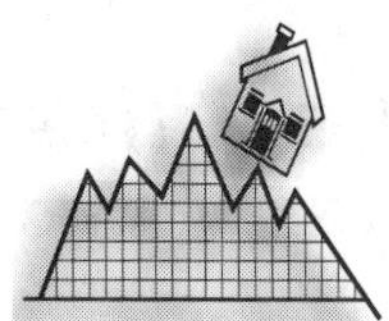

H. THE NATIONAL HISTORIC PRESERVATION ACT OF 1966

This act provides the procedure for registry of historical building sites or historical landmarks. The act also provides for the protection and restoration of historical sites and historical districts.

The economic effect of having a dwelling on the registry of historical structures is generally be very positive. Such a designation makes the property attractive to a great many potential buyers. However, a designation as an historical landmark could make it difficult to demolish the structure should the site value exceed the building's value at its current use.

I. HISTORIC DISTRICTS

Courts have upheld state acts allowing the proper exercise of police power for areas to be designated as historic districts in that they promote general welfare. By designating an area as a historic district, the exterior architecture of an area can be maintained and the appearance of new structures can be controlled.

Having a historic district designation could not prevent change. It would help in shaping changes that enhance the historic assets of the district. Local zoning codes would establish a design review process and a certificate of appropriateness showing that any exterior building change was compatible with the district before any building or demolition permit was issued.

A historic district designation adds a sense of panache to the area and creates an interest for upscale shops as well as persons interested in the arts. In some areas, improvement districts have been formed for antique-style street lighting, cobblestone walks, etc. By providing funds for restoration loans, declining areas can not only be stabilized, but can also become highly sought after for business as well as residential use.

J. RIVERFRONT DEVELOPMENT

In most major cities, riverfronts were formerly ugly places that people avoided. However, some cities like San Antonio, Texas have made their river areas major attractions for tourists and local citizens. San Antonio's river-walk with promenades, cruises, restaurants, music, and shops has been highly successful.

By the time Beerline River Homes had a ground breaking along the Milwaukee River, they already received reservations for 33 of their first 43 units.

Pittsburgh intends to develop Three Rivers Park, a development covering 10 miles of riverfront. Cincinnati has a billion dollar riverfront program. Other cities developing riverfront areas are Minneapolis and St. Paul, Hartford, Sacramento, Louisville, Omaha, and Peoria.

An idea common to riverfront developments is that the waterfront should belong to the people. It should be a place people want to go to as an antidote to urban sprawl and encourage city living.

K. BROWNFIELDS

Developers often avoid Brownfield developments because of possible liabilities from unknown soil contamination. In Los Angeles, construction of Belmont High School was delayed for a long period because it sits on abandoned oil field land where explosive methane gas and toxic hydrogen sulfide were rising from the site.

In order to encourage redevelopment, several states now offer liability protection to developers of Brownfield sites.

Several states as well as cities also offer financial incentives such as tax moratoriums for site cleanups. In addition, some communities offer simplified fast-track approval process for cleanup and redevelopment.

The 2002 Federal Small Business Relief and Brownfields Revitalization Act provides liability protection for innocent owners, limits liability of persons who did not deposit a significant amount of toxic material in the soil, as well as provides financial assistance for Brownfield cleanup. This program, which is business friendly, should help in cleanup and redevelopment of Brownfields.

L. GRAFFITI

Tagging or spray painting symbols, paintings, or just childish scrawls on buildings, walls, and bridges are defacing many of our communities.

It is illegal in many communities for stores to sell spray paint cans to minors. This has had little or no effect on the elimination of graffiti. A manager of a large discount store solved the problem by having a maintenance person roller over the graffiti with paint that matched the building each morning. By opening time, no graffiti was evident. After awhile, taggers activity decreased to the point where repainting was required only several times a month.

In other cases, areas subject to graffiti have been sprayed with coatings so that spray paint will not adhere to the surface and can be easily hosed down or pressure washed.

Some communities offer artistic taggers an opportunity to present their work to the public. They designate areas for spray painting, often construction barricade walls. Competitions and prizes have even been offered where taggers can apply for and be given a site to paint. Graffiti activity has not been prohibited but rather channeled in a constructive direction.

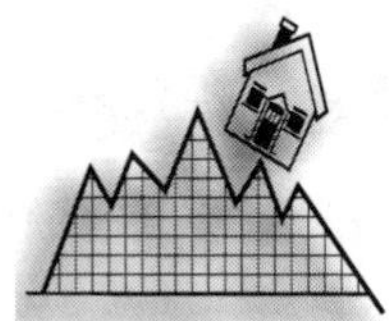

IV. Assistance to Buyers

As of October 1, 2000, families receiving federal rent assistance vouchers can purchase homes for the same amount that they pay in rent. According to Andrew Cuomo, then Secretary of HUD, the goal of this program was for 1 million working families receiving Section 8 rent assistance to become homeowners.

The plan is available to first-time buyers with household incomes of at least $10,300 and who have one household adult member who has been employed for one year or longer. The families must attend financial and homeowner counseling sessions before, and sometimes after, purchasing their homes. Buyers who qualify will have their Section 8 aid applied to the mortgages.

Participants choose their own lenders but purchases must be inspected and approved by a local housing authority as well as an independent certified home inspector.

It is hoped that homeownership will mean better maintenance of older housing stock and that aid recipients will also inherit an improved self-image and strive for greater economic success. Critics of the program point out that new homeowners have no equity in their homes, which can serve as a disincentive to keep up the property.

A. BROKERS AIDING OWNERSHIP

Real estate brokers can play a role in central city rejuvenation by helping to increase the percentage of homeowners.

In some communities, brokers publicize in their ads low-income ownership programs available in their community, as well as work through church groups and local organizations to inform residents of the possibilities of obtaining homeownership.

Living in the community helps to sell in the community.

To communicate with area residents, some brokers seek out individuals living in the area for license training and then provide office training for proficiency in their profession. Some brokers believe this helps to create more homeowners and establish community relations. Of course, a higher percentage of homeowners means that properties will be better cared for.

B. PRIVATE LOAN FUNDS

Experience has shown that urban blight can be halted and the process reversed when the ratio of owner-occupants to tenants is increased.

The Enterprise Foundation, created by shopping center developer James Rouse and Baltimore Federal Financial, has established a private loan fund to enable low-income families to purchase homes. Individuals, charities, and corporations are encouraged to open federally insured accounts bearing low interest. These accounts, administered by Baltimore Federal Financial, allow the fund to make 15-year, six percent loans for home purchases. To keep payments down, the amortization period is set at 25 years (15-year balloon). The fund has received a ruling from the IRS that depositors will be taxed only on interest received and not on imputed interest. To qualify for a loan, the homebuyers must have an income 45 percent or less than the local median income.

Under the **Community Reinvestment Act**, federal regulatory agencies must take into consideration, when deciding whether to approve a branch office or merger, the financial institution's record of community service.

Many banks have established community development subsidiaries to invest in revitalizing deteriorating neighborhoods or buildings or rehabilitating low-income housing.

C. URBAN HOMESTEADING

Wilmington, Delaware adopted the First Urban Homesteading Act in 1973.

After rehabilitating a structure and living there three years, the homesteader received title. Wilmington further encouraged homesteaders by offering low-interest loans and allowing them to deduct 50 percent of repair costs from the assessed value. Most of the homesteaders in Wilmington were middle-class couples.

In 1973, Baltimore also began homesteading city-acquired properties, primarily by tax sale. These were given to homesteaders for a fee ranging from $1 to $200. The homesteader was required to complete major renovations within a stated period of time, usually six months. After 18 months the occupants received the deed. The homesteaders, in many cases, were provided with low interest loans as well as technical assistance.

While the number of homes involved in Baltimore was insignificant (only about 600), the program is credited with significant results. The harbor area known as Harbor Place now has a strong real estate market, credited in great part to urban homesteading. Urban homesteading also served to stabilize and strengthen neighborhoods. Camaraderie developed among homesteaders, spreading to the development of neighborhood pride. The success of several urban homestead programs has been due, in part, to homestead sites being grouped together, making support groups possible. Demonstration teams offered technical assistance in some communities as well.

Other cities that have followed Baltimore's lead have been Denver, Washington, D.C., Philadelphia, and New York.

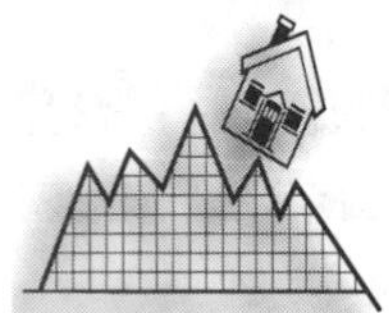

With the increase in value of real estate and gentrification in many cities, fewer properties are being taken for nonpayment of taxes, so the opportunities for new buyers have tightened up.

D. THE NEHEMIAH PLAN (Downpayment Assistance)

The Nehemiah Plan takes its name from the Old Testament prophet who led the rebuilding of Jerusalem in the 5th Century B.C. A consortium of black churches financed the plan, which aids in the down payment for low and moderate-income families.

The program does not give mortgages but makes gifts or loans for down payments and constructs housing units. They work in groups to build homes, which keeps costs down. The land is provided at little or no cost by communities interested in new development in their inner cities as well as placing properties back on their tax rolls. However, the program primarily involves existing homes. Buyers under the Nehemiah Plan must invest 1 percent of the purchase price in the transaction or have it available as a financial reserve. This money can come from another gift source. The home seller of a home must agree to pay Nehemiah a fee of 4 percent of the selling price. The property must meet or exceed FHA guidelines and sellers must also give a one-year home warranty and a 2-year roof certification. The 4 percent from home sellers allows Nehemiah to finance other buyers.

The Nehemiah program has helped more than 60,000 families with $200 million in down payments. The founder of the program, Don Harris, realized that while other programs were available to the poor, a lot of families with good credit and steady incomes were caught in the middle by not having enough for the down payments on homes (**www.nehemiacorp.org/nehemiahnew/072903.htm**).

E. HABITAT FOR HUMANITY

Because of President Carter's active involvement, almost every American adult is familiar with Habitat for Humanity, a nonprofit ecumenical Christian housing ministry dedicated to eliminating substandard housing and homelessness on a worldwide basis. Habitat for Humanity primarily uses donated material and volunteer labor and even has a program for students who wish to help during Spring breaks.

An international organization, Habitat for Humanity relies on little if any government support. In 1997, only one-half of one percent of their income was derived from government sources. While no government funds are accepted for actual construction, the organization will accept land donations from government units for homes. These are often vacant inner city parcels.

Habitat for Humanity has built 175,000 homes around the world in 3,000 communities. This makes the organization one of the largest homebuilders in the world. The organization realizes that owners are more likely to maintain their homes than are renters if the homeowners have an investment, if only hard work.

Habitat for Humanity selects families for these homes based on:

1. need for decent affordable housing.
2. ability to repay a no interest mortgage.
3. willingness to be a partner in redeveloping the neighborhood.

Applicants are trained and are expected to make a sweat equity contribution of 500 hours. After a one-year lease the applicant buys the house.

F. GARDEN PLOTS

In Great Britain, housing authorities have allowed residents use of designated areas for individual garden plots. These plots are highly sought after especially by retirees.

Some U.S. cities adopted this idea and turned city-owned vacant property into community garden spots. Besides the obvious aesthetic value of using formerly vacant lots for gardens, it also brings neighbors together fostering a sense of community.

G. CENSUS FIGURES

Most statisticians feel that our count-every-nose census approach is not only expensive but is also inaccurate. The belief is that city populations, especially when dealing with minorities and recent immigrants, can be better-estimated using sampling techniques rather than counting every human head. A larger count will mean greater Federal aid for programs that can fight blight.

V. CHAPTER SUMMARY

Many of the problems of the cities, which were once thought to be beyond solution, are now being solved by private as well as government action.

New development, restoration, code enforcement, rebuilding infrastructure and solving other city problems can help to avoid white flight.

Sprawl can be limited by smart growth that includes in-fill development, redevelopment and encouraging industry to create jobs.

Crime can be reduced by police involvement in the communities, parent and community involvement and most of all by job creation.

Traffic problems can be alleviated by encouraging flextime work, off-peak workweeks, toll road pricing, one-way streets, coordinated traffic signals, encouraging car and van pools, bicycle friendly environment, trip reduction and encouraging the use of public transportation. Better parking has an opposite effect in that it encourages private vehicles. **Light rail** has not been generally successful and building wider roads simply brings in more users.

Shelters for the homeless are primarily run by charitable organizations. However, many homeless avoid the shelters for a variety of reasons. **Single-room occupancy** facilities seem to better meet the needs of the homeless.

A great deal of the revitalization of cities has come about because of economic reasons rather than government action. Transportation problems have led to revitalization of central areas.

Many new developments include low-income housing because of **tax credits, special financing**, or **inclusionary zoning**.

Communities are competing with each other to give subsidies, tax incentives, or other benefits in order to bring in or retain industries.

By providing city-owned vacant lots to developers at no or low cost, cities are able to get **in-fill developments**.

Blight is being fought in a number of ways, including tough code enforcements and bringing landlords to court, improved policing, encouraging homeownership, community development corporations, community development block grants, empowerment zones, enterprise zones, historic designations, and providing immunity for development in **Brownfield** areas.

Homeownership has been encouraged through the use of **rent vouchers** for home purchases, private loan funds for low income housing ownership, urban homesteading, the **Nehemiah Plan** and **Habitat for Humanity**.

VI. GLOSSARY OF KEY TERMS

Christmas in Action – A nonprofit organization that rehabilitates homes of low-income owners.

Community Development Block Grants – This program gives large grants to entitlement communities for revitalization.

Community Development Corporations – Nonprofit corporations formed to revitalize economically distressed areas.

Empowerment Zones – A HUD designation that allows business in the zone to a quick write-off of investments and credit on taxes for a portion of wages of new hires.

Flextime Workers – Allowing workers to set their own work schedules.

Habitat for Humanity – Nonprofit organization that uses volunteer labor to build homes for low-income buyers. The organization does not give purchase loans.

In-Fill Development – Developing vacant lots within the city.

Light Rail – Electric passenger trains.

National Historic Preservation Act of 1966 – Federal act which provides for the registry of historic buildings and historical districts.

Nehemiah Plan – A nonprofit program where buyers without much savings can buy a home.

Smart Growth – Growth that restricts sprawl.

Urban Homesteading – The sale of city-owned housing to private owners at low cost with the requirement that the housing be rehabilitated.

VII. CLASS DISCUSSION TOPICS

1. In what ways have you noticed improvements as to problems facing your city over the past 10 years? What factors or forces affected these changes?

2. Identify areas that have experienced white flight as well as areas that are integrated and are considered desirable areas by both whites and African Americans. Analyze the differences as to these areas.

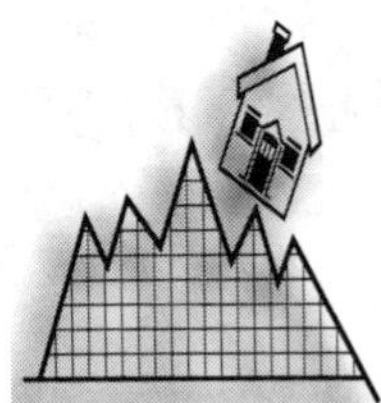

3. What efforts, if any, have been made to reduce sprawl in your community?

4. What has been done and/or can be done to alleviate traffic problems in your area?

5. Is any major public transportation expansion planned for your community? If yes, what results do you expect from the project?

6. What areas of your city have seen economic revitalization? What factors led to this revitalization?

7. What new industries or expansion has come to your city? What types of jobs have been created?

8. Give examples, if any, of gentrification in your community.

9. Do you see evidence of smart growth within your area? Where?

VIII. CHAPTER 6 QUIZ

1. An example of smart growth would be:
   a. in-fill developments.
   b. building more freeways.
   c. leapfrog development.
   d. use of annexation to grow.

2. Which of the following employer actions would contribute to traffic problems?
   a. Allowing home-based workers
   b. Implementing trip reduction programs
   c. Using an off-peak workweek
   d. Providing for free employee parking

3. Traffic management could include all except:
   a. toll road pricing.
   b. coordinated traffic signals.
   c. larger parking facilities.
   d. one-way streets.

4. A costly and taxing transportation system embraced by many communities is:
   a. employee van pools.
   b. light rail transit.
   c. one-way streets.
   d. bicycle paths.

5. Blight can be fought by:
   a. raising taxes.
   b. reducing criminal sentences.
   c. bicycle paths.
   d. strictly enforcing codes.

6. An empowerment zone designation:
   a. provides for employer tax credits for new hires.
   b. makes property exempt from property taxes.
   c. allows for duty free imports.
   d. provides for federal control of local government.

7. Urban homesteading provides that:
   a. a person can claim 160 acres of government land.
   b. homes be built with donated labor.
   c. homes be given to persons who will rehabilitate them and live there.
   d. homes will be given at half price to police officers and teachers.

8. The Nehemiah plan provides for buyers to have 1 percent down payment and:
   a. the seller to pay 4 percent of the selling price as a fee.
   b. contribute 500 hours of construction time on their home.
   c. the seller to carry the loan balance on a land contract.
   d. be either a teacher or police officer.

9. Real estate brokers can aid in community revitalization by:
   a. encouraging residents to move from the center of the city.
   b. helping residents to become homeowners.
   c. handling rentals as well as sales.
   d. encouraging absentee buyers.

10. To develop "brownfield" locations, developers would want:
   a. tenant partners.
   b. minimum leverage.
   c. liability protection.
   d. FHA insured loans.

ANSWERS: 1. a; 2. d; 3. c; 4. b; 5. d; 6. a; 7. c; 8. a; 9. b; 10. c

LEARNING OBJECTIVES

This chapter covers the origin and growth of suburbs as well as development beyond the suburbs. You will understand factors affecting suburban formation and growth as well as the problems. You will also learn about changes in exurbia, the land beyond the suburbs. By understanding suburban growth and its problems, you will have gained a valuable tool to aid in your predictions and planning as a real estate professional.

This chapter covers the origin, growth and development of suburbs.

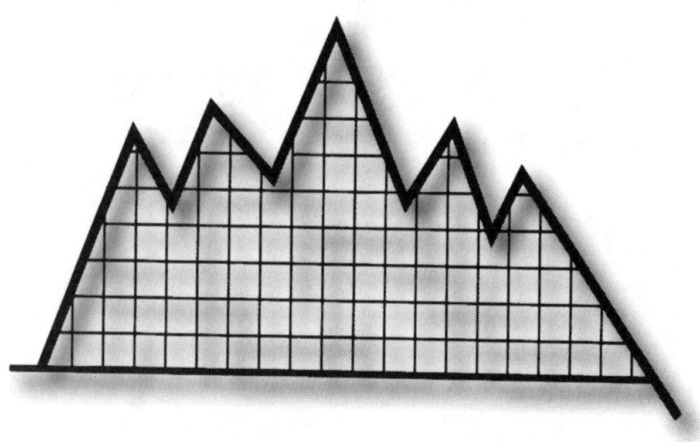

Chapter 7
The Suburbs and Beyond

I. What is a Suburb?

One of the Latin words for cities is "urbs"; city people were urbane. The word "sub" means under, near, or subordinate to. A ***SUBURB**, therefore, describes a community near and subordinate to a central city*. Suburbs depend on cities. You cannot have a suburb without a city.

The U.S. Census Bureau classifies any community outside the central city that exists within a metropolitan statistical area as a "suburb."

Suburbs are communities that skirt cities within commuting distance, which were generally founded and/or grew because of an economic reliance on the city for jobs and/or services.

A. CHARACTERISTICS OF SUBURBS

Income tends to increase with the distance from the city center.

This can be explained because new homes appealing to the wealthy tend to be built in newer communities on larger sites, which generally means farther from the city center. In addition, transportation costs to city employment precludes the very poor from moving to the suburbs.

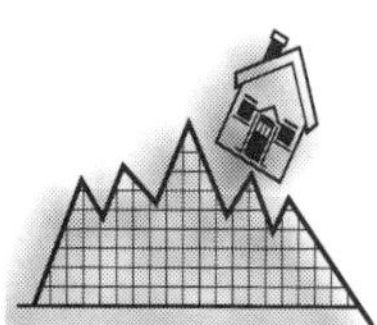

Chapter 7

CHAPTER 7 OUTLINE

Many suburbs attracted large developments where whole communities were planned, mainly due to the lower priced land. Developers were able to modify the usual rectangular street patterns of the city. Curved streets and cul-de-sacs, and even cluster patterns with large open spaces, helped make suburban living attractive.

With only a few exceptions, suburbs were formerly all-white enclaves. In fact, a Federal Housing Administration policy opposed what it referred to as "inharmonious racial and national groups" in the suburbs. This policy did not end until 1950. Despite our fair housing legislation, suburbs are still primarily white. Suburbs generally oppose low and moderate-income developments as well as smaller lot sizes that would allow lower income residents as well as a greater minority presence in the suburbs.

Suburban dwellers are more likely to have a traditional household and more education and income than central city residents.

Besides having average incomes greater than those in the central city, suburban dwellers also have more education, on average, than central city residents. They are more likely to reside in a traditional household (married couple with or without children) than those living in the central city. Same sex couples are more likely to suffer neighbor animosity in a suburban neighborhood of families living in single-family homes than they would living in a central city area apartment or loft. Suburban families are also more likely to be homeowners than city families, and the housing turnover rate is lower in the suburbs than in the central city. A reason for this is that renters are more likely than owners to relocate.

In the late 1940s and '50s, vast developments were built with identical or near identical homes. With the huge market for housing, aesthetics were not a primary concern of many builders. Alda Louise Huxtable, a New York Times architectural critic, called the suburbs a new kind of slum and coined the word "slurb." He was referring to the monotony of suburban architecture.

There was a feeling among many sociologists that suburban residents tried to conform to preconceived behavioral patterns and that this stifled thought. Studies, however, indicate that this perceived lockstep suburban mentality is more myth than reality. The homogeneity of the suburbs is mostly economic. In California, Orange County suburbs are known for their conservatism and as Republican strongholds. Moving to Orange County will not turn a liberal into a conservative; however, a high mortgage, high income, and high taxes might tend to make a homeowner more conservative in both thought and voting.

Because most new suburban developments have residents of similar economic backgrounds and interests, there is often more socializing in the suburbs than in the central city.

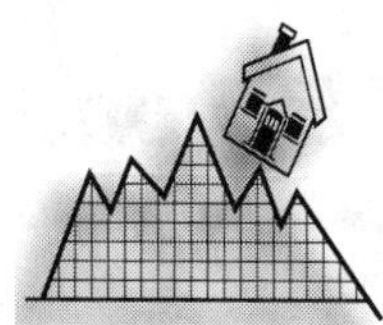

Prior to the growth of two working-parent households, the longer commuting time of suburban living made households more matriarchal in the suburbs than in the cities. Some sociologists regard today's suburbs as more insular than cities. Residents (often two income households) place great emphasis upon themselves and their possessions and little on their community. Others feel that this is a change in values that is not particularly related to suburbs but more to a consumer-oriented lifestyle.

A patch of green characterizes almost all of our suburban homes. Most homes have a front lawn, which is not used but is carefully manicured by the owner and watered to be aesthetically pleasing. While this is economically wasteful to both land and water, it is doubtful that the front lawn will be eliminated.

From the street, the garage for two or more vehicles is a dominant feature of most suburban homes. Garage doors are not aesthetically pleasing.

Many suburbs don't have sidewalks, so they are not pedestrian friendly. Children and the elderly primarily use suburban sidewalks. Journeys with a purpose are generally by vehicle even when only a block away.

Suburbs are NOT just an American phenomena.

They are found throughout the world. In some areas they are formed for reasons similar to those that resulted in our suburbs, but in some countries suburbs are the housing of the poor.

II. A History of Suburban Growth

Many of the earliest suburbs were hovels for the poor outside the city walls.

In early Mesopotamia, laborers lived outside the city walls. During the great peace of Rome ("Pax Romana"), city walls were not needed for protection. Wealthy Roman citizens escaped to the suburbs to avoid the noise and the smell of the city. They sought a rural, healthier lifestyle, which even today is a major attraction of the suburbs.

During the "Dark Ages" the suburbs outside the walled cities became walled also, so several walls protected the central city.

The introduction of gunpowder made city walls obsolete, because security was no longer assured. Hence, a wider suburban growth was seen, limited by transportation.

In London, the opening of the first London Bridge across the Thames opened up a vast area for suburban growth sparked by lower land costs. In the 16th century, the high price of London land caused the growth of low-cost housing to the south and east of London.

Many of our early modern suburbs were within walking distance of the city. In Boston, the suburbs of Roxbury, East Boston, and Charlestown, established in the early 1800s, were within easy walking distance of the central city. Horse-drawn trolleys of the mid-1800s allowed greater commuting distances.

Industrial suburbs emerged in the 19th century because, even then, manufacturers were having difficulty assembling the contiguous lots needed for factories in the cities. Examples of this type of suburb could be seen around Boston, where the suburbs became home to factories and workers. By 1900, half the population of greater Boston lived in suburbs.

Other early suburbs included Lynn, Massachusetts, which was a colonial resort suburb. Newport, Rhode Island, was a residential suburb prior to 1700.

Long before the automobile, the railroads opened suburban areas to city workers.

Passenger trains in the second half of the 19th century led to the establishment of many railroad bedroom communities. ***BEDROOM COMMUNITIES*** *are residential communities where the inhabitants commute to work in other areas.*

Shaker Heights was an early Cleveland railroad suburb. Grosse Point was a railroad suburb of Detroit. Other railroad suburbs flourished around New York, Boston and Philadelphia. Railroad suburbs were generally home to the wealthy.

In 1864, the adoption of lower fares on suburban rail lines for working men and women resulted in a tremendous growth for London suburbs.

Between 1901 and 1920, Henry Huntington laid 1,200 miles of track for his "red cars," which connected most of the small cities in the Los Angeles Basin (see **Figure 7-1**). Land served by the system became desirable and increased tremendously in value. The red cars allowed these small cities to become bedroom communities of Los Angeles. Prior to bringing in his red cars line, Henry Huntington would purchase land throughout the area to be opened by his low-cost transportation.

A great many areas saw suburban growth patterns in an axial form, following trolley lines.

Much of this early development was limited by walking distance to the trolley or rail lines. As the land filled in between the trolley lines, buses took over, delivering people to the fixed rail lines.

The economics of assembly line production led to lower automobile costs, which in turn increased automobile ownership.

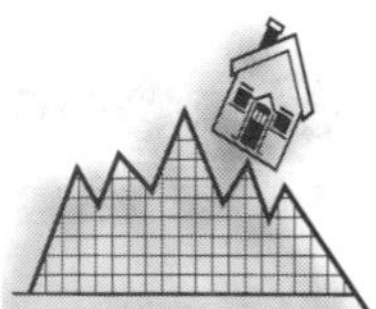

Figure 7-1

Red Car Line

The red car system started in the 1880s with the new technology of the day: electric trolleys. Henry Huntington built and extended the red car line until it stretched over a large portion of Southern California. Huntington would have his agents purchase a large number of parcels at comparatively low prices before he extended his line. After the tracks had been laid, the parcels sold for $350 a block away and $250 three blocks away, creating a huge profit for Huntington.

The Huntington Land Company was created to consolidate real estate growth along the tracks, which were sprawling throughout Southern California. Thousands of Los Angeles migrants eagerly purchased homes only a ten minute ride to Los Angeles.

This large metro system came to an end in the 1950s when red line authorities decided to switch to buses and sell the property underlying the red car lines.

Although industrialization brought people to the cities, the automobile allowed them to move out from the cities. Automobiles allowed for suburban growth wherever there was a road. In the 1920s, for the first time, suburban growth rates exceeded city growth. The Great Depression slowed the growth of the suburbs to about 1.4 percent per year in the 1930s, compared to the 2.8 percent growth of the 1920s.

Freeways/expressways allowed people to commute greater distances than previously would have been possible.

After World War II, the popularity of the automobile caused a decline in public transportation use. The two-car family was no longer a rarity. Most light rail lines were removed. The central city shopping areas were not planned for automobiles. Street congestion, coupled with the lack and expense of parking, led to the growth of suburban shopping areas, and the decline of many central shopping areas.

Road transportation has allowed industry to locate away from rail lines.

Assembly line production created the need for sprawling one-story factories. Because of the need for large low-cost sites, many industries located far from city centers. Improved transportation allowed a greater mixture of residential neighborhoods and commercial and industrial uses.

In the 1800s, the influx of foreign-born people to our cities served to encourage suburban growth. Cities were becoming a conglomerate of separate ethnic enclaves. Wealthier people sought to distance themselves from "foreigners." Similarly, African Americans have indirectly played an important role in the growth of suburbs. In 1940, over 75 percent of the nation's African Americans lived in the South. About 70 percent of these Southern African Americans lived in rural areas. The labor needs of World War II started a migration of African Americans to our Northern cities. In the 1940s, the nation's African American metropolitan population grew 65 percent, while the white metropolitan population experienced only a 16 percent growth.

This African American migration helped to stimulate suburban growth. Due to fear, prejudice or both, many whites moved to suburban areas where they could live separated from African Americans, and where their children would not be educated with African Americans.

Because of relatively high land costs and the absence of low-cost housing in many suburbs, our free enterprise system actually serves to perpetuate the exclusion of the poor or minorities from desirable suburban areas.

We do, however, have non-white suburbs. Kinlock became an African American suburb of St. Louis in the late 1800s. Robbins was a pre-World War I suburb of Chicago. Formerly, Compton was primarily an African American suburb of Los Angeles. Now, it is primarily a Hispanic suburb. Los Angeles also has Mexican-American suburbs, such as Pico Rivera. The population of the formerly Mexican-American suburbs of Alhambra and Monterey Park now have a significant Chinese population. The city of Glendale, California currently has a significant, growing Armenian population.

When racial and ethnic minorities move into a suburb, others of their racial or ethnic group will often decide to locate there. The result is racial and ethnic enclaves within the suburb. In some cases, the entire community has become dominated by one group of minority citizens. Monterey Park, California, is known as "the Chinese Beverly Hills," "Mandarin Park," or "Little Taipei." Two-thirds of the businesses in Monterey Park are now Chinese-owned and Chinese people make up 62 percent of the population. The desirability of Monterey Park by an affluent group resulted in a significant increase in property values throughout the 1980s, 1990s, and continuing to the present day.

Immigrants formerly would go to the cities where there were racial and ethnic enclaves. Because these enclaves might now be in the suburbs, a greater number of new immigrants are initially locating in the suburbs.

In the 1960s, Roosevelt, Long Island, was hailed as an example of how integration could work in the suburbs. The middle and higher income community had a 30 percent African American population, a low crime rate and a school system where most of the high school graduates went on to college. This idyllic integrated community changed as more African Americans purchased homes to become part of this lifestyle. Rapid increase in the African American population led to white flight of residents and many businesses. When the community became primarily African American, it lost much of its desirability to more affluent African Americans and property values declined. Lower property values led to a decline in community services. Purchases by speculators resulted in more absentee ownership and rental homes. Changes in demographics also resulted in a population increase that placed a further burden on municipal services.

Suburban growth is directly related to population loss in central cities. In Buffalo, New York, 81 percent of the city's suburban growth was attributed to loss of population in the central city (**www.demographia.com**).

A. WORLD WAR II CHANGED HOUSING

Prior to World War II, building companies were relatively small concerns.

Many prospective homeowners would purchase a lot and then contract with a builder. This resulted in varied developments. The real boom in suburban growth did not occur until after World War II. There was a tremendous housing need. We had to house the returning veterans and we were entering into the baby boom period. Housing construction from 1930 to 1945 had been very limited because of the Depression, followed by World War II. The G.I. Bill of Rights provided low-interest, no-down payment VA loans and brought white collar as well as factory workers to the suburbs. Homebuilders could sell everything they built because of the pent-up demand. ***PENT-UP DEMAND*** *is the build-up of unsatisfied wants and needs.* Homebuilders expanded to the suburbs, where they could obtain low-cost land, as well as benefit from the economics of scale with large developments. For example, the cost (per unit) to build a home is significantly reduced when it is built in multiples within a large housing project.

Veterans moved to the suburbs because housing was available with low-cost VA loans.

After World War II, William Levitt revolutionized home construction by building huge communities complete with curvilinear roads. He built clusters of homes that included village centers. Homes were available that buyers yearned for at prices they could afford. He sold the homes with a $10 deposit and $90 at closing for a total down payment of $100.

Levittown, Pennsylvania, covered 5,500 acres and consisted of 17,311 single-family homes. The New York Levittown totaled 17,447 homes while the New Jersey Levittown had 11,000 homes.

Levitt used an assembly-line process where a separate crew performed each task and the crew moved from house-to-house with work carefully timed. Workers were paid wages by piecework and construction workers were eager to work for Levitt. Material was all accounted for and delivered as needed. Levittown, New Jersey, was able to complete 36 homes per day. In New York, Levitt claimed to have completed a home every 16.5 minutes.

Pete Seeger, a popular singer and songwriter of the 1950s, mocked Levittown-type housing with the words of a popular song, "They are all made of ticky-tacky and they all look just the same." He also mocked the residents and their children as he thought these subdivisions resulted in homogenized residents all just the same.

Levittowns were all white communities. While William Levitt indicated he would like to sell to blacks, he said that if he did so, he could never sell out to whites. The first black in a Levittown community was met with a riot.

Later suburban growth would primarily be due to lifestyle choices, although present suburban growth in Riverside County in California, is primarily based on lower prices.

Between 1960 and 1970, the 25 largest cities in America gained only 710,000 people, while their suburbs gained 8.9 million. From 1950 to 1980, the suburban population grew from 35.2 million to 101.5 million. This is about 45 percent of our nation's population.

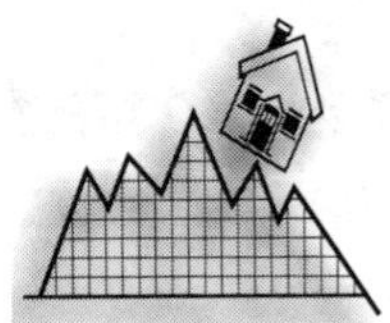

More people lived in suburbs by 1981 than lived in the entire United States in 1920.

The 2000 Census indicated that 140.6 million people lived in suburbs. This was about one-half of our nation's population at the time.

Suburban dwellers in most metropolitan areas outnumber those living in the central city. Less than 20 percent of our nation's population now lives in central cities. In most areas average suburban housing costs exceed city costs, so the growth of suburbs today is generally rooted in lifestyle choice rather than in economics. However, there are some central areas, such as Manhattan and San Francisco, with such high housing costs that many workers choose a lower-cost suburban lifestyle.

III. High Growth Areas

Suburban areas of greatest growth have a number of factors in common:

1. They are outside of cities or other suburbs that have vibrant economies.
2. They have a supply of relatively inexpensive land.
3. They have good transportation routes to the areas' economic centers.
4. The local political climate is friendly to development.

Continued growth has resulted in the suburbs becoming part of continuous urban sprawl.

Suburban growth patterns tend to duplicate city growth. While there are governmental divisions, the megalopolis or metropolis tends to become a singular, physical community.

Historian Frederick Lewis Allen categorizes suburban growth in the United States into five distinct historical phases:

1st: Country homes for the wealthy, reached by horse and buggy; originally occupied seasonally, later used year-round as the suburbs grew.
2nd: Railroad and streetcar suburbs from the 1800s through the 1920s. The automobile allowed for greater growth beyond the rail lines.
3rd: The Depression, which was a period of no-growth that set the stage for suburban post-war boom.
4th: Post-war housing boom.
5th: The movement of business and industry to the suburbs.

A. OTHER GROWTH FACTORS

The main factor contributing to the growth of suburbs was, and still is, transportation.

However, other factors affected residential and commercial relocation to the suburbs.

Without the septic tank system, our suburban growth would have been severely hampered.

The septic tank system allowed the development of land beyond city facilities. It allowed for leap frog development rather than contiguous development.

In recent years, groundwater pollution problems linked to septic tanks have slowed significant developments in many areas of the country where the development is beyond available sewer lines.

The telephone also played an important part in suburban growth.

Prior to the telephone, business was conducted either face-to-face or by letter or telegram. The telephone not only allowed businesses to leave a central area, it gave suburban dwellers a convenience of lifestyle that increased the desirability of suburban living.

Fax machines, along with the proliferation of personal computers and the Internet, are currently making location less important for many firms and is allowing relocation closer to more desirable living areas.

IV. Taxes and the Suburbs

Modestly priced ranch homes on large lots in spread out suburban areas can result in a low tax base, which means higher tax rates. When added to the high cost of schools and other services associated with a spread-out area, it is easy to see that suburbs are likely to be faced with financial difficulty. High density apartments, more expensive homes, smaller lots, and commercial and industrial development, on the other hand, would increase the tax base.

Property taxes are based on the value of improvements, so the higher the value, the greater the amount paid in property taxes.

Compact, highly developed areas also have lower cost-to-service per resident than less intensively developed property. In a compact area, the street, sewer, water, police, fire, etc. costs are less than in a more widely dispersed area. While large lots and winding streets provide a pleasant lifestyle, they do not provide a healthy tax base.

City dwellers feel they are being taken advantage of by suburbanites. Cities provide hospitals, stadiums, universities, parks, airports, zoos and cultural centers, as well as take on the burden of caring for the poor, while the affluent live and pay property taxes in the suburbs. Suburbanites shop in suburban malls, giving their business and sales tax to the suburbs.

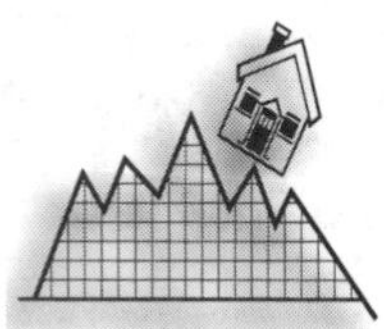

Because suburbs refuse to provide aid to the cities, some cities have found ways to tax suburbanites.

Washington, D.C. has an eight percent sales tax on meals. Los Angeles, Philadelphia, New York, and Detroit have payroll taxes aimed at making suburbanites pay their share of city services. City payroll taxes can have a negative effect, making it difficult for employers to find qualified employees and also providing another reason for business and industry to leave the city.

A. SUBURBAN PRICE ESCALATION

The market forces of supply and demand have resulted in escalating housing costs in many suburban areas. A negative effect of high housing costs is that many employers in such communities have difficulty in filling positions, since new employees simply can't afford the available housing.

V. Nonresidential Growth

People moving to the suburbs created the need for service jobs and shopping. The growth of non-residential suburban development is an example of supply chasing the demand of suburban residents for goods and services.

Suburban shopping was, and still is, based on the automobile. Shopping centers and malls, therefore, tended to be located along major streets and highways rather than concentrated in a central business district.

To gain revenue (property and sale taxes), many suburban areas have been courting large regional shopping centers.

Suburbanites love regional malls. Besides increasing the property tax base and providing employment, these centers can provide millions in sales tax revenue directly to the community. Many cities, such as Denver, are upset because large shopping centers have been built in the suburbs, taking away tax dollars the city believes should rightfully flow to it. Besides shopping centers, suburbs are also courting office complexes.

Non-residential growth has been increasing in the suburbs with the greatest rate of increase in established residential suburbs.

The more pressing increased revenue needs have been, the less selective suburbs have become as to what businesses and industry they are willing to allow. They have thus made trade-offs as to life style for tax dollars.

In the 1970s, California's Orange County planners were worried that they would become a high tax rate bedroom community. They re-zoned 700 acres from single-family residential to commercial and industrial use. Orange County has many industrial parks today. Primarily facilities of high technology and research and development, they are clean industries that offer high wages. Non-residential growth in many suburbs has been aided by growth limitations in other nearby areas.

Closer-in suburbs that have been fully developed require redevelopment to increase the property tax rolls. Redevelopment for business and industry in the suburbs has led to ***SINGLE PARCEL SALES****, where homeowners get together and offer multiple properties (at times an entire subdivision) for sale*. Prices received for property are often much more than the market price for homes. Parcel sale agreements for multiple lots have been used in suburbs in Washington, D.C., Houston, and Atlanta. Because of holdouts, developers are usually not interested in assembling large parcels requiring individual purchases, but when the homeowners themselves reach an accord as to what each will receive, the development becomes much more practical.

In a single parcel sale, neighbors put pressure on neighbors to sell. Some parcel sales have resulted in prices from two to four times the market value for the homes. Several parcel sales in Texas have resulted in homeowners getting over $1 million for unpretentious homes. One problem with these neighborhood sale packages is that after the neighborhood agrees to offer the neighborhood for sale, the owners tend to neglect maintenance and repairs, since they feel their homes will be torn down anyway.

Commercial and industrial development of the suburbs has been accelerated by the need for space and a quality work force.

The suburbs can meet both these needs of space and a quality work force.

An advantage the suburbs are able to offer business and industry is a trained, educated, female work force. To attract these female workers to the central city would require significantly higher wages than those paid in the suburbs. In addition, there is still a marked difference in the wages that many employers pay female employees compared with male employees.

Besides businesses relocating to the suburbs, the affluent suburban population has created a boom in service industry jobs.

Many suburban areas are boom towns with rapid job growth and dozens of new park-like office complexes, hundreds of new companies and thousands of new workers. It is expected that this job expansion will continue at least through 2010.

The Internet has changed the locational needs for both business and employees.

Locational advantages of central city sites are expected to decline in future years. Large businesses are likely to retain a token central city office but delegate much of the

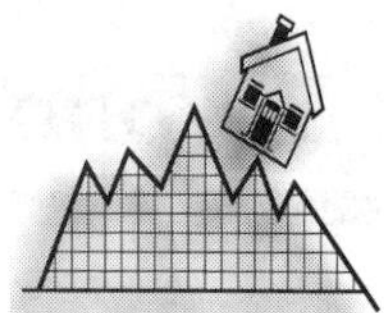

operational work to less expensive locations having a trained workforce. These locations are likely to be in suburban areas.

The suburbs are turning into large cities. The suburban downtown areas of many cities have office towers and central city-type rents coupled with traffic problems. The differences between suburbs and central cities seem to be rapidly disappearing. What is happening is the cities are being brought to the suburbs.

In bringing high-rises to the suburbs, developers have been using an "Urban Village" concept to describe their planning. While the words create a pleasant image, it means increased density and greater height.

In some cases, the increasing popularity of the suburbs as a job site has negatively affected inner city property values as well as contributed to high city unemployment.

Due to the expense of suburban housing and the time and cost of commuting, suburban employers often have difficulty in obtaining and keeping unskilled minimum wage employees.

As suburbs become business and industrial centers, they tend to become economically self-sufficient and to develop their own bedroom suburbs farther from the central city.

VI. Planned Suburbs

Most of our suburbs were the result of private development without much planning for the future.

Suburban planning, however, is not a recent phenomenon. The idea of towns separated by greenbelts was proposed by Ebenezer Howard, a London resident, in *Garden Cities of Tomorrow* (1898). Howard believed cities should be small. He proposed cities of 30,000 people—the same size that Leonardo de Vinci set forth in the 16th century as the ideal city size. Howard felt that a greenbelt was essential or the city would continue to grow and ***SCATTERATION**, or unchecked sprawl*, would be the result.

"Scatteration" is prevented by designated farm, forest and park areas, which keep the cities from fusing together.

Several garden cities were promoted by Howard, including Letchford, which was developed between 1903 and 1904. It was the first garden city, but was not successful because of its great distance (35 miles) from London. It was unable to attract sufficient commuters. However, later developments were successful.

Le Corbusier, a French urbanologist, had the idea that suburbs should be cities within parks: a group of high-rise complexes within a green belt or park. Le Corbusier's critics claimed what would be achieved would be a city within a parking lot.

Frank Lloyd Wright, the famous architect, proposed the abolishment of cities in favor of suburban towns where everyone would have at least one acre. He believed cities made people artificial. He named his ideal town Broadacre City. While some suburbs seem to follow Wright's ideas, cities such as Wright proposed would be a poor use of our land resources, resulting in vast scatteration and costs that would exclude the poor.

In the United States, Garden City and Forest Hills were early garden cities aimed at middle-income people. The idea of a greenbelt city has also been successful in the Netherlands and in Germany's Ruhr Valley.

Franklin Roosevelt's Resettlement Administration established Greenbelt, Maryland, Greenhills, Ohio, and Greendale, Wisconsin. These new towns served the dual purpose of providing low-cost housing in a rural setting and creating construction jobs. The projects had residential super blocks; foot paths and homes facing greenbelt interiors. The towns failed to protect their exteriors and other areas built around them. Greenbelt, Maryland was even bisected by several freeways. Clarence Stein, the architect of these greenbelt communities, later said he learned a new town cannot be planned by itself. It must be just one part of a regional plan.

Los Angeles County planners are embracing the urban village concept—communities where homes, offices and stores are to be intermingled on the same block. The planners are seeking to return to a community of front porches and twilight strolls, community parks and walking to the store and to work. Besides the obvious nostalgia effect, planners hope to maximize use of a shrinking land supply.

Richard Weinstein, Dean of the University of California's (Los Angeles) School of Architecture and Urban Design, warns designers to beware of "hokeyness." He states, "There is an element of contrivance, as if we're trying to get people to live in theme parks. I'm still not sure how well the trend is going to go over."

A. RESTON, VIRGINIA

A ***NEW TOWN*** *is an artificial creation by entrepreneurs, designed to attract people, rather than a natural creation springing up on its own.* Reston, Virginia, is a planned, privately funded "new town" on 6,800 acres 18 miles west of Washington, D.C. Robert E. Simon, Jr., an idealistic millionaire, started it in 1962. While critically acclaimed, initial sales at Reston were poor. Gulf Oil took over the project and invested enough funds to insure success. It is one of the few new towns that have fulfilled the planners' dreams. In 20 years Reston grew from zero to 56,000 residents.

Planned as an integrated community, one of the goals for Reston was to have an economic and racial mix. Reston's population in 2005 was 73.62 percent white, 9.12 percent African American, and 10.1 percent Hispanic. Reston has maintained a relatively steady population balance.

One danger is that higher housing costs might result in fewer African Americans. Many fear Reston will become a "yuppie" community, with growth of high technology industry along the Washington, D.C. to Dulles Airport corridor. New residents may not be as socially committed to the ideal of a diversified social experiment, as were the original residents.

The concept of placing city density housing in clusters of high-rises, townhouses, and single-family homes, and to provide for large, wooded, open spaces, was a revolutionary idea. It looks like a campus environment when compared to conventional housing.

By developing its l, 000 commercial acres for high tech industry employing 18,000 workers, Reston fulfills the developers' dream of providing work and living in the same community.

Reston is tightly controlled. An architectural review board has veto power over even minor home remodeling. Planners discourage incorporation because it would result in the residents deciding their own future. The developers feel this would not be in the best interest of thousands of future residents.

B. OTHER PLANNED SUBURBS

In 1928, Radburn in Fair Lawn, New Jersey was one of the nations most ambitiously planned communities. Radburn predates Reston, Virginia and Columbia, Maryland. It consists of 500 homes, 50 townhouses and 98 apartment units clustered together on small lots. Cars parked on narrow streets outside of back doors. Front yards connect to neighbors on three sides with pedestrian paths. The development includes parkland and community recreational facilities and a small business square. The last housing units were built in 1936. The community was actually planned to be ten times as large but the developer went bankrupt.

The Radburn design has been instrumental in developing a strong sense of community. Many of its design ideas such as linkage of common areas have been duplicated elsewhere. Residents of Radburn seldom move unless forced to because of family or economic reasons.

King Farms in Rockville, Maryland, is a close-in Washington D.C. suburb that offers a mixed use of single-family housing, multi-family housing, and office and retail space, coupled with significant green areas. Although designed to curb traffic congestion, suburban communities such as these fail to do so because residents most likely still hold jobs elsewhere.

It is interesting that the planners are intent on higher density villages while "no growth" is the battle cry in many communities.

C. NEW COMMUNITIES ACT

Congress approved Title VII of the New Communities Act in the early 1970s. The ***NEW COMMUNITIES ACT*** *allowed the government to guarantee developers loans to develop new towns for the purpose of moving Americans out of congested urban areas.* Thirteen new towns won approval. Only one town succeeded however, in that it has met its financial obligations. All the others ran into loan difficulties and were sold.

The one exception was The Woodlands, a city developed in an east Texas forest north of Houston, which is now home to over 56,000 people. Its success was due to a boom in oil exploration. The developer claimed that the other developments failed because they were too great a distance from cities, and in locations where no one would go in the first place. According to the 2000 U. S. Census, The Woodlands population was 92.3 percent white and only 1.75 percent African American.

Without some economic reason for existence, a new town is certain to fail.

D. CULTURE IN THE SUBURBS

For many years demographers believed that cities would still remain cultural hubs, and the suburbs would rely on the city for performing arts, museums, etc. Suburbs today are getting culture. Concord, California, has an 8,000 seat pavilion. Costa Mesa, California, has a $54 million performing arts center. Professional sport teams are even moving to the suburbs to be closer to the affluent ticket-buying sports fan. (The Detroit Lions are in Pontiac, Michigan.) This trend will likely continue and the importance of many cities as cultural centers will decline.

VII. Suburbs and Minorities

The rapid growth of many suburban areas served to open up housing to minority groups.

The principle of filtering down made more housing available at lower economic levels. The increase in the supply of lower-cost housing also served to reduce or keep housing costs low.

Restrictions on lot and home size have closed many communities to the poor, which also means most minorities. A recent issue of the *Journal of American Planning Association (JAPA)*,

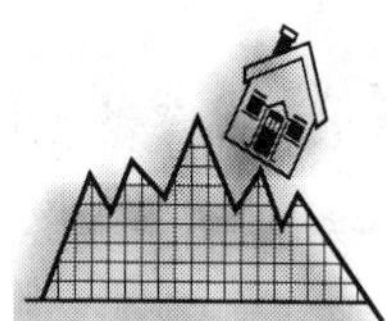

includes a Cornell University study that provides evidence that low-density zoning has an exclusionary effect on housing choices for African Americans and Hispanics in major metropolitan areas. In areas with lower zoning densities, the study indicates there were about half as many African American and about two-thirds as many Hispanics as there were in similar higher-density areas.

What this study reveals is an obvious fact—higher priced homes exclude persons of lower incomes. Because minority incomes have not caught up with the rest of society, it is natural that there would be fewer minorities in higher-cost areas.

Density bears a direct relationship to housing costs—lower density housing means higher costs.

Lower density housing requires more land and land is a significant portion of housing costs.

The study could just as well have compared waterfront property or view lots to minority placement. Again, higher costs for the site would have resulted in fewer minorities. While the study might be construed as indicating discrimination, our fair housing laws provide only for the equal opportunity to obtain housing. The same economic restrictions exist regarding housing as it does on all consumer goods.

Minorities living in many of the suburbs tend to be professional people.

While suburbs offer skilled employment, suburban jobs available to unskilled workers are usually in low pay service industries.

Many communities have large lot size requirements, sometimes several acres. Some communities have raised the minimum lot size requirements. The reason given is usually "protection of the environment"—more green areas for animals and birds as well as less pollution from septic tanks and automobiles.

It is more socially acceptable to preserve the environment by requiring low-density housing than to keep suburbs predominantly white because of racial prejudice. Protection of the environment keeps out the poor.

The Secretary of Housing and Urban Development set up a demonstration program of how to produce low-cost housing. In six of eleven demonstration sites, area residents strongly opposed the program. HUD concluded that local zoning, not high construction costs, was the reason suburbs have become white belts around minority areas.

Today, many formerly all-white suburbs are racially and ethnically diverse populations of middle-class families. The population of the city of Irvine, for example, is now 18 percent

Asian, while more than 6 percent are Latinos, and almost 2 percent are African Americans. Nearly one in ten of the residents of Thousand Oaks are Latino.

Former Senator Ribicoff of New York unsuccessfully proposed legislation that would have required significant racial integration of housing patterns in all the nation's suburbs. The proposal would have forbidden a government agency or government contractor from locating in a community unless there was sufficient low and moderate-income housing to accommodate all employees of the agency or industry. Suburbs would have had to modify restrictive zoning if they wanted industry, since most large firms have government contracts.

Regardless of the reasons for exclusion, the courts are now mandating the opening of suburban areas to the poor.

In *Hope, Inc. v. County of DuPage*, DuPage County, Illinois, was ordered to develop a plan to increase housing for the poor. The court prohibited an ordinance, which required special-use permits for low-cost housing. DuPage County was reputed to be the fourth richest county in the nation (based on average income). It is a bedroom community for Chicago executives. The court held that the county had intentionally excluded minorities by regulating lot size, parking, setbacks and trailer parks.

With passage of the 1994 pubic housing law, HUD permitted big-city housing authorities to build new units in the suburbs. The purpose was to reduce an inner city density of public housing. This law was met with resistance by the suburban middle class.

Minority presence in the suburbs is growing. In 2000, one-in-four suburban residents was a minority group member, up from one in ten in 1990. In 2000, 38 percent of the African Americans in metropolitan areas lived in suburbs, up from 27 percent in 1980, and 48 percent of metropolitan area Hispanics lived in suburbs in 2000, up from 40 percent in 1980.

While very few suburbs are still all white, usually suburbs of small mostly white cities, whites do prefer suburbs to cities. In 2000, 71 percent of non-Hispanic whites resided in suburbs, up from 65 percent in 1980.

Little evidence exists today as to exclusion from buying in a suburb due to discrimination. However, discrimination still plays a part in excluding minorities from suburban rentals. Discrimination in rentals is likely to be subtle. Examples would be the failure to mention to a minority group member that the owner has been offering one month's free rent or other concessions to a renter. Also, failure to follow up with calls or e-mails to minority group persons who visited or requested information on rentals, failure to show all available vacancies to a minority group member, or failure to inform a minority group member of units not yet vacant but would become vacant. All of the above acts or failures would be illegal under fair housing legislation if white applicants were treated differently with disclosures.

A. INCLUSIONARY ZONING

In order to have a more balanced community, some communities require developers to include a specified percentage of housing units for low or moderate-income housing.

Palo Alto, California uses a stick approach and requires developments of 10 or more units to include units for lower or moderate-income families. Montgomery Country, Maryland, uses a carrot approach for the same end. If a developer will build affordable units, they will reward the developer with waiver of fees and by allowing greater density.

Providing housing for all economic levels can be accomplished with a carrot or a stick.

VIII. No Growth or Limited Growth

The term ***GROWTH MANAGEMENT*** *is used by planners to describe restrictions on growth.*

Many people living in small communities do NOT want to see their lifestyle changed by massive growth.

NO GROWTH *or* ***LIMITED GROWTH*** *is the mentality of some suburban and small city dwellers, which seeks to restrict new residential and commercial construction.*

Many feel that continued growth will take away the attraction that brought them to the suburbs. This is known as the "pull up the drawbridge" mentality. In addition, the sewage, water, and school facilities in many communities cannot support rapid growth.

There are real ecological reasons for limiting growth. In many areas, shortage of water exists due to peoples' need to have their greenery, which has significantly lowered water tables. Septic tanks have affected water quality, along with lawn fertilizers and insecticides that are considered normal for a suburban lifestyle.

Petaluma, California, has set a limit of 500 new units per year. At an estimated 2.5 persons per unit, this provides for an annual increase of 1,250 people. Limited growth resulted in higher housing costs in Petaluma. This was due to a more limited supply of approved new home sites and a decrease in land values of unimproved home sites. This is because development of unimproved home sites could be many years away, based upon a permit system. The communities around Petaluma that did not limit growth had great development activity.

Some communities have placed moratoriums on building permits because of overloaded services, such as sewage systems, or to re-evaluate planning.

In order to control growth in California's Napa County, a Residential Urban Limit Line (RUL) was put into effect. Public service would not be provided beyond these boundaries. The result was that prices for undeveloped land within the boundaries increased immediately while land outside the boundaries declined in value.

Other communities have limited growth by increasing minimum lot sizes, which makes over-development uneconomical.

More than 20 suburbs in the San Francisco area have growth controls. In order to restrict commercial development, Walnut Creek, California, requires a ballot approval for any building over six stories. Walnut Creek voters also barred commercial construction of buildings over 10,000 square feet until the traffic at 70 congested intersections is sharply reduced.

Nantucket Island has discovered a way to reduce growth. The local government set up a "Land Bank" to buy property that is to remain free of development. It is financing the land bank by a two percent real estate transfer tax. In 2004, $20 million was raised. The goal was to set aside 4,500 acres. By 2005, 2,450 acres had been purchased. By issuing bonds to buy land now, to be paid out of the transfer fees, the community obtains land at the present prices. Other areas, including Martha's Vineyard, Cape Cod in Massachusetts, Hilton Head, South Carolina, and the Hamptons in New York, are considering similar measures.

The no-growth people see the "Land Bank" idea as a cure-all.

By not leaving any land for development, the community cannot grow. This also results in keeping prices high and keeping the poor and minorities out.

IX. The Graying of the Suburbs (Becoming Older)

GRAYING OF THE SUBURBS *is a phrase that means the average age of the suburbs is rising.* Suburban developments attracted many young families after World War II because suburban land costs were lower. The age of the average suburban dwellers was once significantly less than that of the average city dwellers.

We are now experiencing a graying of many suburbs, with a significant increase in the age of the average resident and the age of the head of the household.

The tremendous appreciation in value of existing homes in many suburbs has placed home ownership in many communities beyond the economic means of most younger couples.

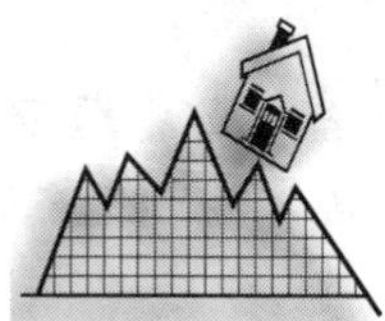

When suburban families lose their children, much of the neighborhood often loses its cohesiveness. This is because a large part of what goes into making a strong neighborhood revolves around children, such as schools, scouts, little league, etc. Many of the older suburban communities now have excess school facilities resulting from the graying of the population, while at the same time growth suburbs have overcrowded schools.

Many suburbs are working hard to retain their elderly population as well as attract new elderly residents. This is not because they like older people; it is purely economic. When families move in, school costs per child are around $10,000 per year. In addition, garbage pickup and disposal costs increase, more vehicles are on the streets, and there is a greater cost for almost all services. Communities wishing to retain elderly will find that they can fund senior centers and senior activities at far less than it would cost for new families. *Some communities provide senior transportation services and even daily calls to residents to make certain everything is all right. The result is a* ***NATURALLY OCCURRING RETIREMENT COMMUNITY (NORC)****.*

X. Deterioration of the Suburbs

Many suburbs have increasing crime, deteriorating housing, loss of tax base and all of the urban problems typically associated with the cities.

Suburbs with a close proximity to central cities in the East and Midwest have become the heir to the problems of the cities. Many Los Angeles suburbs have more severe problems than Los Angeles itself.

The decline of suburbs isn't as visible as the decline of cities. There are small, out-moded homes, many of which have become rentals. The infrastructure is in bad repair and in many older suburbs, there has been a decline in median family income. These suburbs have become home to the poor. The most severe problems are in first-ring suburbs adjacent to central cities. These older suburbs are unable to attract big-box retailers or malls because residents lack the purchasing power necessary for the large retailers that could prop up the tax base.

Suburbs do not have the taxing ability of larger cities, such as taxes on cigarettes and hotels. Their primary funding is property tax and sales tax revenues. With cutbacks in federal revenue sharing and other federal aid, many cities as well as suburbs are in serious financial difficulty. Suburbs, like cities, have become accustomed to federal aid.

Highland Park, a African American suburb of Detroit, went bankrupt a number of years ago. The city laid off one-third of its employees and suspended pension benefits for months. In a Rochester, New York suburb, hundreds of residents lined up for free government cheese.

As suburbs melt into the cities, close-in suburbs are now experiencing white-flight and all the problems of the cities. Economic development and/or redevelopment will be necessary to answer many suburban problems. In Huntington Park, California a developer filled a half vacant retail district with 500 relocated families, through a redevelopment program.

XI. Transportation Problems of the Suburbs

The problems of the suburbs go far beyond crabgrass. Explosive and unplanned growth has flooded the city fringes with cars the highways cannot accommodate.

Traffic congestion is no longer limited to rush hours. Traffic gridlock is becoming a major problem of the suburbs.

Pleasanton, California, a San Francisco suburb, enacted an ordinance requiring employers to devise plans to reduce employees' car trips by 45 percent over four years. In Rancho Penasquitos, workers complain that at rush hour it takes 40 minutes to drive two miles to a freeway entrance. In Southern California as a whole, drivers on major arteries spend approximately 10 percent of their time either stopped or barely moving. That proportion is expected to reach 50 percent by 2010 unless something is done to reduce congestion.

In 1990 California voters approved a project that raises the state sales tax 1/2 of 1 percent in order to increase available transportation. The Century Freeway (route 105) has been completed. Money spent on widening the freeway was well-spent because the flow of traffic has been increased.

In Southern California's Orange County, growth control advocates are urging that development be tied to traffic. Orange County has built toll roads that parallel freeways.

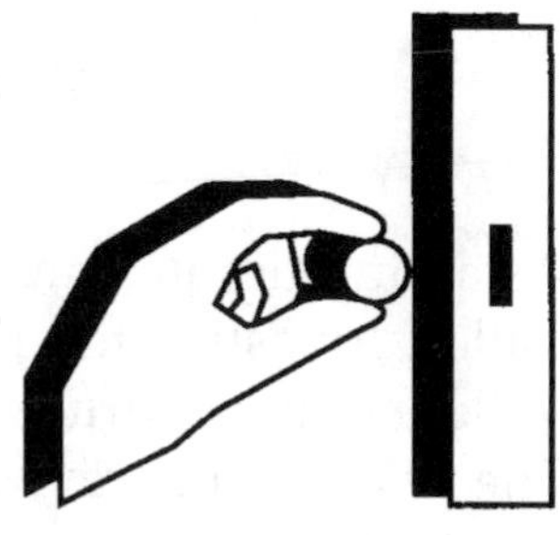

Because suburban shopping areas are spread out and people drive from shop to shop, traffic problems are increased. Most suburban communities provide relatively sparse public transportation systems. This tends to keep out people without vehicles.

Transportation networks were designed to take people from the suburbs to the cities. Typically, planning was NOT for suburb-to-suburb traffic.

Major highways radiate from cities to the suburbs where early planners expected them to be employed. These routes are like the spokes of a wheel and planners didn't foresee the need to travel between the spokes. However, businesses and industries created jobs in the suburbs and suburban residents must travel a road system not designed for suburb-to-

suburb commuting. The connector roads between suburbs, often old farm roads, cannot meet demand. Because drivers start from many thousands of points and travel to many hundreds of points, it is unlikely new multi-lane highways would meet a high percentage of commuter needs, even if funds were available to build them. Multiple points also rule out light rail transportation.

More than 30 million Americans commute from one suburban area to another and this number will grow. This is approximately twice the numbers who commute from the suburbs to central city jobs and the gap appears to be widening even further.

Traffic problems have been intensified by the fact that in the majority of households both spouses hold jobs. This usually means two cars going in different directions. It also increases the likelihood that the household will fail to relocate closer to employment, as it is unlikely both spouses work in close proximity.

The high cost of housing in many areas makes relocation closer to work sites economically impossible for large numbers of workers. Thousands of residents of California's Riverside County, where housing is relatively inexpensive, take to the freeways daily for jobs in Los Angeles and Orange Counties, where they are unable to afford comparable housing. Many Californians spend four hours or more in their vehicles every day.

Some land planners criticize suburbs that allow wide growth without coordinating development with the whole area. A future solution may be compact suburbs combined with high-rises, so public transportation or walking would make sense. This solution is unlikely in the near future, as most people want single-family homes. We are a demand economy where purchasers vote with their dollars.

XII. Revitalization of Suburbs

Asian immigrants are changing the character of a number of suburbs in the San Gabriel Valley. An estimated 150,000 Asians, primarily Chinese, moved into western San Gabriel Valley suburbs during the 1980s and 1990s, which had previously been primarily Caucasian. The Asian influx revived business areas, caused vacant parcels to be developed, and the demand placed upward pressure on real estate prices.

In many cases, close-in suburbs resemble the central city and have similar problems. Many suburban communities now have redevelopment agencies. They offer tax and other incentives for redevelopment and new businesses that will benefit their sales tax revenues and/or property tax rolls.

Minnesota instituted a "This Old House" program that provided property owners tax breaks for investing in revitalization of older properties. The value of improvements was excluded from taxes for 10 years. There are a number of communities offering home enhancement loan programs for owners of older property.

Revitalization makes sense. The cost to update a 50-year old home is far less than the cost to demolish and replace it.

Many communities have taken a smart growth approach in revitalizing suburbs by requiring greater density for redevelopment and new developments. Smart growth is really a command economy telling people what they can have rather than letting them have what they want. By ignoring the preferences of buyers and renters, smart growth tends to push up prices of traditional suburban housing.

George Sternlieb, Director of the Center for Urban Policy Research, believes that many older suburbs will be rediscovered and revitalized.

XIII. Boomburgs

The term ***BOOMBURG*** *has developed to describe fast-growing suburbs.* According to the Fannie Mae Foundation, a boomburg is an area that has more than 100,000 people and double-digit rates of population growth in each recent decade but is not the largest city in the metropolitan area.

There are 53 Boomburgs in the United States today.

Boomburgs are located in 14 metropolitan areas surrounding Phoenix, Los Angeles, San Diego, San Francisco, Denver, Miami, Tampa, Chicago, Las Vegas, Portland, Dallas, Salt Lake City, Norfolk, and Seattle. Boomburgs, because of there size, tend to have more population diversity than smaller suburbs.

XIV. Exurbia (Beyond the Suburbs)

"Exurbia" is the land beyond the suburbs.

EXURBIA *is characterized by smaller-sized farms, homes on acreage and a scattering of subdivisions.*

"Beyond exurbia" is farmland, forests, or wasteland.

We have been experiencing a nationwide ruralization trend. So many people have moved to rural areas that, in some cases, they have had to be reclassified as urban.

In the 1960s, ***FOOTLOOSE INDUSTRIES****, those not tied physically to a particular market location, or suppliers,* began to move to exurbia. Advantages to industry were low costs as well as a less expensive lifestyle. Retirees also fueled the movement beyond the suburbs. Advantages to retirees were less fear of crime and lower costs for housing and services. Retirees often find exurbia can provide a quality of life unaffordable to them within the cities or suburbs.

Chapter 7

The housing increase in exurbia has generally exceeded suburban and urban increases.

According to the 1990 U.S. Census, non-metropolitan counties grew by more than 15.5 percent during the 1980s, but metropolitan counties grew by only 10 percent. The 1990s saw a continuation of this growth pattern. The 2000 U.S. Census found that non-metropolitan areas contained 56.1 million residents, a gain of 5.6 million since 1990. Most of this gain came from migration.

This recent upsurge in rural growth is the first time since 1820 that rural growth has exceeded urban growth.

Newcomers to rural areas tend to be better educated than previous rural residents, and they tend to have above-average incomes. Today, less than 10 percent of rural residents live on farms.

To find a suburban lifestyle, you must go beyond the suburbs.

The attractiveness of living in a rural area has increased both economically and socially. Many people have become disenchanted with the cities and suburbs, spawning an anti-city, anti-suburban movement. Some people want to escape the crime and dirt of the cities. Others just seek a less hectic way of life. Thomas Wolfe said, "You can't go home again," but many are trying. They want a simpler way of life.

This is NOT an entirely white, middle-class phenomena.

The number of African Americans leaving small Southern, rural communities is almost matched by other African Americans moving back into these areas.

The poor are also discovering smaller urban and rural areas. The biggest increases in welfare case loads are occurring in rural areas. The poor have discovered the advantages of low housing costs.

This migration and increasing numbers of welfare recipients is a strain on rural county resources.

A. OTHER URBAN PLACES

Because of lifestyle, many small urban areas are able to woo attractive industries from both central cities and suburbs. Advantages of industries moving to smaller cities is that they are less likely to be unionized, wages are generally lower than in large urban areas, employee absentee rates tend to be lower, and employee retention is greater.

Call centers, handling orders and technical assistance, formerly sought large city locations for their labor-intensive operations. Because of low unemployment during the late 1990s, call centers began operating in less populated areas where there was little competition from other employers. Employers found that they could increase employee retention and employ educated and dedicated employees in smaller communities. By 2006, these call centers had relocated to India and Bangladesh because of lower costs.

XV. CHAPTER SUMMARY

Most **suburbs** were originally **bedroom communities** established to provide a more rural lifestyle for those commuting to the cities. They were generally economically reliant on the city for jobs, material, and services.

Essential to the growth of suburbs was **transportation**. The railroad fostered the growth of many of our first suburban communities. In the Los Angeles area, the **"red car"** line aided suburban growth. Freeways, low-priced cars and septic systems allowed for an era of **suburban sprawl**.

Suburbs today are faced with many of the same problems as the central cities. Many suburbs are now courting commercial and industrial development to increase the property tax base.

Some suburbs have opposed growth in an attempt to maintain a particular lifestyle. They have placed **moratoriums** on construction or placed limits on growth to achieve this result.

Because of housing cost increases, fewer young people can afford housing. This has accelerated the **"graying"** of many suburban communities. In many areas, older residential communities now have unused school facilities. At the same time, many new communities do not have enough schools.

The lack of public transportation, zoning, and private restrictions have all served to keep minorities to a minimum in many suburbs. However, the suburbs are now generally integrated. A number of communities now have inclusionary zoning, requiring subdividers to provide for low-income or moderate-income housing, which should help to integrate these communities.

Boomburgs are large, fast growing suburbsof more than 100,000 people.

Exurbia is the land beyond the suburbs. We have experienced a rapid population growth in these areas. People moving to exurbia are generally better educated and have higher incomes than other rural residents. Problems of both the cities and suburbs are making rural life more attractive. For these reasons, small cities and towns beyond the central city and suburbs have been experiencing exceptional growth.

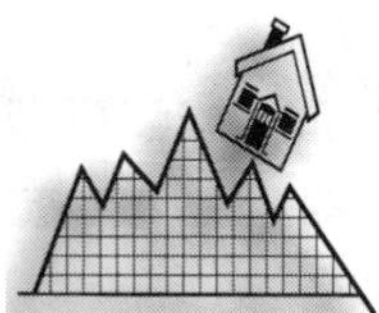

XVI. GLOSSARY OF KEY TERMS

Bedroom Community – A suburban community whose residents commute primarily to and from work in a central city or other suburban community.

Boomburg – A suburb of more than 100,000 people with double-digit growth each decade.

Building Moratorium – A cessation of construction, usually for a set time, in order to revise planning.

Clean Industries – Industries that do not pollute water or air.

Exurbia – The land beyond the suburbs, characterized by homes on acreage, undeveloped land, farms, and small communities.

Footloose Industries – Industries that are not dependent upon particular locations and can readily relocate.

Graying of the Suburbs – The increase of the average age of suburban dwellers.

Hope, Inc. v. County of DuPage – The federal case that held communities, through planning, cannot exclude the poor and minorities.

Inclusionary Zoning – Zoning requiring the inclusion of a feature such as low-cost housing in future developments.

Land Bank – A land reserve to be kept free of development.

Naturally Occurring Retirement Communities (NORC) – Communities that have changed from family orientated to retirees.

New Communities Act – Federal act that provided federal aid for planned suburban communities.

New Town – A planned community that was started from nothing, rather than from the growth of an existing community.

No Growth Legislation – Legislation that limits or excludes future development.

Scatteration – Dispersed development resulting in unchecked sprawl.

Single Parcel Sales – Sales by suburban landowners, as a group, to developers for commercial redevelopment.

Suburb – A community outside the central city that originally grew as a result of economic reliance on the city.

Urban Village Concept – Urbanization of the suburbs characterized by concentrated commercial growth.

XVII. CLASS DISCUSSION TOPICS

1. Identify suburban growth in your area.

2. Identify changing trends in the suburbs in your area.

3. Where in your area do you envision the greatest future suburban growth? Why?

4. Give examples of the filtering down of housing in your suburban areas.

5. How do your local suburbs encourage or discourage minorities and the poor?

6. Where does exurbia begin in your area?

7. What groups would be most likely to favor suburban growth in your area and what groups would be most likely to oppose growth?

8. How can suburban greenbelts be maintained?

9. What big city problems have emerged in suburban communities in your area?

10. Identify another urban place within 150 miles of your home. Would you like to live there? Why?

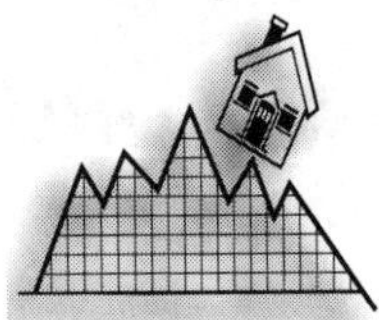

XVIII. CHAPTER 7 QUIZ

1. What is the definition of a suburb?

   a. A rural community
   b. A self-sustaining community
   c. A community near and subordinate to a central city
   d. A residential community without significant commerce or industry

2. Suburban dwellers differ from central city dwellers because, on the average, suburban dwellers:

   a. have greater income.
   b. have less education.
   c. are more likely to be single-person or single-parent households.
   d. are more likely to be renters.

3. The following factors are conducive to suburban growth, except:

   a. a political climate friendly to development.
   b. being outside a city with a deteriorating economic base.
   c. a supply of relatively inexpensive land.
   d. good transportation routes to economic centers.

4. A development that allowed suburban growth beyond city facilities was the:

   a. television.
   b. fax machine.
   c. septic tank.
   d. personal computer.

5. Suburbs can keep property taxes down by:

   a. keeping industry out.
   b. not allowing shopping centers.
   c. promoting lower cost homes.
   d. denser development.

6. Central city office locations are not as necessary as they once were because of:

   a. the Internet.
   b. electric elevators and structural steel.
   c. redevelopment programs.
   d. sprawl.

7. Assemblage is made easy for redevelopment when homeowners get together and:
   a. offer their neighborhood in a single parcel sale.
   b. develop CC&Rs.
   c. use political pressure for code enforcement.
   d. restrict street traffic.

8. Frank Lloyd Wright's approach to suburbs would have resulted in:
   a. compact communities.
   b. vast scatteration.
   c. ready housing for the poor.
   d. larger central cities.

9. A privately funded new town was:
   a. Greenbelt, Maryland.
   b. Greendale, Wisconsin.
   c. Reston, Virginia.
   d. Greenhills, Ohio.

10. The rapid growth of suburban communities helped:
   a. to improve traffic.
   b. in opening city housing to lower income and minority groups.
   c. to reduce city crime.
   d. reduce pollution.

ANSWERS: 1. *c*; 2. *a*; 3. *b*; 4. *c*; 5. *d*; 6. *a*; 7. *a*; 8. *b*; 9. *c*; 10. *b*

LEARNING OBJECTIVES

While regulations can be used to promote the health, safety, welfare and public good, they can also have positive or negative effects on the real estate market. You will also understand how our tax laws (and changes in them) can affect the real estate marketplace.

In this chapter, you will learn the origin and growth of government regulations.

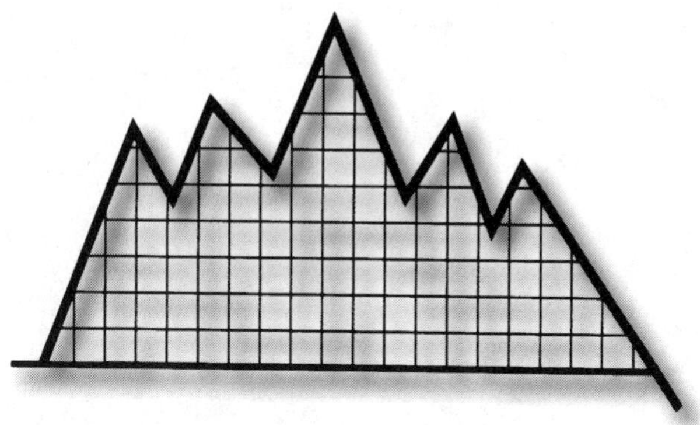

Chapter 8
Government Regulations and Taxes

Government serves many purposes. Among these are:

1. Providing improvements and services.
2. Providing for the national defense.
3. Providing for the needs of those unable to care for themselves (social programs).
4. Protecting the economy.

I. Local, State, and National Regulations

Government regulations, at the local, state and national levels, can have a significant economic impact on the real estate marketplace.

A. BUILDING CODES

Many cities and counties have additional, more stringent construction standards than are required by state law. The ***BUILDING CODE*** *is the basic minimum construction standard for a structure. This includes regulation of all the basic methods, materials and components of a structure, from the foundation to the plumbing and electrical system.* Local building inspectors enforce both the state and local building codes.

The local building inspector enforces construction standards (codes).

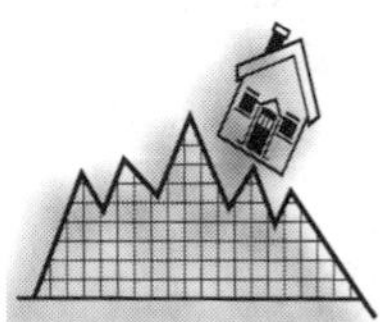

CHAPTER 8 OUTLINE

New construction or building alterations require a building permit. A ***BUILDING PERMIT*** *is an approved building application that includes plans, specifications, and a plot plan.* After an examination of the application, plans, and any revisions of the plans, the building permit is issued. No construction or alteration can be started until the building permit has been issued.

The earliest building code was the Code of Hammurabi, ruler of Babylon.

Code of Hammurabi 1780 B.C.

"...if a man builds a house badly, and it falls and kills the owner, the builder is to be slain. If the owner's son was killed, then the builder's son is slain."

1. Building Codes Protect the Public

Building codes protect the public by insuring that all structures meet minimum safety requirements.

Building codes are enforced under police power. ***POLICE POWER*** *is the authority of any governmental agency to enact legislation or provide rules for the health, safety, moral and general welfare of the public.*

There are a number of standard industry building codes (models) in use, including:

1. **BOCA Code** (Building Officials and Code Administrators, International, Inc.)
2. **Uniform Building Code** (International Conference of Building Officials)
3. **Southern Standard Building Code**
4. **National Building Code** (American Insurance Association)

Some cities have adopted standard industry building codes intact; others have made modifications to the standard codes; and others still have their own special codes.

There are two basic types of building codes:

1. **Specifications Codes –** These codes set forth exact specifications as to material to be used and/or how it shall be used.
2. **Performance Codes –** These codes are based on standards that must be met.

Specification codes can lead to excessive costs since builders are restricted as to material and method. Less costly alternatives are precluded.

Within a single metropolitan area, builders and subcontractors could be subject to standards that differ greatly because of individual codes.

There are also individual codes for specific trades, such as electric and plumbing codes. This diversity of codes makes standardization of building materials and methods impossible and serves to increase costs. It is estimated that codes unnecessarily add an extra five to ten percent to construction costs. Codes become particularly cumbersome when remodeling, restoring, or rehabilitating a property.

B. MASTER PLAN

Cities and counties have a Master Plan and a planning commission.

The purpose of a master plan is to unify city planning considering land use, transportation, parking, employment, recreation, health, schools, shopping, pollution, sanitation, flood control, and public services including police and fire protection. It is a plan for the future.

Entire new cities can be pre-planned so that zoning laws exist only to enforce and execute the city's master plan. The ***MASTER PLAN** is a comprehensive guide through which zoning establishes an ideal plan for the city's development in the future.*

Governmental action often works against providing additional housing units to meet the needs of private ownership by:

1. Zoning restrictions as to density.
2. Building codes that make rehabilitation and development more costly.
3. Rent control or the fear of rent control.
4. Developmental impact fees.
5. Additional government regulations.

C. ENVIRONMENTAL CONTROL

The ***NATIONAL ENVIRONMENTAL POLICY ACT OF 1969 (NEPA)*** *requires both public and private sectors to conform to certain environmental standards.* The NEPA's stated objectives include not only the environment but also insuring an aesthetically pleasing surrounding to protect health and safety, preserve historical and cultural heritage as well as preserving natural resources.

NEPA's goal is to "encourage productive and enjoyable harmony between man and his environment, to promote efforts which will prevent or eliminate damage to the environment and biosphere, and stimulate the health and welfare of man..."

Every federal agency is required to submit an ***ENVIRONMENTAL IMPACT STATEMENT (EIS)*** *for any program likely to affect the quality of the surrounding environment.* Examples of such projects would be new highways, rerouting highways, dams or allowing recreational development on federal land.

The EIS covers positive as well as negative impacts of proposed actions. The EIS does NOT force the government to take the most environmentally sound alternative action.

State governments have followed the federal lead and have passed statutes to require ***ENVIRONMENTAL IMPACT REPORTS (EIRs)*** *for projects likely to have an effect on the environment.*

The Environmental Protection Agency and the U.S. Corp of Engineers have established a wetlands preservation program encompassing 95 million acres. Designated wetlands are protected against development.

epa.gov
(Environmental Protection Agency)

D. HAZARDOUS WASTE

The federal ***COMPREHENSIVE ENVIRONMENTAL RESPONSE COMPENSATION AND LIABILITY ACT (CERCLA)*** *allows the federal government to respond to releases or threatened release of hazardous substances that may endanger public health or the environment.*

CERCLA created a superfund to clean up abandoned hazardous waste sites. The act also makes the person responsible for the release liable for clean up costs. The liability can extend to future owners of the site.

An owner can be liable even when the owner did not know the tenant was using hazardous materials or the materials were only later determined to be hazardous. Buyers of property can escape liability under federal law only if the buyers can show they conducted appropriate inquiries prior to acquiring the property.

Before purchasing a property where hazardous substances could be a problem, get expert analysis of the soil.

Besides federal laws that could require environmental clean up, there are also state laws dealing with environmental problems.

E. OCCUPATIONAL SAFETY AND HEALTH ADMINISTRATION (OSHA)

The mission of the Occupational Safety and Health Administration (OSHA) is to prevent work-related illnesses, injuries and deaths by making and enforcing rules for the workplace.

States have their own safety and health standards for the workplace that are separately enforced.

OSHA's regulations are of particular concern to builders and property managers where there are many safety concerns and applicable regulations. However, OSHA also reaches into offices with lighting, noise abatement, air quality, ventilation, eyestrain, and fire prevention criteria. Congress repealed Ergomatic standards. Businesses that never considered OSHA applicable to their workplace have been fined for violation of OSHA regulations.

Because of complaints of excessive regulations, the ***SMALL BUSINESS REGULATORY ENFORCEMENT FAIRNESS ACT*** *was passed in 1996. Regulations must consider small businesses and there must be fairness to small businesses in OSHA's enforcement.* New regulations must be written so small business owners can understand them. A regulatory ombudsman position was established. Although OSHA believes the act has restricted their ability to issue protective regulations, the Small Business Administration feels that the act was needed to protect against bureaucratic abuse of small business.

F. AMERICANS WITH DISABILITIES ACT

The ***AMERICANS WITH DISABILITIES ACT*** *requires owners and operators of places of public accommodation make their facilities accessible to the handicapped to the extent that is readily achievable.* "Readily achievable" means achievable with a reasonable expenditure.Places of public accommodation include offices, stores, and places of recreation. What is reasonable would be related to the ability of the owner or operator to achieve it and the rental value of the property.

The act also requires that new construction meet accessibility requirements.

Examples of requirements for a typical real estate office might be:

1. Lowering of counters
2. Widening of aisles
3. Hand rails in hallways
4. Widening washroom doors and cubicle doors
5. Support rails in washrooms
6. Sinks and faucets to accommodate wheelchairs
7. Cup dispensers for water fountains

Because the act provides compensation to the person discriminated against, as well as fines, some individuals have been making dozens of complaints of accessibility.

G. LANDLORD-TENANT LAW

Rights of landlords as well as tenants are set forth in state statutes. Most states have adopted all or part of the ***UNIFORM RESIDENTIAL TENANT ACT*** *that regulates landlords' rights to enter the premises, security deposits, notice periods, duty to make repairs, responsibility for garbage, keeping the premises habitable, right to evict, etc.*

H. LICENSING REGULATIONS

Every state requires real estate agents to be licensed and most states require contractors to be licensed.

Licensing requires meeting personal standards, educational and/or experience requirements and/or passing a written test. It is not a free market, as everyone who wants to be a real estate agent or contractor might not be able to obtain licensing.

I. DISCLOSURE REGULATIONS

Every state requires disclosure to a buyer of defects known to the seller.

There are also disclosures as to agency relationship. **Federal Disclosures** are required by the **Truth In Lending Act** and the Real Estate Settlement Act. There is also a **Lead-Based Paint Disclosure** required by Federal Law. Failure to make disclosures could mean the buyers would be able to rescind the transactions, fines and compensatory damages. It is imperative that persons dealing in real estate know the disclosures required in their state.

J. ZONING

ZONING LAWS *regulate the use of property by prescribing what uses land can be put to, and by establishing uniformity throughout the community.* For example, zoning laws may indicate that a specific property can be used only as a single family home, or as multiple-family housing, or commercial or industrial use. It is possible for the planning commission to change zoning.

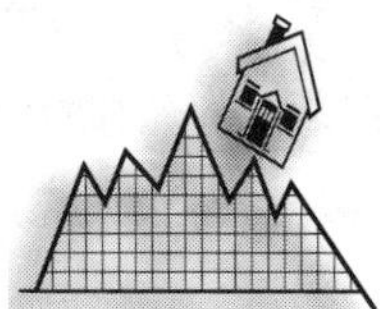

Government control of land use allows for the reasonable utilization of our land. Combined with city planning, zoning can look ahead to meet the future needs of a community.

When insufficient land is zoned for a use, the price of that land will be higher than if sufficient land was zoned for that use.

Conversely, when more land is zoned for a purpose than would reasonably be expected to be utilized, prices decrease.

A favorable change in zoning generally increases value and demand for land. Even the possibility of a favorable zoning change would tend to increase the market value of land.

Downzoning to a less intensive use (changing the zoning from R-4, multiple apartments, to R-1, single residences) would reduce the market value of land.

DOWNZONING *is the governmental act of changing use to a less intensive use.* Downzoning causes a decrease in demand for the land, which in turn causes a decline in its selling price.

UPZONING *is the governmental act of changing the zoning to a more intensive use.* Zoning that increases the density allowed would reduce costs per unit so would increase the demand and value for the land.

II. Public Housing

PUBLIC HOUSING *is residential housing owned by a government agency and rented to the poor.*

Public housing was NOT originally intended to be a permanent government program.

As proposed in the 1930s, it was designed as a way to give construction jobs to unemployed workers and provide them with a temporary shelter until they could afford private sector housing. During the 1930s and 1940s, residents were primarily working class white families. By the 1950s, the urban working classes were not as needy. Federal law set rent for public housing at one-quarter of a person's income. Workers could get superior housing on the open market for this amount of rent. The people who wanted public housing were further down the economic scale. At the same time, most public housing authorities stopped screening applicants. The result was a ghettoization of public housing developments. They became a concentration of the poor.

While most low-income housing units are privately owned, there are approximately 1½ million units in 13,000 public housing developments in 3,400 communities in the United

States. Public housing is federally subsidized but is operated and maintained by local governments. It is estimated that less than 1 percent of our population now lives in publicly owned units. Individual families in public housing usually pay 30 percent of their adjusted monthly income for rent. HUD makes up any shortfall.

Because federal public housing was only built with the approval of local government, public housing was primarily constructed in inner-city areas.

Due to a lack of a profit motive, the difficulty in firing incompetent government employees as well as problems evicting undesirable tenants, public housing has been grossly mismanaged.

A. PUBLIC HOUSING COSTS TOO MUCH

Government construction costs generally exceed the cost of similar housing built by the private sector. Government projects cost more because rigid specifications and bidder requirements actually reduce the competitiveness they were designed to foster. Government construction cost per unit is considerably more than what private developers pay to build apartments for themselves. In addition, there is no incentive to design for cost efficiency.

Besides being expensive and often unattractive, public housing takes property off the tax rolls (federal public housing does not pay city property taxes) and creates a significant increase in the need for community services.

B. FAILURE OF PUBLIC HOUSING

Very little planning has gone into some very expensive government projects. In St. Louis, the Pruitt-Igoe complex of 43 buildings, each 11 stories, was built at a taxpayer cost of $52 million dollars. There were 2,870 apartments in this huge complex, which was heralded as an imaginative advance in urban living. Housing and Urban Development (HUD) poured many more millions into the project. Eventually the project was dynamited, leaving behind $32 million in bonded indebtedness, which remained on HUD's books. Vandalism made the project uninhabitable. The elevators and hallways were not safe. The project became an institutionalized ghetto, without an element of cohesiveness or neighborhood pride.

Some attempts to salvage the project included rehabilitation, attempts to improve living conditions, hiring additional security guards, tenant participation in management, tenant counseling, and even lowering the density and increasing open space by tearing two buildings down. A modernization attempt was abandoned after $5 million was spent because vandals were destroying the buildings faster than workers could repair them.

The problems in St. Louis are not unique. In 1995, 60 percent of Detroit's public housing units were unoccupied because of habitability problems. HUD estimates that it will take $30 billion to repair the present public housing stock.

When the Robert Taylor Homes project was completed in 1962, the Chicago housing project was the largest in the world, with 28 buildings each 16 stories high. Since then, 25 of the buildings have been demolished. The plan is to move the residents out of the remaining three buildings by 2006. Drugs, violence, and the inability to manage the units doomed the project.

Another Chicago project that failed was Cabrini Green. It opened in 1958 close to several affluent neighborhoods. It became the poster child for what is wrong with public housing. Porches had to be enclosed with wire mesh after too many children fell. Roach infestation, garbage throughout the hallways, the smell of urine, graffiti, backed up and leaking plumbing, elevators that failed to work, and residents afraid to leave their apartments led to its demolition.

The future of public housing appears bleak for a number of reasons, including crime, graffiti, and poor property management.

In the period of civil unrest during the '60s, local housing administrations increased services and were reluctant to evict. Attempts to raise rents were often met by tenant strikes, some of which were supported by the Federal Office of Economic Opportunity.

In 1969, the Philadelphia local housing authority signed an agreement with a tenant organization, which provided that constables would not be used to collect rent. This caused a moratorium on evictions, and delinquencies increased 600 percent.

Without an owner who is profit motivated, public housing lacks the incentive for proper management. Public housing competes directly with efficiently run private developments.

Despite the hundreds of millions of dollars spent for these projects, public housing meets the needs of only a small fraction of the poor. Rather than the government being a developer, it would be cheaper for the government to provide cash subsidies to the poor than to attempt to take over their housing needs.

As public housing ages, a great many problems have surfaced. Often built to meet minimum construction standards, public housing units are showing the effects of age, hard use, and in many cases, poor management and maintenance.

In Washington, D.C. a 286-unit building had to be abandoned because repairs would have been too costly. Missing gutters and broken pipes allowed water to seep beneath the foundation, causing the building to tilt. The Philadelphia Housing Authority closed two high-rises only 15-years old because repairs would have cost $18 million in unavailable funds.

The Department of Housing and Urban Development claimed that 70,000 public housing units were unfit for occupancy in 1986. Critics of public housing claim that problems primarily relate to unbelievably poor management. Some housing authorities, such as Phoenix, Arizona, have managed to maintain their stock of public housing units while complying with local codes.

As of 2000, 10 percent of the nation's public housing stock was slated for demolition. The structures being demolished are the high rises, similar to the St. Louis Pruitt-Igoe complex. High-rise projects were heralded as the answer to low cost housing needs during the 1950s and 1960s. Instead, they have become a breeding ground of poverty and crime. Residents feel isolated from society.

In just a few cities, such as New York, high rises are not slated for demolition because management did not allow physical deterioration and other problems to occur that are prevalent in most high-rise projects.

Resources are best allocated when left to the free choice of an open marketplace.

A profit-oriented economy works far better than an economy dictated by the government. The private sector will provide new housing for the poor, but there must be sufficient economic rewards to do so.

Economist Milton Friedman, credited with creating the theory of monetarism, believes public housing is an evil. Friedman believes public housing encourages ghettoization, discourages private housing investment, reduces the quality of life of its residents by fostering gangs of juvenile delinquents, and causes other social ills. He also believes public housing also tends to stifle personal initiative and promote the welfare state mentality of "we deserve it."

III. Subsidized Housing

HUD provides two types of subsidies: "project-based" subsidies and "tenant-based" subsidies.

Project-based subsides were given to owners or developers who agreed in advance to rental schedules. These subsidies were either in the form of low interest loans or special tax credits. Most of these programs are no longer available, but the units created still provide subsidized housing for low-income families (tenant-based subsidies).

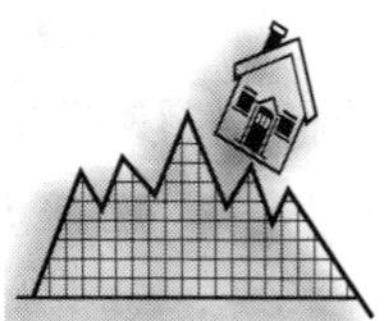

Chapter 8

Under federal housing programs that began in the 1960s, investors who obtained low interest mortgage loans for low-income housing were strictly regulated as to the rents they could charge. The initial investments were primarily made for the tax benefits of the depreciation and not for cash flow. Under the terms of the loans, after 20 years, the borrowers could pay them off and be released from the rental limitation. The 20-year escape hatch for many of the units was between 1986 and 2003. In some cases, the controlled rents charged are only about one-third of the market rent. Owners escaping the rent control programs have raised their rents substantially, which significantly reduced the nation's stock of low-income housing.

"Section 8 housing" provides tenant-based housing subsidies through certificates or vouchers.

Families living in subsidized housing developments pay rent equal to 30 percent of their adjusted gross income and HUD pays the balance. The maximum income requirement for subsidized housing varies by household size and location.

Certificates are given out by local public housing authorities to tenants who then look for housing that meets government quality standards and a landlord who is willing to sign a ***HOUSING ASSISTANCE PAYMENT (HAP) CONTRACT***. *The certificate covers the difference between the 30 percent of the tenants' income and fair market rent*. If the local housing authority sets fair market rent below the rent the landlord demands, the tenant must make up the difference. Because of approval requirements, many Section 8 housing units have rents that exceed non-subsidized units.

Some 2.6 million Americans, less than 1 percent, live in Section 8 housing.

Vouchers are given to needy families who seek private market housing. Unlike certificates, they do not restrict users to a specific rent level or limit their rent expense. Voucher holders choose their own housing and pay the difference between the voucher amount and rent. Current federal funding provides for a voucher plan to help families who are going off welfare but still require some aid.

Vouchers have pretty well replaced construction subsidies and new public housing programs. However, vouchers do not encourage developers to increase the stock of low-income housing. Incentives such as rapid depreciation benefits could fulfill this need.

Vouchers have failed to bring lower-income housing to the marketplace. They have failed to do the most important thing—increase the supply of units.

IV. Anti-Trust Laws

A number of anti-trust laws were enacted to prohibit unfair and coercive tactics by big business. The acts were intended to help small businesses as well as consumers. The most important anti-trust act was the **Sherman Anti-Trust Act**.

Anti-trust laws apply to the real estate profession.

The Sherman Anti-Trust Act prohibits:

1. **Price Fixing** – It would be a violation of the Act for a group of brokers to agree that they would not take a listing at less than a particular rate of commission.
2. **Market Allocation Agreements** – It would be a violation of the Act for brokers to divide a market geographically or by type of property and agree not to compete against each other.
3. **Tie In** – It would be a violation of the Act for a broker to require buyers to contract for services with the broker as a condition of placing an offer to purchase.
4. **Group Boycotting** – It would be a violation of the Act for a group of brokers to agree not to do business with a particular firm or individual.

In addition to federal laws, there are also state anti-trust laws.

V. Rent Control

A. THE HISTORY OF RENT CONTROL

Rent control ordinances presume a market that fails to meet housing needs and fails to add sufficient additional housing units.

During World War II we had national rent control as a wartime measure because there was a shortage of housing. The end of hostilities generally ended rent control, although it continued in New York City under a 1947 ordinance.

Nationwide, less than 10 percent of apartments are subject to rent control.

While city and county governments have been reluctant to enact rent control, voter initiatives have placed rent control on many ballots. It is very popular politically in areas where renters are in the majority. In a city with a high percentage of renters, rent control ordinances are likely to pass. Any legislation against rent control has to occur at the county or state level. Otherwise, it would be defeated in areas having a high percentage of renters. Once enacted, rent control is almost impossible to remove.

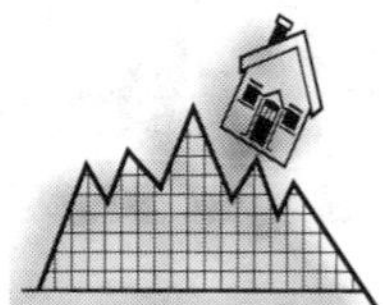

In 1971, an attempt to end New York's rent control by attrition failed after strong opposition by renters.

Fifteen states have passed legislation prohibiting rent control.

Rent control ordinances generally set the current amount of rent charged at a particular date as the base rental price. This penalizes owners whose rental units were at or below market rates when rent control is enacted. Owners who gave rental concessions in the form of several months' free rent in order to obtain a higher rent generally received an advantage under rent control.

In some manufactured home communities, huge rent increases acted as a stimulus for rent control. Without rent control, unit owners were forced to pay rent increases or sell their units to others who could pay. Purchasers of manufactured home parks knew they could create a positive cash flow by simply raising the rent on their captive tenants.

B. EFFECTS OF RENT CONTROL

In New York, owners of buildings having large flats or apartments found a way to increase revenues despite rent control. As units became vacant, they broke up the large units into several smaller units and charged rent for each of the resulting units. This increased the population density in many areas, contributing to a rapid decline. "Brownstone" areas, those with apartment buildings of multiple floors constructed of brown brick and once highly sought by the middle class, became slums.

Rent control has also led to the conversion of rental units to condominiums and cooperatives.

If an owner is faced with decades of rent control, it becomes more economical to convert the apartments into condos and sell them. When rent control precludes the eviction of a tenant after conversion, we have seen an unusual type of speculation. Purchasers are buying with the knowledge that the unit will increase greatly in value when the present tenants relocate or die. The age of the tenants has, therefore, affected the sale price of rent-controlled units after conversion to condominiums or cooperatives. Rent control offers protection to a tenant (in possession) against others who might be willing to pay more for the premises.

In communities where rent-controlled property rents are significantly less than free market rents, families will be reluctant to move even when their needs are not properly being met. Tenants under rent control are not moving up, which creates another problem. The process of filtering down, whereby housing becomes available to lower economic levels, is thwarted by tenants who are reluctant to move.

With no filtering down, minorities, recent immigrants and young married couples are actually kept out of areas as a result of rent control.

In the period from 1950 to 1960 the growth of one-person households in rent controlled housing in New York increased from 12.1 percent to 22.6 percent, an increase of 86.8 percent, compared to a 68 percent increase in all metropolitan statistical areas. This indicates the reluctance to give up an advantageous rental after death of a spouse or a divorce. Rent control thus results in poor space allocation. There will be people with units larger than they need and people with growing families in too little space with both groups unwilling to give up a rent-controlled unit.

Rent control usually results in reduced owner services. If better services cannot be reflected in rents, a profit-motivated owner will strive to only make those repairs and services necessary to protect the value of the property. In some extreme cases, rent control has contributed to buildings being abandoned by their owners. It is common for tenants in rent-controlled structures in New York to take care of much of the maintenance that owners formerly provided because they know it will not be done if left to the owners.

Rent control also leads to reduced city services because property values will be depressed, reflecting the suppressed income which will in turn mean reduced assessed values and lower property taxes. Rent control also results in rent inequality between tenants in controlled rentals and those forced to compete in a free rental market.

Rent control acts as a disincentive to development by putting a cap on profits but NOT on losses.

Even the fear of future rent control will stifle development. Investment of risk capital in apartment buildings requires a high return or market appreciation. When one area limits profits, risk capital investors will go elsewhere. Rent control thus insures rental shortages if the population increases. Rent control was ended in 1975 in Stockholm, Sweden because it was stifling the development of new housing by the private sector. Landlords feel that rent control unfairly shifts the burden of subsidizing renters from the government to the landlord. They feel that rent control is being used as an alternative to public housing. In New York, rent for rent-controlled apartments is about a third of the rent for non-controlled units.

In the '70s, New York tried to encourage the building of apartment complexes. Builders were told that their new units would be exempt from rent control. New York later retroactively put the properties on rent stabilization. This has deterred the development of new apartments.

C. RENT CONTROL IN SANTA MONICA, CALIFORNIA

Rent control in Santa Monica, California was promoted to help the poor. Santa Monica residents tend to have upper level incomes. The apartment association of Los Angeles claimed that the average income of a Santa Monica renter was $50,000 in 1984 (it was estimated at over $70,000 in 2000). There seems to be no social purpose in Santa Monica's rent control. It simply means that rents of those able to pay a prevailing rent are protected against rent increases at the expense of the owner. Santa Monica had few new units being built and sales were down for existing units.

Eighty percent of Santa Monica's residents live in apartments.

Santa Monica has an elected, five-person, rent control board. The board not only controls rents but also conversions and demolitions. In one five-year period, the legal staff of the Santa Monica rent control board spent about $700,000 defending 300 rent control lawsuits.

While real estate values in Santa Monica have remained relatively stable since the start of rent control, values in the rest of West Los Angeles have more than doubled during the same period. In 1984, the city of Santa Monica claimed that 6,000 apartment units needed rehabilitation or replacement. Maintenance complaints by tenants have more than doubled since rent control.

Because of the great difference between the cost of rent control and free market apartments, a black market existed in Santa Monica rent-controlled apartments.

To obtain rentals in Santa Monica, rental agency fees in the thousands of dollars were not uncommon. Owners have also become very selective in choosing tenants. Few units actually reach the vacancy stage.

When rent control was first enacted, Santa Monica had 38,000 rental units. But by 1991, the rental stock had diminished to 28,000 rental units; 26 percent of rental units had been lost.

In 1979, Los Angeles passed a rent control ordinance, which covered half a million rental units. The Los Angeles rent control ordinance allowed up to a seven percent annual increase, additional increases of one percent each for gas and electricity, and an increase for capital improvements. When a tenant moves out, the landlord can raise the rent to market rent level. Santa Monica did not allow a new rent to be set when property is vacated.

Rent control increases the value of a leasehold estate; when the unit is leased at below market rental value.

This value was considered in marriage dissolutions, particularly in the Santa Monica area. According to an area attorney, the right to retain an apartment was traded off for the community property rights in a BMW in a marriage dissolution.

Santa Monica repealed its rent control ordinance, as it applied to new tenants, in 1999. It was a case of "I got mine—forget about you." The existing tenants retained a rent bonanza at the expense of the landlords. The repeal of rent control as to new tenants fostered an apartment construction boom.

VI. Development Subsidies and Fees

Charging fees to developers on new projects does not appear to taxpayers as a tax increase but the fees result in the same net effect to the community. Developer costs are passed on to the users in terms of higher costs or rent.

San Francisco collects millions of dollars in fees from developers of offices to subsidize new and rehabilitated housing.

A. SUBSIDIES

DEVELOPMENT SUBSIDIES *are amounts paid to governmental agencies in order to get approval for a construction project.* Developers pay without complaint because they know the city has many ways to stop or delay a project. The developer subsidizes another project.

The city of Santa Monica demanded that a developer of a $150 million hotel/office/retail center pay $3 million toward 100 units of low income housing, a daycare center and parks. Some developers consider these fees to be extortion. The fees are not related to the added costs to the city caused by the development or to the number of people displaced by the development. New developers feel that they are being burdened with costs, which should be borne by all.

Many cities are using the term "linkage." **LINKAGE** *refers to the idea that developers of desirable central city office structures should provide funds to help improve less desirable areas of the city.*

Los Angeles built a $23 million museum devoted to contemporary art with cash from developers who wanted approval for an office complex. More and more planners are linking project approvals to commitments from developers to provide jobs, create new business, build childcare facilities, and low-income housing, etc.

B. DEVELOPMENT IMPACT FEES

Development impact fees are not new. They were first used in the 1920s. Because of difficulty in passing bond issues, they have become extremely popular in recent years.

DEVELOPMENT IMPACT FEES *are one-time charges to offset the public service costs of new developments.* The purpose is not to maintain or repair existing facilities but to cover expanding needs of the communities with new facilities.

Most communities use the term fee, but it is plural—"fees." There might be separate fees for sewer, water, roads, public transportation, schools, parks, etc. By charging the builder fees that are passed on to the buyer, existing residents don't have to pay for the expanded services.

Various fees may be based on front footage, lot size, square footage of the structure, number of bedrooms, number of baths, etc. Different fees might have different criteria. Fees in the $10,000 to $20,000 range for a singe-family home are common. The fee is usually paid when the building permit is issued.

The higher the fee, the less affordable the home to the homebuyer, as the fee becomes part of the purchase price.

High-impact fees are favored by slow-growth and smart-growth advocates, as the costs act as a deterrent to development and thus slow urban sprawl. If a developer can find similarly desirable property for the same cost in a community having lower fees, the developers will go there.

VII. Property Taxes (City and County Taxes)

Taxation of real property takes several forms. It is important to understand what governmental agency (federal, state, county, or city) is collecting the taxes and for what purpose these taxes are being used.

A. PROPERTY TAXATION (City Taxes on Property)

Real estate taxation is one of the oldest forms of taxation. Ancient Egypt taxed land by what it produced. Rome taxed land by area. The real estate property tax is one tax that cannot be avoided. It pays for upkeep of the streets, police, fire protection, and schools, which contribute benefits to those living on the property as well as helping to maintain the value of the property. Property taxation, however, is not necessarily equitable. The tax paid bears no relationship to either the benefits received by the taxpayer or the taxpayer's ability to pay. It is based only on the value of the real estate owned.

Property tax CANNOT be avoided because land can't be hidden.

The ***BENEFIT PRINCIPLE OF TAXATION*** *is that people should be taxed based upon the benefits they receive from the government*. While in theory it may sound fair, it is just not practical. Generally, the poor receive the greatest benefits from the government in the form of schools and social programs. The poor could not possibly, however, bear the burden of their benefits.

Property tax is the only major income source for local government.

The federal government has income tax and the state government has income tax as well as the bulk of the sales tax.

Chicago has a commercial tax rate designed to please voters. It is 2.5 times higher than the residential rate. While it helps to keep residential taxes low, the effect of this differential has been to discourage manufacturers from locating in Chicago and encourages others to leave. Chicago suffered a declining population because of the loss of jobs during the 1980s and 1990s.

Arizona's taxes are based on:

1. 11 percent of assessed valuation for owner-occupied property,
2. nonowner-occupied residential property taxed on 18 percent of assessed valuation, and
3. nonresidential property taxed on 25 percent of residential value.

While this tax differentiation is not based on tax benefits, it is easy to see the political justification for this tax differentiation. The majority of the population has lower tax rates than those who own rental property or other than residential property. These owners are deemed to be able to afford higher taxes.

In some areas of the country, property is only reassessed upon sale.

Developers have been encouraged to tie up property with purchase options they intend to exercise rather than make a purchase, because property taxes are NOT increased until the property is sold.

In this way, the seller who has title pays what is likely to be much lower taxes during the approval and engineering period.

B. TAX EXEMPT PROPERTY (Non-Profit Organizations)

In Colonial America, life in many communities centered around the church. The decision was made not to tax the church, as this would be taxing themselves. The idea of tax exemption for churches has been expanded.

Religious institutions, schools, and government-owned property are exempt from property taxation. Charitable and fraternal organizations may also be exempt.

Because of this exemption, a large number of landowners pay no property taxes. When a great deal of land within a community is exempt from taxation, the remaining taxable property must carry a larger burden. Since property tax revenue goes for street maintenance, public transportation, police, fire, health department services, etc., the

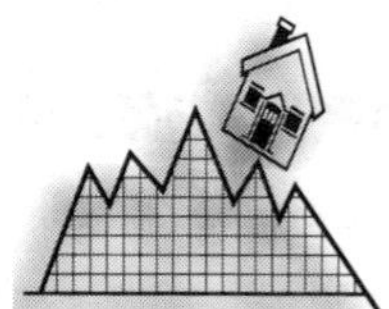

exempt property owners benefit, as well as tax-paying property owners. Exemption laws particularly adversely affect some capital cities and university towns because so much of their property is tax exempt.

In New Jersey, 13.5 percent of the land and building value in the state is exempt from taxation.

While property taxes are operating expenses for private investors, they provide revenue funds for government expenditures. Reduction in tax revenues due to property tax exempted land and buildings will cause government cutbacks and reduced services.

Maximum property taxes are obtained from a compact, highly developed lot due to the high value of buildings.

Communities that are spread out and have a great deal of vacant property have increased expenses for services as well as a lower tax base.

C. PROPERTY TAX EXEMPTIONS (Special Cases)

County tax exemptions are sometimes offered to developers in order to encourage industry development.

County ***PROPERTY TAX EXEMPTIONS*** *are reductions given to corporations that move their business to that county.* New York City has given attractive tax exemption packages to developers to encourage both development and redevelopment. The city of New York aided the development of Trump Tower by agreeing to a long-term tax abatement because it was a redevelopment of under-used real estate.

In addition to special tax benefits for particularly large projects, New York has a program which stimulates housing rehabilitation by exempting increases in value due to rehabilitation for a number of years. New York also gives tax credits of 8.33 percent of the improvement costs each year for 12 years with up to a 90 percent recovery possible.

One justification for granting tax exemptions by many cities is that the benefits of large payrolls greatly offset the additional costs of services for a development. In some areas, historic landmarks are given tax abatement to keep the structure from being demolished. This is considered a socially desirable goal.

Since property taxes are actually a small percentage of total business expenses, some economists believe tax incentives do NOT generally affect businesses' real estate decisions.

Cutting regulatory time for approvals might be a better incentive than favorable property tax treatment.

D. HOMEOWNER TAX EXEMPTION

In many states, a homeowner is eligible for an exemption on his or her residence.

This exemption, while effectively reducing the tax rolls, encourages homeownership. Lost taxes are subsidized by nonresidential and rental property, in which owners pay their full share of taxes.

VIII. Agricultural Property Tax Regulations (Special Treatment)

Farmers have or have had a great deal of political influence in many states.

Agriculture has been treated favorably by most states and the Federal Government.

In many sates, land used for agricultural purposes must be taxed on its agricultural use value rather than the market value for land in the area. This allows land to be kept in agricultural use. If the land were taxed at market value, the taxes could force a family to sell their farm.

Other states allow farmers to contract where they agree to keep the land in agricultural use for a stated number of years in exchange for a lower tax rate.

A. BUYING DEVELOPMENT RIGHTS

In Massachusetts, the state can buy a farmer's development rights. ***DEVELOPMENT RIGHTS*** *are the legal rights to build upon a property*. This means the land must remain as farmland. By the end of 1985, the state had purchased the development rights on 16,000 acres. The farmers thus are able to realize the appreciation in value of their land but continue to own the land and farm. Money for development rights allows farmers to retire their debts.

The state of Ohio has been paying an average of $2,000 per acre for development rights. Since state programs are funded largely by federal funds, it is expected that the program will be significantly reduced in the future. Without development rights, the land must be taxed based on its agricultural value.

B. AGRICULTURAL PRODUCTION

The government has kept marginal agricultural land in production through various subsidy programs.

The benefits of these various subsidies affect farmers' decision making regarding the potential agricultural use of their land. A stated purpose of subsidies is to help maintain small farms. However, the bulk of farm subsidies go to large corporate farms. The top 8 percent of the farms in income receive 40 percent of the federal subsidy payments. In California, the 10 largest farms receive from $1.5 to $2.7 million in subsidies.

C. PUBLIC WATER PROJECTS

Federal and state governments have subsidized many major water projects. This has resulted in water being available for agricultural users at less than its free market cost.

This water availability has, in turn, increased the value of the land receiving the water as well as the profits from the land. The increased land value and profits are reflected in property taxes and income taxes.

IX. Income Taxes (Federal and State)

Real estate investments offer favorable tax treatments that encourage real estate ownership.

A. CAPITAL GAINS

Profit on the sale of a capital asset, such as real estate, is taxed at a rate lower than that used for other income. If a property is held for more than 12 months, it is taxed at a rate of 15 percent of the gain (5 percent if the taxpayer is in the 10 or 15 percent tax bracket). In 2008, capital gains rate for these lower tax brackets will be zero.

If a portion of the capital gain were due to depreciation taken, then that portion of the gain would be taxed at a rate of 25 percent.

As an example, if a property cost $200,000, was depreciated $50,000, and then sold for $225,000, the seller's cost base would be $150,000 and the gain would be $75,000. The $50,000 of the gain attributable to depreciation would be taxed at the 25 percent rate and the $25,000 remainder of the gain would be taxed at the 15 percent rate.

B. HOMEOWNER EXEMPTION ON CAPITAL GAIN

Homeowners have an exemption from taxation on the gain from the sale of their principal residence of:

$250,000 – single person
$500,000 – married couple

(Unmarried co-owners could each claim their $250,000 exemption.)

To be eligible for this exemption, the homeowner must have occupied the property as a resident for at least 24 months during the 5 years prior to the sale.

This exemption can be taken again and again, unlike prior tax exemptions, it is not a one-time exemption.

This exemption has resulted in renewed interest in fixer-upper properties. Investors are buying such properties, fixing them up while living in them and then selling at a non-taxed gain after two years and then repeating the process.

A loss on the sale of a personal residence can be deducted if it has been turned into income-producing property (by renting it).

The only way to deduct a loss on a personal residence is to turn that property into income producing property by renting it. Then a loss based on its sale may be deductible because it is income-producing property, not a personal residence. (It is strongly recommended that a tax attorney or accountant review any plan to change a personal residence to income property.)

C. DEDUCTIONS

Homeowners who don't take the standard deduction can annually deduct these three items from their income tax report, based on their personal residence:

1. Mortgage interest on loan (trust deeds);
2. Property taxes; and
3. Prepayment penalties.

Homeowners also have a capital gains exemption.

Investors of income-producing properties can annually deduct two additional items from their income taxes:

4. Operating expenses;
5. Depreciation of improvements.

According to popular thinking, homeownership makes for a stable population of concerned citizens. Therefore, the government encourages the goal of homeownership.

The government encourages homeownership by making real property taxes and interest expenses deductible on both federal and state income taxes.

In the early years of an amortized loan, almost the entire monthly payment is interest. This deduction is, therefore, substantial, and the net effect in many cases is to make homeownership more economical than renting, as illustrated in the following example:

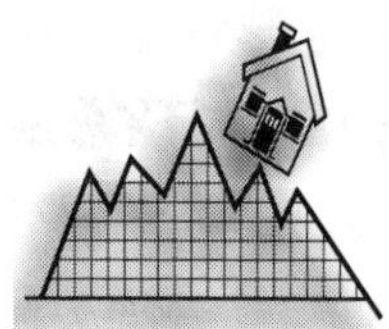

If a renter were paying $1,200 per month in rent, that renter would get no tax credit for any of the rent paid. Assume that renter were in the 38 percent tax bracket (combined Federal and State income taxes) and decided to purchase the same property with a monthly payment of $1,600 per month including taxes. Of the $1,600 payment, $1,500 would likely be tax-deductible interest and taxes. The taxes saved (38 percent of $1,500) would mean savings of $570 or a true monthly cost of $1,030 ($1,600 - $570).

The effect of the deductibility of interest expense is to lower the effective interest rate paid by the taxpayer.

The desire by many to own a home is so strong that the elimination of tax benefits does not materially affect homeownership. A survey by Harvard-MIT Joint Center for Urban Studies found that 76 percent of people who purchased homes definitely or probably would have purchased even if there were no tax breaks.

In Canada, interest and property tax payments are not deductible, yet the Canadian rate of homeownership is only about 5 percent less than the United States rate.

D. DEPRECIATION

***DEPRECIATION FOR TAX PURPOSES** is a yearly tax deduction for wear, tear, and obsolescence on investment property deducted from the income tax report.* This deduction applies only to investment property or property used in a business, **not on a taxpayer's personal residence**. Apartment buildings, commercial buildings and any building improvements to investment property can be depreciated. The land itself cannot be depreciated.

Only buildings and other improvements can be depreciated, NOT the land.

One can only depreciate improved property. Currently, the straight-line method is the accepted way to depreciate buildings and other improvements. ***STRAIGHT-LINE DEPRECIATION** is a method of computing depreciation for income tax purposes in yearly equal installments over the life of the building.*

Residential property (homes and apartments) depreciation schedule:
A minimum of 27.5 years (straight-line).

Commercial improvements depreciation schedule:
A minimum of 39 years (straight-line).

The ***ECONOMIC TAX RECOVERY ACT OF 1981** provided for the **ACCELERATED COST RECOVERY SYSTEM (ACRS)**. ACRS allowed a 15-year depreciation in order to stimulate development.* In 1984, the depreciation period was changed to 18 years, and in 1985, it was lengthened to 19 years. Under the ***TAX REFORM ACT OF 1986*** *the depreciation period was set at 27.5 years for residential property and 31.5 years for nonresidential property.* This lengthening of the depreciation period means that it takes longer for investors to recover their investment. It is a disincentive for real property investments. The ***REVENUE RECONCILIATION ACT OF 1993*** *increased nonresidential property depreciation to 39 years.*

The effect of increasing the depreciation period has been to discourage development of affordable apartments. Politicians should be reducing the years, NOT increasing them.

The amount of depreciation by current law must be spread uniformly over the useful life of the property, with the same amount deducted each year (straight-line depreciation). Since most buildings in these inflationary times actually increase in value, depreciation postpones taxes until the property is sold.

A property owner can deduct depreciation on income, trade, or business real property, but NOT on his or her home.

E. TAX SHELTERS

Depreciation is a paper expense but it can be used to shelter income from taxation. Depreciation can be used without limit to shelter income from property. If depreciation results in a loss that loss can, in some cases, be used to shelter active income, such as wages, from taxation. Up to $25,000 worth of other income can be sheltered from taxation by taxpayers who have an adjusted gross income of $100,000 or less. For taxpayers with adjusted gross income between $100,000 and $150,000, the $25,000 shelter is reduced by $1 for each $2 of adjusted gross income exceeding $100,000.

At one time, there was no limit as to the active income that could be sheltered. Investors were buying property with negative cash flows that were more than offset by using the losses to shelter other income from taxation.

F. FEDERAL TAX RATES

As the old saying goes, "There's nothing surer than death and taxes." One other certainty is the constant change in federal tax rates. Currently, we have five basic tax brackets. People in the lower brackets pay 10 or 15 percent, the middle bracket pays 28 percent, and the higher brackets pay an income tax rate of 33 or 35 percent. The cutoff between these five rates depends on the taxable income and marital status tables designed by the Internal Revenue Service.

Income tax rates are progressive: Tax rates increase as the amount of income increases.

The **Tax Reform Act of 2003** established the lower tax rates as follows:

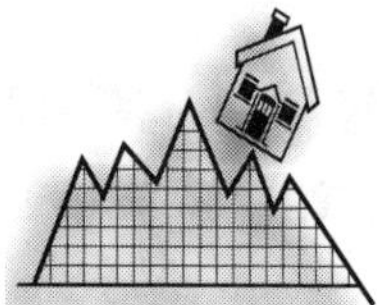

Lowest Bracket	10%
Lower Bracket	15%
Capital Gains Rate	**5-25%**
Middle Bracket	28%
Higher Bracket	33%
Highest Bracket	35%

G. ACCOUNTING FOR THE SALE OF REAL ESTATE

The method of determining a profit or loss on the sale of real property is spelled out by the Internal Revenue Service. Steps 1 and 2 must be completed before determining the profit or loss on a sale (Step 3).

Accounting formulas:

(1) Cost Basis (Purchase price)	$500,000
+ Improvements	200,000
	$700,000
- Depreciation	30,200
= Adjusted Cost Basis	$669,800
(2) Sale price	$1,000,000
- Sales Expenses	32,500
= Adjusted Sale Price	$967,500
(3) Adjusted Sale Price	$967,500
- Adjusted Cost Basis	669,800
= Gain	$297,700

Cost is the basis. It is the base cost, plus capital improvements, minus depreciation. A broker's commission is an expense of the sale.

The gain is taxed at the same rate as regular income if the property was held for one year or less. If the property was held for more than one year, the gain would be taxed at the long-term capital gain's rate.

H. TAX CREDITS (Reduction from Taxes)

In 1994, tax credits, an incentive for private development of low-income housing, were made a permanent part of the tax law.

A ***TAX CREDIT*** *is a direct reduction from taxes owed; but a deduction is only a reduction from the gross income.* A credit, therefore, is highly desirable. Tax reform has reduced rehabilitation credits for old structures from 15 percent, 20 percent, and 25 percent to 10 percent and 20 percent. The 10 percent credit is for buildings originally placed in service before 1936, and the 20 percent credit is for rehabilitation of certified, historic structures.

Government subsidized low-income housing is attracting new interest because it offers a tax credit. Investors can get an annual tax credit (not deduction) of 9 percent of the cost of the building for 10 years when they construct or rehabilitate a structure for rental to low-income residents. They can get a 4 percent credit for 10 years if they acquire a building and rent it to low-income residents. Because investors borrow part of the investment funds, the credit can exceed 9 percent of the cash investment. To qualify, an investment must be held for 15 years. Rents are controlled so there is a low cash flow even when no leverage is used.

X. Installment Sales and Exchanges

Installment sales and exchanges are alternatives to selling a property. Gains on a sale may be reduced, postponed, or delayed by proper planning.

A. INSTALLMENT SALES

An ***INSTALLMENT SALE*** *is the sale of real estate where the payments for the property extend over more than one calendar year*. Installment sales are used to spread a gain over two or more calendar years so that the entire gain is not taxed all in the first year.

By spreading the gain, the seller avoids the disadvantages of paying for his or her entire gain in one year. It postpones rather than avoids taxes. This method is usually used when selling large tracts of land held for a period of time, or large buildings owned by one individual.

Installment sales are used because a gain is only taxed in the year that it is received.

B. TAX-DEFERRED EXCHANGES (Federal and State) (Section 1031 of the Internal Revenue Code)

In an exchange, the adjusted cost basis of the old property becomes the basis of the new property.

An ***EXCHANGE*** *is a transfer of real estate, where one party trades property for another's property*. The property must be of "like kind" in nature or character, not in use, quality, or grade (as an example, a lot could qualify for a tax-deferred exchange for an apartment house since they are both real property). The exchange may be a straight trade (tax-deferred) or one party may receive cash in addition to the property (partially tax-deferred). An exchange can be income tax deferred, partially taxed, or fully taxed, depending on the cost factors in each particular exchange. Exchanges are too detailed to explain here, but it is a way of deferring or possibly eliminating income taxes on the transfer of real estate. The payment of taxes is deferred until a later time. Since you can move your equity to another property, it is almost like buying and selling without paying income tax.

If there is NO boot in an exchange, the old basis is the new basis.

Any net cash or net mortgage relief that a participant in an exchange might receive in addition to the actual property is known as **BOOT**. All boot is taxable to the extent of the gain in this partially tax-deferred exchange.

In a tax-deferred exchange, boot is defined as cash or mortgage relief given in addition to the property. Boot is the amount received to balance the equities in the exchange. Brokers often encounter the term "boot" when talking with a client about income taxes.

The person receiving the boot has a net gain and has to pay taxes on it. When no boot is given or received, the basis remains the same.

C. DELAYED EXCHANGES

The internal revenue code allows for a delayed exchange, commonly referred to as a **STARKER EXCHANGE**. A seller can sell a property and later identify a property he or she wishes to obtain in exchange. For a valid tax-deferred Starker Exchange, a number of requirements must be met:

1. At the time of the original sale the seller must identify the transaction as a delayed exchange.
2. The seller must not receive the proceeds of the sale.
3. The seller must identify the exchange property within 45 days of a sale.
4. The transaction must be completed within 180 days of the sale.

Because it is possible to earmark sale proceeds for a possible tax deferred exchange, many sellers do so in the hope of finding a property they would like to own.

XI. Is the U.S. Heading Toward Less Government?

The 2000, 2002, and 2004 elections at both the state and federal levels seem to be a mandate from the electorate that the politicians should put a lid on government spending and regulations. Voters have elected many politicians who ran on lessening of government involvement in many areas and who proclaimed a belief in the benefits of a free market economy. The benefits of reducing government involvement is a harder concept to grasp than simply having the government make a law which is not efficient but appears to be a quick answer.

While there may be a mandate for less government, we have yet to see significant reduction in federal or state regulations as they apply to any aspect of real estate.

XII. CHAPTER SUMMARY

Government regulations have a significant effect on the real estate market and real estate decision making.

Building codes set minimum standards. Unreasonable codes mean additional costs.

The **zoning** or possibility of zoning changes has an effect on the value of land. Poor planning with too much or too little land allocated for a particular use would also affect value.

Public housing has had many problems. Poor management has been pervasive. The future seems to be with **vouchers** or subsidized programs.

Rent control can be an owner's worst nightmare. It is often caused by large rental increases. Rent control has resulted in fewer units being developed, people not moving up in housing, poor maintenance of existing units, and lower tax bases.

Development subsidies make developers pay to subsidize other off-site improvements. It is a way to raise revenue that is not precluded by Proposition 13. Development subsidies are likely to increase in use in the future.

Property taxes are the principal source of city and county revenue.

Homeowners have **tax deductions** of home interest and property taxes.

The gain on the sale of real estate is taxed at a lower (**capital gains**) rate providing the property was owned for more than 12 months.

Property held for **business** or **investment** can be depreciated. **Depreciation** is an expense for tax purposes and, within limits can be used to shelter other income from taxation.

Homeowners have a **$250,000 exemption** from capital gains on the sale of their residence ($500,000 for married couples), providing they lived in the property for 24 months in the 5 years prior to the sale.

Additional tax benefits are possible using **installment sales** and **exchanges**.

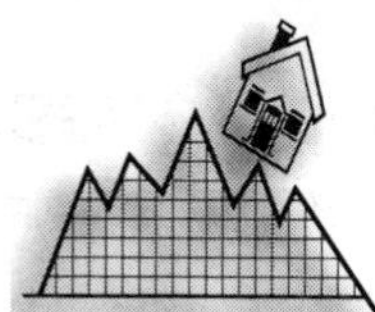

XIII. GLOSSARY OF KEY TERMS

Benefit Principle of Taxation – The principle that people and property should be taxed based on public benefits received.

Boot – Any net cash or net mortgage relief received in addition to the actual property in an exchange.

Building Codes – Codes setting construction standards with material or performance specifications.

Capital Gain – Gain on the sale of a capital asset, such as real estate.

Department of Housing and Urban Development (HUD) – The federal agency that administers government housing programs.

Depreciation – A loss in value; for tax purposes, depreciation is treated as an expense.

Development Rights – Rights to develop property, which in some cases can be separately transferred from the property.

Development Fees – Requires developers to pay fees to offset the effect of their development project on the community.

Downzoning – A change in zoning to a more restrictive use.

Environmental Impact Report (EIR) – Required by state law when projects are likely to effect the environment.

Homeowner Tax Exemption – An exemption from the tax assessment for homeowners.

Linkage – Requires linking development of desirable property with the development of less desirable property or public property.

National Environmental Policy Act of 1969 (NEPA) – Federal act that requires an environmental impact statement for federal projects effecting the environment.

Property Tax – Tax on real property.

Public Housing – Low-income, government-owned housing.

Rent Control – Legislation that limits an owner's ability to increase rent.

Rent Vouchers – A system whereby a voucher holder can apply a public voucher toward rent on the open market.

Section 8 Housing – Subsidized low-income housing.

Sherman Anti-Trust Act – Federal act prohibiting unfair trade tactics.

Starker Exchange – A tax-deferred delayed exchange.

Subsidized Housing – Private housing developed with government incentives such as special tax benefits or loans. The government then controls rents.

Tax Shelter – Using depreciation to shelter income from taxation.

Upzoning – Zoning change that expands the use.

Zoning – Public restriction on land use under police power of the state.

XIV. CLASS DISCUSSION TOPICS

1. Identify local "publicly owned" housing projects and discuss their effectiveness in meeting the needs of the poor.

2. What development fees are assessed in your area?

3. Do you have rent control in your area? If so, what are its provisions and what effect has it had on local values and development?

4. What effect, if any, have changes in the tax laws had on the real estate marketplace in your area?

5. Discuss any exchanges you know of and the reasons for the exchange.

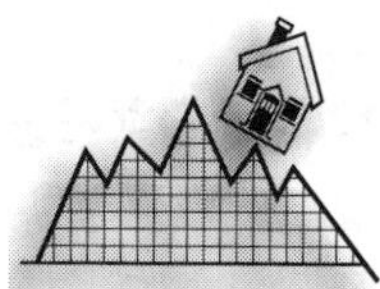

XV. CHAPTER 8 QUIZ

1. Building codes are customarily enforced by:
    a. the local building inspector.
    b. HUD.
    c. the State Department of Health.
    d. the Department of Commerce.

2. When an insufficient amount of land is zoned for a use:
    a. developers may use adjacent land for that use.
    b. the price of the land so zoned increases.
    c. the zoning would likely be declared illegal.
    d. less restrictive private covenants would take precedence over the zoning.

3. An example of downzoning would be to change zoning from:
    a. residential to commercial.
    b. multiple family to industrial.
    c. multiple family to single family.
    d. office use to industrial.

4. As to public housing, it is regarded as:
    a. one of our government's great successes.
    b. helping to keep local values up.
    c. being well managed.
    d. being in very sad shape.

5. Section 8 vouchers would be regarded as:
    a. a project-based subsidy.
    b. a tenant-based subsidy.
    c. a public owned housing project.
    d. an entitlement certificate for public housing.

6. A group of brokers agree not to do business with a particular title insurer. This is an example of:
    a. an illegal tie-in sale.
    b. a market allocation agreement.
    c. a group boycott.
    d. conduct permissible under the Sherman Act.

7. Who would benefit from rent control?

   a. Local governments
   b. Landlords
   c. Only poor tenants
   d. Both rich and poor tenants

8. Cities like property taxation because:

   a. it provides a fair distribution of costs among users.
   b. it cannot be evaded.
   c. it taxes based on ability to pay.
   d. it taxes based on benefits received.

9. The homeowner exemption for a married couple on a sale of a residence that the owners lived in for at least 24 months during the 5 years prior to the sale is:

   a. up to $25,000.
   b. the first $125,000 of the gain.
   c. up to $250,000.
   d. $500,000.

10. Only $10,000 on an otherwise tax-deferred exchange was subject to taxation. The tax applied to:

   a. overage.
   b. depreciation.
   c. boot.
   d. the marital deduction.

ANSWERS: 1. a; 2. b; 3. c; 4. d; 5. b; 6. c; 7. d; 8. b; 9. d; 10. c

LEARNING OBJECTIVES

Besides gaining an insight into single-family homes, you will gain an insight into ownership trends and the factors influencing homeownership. You will learn about housing needs and special markets. The understanding you will gain will help you meet the needs of buyers in your local marketplace.

More Americans than ever before are living in their own homes—the American dream.

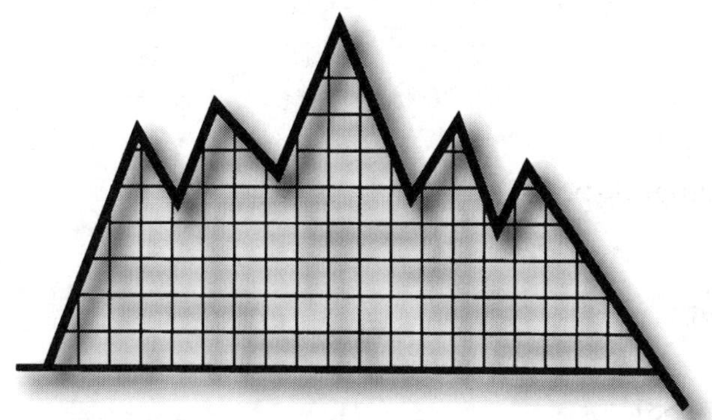

Chapter 9
Housing

I. Homeownership

The majority of Americans want to be homeowners.

A. HOMEOWNERSHIP STATISTICS

In 1940, when America was coming out of the Great Depression, 43.6 percent of American households (family units) owned their own homes.

Despite dips during periods when interest rates have been high, the household homeownership rate reached 67.5 percent in 2000 and 69 percent in 2003. This all-time high was achieved with a period of general prosperity and relatively low interest rates. According to the U.S. Department of Housing and Urban Development, the majority of urban city residents were homeowners in 2000.

Our new millennium is ushering in a period of unprecedented urban homeownership.

According to HUD, most of the increase in ownership between 1995 and 2000, reflected higher ownership among minorities.

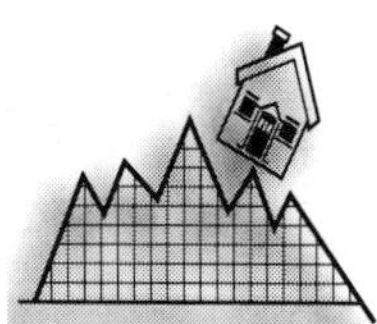

CHAPTER 9 OUTLINE

In 1995, 41 percent of those defined as "poor" by the Census Bureau owned their own homes. This figure included many retirees living on pension benefits.

The relatively high ownership figure is an average of all households. In 2000, ownership broke down as follows:

1. Married couples: 82.4 percent.
2. Single male head of household: 57.5 percent.
3. Single female head of household: 49.1 percent.
4. One person household (male): 47.4 percent.
5. One person household (female): 58.1 percent
6. African American households: 49 percent.
7. Hispanic households: 48 percent.
8. Non-Hispanic, White households: 76 percent.
9. Asians/others: 58.6 percent.

Homeownership rates vary by communities. West Virginia has the highest rate of homeownership at 75.2 percent while Washington, D.C., has the lowest rate at 40.8 percent.

The rate of homeownership has risen in every decade since World War II except during the 1980s. Low interest rates and low down payment requirements have contributed to a continuing rise in percentage of homeownership.

Age bears a direct relationship to homeownership. In 2003, 25 percent of families with a head of household under 25 owned their homes, but at under the age of 39, the figure was 65.2 percent.

In 2004, 40 percent of the homes were sold to first-time homebuyers. These homebuyers allow sellers the opportunity to relocate or to move up in housing.

HUD hopes to boost ownership rates among African Americans and Hispanics to over 50 percent. This may be possible if we continue to have high employment, low inflation and reasonable mortgage rates.

While individuals with what are considered Spanish surnames show a below-average rate of homeownership, they have an above-average rate of homeownership at higher income levels. This would indicate that homeownership is a priority that will probably be realized when income allows fulfillment.

Single person households are on the rise and are expected to grow faster than all other households. Currently, 1-in-4 is a single person household. This growth translates into single persons having a larger presence in the home purchase market.

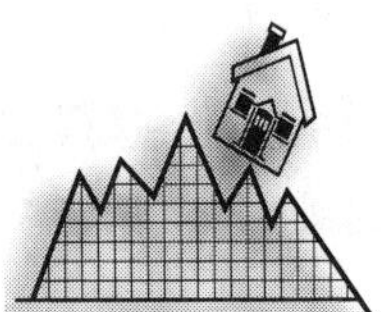

Homeownership and Occupancy

Sherman Maisel, a former member of the Board of Governors of the Federal Reserve System, studied homeownership and occupancy. His Essays *In Urban Land Economics*, published by the University of California Press, concludes that:

1. Single people move more often than families. (This is because they have fewer ties and possessions. They often live in furnished units.)
2. Older people are less likely to move than younger people. (They are less likely to move because of job changes or children's needs.)
3. Seniors are also less likely to sell their homes and buy another one (move up or down in the price of a home) because of changes in income.
4. Housing turnover varies in the marketplace, but the highest turnover occurs during an owner's younger years (often resulting from changing employment and/ or income).

Younger households are becoming homeowners. In 1999, 11 percent of first-time homebuyers were under the age of 25. This percentage was up from 9 percent in 1989. A strong economy, higher salaries, and low down payment requirements have been credited with the growth in young homeowners.

The on-line real estate portal, homescape.com, has been placing ads in Rolling Stone Magazine to target young singles.

While more young people purchased homes during the 1990s, the average age of homebuyers increased from 34 to 39 years of age. While this may seem at odds with the fact that more young people are first-time homeowners, it can be explained by the increase in retirement communities. More elderly are seeking housing more conducive to their needs and lifestyles. Elderly buyers are generally repeat buyers. The average age is 45 among all repeat buyers.

In 2003, the median age of first-time homebuyers was 31 with household income of $54,500, but for repeat buyers, the age was 45 years old with household income of $79,100.

In 2005, 8 percent of buyers were unmarried couples. Thirty years ago this number would have been much smaller. In 1995, 70 percent of homebuyers were married couples. By 2005, the percentage of homebuyers who were married couples had declined to 59%. This decline was due to more singles and unmarried couples entering the homebuying market. Single women purchase close to 20 percent of homes sold while single men purchase slightly more than 10 percent of homes sold. In 2003, 83 percent of buyers identified themselves as "white."

The nation's housing needs are expanding with population growth.

The highest percentage of ownership is among smaller-sized families. At first, this might not appear logical; however, a great many low-income homeowners are retirees, which means small families. Large families at the lowest levels of income often cannot afford homeownership.

Ownership levels are higher outside the central city. Central cities have high land costs, which means a greater percentage of apartment units. The central city is also home to a large number of low income level families.

Ownership is directly related to income. The probability of a family purchasing a home increases dramatically if their income goes up. (A strong desire for home ownership exists and the desire is likely to be filled as soon as it is economically feasible.) There is a large demand for ownership that is not being met, but that demand will not be satisfied until it becomes coupled with purchasing power.

Higher income people are more likely to change their housing than lower income people.

Relocation is less burdensome for people with higher incomes. They view moving as a career move and, in addition, the employer often pays for moving expenses. They are also more likely to relocate because of job transfers, retirement or lifestyle changes.

Homeowners are relatively stable, but renters are often not satisfied with renting and desire ownership. A present tenant is 50 percent more likely to buy than a present owner is to sell and buy another home.

Buying a home is one of the last ways to take advantage of income tax benefits.

Most homeowners have the majority of their net worth in their homes. Despite the huge increase in stock values during the 1990s, the home equity of most Americans still amounts to most of their net worth. The Joint Center for Housing Studies at Harvard University determined that even among homeowners who also owned stock, 59 percent had more equity in their homes than they had in their shares of stock.

Despite problems with our housing stock, we have been experiencing definite improvements in our housing.

Between 2000 and 2010, the U.S. population is expected to increase by 30 million people. This means that 1.3 to 1.5 million new homes must be built annually to keep up with demand and offset our obsolete housing stock. (In 2004, housing starts totaled 1.95 million units.)

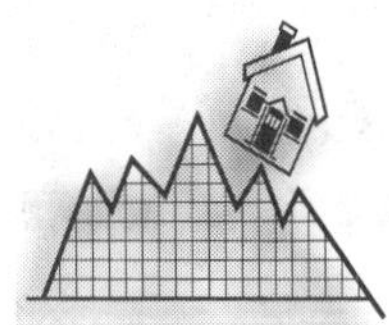

Of these new units, 1.61 million were single-family dwellings and 34 million were apartment units. The population clock keeps ticking. In August 2005, the U.S. population was approaching 279 million people (**www.census.gov/main** and **www/popclock.html**).

HOUSING TURNOVER *is the number of times the inventory of housing is sold within a year*. Nationally, there is about a 10 percent annual turnover among people ages 35 to 45, but the rate decreases to about 7.5 percent for ages 45 to 65.

People are unlikely to move from a house that meets their needs, unless they are forced to do so. (Owners are relatively stable.)

Even low-income Americans have more living space than the average citizen of Western Europe.

In 1940, 20 percent of housing units were considered crowded (defined as less than one room per occupant). By 1990, the percentage of crowded units had declined to only 5 percent. In 1950, 25 percent of all American housing units did not have a flush toilet within the unit. By 1990, only one housing unit in 100 lacked complete plumbing.

B. BENEFITS OF HOMEOWNERSHIP

Confidence – A national study by Rossi & Weber concluded that homeowners had a much greater level of personal confidence than renters.

Stability – Homeowners are more likely to remain in their homes than renters are to remain in their rental units. Owners stay in the homes an average of almost 12 years while renters average just over 3 years.

Wealth – Homeownership builds net worth. Because of appreciation in value, there is a major disparity in net worth between renters and homeowners having similar incomes. The longer a person owns a home, generally the greater the net worth.

Children – Children of homeowners have a 59 percent greater chance of becoming homeowners than children of renters.

Children of homeowners are 25 percent more likely to graduate high school and 116 percent more likely to graduate college than children of renters. (These figures are probably more the result of economic status than homeownership.)

II. The Housing Marketplace

The sale of a house is NOT usually an isolated event. It is normally part of a chain of real estate transactions.

The buyer is very often a seller of other property and the seller will generally be a buyer of another property. A single decision to sell or buy generally leads to a chain reaction involving numerous buyers and sellers. According to a 1997 study by Chicago Title Company, every home is hypothetically sold every 11.6 years.

Real estate housing markets are localized; prices vary from neighborhood to neighborhood. Prices of similar housing will vary considerably over a 50-mile area. Within each local market, each real estate broker handles a small marketplace where buyers can shop and compare. As covered in Chapter 2, a multiple listing service expands a broker's market to include homes controlled by other brokers. The larger marketplace, thus created, reduces the incidence of significant price differential for equally desirable housing.

Housing prices vary greatly across the country.

Differences in land costs, construction codes, construction costs, as well as supply and demand in each marketplace affect home prices.

Buyers, not sellers, ultimately determine housing prices. Buyers determine what they will pay. In order to sell homes in a marketplace where there are more sellers than buyers, sellers will have to become competitive in pricing to sell. However, when there are more buyers than homes, sellers will attempt to maximize their profits by raising prices.

The median price of homes sold is not the average price. In June 2005, the median price of homes sold in the U.S. was $214,800, which means that an equal number of homes were sold above and below this number.

The median price for the nation can be far more or far less than for a specific locale. In June 2005, the median home price in Rochester, New York, was only $106,200, but in areas such as San Diego, the median price was pushing $500,000.

In February 2005, the average price of homes that were sold was $282,100. The average price includes very expensive estates as well as minimal housing.

A. LOCAL ECONOMIC CONDITIONS AFFECT DEMAND

According to former HUD Secretary Andrew Cuomo, two million new high tech jobs in the late 1990s provided a real estate bonanza to the real estate and building industries at the expense of others who sought to buy or lease housing in areas of high tech industries.

The housing market is a segmented market.

The housing market could be strong in one price range of homes but weak in another market segment. As an example, we have had periods where the market was relatively

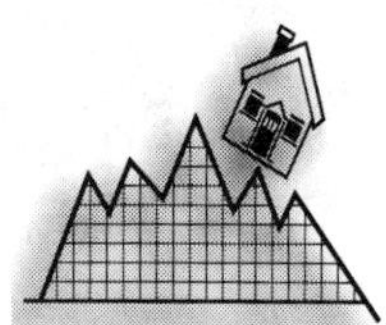

active for homes under $100,000 and homes over $700,000 but relatively weak in the middle.

While there are always some rich people and always secure lower-wage earners, the middle portion of the market seems to be the area most subject to economic conditions. Many middle-income families tend to curtail debt expenditures when the economy is in a recession.

Silver strikes in the 1880s and 1890s, resulted in instant riches for many Americans. This was reflected in a boom in mansions in Nevada and California. For a period of time, the grander the home the greater the desirability to buyers.

The instant riches in computer related and dot com companies in the late '90s resulted in another boom for the top-of-the-line housing. Homes that were considered "white elephants" on the market were suddenly subject to multiple offers.

Recent housing price increases exceed inflation.

From 1992 to 2000, housing prices have climbed nationally at double the inflation rate and rents rose 50 percent faster than inflation. From 2000 to 2006, housing prices accelerated at a far greater rate.

It is the nature of the real estate marketplace that home sellers will set a higher asking price than they are willing to settle for and buyers will offer less than they are willing to pay. Price, terms, and personal property generally are subject to negotiation. For larger new home projects, there is more likely to be a one-price policy with little or no deviation.

As a general rule, the longer a property has been on the market, the more willing the seller is to make concessions.

This would apply to motivated sellers and not "will-sell-if-I-get-my-price" sellers. ***WILL SELL SELLERS*** *are not strongly motivated to sell but will sell at a particular price.*

The time it takes to sell property is related directly to the relationship between list price and market value.

Property listed considerably above its market value will take longer to sell, and the final sale price is likely to be substantially less than the list price. Property listed closer to market value will create greater interest among both potential buyers and real estate agents (salespersons/brokers) and will sell much more quickly.

The real estate marketplace is not a "perfect market." Homes sell for a range of prices, and it is not possible to accurately predict what buyers will pay or what sellers will accept. Reasons for this imperfect market are detailed in Chapter 3.

Builders tend to be optimistic. They often fail to recognize an economic trend and continue to build. Other builders will continue to build as long as they have construction money. In addition, many projects take years before they are ready to be sold. Builders often have so many dollars invested in projects they cannot afford not to go ahead with them. After builders are committed, there is little to do but hope for the best.

The economy drives the market.

Builders are at the mercy of the economy. Changes in interest rates as well as changes in the general economy will affect buyer decisions.

Builders lack "perfect knowledge" of the marketplace. Due to the time it takes to build, many units are completed in a segment of the market that already has a great many unsold units. Builders should be wary when the time it takes to sell speculative homes shows a steady increase. An increase in selling time usually means decreased demand, or supply growing faster than demand.

People are slow to adjust their housing needs (requirements) to changed conditions. Many people occupy housing that does not adequately meet their needs or fails to reflect their present social or economic standing. These are people who might move. This group exerts pressure on the marketplace, because they will react to favorable changes in the market.

Retired and active military personnel have a strong effect on housing around military installations by creating a steady housing demand. Military retirees like the close proximity to bases to utilize their Base Exchange and club privileges, as well as medical services. The housing market around Oceanside, close to both Camp Pendleton (Marines) and the San Diego Naval Bases, was relatively strong throughout recessions in the housing market.

Because of high area housing costs, some businesses have to offer incentives to lure employees.

Corporate employees resist downgrading their standards of living because of a job transfer. Even with a raise, a move to a high cost housing area can mean an economic backward step.

To obtain as well as retain employees, firms in Northern California, New York, Boston, and Washington, D.C., and other high housing cost areas, offer employees incentive packages that might include housing allowances, attractive mortgages, travel allowances, per diem housing costs for a relocation time period, moving allowances, payment of lease cancellation penalties, and even stock options and/or bonuses.

A number of firms offer a home purchase plan to induce employees to relocate. They will buy the employee's home if the employee is unable to sell it so that the employee does not take a loss. In recessionary periods, some corporations have taken significant losses. Because of these losses, some corporations have been less likely to relocate employees when the real estate market was down.

Housing costs in California's Ventura County rose 28 percent in 1988 and created a disaster zone for employees. Proctor and Gamble designated Ventura as one of seven communities nationwide that qualified for housing assistance. Chevron offers cash bonuses to employees moving to the area.

School districts are offering housing incentives to obtain teachers.

In early America, teachers often received housing in addition to a very modest salary. This old tradition is being revived. Communities with high housing costs are having difficulty attracting teachers. San Francisco constructed federally subsidized housing for teachers. With the median Bay Area housing cost exceeding $500,000, teachers simply cannot afford to live in or even near the communities that they work in. San Francisco built a 43-unit rental apartment building. Teachers pay $700 per month rent compared to a fair market rental for the units at around $1,900 per month rent. Other cities are planning municipal housing for teachers as well as other municipal employees, although tight funding will likely mean most projects will not be built.

In New Mexico, the Santa Fe School District has purchased rental housing for teachers. They have also asked the state legislature for funds to build low-cost housing for teachers.

High housing costs in one area can make other areas more attractive to businesses.

The growth of industries in small towns and cities has been fueled by the economic advantages of low cost space for the enterprise as well as relatively low costs for labor and housing.

People will not acquire a house unless they have the purchasing power to do so. This includes available credit, down payment, and ability to make required monthly payments.

The reality of our housing market today is that, while people are sheltered, many are NOT satisfied.

B. FILTERING DOWN IN ACTION

The *housing* **FILTERING DOWN** *process is much like hand-me-down clothing, which passes to younger family members.*

Housing passes from higher to lower economic groups. Filtering down in housing starts at many levels, based on where new units are added to the inventory.

There are many more households at the lower end of the housing ladder than at the top. For filtering down to significantly meet the needs of the lower end, it would take a tremendous turnover of homes at the top. Therefore, the poor are the last to benefit from the filtering down process (see **Figure 9-1**).

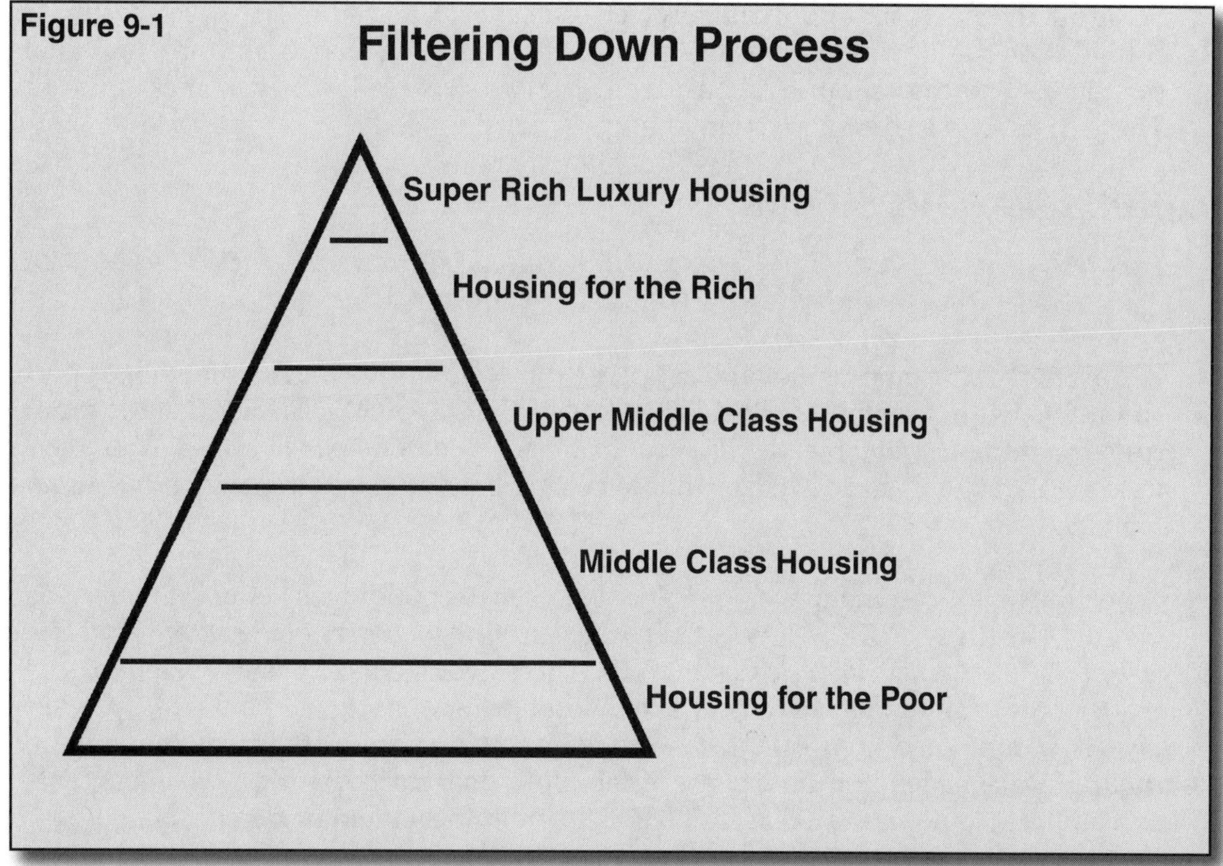

When you think of filtering down, think of a pyramid. As new units are added at any economic level, other units at that level tend to drop to a lower level, unless the demand is such at that level that it can absorb the additional supply of units.

If an economic model with a fixed demand existed, the addition of housing units at the upper end of the housing scale should result in housing at the lower end becoming vacant and/or demolished. The filtering down process takes time. The time between the addition of a unit and the demolition of a vacant unit could be many years. The worst housing remains rented due to new immigration and natural increases in family formations (marriages or living together). Some areas have not seen any filtering down at the lower end of the housing market for generations. The same general group has occupied the poorest units.

When housing deteriorates, low-income tenants will move to more desirable housing, if available.

A high vacancy factor can result in the property suffering a loss. In such a case the owner should either demolish the structure or rehabilitate it. If there is no housing surplus, low-income people are likely to remain in the housing and the owner can continue to rent the building without rehabilitation.

Selling a home costs approximately ten percent of its value in direct costs, i.e., commissions and various closing costs. When moving expenses and immediate purchases for the new home are considered, the cost to the seller can become significant. These costs tend to discourage moving up in housing.

C. HOUSING DEMOLITIONS

Income housing has fixed costs, such as taxes, and variable costs of operation, which include utilities, maintenance, etc.

If a property's income cannot at least cover the Average Variable Costs, the property should be left not rented. ***AVERAGE VARIABLE COSTS (AVC)*** *are operational average costs that vary depending on whether real estate is occupied by one or many.* These costs in real estate are usually small. Variable costs include utilities, repairs, services, and management.

When the rent exceeds the Average Variable Costs, the building is better off rented than vacant. ***AVERAGE FIXED COSTS (AFC)*** *are the difference between the Average Total Costs (ATC) and the Average Variable Costs (AVC).* These average fixed costs must be paid no matter how many units are rented. Fixed costs include mortgage payments, property taxes, insurance and licenses. If the Average Fixed Costs can be reduced by demolition (taking into consideration the expense of demolition) so that the savings on fixed expenses exceed the income less variable costs, then the building should be demolished.

The tax benefits of depreciation will affect a pure economic market, in that a cash loss could be more than offset by depreciation, making it economical to maintain a building that otherwise should be demolished.

The largest losses due to demolition are in manufactured homes, where pre-HUD Code units are taken out of use.

Buildings will also be torn down and the sites redeveloped when the value of a property in its present use is less than the value of the land. As an example, assume there is an 8-unit garden apartment building on a lot zoned for a 40-unit mid-rise structure. Assume the 8-unit building had income that indicated a value of $600,000. If the lot itself had a value of $1,600,000 to a developer, then the economic decision would be to demolish the building and build a 40-unit structure.

More buildings are torn down than wear out.

III. The Rental Marketplace

Renters are generally more informed about the current market than home buyers.

Renters seldom pay more rent than necessary for a property of similar desirability.

The rental market is only concerned with vacant units.

There is no competition between unavailable leased units and vacant units in the rental market.

Rental costs did not rise as much as inflation during the 1970s and 1980s. This resulted in an actual decline in the real costs of rents compared to income. We are now seeing rental increases that are closing the gap in a period of only slight inflation. The fact that few new structures were built due to low rents actually made these rent increases possible. Higher rents spur future rental construction.

Increased rents, coupled with lower interest rates, should result in more units being built and more rental units being rehabbed.

Investors suffered a loss of some tax benefits under the Tax Reform Act of 1986. Kenneth Leventhal & Company officials indicated that apartments previously built to generate tax losses require rent increases of 20 to 30 percent to produce the same return on investments. These tax law changes as to depreciation period and use of passive losses have reduced the number of investors interested in apartment units that, in turn, served to keep sale prices down. It also reduced the number of new apartment units built.

When single-family homes are rented, it is generally because the owner could NOT find a buyer.

Many owners are financially unable to leave a property vacant for what could be a number of months. The pressure of making two house payments often results in a decision to rent. When there is a strong sales market, owners are less likely to rent their single-family homes.

First-time homebuyers, most frequently mentioned the reason for buying a home is "we are tired of renting."

A. RENTAL NEEDS

A study funded by the Education and Research Fund of the California Association of Realtors® estimated that the production of new housing units in California in the

early '80s was 350,000 units short of housing formations (new homes). Rent levels were also considered close to the critical rent level. The ***CRITICAL RENT LEVEL*** *is that level at which no new rental housing will be built*. The rents were low in relationship to cost of construction, land costs and the interest rate charged for borrowed funds. A lowering of interest rates lowered the critical rent level. This in turn stimulated additional construction.

Many of the units built in the early '80s were built by developers who already owned the land. This reduced the critical rent level by whatever the capital required. Even when rentals are insufficient to make apartment buildings a viable investment, units will continue to be built and purchased by those counting on future rent increases and appreciation in value. The latter is no longer viewed with the certainty of the past, so investors are tending to make larger down payments. This is done in order to obtain positive cash flows, rather than counting on income increases to make their payments.

In some areas, conversion to cooperatives and condominiums has significantly reduced the rental supply, resulting in higher rents.

B. COMPETITION IN THE RENTAL MARKET

Landlords compete by offering tenants more amenities.

Some of the amenities offered in new apartment units are built-in wine racks, vaulted ceilings, valet cleaning with on site pickup, etc. Some units have pet corrals and even individual tenant garden plots. One Florida apartment community offers boat slips for tenants from $300 to $500 per month. Gables Residential Trust provided a free personal fitness trainer at a Houston complex. In Seattle, one complex provides a tanning room for tenants, and in San Diego, one apartment community offers full service car washes for its tenants.

Renters are demanding more and more amenities but are willing to pay for them. By providing amenities, apartment owners are increasing their revenue. In addition, satisfied tenants remain for longer periods, which means a lower vacancy rate and lower refurbishing costs between tenants.

Being wired for high speed Internet can attract tenants.

Velocity HIS offers installation of high speed access and web content equipment to apartment owners. They then work with the owners to sell the services to the tenants with the apartment owner sharing in the fees.

Because of the fact that both Internet and cable TV can be a profit center for apartment owners, six apartment REITs have formed a broadband company to offer high-speed Internet access and digital cable television service to tenants.

C. VACANCY RATE

Many vacancies are NOT really available for rental.

Some vacancies occur when properties are being held for sale, and some are already sold and being held for escrow. Others are held for legal determination, such as in estates, while still others have been rented but have not yet been occupied. It is estimated that approximately 50 percent of apparent vacancies are not actual vacancies.

The Department of Housing and Urban Development (HUD) believes a city vacancy rate of 5 percent or less indicates a housing crisis in that city.

A vacancy rate of 5 percent or less usually means the vacancies are short-term between tenants. The vacancy period might be due to owner refurbishing units. A 5 percent or lower vacancy rate can be expected to result in demand-pull inflation.

Vacancy rates are customarily obtained from postal authorities and utility companies.

Vacancy rates of the two above-named sources are generally different. Often utilities are kept on in a vacant unit or utilities may be off even though the unit is occupied. In one area, the Federal Farm Home Loan Bank said the apartment vacancy rate was 1.4 percent based upon postal carrier reports. Water and power figures showed a 4.6 percent vacancy rate in the same area.

When there is a low vacancy rate for an area, conversion of apartments to condominiums or cooperatives generally means a substantial number of the units will be sold to the current tenants. Tenants are really forced to buy if they wish to remain living in the area. Some conversions to cooperatives and condominiums have resulted in over half the tenants becoming owners to avoid moving.

D. FAMILY RENTALS

Despite court decisions prohibiting rental discrimination against children, discrimination still exists.

Discrimination against children is much more prevalent and open than racial discrimination. The California Association of Tenants estimates it receives 1,000 annual reports of discrimination against families with children. This is far more complaints received than those of racial or ethnic discrimination. A reason for continuing discrimination appears to be the reluctance of city, state, and federal authorities to prosecute violators.

Many apartment owners place restrictions on children, which can discourage families from renting. Restrictions could include no bikes, skates or skateboards on walkways

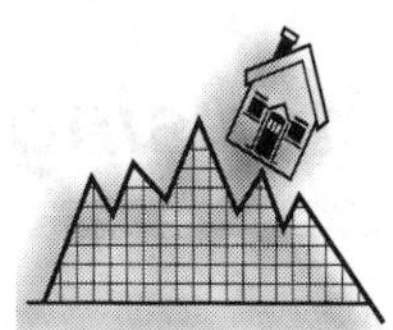

or driveways, no playing or running in halls and stairwells, limited hours and required supervision of children using pools and other recreational facilities. Restrictions based on safety reasons are legal. The courts also uphold restricting units to a specified number of occupants if the restriction is considered reasonable based on the size of the units.

A landlord cannot charge an extra fee, higher rent, or higher security deposit because of children although some landlords feel this is unfair. They feel that greater occupancy, especially children, means greater wear and tear on their property.

The effect of rental discrimination against children is to encourage families to purchase instead of rent. The same could be said of dog owners.

E. PRESENT RENTAL MARKET

Low interest rates, low down payments, and a high level of consumer confidence has led to a strong sale market for homes. Many of these homebuyers were formerly renters, which has led to higher vacancy rates in the upper and middle housing rental market. The low end of the market remains strong with a high demand that has been fueled by the increased information of new housing units as well as by legal and illegal immigration.

In 2003 and 2004, the apartment vacancy rate rose, but in the first quarter of 2005, the rate fell from 7.1 percent the previous year to 6.6 percent (based on the top 64 metropolitan markets). While this drop is small, it is significant since it is a change in an upward trend of vacancies. As the cost of owning starts to exceed the cost of renting, renting vacancies decline.

During the first quarter of 2005, effective rents increased. ***EFFECTIVE RENT** is the rent actually collected*. The effective rent rose by .6 percent from the previous year to an average of $882 per month in the 64 markets surveyed. (These figures are based on a *Wall Street Journal* report.)

Speculators buying new single-family residences want to hold units for at least a year to realize appreciation in value, and to take advantage of long-term capital gains rates. They place their purchases on the rental market to offset part of their holding costs. This glut of new homes being offered for rent has resulted in owners offering free or lower rent to attract tenants. It has become a home renters' market in areas of the country where there has been a great many units sold to speculators. In Fairfield County, Connecticut, the excess supply of new homes on the rental market in 2005 resulted in a decrease in home rental rates by 20 percent.

The rental marketplace, like the sale market, is really thousands of local marketplaces with prices varying because of costs as well as supply and demand factors. Average apartment rent asked in New York for April 2005 occupancy was $2,316. In Memphis, Tennessee, the average for the same time was $538.

While an equal number of units are being built for the upper and middle segments of the housing market, very few units are being built for the lower segment of the market, although this segment is important for affordable housing. The lower end of the market offers the fewest choices for renters.

The Department of Energy is concerned that both existing types of rental properties have failed to become more energy efficient. This is the case where tenants pay energy costs. There is no economic advantage for the owners to spend money for energy efficiency, and the renters are not about to invest in property owned by their landlords.

Most landlords keep their properties well maintained. Exceptions are owners who intend to demolish their units and rent-controlled units where there is no benefit other than to do minimum maintenance.

The National Low-Income Housing Coalition concedes that 95 percent of renters live in housing with no severe or even moderate physical problems.

Besides the rental marketplace, there is a market for renters to sublease their housing units. There are firms that specialize in subleases (see **www.sublet.com**).

IV. Special Housing Markets

There are a number of special markets and market factors that affect the housing marketplace.

A. CENTRAL CITY MARKET

GENTRIFICATION *is the process where inner-city and working class neighborhoods are converted to housing upwardly mobile young people who want the social benefits of living in the central city.* Instead of filtering down, housing filters up. Most of these new residents are single, married, or unmarried couples without dependents. Demand for central city properties tends to crowd out the poor.

In recent years, lofts and apartments in the central city areas have become highly desirable, which has been reflected in rising prices. While developers have generally met with success, the central city success has not been universal. As an example, the downtown lifestyle has been difficult to sell in Phoenix. Nine months after completion, a 330-unit apartment complex in central Phoenix was still half empty. The feeling is that the resort climate as well as the layout of downtown Phoenix is not conducive to an urban lifestyle.

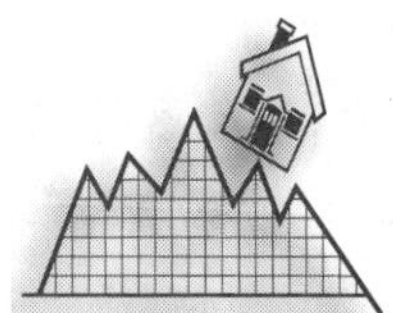

B. UNIQUE REAL ESTATE MARKETPLACE

With upscale shops, restaurants, and entertainment, Las Vegas has become more than a place to visit, it is now a place to live. Las Vegas has become a premier retirement area as well as home to those dependent upon the gambling resort business. The fact that Las Vegas has no state income tax is a factor encouraging permanent residency. In many cases, residents' housing costs are largely paid for by the tax savings they receive. Besides modest priced homes, Las Vegas has experienced strong growth in extravagant housing, including multi-million dollar condominiums.

Las Vegas is just one example of a market driven by local economic factors. Many hundreds of communities have unique real estate marketplaces.

C. FOR SALE BY OWNER MARKET

According to the National Association of Realtors®, 14 percent of sellers sell without an agent. Approximately one-third of these sales were to a buyer known to the seller before a decision was made to sell the property. Therefore, one-third of the sales were never placed on the market.

The median selling price of homes sold without an agent was reported to be 15.4 percent less than the median selling price when an agent was involved in the sale.

Likely factors in the lower selling prices are sales by sellers who underestimated the strength of the market and sales to friends or relatives where the seller, who, for some reason, did not wish to maximize the selling price.

D. ILLEGAL ALIEN HOUSING MARKET

Illegal aliens are believed to constitute over five percent of California's population.

In Santa Ana, California, it is estimated that one quarter of the entire population is composed of illegal aliens. Many other states have large illegal alien populations. Many property owners take advantage of illegal aliens. They provide minimum maintenance and repairs and charge high rents for small, overcrowded units, because illegal aliens pay their rent and do not complain to authorities about the conditions of the premises.

Illegal aliens do buy real estate. More than 10 percent of California homes are purchased by legal and illegal aliens.

Many illegal aliens move in with relatives or friends until they are able to find their own housing. Most will enter the rental housing market at the lower end of the rental scale. They are more likely to live in substandard conditions than other renters.

Many developers and real estate agents actively seek illegal aliens as buyers. In a home purchase, the legal or illegal status of the buyer is usually not an issue.

Competition for home loans has encouraged banks to make home loans to illegal aliens. The FDIC encourages banks to invest in under served market segments regardless of immigration status. Illegals are allowed to use taxpayer identification numbers (TIN) instead of Social Security numbers.

In the rental market, many counties do not check legal status for housing subsidies.

We seem to have a conflict of policies, one to keep out and refuse benefits to illegal aliens and one to help illegals meet their housing needs. There are now so many illegals in the nation that their removal would play havoc with our economy, including the real estate marketplace.

A study by Kenneth Leventhal Group predicts that two-thirds of U.S. population growth until the year 2050 will be from immigrants and their children. This includes legal immigration as well as illegal immigration.

E. THE AUCTION MARKETPLACE

Real estate auctions have been common marketing tools for many years in England, Ireland, and Australia.

However, until recently, auctions in the United States were limited to farms and distress sales. See **Figure 9-2** for the different types of auctions.

Because of the large number of prequalified, potential buyers, the sale prices at auctions are likely to be about the same as market prices. Builders like auctions because they can quickly liquidate developments after the initial sales momentum has worn off. Quick liquidation means greatly reduced holding costs as well as the cash to continue with other developments.

During the savings and loan crisis, the Resolution Trust Corporation (RTC) auctioned off many foreclosed projects. Since then, auctions have not been a significant marketing tool for residential property.

In the summer of 2000, Kaufman and Broad, one of the nation's largest homebuilders, held the first significant auction of new residential property on the Internet. They sold 10 homes at prices ranging from $159,000 to $174,000 and 9 lots between $53,000 and $57,500.

Kaufman and Broad held the auction to cut marketing costs and marketing time. According to Kaufman and Broad, the auction was a success in achieving their goals

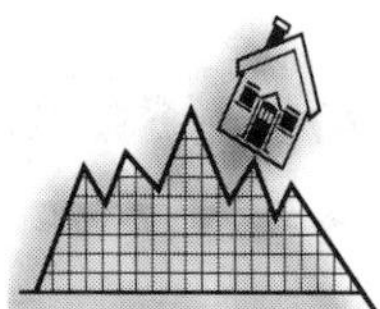

Figure 9-2

Three Major Types of Auctions

Without Reservation (absolute) – The seller is obligated to accept the highest bid. This type of auction will likely result in the greatest buyer interest.

Minimum Bid – The owner must accept the highest bid over a set minimum amount. In order to attract interest, the minimum should be significantly lower than the property's generally perceived value.

With Reservation – The owner is allowed to reject any or every bid. This type of auction will result in the least interested potential bidders, as the likelihood of a bargain is reduced.

Today, auctions are being used as a marketing technique for more than desperation sales. Auctions are heavily promoted and a great many potential buyers are attracted by the possibility of bargains.

even though some homes sold for as much as $15,000 less than the sellers felt they were worth.

To protect customers, Kaufman and Broad required bidders to register and clear a credit check in advance. Each bidder was given a bidder code and bids, when made, were posted on the website. To accommodate persons hesitant to bid at home the sellers also could view a closed circuit version of the auction on video screens and computer terminals at a local hotel. Kaufman and Broad set minimum bids to avoid taking a loss, but all properties were sold. Properties were sold when no higher bid was received for 3 minutes.

Some large builders have indicated that they are not yet willing to use Internet auctions. Pulte Corporation, a national builder, indicated that it did not like the idea of selling similar homes at different prices. However, other large builders are considering Internet auctions based on the success of Kaufman and Broad.

One Real Estate Investment Trust (REIT) that develops apartments is supposedly considering an auction where prospective renters would bid the rent that they will pay for the first 12 months. Thereafter, the rent would be according to the rent schedule. The advantage for the REIT would be marketing time, since it often takes 6 months to lease up a large project, significantly lower marketing costs, and immediate rent for all units. It is an interesting concept and the authors would like to see it happen. It will make economic sense if other savings make up the loss in rent from reduced one-year auction rent. Another consideration is how many tenants will move at the end of their one-year bargain rent.

Home Auctions Online will handle auction sales of individual homes. The auction consists of ads for 3 weeks in local papers of the auction and on the website. The website includes photos and specific information as well as viewing opportunities. The auction is handled by the service for a rather modest fee (**www.nolanrealty.com**).

F. MINORITY HOUSING MARKETS

Minority housing markets are still a reality.

Today, the reason for separate markets is due more to economic reasons than racial prejudice. Few minorities live in many non-minority markets because only a limited number can afford the housing. The net result is segregated or very limited integrated housing.

Because of prejudice and/or fear, anglos will seldom rent or buy housing in minority areas. White owners, when selling to minorities, are much less likely to make price concessions than they would be for white buyers.

White owners are also less likely to provide owner financing to minority buyers than to buyers of their own race.

There is still some racial prejudice, despite legislation making it illegal. Discrimination often takes the form of how much effort is put forth by the seller or landlord as to a sale or rental.

Discrimination in renting tends to be more common than sale's discrimination.

Using testers, HUD has found that owners are much more likely to give additional information about units coming available as well as to ask for deposits when dealing with anglo prospective renters than they will when dealing with African American prospective renters.

G. JAPANESE IN THE HOUSING MARKETPLACE

The Japanese, who formerly purchased only investment-type properties in the United States, went on to buy houses in Hawaii, and by the 1990s, had become a significant factor in the marketplace.

The Japanese invested heavily in homes and condominiums until the early 1990s. These purchases were primarily made by individuals rather than large corporate buyers. It became a status symbol in Japan to own Hawaiian real estate. This buying trend started in 1985, due in large part to the rising value of the yen. While Japanese money certainly aided the Hawaiian economy, it also significantly increased real estate values.

Japanese individuals and firms at one time owned over $7 billion in Hawaiian real estate, according to Kenneth Leventhal & Company, a CPA firm specializing in real estate. According to local broker reports, 41 percent of the condominiums sold in Waikiki Beach and 27 percent of the homes sold in Kahala (an area of fine homes) were purchased by Japanese buyers in 1987.

While some owners were delighted with the positive effect Japanese buyers had on property values, many others had deep concerns. Higher values led to much higher tax assessments and tax bills. Many Hawaiians were concerned that their children would be unable to afford to live in Hawaii. Japanese buying created an anti-Japanese climate among a great many Hawaiians. The Japanese house-buying spree also created a new group of homeless: those who sold for huge profits but found replacement housing difficult to obtain.

As a backlash to Japanese purchases, a bill was introduced in the Hawaiian Legislature, which would have barred Japanese purchases of residential and farm property. Other states limit foreign ownership. Mississippi has a complete ban on ownership by foreigners; Wisconsin and Nebraska also have some restrictions on foreign ownership.

The strengthening of the dollar, coupled with the collapse of the Japanese stock and real estate markets, had significantly reduced the Japanese presence in the Hawaiian real estate marketplace by the end of 2001.

H. RESIDENTIAL LOT MARKET

Builders accumulate lots in periods of building activity and when they believe there will be significant activity in the near future.

Private homeowners may buy a lot to build their home on long before they intend to build. Reasons can be to lock in a large part of their total home cost at present prices or to hope for lot appreciation and then use their lot equity as a down payment for their home loans.

While lenders fund homes, lenders are reluctant to fund lot purchases, except in cases of major builders. However, sellers are more willing to carry the mortgage on lots than they would be for home sales. Sellers usually own lots free and clear so lender due-on-sale provisions would not apply. Lot ownership requires expenditure of cash for taxes, so a sale reduces owner expense. Lots are often an illiquid investment, meaning it can take a long time to sell and turn the lot into cash. The housing market is much more liquid than the market for lots.

In areas where the weather prohibits building in winter, lot sales slow as fall approaches and the market begins to heat up in late winter.

When there is great building activity and rising prices, speculators will enter the lot market. Generally, they will want to sell as soon as they buy rather than try for long-term capital gains.

At times, a situation will develop where the selling price of new homes has escalated to exceed the present selling price of comparable lots plus all construction costs. When this happens, speculators will buy up every lot they can get their hands on because lot prices will be forced up as more homes are built.

I. FIXER-UPPER MARKETPLACE

Generally, homebuyers want homes ready to be lived in.

FIXER-UPPERS *are homes or condominiums in rundown condition or with physical problems that can be purchased at a reduced price.*

Many are not interested in property needing extensive repairs. Since few people are willing to purchase property not in live-in condition, it gives those buyers who are greater leverage. They can often buy such property at great savings in price and terms. In addition, by doing the work themselves, they develop additional sweat equity in the property. ***SWEAT EQUITY*** *is the actual, physical work owners do to their house in order to increase its value. Because of the profits possible on resale, there are now many people who buy, fix and sell houses for a living or to supplement their income.*

In some areas, fixer-uppers have been popularized by seminars and news articles to the point that there are many more buyers for this type of property than sellers.

The increased number of buyers can result in higher prices and a decreased economic advantage in purchasing a fixer-upper. Owing to their popularity, some owners advertise property as fixer-uppers when they do not actually fall into that category.

Fixer-uppers can be found in every price range.

A nationally known syndicated real estate columnist regularly invests in fixer-uppers in the half million dollar to million dollar range. He looks for property where he feels he can at least double the dollars necessary to make the property desirable plus holding costs, a return on his cash investment and the costs attributed to selling. He has indicated to the authors that he finds more property meeting these criteria than he could possibly buy.

The changes in the tax laws have created a unique opportunity for fixer-upper buyers willing to live in a property for two years. The $250,000 single person exemption ($500,000 for a couple) can mean a significant profit for a fixer-upper buyer that would be exempt from federal income taxes.

J. CONDOMINIUM MARKETPLACE

***CONDOMINIUMS** are vertical subdivisions in which the interior space of units is individually owned and land and other common areas are owned in common with other dwellers.* In a ***COOPERATIVE**, the owners own stock in a corporation, which holds the title.* Each shareholder has a lease with the corporation that provides for the occupancy of a unit.

In the late 1960s, condominiums were hailed as the housing of the future, a logical solution to high land costs.

Many people have become disappointed with the "condo" lifestyle. The complaints of condominium owners are the same as those cited by apartment dwellers. Lack of privacy, noise, shabby construction, and disagreements with neighbors and associations are often given as reasons why they want to own their own home site. Cooperatives and condominiums are more an alternative to apartment living than homeownership.

The slowing of interest in condominiums in the late 1970s and early '80s, coupled with high interest rates, resulted in a significant deflation in value in some areas. Another reason for the deflation in value was that builders overbuilt. Savings and loans suffered, taking major losses. It is estimated that 43 percent of Florida condominium sales from 1978 through 1980 were to speculators. The bubble burst and many buyers defaulted, leaving lenders with many units returned to them because of foreclosures.

Condominium values did not experience the growth that single-family homes did in the '80s and '90s. Condominium values declined in many markets in the mid '80s and the number of unsold condominiums reached record highs. However, condominium values surged in many areas beginning around 1988.

Higher prices for single-family homes in the late '80s led many to consider condominiums a housing bargain.

Lower interest rates allow young families to move from condominiums to single-family homes. Condominiums are still regarded by many as the "second best" choice. Lower cost will, however, make many existing condominiums available for first-time homebuyers.

Condominiums have gained acceptance for retirement living because of freedom from maintenance related problems as well as the recreational facilities offered by many condominium developments. Condominiums have also gained acceptance as second homes for the same reasons, as well as the ability of the owner to simply lock and leave. Condominium prices have surged tremendously in resort and retirement areas since 2002. In Florida, over 50 percent of condominium sales are to speculators.

1. Condominium Conversions

Condominium conversions make economic sense.

During the 1970s, investors discovered that apartments could be sold for far more as separate condominium units than as multi-unit rental properties. In many cases, apartment buildings were purchased for prices under $20,000 per unit and resold as individual units for twice the purchase price.

Condominium conversions became the hot item in real estate. The demand for apartments for conversion purposes increased the prices that had to be paid for the units, but at the same time, prices for individual units were increasing.

While low interest rates have had a negative effect on apartments, since many former renters have become homebuyers, low interest rates, low rent, and buyer demand has encouraged the conversion of apartments to condominiums in the last few years. Large profits are still possible considering the unit value as an apartment and as a condominium unit. As long as interest rates remain relatively low, conversion activity will likely continue. Many renters of recent condominium conversions became buyers of their units when the seller showed them how easily they could become owners.

It is not just apartments being converted to condominium housing. In San Francisco, the top half of the 40-story Chevron Texaco building was converted to 140 condominiums. The Public Health Hospital at the Presidio was converted to 300 units. In Fort Lauderdale, Florida, the Double Tree Guest Suites are being converted to condominiums.

The planning boards in some communities have opposed condominiums conversions since they lower available rental stock.

Significant value can be created by converting apartments to condominiums. In 2000, Gables Residential Trust, one of the nation's large real estate investment trusts, sold apartment buildings in Houston and Dallas to condominium converters for $41 million. According to Gables chief executive, as rental units the property sold was worth no more than $37 million. The purchaser paid what Gables regarded as a 10.8 percent premium price. The buyers were apparently willing to pay the premium because the units were conducive to condominium conversion and the political climate would allow such conversion. By 2004, several REITs were handling their own condominium conversions and the marketing of the units.

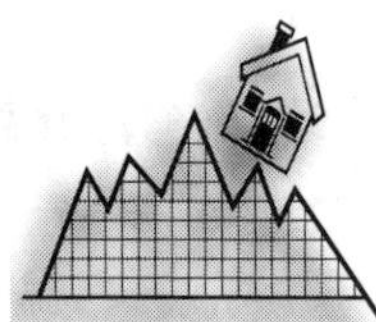

Sixty percent of all households currently have two-adult incomes. These families tend to have less time for maintenance, which could help fuel interest in condominiums, attached housing and homes with smaller lots.

V. Facts About Home Buying

A. TWO-INCOME FAMILIES

In the 1950s, it was the norm for a married woman, after giving birth to her first child, to leave the workplace and become a full time homemaker. By the millennium, this changed, and two-income households became the norm. A number of factors contributed to this change including:

1. weakening of unions, which led to lower wages in the manufacturing sector;
2. growth of service industries that in many cases, offered lower wages than manufacturing positions;
3. loss of manufacturing jobs, which had traditionally been higher paying jobs, to foreign manufacturers;
4. growth of higher technology jobs where gender has no effect on performance;
5. growth of the idea of a liberated woman who was a full partner, not just a mother and spouse;
6. a desire to have more and better consumer goods now.

The two-income household has resulted in a number of economic changes including:

1. families that have greater protection against loss of jobs and income. If one family job is lost, the family would still have one income, plus unemployment benefits so that the family unit would be less likely to face financial devastation;
2. greater income allowed families to pay a greater proportion of their income for housing, often 50 percent or more;
3. many families have opted to spend a large portion of a second income toward better housing.

B. FIRST-TIME HOMEBUYERS

First-time buyers have a difficult time entering the housing market when there is a wide affordability gap between income and housing costs.

In 2004, the typical first-time buyers were younger than repeat buyers (32 vs. 45 years old), had a lower income ($54,500 vs. $79,100), buy a lower-priced home ($139,000 vs. $209,000), and make a lower down payment (3 percent vs. 22 percent).

In 2004, 40 percent of homebuyers were first-time buyers. During the 1981 recession only 13.5 percent of buyers were first-time buyers. High interest rates that year prevented most first-time buyers from purchasing. Buyers were primarily those who had owned before and had enough of a cash down payment to manage high interest payments. Lower interest rates in 1983 and 2001 resulted in more first-time homebuyers entering the market.

Affordability of homes is related to interest rates as well as housing costs. Changes in interest rates significantly affect housing affordability.

First time buyers are more likely to purchase housing units with two or fewer bedrooms than are repeat buyers. The reason for larger numbers of smaller units among first-time buyers is related to affordability and the greater likelihood that first-time buyers are nontraditional or single-person households with less space needs. We will probably see this trend continue.

Of repeat buyers, approximately 30 percent sold and purchased to get a larger home, approximately 20 percent moved to get a better location, and approximately 15 percent relocated because of a change in employment. Other reasons can be lifestyle needs, such as retirement communities, desire to cut maintenance costs, desire for less or greater yards, social reasons, such as being close to another person or facility, monetary needs, etc.

C. LOW DOWN HOME PURCHASES

As prices of homes have risen, lenders have found ways to keep them affordable as to payments and or down payments and to allow more persons to qualify for home ownership.

1. **40-Year Loans** – By going to longer loans, the monthly payment is reduced because less is paid on loan principle.
2. **80-20 Loans** – This loan is really two loans: One loan for 80 percent of the purchase price at a relatively low rate of interest and a separate equity loan of 20 percent at a significantly higher rate of interest. The result is 100 percent financing at a payment that may be manageable.
3. **Adjustable Rate Loans** – Loans having "teaser rates" at low interest can qualify buyers who could not qualify for fixed rate loans of the same amount because a below-market interest rate is used for loan qualifying purposes.
4. **5-25 Loans** – There are a number of formulas used whereby on the first part of the loan, in this case 5 years, is a very desirable fixed rate of interest, but after the initial period, the loan is adjustable at likely higher payments.
5. **Interest Only Loans** – These loans keep payments low since no principal is paid on them. However, a day of reckoning will come when the loan converts to an amortized loan or must be paid in full.

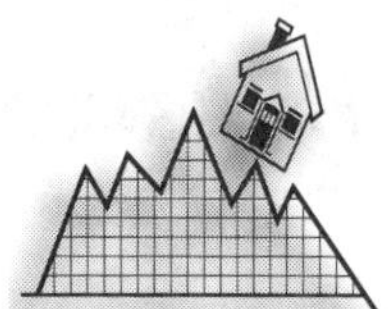

6. **Option-Adjustable Rate Mortgage –** This loan offers the lowest payments and has been pushed by some lenders. In California, 87 percent of Downey Financial ARMs are option arms. This product is often sold to high-risk buyers. The buyer, under an option arm, has the option to make minimum payments. The payment can be less than the monthly interest that accrues. The result is negative amortization with the amount of principal that increases each month. In an amortized loan, the principal decreases. While the balance keeps on going up the purchaser hopes that the property will appreciate in value at a faster rate. If it fails to do so, the buyer and the lender could be in trouble. The loan does have a date when it must be paid off or converted to an amortized loan.

D. HOUSING COSTS VS. INCOME

An old rule of thumb is a person should NOT pay more than two and a half times his or her annual income for a home.

This does not consider the purchaser's down payment. A more realistic rule of thumb is housing debt (not housing cost) should not be more than twice the borrower's gross income.

Another rule is housing costs should not exceed 25 percent of gross income. In recent years we have learned rules such as these have little validity. There are many families paying 50 percent or more of their income to live in desirable areas. $2,000 house payments on a $4,000 per month income are not uncommon.

As of 2000, an estimated 5.4 million households spent more than 50 percent of their income on housing. Since 1995, this number has increased each year. In considering what families can or cannot afford, the size of the family is important. The number, and even ages, of children affect the amount of income a family will be able to allocate for housing.

Previously incurred consumer debt is very important, since the amount of income that must be allocated for debt services reduces the amount available for housing. Many families have discovered they cannot buy a house and drive new, luxury automobiles that require high payments. Their priorities determine if they will become homeowners.

In general, white-collar workers have higher housing priorities than blue-collar workers of similar incomes.

Higher-educated people tend to spend more for housing than lower-educated people with similar incomes.

SCHWABE'S LAW *states that lower income people pay a higher percentage of their income for housing than higher income people.* We can see this is just common sense. While a person making $25,000 per year would likely pay 35 percent for housing, which would be $8,750 per year or $730 per month, a person making $250,000 per year would not be likely to pay $87,500 annually or $7,291 per month for housing. Higher income families have more discretionary income.

People with high incomes will likely pay proportionately less for all necessities, such as housing, food, clothing, and medical expenses.

1. Affordability Index

Affordability Index figures, while widely quoted, are not really a true measure of housing affordability for several reasons:

1. The ***AFFORDABILITY INDEX*** *is based on the median price of homes in an area as well as the median income.* There are just as many homes priced under the median price as are priced over the median price. Just as many households exist with income above the median income as exist below the median income. Therefore, housing matchups are possible even when the index indicates a small percentage of buyers can buy the median price home.
2. The affordability index allows a household to use 30 percent of its monthly gross income for housing expense, while in 2005, the major lenders were allowing homebuyers to spend up to 55 percent of their income for housing. The mortgage industry apparently feels that such loans are safe with these higher housing payments.
3. The affordability index is based on a 30-year fixed mortgage. This is not necessarily the lowest payment mortgage available to the homebuyer.

E. DOWN PAYMENT REQUIREMENTS

In a period of rapid real estate inflation, lenders feel safe in making high loan-to-value (LTV) ratio home loans.

The natural appreciation brought about by inflation provides a safe margin of owner equity within a relatively short period of time.

From 1989 until 1991 real estate prices fell in many areas. A rash of foreclosures occurred. Subdivisions where buyers had low down payments suffered abandonments as equities of homeowners disappeared. Abandoned homes were invitations to thieves, who stole appliances, plumbing, carpeting, and even air conditioning units.

Owners could not see the value in continuing payments on homes where they owed more than the houses were worth, especially in instances where deficiency judgments (losses of the lender, to be paid by the seller) were not possible. In other cases, increased unemployment caused foreclosures. Lenders, therefore, decreased the loan-to-value ratio on their home loans.

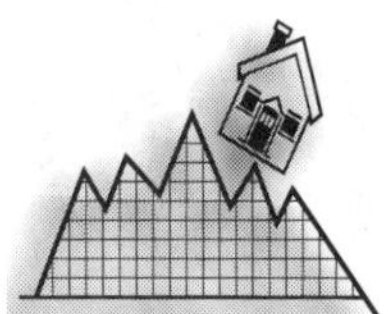

Larger down payment requirements particularly affect first-time home buyers.

A factor contributing to the difficulty of young people to save for a home has been the yuppie (live at or above your income level) emphasis on consumer consumption. The perceived need to have things "now" and easily available consumer credit make saving for many very difficult.

An estimated 30 percent of renters pay over 35 percent of their income toward rent. This makes it harder to save for a down payment.

By 2000, lenders were again making conventional loans with 3 to 5 percent down payments and even zero down. Lenders as well as homebuyers were showing great confidence in the economy.

F. SIZE OF HOMES

In a market that accommodates both small, moderately priced homes and large, expensive homes, economically motivated builders will build the more expensive, larger homes.

More expensive homes offer a greater profit percentage than more economical homes because high-income people will pay more for a beautiful, well-designed house under the right conditions. For example, a builder who has $1,200,000 in a home might net $180,000, a profit based on 15 percent of cost. A builder who has invested $900,000 in a home might net $300,000, which would be a profit based on 30 percent of cost.

Larger, expensive homes may provide greater profits, but they also incur greater risks. They are built for a smaller segment of the market and there is often a longer holding period before a sale. The cost of holding several expensive homes can be considerable. An economic downturn could have a significant effect on the luxury home market.

Much of the demand for luxury homes comes from move-up buyers who have established substantial equity in their current homes.

If first-time buyers are priced out of the market, eventually it will have an effect on more luxurious housing.

When the economy rebounds from a recession, the demand is for larger, more expensive homes. Homes have increased in size since World War II. In 1950, an average size home was 1,100 square feet with one bath. In 1980, half the new homes had 1,600 square feet or more and 75 percent had two or more baths. Size did not increase because of need, as family size declined during this same period. Size increased simply because buyers wanted and could afford larger homes.

To keep house payments down during the high interest period of the early '80s, builders reduced the size of homes. The percentage of homes with four or more bedrooms and fireplaces declined. According to the National Association of Home Builders, the median size of a new, single-family home shrank 3 percent to 1,605 square feet between 1978 and 1985. This short-lived trend for smaller and bare-bone construction has disappeared.

STRIPPED-DOWN HOMES *are homes with few amenities.* For example, single bath homes are a rarity because buyers want more than one bath and the market reacts to buyers' demands.

The present trend is toward more expensive housing.

The medium size of a new home, according to the Census Bureau, had risen to 1,815 square feet by 1988. In 1984, 28 percent of the new homes had more than two baths. By 1988, this had increased to 42 percent. Similarly, in 1988, 26 percent of new homes had four or more bedrooms; up from only 18 percent in 1984. The demand for larger homes and greater amenities meant higher prices, larger down payments and higher monthly payments. Surveys of homeowner preferences by the National Association of Home Builders indicates consumers are not willing to settle for stripped-down homes.

The average household lost one member between 1950 and 2005, but by 2005, the average new home size increased to 2,200 square feet. Buyers have been demanding bigger homes with more amenities. This is a factor in the increase of the median price of homes. The increase in home size also applies to garages, which have been steadily increasing in size.

According to Witold Rybcznski, architect and writer of *Home: A Short History of an Idea,* most people are very much influenced by the notion that a comfortable and impressive home must be large, or at least feel large. Mr. Rybcznski claims this notion is an American trait and Americans have yet to come to grips with the idea they might have to live in smaller houses.

G. LOT SIZE

A 1980 survey by the National Association of Home Builders showed 90 percent of consumers preferred single-family, detached homes. The home preferred by consumers was three-plus bedrooms, two and a half baths and 1,800 square feet. Forty percent of those surveyed indicated that a large lot was essential to their home choice. In 1985, a similar survey showed almost identical housing desires with the exception that only 23 percent indicated a large lot was essential.

Willingness to accept a smaller lot appears to be an economic compromise based on priority of consumers' wants.

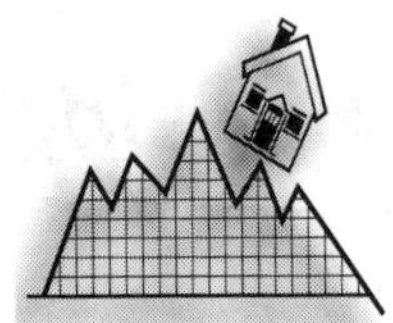

According to the National Association of Home Builders, land costs increased from 11 percent of the total cost of homes and lots in 1965, to almost 24 percent by 1985. Land costs exceeding 50 percent of total home costs in highly desirable locations are no longer a rarity. According to a study by Washington-based Urban Land Institute, undeveloped residential land prices have been increasing at twice the rate of inflation.

Builders have been reducing lot sizes in many areas of the country.

The long, ranch style home with attached garage set parallel to the street, formerly the standard suburban home of the 1960s, will not be duplicated in many areas of the country because of higher land costs.

In Riverside County, California (in 1986), a specially zoned area of small lots was developed for homes having 800 to 1,400 square feet, priced from $50,000 to $74,000. They were sold out immediately, the people having waited all night in line to buy. This indicates that people will buy less than they wanted, when what they want is beyond their financial ability.

When the choice is less or nothing, people will settle for less.

The half to one acre suburban sites of the 1960s are now found primarily in high-priced developments. While cutting lot sizes, builders have devised means to make lots appear larger. Building two-story homes can leave more space between houses. Two-story homes take one-half the land area of one-story homes of the same square footage. In addition, they offer lower construction costs per square foot because one foundation and roof can serve for double the square footage.

ZERO BUILDING SETBACK *means a building is built on the property line.* By use of zero building setbacks on one side, a large side yard is possible on the entrance side of the home, which gives a feeling of spaciousness.

Z-shaped lots are gaining in popularity with houses set at angles, to provide better views as well as yard space that can be utilized. A ***Z-SHAPED LOT*** *resembles a Z, compared to a normal, rectangle-shaped lot.*

Alleys allow narrow lots and provide access to rear garages.

Smaller lots provide for a greater density of population, which also allows lower costs per family for municipal services. A denser population also means higher tax rolls per acre. Drawbacks to greater population density include increased traffic and parking congestion.

Surveys conducted at the National Association of Home Builders' National Conventions indicate most home builders intend to build larger homes on smaller lots. They also indicated that builders intend to include more luxury features in their homes. Almost two-thirds of builders indicated they would be building for the move-up market; only 29 percent indicated they expected to be marketing homes to entry-level homeowners.

In catering to this trade up market, builders intend to increase size and amenities such as fireplaces, spa tubs, etc. To keep costs down, they intend to use smaller lots.

Builders react to the marketplace. In periods of high interest costs, the affordability index falls. To have products that entry-level buyers can afford, many builders exclude fireplaces, hardwood flooring, and other costly amenities that they would have included under better economic conditions.

Home building has a dramatic effect on our entire economy. During a typical year, residential construction accounts for 5 cents of every dollar spent in the U.S. economy. Homebuilding is therefore one of the largest U.S. industries.

In addition to homebuilding costs, a home purchase also means purchases for a myriad of other goods and services. One person moving into a new home usually means someone moving into that person's home and on and on. Each move involves purchases of additional goods and services.

VI. New Home Speculation

Whenever buying and selling any commodity offers profit potential, you will find speculators.

When speculators purchase new homes, they also create a hidden supply of housing that can hurt developers when the supply is later placed on the market. Because speculators want the lower tax rates of long-term capital gains as well as appreciation, they tend to hold properties off the sale market for at least a year.

Because of the great housing demand between 2003 and 2006, builders raised prices of new homes again and again. Pulte Builders did not restrict speculator purchases and a great many units in Indio, California, and in Las Vegas, Nevada (Del Webb Communities), were sold to speculators. Speculators placing their homes on the marketplace were able to undercut Pulte pricing. The result was that Pulte reduced prices on some new units by over $100,000. Speculators saw significant gains disappear overnight. Many speculators who had not completed their purchases walked away leaving Pulte with a sudden inventory of unsold units. Other home buyers who purchased homes at higher prices have sued Pulte.

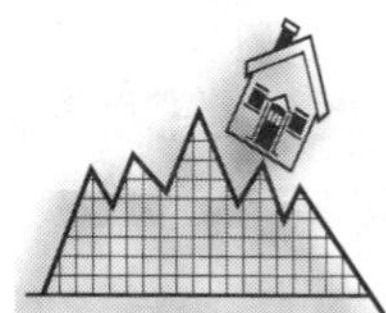

A survey of residential builders by the National Association of Home Builders indicated that builders were very concerned with speculator purchases. The survey showed how builders were dealing with their concerns.

1. 82 percent of builders indicate that they will only sell for owner occupancy.
2. 64 percent prohibit buyers selling or assigning the contract to another buyer prior to the close of the purchase transaction.
3. 55 percent have restrictions on resale in the first year.
4. 36 percent require that the builder be given a first right of refusal for sales during the first year.
5. 39 percent limit the number of investor sales per phase of development.
6. 18 percent indicated they would only sell one home to buyers with the same last name.
7. 18 percent indicated they had additional ways to discourage speculation including a first-year sale fee. Fees of up to $50,000 were indicated.

When a buyer indicates the home purchase is for investment purposes, the interest rate would be higher as would the down payment than for owner occupancy. Because of this, many buyers have indicated the purchase is for their occupancy but later "changed their mind."

Because speculators only intend to keep title for a few years, they want loans with the lowest payments. Many investors have purchased with adjustable rate loans having lengthy teaser rate periods.

Different organizations show different numbers as to the extent of investor speculation in home sales. In 2005, a mortgage industry survey indicated that nationally almost 10 percent of homes were purchased by speculators. A building industry figure was only 3 percent.

Most analysts believe, however, that the rate of speculator purchase of new homes is in the 20 percent range, with 23 percent usually quoted for 2004. Investor speculation as to existing homes is also significant.

In 2004, the FDIC identified 55 metropolitan areas where price increases had reached "boom" proportions because of what they perceive to be speculator purchases.

VII. CHAPTER SUMMARY

The United States has the highest percentage of homeownership in the world. A high percentage of homeownership tends to provide a stable society.

Within our real estate marketplace, which tends to be localized, segregation of housing is probably based more on economics than on racial prejudice. **Racial prejudice** appears to play a greater role in segregating our rental markets. We also have ethnic markets that are segregated to a large degree by choice.

Housing markets are **local markets** and prices vary by marketplace. The housing market is also segmented with different demands at different price ranges. Home sales are also likely to be a chain reaction with sellers becoming buyers.

The economy and interest rates drive the real estate market. Possible changes in the market increase builder risk.

Filtering down is a process where housing tends to pass down to lower economic levels.

A number of special markets exist in real estate such as the **auction marketplace**, **minority housing market**, **foreign buyer market**, and **rental market**.

A **vacancy factor** of 5 percent or less is indicative of a critical housing need.

First-time homebuyers tend to be younger and less likely to be a traditional married household.

Illegal immigrants tend to fill the vacancies at the lowest housing levels and keep units from being demolished.

The **tax exemption** on capital gains for homeowners has made **fixer-uppers** attractive for investors willing to occupy the home.

Condominiums have the advantage of lower prices but are more of an alternative to apartment living than single-family homes.

Two-income families have allowed buyers to pay a higher percentage of gross income for housing.

To keep prices down, the size of lots have been reduced. In the future, affordability might result in lower size homes, although the trend has been to larger homes.

Speculators holding homes for resale create a hidden supply of housing.

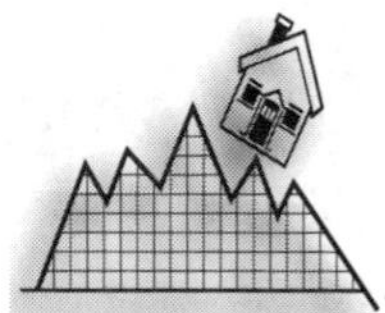

VIII. GLOSSARY OF KEY TERMS

Amortized Loan – Loan that pays off principal during the period of the loan.

Condominium – A vertical subdivision in which an owner owns the interior space of his or her unit, but common areas and the land are owned collectively by all of the unit owners.

Condominium Conversion – Converting property to condominiums.

Cooperative – Ownership by a corporation; individual stockholders have a right to occupy a unit with a lease.

Critical Rent Level – That rent level at which no new rental housing will be built.

Echo Boom – A baby boom caused by children of a previous baby boom having children.

Fixed Costs – Costs such as taxes and insurance that remain unchanged by property operations.

Fixer-Upper – Property in need of renovation or repair that can be purchased at a lower price.

Housing Turnover – The number of times an inventory of housing is sold within a given period of time.

Loan-to-Value Ratio – The percent of appraised value which lenders will lend on a property.

Negative Amortization – A loan where the payment does not cover interest so the principal increases.

Option (Adjustable Rate Loan) – A loan where the borrower has the option of making a minimum payment.

Overbuilding – Reaching a point in construction where the supply exceeds the demand at the price offered.

PCBs – A carcinogenic found in hydraulic and electrical equipment.

Perchlorate – Used in propellants and explosives it contaminated soil and water in former military and ordnance sites.

Real Income – Income adjusted according to cost of living changes.

Schwabe's Law – The rule that lower income people pay a higher percentage of their income for housing than upper income people.

Sweat Equity – Homeowner equity resulting from improvement or repairs personally made by the homeowner.

Toxic Mold – Mold that creates health problems and can be difficult to remove.

Vacancy Factor – Percentage of vacant units or space.

Variable Costs – Costs relating to operation, which can be deferred or changed.

Weeks on Market – The median (average) number of weeks a home will be listed with the multiple listing services before it is sold.

"Will Sell" Sellers – Sellers who are not strongly motivated to sell, but will sell at a particular price.

IX. CLASS DISCUSSION TOPICS

1. Identify and discuss local minority housing areas as well as mixed housing areas.

2. Identify examples of filtering down within your community.

3. Give examples of overbuilding in your area.

4. Have condominiums in your area increased in value proportionally to appreciation of single-family homes?

5. Identify areas of unfulfilled housing needs within your housing market.

6. Do you perceive any housing discrimination in your area? Explain.

7. What if any housing has been demolished in your area? Why?

8. Have there been any real estate auctions in your area? If so, what do you perceive as the motivation for auction sales?

9. What effect, if any, do you think that speculators have had or will have on housing prices in your area?

X. CHAPTER 9 QUIZ

1. Which of the following is a true statement?
   a. Families tend to move more often than single persons.
   b. Non-hispanic whites are more likely to be homeowners than are African Americans.
   c. Older people are more likely to move than younger people.
   d. Repeat buyers tend to have lower incomes than first-time buyers.

2. Which of the following is a true statement?
   a. Homeownership rates are higher within central cities than in suburban areas.
   b. The likelihood of homeownership is inversely related to income.
   c. A single sale normally is part of a chain reaction.
   d. Most renters live in property having severe physical problems.

3. A proper description of the housing market would be that it is:
   a. segmented.
   b. a national rather than a local market.
   c. an economically perfect market.
   d. a market with inflexible pricing.

4. The filtering down process explains housing passing from:
   a. rich to super rich.
   b. poor to upper middle class.
   c. middle class to upper middle class.
   d. middle class to poor.

5. An auction without reservation means that:
   a. a minimum bid is required.
   b. the owner has the right to reject any bid.
   c. the owner must accept the highest bid.
   d. bidders are not required to prequalify to bid.

6. Discrimination in housing today is most prevalent in:
   a. instances where anglos attempt to move into minority areas.
   b. the rental market.
   c. cash sales to minority groups members.
   d. government housing.

7. Which of the following is a true statement regarding the housing rental market?
   a. Prospective renters are less informed as to market conditions than prospective sellers.
   b. Competition in the rental market is between vacant units.
   c. Most owners of single-family homes would prefer to rent rather than to own.
   d. Increased rents and lower interest rates discourage building new rental units.

8. Variable costs to operate income housing, would include:
   a. taxes.
   b. insurance.
   c. mortgage payments.
   d. tenant services.

9. A reason why apartment buildings have recently sold at prices that could not be justified by anticipated rental rates was:
   a. depreciation.
   b. the deductibility of rent payments.
   c. the possibility of condominium conversions.
   d. the Section 8 housing program.

10. High land costs have led builders to build:
    a. on smaller lots.
    b. larger houses.
    c. on acreage parcels.
    d. rambling structures.

ANSWERS: 1. *b*; 2. *c*; 3. *a*; 4. *d*; 5. *c*; 6. *b*; 7. *b*; 8. *d*; 9. *c*; 10. *a*

LEARNING OBJECTIVES

When we speak of traditional housing, we refer to "stick built" single-family detached housing and rental units. Stick Built refers to housing built with on-site labor.

Nontraditional Housing, for the purpose of this text, includes:

1) unconventional construction methods, 2) types of housing, 3) non-family living arrangements, and 4) special need housing.

Much of what we regard as nontraditional housing stems from rising land and construction costs.

Other nontraditional housing has evolved to meet special needs.

In this chapter the growth of nontraditional housing will be examined in relationship to meeting special needs. This material will aid in recognizing unfulfilled housing needs within your community.

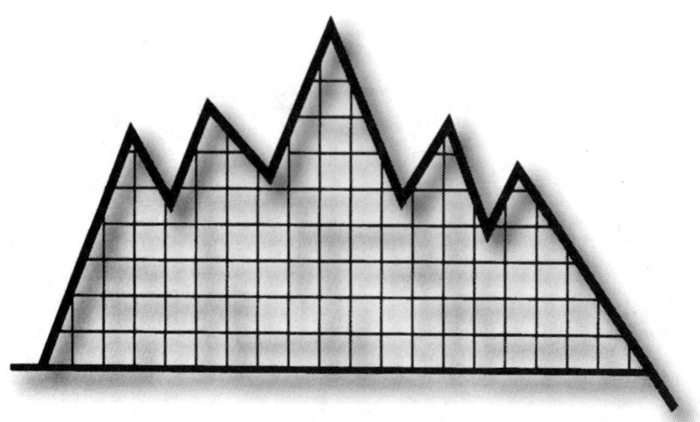

Chapter 10
Nontraditional Housing

I. Manufactured Homes

Manufactured Housing is what the public often refers to as "mobile homes." This commonly used term is NOT used by the government.

Congress, in 1980, changed the official description in all federal laws and descriptions to "Manufactured Housing." While this was done at the request of the industry, it is a more accurate description of this type of housing. There is nothing that is at all "mobile" about this type of housing. Generally, manufactured homes are permanently set on foundations and all tow bars, wheels, and axles are removed. Many newer manufactured homes range from 1,400 to 3,000 square feet and have attached garages and patios. Such structures are no more easily moved than any other house once they are in place. In fact, it is not economically feasible to move them.

A ***MANUFACTURED HOME*** *is built in a factory and has a steel chassis frame that is an integral part of the structure.* The frame adds strength and structural integrity to the house, and allows the home to be transported to its site on removable wheels.

The industry also likes to use the term "off site built housing" to describe their product.

Chapter 10

CHAPTER 10 OUTLINE

This is perhaps the most accurate description. Imagine that you are going to build a thousand homes. In conventional construction this means that you have to assemble your plant and workers at the site as well as bring in the materials. The plant is outdoors and the building materials are at the mercy of the elements. The plant cannot operate during inclement weather and there are often delays in construction. When you have finished and are ready to go elsewhere, the plant and workers have to be moved to a new site. This is inefficient and costly. Manufactured housing, on the other hand, is assembled at a central location, indoors, and construction goes on in all weather conditions. Materials are not exposed to the elements and the work force tends to be stable. This allows the industry to provide housing that is equal or better in quality, for less cost, to the consumer.

Manufactured homes must be built to The Federal Manufactured Home Construction and Safety Standard adopted in 1976. The code includes insulation and energy efficiencies. Conventional construction is only governed by state or local codes.

The original code went into effect in June of 1976. HUD requires all manufactured homes to be built to this code and requires continuous inspection of the housing as it is built in the factory. The code requires tested standards. This means that if an engineer calculates that a roof design will stand up to a wind force of a 100 miles per hour then the roof has to be tested at that wind force to prove that it will.

The HUD code is mandatory for all manufactured housing.

A local jurisdiction may not interfere with the HUD Code by federal law. The code is updated yearly to incorporate the latest safety and technology developments. This has the effect of providing "cutting edge" housing to consumers.

See **Figure 10-1**, which lists the advantages of manufactured housing over conventionally built housing.

While most manufactured housing is located within manufactured home parks or subdivision developments, some are sited on individual lots or acreage.

Manufactured home parks are popular with many senior citizens, particularly, in the sun belt states. Indeed, many seniors prefer manufactured homes even though they can afford other types of housing. While there are still many older parks with closely packed housing, the trend has been to increase lot sizes and park amenities to attract this affluent age group. Another trend has been to convert parks from rental spaces to either condominium units or to fee simple ownership (Planned Unit Development). This has developed as a result of tenant resistance to higher rents, rent control ordinances, and community resistance to more rental parks.

Figure 10-1

Advantages of Manufactured Housing

Manufactured housing has a significant economic advantage over conventionally built housing. Reasons for the cost advantage include:

1. No weather delays because manufactured homes are built in a factory.
2. Factory construction eliminates site theft and vandalism.
3. Manufactured homes are generally built in a few days, significantly reducing interest costs.
4. Insurance costs are significantly less than conventionally built housing, due to reduced construction time and factory protection from on-site vandalism and theft.
5. Manufactured homes are built to basic modular plans, significantly reducing wasted material.
6. Material handling costs are reduced when materials are delivered to the factory site.
7. Because of a single site factory, significant discounts are possible with quantity purchases of material.
8. Factory construction allows use of maximum automation in building, such as jigs to form wall units and automated nailing machines to nail large sections in a single operation.
9. Workers' time is used more effectively, as they do not move from site to site and need not wait for material or other contractors to arrive.
10. Supervision and communication in a factory is constant and problems can be solved quickly.
11. Workers are in an assembly line setting, thus the need for highly developed skills has been lessened. Workers repeating the same tasks with specialized equipment under supervision generally do not need anywhere near the skills required for on-site construction. In many cases, factory wages for manufactured housing construction are at rates less than 50 percent of the prevailing labor rates for on-site work.

Manufactured homes make excellent weekend or vacation homes because of low exterior maintenance costs and the idea that an owner can lock and leave.

The 2000 Census found that there were 9 million manufactured homes in the U.S. This figure doubles the figure for 1980. Greater community acceptance, more conventional appearance, improved parks, and better financing have been factors in the significant growth in manufactured home living.

In the year 2000, manufacturers shipped 250,550 new manufactured homes. Manufactured homes accounted for about 1 in 7 new homes.

In 2000, the average price for a manufactured home was $46,500. That compares with $162,300 average cost for a new home excluding lot. The manufactured home cost does not include foundation costs or cost to site it on the foundation. When comparing sited manufactured homes with similar size conventional homes, the cost savings for manufactured homes will run from 15 percent to over 30 percent.

Some lenders, communities, and prospective homebuyers are unaware of the changes within the industry that have made manufactured housing in many cases superior to the average site-built product.

> *Use of terminology by real estate professionals such as "mobile home," "coach," and "trailer park" does not help allay their fears and suspicions of this alternative housing.*

Aggressive lawsuits by manufactured home builders have in many cases overturned zoning laws attempting to keep manufactured housing out of communities. Such suits were often able to prove that the manufactured housing was built to stricter standards than prevailed in the community.

Lower costs make manufactured homes an attractive housing choice for lower income families. The cost of owning a manufactured home includes park rent, which varies greatly across the country from about $100 per month in some rural area parks with few amenities to over $2,000 per month in some ocean front parks.

Surveys carried out by A.M. Best have indicated a number of interesting facts. Manufactured housing appeals to both young families and seniors. The majority of manufactured homebuyers indicate that they would buy another manufactured home rather than a site-built home. In times of recession, as well as in times of high interest rates, manufactured housing sales increase. This occurred in the mid-1990s, when 37% of all housing starts were manufactured housing.

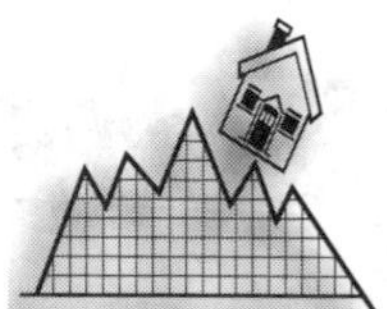

Manufactured Home Lending Changes

Lenders in the secondary market have had loss problems recently with manufactured housing. Most of the problems resulted in states where it is difficult or not possible to convert manufactured housing to real property. Florida, Georgia, and Ohio were noted as problem areas in a bulletin sent out by "Fannie Mae." It seems appraisers and lenders in these states appraised and made real property loans on housing that was personal property and then sold these loans into the secondary market. The secondary market has suffered losses in those areas. This has caused what many in the national manufactured housing market consider an over-reaction on the part of "Fannie Mae" and "Freddie Mac." "Fannie Mae" has gone so far as to attempt to redefine a manufactured home as "any home built on a steel frame or chassis." This definition is obviously incorrect. It, of course, leads one to wonder just how much the people at "Fannie Mae" really know about the home construction products they are buying. "Fannie Mae" has developed a new appraisal checklist form for appraisers and they require the appraiser to certify that he or she is familiar with appraising manufactured homes. The appraiser now also has stricter guidelines regarding what "Fannie Mae" considers comparable as well. "Fannie Mae" has also made getting a loan on manufactured homes more expensive to the national consumer by increasing the rate and term requirements for such housing. "Freddie Mac" correctly defines a manufactured home as one built to the HUD Code, but goes along with "Fannie Mae" in adding forms and loan restrictions. All of these changes have been made to "protect" the consumer, according to "Fannie" and "Freddie." HUD/FHA has made no changes.

The appreciation in land values has caused many mobilehome parks to evict residents and develop the land for a more productive purpose. In 2004, over 900 residents were evicted from Beach Mobile Home Park in Hampton Road, Virginia, so the land could be developed for luxury housing. There has been community concern about park redevelopment since most residents cannot find parks that will accept used units. In addition, the cost to take apart a double or triple wide unit, transport it, and site it on a new foundation can exceed the value of the unit.

To protect owners of units, some communities are enacting zoning for manufactured home parks that exclude other uses.

Because a *mobile* home is no longer *mobile*, investors like mobilehome parks because they provide a steady income with little risk. Major owners of mobilehome parks include Real Estate Investment Trusts such as Sun Communities.

A disadvantage of manufactured homes is that they don't experience the appreciation conventional housing has experienced. Manufactured home appreciation is strongly tied to the desirability of the park or site where it is situated.

II. Modular Homes

The difference between manufactured homes and modular homes is the HUD Code and the use of a steel chassis.

MODULAR HOMES *are constructed to comply only with state and local building codes.* These may be either equal to or inferior to the HUD code.

While manufactured homes are built and transported on a steel chassis, much like a vehicle, modular homes are built without a chassis and shipped on flatbed trucks. For a 24-foot wide unit, they would be in two 12-foot wide sections and lifted and set by a crane. Because modular homes are factory built, the same savings apply as are common for manufactured homes.

Far fewer modular homes are built than manufactured homes. In 2002, 36,000 modular homes were shipped. While this was an 11 percent increase from 2001, the number is not very significant as to our housing needs.

The figures for new housing units and housing starts do not seem to match. One reason for the difference is that building permits are not always required for placing a manufactured home on its site.

State laws and/or local ordinances could effect the need for a building permit, if a unit is placed on a permanent foundation, as well as if the axles and wheels have been removed.

III. Prefabricated Homes

Even ***STICK BUILT HOMES*** *(homes built at the site)* have some degree of prefabrication. ***PREFABRICATED HOMES*** *are generally referred to as "panelized housing components built in factories and assembled on-site."* Like manufactured and modular homes, most of the labor is performed in a factory. The same economic benefits also apply to prefabricated housing as in manufactured and modular homes.

Panelizing housing components are not new. In 1624, panelized housing components were manufactured in England and transported to the New World as housing for settlers. While there were a number of early attempts at panelized construction, prefabrication did not attain significant status until after World War II. A great many firms went into prefabrication, including U.S. Steel, National Homes, Lustron, Wausau Homes, etc. Some of the homes were built in eight-foot to 16-foot wall and ceiling panels and were assembled using cranes and bolts. Some had prefinished interior and exterior walls. Others were finished at the site. Some units were completely wired and plumbed at the factory, while others had these tasks performed at the site.

Variations in local building codes, plus construction trade opposition, hurt early prefabricators.

In some states, prefabricated as well as modular housing is inspected at the factory so it does NOT have to be torn apart for local on-site inspections.

A problem with prefabrication and (modular or manufactured housing) is it requires a very large investment in construction plants and equipment. While tremendous savings are possible if the plant can operate at a steady level, the home construction industry is subject to cycles. Many prefabricators and modular home manufacturers have gone bankrupt during recessionary periods. Because the prefabricator has a huge investment in plant and equipment they have a continuing overhead. Unlike conventional builders, cutting all production does not eliminate most of the overhead. (The manufactured home industry has not been hurt as much in economic downturns.)

In Sweden, prefabricated homes are built with seven-inch miniature "I" beams in the walls instead of studs. The "I" beams, constructed of hardboard and wood, allow for tight fitting insulation. These Swedish homes are considered to be among the finest quality built homes anywhere. The homes use from 30 to 60 percent of the energy required for similar size stick built homes in the United States.

Even penthouses can be prefabricated.

A Swedish firm is producing prefabricated living units to be installed on top of existing structures by use of cranes. These instant penthouses have been installed atop the historic Albert Court apartments in London. The units are being marketed at between $3.9 million and $5.5 million. The development company, which buys a long-term lease on the buildings roof, finishes the exteriors to blend in with the existing structures.

In Japan, prefabrication has been perfected with automated plants. By using concrete panels, Misawa, one of Japan's largest builders, claims prefabrication costs 70 percent less than conventional housing. Misawa claims to be able to produce a home, which is 85 percent complete in less than one hour. It uses Precastable Autoclaved Lightweight Concrete (PALC), which is stronger than normal concrete but about one fourth the weight. Even so, because of weight, these homes are seldom built more than 100 miles from the manufacturing site. It is doubtful U. S. buyers would accept this type of concrete home marketed in Japan.

An advantage cited by manufactures of prefabricated homes is that buyers can save from 20 percent to 50 percent compared to the price of a stick built house if they act as their own general contractor. The manufacturer usually sets up the panels. One Idaho prefabricator claims it can set up exterior and interior wall sections for a 2,000 square foot home in 4 hours. Buyers then deal with the subcontractors. Several manufacturers maintain lists of subcontractors they work with by area and can help buyers contract for home completion.

Prefabrication never lived up to early predictions that it would be the wave of the future, but prefabrication ideas and techniques have had an effect on our stick built housing, which includes:

1. acceptance of drywall instead of plaster.
2. factory built trusses.
3. prehung doors.
4. factory built fireplace inserts.
5. greater use of plywood.
6. factory built cabinets.

IV. Precut Homes

In the late 1800s, home pattern books were in vogue and precut home kits could be ordered. The ***PRECUT HOME KITS*** *included all material and directions.* Even the giant, Sears Roebuck & Company, included precut homes in its catalog. Sears Roebuck offered bungalows starting at $595 and an antebellum styled mansion for $5,000. For $39, a customer could buy a precut privy (toilet). By the time Sears Roebuck & Company discontinued their line of homes in 1937, they had sold more than 100,000 units.

Today, a number of firms sell precut sheds, garages, and homes. Anyone with a basic understanding of hand tools can assemble the package from the directions. There are even precut geodesic dome and log homes.

One of the problems with precut homes is the lack of financing unless a contractor is used.

Lenders are hesitant to make loans to unskilled homeowners who wish to build with their own labor. Lenders do not want to foreclose on a partially completed or poorly constructed home. The result is some large sellers of precut homes have set up their own construction financing, while others rely primarily on cash sales.

While precut homes offer buyers an opportunity to obtain sweat equity, it is doubtful they will ever capture a significant portion of the market.

V. Shell Homes

A number of builders and developers offer shell homes. The ***SHELL HOME*** *has an exterior that is generally completed with windows, siding, and roofing, which is set on a foundation, but the interior is incomplete*. The interior walls, although studded, are unfinished. The buyer is responsible for installing plumbing, electrical, and heating systems, as well as finished flooring, doors, cabinets, insulation, and a finished interior.

These homes are sold at a low cost. A number of recreational land developers offer the option of a shell home, complete with lot.

Many buyers "camp" in their shell homes while they do the finishing work.

Besides vacation housing, shell homes are popular in some rural areas. The heavy work has been completed, allowing the buyer to finish the job as time permits.

Shell homes, like precut homes, have a financing disadvantage. Unless the borrower has demonstrated construction skills and has other collateral, lenders are generally unwilling to make loans on shell homes.

VI. Accessory Dwelling Units (ADUs) (Granny Flats)

One of the answers to sprawl the ***ACCESSORY DWELLING UNIT (ADU)***. *These units are built on land already containing a housing unit*. Because no new land need be purchased, the cost for an accessory dwelling unit is 25 percent to 40 percent less than would be needed if land had to be purchased.

Ordinances are needed to allow ADUs in single-family areas. Approvals are more likely in areas of older housing than in newer areas. Residents are likely to strongly oppose zoning changes.

Residents of the area fear that accessory dwelling units could lower property values. This "NIMBY" (not in my back yard) attitude can be difficult to overcome.

Statistics in many areas indicate additional units will not really overcrowd communities. While single-family zoning was built around the idea of families with children, demographics are changing. There are fewer persons per household. This is the result of an aging population as well as social changes and affluence where more singles and unmarried couples have purchased homes. There are also a great many persons over the age of 65 who live alone.

In 1960, Washington D.C. had 3.09 persons per dwelling unit, but by 1990, it was down to 2.53 persons per dwelling unit. This number is now just above 2 persons per household.

According to HUD, one or two persons occupy 32 percent of homes having five or more rooms. This percentage can be expected to rise.

ADUs could increase our stock of affordable housing without the necessity of government subsidies. If just one in every 10 single-family owner occupied homes built before 1975 were to incorporate an accessory unit, over 3.8 million rental units would be created. This would be a more efficient use of our housing stock and would help to restrain sprawl. ADUs actually help neighborhoods as a rental unit allows elderly owners the additional income to remain in their homes. Sometimes the owner will move to the smaller ADU and rent the main unit.

ADUs can be attached or detached units.

During World War II, the need for housing created many ADUs. Units were broken into two or more units and garage, attic, and basement spaces were converted for dwelling purposes. Many of these units were "bootleg" units, contravening zoning laws. There are still many illegal units in use today. Some of these bootleg units were built for family members such as in-laws.

In many older areas, duplexes were turned into triplexes by finishing basements as separate living units. Because many duplexes had common entrances and stairs to the basements off the central entrances, conversions to separate units were relatively easy. Owners tend to advertise a basement apartment as an "English Apartment." People don't want to live in a basement, but an English Apartment is more acceptable.

Don't confuse an ADU with a room rental. While smaller than the primary unit, an ADU has its own kitchen, living space, and bath and usually has a private entrance.

To avoid overcrowding, some communities have an age requirement or limit ADUs to the elderly. Some cities have limited the rent for ADUs in order to make certain the units will remain affordable. Some cities regulate by relationship of the residents.

In California, every city must have an ADU ordinance.

VII. Elder Cottage Housing Opportunity (ECHO)

"ECHO housing" is an accessory dwelling unit for seniors.

Also called "granny flats," ECHO housing is an affordable option for seniors. A common requirement is that the occupant be 62 years of age and meet relationship requirements. Some communities allow a temporary unit to be brought in while others require the unit be stick built and/or be attached to the house. If the ECHO unit is a permanent unit, some communities allow it to be rented after the departure of the original family member occupant.

The original echo units were manufactured or modular units brought onto a lot for a family member. Australia introduced the echo concept.

VIII. Multigenerational Housing

Once the norm, multigenerational housing all but disappeared in the 1960s-1970s. Large houses used to hold parents, grandparents, brothers, and sisters, as well as their families. Many large farmhouses had numerous additions that were added to accommodate an extending family.

Today we are seeing more multigenerational housing, especially in areas where there are a great many immigrants and first generation Americans. The U.S. Census Bureau figures indicate that there are 4 million housing units in the U.S. that serve as home for 3 or more generations of family members.

Multigenerational families often seek large homes with guest houses or suites.

IX. Co-Housing

The co-housing concept originated in Denmark. A ***CO-HOUSING*** *unit consists of a common building with a large dining area, commercial kitchen, childcare area, library, recreational areas, and workshop. Residents live in separate small buildings.* Residents own and run the facility and decisions are made in common.

The typical co-housing development would have 20 to 30 family buildings. The basis of co-housing is to allow families to retain separate lives and have a community that strengthens and supports the family units.

There are co-housing developments throughout the country. There is a co-housing association of the United States (**www.cohousing.org**).

X. Group Homes

GROUP HOMES *are supervised housing units for a number of unrelated individuals who have a common problem.* While most group homes are for mentally challenged citizens, there are also group homes for alcohol and drug abuse, troubled teenagers, and even released prisoners.

Communities resist group homes as a NIMBY (Not in my back yard) reaction. However, the mentally challenged, as well as alcoholics, are protected classes under our fair housing laws, so local ordinances cannot exclude them.

> *Group homes are run as businesses by individuals as well as by nonprofit groups.*

XI. Lofts

Areas once used for storage above retail stores, as well as old multi-storied factories, were sought by artists because of the low rental cost. Because of high ceilings, light from large windows, and low rent, they met artistic needs. Artists started to live in their studios, and in many instances, added an elevated platform for sleeping. These unusual workspace dwellings became chic and were sought by affluent singles and couples who desired these avant-garde living spaces.

> *The economics of converting a sound structure into loft units for rent or sale as condominiums makes sense.*

Today, owners and developers are catering to the desire for loft units. They are converting factories, upper levels of retail stores, schools, office buildings, and warehouses to lofts.

Loft units can be produced at far less cost than a conventional apartment. Some units are sold with just the plumbing stubbed in, while others have completed baths and kitchens. Many large structures include interior security parking and key operated elevators.

In Milwaukee, a large hosiery factory has been converted into lofts; a piano factory in Boston, glove factory in Indianapolis, hat factory in Cleveland, and a hardware factory in Pittsburgh have all become loft units. Midwest and Eastern cities offer the best prospects for loft conversion with many narrow, multistoried structures in their commercial areas.

Cobbler Square in Chicago is a $25 million project covering seven buildings over a two-block area. It was formerly the home of Dr. Scholl's foot products. Spaces ranging from around 600 to over 1,500 square feet now rent from $1,000 to $1,770 per month.

Early developers of loft space originally found that difficulty in finding lenders was their biggest problem, followed by the reluctance of planning departments to approve rezoning from industrial and commercial to residential. The demand for loft apartments prompted factory owners in Chicago to ask that such conversions be brought to a halt. They pointed out that loft conversions have resulted in higher rents for industry, which must now compete for space with residential developers. Factory conversions to loft space have also reduced the number of manufacturing jobs in central city areas.

In the mid-1990s, when downtown Manhattan had a glut of vacant office space the New York legislature provided tax benefits for developers who would convert office space to residential use. By 2000, the glut had disappeared but the legislature extended the program for 5 years. Political considerations were the reason for this seemingly senseless extension.

XII. Build-Up Units (Adding a Second Floor)

Many neighborhood commercial areas have primarily single-story buildings. When the structure is able to support a second story, building apartments above commercial structures becomes cost effective.

Adding a rental as a second story is far less costly than building a rental unit elsewhere, because the land costs, site improvements, and foundation are NOT factors for the present property owner.

Many of these build-up units are sought after because they offer privacy, and in some cases, amenities such as roof gardens.

Problems associated with adding rental units over existing commercial units have been planning commissions' reluctance to allow residential additions, lender hesitancy, and high interest rates for the second mortgages generally required to pay for the additions. Also, build-up units require rear stairways for access and, in some areas, fire escapes.

When built over offices, residential units do not have much of a negative impact on parking because the hours of office use and dwelling occupancy seldom overlap.

XIII. Shared Housing

Chances are that the classified section of your local newspaper has a category for shared housing.

The number of unrelated people living together has increased dramatically in recent years. Besides romance, shared housing is often based on economic necessity.

Owners or tenants who do not have a problem with their housing costs are generally unwilling to share their dwelling, as privacy is valued as long as it can be afforded.

Single persons are more likely to share a home with another single person than with a family unit. Single owners or renters are more willing to share occupancy to reduce their ownership or rental expense.

> *Whole family units involved in shared housing are most likely to do so with relatives.*

Shared housing among non-related family groups, though not common, is more prevalent in lower income groups. It is more common among single mothers with children than it is with traditional family units. The reason for sharing is economic. There is a greater tendency toward coupling of family groups in times of low employment and an uncoupling in times of high employment.

Senior citizens share housing for a number of reasons. Besides the obvious economic benefits, senior citizens also gain companionship and assistance. Shared housing has kept many senior citizens out of nursing homes.

In Pinellas County, Florida, the number of seniors cohabitating with non-relatives increased 32 percent from 1990 to 2000. In Hillsborough County, the increase was 60 percent.

Alternative Living for the Aging, a Los Angeles-based nonprofit organization, pairs senior citizens for shared living. The organization also operates its own shared housing units.

At least one California retirement development advertises "companionship suites," which simply means two unrelated persons occupy a unit.

www.nationalsharedhousing.org will help match share partners.

There are also programs where a number of unrelated persons will share living space as well as programs for families.

XIV. Single Room Occupancy (SRO)

In the past, low income singles and couples who could not afford a home or apartment were able to rent rooms in a room and board house, rooming house, or in a private residence. Prior to 1960, most daily newspapers had a rental category in their classified ads for rooms for rent.

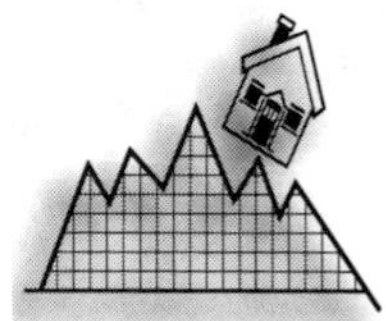

Chapter 10

Old residential hotels and low-cost YMCA hotels existed in most major cities where residents sometimes remained for years. It was really single-room occupancy housing. Many of these facilities have since been demolished for redevelopment.

> *Today, there are very few traditional rooming houses and even fewer room and board houses.*

Family units are far less likely to rent a room to a stranger than they were in past years. In fact, even homeowners in foreclosure appear to value their privacy above ownership. Even when the additional income would allow them to save their homes, few homeowners with financial difficulties will rent rooms.

> *The result is that to be single and poor might mean being without housing.*

The lack of single-room housing is likely a contributing factor to the homeless problem in our cities.

In Los Angeles, a private nonprofit organization, Single Room Occupancy Housing Corporation, has been purchasing old transient hotels and renovating them for permanent housing for the homeless. It pays from $7,000 to $15,000 per room and generally spends in excess of $10,000 per room for renovations. The organization rents the rooms for $150 to $240 per month for singles and couples. (Section 8 housing vouchers are available for SROs.) It has been able to pay back city loans from its operating income.

Social services, nutrition, and transportation are also provided for the mostly elderly residents.

> *Some private investors have seen this need and have also turned under utilized transient hotels into permanent residential hotels.*

An advantage of permanent guests is that many hotel services are no longer required, which reduces operating expenses.

Because of increasing budgetary problems at the national, state and local levels, these housing needs are unlikely to be met by the public sector. The private sector could meet these needs if it were economically advantageous to do so. Possible incentives for the private sector include low interest rate loans (from bonds) and public land and/or property tax moratoriums on new construction.

Dubuque, Iowa, has a Single Room Occupancy Rehabilitation Program that provides low interest loans for owners of rooming units rented to low and moderate-income tenants.

XV. Recreational Vehicle Homes (RVs)

A great number of people spend a considerable portion of the year living in recreational vehicle homes. ***RECREATIONAL VEHICLE HOMES (RVs)*** *are campers, small trailers and motor homes.* While the majority of recreational vehicle owners have a permanent home, a growing number have no permanent home. Some live in recreational vehicle parks, while others are more nomadic and drift between several locations.

East of Niland, California and near the Salton Sea, over 3,000 people settle every winter in an area known as "Slab City" (**www.slabcity.org**). The slabs are all that remain of World War II Camp Dunlap, which was used for Marine training. These people use post office boxes as official addresses. Because Slab City is on the federal Bureau of Land Management land, they pay no rent. Most residents are senior citizens. There is a sense of community in Slab City. Residents built an 18-hole golf course on sand and even have a library. While a few remain year-around, most migrate back to permanent homes or to other locations to escape the summer heat. Many of these permanent trailer people travel in caravans to their summer locations.

While for some this is a lifestyle choice, it is believed the majority choose this way of life out of pure economic necessity.

XVI. Rental Rooms

At one time, when a single person moved to a community, he or she would look for a room to rent. Rental rooms were readily available in boarding houses as well as in private residences. People would not think twice about renting space that they didn't need. It made economic sense. Today, the only areas where room rentals are really common are those in close proximity to colleges and universities.

Privacy issues are one of the reasons that fewer people are willing to rent unused space in their homes. We tend to live in cocoons and not get too involved with others around us. Fear is another reason why people resist renting rooms. They view horror stories almost nightly on television and resist taking strangers into their homes. The exception seems to be college students, who are often welcomed.

We have a huge available housing stock within our present housing inventory but it is doubtful if it will be utilized. Most owners will not share their homes with others.

A. COLLEGE HOUSING

Children of baby boomers (an echo baby boom) have been hitting colleges in record numbers, resulting in schools being unable to provide campus housing for a great many students. Students have been spilling over into nearby communities, which

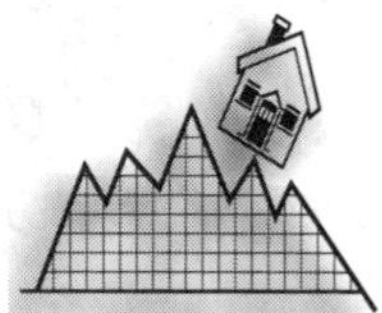

has resulted in increased rents. Home prices have also gone up because of the strong rental demand in college areas.

The worst is yet to come. The Department of Education indicates that college enrollments, which were at 14.9 million in 1999, will hit 16.3 million by 2009.

Landlords in many communities favor students over families since they can rent a unit to a number of students at double the rent a family could pay. Investors have been buying residential property for student rentals.

Some investors are building apartments, as well as dormitory type structures, where zoning allows for student housing. It appears to make economic sense.

Because of the profitability of college housing, Real Estate Investment Trusts have been formed to buy and develop college housing units. They include GMH Communities Trust and American Campus Communities. Both of these REITs are listed on the New York Stock Exchange.

Some parents have used the housing shortage as an opportunity. They will buy a house, condominium, or even an apartment building and let their child live there and rent rooms or units to others. They give their child a free room for the management as well as a management fee. They get the equivalent of a tax deduction for their child in college as well as the tax benefit of depreciation on the property. When the child graduates, they sell the unit, possibly to another parent and hopefully at a profit. They then pay a reduced capital gains tax on their gain.

A few campuses overbuilt their dormitories. The University of Michigan had to aggressively market their 5,500 dorm rooms. While graduate students normally tend to seek off campus housing, the University of Michigan was able to raise their dormitory retention rate by offering students high speed Internet access in their rooms. The university was pleasantly surprised at the difference this offering made in dormitory demand. This amenity could likely be used to increase the desirability of private student housing.

XVII. Retirement Housing

Most retirees remain in their home communities.

A 2003 survey indicated that 59 percent of baby boomers plan to relocate when they retire, but a majority of those who wanted to relocate indicated they were not sure they would be able to afford to do so.

Retirees who relocate are generally well off financially. According to the American Association of Retired Persons (AARP), 80 percent of senior homeowners have paid off their mortgages. When they sell their homes and take advantage of tax exemptions, they are in an excellent cash position.

Residents of retirement communities tend to be white, middle and upper class couples.

A great many are receiving private and corporate retirement annuities in addition to social security and personal savings.

Large retirement communities sell a way of life, as well as housing.

They generally have extensive recreational facilities as well as planned activities.

Fifty years ago, Del Webb pioneered active adult communities with the first Sun City development in Phoenix, Arizona. Sun City, Arizona is the nation's largest senior development with 50,000 residents.

Del Webb discovered an untapped market among an affluent graying population. Del Webb now has communities under development or in the sale stage in 19 states. While formerly limiting his retirement cities to the sunbelt, Del Webb has built near Chicago and is looking for other Northern markets. The Northern developments appeal to retirees who wish to remain close to families.

The National Association of Home Builders estimates that by the year 2010, people 55 to 74 years of age will be buying 281,000 homes annually, up from 189,000 in 1995. The baby boomers that followed World War II are coming into the retirement marketplace and are expected to be a vibrant market for many years to come.

XVIII. Assisted Care Facilities

One of the hottest areas for real estate investors had been assisted (limited) care facilities. These facilities offer residents their own dwelling unit, which might have a kitchen. Unit size varies from around 400 square fee to over 1,500 square feet. The residents generally furnish their own units. The facilities offer meals, which may be optional, planned daily activities and transportation to shopping, medical facilities and recreational events. Maid service is usually optional. They generally have emergency buzzers in the rooms and personnel available 24 hours. They are designed to keep ambulatory persons out of nursing homes.

They provide the elderly a pleasant lifestyle. Generally, they are chosen by persons who are not as active as those in retirement communities.

Rents are often twice what a similar size and quality unit would rent for in an apartment building. Many new assisted living units have been built aimed at the affluent elderly.

XIX. Life Care Facilities

While Leisure World and Sun City type developments are aimed at more active retirees, there is a growing interest in life care facilities for affluent seniors with health concerns.

The facilities are two basic types; those offering prepaid nursing and medical care guaranteed for life and those excluding nursing and medical care. Life care facilities guarantee residents that they will be taken care of for life. Some facilities are simply converted hotels or apartment structures, but most of the new facilities have been specially built.

Most of the first life care facilities were nonprofit and developed by church groups for their members. Today, most life care facilities are being built by private developers.

Private developers are encouraged by demographics showing an aging population. As an example, according to the Census Bureau, in 1985, 7.3 percent of Americans were over 75 years of age. By the year 2000, this number exceeded 11 percent, making the senior citizen (over 75) the fastest growing segment of our population.

Currently, there are about 1000 life care facilities in the United States. The numbers are expected to grow as more developers enter the field. Private hospital corporations have been expanding into life care facilities.

The first life care facilities required a buyer to pay about $200,000 as an initial fee. In addition, monthly fees varied, up to $2,000 per person. Since the initial fee was not refundable in the early developments, a unit could be sold again and again as its elderly occupants passed away.

Due to sales resistance, most life care facilities now offer either a return of the initial investment or a partial return upon death. The developer thus gains interest-free use of all of the initial investment plus any of the nonrefundable portion.

Some facilities offer a variety of services ranging from one, two, or three meals per day, daily or weekly housekeeping, as well as health care. Often there is a full-service nursing home on the premises.

The average buyer of a life care unit either has serious health problems, or is worried about health problems and does NOT wish to become a burden to family members.

An aging, affluent population, coupled with the fact that fewer parents reside with their children, would seem to indicate a significant increase in life care facilities for the future.

XX. Vacation Homes

Responding to a survey, 44 percent of American families indicated that they hoped to buy a vacation home within 10 years.

In 2000, there were an estimated 3.5 million seasonal homes, an increase of 1.2 million since 1980. This amounts to 3.1 percent of our housing stocks. The number increases by about 190,000 new vacation homes marketed each year.

VACATION HOMES *are second homes for seasonal or occasional use.* These do not include investment homes held primarily for rental on a year-round basis.

The majority of vacation homeowners also own their primary residence.

As might be expected, the likelihood of a household owning a vacation home increases with the increase in household income. In 2003, a survey of vacation homeowners revealed that the typical owner was 61 years of age and had owned the vacation home for 9 years. Average income of vacation homeowners was $76,900.

An unusual ownership statistic: ownership of a second home among households of similar income is greater in small or midsize urban areas than in large urban areas.

Several possible explanations offered include the supposition that because expenses tend to be higher in larger metropolitan areas, residents of these areas have less disposable income than residents of smaller urban areas. Another hypothesis is that people in small and midsize urban areas tend to have a higher rate of participation in outdoor recreation, and, therefore, place a higher premium on vacation home ownership.

Vacation homes are not a necessity so prices tend to swing more drastically with economic ups and downs than other housing. Having the money, many families are fulfilling their wish list.

The stock market success of many investors during the 1990s has had a tremendous effect on the vacation home market. According to the National Association of Realtors®, vacation home prices went up about 50 percent from 1991 to 1999. In many areas, prices have more than doubled. In the Bayhead, New Jersey area, a typical beachfront tear down home had increased in value from the $900,000 range to $2,000,000 in the three-year period from 1997 to 2000. Even at what we consider premium prices, modest vacation homes are now being torn down and opulent vacation homes are being built on their sites.

The rapid appreciation in real estate values from 2000 to 2006 brought a great many people into the vacation home market. They were able to use their equity in their primary residences to buy a vacation home. Many of these buyers expect similar appreciation in value for their vacation homes and are making the purchase as much for investment purposes as for lifestyle benefits.

The massive baby boom generation is now between 40 and 55 years of age. This is the period when people desire and can afford a second home. The median age of second homebuyers in 1999 was 43, which is an age when people begin to think of their retirement. Every year, 4.1 million people reach the age of 50. These people are likely interested in vacation homes.

A number of years ago, the government prohibited owners who occupied homes for 15 days or more per year from taking depreciation on their vacation homes. This materially reduced the economic incentive for owning vacation homes. The real estate industry predicted dire consequences for resort area values, but the predictions proved to be untrue. Vacation home values and sales did not vary significantly despite the tax change.

Various proposals have been presented to eliminate deductibility of interest connected with vacation homes.

This is a "soak-the-rich" approach to taxation.

If this is ever done, it would likely have significantly greater effect on values than the loss of depreciation benefits. Some analysts predict it would be a disaster for lower and mid-price vacation homes, but it would have less effect on higher cost homes. Other analysts point to Canada, where interest is not deductible. They point out that vacation homes are still sought by Canadians even though there is no economic advantage in purchasing them. Vacation homes are purchased simply because the purchasers desire the lifestyle that vacation homes offer.

The vacation home market is less perfect than the primary home market because a wider price range exists for similarly desirable vacation home property.

The explanation is that many buyers purchase vacation homes without in-depth market knowledge. Hasty emotional decisions are often the basis for these purchases.

Lender requirements for vacation home financing are tighter than primary residences.

Lenders not only want a higher down payment but higher interest as well, to compensate for what they view as a greater risk.

Like any other type of housing, the most important criteria in choosing a vacation home should be location.

A good location will show the greatest appreciation in periods of growth, the least value loss during recessionary periods, and require less resell time than properties in less desirable locations.

XXI. Condotels

CONDOTELS *are hotels that have been converted or built as condominiums.* Individual rooms are sold to private owners. The management company rents the unit when the owner is not present. Some units have resold for considerably more than original sale prices and have had sufficient income to not only make the payments but also provide a positive cash flow.

Condotels are resort hotels and major hotel operators, such as Outrigger Hotel & Resorts and Marriott have developed and operate condotel properties. Some developments limit the time that the owners can use their unit so the hotel operation has the room for rent. The developer gets the investment plus profit from the sale of the units, and receives a risk-free management income from a generous portion of the rents.

XXII. Timeshares

Timeshares are exclusive occupancy rights in a vacation property for a set period of time each year.

While almost all timeshare developments are in resort communities, there have been two exceptions, the Manhattan Club in New York and a Marriott resort in Boston.

Timeshares may be a leasehold interest for a stated number of years or an ownership interest. With an ownership interest, the timeshare owner is generally a tenant in common with the other owners.

The timeshare concept originated in France in 1967.

The first U.S. timeshares were not marketed until 1970. Developers in the U.S. first used the timeshare concept to market unsold condominiums in desirable resort areas.

Investors were intrigued by the timeshare markup. For example, a unit purchased or built for a cost of $100,000 might be sold as 50 one-week periods at average sale prices ranging from $8,000 to $12,000. This means a gross return per unit from $400,000 to $600,000. (Most timeshare operators keep two weeks free for renovation.)

A timeshare might require 50 separate sales; therefore commissions and marketing costs in many cases exceed 50% of the gross sales price.

Some timeshare developers hire private marketing firms to bring in potential buyers at a price "by the head," maybe $100 per person, for each prospective buyer who will attend a sales presentation.

Timeshare developers frequently offer free gifts such as luggage, weekend vacations, televisions, or a Calloway golf club for persons who will attend seminars. Timeshare salespersons are often masters of persuasion and high pressure tactics.

High marketing costs and great profit potential have contributed to many timeshare operators using hard-sell tactics, where buyers actually felt coerced into buying.

This has led to restrictions on timeshare sales. In several states, buyers have a right to rescind their timeshare contracts within a set period of time after signing a purchase contract.

Today, many timeshares are sold based on the owners' ability to trade weeks, often at exotic locations.

Large timeshare operators either handle the trading themselves or belong to a group where unused weeks can be traded on a worldwide basis. Trades are restricted to similarly valued weeks and/or units.

Timeshares are NOT to be regarded as sound investments.

They are simply the purchase of a vacation lifestyle. The small dollar value of one or two-week timeshares makes it difficult for owners to find brokers willing to actively pursue selling a timeshare. Resold timeshare units are generally at a significantly lower price than the original cost. In most cases, an owner who is able to recoup 50 percent of the cost would be regarded as extremely fortunate.

Several firms list timeshares nationwide. Only 10 to 12 percent of the "for sale inventory" are estimated sold each year. A survey by Resort Property Owners Association (timeshare owners' group) revealed 38 percent of the approximate 1.3 million timeshares in the nation are for sale.

www.timesharevalues.com sells timeshares for owners through an Internet auction.

A number of timeshare developers have sold quarter ownership, giving each owner three months of occupancy each year (one month during each of three periods). This concept has worked out well in the Palm Desert, California area. The concept was well received by buyers, and expensive giveaways were not necessary to bring in prospective buyers. The developer was able to market $100,000 range units for approximately $39,000, a one quarter ownership. Marketing time was reduced to several months rather than the several years required for many weekly sale projects. The quarter concept appears to make sense to both developers and buyers. So far, quarter ownership has proven to be more marketable on the resale market without the large discounts required of weekly timeshare periods. Major hotels such as Four Seasons, Disney, Hilton, Westin, Hyatt, and Marriott have all gone into the timeshare market. The entry of these firms will hopefully add respectability to a tarnished industry.

XXIII. Marina Living

Our recent economic boom has resulted in people being able to fulfill dreams by buying a yacht. Many of these are used for weekend homes but some people live on their boats year round. While it might seem like low cost living, this is not the case. Besides the costly maintenance generally required, the cost to berth a boat has skyrocketed. Marinas that allow living on board charge a premium fee. Living aboard is fairly common even where it is not allowed.

A factor in high berthing fees is the fact that environmental concerns have slowed the development of new marinas. In many areas of Florida, concern with maritime habitat (in particular the manatee) has virtually stopped marina construction.

Even when boat owners have their own dock, if they want dockage overnight for a cruise, they must pay dearly. The Nantucket boat basin now charges $200 a night dockage for a berth that would have cost $15 or $20 about 20 years ago.

The shortage of docking facilities has led to the development of luxury condominiums that includes a dock with the unit. In some cases, the condominium does not even include the house. The owner simply buys his or her dock space and the condominium association manages the marina. Investors have successfully purchased marinas for condominium conversion possibilities. In some cases, most of the units were sold to the wealthy boat owners renting the slips. They were faced with buying or having no place to dock their boats.

Living Abroad magazine sells the lifestyle of boat life and discusses its problems (**www.livingaboard.com**).

XXIV. CHAPTER SUMMARY

Nontraditional housing includes unconventional construction methods; types of housing, non-family living arrangements, and special need housing. Nontraditional housing has evolved from both higher land and conventional construction costs, and special needs.

Manufactured homes (no longer called mobile homes) are homes built to HUD Code standards and transported to a site on their own chassis. They are placed on rental sites in parks or on an owner's lot. Once sited, manufactured homes are seldom relocated for use as housing. The advantage of manufactured housing is primarily the cost savings made possible by factory construction. Primary purchasers of manufactured homes are young families and retirees.

Modular homes differ from manufactured homes in that they are not built to the HUD Code. They are delivered by truck to a site, generally the owner's. Modular homes enjoy the same economic advantages of manufactured homes.

Prefabricated homes are panelized homes in which the segments are factory built for economy, but assembled on-site.

Precut or **kit homes** are primarily sold for construction by the buyer. One problem has been the reluctance of lenders to make loans based on a borrower's ability to properly complete the home.

Shell homes, where the buyer is responsible for all interior finishing as well as the basic systems, allow the owner to build his or her own home at a reasonable cost. Shell homes are primarily sold in rural or vacation areas. The disadvantage of shell homes is similar to precut homes in that lenders are often unwilling to make a loan where the owner is finishing the work.

Accessory dwelling units could help to fill a housing need. They allow greater density and can be built at a reasonable cost since the land is already owned.

ECHO housing units are accessory units used primarily for elderly family members.

Multigenerational housing, **co-housing**, and **group homes** all have aspects of sharing space.

Loft apartments and **condominiums** have become sought-after housing, making the conversion of commercial and industrial space to residential use economically feasible.

In many areas, additional low-cost housing would be possible by adding a **second story** to single-story commercial structures. While this use is cost effective, problems have been both lender hesitancy to finance this unorthodox use and planning commission reluctance to allow residential use in commercial areas.

Unrelated persons and families often share homes and apartments for purely economic reasons. Senior citizens often share housing to maintain independent living, as well as economic considerations.

Due to the reluctance of families to take in lodgers, as well as the virtual disappearance of rooming houses in many areas, low income singles and couples have difficulty in locating housing. Some older hotels have been profitably converted to permanent residency, but the need for **single room occupancy** has not been met. To meet this need, private developers would require some sort of economic incentive.

We have a new class of "homeless on wheels," those who live permanently in **recreational vehicles**. Many of these people are retirees who live in their recreational vehicles for economic reasons.

Homeowners are reluctant to rent unused rooms, except in college areas.

While most retirees remain in their home communities, many relocate, primarily to smaller communities offering clean air and safety. Because a great many retirees are affluent, communities are being developed to tap into this retirement market. Large **retirement communities** sell a way of life as well as housing.

With the increase in senior citizens (over 75), we are experiencing a growth in **assisted living** and in **life care facilities**. These facilities offer housing, some degree of maid service, transportation and meal options. Some facilities include guaranteed nursing home care as part of their fees. Life care facilities might require a large initial fee (which may be partially or fully refunded to the buyer's estate upon their death), as well as monthly fees.

With six percent of households owning vacation homes, this is a significant market area. **Vacation homes** are often purchased based on hasty, emotional decisions, which result in a wider price range for vacation homes than for primary residences. Lender requirements are more stringent for vacation homes than for primary housing because lenders feel values are more likely to drop in recessionary periods.

Timeshares are a type of vacation home in which a buyer holds a fractionalized ownership (or lease interest) with exclusive occupancy rights for a stated period of time. A problem for developers has been the high marketing cost of selling 50 one-week periods for each unit. Buyers have difficulty in reselling their units. Some timeshares now sell one quarter ownership shares, which reduce sale costs and allow a lower markup.

In the past, abusive sales tactics have hurt the timeshare concept image. Several major firms now entering timeshare development should help the image of both the concept and the industry.

Some people live on boats and there has been an increased demand for **marina space**.

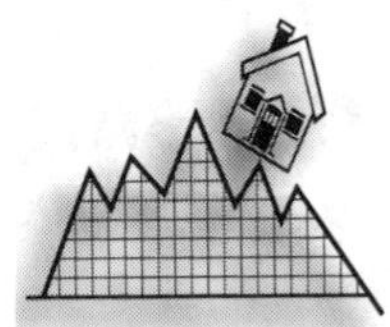

XXV. GLOSSARY OF KEY TERMS

Accessory Dwelling Unit (ADU) – A unit built on a lot already having a single-family home.

Assisted Living Unit – Apartment unit with 24-hour assistance available. Meals are included or optional.

Co-housing – A Danish concept of a central community living building with separate buildings for each family.

Condotel – Hotel where rooms have been sold as units.

Group Homes – Supervised homes for a group of at-risk persons having similar problems.

Life Care Facility – Specialized developments for the care of dependent seniors. They are of two types; prepaid nursing care guaranteed for life and those excluding nursing care.

Loft – Areas that were once factories or storage areas. Lofts are often referred to as artist's lofts. The landlord partitions the space into large, high-ceiling rooms with exposed plumbing and ducts. The simplest of bath and kitchen facilities are provided.

Manufactured Home – A factory built house constructed to the HUD Code.

Modular Home – A factory built house constructed on a wooden floor system and delivered on trucks in either pre-assembled form or in units put together on-site.

Multigenerational Housing – Homes that house extended families.

Precut Home – A kit that includes all materials and directions to build a house. The buyer assembles the home.

Prefabricated Home – "Panelized" housing components built in factories and assembled on-site.

Shared Housing – Single people or families sharing living space, often based on economic need.

Shell Home – A home with the exterior generally completed (windows, siding, and roofing) and set on a foundation. The buyer completes the interior work (including plumbing, electrical, and heating).

Single Room Occupancy – Hotel type rooms rented for permanent occupancy.

Stick Built – A term that refers to conventionally built housing fabricated primarily with on-site labor.

Timeshare – Exclusive occupancy rights in a vacation property for a set period of time each year.

Woodall Rating System – Pertains to manufactured home parks. Varies from one star to five stars, with five stars the most desirable park.

XXVI. CLASS DISCUSSION TOPICS

1. Identify several area manufactured home parks you have visited. Who would each of the parks appeal to?

2. Identify any manufactured home parks in your area where lots are for sale. What are the park amenities, lot sizes, and prices?

3. Identify prefabricated and precut kit home dealers and/or manufacturers in your area.

4. Identify shell homes advertised in your area.

5. Identify structures in your community where loft style housing could be developed.

6. Assuming zoning would permit, where in the community could apartments be placed above one-story commercial property? Would it be a good idea?

7. Identify group and shared housing situations within your community. What are the reasons for sharing?

8. What single-room housing is available in your community? Is there an unfulfilled need?

9. Are there people living permanently in recreational vehicles in your area?

10. Identify retirement housing projects within your area. Do they differ from other housing developments? If so, how?

11. Does your community have any life care facilities? If so, what are the costs? Is nursing home care included?

12. Do you own or desire to own a vacation home? If yes, where? Why?

13. Have you ever visited a timeshare development? If yes, describe the marketing. Are there any timeshares in your area? If so, what time period is being sold? What are the prices?

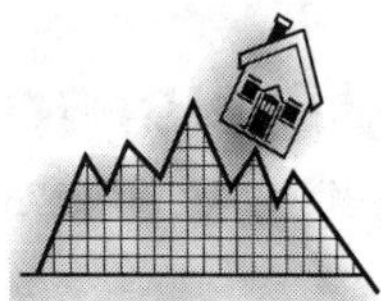

XXVII. CHAPTER 10 QUIZ

1. The term "stick built" refers to:
    a. flimsy construction.
    b. housing built at the site.
    c. manufactured homes.
    d. factory built housing.

2. The term that HUD Code home manufacturers prefer their product to be called is:
    a. stick built housing.
    b. conventional housing.
    c. prefabricated homes.
    d. manufactured homes.

3. The term "modular homes" refers to homes:
    a. built to HUD Code.
    b. factory built homes transported on trucks.
    c. conventionally built using all standard components.
    d. that are all identical.

4. An accessory dwelling unit would be:
    a. a room rented in a home.
    b. a duplex.
    c. an additional unit built on land already containing a home.
    d. shared housing.

5. All of the following are true regarding retirement communities, except:
    a. residents tend to be white.
    b. residents tend to be from middle and upper income class.
    c. residents buy a way of life as well as housing.
    d. they are aimed at seniors with serious physical problems.

6. Vacation homes differ from primary housing because:
    a. interest payments on second homes are not tax deductible.
    b. vacation home prices do not react as much as primary home prices to economic swings.
    c. lender requirements for vacation home financing tends to be tighter than for primary residences.
    d. location is not as important a factor for vacation homes as it is for primary housing.

7. The following are true statements regarding timeshares, except:
   a. timeshares are regarded as excellent investments.
   b. the price of all timeshare weeks greatly exceeds the unit value.
   c. timeshare developers have high marketing costs.
   d. timeshares are often sold based on the ability to trade weeks.

8. Housing where residents are required to pay an upfront fee that exceeds several years' rent and also pay rent would most likely be:
   a. single room occupancy.
   b. a life care facility.
   c. a timeshare.
   d. modular housing.

9. Privacy as well as fear are reasons many people do not want to rent:
   a. their vacant apartment.
   b. a vacation home.
   c. their timeshare unit.
   d. a spare room in their home.

10. In the late 1800s, and in the early 1900s, Sears Roebuck & Company sold homes. These homes were:
   a. manufactured homes.
   b. modular homes.
   c. precut homes.
   d. loft homes.

ANSWERS: 1. b; 2. d; 3. b; 4. c; 5. d; 6. c; 7. a; 8. b; 9. d; 10. c

LEARNING OBJECTIVES

As the romantic ideal of the individual owned traditional family farm fades into national memory and "big farm" ownership increases, we are reminded that the trends of farmland real estate are a mirror of American history.

Farmland has undergone volatile shifts in the real estate marketplace in the past few decades. A 245 percent increase in farmland prices from 1970 to 1980 led to increased production, which eventually led to surpluses and sharply reduced agricultural prices. The fall in profits led to an excess of farms on the market and a significant drop in farmland prices. Farming of today has left behind the traditional small family farm in favor of technologically advanced large family enterprises, partnerships, or corporate agribusiness ventures. The trend toward large farm management is expected to continue, while smaller farmland parcels are sold for hobby, retirement farming, or recreational use.

In this chapter you will learn about the factors determining farmland value.

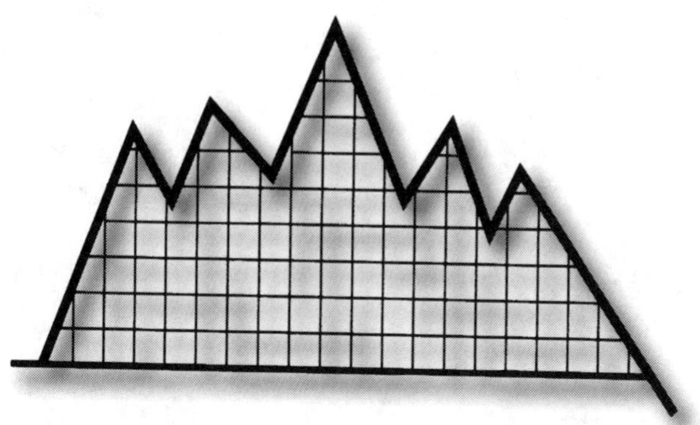

Chapter 11
Farms and Land

I. Farmland in the United States

As described by the U.S. Department of Agriculture (USDA), a ***FARM*** *is an enterprise having agricultural income of $1,000 or more.* The definition of a farm does not include farms having an income less than $1,000. Ironically, it does include some wasteland and forests with income just over $1,000. To give some perspective to this amount of acreage, it is estimated that all cities and suburbs occupy only 26 million acres in the United States.

In 2002, the United States had 936 million acres in production (almost one billion acres). This is 41 percent of the total U.S. land area of 2,263 million acres

Some 30 percent of all farms produce 90 percent of all U.S. crops and livestock. Only 5 percent of all farms sell $250,000 or more of agricultural produce each year.

According to the U. S. Department of Agriculture, the number of farms in the U.S. declined from 7 million in 1935 to 2,176,860 in 2003. Only 400,000 of these remaining farms are full-time farms where the household is not dependent on nonfarm income. Some 90 percent of rural workers hold nonfarm jobs, as farming accounts for only 7.6 percent of rural employment.

CHAPTER 11 OUTLINE

While the number of farms in the United States has been decreasing, the number of large farms with gross incomes exceeding $1 million has increased. About 112,000 large farms (equivalent to the number of farms in Minnesota) produce half the nation's food and fiber.

U.S FARM SIZE	% OF U.S. FARMS
99 acres or less	51%
100-499 acres	33.1%
500-999 acres	7.6%
1,000-1,999 acres	4.7%
2,000 acres or more	3.3%

Economics of scale make larger farms more productive in terms of product per acre as well as production costs. Large farms keep food prices low for consumers.

The average size farm in the United States is 500 acres. This is NOT a median size farm, which would be much smaller.

According to the U.S. Department of Agriculture, agriculture makes up over 15 percent of our gross national product and generates $1 trillion per year in economic activity. One in six Americans works in some aspect of the food and fiber economy while every American benefits from U.S. agriculture.

Figure 11-1 shows the leading agricultural states.

Figure 11-1

Leading Agricultural States

1. California
2. Texas
3. Iowa
4. Nebraska
5. Kansas
6. Illinois
7. Minnesota
8. North Carolina
9. Florida
10. Wisconsin
11. Indiana

II. The Farmland Real Estate Market

The farmland real estate market is a local market with the excess of farmland purchases made by buyers from outside the area.

When the farmland prices in any area fall low enough, farmers from other areas will enter the market. When farm prices in an area rise above those of other areas, potential farmers will leave the area.

Farm catalogs have made national price information readily available to farmers and broadened the farm market. The Internet is now the primary source of farm price information. A potential buyer can now compare farms from a worldwide perspective.

Many local, state, and regional Internet sites are available for farm price information. **www.landandfarm.com** is the largest listing service for farms, timberland, and rural properties. Farms are even being listed for sale on **e-bay**.

A great deal of transferred (sold) farmland is never placed on the market.

Farms are often given or sold to family members or sold to friends or neighbors. Sales to family members are often at prices and terms below those offered in the marketplace.

Farmland prices are affected by market location, transportation and development, available water quantity and quality, soil quality, topography, structures, financing, the market forces of supply and demand, and even the shape of the parcel (rectangular, relatively flat parcels lend themselves to efficient farming). The possibility of uses, other than agriculture, can have a significant effect on value.

While the majority of farms with incomes over $100,000 are owned by farmers, investors, hobby farmers and developers also purchase farms. Non-farmers (people who do not rely on farming income) own approximately 40 percent of farmland.

Some Amish farm communities have a problem in that they are too quaint. City people want to live in these idyllic communities and have pushed farm prices up to the point where Amish families have not been able to afford to buy farms for their children. They have either had to leave farming for other activities or seek other communities. While Thomas Wolfe wrote, "you can never go home again," every year tens of thousands of Americans try to do just that. They buy a home with a few acres trying to recapture the idyllic life of long ago.

More than 300 Amish moved from Eastern Pennsylvania to the area around Fennimore, Wisconsin, one of many communities attracting Amish farmers. They are purchasing Wisconsin farms for approximately $1,800 per acre compared to Pennsylvania prices that have risen to $10,000 to $15,000 per acre in Lancaster County, Pennsylvania. Pennsylvania farms are being driven up in price by wealthy "gentlemen farmers." With 42 Amish settlements, Wisconsin now ranks second in the nation behind Pennsylvania, which has 48 settlements.

A. RATE OF FARM TRANSFERS

Farm sales declined from an estimated 280,000 in 1950 to 83,000 in 1991. Much of the decline was due to the reduction in the total number of farms.

Normally, no more than five percent of farmland is on the market at any one time.

Not all farmers who sell intend to leave farming. Many have sold part of their land to reduce debt. Frequently, the farmer then rents the same land or a similarly sized parcel.

When adjoining property is developed, farmers seem more inclined to place their property on the market, even though they may have previously rejected offers to purchase.

When nearby development comes too close, farmers realize the land cannot economically remain in farm use or it becomes too valuable to keep. When farmers believe their land will be urbanized they will resist making long-term capital improvements. This hastens the decisions to sell out to speculators or developers.

B. LARGER FARMS (Mega Farms)

The U.S. Department of Agriculture estimates that approximately 60 percent of national farm purchases are for the purpose of farm enlargement.

Ralph Nader reported that a total of 29 firms owned 21 percent of California crop land and 75 firms owned another 27 percent. The high cost of irrigation coupled with large, level land expanses has encouraged California's huge corporate (mega) farms. **CORPORATE MEGA FARMS** *are huge farms owned by corporations with the objective being to maximize profit*. Family-held corporate farms average 969 acres while non-family corporate farms average 1,647 acres.

The largest corporate farms are in cattle and poultry production. Animals lend themselves more to industrial type management than crop production. An example of a large operation is Smithfield Foods with 695,000 sows.

Corporate farming has duplicated corporate America in that the larger farm corporations are getting larger by buying out competitors. Corporate farms are now

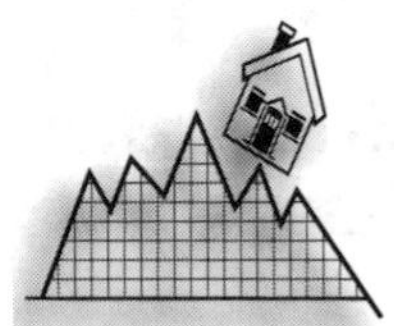

heading for direct marketing. An example is Tyson, which raises and markets chickens. Smaller farms use marketing cooperatives to be able to keep prices at profitable levels.

Some direct marketers, such as Simplot and ADM, contract with farmers to produce crops or cattle that they process and market. While they keep small farmers in business, the farmers in reality are hiring out their land and labor.

Price support systems, new technology, relatively low-cost land, tax advantages of depreciation, and economies of scale also encouraged large corporate farms starting in the 1950s.

Non-farm corporations also became interested in farming. Companies such as Purex, Tenneco, and Ralston Purina entered farming. While some non-farm corporations were successful, others, like Purex, left farming after suffering losses. Poor management was the reason cited most often by non-farm corporations for their problems. The companies were unable to react to the changing farm market with their non-farm-oriented corporate structure. It is doubtful that many more non-farm corporations will enter farming, considering the experiences of Purex and others. An exception to the failure of non-farm corporations is Tenneco, which has been very successful.

Farming is a specialized industry; outside corporations that purchase farms often find it difficult to adjust profitably to agribusiness because of an ill-suited and inflexible business plan.

C. SMALLER FARMS

There is a huge demand for rural land with a home and a few acres for retirement, hobby, or self-sufficiency farming. Seldom do such parcels lend themselves to profitable production agriculture.

Breaking large farms into 40, 20 or even 10-acre parcels has the economic advantage of opening sales to a greater number of buyers, which in turn results in a higher price per acre.

Soil fertility is NOT as important a consideration for hobby farms as it is for commercial farming.

Hobby farms are sold more as a way of life than for what they can produce. In many areas, the beauty of nature, such as great vistas, has become a greater determinant of value than productivity.

Because retirement or hobby farm owners are seldom commercially motivated, they do not achieve anywhere close to maximum production. Owners are more likely to have a small orchard, a few steers, and a small garden rather than a single-crop farm.

When land is broken into small farming units, land productivity is drastically reduced, which has almost the same effect as the land being taken out of production.

Some small parcels are used for highly intensive agricultural enterprises (ie. greenhouses for flower production, specialty crops like ginseng, as well as aquaculture) that can very profitable.

What is important to many small farm owners is the psychic income that comes from pride of ownership and self-sufficiency. The joy of homemade bread baked fresh from wheat sown and harvested by the farmer's own hands is often greater than a cash return on their investment.

D. THE FAMILY FARM

The ideal of the traditional family farm is rapidly becoming more of a nostalgic myth than reality.

The ***FAMILY FARM*** *is the traditionally family owned and operated farm passed on from one generation to the next.* The agricultural revolution of the 1920s marked the decline of this tradition, with better equipment (such as large tractors), lower-cost fertilizers, and higher yielding crop varieties. These factors, as well as a shift toward single crop farming, dramatically reduced labor hours per acre and thus the need for large families.

The trend toward greater efficiency in food production continues to this day. Genetic engineering will significantly affect farm production in the future despite present resistance. Besides increasing production per acre and more meat per animal in a shorter time, we should see crops and animals that are more resistant to disease.

At the present time, farm animals are being given hormones to increase production. They are given antibiotics to prevent disease. While these practices are accepted here, European nations will not import the meat from these animals because of fear of possible long-term health dangers.

The decline in the number of people living and working on farms should have resulted in the decline of the political influence of farmers. Only two percent of Americans are really farmers. Despite their relatively small numbers, the nations politicians have been reluctant to do away with farm subsidies. While subsidies were originally begun to aid the small family farmers, most of the government money for subsidies actually goes to the large farms.

The capital requirements of land and equipment have made entry into farming difficult. In fact, today many younger farmers lease rather than buy their land. Since a farm's value is based on its production rather than its physical size, the modern farm does have advantages over the traditional family farm, which relies on a fixed amount of land and the size of the family. The traditional family farm is not an efficient economic unit because labor and land are fixed factors. Professional farmers will hire more workers and lease more land if it is profitable. Traditional farms make only adjustments relative to production—what crops should be planted.

A number of states have passed anti-corporate farm legislation that generally places restrictions on farming and landholding activities of non-family corporations. These laws were passed to maintain family farming. Economically, these laws are counter productive. A free market would allow better utilization of our resources.

With the decline in traditional family-owned farms, there has been growth in investor professional farm management. Farmers National Company manages 3,600 farms across the country (**www.farmersnational.com**).

Despite the decline, the family farm is not dead. Today's family farms are modern operations with capital investment that is often well over $2 million. The farms are also much larger than they were several generations ago.

Of the farms that have more than one operator, one-quarter of them are operated by multigenerational operators. This will probably ensure the continuation of the family farm.

III. Changes in Agricultural Use

Higher land costs have caused many farmers to change to more profitable crops to justify the investment.

In areas of high land costs, farmers have switched to more intensified uses of the land. For example, vegetables and fruits have replaced grains and grasses.

Higher yields, due to new hybrid varieties of crops, as well as fertilizers and irrigation, have also reduced the amount of land required.

Changes in our nation's eating habits are affecting land use.

Lowered red meat consumption means less land necessary for grazing or feed crops. Cattle, while not labor intensive, require a great deal of land. The demand for poultry is up, but it requires fewer land resources.

The health food movement toward fish coupled with a declining fisheries industry has resulted in the growth of aquaculture. While little land is required, except for feed, it has been extremely successful. Trout, salmon, catfish, striped bass, etc., are being raised with economic success.

A. SUBSIDIZED PRODUCTION AND TRADE BARRIERS

Farming is the most subsidized business in the United States, as well as in the rest of the world.

In 1999, the U.S. support to farmers totaled $54 billion, which was 24 percent of gross farm revenues.

Subsidies were started in the depression with a noble purpose, to preserve the small farm by helping them in difficult times, but have become a way of life. Subsidies have been ineffective at best and today result in the bulk of federal aid going to large million dollar or larger farms. In recent times, the stated purpose of subsidies was, "to encourage production." It has actually served to encourage over-production. Subsidies have altered the free market with part of the production costs transferred to the government. George W. Bush has indicated that the solution to the farm problem is not in subsidies, but in opening foreign markets.

While the U.S. government has taken the position for years that there should be a global reduction in nations supporting farm production, the total U.S. dollar support has actually been increasing.

Farming subsidies are welfare payments for the rich.

The case against subsidies is strong in that the means doesn't appear to lead to the desired end. The result of farm subsidies has been to encourage overproduction of products and to depress prices.

The top 10 percent of farm subsidy recipients received 65 percent of all farms subsidies. The bottom 80 percent of subsidy recipients receive only 19 percent of federal subsidies. There were 78 farms in 2002 that received over $1 million in federal subsidies. These large subsidy programs have helped and encouraged large corporate farms to become even larger.

58 percent of farms receive no federal subsidies.

While originally intended to help poor depression era farms, some of the recipients of subsidies in 2002 were David Rockefeller, Ted Turner, and Kenneth Lay. Twelve

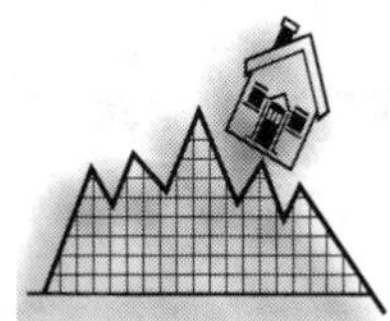

Fortune 500 companies received subsidies because of their farming subsidiaries. John Hancock Mutual Life Insurance was the recipient of $2.3 million in agriculture subsidies.

Subsidies go primarily to just a few crops. Corn, rice, cotton, wheat, and soybean growers get 90 percent of agriculture subsidy dollars; growers of most other crops get nothing.

Getting rid of subsidies would undoubtedly hurt many thousands of farmers and many farms would cease to be family owned. The end of subsidies would also effect farmland prices. Prices would drop for farms that can only be sustained with government aid.

Proponents of subsidies point out that subsidies and price supports keep our production high and protect America against food shortages.

The World Trade Organization wants to eliminate all agricultural subsidies. If we eliminate them, the reason will more likely be budgetary in nature rather than meeting the goals of the WTO.

The purpose of trade barriers and tariffs is to protect our agricultural industry from foreign competition. It isn't just the U.S.; other countries have barriers to the impact of U.S. Agricultural products. The U.S. Tariff on food coming into the country averages 12 percent, but world wide, food tariffs average 62 percent.

Agricultural subsidies accomplish the same results as tariffs in that they give the domestic product a competitive edge. Japan and the European Union subsidize agriculture far more than the United States. We actually have an agricultural trade deficit with Europe because of tariffs and subsidies.

Because of increased foreign agriculture production due to the adoption of modern methods, high production seeds, fertilizers, and insecticides, countries that were net food importers have now become exporters. The U.S. agricultural balance of trade is rapidly declining. In 2004, we had a positive balance of $9.6 billion with exports of $62.3 billion, and imports of $52.7 billion. In 2005, our surplus was estimated at just $1 billion based on an estimated $59 billion in exports and $58 billion in imports. Once a positive area in our balance of trade, we are expected to show a negative agricultural trade balance by 2006.

Much of our imports consist of off-season vegetables and fruits to meet consumer demand for fresh products. However, a significant portion is exotic and ethnic foods.

Besides foreign subsidies and tariffs that affect our ability to compete with our exports, American agriculture is faced with non-tariff barriers to trade. As an example, China requires high sanitary standards and agricultural quarantines which affect our ability to market our products. Europe blocks imports on genetically modified corn and soybeans, two of our major exports, although there is no clear scientific reason for these decisions.

B. PRODUCTION CYCLES

When prices are high for a crop, farmers tend to put more land into production. They are willing to pay higher prices for additional land. A shortage and high prices in one year would customarily be followed by a surplus and lower prices the next. This is not as true as it once was because farmers have more marketing opportunities now and they engage in more sophisticated techniques, such as hedging agricultural products on the commodities exchanges (can forward contract or sell on a storage contract).

There is a great deal of time between planting and harvest. The farmer plants with limited knowledge of what other farmers are planting. By the time the Department of Agriculture comes out with its estimates of acreage in various crops, the farmer is already committed to the crops he or she has planted. Overproduction often results in lower cash yields from the land and, therefore, more farmland offered for sale. The increase in sellers results in lower land prices.

When low market prices cause a farmer to have a disastrous year with a particular commodity, many will switch to different crops the next year.

This may result in lowered production and higher prices for a crop that was overproduced the year before. One of the biggest challenges to farming is the balancing of production and market factors.

Weather plays a part in production decisions. Several years of good weather can mean high production for a crop and prices will fall. Falling prices encourage farmers to switch crops or take land out of production. Conversely, bad weather can raise crop prices, which encourages greater production.

Orchards and grapevines create a special challenge due to the number of years required between planting and production. The problem intensifies when additional acreage comes into production long after a surplus situation has been realized. An advantage of grapevines and orchards is that they have special appeal to gentlemen farmers who will often pay more than the economic value of the land.

Growing export markets have created opportunities for farmers, but many nations protect their own farm industries with import restrictions.

MARGINAL LAND *is land where income and costs are a trade-off. It becomes* ***SUBMARGINAL LAND*** *when benefits will not cover production costs (variable cost).*

Marginal land will be taken out of production when there is a surplus and it cannot be economically farmed. It will be put back into production when there is a crop shortage that causes crop prices to rise. **Figure 11-2** illustrates the different classes of farmland available for use and the value each has per acre.

Rental land is more likely to be taken out of production than farmer-owned land.

If the market appears poor, farmers will not rent land. However, if they own the land they are more likely to farm it, even when the operation may be marginal. In this case, the farmer already has the fixed cost of ownership. If the farmer feels the crop income will exceed the variable costs associated with farming, the decision to farm becomes an economic decision. Often decisions to farm marginal land are made on the chance that adverse weather conditions in another part of the country will decrease the supply so that significant profit will be possible. The farmers in such cases are gambling on a possibility rather than a probability.

Taking land out of production to reduce surpluses and increase prices is only a temporary solution, because the land remains with us and can again be put into production.

If farming becomes economically viable again, the idled land will again be placed into production, and surplus could return if market demand has not increased proportionally.

C. GOVERNMENT ENCOURAGEMENT OF FARMING

Despite the dwindling political influence of farmers, the government encourages farming in numerous ways other than crop subsidies.

A call to the federal Agricultural Stabilization and Conservation Service can provide information as to what programs are available.

The ***FARMERS HOME ADMINISTRATION (FmHA)*** *makes and insures loans to farmers who are otherwise unable to obtain credit.*

FARMER MAC *is an organization created by Congress to provide a secondary market for qualifying agricultural real estate loans.*

A number of states provide for reduced property taxes on agriculture property.

The government has subsidized irrigation for farmers through various water projects.

Figure 11-2

Value of Different Types of Farmland

The value of agricultural land generally depends on the annual value of crops that can be produced in that type of soil. The following diagram illustrates what types of land use bring the most money per acre. Other factors affect value, like long-term soil quality and location, but are not considered here. Commercial and industrial land generally commands the highest dollar per acre, while wetlands and wasteland bring the lowest price per acre. This is a useful tool to see the relative value for all different types of land uses. But remember, it is just a rule of thumb.

The estimated market value of a specific property should be made by an appraiser with the necessary education and back ground, who does an in depth analysis of that specific site.

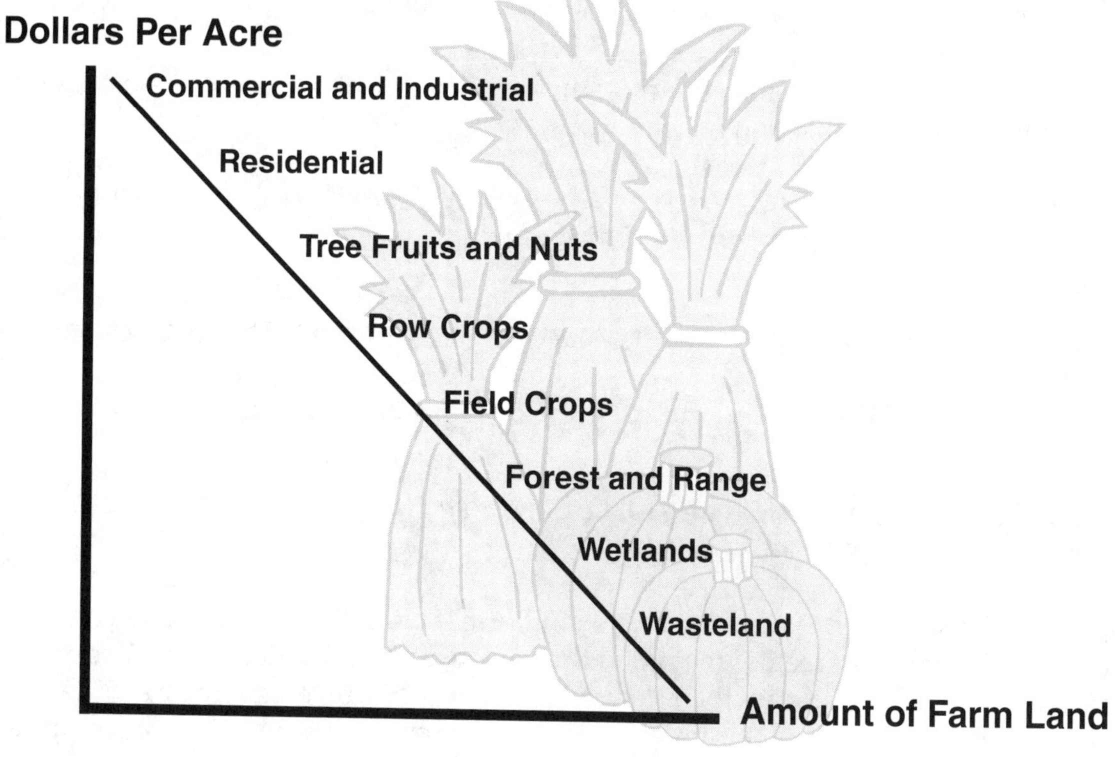

Dollars Per Acre
Commercial and Industrial
Residential
Tree Fruits and Nuts
Row Crops
Field Crops
Forest and Range
Wetlands
Wasteland
Amount of Farm Land

A special thanks to Stephanie Swenson Field, who helped with this chapter, she is a freelance writer for agriculture magazines.

Field & Associates, International
458 Bonnyvale Rd.
Brattleboro, Vermont 05301

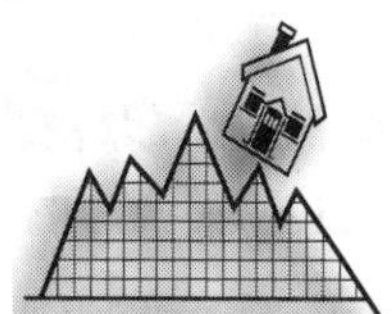

Without government and family help, high water costs would make it almost impossible for young people to enter farming. In order to keep the land in production, Oregon prohibited splitting farms into uneconomical farming sizes. State marketing boards as well as marketing restrictions and price supports help to keep agricultural prices high and aid farmers (see **Figure 11-3**).

Figure 11-3

State Farm Programs

A number of states have programs to aid their state agriculture.

California has several state "market order" programs to help increase the marketing of farm products. The following are examples of California market orders:

1. Oranges must be over a certain size or they cannot be sold in California.
2. Whole milk must be sold in California to processors for a set minimum price per gallon.
3. Raisins must be advertised (marketed); a portion of all California raisin sales must finance this marketing activity.

The California Raisin program "I heard it through the grapevine," was part of this television market order advertisement.

IV. The Farm Crisis of the '80s

Financial leveraging allowed farmers to use their farms as collateral in order to purchase more farmland.

During the mid-1970s, many farmers felt that land prices would continue to go in only one direction—up. There was a feeling that good times were ahead. Farmers were encouraged by lenders to use the equity in their farms to expand. Farm magazines extolled the progressive farmers who used their financial leverage to create personal farming empires. The result was that farm debt-to-asset ratios grew.

The demand for more farmland by both farmers and investors caused the price of farmland to rise by 245 percent between 1970 and 1980. (The rise in prices between 1950 and 1980 was over 900 percent.) Increased land value provided farmers with increased equity, making expansion by further borrowing relatively easy. Optimism about the future caused additional land to be placed into farm production. This increased production, coupled with the Russian grain embargo, resulted in surpluses, lower prices, and sharply reduced agricultural revenues (see **Figure 11-4**). At the same time, interest rates escalated. Many farmers had short-term or adjustable rate interest loans and their production could not justify paying rates that, in some cases, were over 20 percent.

Figure 11-4

Using Food as a Weapon

Former President Carter imposed a grain embargo against Russia as well as restricted U.S. athletes from participating in the 1980 Olympics. This action was in retaliation for Russia's action in invading Afghanistan. The embargo devastated U.S. grain producers. Russia made up for the shortfall in grain by importing grain from Australia, Canada, and South America. The long-term results have been that U.S. farmers and farm lenders were hurt and foreign growers were encouraged to compete in the world grain market. Besides, U.S. athletes were denied a chance to compete. It is apparent that we can punish ourselves more than others when we attempt to use a food as a weapon.

In California, avocado investments were touted in the '70s and early '80s as "green gold," with prices of $25,000 an acre common.

Due to an oversupply of avocados, however, foreclosure sales in 1986 were in the $5,000 to $6,000 per acre range.

Many farmers had to sell part of their land to pay debts. All of these factors resulted in a rapid decline in farmland values, creating a buyers' market.

Whether selling voluntarily or being foreclosed, the effect of a great many farms being placed on the market during a time when farm commodity prices were down caused farm prices to fall more drastically.

Speculators, who had helped bid up the value of farmland, were some of the first to try to unload their land holdings.

The drop in land values hurt two other groups: farmers who tried to expand on credit, and younger farmers who were financially leveraged and had heavy debt-to-asset ratios.

With adjustments for inflation, the average drop in farmland value from 1981 to 1986 was 50 percent. In some areas, the unadjusted drop in farmland value was over 50 percent. In 1985, farmland values fell an average of 12 percent.

The average farmland price per acre in California in 1981 was $1,732. In 1986 it had declined to $1,517. Thus, a 9 percent decline (when adjusted for inflation) was equivalent to an actual drop of 31 percent. In order to increase with inflation, the value of California farmland would have had to increase to $2,269 per acre. Over the same period, the actual drop in national farmland prices amounted to 56 percent.

In 1988, prices of farmland in many areas of the nation showed the first evidence of increase in over six years, according to the U.S. Department of Agriculture. Since that time California farmland values have steadily increased.

Foreclosing lenders had a huge stock of farms. Many were being held in the hope that values would increase.

As of September 30, 1986, the Federal Farm Credit System and the Farm Home Administration held a combined 3.4 million acres of farmland. Commercial banks and insurance companies were believed to have held at least another 1.8 million acres. The sale of this lender inventory further depressed farm prices.

Over 11 percent of farm loans were with insurance companies. In 1985, over 15 percent of insurance company farm mortgages were in a delinquent status. Because of market conditions, many insurance companies delayed foreclosure if it was felt the loan might attain a performing status again.

The insurance companies with the largest inventory of foreclosed farms were Metropolitan, Prudential, Travelers, John Hancock, and MONY. These companies, though not by choice, became the nation's largest farmers. Metropolitan, Prudential, and MONY all purchased farm management firms to handle their inventories. Metropolitan purchased Farmer's National (Omaha), which was managing 4,000 farms.

These insurance company foreclosures primarily involved larger farms. Most insurance company farm loans were for at least $250,000.

Outside management companies rented many farms that were too small to support professional management. About 40 percent of Metropolitan foreclosures were rented to the original owners. Metropolitan, in many cases, sold back the farms to the original owners who had become tenants. An advantage of such a rental arrangement was that the farm would likely be well maintained.

In order to dispose of farmland, Farm Credit Services of St. Paul, Minnesota, offered a money back-guarantee. A buyer could return farmland by an agreed-upon date and get all principal payments returned. (This was actually little more than the down payment, since most of the mortgage payments cover the interest, which was not refundable).

The purchasers at foreclosure sales generally were not speculators who had been scared from the market, but other farmers who were in a good cash position and able to take advantage of distressed sale prices.

The severe drop in farmland values seriously affected farm area banks.

According to the First National Bank of Chicago, of the 90 banks that failed in the first half of 1986, 43 were classified as farm banks.

The farm problem did not affect all farmers. A great many farmers resisted easy credit.

30 percent of U.S. farms were debt-free at that time.

A. FOREIGN FARM INVESTMENT

In the mid 1970s, there was a fear among many that foreign nationals would end up owning all United States farmland. Many Dutch and German investors purchased farms in the Midwest. French and Italian buyers purchased in California. Despite worry about Arab control of American food production, the citizens of OPEC countries have made only minimal land purchases in the United States.

In 1998, Japan signed the Beef Market Access Agreement with the U.S. and Australia. Since then, several Japanese firms have purchased U.S. ranch property as well as meat packing facilities to export beef to Japan. In this way, Japanese imports from the U.S. will be largely Japan shipping to Japan.

Foreign purchases were generally made as long-term investments to hedge against inflation and were usually quality farms with professional management.

Foreign nationals were attracted by American political stability and by U.S. farm prices, which appeared to be a bargain compared to European land prices. Many of these foreign purchasers paid top dollar, coming in at, or close to, the market peak in the late '70s. These additional buyers probably helped to escalate farm prices.

With the decrease in farm income in the early '80s, as well as a period of high interest rates and unfavorable exchange rates caused by the strength of the dollar, foreign interest in purchase of U.S. farmland all but disappeared by 1982. It is estimated that less than one percent of farmland is currently foreign-owned, with Canada having the greatest ownership.

B. SPECULATORS AND THE MARKET

Land with potential urban development might sell for several times the farmland prices, even when urban development is not assured within the near future.

The average cost of New Jersey farmland is the highest for any state because investors envision future development for virtually the entire state. Open land in California somewhat close to populated areas has been increasing in prices because of urban sprawl.

Former capital gains benefits, as well as the ability to rapidly depreciate improvements and orchards, helped to make farms attractive to investors. Investors played a major role in fueling the farmland inflation of the '70s. Many purchased and sold to each other on the theory that prices had to go higher.

Except for a few "contrarians" (investors who run contrary to prevailing views), investors generally left the farm market after the tumble in land prices in the early '80s. There has been some resurgence of investor interest, however, primarily from professionals who have a farm background.

V. Modern Threats to Agriculture

A. URBAN THREATS TO CALIFORNIA AGRICULTURE

Santa Clara Valley, California once had 100,000 acres of orchards.

There are probably only 10,000 acres remaining. The loss has been caused by urban sprawl. Both housing and agriculture compete for the large, fertile valleys.

Agricultural land lost to urbanization is usually the most productive land because cities were sited in coastal and inland river valleys having deep fertile soil and an abundance of water. Besides being ideal sites for communities, they were the most desirable agricultural locations.

While land lost by sprawl to urbanization would at first appear to be a significant threat to agriculture, it should be placed in the proper perspective. Over three-fourths of our states have more than 90 percent of their land in rural areas as farms, forests, and wildlife areas. Less than 5 percent of the total land area of the nation is developed. Only one-fourth of the loss of farmland since 1945 is attributable to urbanization.

In California, the rate of withdrawal of prime crop land from agricultural use has been between 60,000 and 150,000 acres per year.

Even though California is one of the most urban of all states, based on the percentage of residents living in its cities, it leads the nation in agricultural production. Irrigation was instrumental in making California our most productive agricultural state.

Contamination from natural and man-made sources has threatened a great deal of farmland. Elevated salt levels in some irrigated areas have had a negative effect on land values. Air pollution has reduced some crop yields.

The University of California has discovered that, due to air pollution, citrus yields in some areas have declined 50 percent over the last four decades.

The consumer fear of contaminated crops has resulted in the growth of organic agriculture where chemical fertilizers and pesticides are not used. Organic farms also shun genetically altered crops.

B. PREMATURE SUBDIVISION

Premature subdivision has taken a great deal of farmland out of production before it is fully developed.

In California, Arizona, Nevada, New Mexico, and Florida, developers subdivided thousands of acres for sale to individual investors. They often used high pressure sales tactics and set sales prices at over 10 times the agricultural value of the land.

In the Antelope Valley of California, miles of alfalfa fields were divided into 2½-acre parcels and sold as investments. The land was effectively taken out of agriculture because of the multiple ownership.

C. IMMIGRANTS AND FARM VALUE

Though U.S. policy prohibits illegal immigration, a great deal of our agricultural industry is based on alien workers. Much of farming is still labor-intensive, requiring row crop workers, citrus pickers and grape pruners and pickers. Legal and illegal immigrants fill the majority of these positions. Each worker is supposed to have a green immigration card to work in the United States.

Estimates are that 60 to 70 percent of California's agricultural workers are illegal aliens, although United Farm Workers claim these figures are grossly exaggerated. Placing criminal penalties on those who knowingly hire illegal aliens did not seriously affect labor-intensive farming. Some sociologists predict a great many farm workers will leave agriculture when they are granted legal status. Inability to find low cost domestic labor has led many farmers to establish Mexican and Central American farms, where labor costs are well below U. S. minimum wage level.

Loss of large numbers of workers would force U.S. farms to produce fewer labor-intensive crops and import many vegetables.

This could in turn have a significant negative effect on farmland values.

D. TAX REFORM AND FARMING

The restriction in our tax laws on tax shelter depreciation had a further negative effect on farm value.

Investors who formerly sought farms for depreciation and large tax shelters have migrated to other investments now, such as the stock market and residential housing.

A loss of high-income investors from the farm market helped push farm values down (due to a reduction in demand). Furthermore, the decreased tax rates reduced any incentive to farm at a loss.

VI. Land

A. FALLOW AND RAW LAND

***FALLOW LAND** is farmland that is idle and not used for crops or grazing for at least one season—sometimes more. **RAW LAND** is land that has never been developed for any purpose (never used for farming) or land that has been taken permanently out of production.* Fallow and raw land has no depreciation and no income, but property taxes must be paid on it. Therefore, holding fallow or raw land generally results in a negative cash flow.

To be an economic investment, the appreciation must exceed the cost of holding the property (interest and taxes), as well as provide a return on the purchaser's equity.

Because fallow and raw land are negative cash flow properties, owners of fallow and raw land have a much higher motivation to sell than owners of income-producing property.

B. RECREATION LAND

Shorter work weeks, longer vacations, earlier retirements, and more disposable income have combined, in recent years, to increase the demand for both developed and undeveloped recreational property. However, the demand has been primarily in wooded, water-related desert and mountain property, rarely in agricultural property.

Boise Cascade was the first major timber company to enter the recreational land development area.

Undeveloped land has typically been sold with low down payment seller financing.

Because of high sales costs, small recreational parcels are generally sold by developers at many times the per acre price of similar property in larger parcels. During the oil crisis of 1974, there was a slump in recreational land sales, but there has been a recovery. Our current high oil prices do not seem to have negatively effected the prices of recreational land.

Many recreational developments are aimed exclusively at campers and/or recreational vehicle owners. Some use cooperative, condominium, or timeshare concepts.

C. OIL LAND

Land with oil royalties, leases, or even oil possibilities were bid up in the '70s after the Arab oil boycott. Many analysts were predicting $100 per barrel oil prices. With the end of this boycott came lowered oil prices and, consequently, far fewer working oil rigs. Lowered oil prices directly affected the demand for oil land. This lowered demand resulted in many cases of collapsed prices for oil lands and leases. The later increase in oil prices in the late 1990s again fueled an increase in demand and prices for oil related property. We are again seeing oil field frenzy with oilmen hopefully predicting $100 per barrel oil.

D. FOREST LAND

Timber prices are tied to the domestic construction industry as well as to foreign demand.

The prices of land having marketable timber rise and fall with lumber prices.

Besides the economic value of timber, timberland prices have, in recent years, been influenced by the possibility of recreational use. A great many acres of timberland have been broken into small parcels that have been sold as recreational home or camp sites. A number of lumber companies have gone into selling recreational land. Recreational possibilities resulted in keeping land prices up even when timber prices happened to be dropping. The strengthening of the housing market in the '90s and the boom market in the 2000s resulted in higher timberland prices.

Increased demand for pulpwood for paper has affected prices of hardwood acreage. Increased oil prices have also affected hardwood demand. In many areas of the country, people are converting to wood stoves and furnaces. This has resulted in a revitalized demand for firewood.

Private timberland tends to be allocated in large parcels that are owned by a few large forest product's companies.

Plum Creek and International Paper are the two largest owners of timberland. Together, they own over 14 million acres of forestland. Plum Creek has invested in planning and has long-term development plans for its holdings.

Due to the thin market, not as much data is available on forest land prices as there is for farmland. However, forest land prices seem to have paralleled farm prices in their increases.

E. RESIDENTIAL DEVELOPMENT OF FARMLAND (Lots)

Prices of improved lots, including farmland, are directly related to construction activity.

In areas of the country where construction is seasonal, more lots are sold in February and March for spring construction than are sold in November and December.

Due to time constraints of approvals for improvements, it often takes several years for raw land to become building-ready lots. Therefore, the price of lots tends to be based more on the supply and demand of the marketplace rather than on the cost of raw land and improvements.

When the demand for lots within an area exceeds the supply, the marketplace will bid up the price of lots. During a period of low demand, lot prices tend to drop.

If, however, owners anticipate a strong future demand, they are likely to keep their prices up.

When the supply of lots is greater than demand and the price is accordingly too high, the result is a surplus, and prices then fall to the equilibrium point.

High interest rates during the late '70s and early '80s kept buyers out of the marketplace, creating a pent-up demand. Lower interest rates stimulated building in both 1985 and again starting in the mid-1990s to the point of creating a healthy demand for lots. Lot prices rose over 25 percent in one year in many areas of the Eastern and Western United States. In hot building areas, the rise in value has been even greater. According to Lomas and Nettleton, a Dallas-based mortgage banking firm, lot prices have been rising faster than home prices.

Historically, land had accounted for 20 percent of total housing costs. Now, on a nationwide basis, it is over 30 percent. In some areas, it is even higher than 50 percent.

Higher lot costs have caused more builders to abandon low or moderate-cost housing in favor of luxury homes.

With high land costs it is difficult to build a salable (desirable) product and maintain profit margins when building for the lower end of the market.

When building activity slows, reduction in demand does not lead to a corresponding reduction in lot prices. This is because the costs to hold a lot are not great. Owners, unless strongly motivated to sell, will resist lowering prices and will hold their lots until the market recovers.

Imperfections in the marketplace create times when homes are sold for considerably more than the sum of the land value and the cost of construction.

Markets existed where the strong demand for housing resulted in market prices that exceeded the cost of lots plus construction costs (including normal markups). In such a market, lot prices tend to rise rapidly to reduce the disparity between building costs (construction plus lot) and the prices for which new homes can be sold.

Growth control can have a devastating effect on lots and land where the value was based on anticipated development.

In areas that only allow a minimum number of building permits and many lots are available, it could take years to sell a lot. In such a market, lot prices would be depressed while prices for completed homes would increase.

F. CONTAMINATED LAND

There is a high degree of concern today over contaminated land. Developers fear another Love Canal (contaminated land area) and massive liabilities, as well as clean-up costs (see **Figure 11-5**).

Contaminated land hurts the owner, lender, and society as a whole because clean-up can be so costly.

Several years ago, PCP-contaminated cattle feed resulted in the contamination of thousands of acres. Herbicides, insecticides, and chemical fertilizers have also contaminated some parcels of farmland. However, the biggest problems have resulted from land used as illegal and legal dump sites. When dumping is suspected, developers have the soil tested prior to purchase.

Cadillac Fairview California, Inc. purchased acreage in Torrance, California and received the seller's assurance that the land had not been contaminated. The corporation later discovered a previous owner had used it as a chemical dump site. While the seller expressed no knowledge of this use, the result was a costly law suit. In another California case, an $8 million price was reduced to $5.5 million when the purchaser discovered diesel oil spills on the land.

Figure 11-5

Love Canal Waste Disposal

As required by the 1976 Resource Conservation and Recovery Act (amended in 1984), the EPA regulates the handling of substances listed as hazardous (not all toxic chemicals are regulated as hazardous). The movement of these materials must be documented from production through ultimate disposal. Disposal sites must meet standards designed to ensure that they do not leak into ground or surface waters or onto the land, and that they will be monitored and maintained for at least 20 years after they are closed.

Such long-term contamination was involved in the disastrous events at the Love Canal near Niagara Falls, New York. ***LOVE CANAL** is known the world over for dangerous ground contamination.* The Hooker Chemical and Plastics Corporation had used an old canal bed in this area as a chemical dump for thousands of tons of hazardous chemicals from the 1930s to 1952. The filled land was given to the city in 1953, and a new school and a housing tract were built on it. In 1971, toxic liquids began leaking through the clay cap that sealed the dump, and the area was contaminated by at least 82 chemicals, including a number of carcinogens: benzene, some chlorinated hydrocarbons, and dioxin. Extremely high birth defect and miscarriage rates developed, as well as high incidences of liver cancer and of a seizure-inducing nerve disease among the neighborhood children. Love Canal was declared an official disaster area; 7,500 residents left the area although most returned after cleanup. The state paid $10 million to buy some of the homes and another $10 million to try to stop the leakage. About 1,000 families had to be relocated. Hooker Chemical originally disclaimed responsibility, however, Occidental Chemical Corporation that purchased Hooker, agreed to pay $129 million to cover federal cleanup costs. The site was cleaned up sufficiently in the 1990s for houses located there to be put up for sale as well as to allow new construction.

New River flows 80 miles south to north, from Mexicali, Mexico to the Salton Sea in California. From Mexico, the river carries untreated and partially treated sewage as well as industrial waste from the many companies that have built plants in Mexico to take advantage of NAFTA (North American Free Trade Agreement). Over 25 metals have been detected in the water leaving Mexico. As the river goes north, it collects pesticides and fertilizer runoff from California agricultural land. While some "experts" claim the river is contaminating the air, groundwater, and even agricultural land on both sides of the river, government officials downplay the dangers from the river, indicating only a slight danger. Environmentalists consider it a time bomb that could conceivably be worse than Love Canal.

VII. CHAPTER SUMMARY

U. S. farms are able to produce more food and fiber than the nation can consume. Both agricultural and land prices have been kept high because of exports, as well as various **government subsidies**. The loss of much of our export market, coupled with a period of high interest rates, resulted in many farm foreclosures and a glut of farms on the market in other states. The excess of supply resulted in a significant drop in farm prices nationally.

The **traditional family farm** is no longer a viable economic unit and has been decreasing in number over the past few decades. Family owned farms today are larger and employ outside labor. Many are run as corporations or partnerships. By contrast, the number of large farms and the use of farm management have increased, and leasing rather than owning farmland has become more popular.

While traditional family farms are declining, a growth in **hobby** or **retirement farms** has kept values up for small non-economic farms.

Many farms have become dependent on legal and illegal aliens for a great deal of their labor.

When prices are high for a commodity, more land is used to produce that commodity. The increased supply tends to drop prices so that less land is placed into production for that commodity the following season. This can cause crop shortages, which result high prices, thus, the cycle repeats itself. **Marginal land** is put in and taken out of production according to these cycles.

Besides farmland, undeveloped land also has value for oil and minerals, forests, and even recreation. Land closest to metropolitan areas has greater value based on the possibility of development.

The demand and price for lots corresponds with **construction cycles**. Rapid appreciation in value of developed property also results in the rapid appreciation in value of lots that can be developed.

VIII. GLOSSARY OF KEY TERMS

Agribusiness – Treatment of agriculture as a profit-generating entity.

Corporate Mega Farms – Large farms operating under corporate ownership, which may or may not be family owned.

Fallow Land (Raw Land) – Land lying barren; land not in agricultural production.

Traditional Family Farm – Farm operated as a family business by family members.

Farm – According to the U. S. Department of Agriculture, any operation producing and selling at least $1,000 a year in agricultural products.

Marginal Land – Land on which income is matched but not exceeded by the cost of production.

Oil land – Land where value is primarily based on oil and/or gas deposits contained or believed to be contained under the land.

Premature Subdivision – The subdividing of land long before it will be developed, taking the land out of agricultural production.

Psychological Income – A non-cash benefit in the feeling of self-worth that comes with (hobby or retirement) farm ownership.

Recreational Land – Land sold primarily for recreational use.

Submarginal Land – Land on which the income does not cover associated costs of production.

Subsidies – Government grants or price supports to farmers.

IX. CLASS DISCUSSION TOPICS

1. Discuss the competition for farmland in your area.

2. What does farmland within 10 miles of your community sell for? What does farmland 50 miles away sell for? What does farmland over 100 miles away from large metropolitan areas sell for?

3. Identify farm purchases by foreign nationals, if any, within your region.

4. Identify former farmland not now in production. Why do you suppose it is not?

5. Identify recreational land that is being offered. Compare the asking prices to prices of similar land, which is on the market in large parcels.

6. What changes in agricultural land use has occurred in your area over the past 20 years?

X. CHAPTER 11 QUIZ

1. Which of the following is a true statement regarding U.S. farms?
   a. The number of farms in the U.S. is increasing.
   b. The majority of U.S. farms have income over $250,000.
   c. The number of large farms with income over $1,000,000 has been increasing.
   d. Twenty percent of Americans live on farms.

2. Breaking up farms into smaller acreage parcels results in:
   a. a higher sale price per acre.
   b. an increase in agricultural production.
   c. more single crop farming.
   d. a better utilization of farm labor.

3. Which of the following is a true statement as to family farms?
   a. The numbers have been increasing because paid labor is eliminated as a cost.
   b. They are not economically efficient because both labor and land are fixed factors.
   c. The low capital requirements allow young families to easily enter farming.
   d. Small family farms produce most of our nation's food supply.

4. Which of the following agricultural activities requires the most land?
   a. Vegetables
   b. Aquaculture
   c. Fruits
   d. Cattle

5. The end of government subsidies to farmers would:
   a. increase farmland prices.
   b. lower consumer costs.
   c. result in more family owned farms.
   d. protect America against a food shortage.

6. Marginal land is most likely to be farmed when:
   a. it is available for rental.
   b. a surplus is predicted.
   c. it is owned by the farmer.
   d. commodity prices are low.

7. What type of farmland would have the highest value per acre?
   a. Rangeland
   b. Field crops
   c. Row crops
   d. Fruits and nuts

8. The U.S. grain embargo to Russia, in retaliation for the Afghanistan invasion, had a number of effects, except:

a. farm foreclosures.
b. losses by farm lenders.
c. encouraging foreign farmers to produce grain for export.
d. higher farm values.

9. The value of forest land is tied closely to:

a. government subsidies.
b. lumber prices.
c. grain prices.
d. the Gross Domestic Product.

10. The most severe land contamination problems are the results of:

a. fertilizer use.
b. insecticide use.
c. animal waste.
d. use as a dump site.

ANSWERS: 1. *c*; 2. *a*; 3. *b*; 4. *d*; 5. *b*; 6. *c*; 7. *d*; 8. *d*; 9. *b*; 10. *d*

LEARNING OBJECTIVES

In this chapter you will learn the different types and uses of non-residential real estate. The importance of analyzing locations will be discussed as well as the benefits and negative aspects of real estate investments. The most common type of nonresidential leases will be reviewed, along with the benefits of rent concessions.

You will study the different types of office buildings and how each type is suited for a particular need. The different types of shopping centers and malls will be identified along with a discussion on how population, demographics, and other factors determine the suitability of each one. What are the best locations for industrial property? How about wholesale and warehouse areas? Finally, a look at foreign investment will show the rise and fall of such investment as market conditions change.

Nonresidential real property offers an entirely different market for the real estate professional—one that requires special skills and a solid understanding of market conditions and trends.

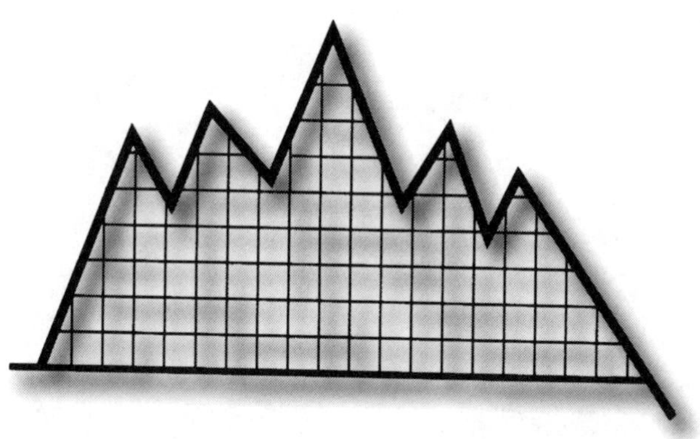

Chapter 12
Nonresidential Real Estate

***NONRESIDENTIAL REAL PROPERTY** consists of offices, retail stores, wholesale and warehouse use as well as manufacturing, but not any type of residential property. Users as well as investors acquire nonresidential real property.* **Figure 12-1** lists the benefits and negative aspects of real estate investments.

Buyers and sellers in the nonresidential real estate market tend to be more knowledgeable than those in the residential real estate market.

I. The Economy and Value

Real estate can benefit by unearned increments to value.

Real estate investors can often benefit by changes in demand and economic changes outside the control of the investor.

During periods of inflation, all real estate tends to increase in value.

The ***CAPITALIZATION RATE** is the rate of return an investor would want for a particular investment*. The higher the risk, the higher the rate of return an investor would want to compensate for the risk. To determine what a property is worth to an investor, the investor

Chapter 12

CHAPTER 12 OUTLINE

would divide the net operating income (do not deduct interest expense or payment on loan principle). As an example, if an investor desired an 8 percent return on an investment property and the property had a net income of $40,000, then the investor would not pay more than $500,000 for the property (Net $40,000 divided by Capitalization Rate of 10 % or .10).

The capitalization rate is tied directly to lending rates. If an investor has to pay more for borrowed capital, the investor's cash flow will suffer. To make up for this loss, the investor will increase the capitalization rate used, which will reduce the price the investor is willing to pay.

During periods of economic slowdown, investors seek investments with higher capitalization rates to offset risk.

Because value moves inversely to the capitalization rate, investors using a higher rate would lower the price that they would be willing to pay for property.

During recessionary periods, retail stores and shopping centers become out of favor with investors. Retail merchants are more likely to default on leases than other types of nonresidential tenants. In order to sell such properties, price reductions that result in a higher capitalization rate become necessary.

Hotel and motel property suffer as well from economic downturns as both business and vacation travel tends to be curtailed.

While not as sensitive to economic downturns, suburban office buildings tend to fall out of favor with investors in periods of recession.

Figure 12-1

Benefits of Real Estate Investments

1. **Income** – Rents or use benefits are sources of income in property investment.
2. **Appreciation** – Real estate has, in the past, appreciated in value in excess of inflation. This has been due to demand for real estate as a hedge against inflation as well as increases in rents.
3. **Preservation of Capital** – Real estate as an investment has less downside risk than investments in stocks or commodities. During inflation periods, real estate investments have preserved the purchasing power of capital.
4. **Depreciation** – Since improvements to income or investment real property can be depreciated, real property depreciation can shelter property income from taxation.
5. **Leverage** – Due to the availability of both lender and seller financing, tremendous leverage is possible for real property investments.
6. **Collateral Value** – Owners can use their equity to borrow money for other uses.
7. **Psychic Income** – Ownership of real property provides an intangible feeling of worth and satisfaction beyond dollar value. This feeling is known as "psychic income."
8. **Capital Gains** – Profit on the long-term gain from the sale of real estate is taxed at a rate less than that of regular income.

Negative Aspects of Real Estate Investments

1. **Risk** – Unexpected expenses, vacancies, collection problems, changes in the area, or even changes in law or governmental regulations could occur. No investment is risk-free.
2. **Illiquidity** – Real estate investments are illiquid in that they cannot be readily converted to cash. At times, sales take many months or even years to complete. Borrowing on equity as well as using borrowed funds can offset the illiquid nature of real property.
3. **Management** – Income property requires management expenses and effort. Tenant selection and operational policies can materially affect value.
4. **Property Taxes** – Real property is a primary source of government revenue. It costs money (in the form of property taxes) to hold real property, even when it is already paid for.

Investments that are most likely to hold their value in recessionary periods are apartment buildings, industrial property, office buildings in better downtown markets, and health care facilities. **Self-storage facilities are actually counter cyclical, as the business tends to increase during recessionary periods**. People and businesses tend to downsize in recessionary periods and there is a strong need for space to store furniture, equipment, and inventory. Businesses that are actually expanding are reluctant to obligate themselves for more space and often will use temporary space for inventory.

II. Location Analysis

It has often been said the three most important determinants of value are location, location, and location. This holds true for all types of property.

Figure 12-2 lists factors that must be considered when analyzing a location.

A. ONE HUNDRED PERCENT LOCATION

***ONE HUNDRED PERCENT LOCATION** is an idiom that refers to the best retail location for a particular type of business within a community.*

The 100% location for an auto dealer might be on a street where competitors are all located (Principle of Conformity).

The one hundred percent location for a men's store could be in a central retail area where the area's finest men's stores are located, while the 100 percent location for women's wear might be miles away in a suburban mall. The 100 percent location for a dealer in orthopedic appliances might be in a medical building having a number of orthopedic surgeons. The one hundred percent location within a community, therefore, varies based on the type of business.

In New York City, Fifty Seventh Street is considered a 100% location for upscale retail trade.

Rents reflect the desirability of the area. Some Beverly Hills stores on Rodeo Drive make more than $2,000 a square foot in sales, although most are believed to have sales of about $700 to $1,000 a square foot. Available space is in great demand by merchandisers. For many exclusive chains, a Rodeo Drive location is very important for image purposes.

Broadway Street in Los Angeles would be considered a 100 percent location for lower income shoppers. Over half of the shoppers arrive by public transportation. Between 3rd and 8th Streets on Broadway, the primarily Hispanic customers provide a sales volume of between $500 and $800 per square foot. Annual rentals are about $120 per

Figure 12-2

Location Analysis

In analyzing a location, a number of factors must be considered.

1. **Neighborhood.** The character of the immediate neighborhood should be examined. Trends in vacancies, population shifts, or land purchases by potential users are very important. The purchasing power of an area is more important to many retail firms than raw population data. The age, social background, and discretionary income of residents within the area, as well as that of employees who work in the area but live elsewhere, are of prime importance to retail developments. Younger families have a higher propensity to spend and a lower propensity to save than older families of similar incomes.
2. **Transportation.** Transportation routes for goods, employees, and customers must be considered.
3. **Parking.** Street and off-street parking must be considered, as well as parking potential for the site itself.
4. **Utilities.** Besides utility availability, adequacy must be considered. Water pressure and volume are important in fire suppression systems and for reasonable insurance rates. Industrial use often requires large water volume as well as sewer capacity. The availability of "three phase wiring" is of great importance in manufacturing use. Large users of utilities are also concerned with cost.
5. **Traffic.** The amount of motor traffic and its speed are important. For example, a location for a fast food outlet where traffic averages 55 miles per hour would not be nearly as desirable as the same volume of traffic with a 25 mile per hour speed average. The lower speed would allow drivers more time to consider stopping and make ingress/egress easier. Besides volume and speed of traffic, hours are very important. If most of the daily traffic is between 7:30 and 8:30 A.M. and 4:00 and 5:30 P.M., it would indicate traffic is primarily people going to and from work. This type of traffic would result in limited stopping for goods and services compared to a spread out traffic.
6. **Accessibility.** Convenient and safe street accesses to the site as well as accessibility to major freeways are very important for most uses.
7. **Cost.** The cost of land and improvements must be evaluated in terms of alternative locations.

(continued)

8. **Exposure.** Corner locations have greater exposure than locations in the middle of a block. They also offer greater signage as well as traffic access on two streets. The closer a retail store is to the corner, the greater its exposure and value for retail purposes. A location adjacent to a well-known location that attracts a great deal of interest is an excellent commercial location. Locations between major consumer destinations are especially desirable.
9. **Government Regulations.** Local rent control, moratoriums on construction, or limits on expansion and lengthy approval processes affect value. Growth limits reduce the value of undeveloped land due to the uncertainty of development. However, such limits would increase the value of developed property because government action limits the supply. Zoning affects use, which has a direct effect on value.
10. **Linkage.** The proximity of suppliers, consumers, or competitors has a direct bearing on property value for a particular use. For example, a site close to a hospital would have great value for medical offices, and a first floor location in a medical office building would be a prime site for a pharmacy.

Competition aids many businesses. As an example, a group of automobile dealers located together will draw more customers than each auto dealer located separately.

Warehouses should be located close to manufacturing or distribution points along transportation routes, and restaurants should be close to work centers for breakfast and lunch business.

For evening business, restaurants should be linked by proximity to middle income and upscale housing areas.

Secretarial services and business services are naturals for large office buildings.

The best location for a tannery might be in close proximity to stock yards and/or shoe factories.

Many industries require each other. Dominant and support industries are really interdependent and location linkage benefits all.

Linkage locations utilize what is available for the maximum benefit of the local industry.

Large chain stores and franchises, by using careful site analysis, have found they can pinpoint those factors important to their success and limit failure.

square foot. The Broadway area, while ignored by many merchandisers, has become one of the fastest growing retail areas in California.

B. BARGAIN LOCATIONS

Low rent locations are not necessarily bargains. In fact, a low rent location could well be the most expensive location available.

Consider the fixed expenses of two alternative retail locations, one renting for $1,000 per month and the other $4,000 per month (see **Figure 12-3**).

Figure 12-3

Bargain Locations May Not Be A Bargain

	Low Cost Location	High Cost Location
Rent	$1,000.00	$4,000.00
Owner's personal expenses	4,000.00	4,000.00
Advertising	1,000.00	1,000.00
Hired labor	4,000.00	4,000.00
Phone and utilities	600.00	600.00
Miscellaneous	500.00	500.00
Interest expense	2,000.00	2,000.00
Total monthly expense	**$13,100.00**	**$16,100.00**

While the rent for the high cost location is 300 percent higher than the rent for the low cost location, the other fixed costs for the high price location are the same as those for the low price location.

The high cost location offers a greater volume of business because of higher traffic, better exposure, linkage with other businesses, etc. The benefits of the high cost location account for its higher cost (see **Figure 12-4**).

Figure 12-4

In analyzing the businesses we find:

LOW COST LOCATION

Income		$24,000.00
Expenses as follows:		
	Fixed Expenses	$13,100.00
	Cost of Goods	12,000.00
	Total Expenses	$25,100.00
	Net Loss of	**$1,100.00 per month**

HIGH COST LOCATION

Income		$48,000.00
Expenses as follows:		
	Fixed Expenses	$16,100.00
	Cost of Goods	24,000.00
	Total Expenses	$40,100.00
	Net Profit of	**$7,900.00 per month**

In this comparison the low cost location is not a bargain. (A retail location with rent several times that of a low cost location is probably able to produce a business volume far greater than twice that of the low cost location.)

In studying this example we can readily understand why lower cost retail locations tend to have higher rates of turnover than higher cost locations.

C. SHOPPING STREETS

Many quality shopping areas are dependent on foot traffic. For maximum values to be maintained on a shopping street, uses should be harmonious.

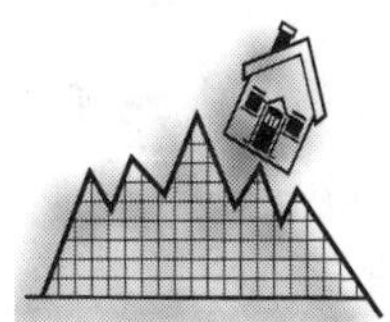

Just as in a mall, stores attract shoppers not just to a particular store, but to other stores as well, a concentration of similar stores will attract shoppers from a wider area. Uses that do not generally contribute to the retail climate of a shopping area are banks, savings banks (S&Ls), real estate offices, churches, etc. These uses attract customers primarily for their particular services and not for general retail sales.

When a block of financial institutions breaks up a pedestrian shopping street, the foot traffic tends to reverse at that point. Shops on the other end of the block will not materially benefit from foot traffic on the other side.

Like residential vacancies, commercial type vacancies compete only with other vacant property, NOT with rented property.

III. Types of Leases

A variety of leases and special lease provisions are utilized for nonresidential property.

A. FLAT LEASE

A flat lease is a lease with a fixed rental amount.

For very desirable space the lessor will normally demand a longer lease, unless the lessor anticipates higher future rents. (Less desirable space might be available on a month-to-month basis.) Rents are normally expressed in a monthly or annual price per square foot although the lease itself would just show a flat rate for the designated space. Longer term leases would generally include an escalation clause, whereby rents would increase with inflation. Leases are often tied to indexes such as the Consumer Price Index (CPI).

If a lessor has an adjustable rate loan, adjustments in interest could result in a negative cash flow. Therefore, the leases should, if at all possible, provide for similar adjustments based upon the cost of money. *Lease clauses allowing rent to be adjusted, based on some criteria, are known as* **ESCALATOR CLAUSES**.

B. TRIPLE NET LEASE (NET, NET, NET)

Under a **TRIPLE NET LEASE** *(usually referred to as a "net" lease), the tenant makes a fixed payment to the owner and pays taxes, insurance, maintenance, repair, and all operating expenses.* The net lease makes real estate a more trouble-free investment. Net leases are widely used by chain stores and franchises, which build the structures and sell them to investors with a long-term leaseback. This arrangement allows for rapid expansion, without capital being tied up in fixed assets. Net leases are generally long-term leases.

In order for the investor to maintain the purchasing power of his or her income, the net amount should be adjusted by one of the indexes, such as the Consumer Price Index.

C. PERCENTAGE LEASE

PERCENTAGE LEASES *are leases where the rental is a percentage of the gross sales.* Generally, businesses with higher merchandise markups pay higher percentages. Trade associations provide data on percentage ranges being charged for various types of businesses.

Shopping centers generally use leases where the rental is a percentage of the gross sales.

Percentage leases generally require the lessees to use a "totalizing type" register that cannot be turned back. The leases usually include:

1. a minimum rent;
2. a covenant to remain in business;
3. an agreement regarding hours of operation;
4. an agreement regarding cooperative advertising;
5. a prohibition against off-site sales (such as warehouse sales); and
6. a provision for mail order and Internet sales.

In addition, percentage leases frequently contain a "recapture" clause, enabling the lessor to regain the premises if the lessee fails to attain or maintain a target gross.

It benefits the lessor if the tenant obtains a maximum gross. The lease can encourage the tenant to maintain sales by providing a lower percentage once a target is reached.

Tenant selection is extremely important with percentage leases.

The lessor wants tenants who not only will provide a high gross, but also will fit in with other tenants. The purpose of this kind of tenant is to provide cross-shopping, which will result in the highest possible gross for the shopping center.

D. RENTS ARE GOING UP

Many markets experienced double-digit rent increases in the first half of 2000. Demand for office space in many urban markets drove rents to historic highs.

According to Torto Wheaton Research, the six-month period from January through June 2000, resulted in office rent increases as follows:

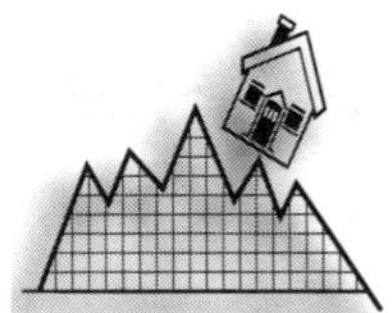

San Jose, CA	23.9%
Washington, D.C.	15.4%
Austin, TX	15.3%
San Francisco, CA	14.3%
Tampa, FL	13.6%
Detroit, MI	13.3%
Portland, OR	12.8%
Charlotte, NC	11.7%
Seattle, WA	11.4%

The rents were driven up primarily because of demand by technology firms. In many cases, old line companies are being forced out of high demand areas.

Because of high rent, Charles Schwab moved 400 employees out of San Francisco to less costly space in Pleasanton.

Firms will move back to more desirable areas if the rent drops to what they consider an acceptable level. As an example, the consolidation in the oil and gas industries led Exxon Mobil Corporation and Texaco to dump 600,000 square feet of office space in New Orleans. This additional space on the market lowered rents to $13 per square foot. Since this was about $8 per square foot less than comparable suburban space, firms that had moved to the suburbs for lower rents moved back to the city.

InfoRocket.com felt priced out of the Manhattan office real estate market. Rather than moving elsewhere, they looked for sources of space from other than developers and property managers. They entered bankruptcy court in Delaware and bid for 22,000 square feet of 7th Avenue Manhattan office space that had 5 years remaining on the lease. They were able to obtain the space at $23 a square foot that was about $15 less than market rent for that space. Leasing agents should realize that leases can be an asset for firms in bankruptcy and can provide an excellent opportunity for buyers of those assets.

After experiencing several years of declining or flat rent, vacancy rates fell in 2004 for most nonresidential investment properties and rents began to rise.

E. HOW HIGH CAN RENT GET?

Nonresidential tenants generally rent space to contribute to profit. If they cannot make a profit, they cannot use the space at the rental price.

The economic ideal for an owner is a rent that allows the tenant to make a reasonable profit and maximizes the owner's net income.

However, there is a point where rents can get too high to be tolerated, even by tenants who are making significant profits. A number of the high tech firms in the San Francisco area have been migrating to the Sacramento area. Even though the Silicon Valley is the center of the tech universe for engineering talent and venture capital, rent for facilities reached the point that many firms were just refusing to pay it. Besides what they regard as exorbitant rent increases, it has become increasingly difficult to bring in new hires because of housing costs.

By moving, firms are able to obtain comparable space from $1 to $2 per square foot around the Sacramento area when they had been facing $7 to $8 per square foot rental rates in the Silicon Valley.

Startup firms that historically had to be in Silicon Valley, are finding that they do NOT have to locate there. By locating in other areas, they are more likely able to stretch their capital until they become profitable.

Firms that have relocated found that close physical proximity to other high tech firms is not as important as they had thought. Communication is not a big problem due to the benefits of the Internet.

To convince key employees to move with them, Insweb Corp. provided sessions for employees with relocation consultants to sell the employees on the personal advantage of the move. Of those the company sought to convince, half the employees agreed to relocate. In addition to commitment to the firm's goals, factors contributing to employee relocation were the high prices possible for employees in selling their homes and the much lower prices for new homes, allowing for a better standard of living.

When the Internet dot-com bubble burst in 2000, many Internet high-flyers went bankrupt because venture capital and bank loans dried up. The result was a high vacancy factor in the Silicon Valley and drastically reduced rents. The exodus of firms leaving the area because of high costs was reversed with relocation to, and back to, the Silicon Valley.

F. RENT CONCESSIONS

RENT CONCESSIONS *are free items given by the landlord in order to keep the rent higher than market.* Owners prefer to provide concessions such as free rent, moving costs, fixture allowance, etc., rather than lower rents. Lowered rents would directly affect owners' equity and borrowing ability, because property appraisers customarily use rent capitalization to determine value.

A problem with providing a lower base rent, rather than a rent concession, is that a tenant might move when rents are increased. The same tenant would be much less likely to move when a new lease remains at the old rent, even though the tenant

may have received concessions that reduced the effective rent to less than the amount stated.

Office leasing usually involves a large amount of dealing. For a desirable tenant, office owners will give rent concessions, extra parking, and even health club memberships. Therefore, office management firms describe rents as "effective rents," not the scheduled rents. ***EFFECTIVE RENT** is the scheduled rent less concessions given.*

In office buildings, developers often use the "structure name" as an inducement for a tenant who agrees to rent a great deal of space.

The tenant's name on the building gives the tenant prestige, which often he/she is willing to pay for in the form of an advantageous lease.

In Chicago, Boeing leased more than one-third of an office tower as its new national headquarters. The Boeing symbol is now prominently displayed on the building's clock tower.

G. STARTUP COMPANIES

Landlords who sign long-term leases with startup companies take greater risk than when renting to a firm with an established history. Some landlords actually seek out startup companies but want extra compensation such as:

1. Higher rent for greater risk;
2. A provision in the lease allowing the landlord to buy stock in the company at the offering price should the firm go public;
3. An equity position in the tenant company in exchange for lower rent.

Because of the phenomenal success of "dot-com" firms in the late '90s, many lessors became intrigued with the possibility of sharing in a tenant's success. Letting the landlord share in success is a two-way street. For high tech firms it is like another source of venture capital. Tenants have been negotiating free or below market rent in exchange for equity and landlords who are able to take the risk have done so in the hopes of exceptional rewards. One Austin, Texas developer has been actively seeking out startup companies and not only providing free space but investing cash as well.

The technological boom of the 1990s offered opportunities for landlords who were able to think outside of the box. They created "business incubators."

***BUSINESS INCUBATORS** are organizations and businesses that support new businesses by offering space plus support services to decrease likelihood of business failures.* Some include technical and financial advice. They serve as mentors to new businesses. The ***NATIONAL BUSINESS INCUBATOR ASSOCIATION** is an organization of incubator developers* (**www.nbia.org**).

Some landlords converted space to the special needs of high tech startup companies. They are renting to multiple tenants with individual space for each tenant but communal use coffee rooms, reception areas, secretarial services, conference rooms, etc. Tenants furnishing needs are kept to a minimum. Tenants love the atmosphere of these creative type facilities. The interaction with other tenants results in ideas, customers, and services for each other. In Greenwich Village, one 40,000 square foot building has 40 such tenants.

S.L. Green Realty outfitted two floors of a New York office building with desks, files, Internet wired offices, recreation area equipped with a pool table, etc. They are renting space to start up companies offering 3-month to 12-month leases, rather than traditional 5-year to 10-year leases. S.L. Green Realty even offers services such as website design.

H. TENANT PARTNERS

Blue chip (top rated) tenants are beginning to realize how important they are to developers.

A developer's risk is reduced when a strong tenant rents a large block of space. This is especially true when the vacancy rate is high for the type of space being developed. A prime tenant will not only attract others because of the prestige factor, but a strong tenant will also result in easier and better financing. When a building has a severe vacancy problem, an owner is likely to look favorably on a tenant equity arrangement.

IBM, in periods of high vacancies, asked for equity positions (part ownership) in projects as a limited partner when it took a major block of space or renewed a lease. IBM rents an estimated 30 million square feet, and has been able to obtain equity positions in about 10 percent of this space. The net effect of having an equity position is giving the equity-holding tenant a reduced rent. A share in the profits and an appreciation in the structure account for the reduced rent.

AT&T realizes that its leases can affect whether or not developers attain favorable financing. It holds formal competitions to choose developers as partners for space. AT&T is willing to give a 20-year lease commitment, but is asking for 50 percent or greater ownership. AT&T has entered into a number of these developer partnerships, including one in Pleasanton, California, and a new regional headquarters in Chicago. In Dallas, AT&T received joint venture proposals from owners of completed projects because so much space was vacant at the time.

I. PARKING

Many buildings will give tenants parking spaces based on the number of square feet leased. Tenants might validate customer parking, paying a fee for those exceeding an agreed upon number.

Some owners lease parking space separately. This allows a psychological advantage of appearing to have a lower per square foot rental.

Parking space in many cities is becoming critical. In Boston, garages are charging up to $30 per day for parking. To be guaranteed a parking space, workers in central business districts must lease a parking space by the month. Average monthly rentals are as follows:

Manhattan	$432
Boston	$375
Chicago	$328
San Francisco	$298

Nationally, the average parking rate in 2004 was $143 per month and $13.07 per day.

IV. High-Rises

Historically, high land costs in metropolitan areas meant maximizing the height of structures to maximize profits. Henry Hyde, the owner of the Equitable Life Insurance building in New York, installed the first Otis Elevator in 1857. However, it was not until steam power was replaced by electricity in the 1880s that elevators became commonly used.

Hyde priced the higher floors at a premium because he thought they would add to tenants' prestige. The rents of high-rise structures still vary by floor. Except for ground floor and mezzanine levels, which generally rent at a premium, the higher (by floor) the rental space, the higher the rent. View and less street noise are factors that affect the rental.

In the past, brick and stone construction was a limiting factor in construction as massive walls and pillars were necessary to support these structures. In 1884, the first structural steel building was built.

The use of structural steel, coupled with the elevator, made the towers of today possible.

In 1890, the 300 foot World Building was constructed in New York. By 1908, the Singer Building was completed at 47 stories and 612 feet high. In 1909, Metropolitan Life built a 50-story structure that topped at 700 feet.

As previously mentioned, upper floors rent for more than lower floors in high-rise structures. While it costs more to build each additional floor, additional costs may be worthwhile because of additional rents. Eventually, however, a point of negative return will be reached when the rentals become insufficient to amortize the additional cost of the last floor (principle of diminishing returns).

Building efficiency is measured by the ratio of rentable space to total floor space. The highest ratios are generally found in residential structures because they contain less area for public services.

If a full floor is rented, all the space is considered and the rent is usually at a lower price per square foot.

Due to the economics of scale in dealing with one tenant and one lease on a floor rather than with many, the owner has benefits that might be passed on to the tenant.

When there are numerous offices on a floor for rent, hallways are not generally considered as rentable space.

A. THE EDIFICE COMPLEX

New world records for height are being broken on a regular basis. The Empire State Building at 1,250 feet in height is still a tall building, but can't compare to Taipei 101 in Taipei, Taiwan, at 1,667 feet. To beat out the Petronas Towers in Malasia, the Taipei builders added a 197-foot spire.

Rather than risk having a title lost by just a few feet, the Burj Tower in Dubai, now under construction, will have 160 floors and top out at 2,600 feet. Completion is planned for 2008.

These new buildings are not being built taller for economic reasons. Developers and their nations want to build taller for national prestige and because they want to show they can.

The September 11, 2001 terrorist attack on the 110-story twin towers of New York's World Trade Center has not led to a major change in attitude about these buildings.

V. Office Buildings

Developing an office complex is something like dealing on the speculative "futures" market. It might be many years after land acquisition before a building is ready to rent. Besides the construction phase, a great deal of time can be spent on design and obtaining all necessary approvals and financing. By the time the building is completed, the needs of the area could have significantly changed. Relocation of firms, the general business environment, as well as new competing structures, are changes that can affect an area's needs. Developers must be optimistic or they will never start a new project.

A. SALE OF OFFICE BUILDINGS

When the real estate market was hot in the late '70s, several Canadian firms, such as Cadillac Fairview and Olympic York, entered the U.S. office building market. They

went on buying binges, which caused prices to increase. Many analysts believed they overpaid in order to get into the game. They were hard hit by the end of the office boom in the '70s. Their rents were, in many cases, insufficient to cover debt service. By selling they were able to reverse the sage financial advice of Bernard Baruch by buying high and selling low.

In the 1970s, Japanese investors went on a buying binge trying to pick off trophy buildings in major cities. By American standards, the Japanese investors overpaid to get what they wanted. However, they did not overpay by Japanese standards. They borrowed their money from Japanese banks at interest rates far lower than U.S. buyers would have to pay. They were, therefore, able to use capitalization rates of 4 to 5 percent, which was less than U.S. borrowers had to pay for funds. While they got their buildings, most were sold at a loss or foreclosed when the Japanese lenders rewrote or called in the loans.

Due to the time lag between land acquisition and space rental, many developers watch for trends that could significantly affect the future. Some builders will start building office space when there is a glut and no one else is building. They hope by the time their building is ready the glut will have disappeared and they will have a new building without competition.

Because of low interest rates between 2004 and 2006, we have seen an escalation in the prices being paid for office buildings, even though vacancy rates are relatively high and rents are not showing significant improvement. Some analysts claim the prices reflect lower future vacancies and higher nets.

There has also been an increase in sales activities for office properties. By 2006, sales were up 41 percent from 2004. There is a lot of capital chasing office property investments and buyers are accepting capitalization rate in the 5 percent range because there are few alternatives. Speculators with deep pockets are entering the office market. The 52-story Bank of America Center in San Francisco was sold in 2004 for $825 million. The buyer placed the property on the market in 2005 for $1.25 billion.

Not everyone shares this enthusiasm for office properties. CALPERS, the nation's largest pension fund and Equity Office Properties, a large REIT, are both sellers of office properties in markets where they have shown rapid appreciation. Apparently, they believe the market has peaked.

B. OVERBUILDING (Recent History)

According to real estate consultant Torto Wheaton Research, office glut is the simple result of too much money chasing real estate.

The overbuilding of commercial property in the 1980s and early 1990s in every area of the country led to:

1. lowering of rents,
2. an increase in the vacancy factor, and
3. a deflation in property value as a result of very high vacancy levels.

In some cases, rent fell low enough to only cover variable costs, leaving nothing for return on capital or debt service.

Office rents in many cities dropped 25 to 40 percent and occupancy rates for certain types of property also plummeted. In areas dependent on the energy business (Houston, Texas), the situation was even worse.

The Frank Russell Company Index, a leading barometer of commercial real estate values, showed a .7 percent fall in values for the first nine months of 1986. Stephen E. Roulac, President of a San Francisco real estate consulting firm, claimed the market for commercial real estate was the worst since the Depression.

The authors predicted in their writing in the mid '80s, "...the national office vacancy rate will remain high through the year 2000." We must eat those words. What can seem as a glut today can be gone tomorrow. We never expected absorption at the rate seen in the strong economy of the 1990s.

We were not the only ones who failed to predict future demand for office space. In Houston, Texas, glass office towers were referred to as neutron buildings in the 1980s because they had killed both the developers and the lenders but left the structures intact. Some local "experts" thought that Houston would take 30 years to absorb the available office space. They were wrong.

Dallas, Texas had an office vacancy problem, and may have even exceeded Houston in office vacancies as new structures were completed. Dallas was believed to have had over 40,000,000 non-rented square feet at the end of 1986. However, Dallas has a more diversified economy than Houston. The majority of the glut in Dallas office space was filled within seven years, but vigorous building led to another glut by 1998.

Solomon Brothers (a stock brokerage firm) set up a mutual fund to buy distressed commercial property. A number of other groups have put together funds for the same purpose. Commonly known as "vulture funds," they sought to take advantage of the misfortune of others.

Many private investors also entered the marketplace looking to buy at the bottom.

The market, as of 2000, was strong and according to CB Richard Ellis Services, Inc., San Francisco became the first American city in seven years to be listed as one of the top ten expensive cities in the world for office space. San Francisco, which was ranked 9th, had average annual tenant occupancy costs of $64.70 per square foot in 2000. This

included utilities, janitorial services, etc. In comparison, central Tokyo had occupancy costs of $155.23. Midtown Manhattan ranked 12th as the costliest at $58.30 per square foot and Silicon valley ranked 13th at $57 per square foot.

High vacancies in Houston and Dallas, as well as other cities, resulted in developers cutting back on proposed projects and lenders reluctant to commit without firm leases for significant portions of the projects. The high vacancy rate also resulted in free rent (as long as two years on a five-year lease).

In Denver, BCE Development Properties assumed the lease of any tenant willing to relocate to its new 56-story Republic Plaza. Owing to a vacancy rate of 30.6 percent in downtown Denver in January 1987, BCE was unable to sublease any of the leased space through conventional methods. It solved the problem of disposing of this space (some on relatively short leases) by auctioning off 200,000 square feet. The auction resulted in bargain leases for some tenants, and a reduction in the lease obligations of BCE.

Anthony Downs, a senior fellow at the Brookings Institute, forecasted continued problems with office space. He predicted:

"In the future, a 10% vacancy factor will be the ideal rather than the 5% of the past."

By the late 1990s, the rental market for office space was strong and only a few markets had a glut of office space. However, in late 2000, the Federal Deposit Insurance Corporation issued warnings as to areas that they felt were in danger of commercial overbuilding. They considered loans in these areas to have greater risk.

Torto Weaton Research (TWR) measures prospective demand from both tenants and from what is being built. Because Torto Weaton Research and the FDIC use different models for at-risk marketplaces, their lists of at-risk cities vary considerably.

In Portland, Oregon, the real estate community considered a 27-story office structure started in the late 1990s to be a folly. They predicted the financial demise of the developer. However, by that time it was completed and ready for leasing in late 2000, the market conditions had changed. It was almost fully leased at the time of completion.

Another example of rapid turnaround in the office rental market is Dallas, Texas. Lenders pretty well abandoned the Dallas market in 1998 because of the fear of overbuilding. In 1999, Lend Lease Real Estate Investments and Price Waterhouse Coopers gave Dallas the lowest possible score for development potential. However, strong job growth resulted in leasing far exceeding expectations in 2000. Rental increases developed even though a significant office vacancy factor still existed (19%). Because developers' plans for new structures take a number of years to complete, Dallas developers went with plans for new structures.

When there is a healthy rate of absorption of vacant office space, it appears that developers believe, "If we build it, the tenants will come."

While 2002 to 2004 were lackluster years for office rentals, in 2004 office vacancy factors had begun to show a slow reduction. Nationally, by the end of June 2005, the office vacancy factor was 15.4 percent, down from June's 15.9 percent. However, rental rates were not improving. Because the pipeline for new office structures had slowed, it was estimated that the vacancy factor will continue to decline and we will see rents starting to increase.

C. B. Richard Ellis has been tracking vacancy rates for office and industrial properties, both nationally and by state, since the early 1970s (**www.cbre.com**).

C. SMALLER OFFICE BUILDINGS

According to a 1986 survey by Grubb & Ellis Company, of the 3,000-plus San Francisco Bay-area firms, 54 percent used less than 7,500 square feet of office space. Seventy-one percent used less than 15,000 square feet of space. These figures indicated a great need for smaller blocks of office space.

Since many smaller firms do NOT want to feel lost in huge office structures, a demand for smaller office buildings that cater to smaller firms exists.

D. IMAGE STRUCTURES

Corporations want more than office space. They want an image as well as a building, one that gives them a distinctive logo. A move away from the monolithic glass towers to more distinctive structures can be seen.

A number of firms have genuine interest in the environment. Merrill Lynch and Company hired Fox and Fowle, a designer of "green" buildings, for a 40-story tower that will incorporate cutting edge technology in the use of solar power, fuel cells for backup generators and recycled building products. However, while more friendly to the environment, green buildings do not make economic sense in that the greater costs cannot be recouped in rent. Therefore, the decision to build a "green" building will likely be based more on corporate image than bottom line profits.

E. SMART BUILDINGS

In order to gain a competitive advantage, office building developers are integrating electronic services. ***SMART BUILDINGS*** *are structures that include centralized data processing, computer networks, high speed Internet, e-mail, teleconferencing, long distance phone services, satellite phones, etc.* Developers allow tenants to enjoy these services at a fraction of the cost tenants would pay if they were to purchase the equipment themselves.

A problem smart buildings have is height. They depend on microwave and satellite dishes for many of their services, and if a location is overshadowed by other structures, the services cannot be provided. Building owners also bear the risk of obsolescence of equipment, but the benefits of higher occupancy, increased rents, and charges for services have made many developers eager to shoulder these risks.

F. OFFICE AUTOMATION

Office automation has led to a reduction in office workers; however, space requirements have continued to grow due to the space requirements of computers and related equipment.

G. SPECIALIZED BUILDINGS

Older buildings have been successful in reducing vacancies and have actually increased rents through tenant selection. By specializing in a particular type of tenant, the structure becomes extremely desirable. As an example, a building that is a wholesale jewelry center might have many tenants, such as sellers of unmounted stones or completed jewelry, polishers and repair people, designers, etc. These tenants create a great volume of business among themselves because of their linkage. In addition, having a large number of wholesalers at one location will attract customers from a wide area.

The Merchandise Mart in Chicago is the most famous of the specialized structures, although California has a number of similar but smaller wholesale centers. (Los Angeles has a Merchandise Mart at 9th and Hill Streets.)

Specialized wholesale buildings for women's wear, interior design, furniture, and even hardware can be found.

H. THE RIPPLE EFFECT

When new office space enters the real estate market, its demand is limited to new firms or the relocation and/or expansion of existing firms.

Due to lease commitments, relocations are limited to those firms whose leases are expiring or the economics is such that it is worthwhile to move despite existing lease obligations.

Relocation to new space means a vacancy at another location. The principle of "filtering down" applies to retail and office space in the same manner as it applies to residential property.

Eventually, the least desirable space will become vacant.

The ripple effect occurs with each new structure. Even a loyal tenant can be lured away through concessions. ***CLASS C OFFICE BUILDINGS*** *are the oldest, least desirable office space.* Owners of Class C space eventually will find themselves in a situation where they must either eliminate their space, convert it to other uses, or upgrade it to Class B office space. A ***CLASS B OFFICE BUILDING*** *is older but has quality space.* A ***CLASS A OFFICE BUILDING*** *is newer office space that has the highest rents and is highly desirable by businesses.*

I. OLDER OFFICE BUILDINGS

Older office buildings can absorb a greater vacancy factor than newer structures because owners generally have much lower fixed loan expenses.

After awhile, as vacancies increase, a point will be reached when the structure must either be renovated, razed, or converted to other uses. Because of low owner costs, older office structures can be renovated to compete with newer structures and still offer a rent advantage. Spending $50 a square foot for extensive renovations in an older structure purchased at $50 per square foot still brings total costs to less than half of what newer space would cost. Renovated space offering significantly lower rents can be kept occupied while other structures suffer.

Restored older space can also offer prestige to tenants. In Milwaukee, the owners of the 105-year-old Mackie Building spent $750,000 to restore the Grain Exchange Room. The restored room was a cultural attraction that also attracted prime tenants.

Prudential Insurance Company bought out its partner's interest in the Renaissance Tower in Dallas. The fully occupied structure had 1.3 million square feet of leases due to expire within a three-year period. Rather than risk a high vacancy rate (Dallas had an extremely high vacancy factor at the time) and sharply reduce rents, Prudential made the economic decision to spend $40 million to give the building a major upgrade, which included a new plaza, remodeled lobby, new facade, etc. The net result was the structure was able to compete with the most desirable new buildings.

VI. Hotels

The tragedy of 9-11 had a devastating effect on the hotel industry. Business travel, the backbone of most hotel business, fell drastically. Hotel REITs dropped in value, in most cases over 50 percent. The sales market for hotels turned around in 2004, with increased occupancy and higher rents.

By 2006, despite the rise in interest rates, investors were buying at lower capitalization rates in the belief that future income would rise significantly.

The risk in hotel investment is effected by:

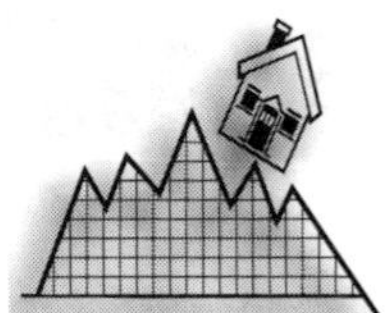

1. The national as well as the local economy;
2. Changes in competition;
3. Social and economic changes in the specific area.

We are seeing a change in the hotel industry at the high end. There are a number of small luxury boutique hotels catering to celebrities and the super rich. Larger luxury hotels are trying to out do each other in terms of luxury as well as expense. They are building or renovating suites to appeal to the super rich. The Mansion at the MGM Grand rents for $5,000 per night, but that appears to be modest compared to the $3 billion Emirates Palace in Duboi. This is the most expensive hotel ever built and offers rooms starting at $625 per night to suites at $13,000 per night plus a 20 percent service charge.

Older quality hotels have been expensively renovated in an effort to upgrade their facilities and maintain or increase occupancy rates and rents.

While renovation is expensive, it still costs far less than new construction. The Chicago Hilton spent an estimated $150 million in renovations or about $100,000 per room. As expensive as this seems, the facility could not be duplicated for less than $200,000 per room. The U.S. Grant Hotel in San Diego underwent an $80 million restoration project and was subsequently able to raise average room rates from $32 to $110. The Beverly Hilton in Beverly Hills is undergoing a $60 million renovation.

VII. Retail Space

The need for retail space within a community is based not only on population within the community but 1) discretionary purchasing power of the residents; 2) demographic considerations, and 3) the drawing power of the area. In a community of older homes and older-aged residents, there would generally be need for fewer square feet of shopping space than in a community of young families, who tend to be greater consumers.

Where there is greater personal discretionary income, a need for more specialty shops exists because they carry the desired luxury items.

Better retail stores tend to follow better housing along major transportation routes. Better stores also tend to locate in areas of other quality stores.

Retail shops with the greatest per square foot sales will tend to dominate prime locations in a free market situation, as they are able to bid more for available space.

Supply and demand of the marketplace determines rental rates. According to Grubb and Ellis, asking yearly rental rates per square foot for the top five retail markets in mid-2000 were as follows:

Manhattan	$85.00
San Francisco	$73.00
Oakland/East Bay	$32.00
Washington, D.C.	$26.00
Boston	$25.00

These rents are modest compared to rentals in 2005 for East 57th Street in New York, which boasts of having the highest retail rent in the world, $700 per square foot. At this rate, a 2,000 square foot store would rent for over $116,000 per month.

A. ONLINE SHOPPING

Many "experts" predicted that online shopping would reduce the need and demand for retail space, which would depress rents. Some experts also wrote of the eventual dominance of online shopping over in-store purchases. They pointed out online advantages of a wider product line coupled with lower rents and overhead allowing more competitive pricing.

While online shopping might eventually have a significant effect on the rental and sales market for retail properties, we have yet to see it.

There were a number of websites for grocery shopping with same or next-day delivery to the door. While it seemed a viable idea, most of these ventures ended in failure.

Disadvantages of online shopping are the inability to actually see and feel purchases, a delay in obtaining purchases, and shipping costs. Online shoppers do not receive the instant gratification of in-store purchases. Another problem for online shopping is the lack of personal or technical advice (although some sites provide it) as well as the absence of social experience. Many people list shopping as an activity they like more than sports.

"Born to Shop" is the experience more than just the purchase.

Websites describing items that can be ordered online and picked up at stores have proved successful. The purchaser has the opportunity to view the item before the sale is completed.

B. SHOPPING CENTERS AND MALLS

A developer of a shopping mall or center should first analyze the market to establish need based on population, demographics, purchasing power of the area, and competition.

To maintain a quality shopping center, a high discretionary income of the people in the area is extremely important.

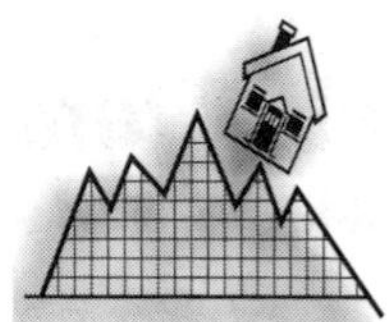

In analyzing areas, understanding competition is vital. White Front, which was a major California discount department store in the '60s, failed to understand its customer base. When it opened a new store in the Riverside area, a significant decrease in business at its San Bernardino store resulted. White Front was, in effect, competing with itself.

In choosing the precise location, size, accessibility, and exposure should be considered.

City approval and planning stages could take several years.

Anchor tenants should be sought prior to construction. ***ANCHOR TENANTS*** *are large department stores located at opposite ends of a shopping center to draw customers between them.* Generally, space is designed based on anchor tenant needs. A major store that signs a lease or a letter of intent to lease will attract other tenants. While a letter of intent is not a binding contract, it indicates a serious intent to enter into lease negotiations.

Developers will often give the first anchor tenant(s) an advantageous lease(s) to insure the attractiveness of the center to other tenants. In a mall type development, other tenants benefit by traffic generated between the anchor tenants and pay premium rents for this benefit.

Having one or more desirable anchor tenants signed up before construction reduces the developer's risks.

In addition, pre-construction lease agreements will result in more favorable construction and permanent financing.

Due to the cost of large centers, insurance companies, mortgage REITs, or pension funds customarily provide permanent financing. Their financial leverage has led to participation loans. In a ***PARTICIPATION LOAN****, the developer receives an equity position (share of the ownership) as well as interest from the loan.*

REGIONAL SHOPPING CENTERS *are larger shopping centers containing several major department stores that generally service a population of 200,000 or more.*

COMMUNITY SHOPPING CENTERS *are smaller shopping centers with only one major department store.* Community shopping centers are usually older centers. They have suffered the most because of the growth of large regional centers.

NEIGHBORHOOD SHOPPING CENTERS *usually have a food store as the major tenant.* Other stores would include a drugstore, variety store and a grouping of neighborhood stores. Most householders will visit a neighborhood center several times per week and many visit these centers on a daily basis. Because it has not been practical to sell groceries in large regional centers (bulky purchases and distances from parking), neighborhood centers have not suffered from the growth of large regional centers.

A number of specialty centers draw from a wide area because of a particular appeal. Examples would be centers that cater to women's fashions or even a more specialized center, such as shoes. We are also seeing a growth in centers catering to manufacturers' outlets and off-price merchandise. Shopping centers can even be developed in existing structures. A prime example of this is Ghirardelli Square in San Francisco.

Some analysts feared that investor interest in large centers could result in overbuilding and a glut would be around for many years. These fears have been realized in many markets, with a decline in sales at older and smaller shopping centers.

C. THE MEGA MALL

Shopping has become more than just a necessary activity to fulfill needs. It has become a pleasurable hobby with many Americans who can indulge either alone or in groups. U.S. shopping centers have grown from an estimated 2,000 in 1957 to more than 30,000 today. The hub of commerce has become the large regional mall. According to Mark Baldassare, professor of sociology at the University of California at Irvine,:

"Malls provide what little civic identity exists in the suburbs. They are places to go if not to meet people, then to see other people, to feel you are a part of things."

Shopping malls have been getting larger and larger. Entertainment can be as much of an attraction as an anchor tenant. South Coast Plaza management found that a carousel was an effective attraction. Ernest Hahn now puts ice rinks in his California centers. In San Diego, Ernest W. Hahn opened Horton Plaza, which includes two live theaters and an art museum. This appeals to more affluent consumers.

The 685,000 square feet Crystal Court addition to South Coast Plaza brought the center to 2.9 million square feet, making it one of the nation's largest shopping centers. In addition to surface parking, a new three-level parking structure, accommodating 2,700 vehicles, will provide free shuttle service to South Coast Plaza.

Close behind are the 2.65 million square foot Del Amo Fashion Center in Torrance and the 2.4 million square foot Lakewood Center Mall in Lakewood.

Most malls, however, seem puny beside the $900 million (Canadian dollars) West Edmonton Mall.

It was developed by four brothers, the Ghermezians, who had previously been in the Persian rug business. In a city of 600,000 people, it is the world's largest mall at 5.5 million square feet.

The Edmonton Mall, with over 15,000 employees, has parking for more than 30,000 cars and approximately 250,000 visitors on an average day (more on weekends). The

mall has been credited with a 70 percent increase in tourism to Edmonton (an estimated six million people), with 50 percent of dollars spent at the mall from tourists. Besides bands, singers, tumblers, etc., the mall has a hockey rink used by the Edmonton Oilers for practice, an amusement park with Ferris wheels, a life-size replica of a Spanish galleon, a Disney-like aquarium with four, 28-passenger submarines, and 836 retail stores, a church, a 142-foot-high roller coaster with a triple loop, a water park with a 120-foot waterfall providing water-skiing and surfing (with man-made waves), as well as a 360-room hotel with each floor decorated in a different theme.

While figures are not available as to its profitability, the developer claims, "It's a license to print money." The mall is apparently very profitable despite gargantuan heating costs. The mall's gross was estimated at over $561 million. This is nearly double the sales elsewhere in North America for the same amount of retail space. The feeling of the Canadian developer is that if an amusement mall is built right, it will dominate the market and effectively wipe out competition.

Other large developers have been studying the Edmonton success. Some developers claim huge mall amusement centers will only work in frigid temperatures. However, a Tustin, California amusement park consultant claims to be working on the planning of amusement park malls in the Southwest.

The Mall of America in Bloomington, Minnesota, a suburb of the Twin Cities, is the largest fully enclosed retail and entertainment complex in the United States. It was built at an estimated cost of $625 million and opened in 1992. The Ghermezian brothers were also development partners of this mall, which is so large it has stop lights in the parking lots, which extend ¼ mile on the sides. The mall has 20,000 parking spaces. The 4.3 million square foot mall, which is 4 stories high and also has stores in the basement, has 4 huge department stores, over 520 specialty shops, bowling alley, a four-story Lego showcase, over 60 restaurants and nightclubs, 14 movie theaters, and a 7-acre amusement park, Camp Snoopy, at its center with over 80 rides, including a roller coaster and Ferris wheel. Underwater World is a 1.2 million gallon walk-through aquarium. The mall even includes a campus of National American University. The Mall of America, located 5 minutes from the Minneapolis airport and 10 minutes from downtown Minneapolis or St. Paul, is claimed to be the nation's largest tourist attraction with more visitors than Disney World. With 40 million shoppers per year, the Mall of America has become an important vacation destination, which is touted by travel agents.

The Woodland Mall in Schaumburg, Illinois, has more shopping area than the Mall of America. In terms of shopping area, it is the largest mall in the United States. Located in a Chicago suburb, it draws an estimated 26 million shoppers each year. Unlike the Mall of America and the Edmonton Mall, The Woodland Mall lacks entertainment facilities and instead must rely on the local area for most of its shoppers.

In Chicago, the amusement center mall concept failed. Old Chicago was the first combination shopping center and amusement park. Analysts point out, however, that its attractions were mediocre and it was built in an area not suited to attract upscale families with children. Another problem of Old Chicago was its failure to control gangs of youths who intimidated and scared off patrons.

D. MINI-MALLS

While shopping centers are growing in size, a growth in small convenience centers (mini-malls) is also occurring.

A ***MINI-MALL*** *is a small strip center that has as an anchor tenant a convenience store such as "7-Eleven."* Other stores include donut shops, fast print shops, one-hour cleaners, delicatessens, quick photo developing, fast food outlets, etc. These centers cater to convenience, where a customer can park close to the door and be in and out quickly. While the huge malls are for people who may wish to make shopping an experience and have time to do so, the new mini centers attract people on their way to or from work, or who otherwise want the convenience of quick shopping.

Mini-mall development took off in the mid '70s, when full service gas stations were being closed. These sites were gobbled up for mini-mall centers. Mini-malls have grown in such profusion that in many areas they have saturated the marketplace, resulting in rising vacancies. They are also encountering resistance from homeowner groups and law enforcement agencies. Mini-malls compound traffic problems and are claimed to "attract undesirable people." Litter from the small centers often ends up in adjacent residential areas.

E. URBAN PEDESTRIAN MALLS

Many cities have tried unsuccessfully to revitalize their central business areas.

Advocated in the 1960s, urban malls became the most promising solution to central blight. One of the first of these projects was the Fulton Mall in Fresno. The mall, which became the model for urban malls in many other communities, was an open street mall for pedestrian traffic only. It included fountains, art work, plantings, benches, playgrounds, music, and outside cafes, covering a 36-acre super block.

Today, Fulton Mall has many vacant shops, and maintenance is needed. The remaining shops include discounters (discount stores). At night, the mall is deserted. This mall failed for a number of reasons, including:

1. The mall was not in tune with our automobile lifestyle; it envisioned a more European lifestyle.
2. The Fresno Fashion Fair (enclosed mall) on the north end of Fresno's suburban growth area practically killed the upscale stores in the Fulton Mall.

3. The mall had only one major anchor tenant, Gottschalks. Without at least two major anchor tenants, the mall failed to stimulate foot traffic. The major chains were not interested in the Fulton Mall because they wanted to be closer to the residences of upscale shoppers. (The major department stores located within the Fashion Fair Mall.)
4. Crime. Stores vacated and shoppers avoided the mall because of crime.

An attempt has been made to revitalize Fresno, California's Fulton Mall with limited success.

There is another Fulton Mall. It is a mostly pedestrian mall located in a twelve-block area of Brooklyn, New York. Unlike the Fresno mall, public transit is allowed. The roadways were narrowed to 18 feet to provide wide walks. The Brooklyn mall seems to be succeeding and is working to rejuvenate the entire area. Streets feature seating areas, vendor kiosks, and high-mast lighting. The success of the Brooklyn pedestrian mall and Fresno's mall failure is likely the fact that Brooklyn area shoppers are less dependent on vehicles than Fresno area shoppers. Also, the Brooklyn pedestrian mall allows public transit traffic along the mall roadways.

A study by the Washington-based Urban Land Institute concluded that:

Pedestrian malls practically "killed business" in 80% of the communities that had them and 21 identified cities were tearing them down.

Besides Brooklyn, urban pedestrian malls seem to be working well in smaller college towns and upscale areas where gentrification has taken place. In Santa Monica, California, a street was blocked off to traffic. It now has successful upscale shops, restaurants, and even street musicians. The year-round temperate climate in Santa Monica and a number of huge parking structures close by attribute to its success. Desirable housing for high-income young singles and families surrounds the shopping area.

Despite problems of open air malls in other areas, Hollywood built the Hollywood and Highland Mall—home of the Academy Awards and upscale stores—as the cornerstone of a redevelopment project. The mall includes two, 235-foot towers (one a hotel and the other for offices), a motion picture museum, open air plazas, walkways, and small shops. Mann's Chinese Theater is incorporated into the project.

F. FREESTANDING RETAIL DEVELOPMENTS

Many firms prefer freestanding big-box stores surrounded by parking, rather than being a part of shopping center complexes.

Off-price discount stores such as Kmart and Wal-Mart appear to prefer such property.

Some of these retailers believe they can generate traffic on their own and do not need shopping centers with their higher costs. Some shopping centers do not want off-price merchandisers because they do not fit in with the upscale image of their other stores. Also, full priced merchandisers would be less likely to lease in centers having off-price merchandisers.

VIII. Industrial Property

Early factories used water power or steam as an energy source. Belts, gears, shafts, and pulleys transmitted power. Vertical factories were most efficient for this transmission of power.

With the advent of electrical power, single-story, clear-span structures became more efficient. These structures allowed assembly line production with the receipt of raw materials at one end and shipping or storage of finished products at the other. Single-story structures also eliminate costly material handling of vertical movement.

Modern transportation has allowed plants to locate at larger sites on lower cost land that can accommodate not only the plant, but ample parking for employees as well.

Many large employers have leap frogged the suburbs to buy large tracts beyond the established bedroom communities. Not only does this result in lower land costs, but also the surplus land purchased will increase in value based on the plant development. The net effect can be getting a site at a reduced cost or for free, and in some cases, making a large profit as well.

In periods of economic recession, a glut of industrial space occurs. In the early 2000s, a weak economy, coupled with outsourcing of manufacturing to areas of the world with lower labor costs, resulted in a great deal of industrial vacancies. These vacancies are now being absorbed as our economy strengthens. In 2004, over 166 million square feet of industrial space was absorbed, compared to only 56.8 million square feet in 2003. At the end of 2004, the national industrial space vacancy rate was 9.4 percent compared to 10.27 percent in 2003.

Investors are now seeking industrial properties. In 2005, a number of industrial REITs developed industrial property, which will show a cap rate of between 7.5 percent and 8.5 percent.

A. INDUSTRIAL SITE SELECTION

The best location for an industrial development will vary with the industry.

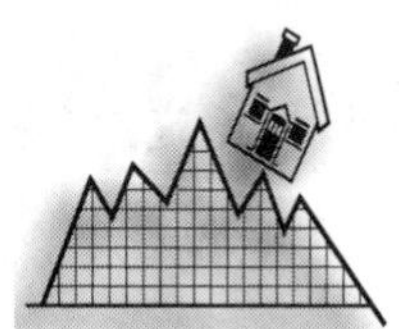

Location can minimize labor costs based on labor rates of the area and unionization. The supply of skilled labor is important for many industries. Besides the size of the labor pool, competition should also be considered. Location in relation to raw materials, markets, suppliers and transportation can affect transportation costs and reduce delays. The availability and cost of required utilities also plays a role in site selection.

The attitude of the local government toward industry is extremely important.

We have seen a growth in modern industrial parks. Besides private investors, many communities developed industrial parks to attract industry because of the need for jobs. Often a final site selection is made based on the benefits offered, which could include free or low cost rent, loans at favorable rates of interest, and/or property tax relief.

Managers are very interested in the quality of life for themselves and their families. They consider cultural aspects of an area, climate, schools, recreational facilities, and the quality and cost of housing.

Facility City magazine is geared to executives responsible for the relocation and expansion of facilities (**www.facilitycity.com**).

B. RESEARCH AND DEVELOPMENT (R&D)

***RESEARCH AND DEVELOPMENT** involves study, design, formulation, sample production, testing and evaluation to produce new products, improve old products, and find new uses for products.*

The ultimate purpose of R&D is to determine commercial feasibility.

R&D facilities include offices, meeting rooms, design areas, laboratories, production areas for sample products, and/or modification as well as testing facilities. Many R&D facilities resemble college campuses.

Because Research and Development is regarded as a clean industrial process and they are staffed with professionals and high-paid workers, R&D facilities are welcomed by most communities.

In the United States, 3.5 percent of industrial revenue is reinvested in R&D, although for some pharmaceutical companies, their R&D expenditures can exceed 40 percent. R&D facilities are often located near colleges and universities because they are a source for employees and consultants.

C. HIGH TECHNOLOGY

While many people regard manufacturing as the huge dirty plants that were the mainstay of manufacturing in the rustbelt, high technology plants are modern and relatively clean.

HIGH TECHNOLOGY *refers to "cutting edge" technology, but has come to mean technology involving computers and other new electronic devices and their components.*

High technology was the darling of investors until 2000. New facilities could not be built fast enough for new companies and expansion of existing ones. The collapse of many firms, as well as outsourcing, resulted in a high vacancy rate for these new facilities.

The Silicon Valley is experiencing a net absorption of space and an actual increase of rents in 2005 to 87 cents a square foot, up one cent—the first increase since the fourth quarter of 2000. Many firms are upgrading space as old leases expire, getting better space for the same or less money.

D. WHOLESALE AND WAREHOUSE AREAS

Wholesale and warehouse areas were historically located close to the central office/retail areas of a city along a rail line, freeway, or waterway.

Because of central traffic congestion and greater reliance on trucks, many of these historical central city operations have left the central area for fringe locations having ready access to major highways.

Nevada has become a warehouse and distribution center for the mountain and Western states because of its tax laws. Besides the absence of state income tax, Nevada does not have a personal property tax on goods stored within the state. The savings possible is significant compared to other locations.

Kansas City has a unique advantage over other cities when it comes to storage space. It has cheap storage space available in old limestone mines. To date, 20 million square feet of space have been developed for storage. This is equivalent to all of the office space in downtown Cleveland. The space, which is dry, also boasts a consistent temperature. Businesses have actually come to Kansas City to take advantage of this unique storage opportunity.

In 2004, the normal vacancy rate for warehouses was 10.1 percent.

Many facilities once called warehouses are now being referred to as distribution centers. A ***DISTRIBUTION CENTER*** *is simply a warehouse that receives goods for business* *purposes and then ships the goods to wholesalers, retailers, or end users.* Their main purpose is distribution rather than storage. Distribution centers require access to transportation, high ceilings for forklifts, loading docks, sprinkler systems, office areas, and parking.

E. STORAGE SPACE (Mini-Warehouses)

Mini-warehouse investments are one of the hottest available investments. Units show exceptional returns. Because of competition as well as higher land and construction costs, the return on investment has declined in some markets. However, most markets remain strong despite new units being added. Even smaller markets have had successful mini-storage developments. Rent for a 10′ x 20′ space will vary from about $50 per month to over $300 per month, depending upon the location.

Mini-storage centers tend to run counter to economic conditions. In recessionary periods, businesses and individuals store equipment and inventory when downsizing. They also hesitate to expand even if their space needs increase.

A number of Real Estate Investment Trusts specialize in mini-storage facilities. Public Storage, a REIT, has a philosophy of seeking valuable sites along major highways for their projects. While their mini-storage facilities bring in a positive cash flow, they have another agenda. Eventually, they intend to sell selected sites to developers at significant price increases. They are therefore seeking income as well as appreciation, which they intend to cash in on.

IX. Changes in Use

In many cities, large Victorian homes are converted to offices.

These offices frequently command premium rents and are sought after by law firms, investment firms, accountants, and other professionals who deal with the public in a position of trust. Many firms feel that offices in these staid, old structures create an atmosphere of strength and dignity. Some of those structures rent for as much as Class A office space.

Large, old homes lacking special architectural appeal are also frequently converted to offices when zoning permits. While these offices usually rent for significantly less than traditional office space, the returns can still be significantly higher than would be possible if renting for residential purposes.

Developers often convert existing homes to offices with the intent of replacing the homes with new, high-rise office structures at some later date.

Motels have frequently been converted to office space. These conversions result in lower operational costs and a more stable income. Even without a greater net profit, office conversions make marginal motel operations more saleable, as they do not require the intensive management effort of a motel.

A pre-Civil War spice warehouse in Savannah, Georgia, a railroad station in Scranton, Pennsylvania, a Federal Reserve Bank in Boston, Massachusetts, and grain elevators in Akron, Ohio, have all been converted to luxury hotels.

There was a strong economic factor responsible for many of these earlier conversions, due to the investment tax credit. If the conversion costs more than the price of the building, the investor could obtain a dollar-for-dollar reduction in his or her taxes. For properties listed on the Register of Historic Places, the credit could equal 25 percent of renovation costs. For non-landmark properties more than 40 years old, the credit was 20 percent. For buildings 30 years or older, a 15 percent tax credit applied. If an investor financed 80 percent of the renovation and had a 20 percent investment tax credit, the government could actually reimburse the total investment by reducing the investor's taxes. For taxpayers who had high tax bills, the investment tax credit offered a unique opportunity.

In Los Angeles, Spring Street owes rejuvenation to the investment tax credit, as does Colorado Boulevard in Pasadena. According to the National Park Service, which certifies historic rehabilitation, almost 15,000 historic structures have been rehabilitated since the Tax Reform Act of 1986 went into effect.

The Tax Reform Act of 1986 reduced rehabilitation tax credits to 20 percent for rehabilitation of certified historic structures, and 10 percent for the rehabilitation of nonresidential buildings originally in use before 1936. Restrictions on qualified rehabilitation require that at least 75 percent of both the external walls and internal framework be retained.

Benefits received by the government far exceed tax credits allowed. Renovation results in permanent as well as construction employment, which means additional federal tax dollars. A higher tax base as well as private funds is being used to preserve and improve the city and benefit the community. Renovations have resulted in businesses remaining in the city and increased tourist dollars.

In some cases, developers have shunned tax credit opportunities. Forest City Enterprises renovated Cleveland's Terminal Tower at a cost of $179 million. It received no tax credits for renovating the 57-year-old beaux art structure because the potential tax credits were less than the additional costs required to meet preservation requirements.

Central city warehouses and factories have enjoyed a rapid appreciation in value based on possible new use as office space. This transformation started in the 1970s. Besides a rental cost advantage, these older spaces with high ceilings and often architectural accouterments encourage flexible work space and have an arty appeal. Graphic firms, Internet commerce, advertising agencies, and other creative business service firms have gravitated toward these structures.

Small industrial firms, in some markets, have not been able to renew leases because entertainment and high tech businesses are attracted to the casual cool image of concrete and brick, high ceilings, open trusses and ductwork, as well as good parking. While lowered ceilings to hide the buildings support and system was formerly in vogue, now tenants want everything exposed and often paint ducts and trusses in bright colors. In desirable areas of Los Angeles, small industrial structures are renting for upwards of $1.35 per square foot. A 3,000 square foot shop would rent for over $4,000 per month. This is more than most industrial firms will pay, so they are being forced to move to areas where lower cost space is available.

A developer spent about $10 million on seven old and ugly airport hangers at Hamilton Field, North of San Francisco, that sat in a field of tarmac. Local real estate professionals thought the developer was out of his mind when he announced plans to convert the old hangers to offices. However, the first hanger was fully leased within one month of completion. While it is not Class A office space and has ceilings as high as 39 feet, the space was nevertheless gobbled up by eager tenants. The developer counted on both the odd appeal of the conversions and the fact that there was a scarcity of office space in Marin County.

Older office buildings in downtown areas were often viewed as dinosaur structures.

One hundred-year-old buildings without distinctive architecture were not being upgraded. Besides loft conversions, many of these old buildings have received a new lease on life because of technology. These old buildings have three things going for them: high ceilings, floors that can take a load factor of from 150 to 250 pounds per square foot, and locations in central areas close to underground fiber optic networks. These buildings are highly desirable for telecom switching centers. High heavy equipment requires the air space of high ceilings for proper cooling as well as floors built to take heavy loads. Modern office buildings do not meet either of these requirements. In addition, the buildings are located in the right areas for connections since underground fiber optic lines, which are the highway of the Internet, generally originate in central city areas.

The need for switching centers has led investors to seek out these older structures for lease to Internet related firms. Q West Communications International Inc. is developing 40 "cyber centers." In New York, it has leased the old Sak's Fifth Avenue distribution center. It expects conversion costs of $100 million to turn the 500,000 square foot facility into a service center for Internet companies.

Old empty shopping malls in many areas of the country were no longer economically viable because of changing demographics and competition from newer malls. Suburban sprawl has left these carcasses behind. A number of school districts are looking at strip malls, supermarkets, and factories as future homes for students. Public school enrollment is expected to rise 15% in the next 10 years with an estimated 47.5 million students.

Existing structures offer a reasonable cost solution.

The Maryvale Mall in Phoenix, that was vacant for seven years, became the Marc T. Atkinson Middle School. In St. Paul, an art magnet school occupies what was once a car dealership. In Phoenix, an abandoned church is an art magnet school. Reno, Nevada, boasts a technical training school that occupies a former factory. An empty research and development facility in Wake County, North Carolina, became the Lufkin Road Middle School.

The trend of converting vacant structures to schools has also helped to revitalize deteriorating neighborhoods and make area housing more attractive.

A. RAZING FOR PARKING

In many cities, there are large, blighted structures close to the central business districts. These structures, due to vacancies and low rent, often produce revenue less than the variable operational costs. Because of the negative cash flow, owners of such structures are often highly motivated to sell. Purchasers of such properties are often long-term investors who raze the structure. ***RAZING** is the removal of existing improvements from a parcel.* When razed the structure is demolished, it is also removed from the tax rolls. The purchaser ends up with a desirable parking lot that can be leased to an operator and will yield trouble-free income. The investor can then wait for anticipated redevelopment in the area to increase value without being under pressure to sell quickly.

X. Nonresidential Investors

Individual investors own many smaller nonresidential properties. While there are some individuals as well as families that invest in major projects, the number of these qualified individuals is limited.

Money from sources other than the savings of a single person or family is required to buy or develop properties that might run into the 10s or even 100s of millions of dollars.

A. SYNDICATES (General and Limited Partnerships)

The higher the price for investment property, the fewer the number of qualified buyers. For investments that require several million dollars in cash, there are relatively few individual buyers.

A syndicate is a group of investors that are often organized as limited partnerships.

Syndicates created a large number of qualified buyers for large projects. Instead of a few buyers for a number of large investments, syndicates created markets where there

are a number of syndicates competing for prime investment property. The supply and demand of the marketplace resulted in substantial increases in sales prices of larger properties.

In the 1970s many syndicates were highly leveraged. In an expanding economy it was economically advantageous to use as much borrowed capital as possible. This allowed the investors to take the maximum benefit of appreciating values. However, a highly leveraged position posed greater risks. Increased vacancies, coupled with high money costs and expenses, resulted in negative cash flow. Because of a depressed market, properties often could not be sold for enough to cover the indebtedness and the properties were foreclosed. With foreclosure, the investors lost their entire investment.

Many syndicates are overly optimistic in their reports to investors regarding the value of their holdings. While this encourages investors to make further investments, appraisers employed by the syndicate do not determine the true value of syndicate property. Only buyers determine value.

The 1986 Tax Reform Act hurt many syndicates that were formed for tax shelter rather than income purposes. The prohibition on use of excess passive losses from syndicates against other investor income resulted in many syndicates liquidating or becoming Real Estate Investment Trusts.

B. REAL ESTATE INVESTMENT TRUSTS (REITs)

Approximately 200 publicly traded Real Estate Investment Trusts exist. They are organized under federal law and must include 100 or more investors, although the larger REITs have thousands of shareholders.

Most Real Estate Investment Trusts (REITs) use only moderate leverage. They are open-ended trusts that are traded on major stock exchanges. The marketplace, not the underlying value of the real estate, determines prices for shares. REITs may sell at a discount or premium to the value of their holdings. Real Estate Investment Trusts customarily often specialize in types of property such as apartment REITs, industrial REITs, mall REITs, etc. Real Estate Investment Trusts are now the biggest players in the real estate market and often hold billions of dollars in assets.

An advantage of REITs over other stock investments is the high cash dividends paid.

Real Estate Investment Trusts (REITs) do NOT pay income taxes if 90% or more of their profits are distributed annually to their shareholders.

Additional information about REITs is available from the National Association of Real Estate Trusts (**www.NAREIT.com**).

C. PENSION FUNDS

Swelling pension funds searching for investment opportunities could be a major force in keeping prices high on large developments.

Pension funds have historically utilized all cash for their investments. With lower interest rates, pension funds have now been borrowing 40 to 50 percent of property value. This is considered leverage without risk, which allows additional real property investments. The net effect of safe leverage for prime properties is an increase of net income and real property holdings.

Because of low returns from bonds, pension funds have increased their REIT investments. Real Estate Investment Trusts and pension funds together have an estimated $320 billion invested in real estate.

D. INSURANCE COMPANIES

Insurance companies invest premiums received so that the money will grow to pay benefits.

Insurance companies are major investors in nonresidential mortgages. They are also direct investors in real estate.

Northwestern Mutual Life invests between 2.5 and 3.5 billion in real estate each year with 79 percent being fixed income (mortgages) and 21 percent in direct equity investments as sole owner or in a partnership role.

Insurance companies like to team up with successful developers and provide financing for projects as well as to assume an equity position.

E. FOREIGN INVESTMENT (Recent History)

Our trade imbalances with China, Japan, Taiwan, Indonesia, South Korea, several Middle East countries, and Germany have led to a great many dollars being held abroad.

Significant foreign investment of these dollars in U.S. dollar securities has helped to keep interest rates in the United States low, with dollars available for investment.

In the '80s, the average price for office space in Tokyo was $4,000 per square foot. Top quality office space in New York was available for around $400 per square foot. This dramatic difference in initial cost, as well as a much greater return in the U.S. on investment property, were magnets for Japanese investors.

In Japan, prime real estate yielded 2 to 3 percent, but prime U.S. property could be purchased showing returns three times those possible in Japan for cash purchases.

The high yields possible, especially when coupled with the depressed value of the dollar, make U.S. real estate extremely attractive to Japanese investors.

Japanese taxes also encouraged American investments. In Japan, the depreciation period on real estate was 60 years, while in the United States it was 15 years on nonresidential property.

Japanese investors typically had loans from Japanese lenders at interest rates of 5 to 6 percent. With low interest financing, they realized positive cash flows on purchase prices, which would otherwise have resulted in negative cash flow situations.

The collapse of the Japanese stock markets and lower Japanese real estate values resulted in financial problems for many Japanese who had invested in U.S. real estate. Their loans were often collateralized by corporate stock and/or Japanese real estate. In addition, the Japanese lenders raised the interest rates on these loans. The results were foreclosures and "fire sales" in the '90s by Japanese lenders.

In 1999, German investors were enthusiastic buyers of trophy properties in the U.S. that included the Rockefeller Center office tower. One of the reasons Germans became active buyers of U.S. property was because the tax incentives for investments in East Germany had expired. Also leasing income from U.S. buildings is taxed in the U.S. and not subject to Germany's higher tax rates. The fact that U.S. property allowed an 8 percent return compared to an average 6 percent in Germany made U.S. property attractive.

In 2000, German interest in U.S. properties dwindled for a number of reasons including:

1. A strong dollar which raised U.S. costs in Deutch Marks;
2. A weak Euro which reduced the value of Euro holdings for U.S. purchases;
3. Rising U.S. interest rates;
4. The competitive lure of the stock market (there were major new public offerings in Germany).

While German buyers seem to have lost a great deal of their interest, German banks have entered our mortgage market. They have been very competitive and are making many large loans, which most U.S. lenders are not willing to make. German banks are exporting their funds. German funds available for lending are currently exceeding domestic demand.

Middle East investors control billions of dollars. U.S. investors have been stymied in attempts to tap these funds; one reason being Islamic law, which prohibits the receiving of interest.

A New York law firm has developed a structure to obtain debt financing without violating Islamic law. They are using land leases where the investors buy the land and receive rent payments for their investments rather than interest. By using a floating rent tied to the London Interbank Offer Rate (LIBOR), the lease payments are the equivalent of interest but remain rent. The plan has been implemented and has been approved by the Shari'ah Committee of Kuwait's Gulf Investment House.

In 2003, according to the Association of Foreign Investors in Real Estate, foreign investment in U.S. real estate rose by 59 percent and was expected to rise another 11.9 percent in 2004. The leading market for foreign investment was New York and Washington D.C. The drop in the value of the dollar has created bargains for European investors. The Association of Foreign Investors in Real Estate is a trade association of non-U.S. investors in the U.S. market (**www.afire.org**).

From mid-2004 to mid-2005, Australian investors purchased $6.8 billion in U.S. commercial properties. This was 37 percent of the foreign capital entering our real estate marketplace. Australia topped Germany as the largest foreign buyers during this period. While the U.S. commercial real estate market is setting records for high prices, low returns, and high mortgages, the market looks good to Australian investors. One reason is the fact that the strong Australian dollar makes U.S. prices seem more reasonable. The investors indicate that even at record prices, the investments in the U.S. are better than could be obtained in Europe or Asia. The money flows in from loans from Australian pensions, which control $1.5 trillion in assets. Historically, Australian pension funds have invested 10 percent of their assets in real estate.

XI. Asbestos Affects Salability

The presence of asbestos insulation has affected the salability of many commercial structures. ***ASBESTOS INSULATION** has been found to cause severe health problems and even death in people who have inhaled large quantities.* By scaring off prospective buyers the result has been lower prices for such structures.

While the federal government has not set any standards for the presence of asbestos in structures, owners are worried about liability for asbestos-related illnesses of tenant employees as well as the cost of removal. A 1987 New York City ordinance requires that a structure must be inspected for asbestos and an abatement plan must be approved before a building permit is issued.

The cost of asbestos removal will normally range from $10 to $30 per square foot. However, in structures where the steel structural frame was coated with asbestos material as a fire insulation, costs could make removal uneconomical.

The sale of the Atlantic Richfield Plaza in downtown Los Angeles provided for an adjustment in price for asbestos removal. It was estimated this lowered the approximate $600 million dollar cost by $40 to $50 million.

Buyers of buildings having asbestos are asking sellers to indemnify them against future claims from employees or tenants. Another problem is that a building owner is considered to be the owner of the removed asbestos even if placed in an approved landfill. An owner could, therefore, have liability for a future, mandated cleanup of the landfill. Commercial brokers report many deals die when the presence of asbestos is discovered.

In New York, Exxon Corporation and Rockefeller Group, Inc. sold their jointly owned Exxon building to Mitsui Fudoson, Inc. for far less than the building had been expected to bring. The reason cited for lower than expected bids was the presence of asbestos, which experts believed would cost from $20 to $40 per square foot for removal. The price for the Exxon building computed to $270 per square foot. This price was a bargain at the time of sale compared to prices in the $500 per square foot range paid for other prime Manhattan property. Prices on asbestos-related buildings appear to have been discounted far greater than the cost of asbestos removal.

Many lenders and investors will not even consider buildings where asbestos was used because of the removal expense and possible lawsuits. Aetna and Prudential insurance companies have indicated they will no longer buy or finance older buildings containing asbestos. However, there are some lenders and investors who see opportunities because of asbestos. General Electric Credit Corporation, a subsidiary of General Electric company, will make mortgages on buildings where it is practical to remove the asbestos if the buyer agrees to set up a fund for its eventual removal. It feels that, while asbestos is a problem, it is a manageable one. Tishman Speyer Properties, a New York builder and investor, has purchased asbestos properties because of the owner hysteria and resultant low prices on structures that contained asbestos.

XII. CHAPTER SUMMARY

Investors are attracted to real property investments for income, appreciation, preservation of capital, depreciation, leverage, collateral value, as well as **psychic income**. Negative aspects of real estate investments include risk, illiquidity, necessity of management, and taxes. Real estate investment risk can be reduced by careful **location analysis**.

Like residential vacancies, commercial vacancies only compete with other vacant property. Commercial property can be leased under **flat leases** like most residential property, as well as under **net leases** or **percentage leases**. **Rent concessions** in a form other than reduced rents are generally in the best interest of the lessor.

As a rental inducement, the building's name is frequently given to a lessor who rents (or leases) a great deal of space. Other owners actually give prime tenants an **equity interest** in the structure in exchange for a long-term lease.

Because of the long time period between planning and completion, office structures often come on the market when vacancies are high. This time delay, coupled with incomplete knowledge of the market and changes in the economy, can lead to **overbuilding**.

New space entering the market has a **ripple effect** that results in higher vacancies in the least desirable structures. Older office buildings can generally absorb a higher vacancy factor than new structures because of lower fixed costs. Many older structures are renovated from Class C to Class B space, allowing them to effectively compete with newer structures.

Overbuilding in some areas of the country has resulted in not only a high vacancy factor, but also deflation in value and in foreclosures. At the present time, values have appreciated because of a general high demand, despite significant vacancy factors.

While **community shopping centers** have been declining, we are seeing growth in **shopping malls** and even **mega malls**. **Mini-centers** of convenience stores are also showing good growth. **Neighborhood shopping centers** anchored by large food stores have retained their value.

The best retail location for a business is known as a **100 percent location**. The 100 percent location for a business will vary based on the type of business. Generally, the lowest cost location for a retail business is the most expensive location in terms of net results.

Industry has been moving out of the central city. The best industrial locations are based on a number of factors, including transportation, relationship of suppliers and markets, labor supply and costs, land costs, attitude of local government toward industry and quality of life.

Many structures are finding new uses based on needs of the marketplace.

Largely because of our trade deficit and the decline in the value of the dollar, we saw a great deal of foreign investment in prime properties, mainly office structures. This has cooled off and many of these foreign owned properties have been foreclosed and sold. However, U.S. real estate is still attracting foreign buyers.

XIII. GLOSSARY OF KEY TERMS

Anchor Tenant – The major tenant of a shopping center who creates traffic benefiting other tenants.

Business Incubators – Organizations and businesses that aid new businesses with services as well as space to reduce the likelihood of a failure.

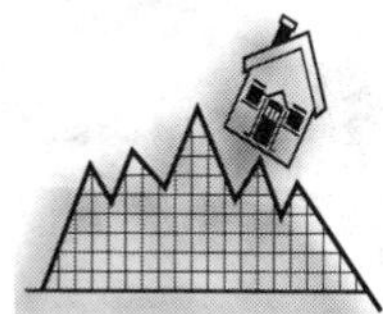

Class A Office Buildings – Newer, most desirable office structures.

Class B Office Buildings – Older, but well-maintained office structures.

Class C Office Buildings – Older, least desirable office structures.

Collateral Value – The loan value of a property.

Community Shopping Center – A shopping center with one major department store as an anchor tenant.

Effective Rent – Scheduled rent adjusted by concessions given.

Escalator Clause – A clause in a lease that allows the rent to be adjusted based on some criteria, such as the Consumer Price Index.

Flat Lease – A lease in which the tenant pays a fixed monthly rental.

Flight Capital – Capital investment from areas of political and/or economic instability, seeking safety.

High-Rise – A multi-storied structure.

Image Structure – A distinctive, usually expensive structure that contributes to the image of the tenant.

Investment Tax Credit – An investment whereby part of the cost is directly credited against taxes owed by the investor.

Letter of Intent – While not a contract, it is an indication that a firm intends to negotiate in good faith (generally to lease).

Mega Mall – A huge, mall-type shopping center.

Mini-Center – Small (or mini-mall) strip center anchored by a convenience store.

Neighborhood Shopping Center – A strip-type development anchored by a major food store.

Net Lease – Also known as a triple net lease, it is a lease in which the tenant pays the lessor a flat rental as well as taxes, insurance, and maintenance expenses.

One Hundred Percent (100%) Location – The best location in a community for a business.

Percentage Lease – A lease in which the lessee pays a percentage of the gross business receipts as rent.

Recapture Clause – Clause allowing lessor to terminate a percentage lease if lessee fails to achieve the required volume.

Regional Shopping Center – A larger shopping center anchored by several major department stores.

Rent Concession – Rent abatement or other concessions given to a tenant as an inducement to sign a lease.

Research and Development Facility – Industrial facility that develops and tests new or improved products.

Ripple Effect – The filtering down of commercial space.

Sale-Leaseback – Usually sale to an investor in which the grantor becomes a lessee. The purpose is generally to free capital.

Smart Buildings – Buildings that offer computer and other electronic services for tenants.

Specialized Buildings – Buildings that specialize in rentals to a particular type of business activity.

Tenant Partners – Making a tenant an equity partner in the structure as an inducement to sign a lease.

Trophy Property – Highly desirable landmark structure.

Unearned Benefit – An unearned increment to value not due to any effort or expenditure of the owner.

Vulture Funds – Investment funds established to purchase buildings in financial difficulty.

XI.V CLASS DISCUSSION TOPICS

1. Discuss the where and why of the best locations within your community for the following:

   a. Retail jewelry store
   b. New car dealership
   c. Medical offices
   d. Real estate offices
   e. Wholesale plumbing supply
   f. Parking lot
   g. Mini-storage
   h. Service station
   i. Fast food outlet
   j. Prestige supper club
   k. Large motel
   l. Auto rental agency

2. What office buildings, shopping centers, stores, etc. in your area have inadequate parking?

3. Identify inefficient structures in your area (ratio of rentable space to total space).

4. Identify specialized buildings in your area devoted to one business or trade.

5. Which office structures in your area have the highest vacancy rate? Why?

6. What areas of your community have had the highest turnover in retail stores? Why?

7. Give an example of blockage of shopper foot traffic in your area.

8. Rate area office structures as Class A, newer/modern; Class B, older/quality space; or Class C, older/least desirable space.

9. Identify housing in your area that could economically be converted to office space.

10. Identify empty nonresidential structures where conversion to other uses might be feasible.

11. Identify any "image structures" in your area.

XV. CHAPTER 12 QUIZ

1. During recessionary periods, the type of property most likely to retain its value would be:

   a. retail stores.
   b. shopping malls.
   c. hotels and motels.
   d. apartment buildings and health care facilities.

2. Benefits of owning a real estate investment include all, except:

   a. income.
   b. appreciation.
   c. illiquidity.
   d. depreciation.

3. The term "100 percent location" refers to:

   a. a triple net lease.
   b. the best retail location for a particular type of business.
   c. the location having the highest rent.
   d. a store where all the space is usable.

4. A lease where the lessee is responsible for taxes, insurance, and maintenance expenses would be a(n):

   a. triple net lease.
   b. flat lease.
   c. percentage lease.
   d. escalator lease.

5. The best quality office building would be Class:
   a. A.
   b. B.
   c. C.
   d. D.

6. Overbuilding of office structures will lead to all, except:
   a. deflation in building value.
   b. an increase in the vacancy factor.
   c. higher office rents.
   d. lender foreclosures.

7. As of 2000, the highest cost city in the U.S. for office rents was:
   a. Washington, D.C.
   b. Los Angeles.
   c. Boston.
   d. San Francisco.

8. The largest enclosed mall in America is:
   a. South Coast Plaza.
   b. Mall of America.
   c. Grand Avenue Mall.
   d. Horton Plaza.

9. The anchor tenant for a mini-mall is likely to be a:
   a. major department store.
   b. large grocery store.
   c. convenience store.
   d. home center.

10. Property that has great demand during recessionary times would be:
   a. office structures.
   b. mini-warehouses.
   c. industrial property.
   d. research and development property.

ANSWERS: *1. d; 2. c; 3. b; 4. a; 5. a; 6. c; 7. d; 8. b; 9. c; 10. b*

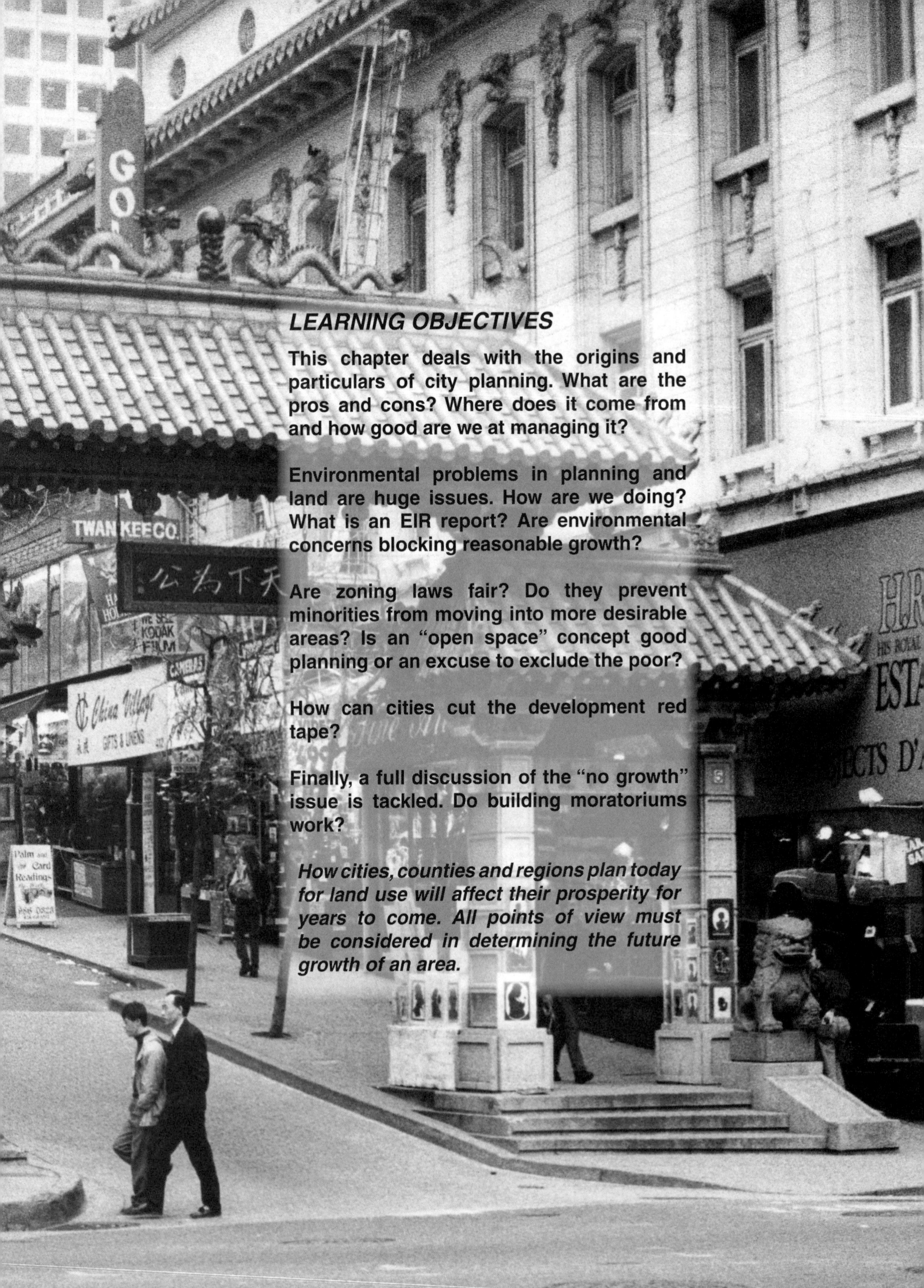

LEARNING OBJECTIVES

This chapter deals with the origins and particulars of city planning. What are the pros and cons? Where does it come from and how good are we at managing it?

Environmental problems in planning and land are huge issues. How are we doing? What is an EIR report? Are environmental concerns blocking reasonable growth?

Are zoning laws fair? Do they prevent minorities from moving into more desirable areas? Is an "open space" concept good planning or an excuse to exclude the poor?

How can cities cut the development red tape?

Finally, a full discussion of the "no growth" issue is tackled. Do building moratoriums work?

How cities, counties and regions plan today for land use will affect their prosperity for years to come. All points of view must be considered in determining the future growth of an area.

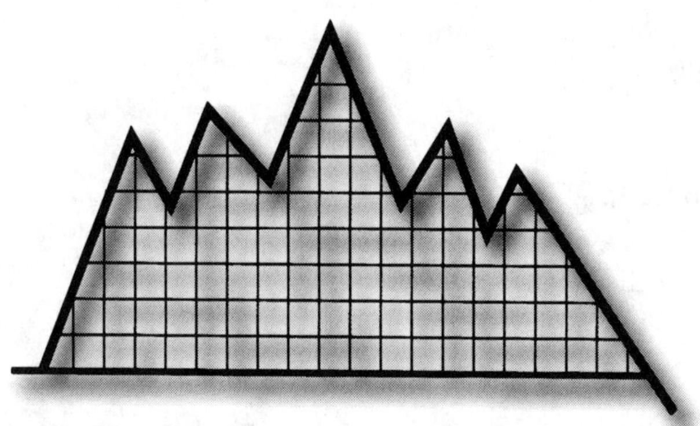

Chapter 13
Planning and Land Control Use

I. City and County Planning

"Plans are nothing: planning is everything." – Dwight D. Eisenhower

A. HISTORY OF PLANNING

Ancient cities show evidence of complex planning. Rome, Italy had a well-planned infrastructure to support the populace.

In the ancient Roman Empire, when a city became too crowded, straws were drawn to see who would be chosen to start a new city at some other location.

1. William Penn (1644-1718)

William Penn started systematic land planning in the United States.

***WILLIAM PENN**, a Quaker reformer, was the founder of Pennsylvania and started systematic land planning in the United States.* In 1681 he obtained from England the province of Pennsylvania. Penn planned to make his new colony the "Holy Experiment." William Penn located the city of Philadelphia between the Delaware

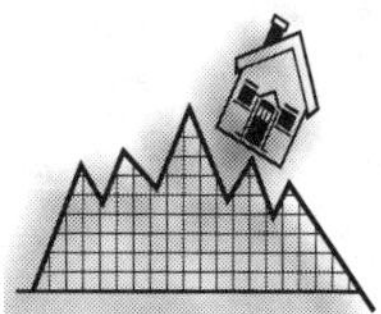

CHAPTER 13 OUTLINE

and Schuylkill (pronounced "Skoo' kl") Rivers. In Penn's architectural plans the entire area between rivers was symmetrical, with noticeable differences between primary and secondary streets, and the provision of public open space.

Penn, shown in **Figure 13-1**, is signing a treaty of friendship with the Indians of Pennsylvania, setting a high standard in relations. He later proposed laws guaranteeing settlers of Philadelphia an elective assembly and religious freedom. He traveled through Europe selling land in his colony and offering religious freedom.

City planning is NOT of recent origin. As early as 1682, William Penn had commissioned a plan for Philadelphia.

Philadelphia was divided into four quadrants, each with a public park. George Washington and Thomas Jefferson both worked on a city plan for Washington, D.C. It was based on a plan devised by Major Pierre Charles L'Enfant. The plan had a grid pattern of streets with wide radial boulevards.

B. WHY PLANNING?

PLANNING *is the design of the physical environment*. The goal is to protect the health and welfare of the citizens. Because the use of a single property can affect other properties, planning can coordinate uses to best serve the welfare of the people.

Some economists believe city planning is NOT necessary.

Those economists believe that, in the absence of planning, we would bargain for land use that results in orderly development, with the highest and best use prevailing for each site. This is an example of economics deciding land use. While this view may sound logical in theory, we do not have a perfect market where every buyer and seller is fully informed and economically motivated. Many decisions are made without

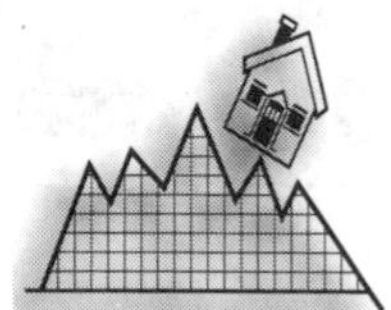

Figure 13-1

perfect knowledge and not in the best economic interests of the owners. Even with informed economic decision making, planning is needed to provide transportation, services and community needs as well as owner benefits. Each parcel of land is part of a whole and planning allows integration of the parcel into a well functioning whole.

Planning forces us to ask, "Where are we now? Where do we appear to be heading?" And, "Where do we want to be heading?" The basic goals of planning are wide distribution of ownership, orderly economic growth, and the wise development and conservation of our resources. Without planning, these goals cannot be accomplished and land will be locked into uses which fail to properly benefit individual citizens and the community as a whole now, and into the future. In the past, American cities have often been shaped by decisions of individual developers based on short-term benefits.

Planning forces long-term goals.

With planning, common usages can be linked to avoid conflict and advantageously serve the users. Examples are industrial and residential areas. Planning can also link areas together for a working whole.

Without planning, growth can become chaotic.

C. THE LIBERTARIAN VIEWPOINT AS TO PLANNING

Libertarians feel that government solutions to land use have been political and that they have imposed unnecessary costs on middle and low-income people. They feel that zoning boosts renter costs, rent control limits new construction, building codes increase costs and public housing hurts rather than helps low income individuals. Libertarians would repeal land use controls, but allow use to be regulated if it was a nuisance. They would encourage private arbitration involving land use and housing. They would also encourage private restrictive use covenants. They want building codes to be voluntary.

Libertarians look to Houston as a model since Houston has no comprehensive plan and no zoning. Houston has grown based on a free market and Libertarians feel that government interferes with the free market. In fact, Houston voted down zoning on three separate occasions, the last time in 1993. Opposition to zoning was based strongly on individual property rights.

Libertarians feel that if left alone, a free market will solve the problems of housing and reasonable land use.

D. CRITICISM OF CITY PLANNING

Planners and their plans have been far from perfect. Some criticisms are listed in **Figure 13-2**.

In a few states, such as Virginia, court decisions lean strongly toward the economic well being of the property owner over the power to regulate for local planning needs.

While the courts have upheld planning as a proper exercise of police power, state legislatures and courts are beginning to place limits on planning power. Texas and Mississippi require compensation for state or local regulations that reduce property values. Similar property rights laws are being considered in other states. In Florida, a 1995 statute not only allows courts to order compensation when regulations reduce property value, but requires payment of damages when the owners were prevented from making the money that the owners could reasonably expect to make.

In the face of growing hostility, planning agencies should be prepared to justify use restrictions as well as impact fees charged. Even with justification, in some states the financial impact should be considered if the regulations infringe ownership rights.

Figure 13-2

Criticism of City Planning

City planners and planning have been far from perfect. Some critics have said:

1. City planners base all planning on the automobile. They do not consider bikes or foot traffic as viable transportation.
2. Planners' answers to transportation needs have consistently been larger freeways that exacerbate other problems.
3. Planners have failed to properly address the pollution problems of air, water and soil.
4. Planning seems to be based more on size rather than quality.
5. Planners seem to want to duplicate what has been done before rather than consider specific needs. The result has been that American cities have a sterile sameness about them.
6. Bureaucratic regulations are overly complicated, often ambiguous, and sometimes have conflicting goals.
7. Planners tend to copy regulations from other communities, without considering possible differences in goals.
8. Lower level government employees tend to accept planning regulations as gospel.
9. Planning boards are not technically oriented and often overrule their technical staff.
10. Planning boards are often politically motivated and influenced by political considerations.
11. There is often little supervision of officials who take an inordinate amount of time processing approvals.
12. Planning boards tend to make decisions based on short-term needs and fail to consider the future.
13. Unreasonable regulations and delays keep costs high and thus discriminate against minorities.
14. Planning is often fragmented with failure to consider area-wide needs.
15. Planning is an infringement on ownership rights.

E. FRAGMENTED PLANNING (Problems of Coordination)

The fragmentation of community government hampers effective area planning.

For example, California's Santa Clara County has 72 local governments all involved in planning (15 cities, 37 school districts, and 19 special districts, as well as the county itself).

This problem of "balkanization" of governments is not unique to California. ***BALKANIZATION*** *is fragmentation from overlapping governmental controls on state, regional, and local entities.* This process occurs due to the lack of a coordinated approach to planning. Metropolitan Atlanta has 53 separate governmental units and Denver has 50. The logical solution would be strong regional governments with little local control.

The St. Louis region consists of 2.5 million people in two states, the City of Saint Louis, eleven surrounding counties, and a multitude of municipalities, school districts, taxing authorities, and government services providers. Former Senator John Danford stated in 1997, "it is a system that encourages jealousies and fosters stalemate. A comprehensive answer to our problems of governance is probably beyond our reach, but the status quo is absolutely unacceptable."

Decisions in one community will affect other communities, therefore we need coordination and control of local planning. City and county planning should be within the context of regional planning, not vice versa.

While we have a number of governmental associations, they lack the power to set regional planning policy. In some cases, cities refuse to join governmental associations. Inter-city coordination of utility needs does not really exist.

Although the American Land Institute's (ALI) code requires regional review of developments of regional significance, even when adopted, the code does not cover smaller projects that could have a cumulative effect on the region.

Because we are beginning to realize that uncoordinated and unregulated growth can have irreversible effects on an entire region, we are beginning to see substantial new legislation in the field of regional planning.

An answer to fragmented government would be to consolidate separate municipalities. Canadian provinces have consolidated cities with several of their suburban municipalities in major metropolitan areas including Toronto, Montreal, Winnipeg, and Halifax. The Canadian merger would not have taken place if it had been up to the municipalities involved. Jealousy and self-interest would have made consolidation impossible. Politicians would never agree to eliminate their own jobs. The provinces

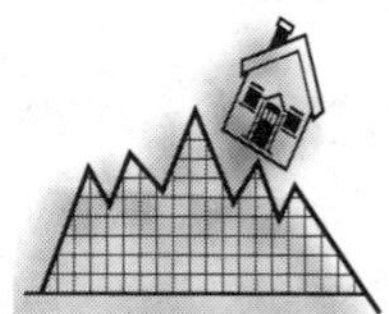

forced the consolidations upon them even after nonbinding referendums showed the people involved opposed consolidation.

Consolidations were easier in Canada than they would be in most U.S. metropolitan areas because county type governments and not the individual cities were handling many of the services.

Sixteen states now have legislation to allow cities to merge, but this would require agreement. It is doubtful that communities would agree to become part of a regional government.

F. TRANSPORTATION AND PLANNING

There is NO easy solution to the conflict between growth and mobility.

In most states, transportation planning is the function of the State Department of Transportation, but land use is under local control.

Multiple planning agencies, as well as the difficulty in coordination of planning over regional and state boundaries, have resulted in both serious traffic problems and less than optimum land utilization.

Some communities have encouraged uses that enrich public coffers such as retail, offices and factories without regard for the effect on the total transportation needs of the area.

Where to build new transportation facilities and what to build as well as new light rail versus highways have become politically charged issues. Citizens groups often oppose new major arteries or improvements in their areas that will increase traffic, noise, fumes and/or traffic speed.

Political pressures determine which projects get funded and which do not, NOT necessarily based on the priority of the Department of Transportation.

In Virginia, the legislature overruled a decision of the Virginia Department of Transportation over a connecting route between I-95 to I-64 and I-295. Politics decided the new route.

Funds for transportation projects often come from bond financing. Where voter approval is required, retirees as well as large property owners and property owner groups will generally oppose bond financing since it will result in higher property taxes. Many owners feel that the highway burden is unfairly levied on property owners when it should be shared by others benefiting from the expenditures. In many states, the gas tax provides funds for new roads and road improvements. It has been suggested that local developments pay a transportation or impact fee to the State Department of Transportation to fund needs generated by new developments.

It is clear that transportation needs and land use are linked together so coordination is needed at all levels. One suggested solution is to give transportation planning the primary role and to require local planning to fit in with the transportation route rather than to require transportation planning to come after the fact and try to meet diverse needs of many communities. Other planners believe that no single element can be planned separately. Transportation and land use are linked together and must be planned together.

In some areas, we have managed to coordinate and control to the point that it is difficult to achieve goals. In the greater Washington, D.C. area, regional responsibility is fragmented with the Washington Metropolitan Area Transit Authority, being the regional provider of public transportation, the Metropolitan Council of Governments which is responsible for coordination of transportation planning, the Northern Virginia Transportation Commission, the Palomar Rappahannock Transportation Commission, the Northern Virginia Planning District Commission as well as state agencies and commissions having a great deal of overlap. To make matters worse, there is no clear definition of what constitutes Northern Virginia.

Coordination of land use and planning on a regional basis is NOT going to be an easy task.

There is a feeling that there should be a single combined regional planning agency having power over both transportation and land use if long-term planning is to be effective. Such a regional agency would have to be given the power to raise money and build projects. This would separate transportation from political accountability and meld it to planning considerations.

A problem with obtaining integrated regional planning is the resistance of local communities to give up control of land use within their communities.

G. GENERAL PLAN

Most states require municipalities to prepare long-term general or master plans for the development of their communities. In California, the general plan must address seven elements: land use, circulation (transportation), open space, safety, housing, conservation, and noise. The general plan is a vision for the future of the community and serves as a guide for improvements and development.

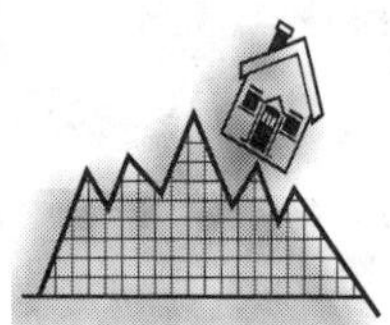

H. CONSISTENCY DOCTRINE

The consistency doctrine, as set forth in some state court decisions, requires that cities and counties must bring their zoning into conformity with their general plan. Courts can invalidate zoning inconsistent with a general plan.

In 1974, Senator Henry "Scoop" Jackson of Washington failed in an attempt to pass a national planning act. Senator Jackson wanted a planning process to be a condition for eligibility for federal grants.

II. Environmental Problems

A. ENVIRONMENTAL PROTECTION

We have had a tremendous interest in environmental matters in the last 30 years. Environmental problems have slowed development and, in many cases, stopped it altogether.

Environmental protection is also used by many to limit growth. The result of limiting growth is higher real estate prices. Growth limitation also has the effect of keeping minorities out of certain areas. Unfortunately, environmental protection is advocated by many whose major concern is to keep out people who, because of race or income, are not wanted in the community.

In periods of high unemployment, environmental concerns often lose out to economic considerations.

Farmers and ranchers have generally been in opposition to an environmental land use agenda. They feel that if land increases in value, they should be able to take advantage of that value based on its highest economic use.

A continuing conflict exists among potential owners who want to maximize the economic advantage associated with ownership and others who feel a use will negatively affect the use and enjoyment of other lands, or have a negative effect on their health. Sometimes there is even a conflict between goals of different governmental agencies.

Murfreesboro, Tennessee, rezoned land for commercial development that would aid their tax base. The land is also being sought by the federal National Park Service to expand the Tennessee Stones River Battlefield from its current 580 acres to 4,000 acres.

Morris Island, S. C., outside Charleston Harbor is the site where the African American Regiment, the 54th Massachusetts, fought the 1863 battle that was depicted in the movie "Glory." In 2005, a developer put the island up for sale on e-bay asking $12.5

million. Historians and preservationists were outraged that planning had failed to protect this famous battlefield from development.

B. ENVIRONMENTAL IMPACT REPORTS (EIRs)

States have been requiring developments that are likely to have an impact on the environment to prepare an environmental impact report prior to approvals.

A developer can file a negative declaration that a project will not have any detrimental effect on the environment. Unless challenged, NO Environmental Impact Report (EIR) will be required.

An ***ENVIRONMENTAL IMPACT REPORT (EIR)*** *is a study of how a subdivision will affect the ecology of the subdivision's surroundings. A* ***NEGATIVE RESULT*** *(nothing found) on an EIR report means it is a good report; a* ***POSITIVE RESULT*** *(adverse impact) means it is bad for the environment.*

Citizens' groups have been challenging negative declarations as well as environmental reports, which they consider erroneous or too narrow in scope. Environmental Impact Reports are required to describe adverse effects, ways to mitigate those effects, and alternatives.

In San Francisco, a group of citizens went to court after the planning commission had certified environmental impact reports for four high-rise buildings in the downtown area. The citizens claimed the report considered the impact of these four buildings and not the cumulative effect of those structures already under construction or approved for construction. The court agreed with the citizens group. The court required new environmental impact reports. Because this project was almost completed, the court decided not to halt construction, but that proper EIRs would be required for future approvals (*San Franciscans for Reasonable Growth v. City and County of San Francisco,* 151 Cal. 3d 61 [1984]).

C. MINERAL KING (Walt Disney's Failed Mountain Project)

Walt Disney was issued a three-year permit in 1965 to study development of the Mineral King area. This was entirely in the Sequoia National Game Refuge, 55 miles east of Visalia on the boundary with Sequoia National Park.

The development was planned in a valley ranging from 8,000 feet to 12,000 feet in elevation and possessing five major streams. It was an area of lush vegetation and the summer range for many animals.

The Forest Service proposed 4 ski lifts and parking for 1,200 cars. Disney proposed a village with 22 to 27 ski lifts, a one-story parking structure for 3,600 cars, housing for 3,300 guests plus 1,000 employees, offices, restaurants, heliport, convention center,

theater, equestrian complex, swimming, skating, a cog railroad, stream control, avalanche dams, water reservoirs, power lines, etc.

Walt Disney proposed to blast and bulldoze so there would be properly groomed slopes. Disney indicated there would be future expansion and, like Disneyland, it would never be finished.

The California Highway Commission approved $22 million dollars for construction of a highway to the project. The Department of the Interior proposed running a 60,000-volt power line across Sequoia National Park to the project.

The Sierra Club brought the proposed project into federal court and was able to stop the Mineral King development. No ecological studies had been made. The Sierra Club showed that the project would adversely affect fishing, stream flow, vegetation, soil, and wildlife.

After intense debate, Mineral King was incorporated into Sequoia National Park to preclude its development.

D. HAMMOCK DUNES

Hammock Dunes is a 2,250-acre coastal project in northeast Florida. In order to begin this 6,670-unit development, the developer has had to:

1. Rebuild and plant groves in the beach dunes due to damage caused by off road vehicles;
2. Agree to preserve 250 acres of dense groves of hardwood trees;
3. Institute a capture and release program for Indigo snakes and Gopher tortoises;
4. Provide a watch so that manatees were not injured during construction of a bridge;
5. Set aside 30 acres of oceanfront for a colony of 10 Florida Scrub Jays;
6. Preserve a 4-acre Indian (Native American) burial ground;
7. Develop a system where wastewater would be reclaimed and used to irrigate the golf courses.

To avoid such costly efforts as were required for Hammock Dunes, other developers are sizing down their projects to escape Florida's requirements of filing a regional environmental impact statement. Smaller projects have resulted in only about five percent of Florida's projects being subject to environmental review.

E. ARCTIC NATIONAL WILDLIFE REFUGE

Our need for oil has collided with environmental issues and, so far, we have a deadlock with neither side ready to give up. Oil interests wish to open the Arctic

National Wildlife Refuge to drilling. They claim that there will be minimum damage to the environment. Over 75 percent of Alaska's residents support oil drilling. Alaska's residents do receive an annual rebate check from the state based on the oil taken.

The opposition to opening the refuge for oil drilling is an array of conservation and naturalists groups as well as many scientists who claim the Arctic tundra is ecologically fragile and drilling and transporting oil will cause irreparable harm.

F. CONTAMINATION

Without expensive cleanup procedures in place, contaminated soil and water from a variety of causes can make sites unsafe for development.

PERCHLORATE, used as rocket fuel and in munitions, was often dumped at military bases and at sites of defense contractors. Perchlorate is now known to be an endocrine disruption that can alter hormonal balances and impede metabolism and brain development particularly among infants. Perchlorate has seeped into the water table in 22 states.

The environmental protection agency and the Department of Defense disagree as to the perchlorate danger and the DOD does not want to be burdened with clean-up costs. Even though a standard of permissible contamination has not been agreed to, state and local authorities have sealed dozens of wells. In some water sensitive communities, this has had the effect of placing a moratorium on development.

G. ARCHEOLOGICAL REMAINS

The discovery by a developer of archeological remains can delay a development and significantly increase costs. In some areas an archeological site inspection is actually required prior to the start of a project.

III. Zoning and the Developer

A. HISTORY OF ZONING

While ownership may be exclusive, it is not absolute. Ownership is subject to use controls for the benefit of the community.

A 1692 Massachusetts law authorized towns to designate the least objectionable areas for slaughter, tanning, and horse stalls.

In California during the 1800s, statutes restricted Chinese laundries to particular areas. The reason for excluding them from other areas was that wash water was dumped in the streets causing mud hazards. Also restricted to specific areas were kilns, livery stables, and carpet beaters.

In 1903, Boston set building height limits by district. In 1909, Los Angeles established seven industrial districts. Everything else was declared residential.

The first comprehensive zoning law was enacted in New York in 1916. It controlled height and use. Like other early restrictions, it was concerned with safety and nuisance control. The New York statute was held to be a valid exercise of the police power of the state by the U.S. Supreme Court in *Village of Euclid v. Ambler Realty*, 272 US 365 (1926).

The U. S. Department of Commerce's Advisory Committee on zoning issued the Standard State Zoning Enabling Act in 1924. The Standard City Planning Enabling Act was presented in 1928. The Enabling Act encouraged local control over land utilization. By 1930 some municipalities in every state were enacting zoning ordinances. Under the present system of zoning, municipalities and county governments have great autonomy in exercising zoning controls.

Zoning is the most powerful tool that local communities have for land use control.

People can only challenge zoning in the courts after they have exhausted their administrative remedies. The courts will not uphold zoning if it is determined to be arbitrary or capricious.

Although zoning has a negative effect on value, that is NOT enough to set zoning aside.

Most courts will not give compensation for any loss in value due to a zoning change; however, federal courts and some state courts have awarded damages under the theory that downzoning is a taking of property. ***DOWNZONING*** *is the process of taking the current zoning and limiting what can be built*. Downzoning, therefore, reduces the value of the property because less development can take place. It is expected that the U.S. Supreme Court will eventually determine if downzoning can be accomplished without compensation.

Business Licensing

Property tax laws, zoning and business licensing are disincentives for disclosure of home-based business activities.

Home-based businesses could be a violation of a community's zoning ordinances and obtaining a license would be a homeowner's admission of such activity. Because of the high licensing fees, and property tax on business equipment, there are probably many more unlicensed business activities conducted out of homes than there are licensed businesses.

Owners don't object to upzoning although neighbors are likely to oppose it. ***UPZONING*** *is the opposite of downzoning in that it changes the zoning to allow greater density or a more intensive use.*

Private redevelopment can be encouraged by changing zoning to allow for more favorable uses.

In this way redevelopment can be accomplished without government assistance. Politicians should be reminded that an area can be rejuvenated by the private sector if the city allows more permissive zoning.

B. INCLUSIONARY ZONING ("Including")

Requiring a developer to add something, such as low income housing to a project, is known as "Inclusionary Zoning."

Inclusionary zoning often requires a percentage of units in a project be built for lower income families. There is usually a provision that requires the units to remain permanently affordable. Some communities allow cash payments, the dedication of other land to the community or developing affordable housing elsewhere in lieu of an inclusion of affordable housing in a project.

San Francisco city officials decided they wanted the financial district to have some activity outside of working hours. In order to obtain approval for an office building, a developer agreed to put 33 condominium apartments on top of a 26-story office tower. Because of the high cost of construction, the units were priced from $400,000 to $2 million. Although the office portion of the project had been successful, the condominium sales were extremely slow which increased marketing and holding costs. While a city can compel a developer to include condominiums in office structures, the city cannot compel buyers to purchase them.

C. EXCLUSIONARY ZONING ("Excluding")

EXCLUSIONARY ZONING *can specifically exclude a stated use.*

Zoning can also be exclusionary, where only one use is authorized, such as agriculture.

Zoning ordinances that completely exclude adult bookstores and theaters are a violation of the First Amendment constitutional right of free speech and are not enforceable.

While adult entertainment can be excluded from an area there must be designated areas within the municipality where they can locate.

Reasonable restrictions on these uses, such as prohibitions within 1,000 feet of a residential zone, schools, churches, parks, or other adult entertainment facilities, have

been held to be valid. Courts have also upheld the validity of a 120-day period to discontinue a preexisting adult oriented business when the zoning was changed.

Nonetheless, the presence of these adult oriented businesses will have a negative effect on other businesses in the area and on property value. Because of the clientele attracted to these businesses, many shoppers will avoid the area.

D. AGRICULTURE ONLY ZONING (Conservation)

Sprawl is turning agricultural land into subdivisions at an alarming rate. Citizens' groups such as People For Open Space and the Greenbelt Congress have become involved in preserving agricultural areas. They have influenced planning bodies to maintain land in agriculture.

The Center for Analysis of Public Issues, a Princeton, New Jersey private research organization, warned that the quality of life in New Jersey could be endangered by the growing influence of land speculators. They recommended requiring municipalities to set aside 65 to 75 percent of their farmland in preserves.

Critics of open space concepts claim the result has been to keep land prices high, housing expensive, and the poor out.

Critics claim the farm preservation movement is only a cover for a suburban elitism whose goal is to keep out affordable housing.

Farmers have generally not been supporters of farm preservation. They like the old ways of farming until profit makes selling irresistible.

Several states and local governments are creating greenbelts by purchasing development rights from farmers. The government assesses the value for farming and the present value for other uses. Farmers are then offered the difference in return for an agreement that precludes the land from development. Farmers like this arrangement, as it allows them to farm debt free without pressure.

Connecticut, Maine, Maryland, Massachusetts, New Hampshire, New Jersey, Pennsylvania, Rhode Island and Vermont are buying development rights. Local programs exist in Colorado, North Carolina, Washington and Texas, as well several counties in California. The advantages of buying development rights are lower costs than if buying properties and also the properties remain on the tax rolls.

E. INCENTIVE ZONING

INCENTIVE ZONING can be a motivation for developers to improve the quality of life. For example, incentive zoning might allow a developer greater density if he includes common areas open to the public. In an area in the city of San Diego, if a developer uses imitation cobblestone driveways and walkways, the city will make concessions on zoning requirements.

F. CUMULATIVE AND NONCUMULATIVE ZONING

CUMULATIVE ZONING allows a lesser use. As an example, if zoning allowed heavy manufacturing, if it were cumulative it would also allow less intensive uses such as warehouse use. *NONCUMULATIVE ZONING allows only the stated use.* Most zoning is noncumulative as it allows greater control over use patterns.

G. BULK ZONING

Zoning for density is ***BULK ZONING***. By setbacks, height limitations, open space and parking requirements as well as minimum lot sizes, communities can zone to limit or increase structural as well as population density.

By requiring large lots and large houses on the lots, zoning serves to exclude the poor from communities.

Minorities are often poor, so the net effect of zoning is to exclude minorities, with the exception of a few professionals.

Being green can have the same effect as discrimination.

DuPage County, Illinois, reputed to be the fourth richest county in the nation, was alleged to have intentionally excluded the poor and blacks by regulating lot sizes, setbacks, parking requirements, yard requirements, and the exclusion of manufactured home parks. The 7th Circuit Court of Appeals affirmed a Federal District Court injunction of enforcement of ordinances and the requirement of special use permits. The county was ordered to develop a plan to increase housing for the poor (*Hope, Inc. v. County of DuPage*, 717 F2d 1064).

For many years Philadelphia had a gentlemen's agreement regarding the height of new structures. No building was to be higher than the hat on the William Penn statue atop city hall. The 491-foot height (forty plus stories) held until very recently, when both the Rouse Company and the city itself proposed higher structures.

As land becomes more valuable, gentlemen's agreements on height limitations are becoming obsolete.

Preservationists are fighting skyscrapers for far more than aesthetic reasons.

Skyscrapers block sunlight, create wind tunnels, cause horrendous traffic congestion, create tremendous service problems for the community, and create a safety problem in the event of a fire. Because of problems generated by skyscrapers, cities across the nation are putting a lid on height. San Francisco has set a height limit of 700 feet in the central area, 550 feet outside the central area, and 50 feet in historically significant or scenic neighborhoods. San Francisco also requires new structures to be tapered to allow greater sunlight.

Boston is considered by developers to be the toughest city in the nation in which to build a skyscraper, with San Francisco coming in second.

In Encino, California, several high-rise office buildings on Ventura Boulevard completely block sunlight because of their massive size. The developers offered to buy out the local homeowners at current market prices before development started. The homeowners refused, and now their homes are always in the shadows.

In the aftermath of 9-11, many cities are rethinking their attitude towards massive towers.

Developers are facing tight controls and design reviews across the nation.

Today zoning considers aesthetics. Washington, D.C. has long had a 13-story building limit. One effect of the limit has been to generate a forest of towers in Virginia, which has no such limitations.

H. VIEW ZONING

VIEW ZONING *is where the zoning regulations of the city protect such views as the ocean, the mountains or the city itself.*

Seattle protects views of its bay and mountains. Austin, Texas protects the view of the state capital by banning high-rises in the area. Cincinnati protects the view of nearby hills by height limitations. Denver prohibits blocking the view of the Rocky Mountains from certain vantage points.

I. AESTHETIC ZONING

In 1954, in *Berman v. Parker*, the U.S. Supreme Court indicated that protecting the general welfare is broad enough to cover preservation of aesthetic values.

We can zone to keep ugly out.

The requirement of approval of architectural review boards prior to issuance of building permits has generally been upheld even though there is subjectivity in approvals.

J. CLUSTER ZONING

CLUSTER ZONING is open space zoning. Open space zoning doesn't necessarily result in greater density, just that there is more open space. The open space is made possible by requiring the housing units to be clustered together on small lots, leaving the rest of the space as a greenbelt or green area.

K. SPOT ZONING

SPOT ZONING is zoning a particular parcel different than adjacent parcels. Spot zoning is often the result of political pressure to benefit a particular owner. Courts are likely to rule against spot zoning as being arbitrary. In many states, spot zoning is illegal.

L. BUFFER ZONES

BUFFER ZONES are zones between significantly different uses such as single-family residential and commercial or industrial zoning. The buffer zone could be underdeveloped green areas or it could be use such as multiple family zoning.

M. REZONING AND ZONING VARIANCE

REZONING is a change in zoning by the zoning board or commission. A *VARIANCE is an exception to the zoning*. As an example, a variance might be given to allow a structure on a 9,500 square foot parcel when zoning requires 10,000 square feet.

N. NONCONFORMING USE

A *NONCONFORMING USE is a use that existed and was a legal use prior to zoning*. Generally, the use will be allowed to continue (grandfather clause), but it cannot be expanded. If destroyed, it cannot be rebuilt and if abandoned, it cannot be again so used. Communities can set a time period for the use to cease allowing the owner to amortize the cost. If nonconforming use is also a nuisance, the municipality can order the use to cease.

O. AIR DEVELOPMENT RIGHTS

In New York, zoning limits the amount of space that can be built according to the size of the lot.

If an existing structure is not built to its maximum, it can sell its air rights to an adjacent property owner. As an example, assume a lot has a 6-story building, but it could support a 15-story building under current zoning. The owner could sell the 9 stories of unused air rights to an adjacent owner.

The transfer of air rights for development has resulted in a tremendous market for air rights.

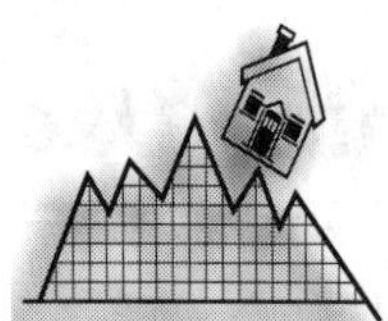

Sak's Fifth Avenue demolished a nine-story building and some brownstones it owns adjacent to its Fifth Avenue store. The new, taller development on the site not only added 100,000 square feet of retail space, but it allowed Sak's to sell 300,000 feet of development rights the existing store is not utilizing.

Besides New York, Illinois and Maryland also allow development rights to be sold. While the concept of transferring development rights could move the density from one location to another, the ability to transfer rights tends to defuse lawsuits by persons denied development or limited in development by downzoning.

The city of Auburn, Washington, is considering selling the development rights over city parking lots. They want the parking to remain but developers will be able to build over the lots. Besides cash from the sale, the development will increase property tax revenue.

P. ZONING AND THE TAX BASE

High-density areas with small lots and narrow setbacks will provide a higher tax roll than would similar lower density areas. However, the greater population would add to the services required for the residents, especially school costs.

Areas of fewer but more expensive homes mean a relatively strong tax base without the added burden of services for a larger population. Lower population means less cost for police and social services. However, a sparse population can mean greater costs per taxpayer for services.

Large industrial and commercial areas also provide a strong property tax base. Many communities welcome large shopping malls because the community directly benefits from the sales tax as well as the increase in the tax base.

Communities often compete for sales tax dollars. They zone for retail uses and often offer incentive for mall or auto sales center developments.

Q. ZONING AND VALUE

When land allocated by zoning for specified uses exceeds or is less than would be delegated for that use in a free market environment, the zoning will then directly affect value.

When less land is available than is required, the competitive marketplace will drive up the price so the users demanding it the most will obtain use. When supply exceeds demand, value will drop.

For residential zoning, the requirement of larger-sized parcels will of course mean fewer units per acre, which will mean higher costs per unit. Where zoning allows more units per acre, the per unit cost of land will drop, but a greater demand for land that can be more intensely used will increase the price per acre.

R. INDIAN LAND (Native American)

Local and state governments, under numerous court rulings, have little control over what is happening on Native American land.

In Parker, Arizona, approximately 100 tons of industrial waste, considered hazardous by California standards, was deposited within one mile of the Colorado River. According to the mayor of Parker, "We don't like it, but there ain't a damn thing we can do about it." The landfill is on sovereign Indian territory owned by the Colorado River Indian tribes. One tribe lobbied for an atomic waste dump on tribal land. Other Native American tribes are being wooed by some of the nation's largest waste management corporations. The result could be to adversely affect the water table and reduce values for a great deal of land outside the reservations.

Because Indian Reservations are theoretically Sovereign nations, the Indians police their reservations. Lack of sufficient police has led to illegal dumping of solid and liquid toxic wastes on Indian lands. In some cases, the dumpers save hundreds of dollars per barrel of dumping costs by simply opening valves and pouring wastes along dirt roads.

IV. Other Planning and Land Control Issues

Zoning is not the only control issue facing developers. There are health and safety codes and proceduress, fire codes, delay problems, citizen opposition, as well as private restrictions, that can all effect development decisions.

A. PRIVATE RESTRICTIONS

In addition to public zoning restrictions, private restrictive covenants can be used to control land use. ***PRIVATE RESTRICTIONS*** *are generally to maintain a quality of life as well as value by keeping out what the owners or developers consider undesirable uses.* This is done by including them in the deed CC&Rs (Covenants, Conditions, and Restrictions). ***CC&Rs*** *limit a property's use.* A covenant is a promise to do or not to do a certain thing; conditions are covenants that, if broken, may actually require the reversion of the property to the grantor; and restrictions limit the property's use in the deed.

While restrictive covenants usually cover much of the same things as zoning, such as use, setbacks, size, etc., restrictive covenants might also cover items such as:

1. landscaping requirements,
2. maintenance requirements,

3. prohibitions against working on automobiles in driveways,
4. requirements that no campers or motor homes be on premises more than 24 hours,
5. paint colors, and
6. architectural approval committees for any additions or remodeling.

When zoning and restrictive covenants differ, the more stringent requirement generally governs.

B. BUILDING CODES AND REGULATIONS

Besides zoning and private restrictions, a developer must meet local and state construction codes and obtain local approval for land splits as well as building permits. ***BUILDING CODES** are the basic minimum construction standards for a structure.*

State construction standards must be met. State health standards cover drainage, water supply and sewage disposal. In addition, there are numerous requirements dealing with environmental protection. If state and local building codes are in conflict, the more stringent code prevails.

C. CUTTING THE RED TAPE OF APPROVALS

Regulations and the approval process are generally regarded as a bottleneck to development.

With multiple forms to complete, regulations, and approvals of various city and county departments, developers often feel they are caught in a bureaucratic flood of paper and red tape.

The city of Simi Valley, California, wanted to encourage commercial and industrial development. The steps it took to do so included:

1. The City Planning Commission was directed to give the highest priority to the review and processing of commercial and industrial projects. (It was able to reduce the processing time by two-thirds.)
2. Adopting a blanket environmental impact report that covered three major industrial and commercial areas.
3. Cutting business and industrial building permit fees to one dollar for a one-year period (this probably had little effect on encouraging development).

Rockville, Maryland, has a solution to the paperwork process that applies to all types of projects. Instead of forcing developers to go from department to department filling out multiple forms containing much of the same data and waiting for separate approvals, Rockville has developed a one-stop approval procedure. It has consolidated various forms and approvals that has not only reduced paperwork, but has also reduced processing time for large projects from an average of three years to a period of only nine months.

D. CONSTRUCTION INSPECTIONS

City and county inspectors inspect construction projects during many phases of the work.

Our inspection process results in construction delays and added labor costs as well as interest expense.

Some solutions proposed by builders are:

1. If the inspector is not present within one working day of the time requested, the builder should be allowed to continue as if the work was approved.
2. Licensed contractors should not be subject to required inspections and approvals unless spot inspections indicate the contractor has not performed in accordance with the codes. (This would have a strong self-policing effect, as contractors would not want to hire subcontractors whose work would require possible approval delays.)

E. COSTS OF CODE COMPLIANCE (Recent History)

American Land Institute (ALI) has developed a model land development code. A study made of code cost compliance estimated that compliance costs $971 per dwelling unit (1979). Because some of these costs would have been present anyway, the net additional cost was estimated at $576 per unit. These costs apply only to state regulations. Local regulation compliance would be additional.

In Florida the total cost for residential compliance with state and local development codes was estimated at $4,698 per unit.

Most of these costs are, however, interest expenses dealing with time delays for approvals.

When various review and approval processes must be in sequence, costs are materially higher than in areas where the review and approvals processes are concurrent.

An Urban Land Institute study in San Jose indicated that between 20 and 30 percent of the housing cost increases between 1967 and 1976 were the direct result of local growth management policies. Because local and state regulations raise prices, they also have the effect of increasing the tax base, which is based on sale prices.

Besides interest costs due to delays, there are costs in the preparing of reports and forms, builder overhead during the working period, costs that should be assigned to

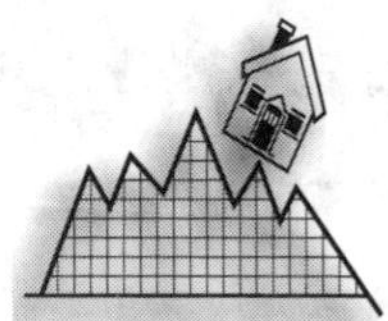

the tied up equity of the developer, and the costs associated with inflation because of these delays.

A study for the Committee on Urban Public Economics Conference blamed local land use regulations and growth moratoriums for a 19 percent increase in housing costs in Bay area communities while most other areas of California had stable or declining prices in the same time period.

F. PREMATURE SUBDIVISIONS

Premature subdividing and sale of lots will result in fragmented ownership, which could block orderly growth at a later date because of the difficulty in assembling parcels for developments.

La Quinta, California, was subdivided into thousands of 50-foot wide lots in the 1920s. The lots were sold to speculators. Fifty years later, several investors started accumulating lots so they could start meaningful development of the area. The process took years and building is continuing as lots are obtained. Most of the area is now developed

***PREMATURE SUBDIVISIONS** are developments built before they are economically viable.*

Premature subdivisions can be discouraged by requiring a substantial number of improvements, such as paved streets, curbs, sidewalks, sewer, water, electricity, telephones, etc.

Cities and counties can also require large payments per lot for community purposes. The economics of high initial outlays per lot would discourage premature subdivisions. The developers would be economically precluded from selling lots with low down payments.

G. OPPOSITION TO DEVELOPMENT

Generally, growth control starts with the belief that the free market will produce too much, too fast, and that this rapid growth will result in both poor planning and pressure on local support services.

Most homeowners are not concerned about the impact of sprawl on our ecosystems. They simply don't want growth in their backyards.

The NIMBY attitude is "Not In My Back Yard."

However, people will favor growth if they feel it is in their best economic interests to do so.

When there is high unemployment, people are more likely to support growth than during a period of low unemployment.

In 2000, a national survey by the PEW Center for Civic Journalism indicated that people ranked sprawl as one of the top problems facing local communities.

People who did not want to see their communities change started growth limitations in the 1970s in upper middle class areas. Opponents of growth limitation consider these people elitists and regard limitations as a "pull up the drawbridge" mentality.

Growth control creates "haves" and "have nots" and results in exclusion. This is abhorrent to many who feel it thwarts the equal opportunity concept of a democracy.

However, in Los Angeles, blacks and Hispanics voted strongly in favor of commercial growth limitations. The ease in which local voter-sponsored measures can be placed on the ballot has spurred the no-growth and slower growth movements in California. Despite strong developer opposition, growth control measures that reach the ballot have had an excellent chance of passing.

In Campbell, California, developers opposed a height limitation and outspent proponents 37 to 1, but were unable to block the measure. Some growth control measures have been challenged in the judicial system, but the courts tend to guard the right of a city to zone itself.

Many voters don't care how growth limitations affect jobs for others because they either already have a job or are retired.

Many people have gone beyond growth control and are now advocating absolute "no-growth."

Growth control is a financial windfall for the owners of homes within the controlled area. Local homeowners can expect both increased value for their homes and the environmental advantages of limited growth. Tenants suffer because of higher rents, as do local merchants who lose the revenue they would have otherwise received from a greater population.

Later purchasers or would-be purchasers also are losers because they must either pay a price based on a more limited supply or forego living in the community.

The local labor force suffers, as service and construction jobs are created elsewhere. The community also loses the tax potential of the area.

In Petaluma, California, growth has been limited to a specified number of building permits annually. This allows the city to plan its expansion and properly provide

resources for controlled growth. The effect of the growth limitation has been to depress raw land prices and increase prices of existing homes. It has also resulted in increased growth in neighboring communities that have not limited their growth.

Some communities have excluded industrial development by high impact fees rather than an actual prohibition. The result has been bedroom cities that must rely on other areas for work. While industry would mean lower tax rates, many communities are willing to trade off higher taxes for the charm of suburbia.

The idea of impact fees is that when a new development puts a financial burden on a community because of infrastructure needs, the development should pay the cost rather than require the entire community to accept the financial burden. In some communities fees associated with a single residence are into the $30,000 range.

San Francisco has a voter-mandated cap on construction of new office space. San Francisco found a solution to going over the cap by use of semantics. Dot com buildings are no longer designated as "office space," they are now "business service space." Nevertheless, the general cap on growth benefits Oakland, which actively encourages technology companies to come "from the city across the Bay." Oakland's Mayor Jerry Brown, who once was considered by some to have an anti-growth bias, pointed out that Oakland has both the space and political will to grow.

While San Francisco's Mayor Willie Brown favored city growth, the 2000 elections for Board of Supervisors was a referendum on the way the Mayor favored growth, especially "dot-coms." (Dot-coms were exempt from having to pay into the affordable housing fund.) No-growth candidates prevailed. The no-growth proponents courted voters with the fear that growth of dot-coms would lead to a city where only "dot-commers" could afford to live.

In Blythe, California, a group composed of local business and real estate people favored a proposed prison for the area. The area has been economically depressed and a prison would mean many jobs. The opposition group was composed of growers, retirees and individuals whose income was not tied to the local economy. While part of the opposition wanted to preserve the small-town atmosphere, others were concerned with the effect of a large, high wage employer on the agricultural work force. In this case, the pro-prison forces prevailed.

The fear of growth control often causes already overbuilt markets to expand.

Ground was broken for over 300,000 square feet of space in Walnut Creek, California in the month preceding the November 1986 election. The city had a voter initiative on growth limitation on the ballot. Developers rushing to start developments met the threat of growth control.

Sentiment for controlling growth collides with a strongly held conviction of the rights of private property owners. Controlling growth is incompatible with the belief in private property rights. Growth control is also incompatible with the belief that communities should foster affordable housing. Growth control leads to high values for property, which tends to keep out families of modest income.

Residential growth control and affordable housing are incompatible.

MORATORIUMS *are a defined time-out period for construction approvals, which allow communities breathing time to evaluate needs and effectively plan for the future.*

In California, moratoriums on construction cannot exceed two years. A number of suburbs around Atlanta, Georgia, placed moratoriums on building permits because they could not provide public services for the new developments as fast as the developers could build.

Building moratoriums tend to depress the land market.

Because of the uncertainty of the length of the moratorium, as well as possible changes in zoning, developers are hesitant to make land purchases during a moratorium period. Developers do not want cash tied up in future obligations without knowing when and if they will be allowed to develop.

The fear of a moratorium on construction will also cause developers to rush to obtain approvals for projects that might otherwise have been delayed until conditions were more favorable. This could result in overbuilding.

H. VOTER PLANNING INITIATIVES

In some states voters can get initiatives on the ballot and bypass planning commissions, city councils, county boards and state legislatures. To get a ballot box initiative or referendum on the ballot requires a specific number of signatures. In the past few years, we have seen many ballot box laws that now restrict growth or land use.

Based on the desire for a "Leave It To Beaver" fantasy lifestyle, the exclusion of minorities, the preservation of the environment, or a concern for the ability to service new residents, growth control measures can be expected to result in strong voter support.

Opponents of voter growth control feel that intelligent planning is not possible at the ballot box.

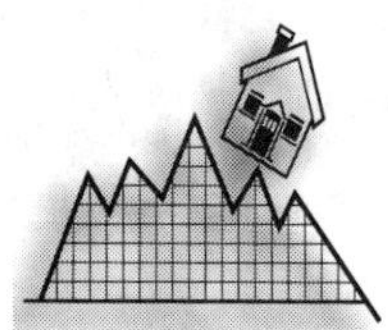

Proponents and opponents of ballot measures often have very partisan interests.

In Yucaipa, California, unions supported a measure to prohibit a Wal-Mart, which is nonunion. However, construction unions strongly oppose growth limitations.

Wealthy owners of beachfront property have strongly opposed hotel and resort developments in their areas.

In Escondido, California, voters passed a 1998 measure that required voter approval for any major project.

In 2000, the voters rejected the eight projects on the ballot. Developers found that it is extremely difficult to get voters to vote yes for a project.

Voters in Colorado (Amendment 24) and Arizona (Proposition 202) defeated measures in 2000 that would have created growth boundaries. While these growth control initiatives received strong public support initially, the National Association of Home Builders, real estate broker organizations and trade unions mounted a multi-million dollar media blitz to defeat the measures.

Several communities have managed to set boundaries on growth by ballot box measures prohibiting annexation. This means that city services of sewer and water cannot be extended beyond city boundaries.

In 2002, Ventura, California voters rejected an initiative to extend city services to hillside areas for a 1,390 home development. Seventy percent of the voters said, "No!"

In 2002, voters in Santa Paula, California rejected a proposal to expand the city's urban growth boundaries by 5,200 acres. Sixty-three percent of the voters said, " No!"

Critics of ballot box measures claim that it is social engineering to keep people out.

To counter ballot box planning, developers and property owners have been using the ballot box to their own benefit. In Burlingame, California, landlords were successful in getting a ballot measure passed which prevented the city council from enacting rent control. Developers who have been turned down for projects have been taking their proposals to the voters. Generally, their results have not been successful. Pro-industry ballot measures are unlikely to pass when the income or taxes of most of the residents would not benefit by development.

Wal-Mart lost a 1999 election in Eureka, California, that would have allowed a Wal-Mart store. In 2004, Wal-Mart tried to bypass the approval process and go directly to the ballot box for approval of a super store in Inglewood, California. Their well-financed campaign failed to get voter approval.

By limiting growth, communities upset the natural market.

While land use control can aid the environment on one hand, it also serves to prevent low and moderate-income families from entering the housing market by increasing prices.

Growth control also results in the loss of jobs in construction.

A side effect of the slow-growth movement is that housing for employees will have to be located at greater distances from their jobs. This further travel will, in turn, cause severe traffic problems.

I. SMART GROWTH

In the past we worried about the problems associated with sprawl, but we lacked a consensus viewpoint as to how future growth should be accommodated. As cities debated solutions, sprawl continued.

Maryland Governor Parris Glendenning coined the term "smart growth." Admitting that growth cannot be stopped, smart growth seeks to channel growth to central cities and older suburbs. Smart growth means less open land will be chewed up for development and investment dollars will not be exported.

The smart growth concept is to minimize problems associated with growth but not to stop it. Examples of smart growth would be:

1. Redevelopment of inner core areas to provide a higher density;
2. Conversion of unused or under used facilities for productive purposes;
3. Allowing auxiliary living units on lots with single-family dwellings;
4. In-fill developments for vacant land and lots;
5. Higher density new developments.

Some communities that are rezoning for more multi-family units, are trying to meet concerns of citizens by hiding parking lots from the street and requiring the units blend in architecturally with the neighborhoods. NIMBYS tend to oppose multi-family developments because of fears of perceived crime, traffic problems, noise, lower property values, etc. In some areas, environmental groups and businesses have found common ground to work together for smart growth. Business owners realize that they cannot draw skilled employees or compete in a grid locked environment. In the Atlanta area, the Sierra Club worked with business groups to create the Georgia Regional Transportation authority that has powers to control sprawl. Other business and conservation groups have worked together for smart growth in Pennsylvania and Maryland.

Unless we smarten up and work together, unchecked sprawl will be our future.

Some planners predicted that higher gas prices would be an impetus for the return to the central city. However, the movement back to the central city areas does not seem to be influenced by gasoline prices. However, if the availability of gasoline was restricted to consumers, then we would expect to see sprawl greatly curtailed and an impetus for smart growth.

J. ANNEXATION (Adding Areas To The City)

Annexation decisions are often based on emotion.

ANNEXATION *is the process by which a city acquires new, adjacent land, which will be under the city's control.* In the United States we often equate size to quality and growth to progress while the terms are in no way synonymous.

Cities should make annexation decisions based on economic considerations, balancing out the costs associated with servicing the new area as opposed to the benefits received (both tangible and intangible).

Tangible benefits would be increases in the property tax base, increased sales taxes as well as increases in other grants and revenues. Intangible benefits include the ability to control the development of the annexed area so that the citizens will be best served, rather than see a development that would be inconsistent with the city's best interests.

Residents in unincorporated areas tend to favor annexation when they want city services such as sewer and water, but if they don't see benefits in annexation, they are likely to want to remain in the status quo.

V. CHAPTER SUMMARY

The goals of **city planning** are a wide distribution of ownership, an orderly economic growth, and wise development and conservation of our resources. Planning must be within the framework of the availability of adequate water and waste disposal.

Fragmented planning has occurred on every governmental level. Greater coordination in future planning is needed. Besides use planning transportation needs must be coordinated on a regional basis.

Growth control starts with the belief that a free market will produce too much too fast, placing pressure on local support services. Besides those who want to slow growth, some people are opposed to all growth. An economic effect of growth control is higher prices for developed property and lower prices for undeveloped property. Both result from the principle of supply and demand in the marketplace.

Zoning is governmental control of land use. **Enabling acts** give communities the power to zone. The courts will overrule zoning if it is arbitrary or capricious.

Zoning can be **inclusionary**, requiring something to be done, or **exclusionary**, which excludes a particular use. Zoning is used to carry out planning for the community. Recent cases indicate zoning may not be used to intentionally exclude minorities.

Private restrictions are those restrictions placed by owners or developers to maintain property values. They are restrictions based on agreement, while **zoning restrictions** are by the government.

The time and cost of meeting various code requirements and obtaining all necessary approvals can add materially to final costs. Today developers are also encountering environmental problems. Citizens can delay projects by challenging an **environmental impact report (EIR)** or the exclusion of a report.

In many communities we are seeing **ballot box planning** where planning can end up being determined more by emotion than need.

Smart growth is growth that limits sprawl by **redevelopment**, **in-fill development**, **smaller lots**, and other means to increase density. Smart growth advocates realize that growth is inevitable but sprawl must be limited.

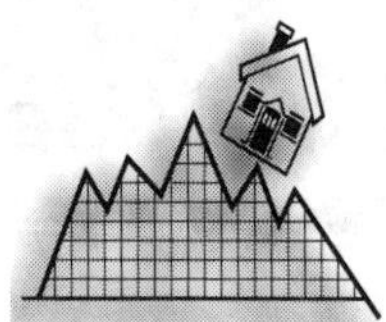

VI. GLOSSARY OF KEY TERMS

Annexation – Generally refers to unincorporated land becoming part of a city.

Bulk Zoning – Zoning for density, using setbacks, height limits, open space requirements, etc.

Consistency Doctrine – The requirement that cities and counties must conform zoning to their general plan.

Cumulative Zoning – Zoning that allows less restrictive uses.

Enabling Acts – Acts passed by states granting cities and counties authority to plan and zone.

Environmental Impact Report (EIR) – A report concerning the negative impact a development will have on an area's environment.

Exclusionary Zoning – Zoning that prohibits a stated use.

General Plan – Comprehensive plan for development of a community.

Incentive Zoning – Zoning that offers a developer an incentive if something is included in the development.

Inclusionary Zoning – Zoning that requires a developer to include a stated feature.

Moratorium on Construction – A prohibition of new construction for a stated period of time.

Noncumulative Zoning – Zoning that allows only the designated use.

Premature Subdivision – The division and sale of parcels of land long before development would be economically feasible.

Smart Growth – Growth that increases density and minimizes sprawl.

VII. CLASS DISCUSSION TOPICS

1. Discuss your community by answering these questions:

   a. Where do we appear to be heading?
   b. Where do we want to be heading?

2. Discuss criticisms of city planning. Are they valid in your community?

3. Give local examples of opposition to development.

4. Identify environmental concerns in your area that can affect development.

5. Identify major traffic problems present in your community. What can be done to alleviate them?

6. Give examples of premature subdivisions in your area.

7. Give examples of what you consider poor planning in your area.

8. Do you think your city would be willing to give up control of its planning and zoning functions in favor of a regional government?

9. How could sprawl be reduced in your community?

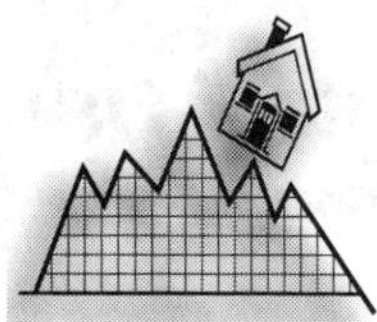

VIII. CHAPTER 13 QUIZ

1. The first city planning in the U.S. was in the:
   a. 17th Century.
   b. 18th Century.
   c. 19th Century.
   d. 20th Century.

2. A group that opposes zoning and controls on new construction is the:
   a. Democrats.
   b. Republicans.
   c. Libertarians.
   d. Greens.

3. An advantage of city planning is that:
   a. decisions are often made based on short-term goals.
   b. planning regulations can help keep costs high.
   c. planning is duplicated so cities have a sameness.
   d. planning forces us to evaluate what is happening and where we want to be heading.

4. When a city considers nonresidential uses that will help in sales and property taxes, they should also consider:
   a. how to spend the revenue.
   b. how the voters will react.
   c. associated transportation needs and problems.
   d. how soon before the additional revenue will come in.

5. Farmers and ranchers generally want:
   a. growth limitations.
   b. conservation zoning.
   c. rent control.
   d. to be able to take advantage of any increase in value for the highest and best use.

6. A developer filed a negative declaration. This means that the project:
   a. will have no detrimental effect on the environment.
   b. will not require any city subsidies.
   c. will be in accordance with zoning laws.
   d. will require a special use permit.

7. A zoning ordinance requires a development to include low-income housing. The zoning would be:

   a. exclusionary.
   b. inclusionary.
   c. cumulative.
   d. noncumulative.

8. Zoning for density is known as:

   a. inclusionary zoning.
   b. view zoning.
   c. incentive zoning.
   d. bulk zoning.

9. A "time-out" period for construction approvals is known as a:

   a. moratorium.
   b. lapse period.
   c. down period.
   d. post-approval waiting period.

10. The following are examples of smart growth, with the exception of:

   a. in-fill developments.
   b. redevelopment.
   c. leap-frog development.
   d. smaller lots.

ANSWERS: *1. a; 2. c; 3. d; 4. c; 5. d; 6. a; 7. b; 8. d; 9. a; 10. c*

LEARNING OBJECTIVES

In this chapter we will look closely at the economics of development. You will begin to acquire the analytical tools needed to understand the factors at work in any real estate project from home improvement to industrial developments.

Development has a direct as well as indirect effect on our economy.

When all jobs dependent on development are considered, development is the largest industry in America.

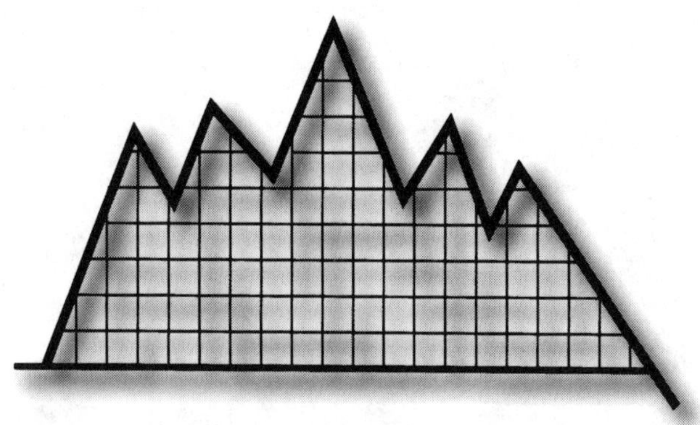

Chapter 14
The Economics of Development

I. Basics of Property Development

A developer adds value to land by improvements. The developer either plans to sell for profit or hold for investment.

Sears has created a corporate villa 30 miles northwest of downtown Chicago in Hoffman Estates. Sears transferred 6,000 of its employees to a campus-type development on 800 acres of rural land four miles from the nearest commuter train. The company moved their headquarters from the landmark Sears Tower in downtown Chicago.

Sears' move did not create a new city, but moving their headquarters resulted in many new developments for housing and peripheral industries. To gain the Sears headquarters, the state gave Sears $33 million for site acquisition and utilities, $20 million for road improvements, $6 million in tax credits and exemptions and $2.1 million in job training and day care funds. In all, Sears received $61.1 million in incentives. This package kept Sears in Illinois where the state feels the various tax revenues will pay for the expenditure.

Hoffman Estates not only gained economic clout for other developments from Sears' move, but also the traffic problems that go with growth. With the Kmart merger, Kmart is expected to sell their 44-acre headquarters in Michigan and relocate in Hoffman Estates, bringing more people and businesses to what was once a rural community.

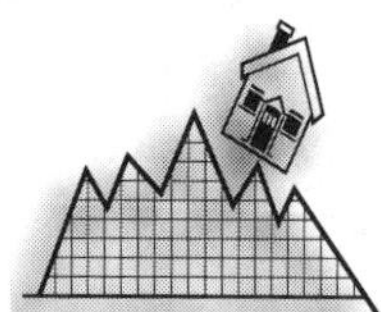

CHAPTER 14 OUTLINE

A. CATEGORIES OF DEVELOPMENT

Development falls into three major categories: 1) residential, 2) nonresidential, and 3) public works.

1. Residential Development

Residential development is affected by housing needs, the availability and cost of credit (loans), the economic climate, and people's expectations of their future.

2. Nonresidential Development

Besides the availability and cost of money, the economy and future prospects for the economy, nonresidential development is also affected by rental rates, vacancies, and anticipated changes in rates and vacancies.

3. Public Works Developments

Public works developments are dependent on the amount of available public money.

President Franklin D. Roosevelt started many projects to employ people and circulate money. "New Deal" projects included housing, public buildings, roads and bridges.

Dwight D. Eisenhower used public money to inaugurate our system of interstate highways.

The government often uses public works as a means to stimulate the economy.

B. REDEVELOPMENT (Old Uses to New Uses)

***REDEVELOPMENT** is developing what had previously been developed by modification, restoration, or by demolition and new construction.*

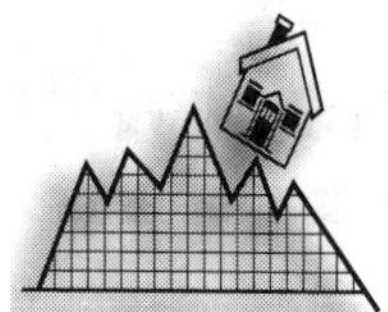

Redevelopment means replacing a property's current use with a more profitable use.

The prior use generally seeks a new location. This can result in a ripple effect where less economic uses are forced to less desirable locations.

C. GROWTH AFFECTS DEVELOPMENT

A single real estate development can change the character of a community and the direction of its growth.

Lower cost housing in an area could preclude high cost housing development just as luxury home development would increase land values in the same area, making low cost development economically impractical. A new college or golf course in an area will act as a magnet, attracting better quality homes to that area (see **Figure 14-1**).

Industrial growth will thwart better quality homes from being built but will attract other similar uses to the area.

A major new industry will bring in supporting industries and increase the demand and the price for industrial sites.

D. DEVELOPMENT AND THE ECONOMY

A single development can have a significant effect on the economy of a community by itself, as well as a cumulative effect with other developments. Beside affecting jobs and population growth directly, there is an indirect benefit as to support businesses and personnel. There is also an increase in the tax base coupled with greater need for community services and public service jobs. According to the National Association of Home Builders, the construction of 1,000 new homes generated 2,448 full-time construction jobs, $79.4 million in wages, and $42.5 million in combined federal, state, and local revenue and fees. For further economic effects of development, see Figure 14.1.

II. The Development Industry

The ***DEVELOPMENT INDUSTRY*** *is made up of builders and subcontractors who are often in and out of business due to changes in the market.* The industry is fragmented, with both large and small developers.

A. SMALL DEVELOPERS

Many firms are undercapitalized and can go out of business with just a modest change in the market. They usually operate as limited liability companies (LLCs) or corporations so that bankruptcy will not affect the principal's other assets. The small developer is then free to form a new LLC or corporation.

Figure 14-1

Economic Effects of Development

Studies indicated that homebuyers can expect a minimum of $6,100 in additional fix-up costs.

Many economists believe private residential building activity can lead the country out of recession and a lack of activity can start the slide into a recession.

Besides direct labor dollars for the construction trade and its multiplier effect, home construction affects the economy of a number of other businesses, such as:

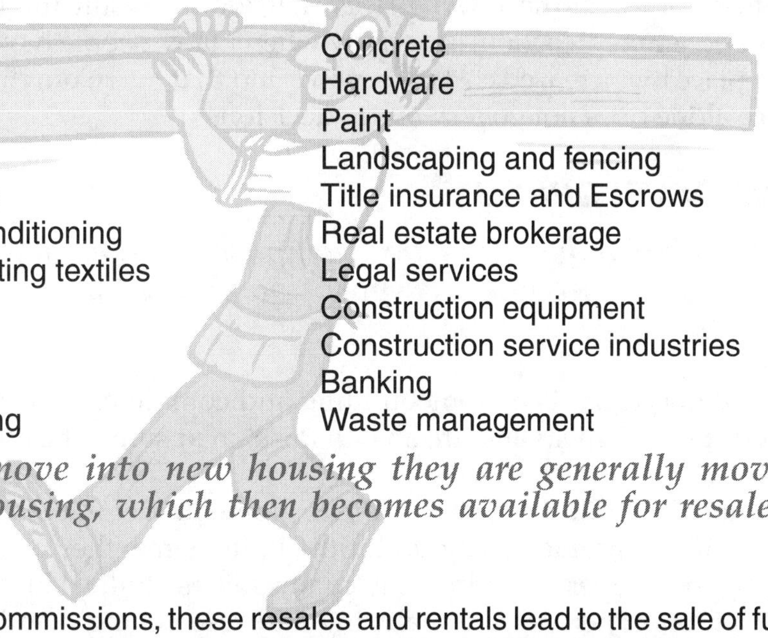

- Lumbering
- Steel
- Millwork
- Electrical supplies
- Plumbing supplies
- Heating and air conditioning
- Drapery and carpeting textiles
- Furniture
- Appliances
- Glass
- Trucking and moving
- Concrete
- Hardware
- Paint
- Landscaping and fencing
- Title insurance and Escrows
- Real estate brokerage
- Legal services
- Construction equipment
- Construction service industries
- Banking
- Waste management

When people move into new housing they are generally moving out of other housing, which then becomes available for resale or rental.

Besides real estate commissions, these resales and rentals lead to the sale of furniture and appliances, increase redecorating services, and can also affect landscaping and fencing. In addition, many purchasers repair, restore, remodel, expand, or install capital improvements, such as pools.

Development is America's largest employment industry, when both direct and indirect results are taken into consideration.

Although development is a huge industry, the nature of the industry allows small builders to compete in the marketplace, especially in the area of custom homes and smaller commercial projects.

Imperfect competition exists within the homebuilding industry because every piece of land is unique and structures vary.

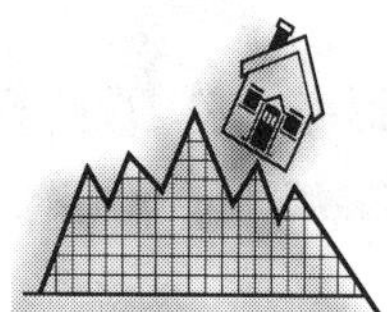

Imperfect competition aids small builders. Homebuyers are influenced by their emotions. Purchases that are economically in their best interest are not necessarily the purchases that are made. A color scheme, a blooming rose bush or a myriad of other factors can influence sales. Therefore, builders who have higher costs than those of builders of comparable properties are often still able to compete. Competition extends to the ambiance of the home itself as well as the price.

Due to the proliferation of small builders, individual designs, and non-standardization of materials and methods, costs are higher than they would be if there were just a handful of large builders and a more standardized product.

Consumers today resist a Levittown concept of sameness. However, because of economies of scale, the lower prices that would result might be enough to create positive consumer reaction, especially when many people have been forced out of the marketplace by increased costs. Keep in mind that home purchases are also emotional, so price alone does not govern buyer decisions.

B. GIANT DEVELOPERS

The building industry is not composed solely of small businesses. Some builders are giant corporations listed on the New York Stock Exchange.

There are many giants in homebuilding and commercial construction. Some of these firms are publicly held and are able to raise great sums of capital.

In revenue, Pulte Homes was the largest homebuilder in the nation in 2004 with sales of $11.7 billion. Besides going under the Pulte name, they also solely own Del Webb, the huge developer of retirement communities. Pulte Homes spend between $10 and $15 million per year in analyzing and researching new homebuilding methods and materials. They have been bypassing distributors and dealing directly with manufacturers to develop reliable sources of critical components such as drywall and concrete. In 2005, Pulte owned or controlled almost 350,000 residential lots. According to management, their biggest problem is the human factor—finding reliable workers.

These large building firms, however, are NOT so much a revolution in technology as they are in management. There are several "vertical conglomerates."

A ***VERTICAL CONGLOMERATE*** *(vertical company) is a very large company that owns the companies that supply it and that it supplies.* In other words, it owns companies in a direct line between the producer and the customer. It not only controls its construction company, but also owns the material suppliers and the mortgage loan companies under its corporate umbrella.

In smaller communities, lumberyards and builders are often under the same ownership. In some cases, they also subdivide to create building sites. Del Webb purchased a firm making concrete roof tile close to Sun City in Palm Desert, California that is a 5,000 home community in which all the homes have concrete roof tile.

Some corporations that have entered the development business from other fields have had serious problems caused by their management philosophies. Corporate approval processes and decisions made by consensus have not worked well in an industry as sensitive to changes in the economy as the development industry.

Disney purchased Arvida, the large Florida developer, and sold it three years later. Disney's management style did not fit in with the development needs of Arvida. Arvida management was reportedly frustrated because Disney shied away from the controversy that accompanies community development and Disney failed to buy new property. Disney was geared to entertainment, not to home building. Arvida was then purchased by JMB Realty Corporation, a large syndicator manager and developer.

In the 1960s, Boise Cascade entered the land business, selling recreational parcels in remote areas. What they thought would be a good profit center turned out to be an economic nightmare. Apparently, Boise Cascade management let managers loose with instructions to make a profit. Properties were misrepresented and court judgments requiring Boise Cascade to buy back properties and pay damages led to Boise Cascade's exit from the land development business.

Some large corporations, such as Santa Fe, Penn Central, and Soo Line, have successfully developed land they own. Exxon is a large corporation that has been extremely successful in development. An Exxon subsidiary, Friendswood Development Company, has been a huge developer of new communities for over 40 years. Exxon has also been active in developments in Washington, D.C., and is looking at other areas. Chevron Land and Development had been a big player in development, but they sold their last 17,000 acres to developers in 1996 to concentrate on their petroleum interests.

Other oil companies like Royal Dutch/Shell Group, Mitchell Energy and Development, and Mobil Corporation, have been active in development.

C. RISKS OF DEVELOPMENT

Oil companies are well suited for real estate development.

Oil companies own vast tracts of land, have deep pockets to hold onto property should the market not be conducive to sales, and understand high-risk ventures (see **Figure 14-2**).

According to Larry Sherry of Kenneth L. Leventhal & Company, a public accounting firm that specializes in real estate, "Real estate is a natural extension of their business. Real estate is entrepreneurial, capital intensive and high risk, the same as oil."

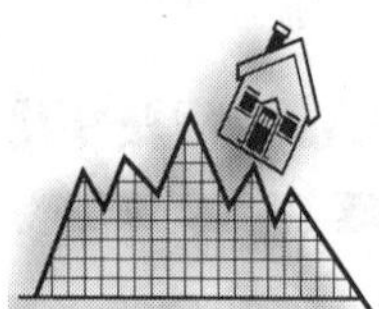

Figure 14-2

Developers' Risks

Developers face many types of risk. These include:

1. **Political risks**, such as zoning changes, construction limitations or moratoriums, rent control legislation, and tax or development fee changes.
2. **Economic risks**, such as changes in the general economy, and changes in interest rates and competition. A developer faces far greater risks when developing in a community whose economy is closely tied to a single employer or industry. As an example, if the economy of a community is closely tied to a single steel plant, then the closure of that plant could effect the developer's ability to sell existing inventory or to raise money.

   Changes in interest rates will effect a developer's costs as well as the sales demand for homes. Many developers have been put out of business by increases in interest rates. While a developer may lock in construction loan costs, permanent financing may be far down the road. An increase in interest rates could change what looks like a good investment into a money pit.

   Developers also risk the availability of money. If a developer cannot obtain permanent financing to replace construction loans, the lenders risk either foreclosure by the construction lenders or high cost interim financing.

   Economic risks can involve tenants. A far greater risk exists when a structure is designed for a particular tenant's use. If the tenant backs out, re-renting could be difficult without incurring significant additional expenses. Some developers insist on rental insurance to protect themselves should this happen. Mort Zuckerman built the 47-floor Time Square Tower in 2002 at a cost of $650 million. It appeared to be a relatively low-risk investment because there was a prime tenant for almost half the space, Arthur Anderson. The giant accounting firm became mired in lawsuits and became "history" before it could take possession.

   Leasing to newly established businesses subjects an owner to greater risks than leasing to a business with a successful operating history. Business failures are at their highest among new firms. Some new businesses, such as non-franchise restaurants, have a first year failure rate of 50 percent or more. Generally, the failure rate for all new businesses is in the 50 percent range for the first three years. Business failures can mean legal expenses, uncollectible rents, vacancies and costs to re-rent. In addition, a high tenant turnover can hurt the prestige of a building and cause other businesses to avoid the location.

3. **Risks of nature**, such as weather delays and natural calamities. Earthquake and flood insurance can be costly and many developers fail to cover themselves for these losses.

(continued)

4. **Physical risks**, such as fire, vandalism, theft, and natural calamities. Most developers insure against these risks and spend money on property security.

5. **Labor risks**, such as strikes, increases in wages, or the unavailability of an adequately skilled labor supply.

   In most of the country, construction unions have been losing strength. Inroads by non-union contractors have resulted in unions allowing more efficient construction practices and dropping "feather bedding" requirements. Labor risks have, therefore, been going down. By 2005, union members in construction had fallen from 80 percent in 1955 to just 18 percent. Real wages (wages adjusted for inflation) fell 25 percent since 1975. The remaining union strongholds are a number of urban centers.

6. **Material risks**, such as the ability to obtain adequate material when needed and increases in material costs between the planning phase and the actual time the material is purchased.

   In 1999, a national shortage of drywall occurred due to demand far exceeding manufacturing capabilities. Long delivery times resulted in costly delays in construction projects. When the drywall finally arrived on the job, the prices had dramatically increased, which cut the builder's profit margin when costs could not be passed on to buyers.

   In 2005 and 2006 in many parts of the country, developers were experiencing a cement shortage that caused delays in many projects. Twenty-five percent of U.S. cement is imported. Thailand and China have been major sources for our cement. Much of Thailand's supply was diverted for rebuilding Southeast Asia areas ravished by a Tsunami, as well as to fill China's growing needs. China has turned from a cement exporter to an importer. Beijing is preparing for the 2008 Olympics and huge structures are being built. In addition, China is making massive efforts to improve its infrastructure with dams and roads. To top it off, relaxing regulations has resulted in frantic construction efforts by private investors. It is unlikely that China will export much cement for many years.

   U.S. mills are working seven days per week at capacity. With the increased U.S. production, railroads are being stressed to meet shipping needs. New U.S. cement plants are not expected to be in production until 2007.

   Rebuilding the damage from Hurricane Katrina should have a negative effect on the availability of all building materials.

7. **Judgmental risks**, such as the ability to sell or lease the units produced at the anticipated sale price or rent.

(continued)

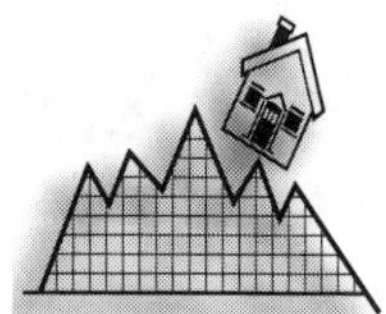

This could be related to a failure of the developers to properly analyze the market, unforeseen competition, or other factors. The design and the site affect buyer and lessee decision-making. Thus, designs and sites that fail to meet buyer and lessee desires can result in a developer's loss.

Unanticipated delays in obtaining approvals, delays in construction, and delays in the sale or rental of a project can also adversely affect costs.

Developers must consider a contingency factor when estimating costs. Things never go entirely as planned. Some homebuilders compute all costs and then add 10 percent for contingencies and claim that without pricing in unknowns, their profits would evaporate.

Developer risk is greater in small and midsize cities because the marketplace will be more easily saturated than in a larger community.

In Nashville, Tennessee, the Trion Group determined that there was a great need in Nashville for additional office space. The city's vacancy rate was around 7 percent and very little new office space was under construction. After breaking ground on an office building, a half dozen competing office structures were started in the area, resulting in a 20 percent vacancy factor and owners offering tenants one year free rent on a five-year lease. Developers have, in this way, created the same problems in smaller markets as they have in many larger cities, only faster.

Many developers have gone bankrupt, not because their liabilities exceed their assets, but because they didn't have current cash assets to meet current cash obligations. They failed to manage their assets in such a way that they would not default on their obligations.

For many years insurance companies have had limited partnerships with developers, where the insurance company supplied the capital.

Insurance companies generally do NOT make good developers.

Several insurance companies set up their own companies to develop office, industrial and commercial properties. Instead of putting up money and just collecting interest or even limited partnership equity in addition to interest, they felt that they should have it all. Results were less than spectacular. Insurance companies involvement as developers are now primarily that of silent partners.

Insurance companies are too rigid in their approach to decision making to make good developers. They cannot think outside the box. In addition, they have shown an unwillingness to delegate authority to make major decisions that result in a sluggish response to opportunities and conditions.

There is software designed for developer risk analysis. Some of the nation's major developers use risk-analysis software to gather information as to proposed projects. Palisade has available one of the better-known programs (**www.palisadeeurope.com**).

D. TAXES AND LAND

High property taxes on land encourage development.

High holding costs force owners to either develop land or sell it. Conversely, low property taxes on vacant property take the pressure off owners. They are more likely to hold land for later development or sale.

E. COMMUNITY TAX BENEFITS OF NEW DEVELOPMENTS

Many developers must dedicate land for community use and pay many types of fees, which benefit the community. The tax burden borne by new homes is proportionately higher than borne by existing property.

Many communities have charged fees for development that exceed the costs of infrastructure needed to support the development.

Timeshares offer unique community benefits.

While as a condominium a unit might have a value of $100,000, when sold as a timeshare of 50 weeks at $10,000 each, in some communities the property can now add $500,000 to the tax rolls if taxes are based on sale price. To avoid these higher taxes, many timeshares are leaseholds rather than fee interests. Because the residents of timeshares are not permanent residents, they require few social services from the community.

III. The Development Entrepreneur

An ***ENTREPRENEUR*** *is a person who builds and owns his or her own business*. When a project is developed, the possibility of profit or loss is accepted by the builder/developer.

An entrepreneur makes things happen.

Equitable Life Insurance maintains that the individual entrepreneur is extremely important. Equitable has been a partner with New York entrepreneur Donald Trump in many projects. The insurance company issued a $20,000,000 life insurance policy on Trump because it believes his loss would have an adverse effect on those projects.

Prudential Life Insurance granted Trump a 49 percent interest in a condominium project without requiring him to invest in the project. It wanted Trump's expertise, so it made him a partner.

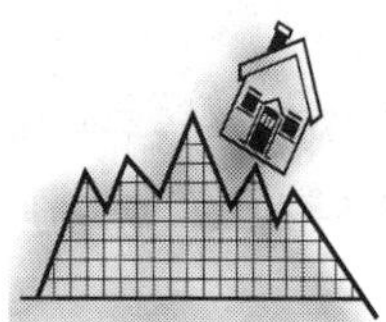

Entrepreneur Trump, despite some difficulties, has managed to manipulate seemingly adverse conditions to his advantage.

Because of their successful track records, developers such as Trump can raise a large quantity of capital. Chase Manhattan Bank told the New Jersey Gaming Commission that Trump had a $35 million personal line of credit payable at the prime rate. It also indicated the $35 million ceiling was flexible.

In the '40s, '50s and early '60s, William Zeckendorf was one of the nation's largest developers and real estate deal maker. Some people classified Zeckendorf as a genius while others said he was a gambler. His Webb and Knapp Corporation engaged in major development projects across the country. Zeckendorf single-handedly shaped the development and redevelopment of many major cities in the United States and Canada. Like other successful developers before and after him, Zeckendorf was a visionary with great faith in his personal abilities and judgment. A number of factors led to the bankruptcy of Webb & Knapp Corporation. These factors included changes in local codes, unforeseen competition, several negative cash flow projects, expenses exceeding estimates, and the fact that Webb & Knapp had expanded utilizing maximum leverage. An editorial at the time said, "He went one dream too far." He was right but his timing was wrong. However, without entrepreneurs such as William Zeckendorf and Donald Trump, our city skylines would be far different than they are today.

Del Webb went on to build huge retirement communities with many activities and amenities. Del Webb's company specialized in building and running active adult communities for persons age 55 and over. One of Webb's successful California projects is called Del Webb's Sun City in Palm Desert, California. It has a 27-hole championship golf course, three multi-million dollar recreation centers and other amenities. It has many floor plans and prices originally started in the mid-$100,000s. When Del Webb sold out to Pulte Homes in 2001 for $1.7 billion, home prices ranged from the $200,000s to over $500,000.

IV. Dangers of Growth Limitations

The city of Camarillo, California and Pardee Construction Company entered into a stipulated judgment that Pardee had vested rights to develop all of the property on a 1,150-acre tract in accordance with an approved zoning and master plan. The city agreed not to adopt any zoning inconsistent with that already approved.

Based on that agreement, Pardee spent approximately $13.5 million on development. A voters' initiative now limits the number of building permits for the entire city to 400 per year. It provided a detailed method of permit allocation.

The California Supreme Court, in *Pardee Construction Company v. City of Camarillo*, 37 Cal.3d 465 (1984), held that the growth control ordinance did not violate Pardee's vested right to complete the project, ruling that it only affected the timing of the project.

Growth limitation rulings such as *Pardee v. Camarillo* can be economically disastrous. No-growth ordinances can make economic development of large parcels impossible and any development costly. The attitude of a given community toward development should always be very carefully studied first by developers.

V. Billboards and Development

Strong public sentiment exists against billboards. Many communities are working to eliminate billboards, which they equate with blight. Besides aesthetics, billboards create a safety problem in that they can distract drivers.

Lady Bird Johnson, wife of President Lyndon Johnson, was instrumental in limiting billboards on Interstate highways. She lobbied for passage of the 1965 Highway Beautification Act. Lady Bird Johnson stated, "Ugliness is Glum."

Developers are now incorporating billboards into their redevelopment projects. If a community wants a project, they must agree to the billboards.

Without the millions of dollars from billboard advertising, many redevelopment projects would not be feasible.

The developers' "take it or leave it" approach has worked and billboards are springing up in high-traffic projects in central cities. In some cases, developers dangle a carrot by giving cities a portion of the billboard revenues. West Hollywood was given 10 percent of the gross revenue from one sign, a giant Jumbotron electric display. West Hollywood should receive over $100,000 annually.

VI. Speculator's Risk and Development

SPECULATORS *are people who take on large risks with real estate investments and developments.* The risks taken are beyond an ordinary investment. Speculators are interested in a relatively quick profit on a sale rather than in operating income.

During boom periods like 1976–1978 as well as in the 1999-2006 period, many new subdivisions were sold out even before the models were completed.

Many of these new sales were to speculators who never intended to take title or occupy a unit.

Builders customarily take reservations (deposits) before completion.

Speculators who placed deposits on units intended to resell their reservations at a profit if the subdivision sold out quickly. In some states, speculators were legally entitled to the return of their deposits prior to signing the final sale contract. The only downside risk for the speculators in these cases would be the loss of interest on their deposit.

Speculators make it appear as if the demand is far greater than it actually is. In some subdivisions it was estimated that two-thirds of the reservations were by speculators. The result was projects appeared to have been sold out and developers were able to get financing and begin new projects before their old projects were completed.

When interest rates rose in the late 1970s, many speculators withdrew their deposits. In some cases over half of the "sold out" subdivisions became unsold. Builders were faced with large inventories in a market that had come to a halt.

To prevent potential buyers from selling their reservations, many developers take non-assignable reservations.

Non-assignable reservations force a speculator to come up with the cash for financing and then to resell the property. Larger reservation fees and limiting reservations to one per buyer also increase the chances that buyers placing reservations are good faith buyers and not speculators. Various prohibitions against resale within an agreed period, as well as prohibitions against renting the unit, are some of the efforts developers are taking to discourage speculators.

According to Forbes, a business magazine, 43 percent of the condominiums sold in Florida in the late '70s were to speculators. In 2004, it was estimated that the percentage of condominiums sold in Florida to speculators were well over 50 percent. In some buildings, the speculator purchase was estimated at 75 percent. The true percentage is difficult because buyers will claim to be buying as a principal residence in order to obtain better financing terms, but have a secret intent to rent or resell the property.

Speculator purchases of condominiums gave a false reading of demand. When the market slowed down and speculators attempted to bail out, the glut of condominiums resulted in significantly reduced prices and a huge supply of unsold units.

The 2000s have thus far been a heyday for speculators who are buying all types of property, but primarily residential, for what they regard as a certain profit. But the one thing that is certain is—nothing is certain.

VII. The Economics of Development – Profit

Developers utilize:

1. capital,
2. labor,

3. land, and
4. management

to develop a finished product for which the selling price will hopefully exceed the total required expenditures. This excess is called "profit."

Developers will build if they believe selling prices will exceed the cost of land and construction. If they overbuild, they must wait for demand to catch up with supply or reduce the price to increase the demand.

A developer who plans well will survey the market, measure present needs, and estimate anticipated profits as well as anticipated risks.

Unfortunately, developers do not always have complete knowledge. Decisions by government agencies, voters, and competitors, as well as changes in interest rates and the local and national economy, can all affect the viability of a project. The risk of development increases with the length of time between inception and completion of a project.

A developer's profit must NOT only provide for a reasonable return on the investment of time and money, it must also be enough to offset the risks involved.

The greater the risk, the greater the anticipated profit must be. Without the possibility of greater profits, developers would not develop high-risk projects.

A. MARKUP

"Markup" is the percentage added to cost to determine sale price.

Many small builders use a simple "10, 10, and 10" system of pricing to cover risks. First they estimate costs carefully, trying to be inclusive and conservative in their estimates. To this figure, they then add 10 percent for unforeseen contingencies. Finally, to this figure they add 10 percent for profit. In the actual construction, builders hope to reduce costs below their estimate. By cutting delays they hope to cut their financing costs by 10 percent. If all this occurs, builders' profits will be significantly greater than 10 percent. This "10,10, and 10" is just a rule of thumb. Builders of more expensive homes try to set profit significantly higher to offset greater risks.

B. TIME AND MONEY

A recent survey has revealed that the percentage of building projects that were completed within a seven-month period dropped from 70 percent to 27 percent.

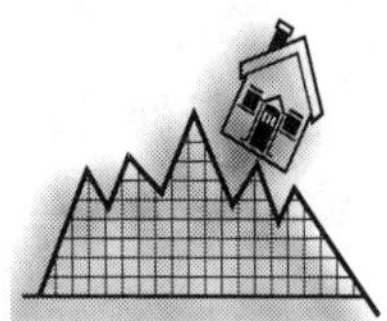

A HUD conference on housing reported that problems were caused not by ordinary construction delays as much as by unexpected political delays. The chance of unexpected delays caused builders to plan higher markups.

Processing time increases the cost of the services of engineers, attorneys and other specialists. Time itself also costs money. Interest on a developer's investment, as well as a project's share of the developer's overhead, can more than double land costs before development starts.

In addition to these direct and indirect costs, inflation during the approval process will result in a significant increase in the final costs.

The percentage of total cost associated with land and financing has been rising dramatically. A major reason for land cost increase has been time delays in approvals.

C. LABOR

Projects can fall behind schedule when there is an inadequate supply of skilled labor available.

Building is cyclical in nature, and when the industry is booming, skilled labor is in short supply. Therefore, homebuilders during boom periods find that due to labor shortages they are unable to build as fast as they can sell.

Not being able to complete speculative housing projects while the market is hot can be disastrous. An increase in interest rates could cool the market and leave a developer with unsold units.

The inability to obtain enough workers in a particular trade is a limiting factor of production.

When increases in costs can be readily passed on to purchasers, builders will pay higher wages.

In fact, builders will even offer extra pay to attract qualified workers. For example, a builder in Palm Springs offered one-hour daily pay above wages, plus a per diem allowance, to attract roofers from other areas. When there is uncertainty in the market, builders will resist labor rate increases because of the developer's inability to pass on cost increases to purchasers.

D. LAND COSTS

The value of land is directly related to the future use of that land. The agricultural use of land sets the floor on land value.

Urban lots are manufactured. They result from the expenditure of a great deal of labor and material for improvements and approvals.

When land is set aside for public use, less land is available to be sold, resulting in higher prices.

Because of the high land cost, developers seek to avoid excess land.

EXCESS LAND *is land that does not contribute to the value of the project.* An example would be more land devoted to parking than necessary. The additional land for parking would not contribute to the value of the completed project.

In order to keep lot costs down, developers use smaller lots. Another method of keeping costs down is to plan longer blocks. Not only does this result in lower costs for street improvements, it also adds more lots to the acre since less land is lost in streets.

Apartment developers often speak in terms of land costs per unit, while commercial developers talk about price per square foot.

Sophisticated commercial developers realize ratios or limitations placed on land costs are meaningless when making an economic decision. The forces of the marketplace determine value. Sophisticated developers believe no price is too high if it can be justified by rent returns or if it can be readily passed on to purchasers. If the land costs cannot be fully recovered in sale prices or rents, then the cost of land would be too high.

The shape of a parcel affects its use.

A ***GORE*** *is a triangular-shaped lot*. For example, if a gore requires a triangular structure, the costs per square foot would be higher than for a rectangular structure. This is because of the high ratio of square feet of exterior wall to the available floor space in a triangle-shaped building. Similarly, a lot that requires a long, thin building would also have higher construction costs per square foot than would a more square structure. Lots that have higher construction costs, therefore, would generally sell for less than similarly desirable lots that would allow more economical construction.

For large, quality residential developments, builders prefer gently rolling land.

The development costs for rolling land are not as high as they would be with steeper slopes and the development will not have the monotonous appearance it would have were it built on a flat surface. Low land is generally not desirable for quality housing unless it is water or view-oriented.

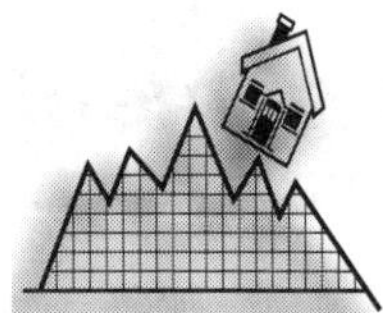

The National Association of Home Builders breaks down housing costs into five elements:

1. Structure
2. Land
3. Financing
4. Overhead
5. Profit

E. SITE SELECTION

While there are still people who develop property because they own the land, a developer will analyze the location and add up the costs of development for the proposed use. If it is not profitable, the developer will sell that site and purchase one more suitable for the intended use.

One of the authors of this text was contacted by a nationally prominent family that owned a huge estate and private golf course. The family intended to expand the golf course and develop condominiums along the fairways. They wished to appeal to weekenders from the Los Angeles area. After reviewing the site and plans, the recommendation was made to sell the property and purchase a large parcel for the development in a different location. The reason for the recommendation was the site owned by the family was relatively isolated from other projects, shopping, restaurants, and quality medical facilities. The author believed it would be difficult to sell the units to the intended market. The advice given was not followed. The result was a premature development, unsold units, foreclosure and family bankruptcy.

Just as a retailer of quality clothing would not want a location in an industrial area, a wholesaler of plumbing fixtures would not need a Beverly Hills Rodeo Drive location.

The supplier of plumbing fixtures would get little, if any, economic benefit from a costly Rodeo Drive location. In fact, traffic and parking problems could likely result in less business than a lower-cost site that allowed better truck access.

Site selection is NOT hit or miss.

Franchisers know that volume can be predetermined for a site based on the demographics of the area, traffic count, speed and time of traffic, signage, access and parking. **LOCATION ANALYSIS** *is an individual economic study to determine the profitability of a development by considering proximity of buyers to their markets, services, employment, transportation routes, shopping, customers, and parking, etc.* A marginal site for a use often requires higher costs to promote the use, and generally results in lower rents or profits.

Location analysis is an individual economic study to determine the profitability of a particular development.

The labor force, housing needs, area demographics, traffic patterns and speeds should all be considered based on the contemplated site use. Of particular importance would be changes or trends in the area. Cost for a location should be analyzed taking into consideration locations of similar desirability.

Because of differences between state income taxes, sales taxes, inventory taxes, and other business fees, cities on state borders have lost industries and business to neighboring states that offer economic advantages to owners as well as their customers.

Some of the nation's largest developers use analysis software for site selection. Geovue software is one such program (**www.geovue.com**).

F. BARGAIN LOTS

Because location is so important to value, the person who looks for a bargain lot to build on could, in fact, be buying the most expensive lot.

A poor location could mean that a property will take many more months to sell or rent than a property in a better location. This could mean thousands of dollars in interest expense. More importantly, the difference between the sales price or rent of the property built on the inexpensive lot, and the sales price or rent of the property built on the more expensive lot, is very likely to be far greater than the savings realized by purchasing the "bargain" location.

G. THE PRINCIPLE OF CONTRIBUTION

The principle of contribution is that an amenity should not be included unless the increase in rents or value justifies the expense.

Some amenities are well worth the added expense. Upgraded tile and carpet, as well as upgraded cabinets, might be more than offset by a higher selling price, in which case including them would be an economic decision.

On the other hand, the difference in cost between a prefabricated steel fireplace insert with stone facing and a solid masonry fireplace might not result in an increase in sales price that covers the additional expense. If this is the case, a decision to include the more costly solid masonry fireplace would not be in the best interests of the developer.

H. WHO TO TARGET

A developer should aim the project, no matter what type will be built, at those who the developer believes will be the eventual renters or buyers. This applies to likely needs and economics.

If a housing developer targets young, upper-middle class families, the developer might provide three or even four-car garages and three to four bedrooms. However,

if the developer is targeting retirees, a two-car garage and two bedrooms and a den might meet the needs of this market.

The decision to include amenities, such as fiber optic hookups, would be based on the needs of anticipated occupants.

I. DESIGN DECISIONS

Cutting edge designs make distinctive structures. Distinctive structures generally add to construction costs, but are highly desired by commercial tenants. The additional costs can generally be recouped by higher rents or sale price.

It is possible to design a building that is too avant-garde which actually then detracts from its rental desirability.

For homes, developers tend to stay with traditional exterior designs and floor plans that buyers approved of in similar developments. Modernistic looking homes may make the cover of an architectural magazine and even win design awards, but in most markets the homes will be hard to sell.

Generally, people like cutting-edge designed homes, but they feel more comfortable buying something that looks more like what they are used to.

When building for speculation, developers should not attempt to reshape architectural taste or impose their architectural design ideas on buyers. Developers should ascertain what buyers in the proper segment of the market want and strive to fulfill that want. However, when building for a buyer, that buyer's taste will determine the design.

J. FEASIBILITY STUDIES

The ***FEASIBILITY STUDY*** *is essential in the decision process for a successful developer. It ties together in a single document the economic considerations of development*. Some of the areas involved in feasibility studies include the following.

1. The Site

Besides site cost and preparation costs, ingress and egress, traffic, parking, area demographics, area use, and alternative sites should be considered.

2. Design/Engineering

In addition to costs, design decisions for maximum profit should be made.

3. Approvals

The difficulty and time required for approvals should be considered.

4. Improvement Costs

All costs of improvements should be calculated. Cost estimating software is available.

timberline.com
realdata.com
hollybar.com

5. Financing

The availability and cost for construction and long-term financing must be considered.

6. Time

Estimates should be made for completion of the project.

7. Cash Flow Analysis

An analysis should be made as to cash requirements and loan payouts as work progresses.

8. Marketing

Marketing time and cost and estimated sale price or rents should be considered.

9. Competition

The effect of other likely projects on this project must be taken into consideration.

10. Profit

The estimated profit must justify the effort and risk involved in the project.

Software is available for feasibility studies. Tract-Pie and Land-Pie are easy to use software programs that address development-planning needs and provide projections for cash flow, loan flow, profit and loss balance sheet and budget analysis (**www.tractpie.com**).

VIII. Financing the Development

A. CREDIT

The availability and cost of credit have far more lasting effects than simply affecting development decisions.

The availability and cost of credit are of prime importance for the tenants and/or purchasers of commercial and industrial developments. When credit is difficult and/

or expensive, expansion or relocation decisions requiring an increase in debt are likely to be postponed.

B. CASH FLOW ANALYSIS

Developers must analyze their cash needs for the total time period of each project.

Progress payments on construction loans do not always correspond to actual cash requirements. A cash shortage can cause costly delays. By predicting cash flow need, arrangements can be made for a line of credit that will avoid a cash crunch.

CASH FLOW ANALYSIS is the analysis of when cash is received and paid so cash loans can be arranged if there is a temporary deficit.

There are a great many financial software programs available to help a developer manage cash flow (**www.projectedfinancials.com**).

C. PROJECT FINANCING

Developers of projects for sale should consider permanent financing as well as construction loans.

Lenders will often agree to grant permanent loans at a future date at interest rates agreed upon in advance. By locking in permanent financing, the builder is protected against a rise in interest rates, which could make sales difficult or turn what was planned as a positive cash flow situation into one where there is a negative cash flow. On the other hand, locking in the interest rate and then seeing rates fall could reduce the salability of a project or cause costly prepayment penalties. When interest rates have fallen, some developers have refused to go through with the high interest permanent financing. In many cases, developers have been successfully sued for damages based on the breach of their agreement. In other cases, to avoid a long legal process, lenders agreed to settlements for less than they felt was their actual loss.

Having permanent financing allows a developer to keep title to a project, and hold or later resell, rather than be forced to sell in an unfavorable market, or lose the project when permanent financing is unavailable.

If the permanent financing rate is tied to the prime rate or other index, an otherwise profitable project could have a negative cash flow. Both sale and holding would be difficult if the prime rate increases significantly.

In developing large projects, William Zeckendorf was a master of finance—able not only to fully leverage a project, but take cash out as well. One of Zeckendorf's methods was called the "Hawaiian technique," since he developed it while on a

Hawaiian vacation. The ***HAWAIIAN TECHNIQUE*** *is the profit realized in the sale of a project by selling the parts to obtain greater revenue than possible from a single sale.* His Hawaiian technique involved separating the project into two basic parts; the land and its lease, and the structure and its lease rights. Based on a master lease he would give, he was able to put first and second mortgages on the land. He would then sell the land with the mortgages to an institutional or private investor. Then he would put a first mortgage on the master leasehold interest.

He would also put a second mortgage on it, whereby the payments and interest were not to start for 25 years, when the first mortgage was paid up. The second mortgage could be sold to private investors who liked the idea of taking care of their grandchildren at a modest cost. He would then sell the master lease with a price based on the strength of the operating leases. The purchaser of the master lease was, in effect, the building owner, who would also take all the depreciation.

D. PACKAGES FOR DEVELOPMENT

Approvals are often difficult to obtain, so some entrepreneurs have taken to packaging projects with approvals for developers. They generally attempt to tie up the land with options or purchase it with a minimum down payment. They obtain zoning changes where necessary, and have the basic engineering work completed as well as necessary designs for approvals. They then offer their packages to developers for immediate construction. Packagers are particularly active in condominium conversions, manufactured home park approvals, higher density housing, and commercial projects.

IX. Recreational Developments

RECREATIONAL DEVELOPMENTS *are projects that consist of recreation facilities.*

Recreational developments have been extremely successful. Fairbanks Ranch near San Diego, California, appeals to horse owners. A number of developments where homeowners own corrals, trails and stables are common. According to the National Association of Home Builders, demand for homes in equestrian communities could support 35,000 units annually.

Boating developments have terrific demand. However, development sites are limited, and coastal zone and local development regulations are strict, which result in relatively few of these developments.

The aging population of this country and the fanaticism of golfers have made golf course development attractive. The National Golf Foundation estimated that there were 17.5 million golfers in 1986. By 2000, the number of golfers in the U.S. was more than 30 million.

Golf courses by themselves have NOT always been a viable investment.

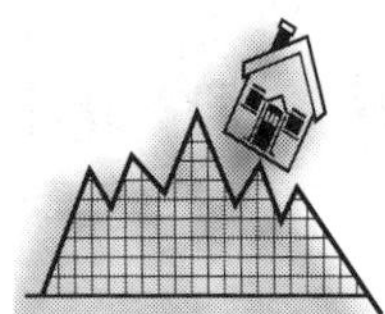

Fees have not always paid the costs. However, real estate-oriented golf courses have generated a significant return to investors so that they are being built as quickly as possible.

By lining fairways with homes and condominiums, highly desirable home sites are created. Golf courses raise the value of housing units. Units overlooking a fairway are sold at premiums. Even units not situated right on a fairway can be sold for higher values because they are near a golf course.

Often, golf courses can be built on land not suitable for homes. In other situations, the presence of the golf course open space allows high density cluster development. This reduces greatly the loss of land for sale. Another consideration for developers is user fees. Frequently, the golf course is separately owned by the developer and membership and user fees can be a profit center.

The development cost per hole of a golf course can be well over $100,000 per hole. This cost has been justified by many developers, particularly in resort areas.

Jack Nicklaus designed or redesigned over 60 golf courses. For approximately a $1 million fee, Nicklaus prepares "signature" course packages that include design, consulting services and promotional efforts. Nicklaus feels that golf course developments are the logical way to meet the increasingly stringent requirements of local planners. The golf course provides the open space (green belt) and allows a developer to meet total density requirements of a parcel and add great value to each home site. Nicklaus believes that the two best ways to add value to residential sites are a golf course and water. The holes created by grading a course become its lakes.

PGA West, a huge development of the Landmark Corporation near La Quinta, California, sold 650 memberships at $30,000 each with its first course, and had a waiting list of over 100 for new memberships at $50,000 each. Sales of condominiums in the $400,000 price range were brisk. Located in a relatively low-cost remote area, land prices in the area have since soared. Golf course residential housing developers have paid over $150,000 per acre for their sites.

Residential developers have paid high prices because they have been able to pass them on to home purchasers.

Buyers in recreational golf course complexes are generally wealthy golfers who purchase the units either as a retirement home, a second weekend home, or a vacation home.

One of the easiest ways to create value is to build a lake.

Quick sales of homes, townhouses, and condos to homebuyers, who often reap high appreciation on resale, make lake developments a wise choice. In some cases, the lakes serve as reservoirs for watering systems and as flood control basins. Artificial lakes maintain an ecological balance with an aeration system. Generally, lake front homes will sell at considerably higher prices than golf course homes.

Tennis courts are popular amenities in both sale and rental developments. While a swimming pool takes less land and accommodates several dozen people, a tennis court can only accommodate a maximum of four people at a time.

Many projects have pools and no tennis courts, but few have tennis courts and no pools. While developers of new resort area projects feel tennis courts are an absolute necessity, the number of courts in new year-round housing projects is declining. Apparently, many developers think they cannot justify the land, construction, and maintenance costs for this amenity.

X. CHAPTER SUMMARY

Development falls into three categories: **residential**, **nonresidential**, and **public**. Development has an indirect, as well as a direct, effect on our economy. Development is the largest industry in America when all jobs dependent on development are considered.

The **development industry** is composed of many large and small builders and developers. Some successful **entrepreneurs** are sought after for **joint ventures** with insurance companies, pension plans, real estate limited partnerships, and real estate investment trusts.

While land costs may seem high, a land price is not high if it can be justified by rent returns or the costs are passed on to a purchaser.

Speculators have at times driven up prices by increasing demand. With many speculators buying, it becomes difficult to assess the actual consumer demand for a development.

Developer risks are many, but risks can be offset by profit. Developers are unwilling to accept increased risks unless the development also offers a higher than normal potential for profit.

Feasibility studies tie the economic considerations of development together in a single document.

Golf developments have been very successful. The golf course provides open areas and the lots sell at premium prices. We are seeing a proliferation of walled, golfing developments.

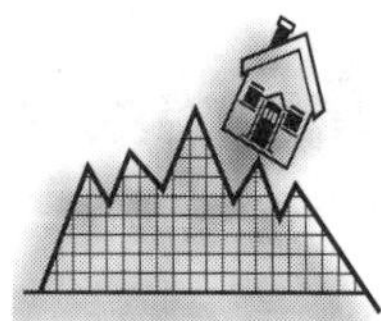

XI. GLOSSARY OF KEY TERMS

Cash Flow – Having cash available when needed to pay costs.

Excess Land – Land which does not economically contribute to a project.

Feasibility Study – Economic study by developer as to the desirability of a project.

Gore – A triangular-shaped parcel of land.

Hawaiian Technique – A technique of financing and sale developed by William Zeckendorf that fractionalized loans and ownership.

Locational Analysis – Economic analysis of a site.

Recreational Developments – Developments where parcels are sold primarily for recreational use.

Speculators – Investors who are interested in a short-term investment. They buy for sale profit rather than income-generated earnings.

Vertical Conglomerate – A number of separate corporations under one corporate umbrella that are economically related by products or function.

XII. CLASS DISCUSSION TOPICS

1. Give an example of a single development in your community that has materially affected land use of other parcels.

2. Name the major developers active in your area. Which market(s) is/are their developments aimed at?

3. Give an example of a subdivision in your area where a high percentage of prospective buyers have placed deposits prior to completion.

4. Identify low-priced and high-priced parcels of vacant land. Why are the prices set as they are?

5. Give examples of speculator activity in your area.

6. Give examples of developed properties that have excess land.

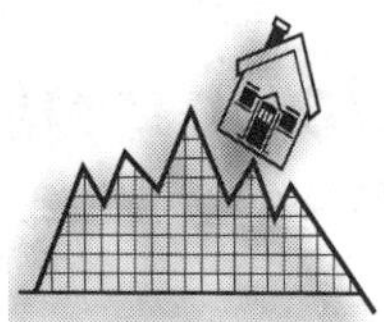

XIII. CHAPTER 14 QUIZ

1. An example of public works development would be:
   a. the Mall of America.
   b. Section 8 housing.
   c. the Interstate highway system.
   d. subsidized developments.

2. Corporations active in other fields have entered into development. Which field offers the flexible mind-set that is necessary for development success?
   a. The oil industry
   b. Insurance
   c. Banking
   d. Steel

3. An owner of vacant land with high taxes would be economically encouraged to:
   a. develop it.
   b. leave it fallow.
   c. let it be foreclosed for taxes.
   d. give it to charity.

4. An entrepreneur is a person who:
   a. gives heavily to charities.
   b. takes unfair advantage of others.
   c. builds and owns his or her own business.
   d. works for others.

5. How do speculators differ from real estate investors?
   a. Speculators normally buy with all cash.
   b. Speculators hold property longer than investors.
   c. Speculators do not plan on selling when buying.
   d. Speculators take greater risks than investors.

6. How would excess land be defined?
   a. It is land not yet ready for development.
   b. It is the available land for development that exceeds demand.
   c. It is land that has yet to be zoned.
   d. It is that portion of a site that does not contribute to the value of a project.

7. A developer wishes to build a large, mid-income housing tract. What kind of topography would the developer prefer?
   a. Absolutely flat
   b. Gently rolling
   c. Low with marshy soil
   d. Steep slopes

8. Which of the following businesses would have the least need for a site on an upscale shopping street?

   a. Men's clothing store
   b. Women's shoe store
   c. Plumbing wholesale supply
   d. Furniture store

9. A developer decided to use ceramic tile rather than more expensive marble in the entryway and baths of an apartment building. In making this economic decision, the developer considered the principle of:

   a. change.
   b. contribution.
   c. substitution.
   d. supply and demand.

10. Developers have found that they can increase land value by adding a golf course and/or a:

   a. fireplace.
   b. front porch.
   c. lake.
   d. family room.

ANSWERS: 1. c; 2. a; 3. a; 4. c; 5. d; 6. d; 7. b; 8. c; 9. b; 10. c

LEARNING OBJECTIVES

One must consider many factors when developing property. This allows a potential investor to evaluate the risks of a project, weigh it against the potential profits, and make an economically sound decision.

This chapter will detail many economic factors when developing a property, explain their importance and give the student the basis to make real estate related decisions.

This chapter will examine fair housing laws from an economic perspective.

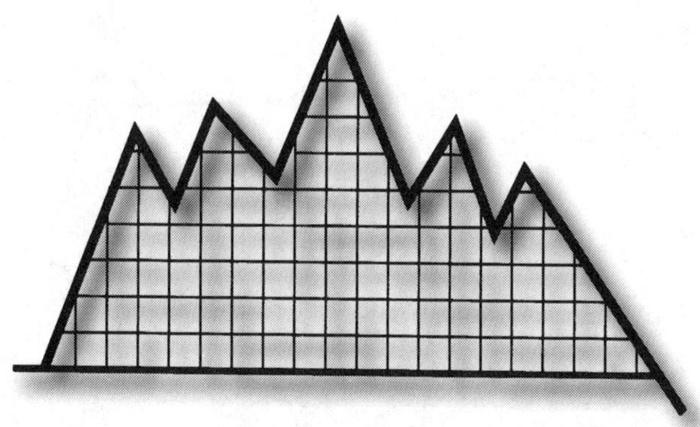

Chapter 15
Economic Decision Making and Fair Housing

A wide variety of economic decisions are continuously being made in real estate.

This chapter will explore the decision making process you may be faced with in the real estate profession.

I. Financial Forecasting

A. MARKET FORECASTS

A developer or investor will not commit capital unless there will be benefit on the investment.

An economic benefit may be in the form of income, appreciation, and tax advantages. The future profit must be worth the present investment. While company image enhancement could be an indirect economic benefit, personal aggrandizement would be a noneconomic benefit that, nevertheless, could influence a decision.

In economic decision making, forecasts must be made with the future in mind.

Chapter 15

CHAPTER 15 OUTLINE

The local as well as national economy must be considered, because the local economy may run counter to national economic trends. A builder who is building for resale is interested in the future measured in months. An investor who plans a long-term hold would consider a forecast measured in years.

Real estate predictions must take into account the general economy as well as the character, direction and amount of growth, population changes, future trends, and so on.

While there are many uncertainties in predictions because of influences outside of the investor's control, nevertheless, the chances of investment success will be enhanced by careful evaluation and reasonable anticipation of actions and trends.

B. BREAK-EVEN ANALYSIS

The break-even point occurs when the income covers total cost (the sum of fixed and variable costs).

Purchasers and developers will calculate their break-even point based on anticipated rents and the required occupancy rate. They must plan for financing until the break-even point is reached in order to cover their negative cash flow (see **Figure 15-1**).

Developers consider contingencies that might affect the desired return. By adding an allowance for both increased costs and rental delays, a safety factor can be built into the calculations. The purchaser or developer can then shoot for a target. The ability to reach that target determines the risk for the initial investment.

The break-even point for building an apartment can be reached sooner by reducing expenses, earlier occupancy, higher rents, or a combination of these methods.

Figure 15-1

Break-Even Analysis

The ***BREAK-EVEN POINT*** *is the point (in dollars and number of units) where total revenue (income) covers total cost (the sum of variable costs and fixed costs).* It is the point where the investor starts to make a profit. Any sales before that point are a loss and sales after that point start to make a profit. Wise investors would prefer a lower or quick break-even point so that the investment would only have to sell a few units in order to start making a profit. If the investors are not selling products, such as new condos in a tract, the same principle applies to services, rental, or commissions, depending on the business.

Total cost is the sum of both 1) variable costs and 2) fixed costs. *Costs that change in direct proportion to changes in volume (units sold) are called* ***VARIABLE COSTS. FIXED COSTS*** *are indirect costs that remain constant and do not vary with each unit produced.* These are expenses that would be incurred even it there were no business activity. Examples of fixed costs are office rent, utility cost, and administration or staff.

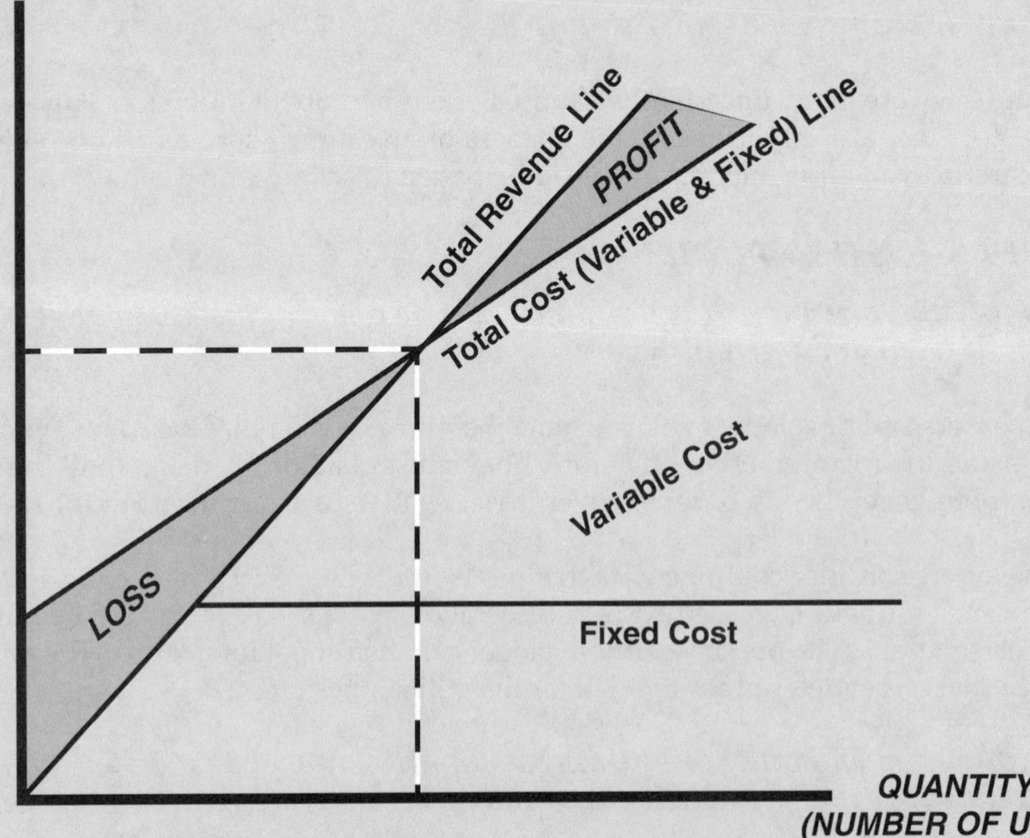

C. IMPLICIT COSTS (Opportunity Costs)

OPPORTUNITY (or IMPLICIT) COSTS *are the income that could have been made if the money was invested somewhere else.*

Opportunity or implicit costs are NOT cash expenses paid, but alternative income that could have been received.

For example, assume a developer has $100,000 equity in a parcel of land he is holding for future development. The taxes and interest on the property would be explicit costs, but if the money could be earning eight percent per annum interest, then the cost of holding the parcel would be increased $8,000 per annum. This $8,000 would be an implicit cost (opportunity cost) caused by not investing the equity.

In economic decision making, the developer weighs anticipated future profits against immediate explicit (direct) costs, and implicit (opportunity) costs.

Many owners do not think in economic terms. As an example, assume an owner wants $100,000 for a parcel of land. Assume also that the owner refuses an offer of $90,000 and says, "I will wait until I get my price, even if it takes 5 years." The owner, in this case, is not considering the implicit costs of holding the property.

Implicit costs are really the time-value of money; the use value of the money now versus the value of a larger sum at a future date.

D. RISK IN INVESTMENT DECISIONS

Developers and investors want a profit to justify the risk.

The greater the risk, the greater should be the anticipated profit. Risk factors include costs, income, and time delays. The narrower the anticipated margin between income and expenses, the greater the risk. In a low cash flow situation, investors would expect appreciation in value and/or future income increases to offset the high risk.

Investors are interested in the ratio of variable costs to total costs. When there is a higher ratio of variable costs there is less risk, because variable costs are related to income, fixed costs continue regardless of income.

E. UNSTABLE INTEREST RATES

Developers often borrow funds at interest rates that are tied to the prime rate.

Because of unstable interest rates, developers cannot be certain about costs. Therefore, a profit margin should be planned to cover the cost of the worst-case scenario. While developers are optimists by nature, the worst-case scenario should be addressed in planning.

If a project CANNOT bear the cost, abandonment or modification of the project should be seriously considered.

F. USE OF LEVERAGE (Borrowing)

In an inflationary market, a wise investor will consider maximum leverage (borrow as large a percentage of purchase price as possible).

Low or no down payment (using borrowed or seller financing) will allow the investor to gain maximum appreciation. For example, if a property was purchased with 10 percent down and it appreciated 10 percent in value, the investor would have increased his or her equity by 100 percent. **Example:** Price $1,000.000; 10 percent down $100,000. If the value goes up 10 percent, the value would go up $100,000. This is 100 percent of down payment, which was the buyer's equity. If that investor had paid cash for the property, a 10 percent increase in value would have resulted in only a 10 percent increase in equity. Another advantage of using leverage in times of inflation is the borrower can pay back dollars borrowed with cheaper dollars having less purchasing power.

As leverage increases, so does risk.

Greater leverage, due to debt payments, decreases cash flow. Unexpected expenses or a loss of income can result in inability to make payments. Should this happen, the lender could foreclose on the property, causing a complete loss of the investment.

In an uncertain or flat market, investors usually avoid high leverage, high risk situations. A high down payment, sufficient to insure a positive cash flow, will reduce risk.

Leverage decisions are based on a trade-off between maximizing profits should values increase, and the risk of a flat or declining market. While problems with foreclosures have led to developers not borrowing (require all-cash real estate investors), this is an overreaction to past problems. Economic decisions should be based on yield from the property, current interest rates, and anticipated appreciation levels.

As an example, assume a property purchased for cash shows an annual yield of 7.5 percent. Assume also that the property has an anticipated appreciation of 5 percent a year. This would mean a 12.5 percent per year real rate of return on an all-cash investment. If the investment could be financed at 10.5 percent, the investor would make a 2 percent return on the portion financed, as well as 12.5 percent on the cash invested. It is possible to calculate the total return for the investor, with various down payments, by using the ***INTERNAL RATE OF RETURN**, which is a mathematical measuring tool used for investment comparison.*

If the finance costs in the above example were 13 percent, then it would appear best for the investor to purchase all cash rather than borrow at 13 percent to earn 12.5 percent. However, if an investor anticipated increases in income above 7.5 percent, then the investor should calculate these increases in making a decision regarding leverage.

A ***NEGATIVE CASH FLOW INVESTMENT** is characterized by a larger cash out-flow from an investment than the cash in-flow.* While highly leveraged investments may result in a negative cash flow, a negative cash flow investment could nonetheless be a good investment based on anticipated future cash flow and profit on sale and/or tax benefits. Of course, if an investor is unable to carry a negative cash flow, then leverage should be reduced to a point where a positive cash flow is assured.

G. LEVERAGE FOR HOMEBUYERS

It is possible for homeowners to buy a home with little or no down payment. The amount of the down payment that the homeowner should use varies with individual circumstances.

In states where buyer default cannot result in a deficiency judgment, a low down payment or no down payment might seem economically sound. In the event of an economic downturn and lower property values, the buyer could walk away from the home without further legal obligation.

In these upside-down situations, where the loan is greater than the property value, instead of walking away that would negatively effect the owner's credit, the buyer should approach the lender to agree to a short sale.

In a short sale, the lender agrees to accept the proceeds of the sale as total satisfaction of the owner's debt.

This agreement makes sense to a lender who saves the cost of foreclosure as well as avoids the possibility of vandalism. Chances are the owner will maintain the property until it can be sold. In a depressed real estate market, the one thing lenders do not want is another property in their inventory.

Generally, a buyer will obtain a lower interest rate for a loan with 20 percent or more down. Also a buyer need not pay a mortgage insurance premium (MIP). For these reasons, if a buyer is able they should make the larger down payment. However, if the buyer is able to obtain an FHA or VA loan then the buyer will generally be better off doing so with a minimum down payment.

If the buyers feel they can get a greater benefit from their cash investments than they are paying in interest, they should consider a lower down payment. However, if a buyer has no safe haven for his or her cash, it would be better if he or she put more cash down and carried a lower loan balance.

For self-employed buyers who may have difficulty in documenting their income, a higher down payment will qualify the buyer for a no documentation loan.

II. Investment Alternatives

Development and investment decisions should not be made in a vacuum. Decisions should be weighed against available alternatives.

Investment decisions should be made based on the needs of each particular developer and investor. In evaluating investment alternatives (which range from other types of developments to stocks, bonds, and certificates of deposit), a number of factors should be considered. These include cash flow, equity appreciation, tax shelter, and security.

Projects that offer several ways of making a profit are particularly attractive to developers.

For example, a townhouse project could be sold upon completion as individual units, kept as a rental project until there was a seller's market, or simply sold as a rental project to another investor, who in turn, would have alternatives. The available alternatives can reduce the developer's risk.

III. Pricing

A. PRICING STRUCTURE

The pricing structure (setting prices) for the sale of real property is extremely important.

In a competitive market, setting too high a sales price in a housing project will result in few sales and a long, costly holding period. The benefits of increased prices (high selling prices) could be outweighed by the costs associated with holding property for a longer period of time prior to sale as well as by greater marketing costs.

Too low a price will fail to maximize profits.

A low price, however, will result in quick sales or rentals, which reduce the owner's risk. In the late 1970s, many residential developments sold out on opening day. Many of the purchasers resold their units or reservations to buy at profits ranging from

$10,000 to $25,000. These quick sales and resales indicate that developers failed to properly assess the demand and priced their units too low. In the later 1990s, a number of projects sold out in one day. Again, this indicates that the price structure failed to maximize profits.

In an active market, a developer's price structure must be competitive with other sale prices unless there is a flaw in the market. In a buyer's market there are few buyers and many sellers, so the price structure should be lowered to ensure sales.

The price structure should be advantageous compared to the competition, unless the owner is somewhat willing to settle for a long holding period.

In a real hot housing market, there are often multiple offers above the asking price. Prices escalate in such a market. During such a market, rather than setting asking prices at prices related to recent sales, it would be in the seller's best interests to ask more than what others have sold their properties for.

B. PRICE VS. FINANCING

Except when there is a flaw in the market, high interest rates result in a buyer's market.

When interest rates are high, many prospective buyers stop looking and wait for interest rates to drop. This, however, is not necessarily the best economic decision.

When interest rates drop, the market tends to heat up, which means higher prices. For example, the weighted average price of a newly-constructed, single-family home in San Diego, as of February 2004, was $602,232—a 145 percent increase from eight years ago. This increase has generally been attributed to lower interest rates.

A purchase made at a high interest rate in a slow market is likely to be the best economic decision.

As an example, a purchase made at 10 percent interest might be made at a price of 20 percent less than if the interest were 6 percent, because there would be very few buyers and many sellers.

If the purchaser had a two-year holding period before refinancing at a lower rate, even considering points and costs, the purchaser would likely be ahead. If a purchase is to be made during a period of high interest rates the buyer should seek a loan that does not have a prepayment penalty, as this penalty can be severe. In many cases, prepayment requires six months' interest as a penalty. On a $400,000 loan at 10 percent interest, this would mean a penalty of $20,000. In many states, prepayment penalties for homes

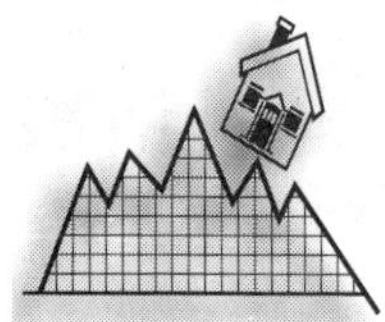

are limited or prohibited by law but they are not generally limited as to commercial property. Adjustable Rate Mortgages usually do not have prepayment penalties.

As long as home interest is an income tax deductible expense, the government would be actually paying part of the interest. For a taxpayer in the 40 percent bracket (total of state and federal income tax brackets) 40 percent of the interest is really paid by the government. Ten percent gross interest would mean a net cost of six percent of the principal.

C. PRICE VS. INTEREST RATE

A higher price with a lower interest rate could result in the same payment as a lower price with a higher interest rate.

There are income tax advantages to a buyer in paying a lower price with a higher rate of interest. Interest expense is fully tax deductible to the buyer. This advantage would be offset, however, if the asset was depreciable, because a lower price would mean less in depreciation deductions.

The Internal Revenue Service (IRS) was disturbed about sales with below-market seller financing. The IRS realized the purpose was to turn regular income (interest) into capital gains income, which has a lower rate of taxation. They will, therefore, impute interest rates in some situations. ***IMPUTED INTEREST*** *is the federal government's requirement that the debt holder pay income tax on interest that should have been charged even if interest was not charged.*

D. EXCHANGE DECISIONS (IRS Section 1030)

A like-for-like exchange (real property for real property) held for income or investment allows an owner to defer income tax. The owner of qualifying exchange property can keep his or her old tax base, which would be increased by any additional cash paid or additional debt assumed. The exchanger wants to avoid cash received (boot) or debt relief as a result of the exchange since boot is taxable as gain.

It is not necessary for a person to have in mind a property to buy when he or she enters into an exchange agreement. A deferred exchange is possible, where an intermediary sells the property, then takes the cash and uses it to purchase a property desired by the seller (see Chapter 8).

A tax-free exchange allows an owner to sell a property and acquire full use of the proceeds of the sale for investment purposes without paying federal and state income taxes.

Assume a person had a lot with a cost basis of $25,000. If the lot were sold for $525,000, there would be a taxable gain of $500,000. Federal long-term capital gain tax would take 15 percent, $75,000 of the proceeds, so the seller would have less money to invest. With a tax-deferred exchange the seller could get the property desired and pay no taxes on the exchange. (State taxes could reduce the cash available to invest even further.)

E. GIFT DECISIONS

There are times when it makes economic sense to give property away.

For example, if an owner gave a part of her property to a charitable organization or a college, the value of the donated portion would be deductible. The presence of the college would add value to the land retained by the donor, which would likely surpass the value of the gift. In one instance, a nationally known celebrity gave 40 acres of a 320-acre tract to establish a major medical center. Before the first phase of the medical center was completed, the value of the remaining 280 acres had more than tripled in value.

IV. Rental Decisions

A. SETTING RENTS

Rents are determined by the supply and demand of the marketplace, NOT by actual apartment construction and/or operating costs.

An overpriced rental will receive the same consumer reaction as any overpriced commodity.

A vacant unit is in competition primarily with other vacant units.

What others are charging in rent is not a determinant of what rent can be obtained, because a vacant unit is not generally in competition with units that have tenants.

There is a direct relationship between the rental rate and the vacancy factor.

Talus Solutions, Inc. of Atlanta is working with a REIT collecting apartment demand data for rent pricing in a similar manner that hotels and airlines use demand data for setting their rates. This will be an attempt to set rents more on actual demand than on what others are charging.

VACANCY FACTOR *is the percentage of rent that is not received due to vacancies.* It takes longer to obtain a tenant at a rent that is not competitive with equally desirable properties than it takes to rent a competitively priced unit. In the same respect, tenants who are paying more in rent than they would pay at similarly desirable properties are less likely to remain as tenants than those who are paying a competitive rent.

If a 10 percent increase in rent results in a 10 percent vacancy factor, the net result is a loss in total rents (10 units at $1,000 per month = $10,000). If rents increased to $1,100 and only 9 units are rented, total rent would be $9,900 per month.

In addition to a loss of rent, vacancies mean greater expenses, such as increased insurance costs spread out over occupied units, rental fees, advertising, utilities transferred to owner, cleaning and decorating expenses, repairs and alterations for new tenants, as well as the danger of vandalism. Insurance costs for a vacant commercial structure could well be 300 percent to 500 percent more than the cost for an occupied structure. In addition, rental concessions (see below) might be necessary.

If a newly constructed apartment project is fully rented before its completion, it means the rent structure is too low. If a new apartment project has vacancies 90 days after the project becomes available to tenants, the rent structure is very likely set too high.

An intelligent owner strives to set rents at a level where the combination of rent and the vacancy factor produce the greatest net income.

B. RENT CONCESSIONS VS. PRICE

RENTAL CONCESSIONS *are non-rent items granted by a landlord, which effectively lower the total rent paid.* Several months' free rent, remodeling allowance, reimbursing moving expenses, free flat-screen TV, and health club memberships are all being offered by owners as incentives for renters to move in. Rent concessions have an advantage over lowering rents. Reducing rents for only one tenant will make other tenants unhappy and more likely to move out at the end of their leases.

Rental concessions offer many advantages over reducing rents.

After the recipient's (rent concessions) lease has expired, that tenant is likely to remain at the same (higher than normal) rent. If a reduced rent were raised at the end of a lease, the tenant would more likely relocate due to the psychological effect of a rental increase. When faced with the prospect of rent control, the owner will want to set the scheduled rent as high as possible and use rent concessions to get the units rented.

Suburban Houston experienced an apartment glut in 2000. Landlords were offering rent-free months and other incentives to fill vacancies. Equity Residential Properties offered free cruises with the leases at a 400-unit complex in West Houston. Renters were given choices of 10 different cruise packages.

Because the value of income property is customarily appraised by capitalizing the net income of that property, higher rents with concessions would make a sale at a higher price more likely and would allow the owner to obtain greater financing on the property. (As a buyer, you would want to know if tenants were given any concession to rent.)

C. LENGTH OF LEASE

A long-term lease with a strong tenant helps owners borrow on their equity because lenders know that a good tenant is hard to find and makes the property attractive to purchasers.

Long-term leases benefit a lessor if the rental market deteriorates. The lessor would have a tenant tied to a rent even though changing economic conditions no longer justify that rent. A long-term lease in a ***LESSEE'S MARKET*** *(more lessors than lessees)* would likely result in the tenant having the ability to obtain concessions from the lessor. In a ***LESSOR'S MARKET*** *(more lessees than lessors)*, the lessor would be able to dictate lease terms.

A large wholesale lessor of office space rented suites to attorneys. He had long-term master leases but kept his tenants on short leases because he believed rentals would rise in the future and he wanted to be able to increase future rents. A ***MASTER LEASE*** *is applied to an entire area of a building and allowed for short-term subleasing*. When the office market became glutted, his vacancy factor dramatically increased. His tenants moved to lower-cost space elsewhere while he was tied-in to long leases. The result was financial disaster. Others used his formula against him. Because they paid lower rent for their space, he could not be competitive.

In cities with a great deal of soot and dirt, apartments must be renovated between tenants. Because of this, owners tend to require longer leases (two to three years) rather than the more customary one-year lease. On the downside, the landlord could be tied into a rental below-market value because of inflation.

Commercial long-term leases customarily provide for rent increases based on an index such as the Consumer Price Index (CPI). *Provisions for rental adjustments are called* **ESCALATOR CLAUSES**. The effect of the rent adjustment is to give the lessor the same purchasing power for each dollar spent. In the late 1970s, some lessors who provided utilities and whose long-term leases had increased based on the CPI, found themselves in difficulty because the costs of utilities increased far more than the CPI. (We are once again heading for significant increases in electricity and natural gas.) Landlords who include heating and/or electricity in their rentals could be in trouble if they have long-term leases. Owners who have adjustable rate mortgages could have similar problems if interest rates increase. With a long-term lease, this could be disastrous.

A long-term lease is a financial obligation of the tenant. When a tenant wants out of a long-term lease, the lessor is likely to demand compensation. The Long-Term Credit Bank of Japan paid more than 12 million dollars to be released from their lease in a Manhattan office building. In this particular case, the owner was able to re-rent the space for $10 more per square foot than the Japanese bank had been paying.

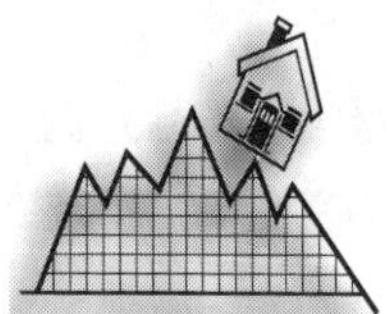

When there is a high demand for space and steadily rising rents, landlords have negotiated agreements with tenants to let them out of their lease. In some cases, landlords have negotiated agreements where the tenants share in any higher rents received for the balance of the lease term.

D. RENT OR BUY DECISIONS

Individual circumstances effect decisions as to renting versus buying. These factors are spelled out in **Figure 15-2**.

Figure 15-2

Rent or Buy Decisions

In making a rent or buy decision, a business should consider the economic advantages to each.

Advantages to rent rather than buy:

1. Rent payment is fully deductible (if a business expense). Payment on loan principal is not deductible.
2. Mobility – since real property is fixed, owning makes it more difficult to expand or relocate.
3. Liquidity – money is not tied up in fixed assets. This is the primary reason for most sale-leaseback arrangements.
4. Tenant has none of the risks associated with ownership.
5. Tenant is not tied to a fixed expense in the event of a recession.

Advantages to ownership rather than rent:

1. Protection against rent increases or arbitrary decisions of owner.
2. Improvements can be depreciated, which shelters other income from taxation.
3. Interest and taxes are tax-deductible expenses.
4. Ownership offers a collateral value. Owner can borrow against his or her equity.
5. Real estate tends to appreciate in value.

E. LEASING LAND

Commercial developers frequently lease rather than purchase land. Leases allow developers to reduce their capital (cash) requirements for the leased land and therefore lower the total development cost.

In addition, property can frequently be leased for significantly less than the value of the property would indicate is a proper return. The reason for this is the owner of the land remains the owner and knows that his or her heirs will end up owning the improvement.

Owners who are hesitant to sell are often eager to lease. Someone else builds a building that will become theirs and the negative cash flow of ownership (taxes) turns into a long-term income stream. The leases are usually triple net leases. A ***TRIPLE NET LEASE*** *is a lease in which the tenant pays the property taxes, insurance, and all operating expenses, and the landlord gets a net rent*. Triple net leases are generally tied to the Consumer Price Index so that the owner maintains the present purchasing power of the rent.

A developer or investor should not turn down an opportunity solely because the improvements being built or purchased will revert to the landlord at some future date. If the income from the property will amortize the investment over the lease period (pay back the investment) plus provide an adequate return on the investment, it makes economic sense.

F. SALE-LEASEBACK DECISIONS

A ***SALE-LEASEBACK*** *is a financial maneuver in which the owner builds a structure, sells it and leases it back on a long-tern lease.* Retail businesses require a great deal of capital to cover inventory, equipment, and accounts receivable. They generally want their capital to be working for them (invested in inventory) rather than tied up in a capital asset (real estate). When capital is tied up in fixed assets, it cannot be used for expansion.

Franchises and large chain stores will build facilities, sell them to investors and lease them back. The store gets the type of building and location it wants, and the investors are assured of a long-term return on their investment, usually with a triple net lease.

Owners can build a structure of their own design, specifications, and choice of materials, and after the sale have no cash tied up in the new facility because they are now leasing it back.

The tenant can sometimes make a profit because the lease terms of a strong tenant (guaranteed payer) have more effect on value than replacement costs (value of the building). By paying more rent, a financially strong tenant can create a greater sales price. Sale-leasebacks can thus give the lessor additional cash to allow for rapid expansion of his or her business.

Sears went through a major expansion after World War II without tying up operating capital. They built new stores and sold them to investors at prices that were justified based on their long-term lease. This technique, which has now been copied by most major chains, allowed Sears to be the dominant player in merchandising for several decades.

V. Housing Development Decisions

New housing is built where the demand for houses (in price, size and location) is greater than the supply.

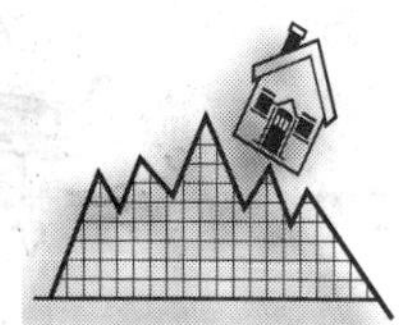

When there are different areas of the market that meet the above criteria, the developer will consider trade-offs between risk and profit. Often lower cost units, because of greater demand, offer lower risks. Higher price units can offer a greater return on investment but offer greater risks since there is a more limited market.

The risk profit trade-off is influenced by the way each developer views the economy and predicts the future.

A. DESIGN DECISIONS

Distinctive designs can attract high-priced renters to commercial structures. The design will stand out and offer greater prestige for the tenants.

While people love to tour housing with different styling, most potential purchasers do not buy unique houses. The majority of consumers prefer to purchase more conservative-style homes.

In the Southwest, a Spanish-style home is likely to require a shorter sale period than an art deco-style home. In the Northeast, Colonial styles are very desirable. In residential developments, people tend toward traditional styling. In office structures the reverse is often true.

Distinctive, contemporary designed commercial structures bring premium rents.

Standout buildings are also desired by major tenants as signature structures, which add recognition to their business through free advertising. The pyramid-shaped Transamerica building in San Francisco is such an example.

B. QUALITY OF CONSTRUCTION

It would not cost much more than current construction costs to build structures that would have a life expectancy of several hundred years. Some of the additional costs would be:

1. More steel in footings and slabs;
2. Greater use of treated lumber;
3. Better quality windows and doors;
4. Better quality hardware;
5. Cast-iron bath fixtures;
6. Hot dipped, galvanized nails or screws;
7. Better attic ventilation;
8. Treating soil beneath structure for termite prevention;
9. Vapor barriers under slabs;

10. Access panels for all plumbing;
11. Use of standardized sizes for replacement;
12. Heavier gauge ducts and flashing;
13. Tile, slate, or copper roofs.

Few structures are built to last centuries because buyers are generally unwilling to pay the extra costs required for extra quality.

Paying additional costs for a structure that will physically last 300 years as opposed to 100 years has little appeal to most buyers.

While builders will meet state and local codes, they will generally only exceed the code requirements when they can see that the increased costs will result in higher profits.

Buyers will react favorably to quality construction that affects operational costs, such as insulation, double or triple glazing, more efficient heating and cooling, and appliances.

Buyers will pay for quality they can see, such as quality wood cabinets, ceramic tile, brick or stone trim, and granite counter tops.

C. EVALUATING AMENITIES

Any amenity added to a development should garner an economic benefit. ***AMENITIES*** *are items people want and are willing to pay extra for, such as a Jacuzzi, tennis court, or beautiful view.* The benefit could be higher rent prices, lower vacancy factors, publicity, faster sell-out, etc. Amenities that are not desired by the public and do not result in direct or indirect economic gain should be avoided.

Owners/builders should only make improvements that will pay for themselves (principle of contribution). Improvements that CANNOT be justified based on net income are NOT economical.

As an example, assume an owner of an apartment building is considering the purchase of an adjacent lot to build a tennis court. Assume the cost for the lot and the construction costs of the tennis court would be $200,000. Assume also that the apartment owner expects a 10 percent return on any additional investment. The tennis court would have to contribute $20,000 a year plus maintenance, depreciation and additional property tax costs before it would be a sound economic decision.

In Britain, new developments are marketed stressing their electronic wired advantages, which has been a successful amenity with the growth of what is referred to as the "telecottage" industry or home workers.

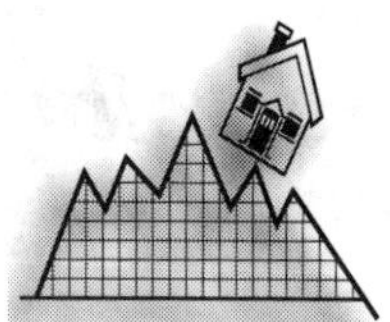

When making property improvement decisions, the vacancy factor should be considered. If the improvement is made to maintain the occupancy rate, then the cost of the improvement should be weighed against how much income would be lost if the improvement is not made.

D. REDEVELOPMENT OR DEMOLITION?

A property that no longer produces income attributable to the improvements alone has exceeded its economic life.

ECONOMIC LIFE *is the period of time that an investment produces higher net income compared to what a property's alternative uses could produce.* As an example, assume a property had a net income of $10,000 and a 10 percent return was a reasonable return for the owner's investment. By capitalizing the net income ($10,000 ÷ .10), we find that the income indicates a value of $100,000. If the land alone has a market value of $150,000, then the improvements are not contributing to income and have exceeded their economic life. The reason a structure exceeds its economic life is generally not physical problems. Instead, it is usually caused by land value increases that make the present use uneconomical.

When a building has exceeded its economic life, an owner or investor has two basic options: 1) making alterations to the structure; 2) demolition of the structure and building a new structure. The cost of demolition should be considered in the decision making.

It would NOT be economical to demolish without rebuilding as long as the property income exceeds variable expenses.

E. EFFICIENCIES OF DEVELOPMENT AND OPERATION

When profits are increasing, inefficiencies tend to increase if care is NOT taken to maximize profits and reduce unnecessary expense. Efficiencies are often the direct result of necessity.

As profits decrease, a greater emphasis would be placed on accounting for the necessity of all expenses. Staffing, purchasing methods, scheduling, and substitution of materials and methods all become closely scrutinized.

F. EMPLOYEES OR INDEPENDENT CONTRACTORS

The decision to hire employees or use contract labor applies NOT only to construction but the provision of services such as maintenance and security as well. The principal advantage of using one's own employees is the control of timing and quality.

One is not subject to the scheduling of independent contractors when one's own employees are used. You have control with your own employees.

There are a number of advantages to using independent contractors. The cost of processing paperwork and the expense of worker's compensation, unemployment compensation, social security contributions, withholding taxes, employee benefits, liability insurance, etc., are eliminated. When contracting for a fixed price, costs are locked in. Use of employees could also subject one to costs associated with unexpected problems.

The federal government has found that maintenance and security by contractors results in significant savings when compared to the use of government employees, because contractors have lower wage scales and are offered less in employee benefits than government workers.

Another advantage of contracting is it frees management from direct responsibility and supervision of employees so that they are available for other tasks.

VI. Financing Decisions

Many important decisions in real estate involve financing.

A. EVALUATING LOANS

While interest rates among lenders might vary only slightly, other loan provisions can vary significantly and should be considered when making a loan decision.

For example, one loan might have a quarter percent lower interest rate than another, but require the borrower to pay two more points (one point is one percent of the amount borrowed). The APR (annual percentage rate) might, therefore, be the same on both loans. If a borrower intended a fairly quick resale, the loan without points might be more advantageous as the total loan costs would be less. For a borrower who intended to hold a property for 20 years, the lower interest rate, even though coupled with more points, would likely be more desirable.

In addition to interest rate and points, all loan costs should be considered.

The borrower should consider appraisal fees charged, title charges, documentation charges as well as presence or absence of prepayment penalties and balloon payments. The borrower should also be concerned about loan assumability.

Many lenders also charge what are known as garbage fees. They're costs that are charged to the borrower for which minimum or no lender costs were incurred. They

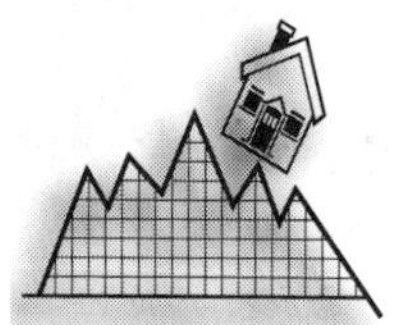

might include transfer fees for documents that were simply moved from one desk to the next desk.

If a borrower believes future interest rates will drop, or if he/she expects to refinance or pay off the loan, a loan without a prepayment penalty would be desirable.

For a construction loan, the borrower should be concerned with the payout schedule. This varies among lenders.

The builder generally wants as much money as possible as soon as possible.

Balloon payments (large ending payment) should be evaluated against the worst-case scenario. Generally, a higher interest rate would be preferable to a balloon payment.

If a borrower believes interest rates will remain stable or decline, an adjustable rate mortgage could be considered if the interest differential was enough to offset the risk of rising interest rates.

If the borrower believes interest rates will rise, then a fixed rate loan is preferable, even at slightly less advantageous terms.

There are a number of software programs that not only allow you to evaluate total costs of a loan, but to also compare various loans.

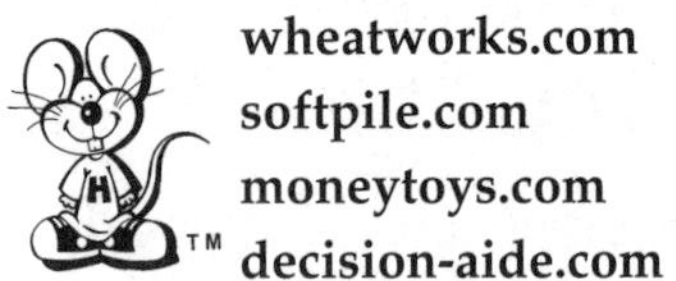

wheatworks.com
softpile.com
moneytoys.com
decision-aide.com

B. ADJUSTABLE LOANS

Because they offer different features, it is difficult for borrowers to compare loans offered by different lenders.

Figure 15-3 shows the many features and variations in Adjustable Rate Mortgages.

C. PERMANENT FINANCING

PERMANENT FINANCING is a long-term loan that pays off a short-term construction loan. In the past, many builders lost their projects because they were unable to obtain permanent financing.

According to the Urban Land Institute, a nonprofit organization for developers, builders continue to start projects without permanent financing. The surveys indicate

Figure 15-3

Adjustable Rate Mortgages (ARMs)

With adjustable rate mortgages, some factors to consider are:

1. Index Used – for California, the most stable index is probably the appropriate Federal Reserve District Cost of Funds Index. Other indexes seem to be more volatile.
2. Margin – the percentage above the Index at which the loan will be set.
3. Cap – the maximum interest that can be charged on the loan.
4. Adjustment Cap – the maximum interest raise for any adjustment period.
5. Initial Rate – as an inducement for an Adjustable Rate Mortgage (ARM) lenders will offer a below market rate for a period of time.
6. Adjustment Periods – how often will the loan be subject to adjustment?
7. Negative Amortization – is negative amortization possible?
8. Points – some lenders have reduced or eliminated points to make ARMs more attractive.
9. Loan Costs – costs vary greatly with lenders; some no longer charge appraisal fees.
10. Assumability of Loan – many ARMs are assumable if buyers meet credit requirements.
11. Prepayment Penalties – generally, ARMs can be prepaid without penalty.

If an owner wanted to refinance a loan but not keep the property for a long period, then the absence of points and lower loan origination costs would be a major factor in a loan decision. For a longer term, holding the interest rate and interest cap would become more important.

that one in five projects are not covered by a permanent loan. The Urban Land Institute warns that this could lead to foreclosures.

The reason builders give for starting without long-term financing is the difficulty in arranging financing years before it is required. They apparently weigh the economic advantages and risks and decide to proceed. Of course, when interest rates are dropping, a delay in permanent financing arrangements can be in the developers' best interest because the longer they wait, the lower their interest rate will be.

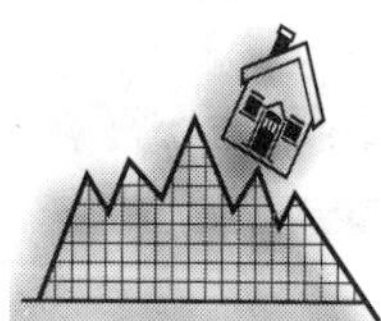

D. REFINANCING

REFINANCING is obtaining a new loan in order to pay off an existing loan. Refinancing real property can provide owners with additional capital at interest rates that may be less than rates charged for commercial or consumer loans. In deciding whether to refinance, an owner should consider all front-end costs, such as appraisal fees, escrow fees, new title insurance, and loan charges. These costs should be considered in determining the actual cost of the money being obtained. As an example, assume an owner could refinance a $500,000 loan and obtain a $1,000,000 loan at the same 10 percent interest rate. If all loan costs totaled $50,000, the borrower would have to consider the effect of $50,000 in costs on his or her interest rate. Because most loans are paid off or refinanced long before they mature, the borrower might be wise to consider a five-year effect. Fifty thousand dollars for a five-year loan of $500,000, without considering a time value factor, would amount to 2 percent per year or a more realistic interest rate of 12 percent for the additional $500,000.

If the original $500,000 loan were for 8 percent, then the new 10 percent rate would mean that the borrower would be paying 2 percent more for the $500,000, which in effect means that the true interest for the additional $500,000 obtained by refinancing is 2 percent greater or, in this example, 14 percent.

When the purpose of refinancing is to reduce interest being paid on a loan, an owner should consider all loan costs to determine savings.

An owner should also consider the likelihood of a sale within a short period of time. If a sale within the next several years is probable, refinancing costs are likely to exceed interest savings.

As a rule of thumb, it is generally NOT advisable to refinance unless there is at least a 2 percent savings in interest.

Many financial advisors counsel against refinancing unless the loan costs can be repaid from payment savings within five years.

(Note: five years was used in the example above to determine actual interest rate. A three-year recovery would mean a considerably higher effective interest rate.)

It is extremely risky to refinance a fixed rate loan with an adjustable rate loan since future interest rates will be unknown.

Software is available that will evaluate the benefits or negative financial impact of refinancing.

filesland.com
interestsaver.com
moneytoys.com

E. REFINANCE OR EQUITY LOAN

Refinancing and taking cash out of a property can obtain the same net effect as putting a second mortgage or trust deed against the property to obtain the cash. While the two methods could yield the borrower the same amount of cash, the costs associated with the two methods could differ significantly.

Refinancing will allow a borrower to obtain a favorable interest rate based on the present market. A second mortgage (equity loan) would have a higher rate of interest than the refinance rate since second mortgages are considered more risky and are less desirable on the secondary mortgage market.

If the existing mortgage is a lower interest rate than the current market rate for the type of loan, then the borrower might be better off keeping the loan and paying a premium rate of interest for the second mortgage. Of course, the total interest cost for first and second mortgages, as well as loan costs, have to be evaluated against the interest on a refinanced loan including loan costs. If a borrower expected to sell the property and/or pay off the loam within a short period of time, then an equity loan might be more advantageous since many equity loans have low down origination fees and no prepayment penalties.

If the interest rate on the existing loan were more than the current rate for loans, then refinancing would, in all likelihood, be the economic decision to make. Of course, in any decision, loan terms, and total loan origination costs must be considered.

F. SELLER POINTS

By paying points, an owner/seller can obtain advantageous institutional financing for purchasers.

In periods of high interest, the ability to offer purchasers interest rates that are substantially less than market rates can be more effective than a lower price.

Builders often buy down the interest rate for a few years, which means an initially lower payment.

In a loan buy-down, the lender is paid in advance for providing a below-market rate of interest.

Many buyers are much more interested in payment amounts than price.

Young, high-income professionals able to afford large payments are attracted to zero interest loans.

With zero interest loans, the purchaser usually pays about one-third down, then makes equal monthly payments for the balance of the loan, often for 60 months. For a $360,000 home, a purchaser would pay $120,000 down and make monthly payments of $4,000 for 60 months. While the purchaser would have tremendous savings as pertains to interest, the price would reflect the seller's costs associated with the non-interest loan. Lenders do not lend without interest. In order to offer a zero interest loan, the seller pays the interest in advance.

G. SUBORDINATION DECISIONS

When a seller agrees to subordinate the sale of real property to another loan, the seller's security position takes a secondary position to the new loan.

Many sellers have lost the equity in their second loan when the new first loan is foreclosed upon.

There are, however, times when agreeing to subordinate could be a wise economic decision. An example would be a subdivider who has a large residential lot subdivision and wishes to sell lots. By agreeing to subordinate one or two lots each to a number of builders for quality homes, the subdivider could obtain immediate construction activity. The risk would be lessened because it would be spread out. The activity would attract other builders as well as buyers to the area. The effect would be that the subordinate loans would directly result in greater sales activity.

To keep risks at a minimum, the loan should be subordinate to a specified construction loan rather than all loans. In this way, the seller's loan would have to be paid off when permanent financing is obtained.

VII. Other Economic Decisions

Besides buying decisions and financing decisions, management decisions and selling decisions should also be made for economic reasons.

A. WHEN TO SELL

A very successful investor came up with a four-step analysis for when-to-sell decision-making.

1. The first question is, "If you didn't own this property, would you want to buy it at the price you think it should sell for? If the answer is yes, then don't sell. If the answer is no, proceed to 2.
2. Determine what you will have left after federal and state capital gains taxes, any loan payoffs, as well as brokerage fees and other selling costs.
3. What would you do with the proceeds?
   a. Buy another property? Identify the property.
   b. Use the money for purposes other than investing?

4. What would you prefer?
   a. Buy the other property and own that property (with likely debt service) rather than your present property.
   b. Have the cash to use for other purposes rather than continue owning the property.

If the answer to a. or b. is yes, then you should sell. If no, then you should not be a seller at this time.

B. DEALING WITH PURCHASE OFFERS

Upon receipt of an offer to purchase, the offeree has three choices:

1. Rejection of the offer. A rejection kills the offer and it cannot later be accepted. The offeree by rejection shows disinterest in the offer and in pursuing any negotiations with the offeror.
2. Acceptance, which forms a binding contract.
3. A counter offer which, while killing the original offer, becomes a new offer by the original offeree. The original offeror is the recipient of this offer and has the same three choices as the original offeree had. A counter offer shows interest in continued negotiations.

Generally, an offer should not be rejected unless it is frivolous and/or it is clear that the offeror is not serious as to a purchase.

If an offer is reasonable, acceptance should be considered. By rejection or a counter offer, the offeror is relieved of any obligation. Many buyers have second thoughts, often referred to as buyer's remorse, and will welcome the opportunity to get out of the offer. For this reason, if an offer is to be accepted, it should be accepted as soon as possible so that the buyer cannot revoke the offer. Even if an offer states that it will be open for a specified period of time, the offeror can revoke the offer anytime prior to its acceptance.

In a seller's market, with many buyers, few sellers and where multiple offers are common, the seller might consider a counter offer even though the original offer was reasonable. In this type of market, the buyer is more likely to accept the counter offer, and even if not accepted, the market will likely produce another buyer.

When the seller decides that an acceptance of an offer is not in his or her best economic interest, he or she should make a counter offer. The counter offer should give the original offeror something, that is, it should allow the offeror some gains in making an offer for less than the property was placed on the market for.

Splitting the difference makes no economic sense, even if it has the appearance of being fair. An offeror who receives a counter offer that is halfway between the offer he or she made and the asking price is likely to regard the counter offer as reasonable even if it is not based on economic reasoning.

Counter offers can cover other than just price. All terms in the original offer can be open to negotiation in a counter offer.

At times, an original offeree will demand the asking price and terms and will give a counter offer that reflects this position showing an unwillingness to negotiate. The buyer will often walk away from the purchase, even if it were economically advantageous, because of the feeling that to accept would be a loss of face. That is why some flexibility would normally be in the seller's best interest.

A buyer who receives a full price and term counter offer should try to treat the counter offer economically rather than emotionally. The buyer should ask, "If the property were priced 10 percent higher than it is and the seller came back with this counter offer, would I accept it?" A buyer should not let the fact that the seller won't negotiate keep him or her from a purchase that is in his or her best interests.

VII. Noneconomic Decisions

Many decisions are not based on the careful weighing of alternatives. Decisions can be made because of:

1. Personal goals unrelated to profit. Many prestigious ("trophy") buildings are purchased for personal reasons, not returns.
2. Current ownership of the land. Misplaced improvements are often made simply because a person owns a particular piece of property.
3. Greed. People tend to desire to own more. They often expand beyond the ability of their capital or the market. At times, there will be more opportunities than resources to pursue them. Limits must be established.

   Another example of greed is the belief that a buyer needs you so badly, the buyer will pay whatever you ask. A good example of this is a case in Wisconsin where a small factory wished to expand. The only feasible expansion required the acquisition of a particular property, which had an old house and barn on it. The property had a market value of about $100,000. Agents for the factory offered $200,000. The owner refused, saying he wanted $500,000. When the agents presented an offer for $500,000, the owner said he wanted $1,000,000, but refused to put this counter offer in writing. The result was that the factory found existing larger facilities within 20 miles for less than the land would have cost them. They were able to lease their small plant to one of their suppliers. The owner of the adjoining property kept ownership of a property with a value of about $100,000.
4. Substantial predevelopment costs and commitments. The developer might be forced to go ahead with a project because of investments and commitments, even though changed conditions have placed its profitability in doubt.

5. Short-term expenses or other immediate needs. They cause property to be sold at less than its value.
6. Personal attachment. Often an above market price is not enough to persuade a person to sell real property. People develop an emotional attachment to land. Even though they could sell at a profit and buy similarly desirable property elsewhere for less, it is often not enough to get an owner to sell.
7. Inertia. The easiest decision is to make no decision. Rents that could be raised are not raised, property that should be redeveloped, developed or sold is left as it is. Many people tend to put off changes in favor of the status quo.
8. The ready availability of financing. When lenders are flush with money to lend, builders may be able to obtain loans that meet or exceed their estimated cash outlays. In such a market, builders are likely to expand and keep building despite any changes in the marketplace. The builder is making construction decisions based on financing rather than the marketplace. Cash out construction generally results in overbuilding.
9. Owners are often unwilling to accept a loss. Even though they could better invest the proceeds of the sale in a better investment, owners often refuse to realize a loss. A wise economical investor would sell if other alternatives were more attractive than the investment owned.

IX. Fair Housing

Fair housing was regarded as bad business at one time.

In 1917, the Chicago Real Estate Board set a practice to keep African Americans out of white neighborhoods. A block had to be filled solidly with African Americans before they would be allowed to move to adjoining blocks. That same year, the U.S. Supreme Court ruled that racial zoning was unconstitutional. To get around that ruling, developers used racial Covenants, Conditions and Restrictions to accomplish the same racial zoning effect. The National Association of Real Estate Boards played an active role in developing these restrictions. Between 1917 and 1948, racial restrictions were upheld in 19 state courts.

In 1948, the U.S. Supreme Court held that racial restrictions in restrictive covenants were void and unenforceable (*Shelly v. Kraemer*). However, this decision did not end discrimination in housing, which continued without much opposition for another 20 years. Discrimination was still regarded as good business.

A. FAIR HOUSING LAWS

1. Civil Rights Act of 1866

Passed shortly after the Civil War, the Civil Rights Act of 1866 was intended to prohibit racial discrimination (applied to race only). It was put on the shelf of

forgotten legislation because the courts refused to enforce the act as written. However, in 1968, the Supreme Court held that the law was valid and enforceable. A person discriminated against could seek compensatory and punitive damages in federal court.

2. Civil Rights Act of 1968

Known as the Fair Housing Act, this act as amended goes beyond the Civil Rights Act of 1866 in that it prohibits discrimination as to race, color, national origin, religion, sex, familial status, and handicap. The act requires brokers and developers to post an **Equal Housing Opportunity Poster**. Failure to display the poster could shift the burden of proof to a defendant who would then have to prove he or she did not act in a discriminatory manner (see **Figure 15-4**).

A property owner or manager who treats prospective rental applicants differently could be in violation of the Fair Housing Act. As an example, calling back white visitors who have seen a unit, but not following up calls to African American visitors would be discriminatory. Similarly, checking references of African American rental applicants and not doing the same for white applicants would be discriminatory.

Unreasonable occupancy rules could be discriminatory, such as allowing a couple to occupy a one-bedroom unit but not allowing a single mother with one child to occupy the same unit. HUD currently has indicated that a two-person limit per bedroom is a reasonable limitation.

Sexual harassment is considered a violation of the Fair Housing Act and owners of rental property should be aware of problems in this area. Sexual harassment goes far beyond demanding sexual favors or groping. What a property manager may regard as a joke could be taken by the tenant to be sexual harassment. Similarly, lewd conversations between employees could be regarded by tenants, and more seriously the courts, as being sexual harassment. A claim of sexual harassment could result in significant legal fees, penalties, and damages, including punitive damages.

Figure 15-5 indicates some fair housing violations.

3. State Fair Housing Laws

Most states also prohibit discriminatory actions by lessors, sellers, and their agents. State laws, even though they may duplicate federal laws, allow aggrieved parties to sue in state courts including small claims courts. The cost of bringing an action is considerably less in state courts.

Besides suing, aggrieved parties may take the complaints to HUD or a state agency, which can investigate and bring legal action against the wrong doer.

Figure 15-4

U.S. Department of Housing and Urban Development

We Do Business in Accordance With the Federal Fair Housing Law

(The Fair Housing Amendments Act of 1988)

It is Illegal to Discriminate Against Any Person Because of Race, Color, Religion, Sex, Handicap, Familial Status, or National Origin

- In the sale or rental of housing or residential lots
- In advertising the sale or rental of housing
- In the financing of housing
- In the provision of real estate brokerage services
- In the appraisal of housing
- Blockbusting is also illegal

Anyone who feels he or she has been discriminated against may file a complaint of housing discrimination:
1-800-669-9777 (Toll Free)
1-800-927-9275 (TDD)

U.S. Department of Housing and Urban Development
Assistant Secretary for Fair Housing and Equal Opportunity
Washington, D.C. 20410

Previous editions are obsolete

form HUD-928.1A(8-93)

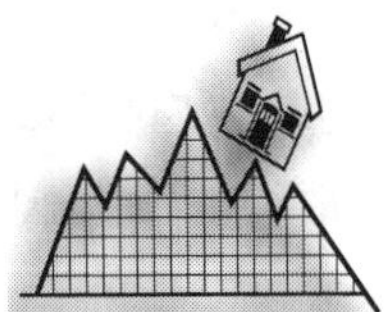

Figure 15-5

Fair Housing Violations

1. **Redlining –** Refusing to loan or insure within designated areas.
2. **Steering –** Directing buyers or lessees to or away from a property based on race, religion, etc.
3. **Refusal to show**, sell, or rent based on race, religion, etc.
4. **Refusal of access** to multiple listing services.
5. **Block Busting –** Inducing panic selling because of fear of lower property values or crime because of minorities' entrance into an area.
6. **Discriminatory Advertising**.
7. **Retaliatory Action** against a tenant for making complaints as to fair housing violations.
8. **Discrimination** as to loan terms.
9. **Coercion** or interference with a persons' rights as to buying selling or leasing.
10. **Refusal to allow support animals** or seeing eye dogs.
11. **Refusal to take reasonable action to accommodate handicapped**.
12. **Refusal to rent or sell to families with children** unless subject to an elderly housing exemption.
13. **Sexual Harassment**.

4. Equal Credit Opportunity Act

This act prohibits lender discrimination in providing credit. It also prohibits the lender to use the source of income (public assistance) as the basis or denial of credit. The act allows a person to know what is in his or her credit file, have wrong information removed or place an explanation in the file.

5. Americans With Disabilities Act

Unlike the fair housing acts, this act has a direct economic impact on property owners.

Owners and operators of places of public accommodation must make their facilities accessible to handicapped to the extent that it is readily achievable.

"Readily achievable" is subjective based on value of the facility and cost to comply.

Accessibility issues create problems with developers, owners, and managers. The codes are vague and often seen to be in conflict as to accessibility issues, which are addressed in federal, state and local codes.

For information on accessibility issues, developers can contact: **www.fairhousingfirst.org**.

B. "NAR" ALSO ENFORCES ANTI-DISCRIMINATION

The National Association of Realtors® Code of Ethics

REALTOR®

The National Association of Realtors (NAR)® Code of Ethics and Fair Practices forbids discrimination against any minority group. Any violation by a real estate licensee could subject that licensee to disciplinary action from the local board of Realtors®.

Article 10 states, "Realtors® shall not deny equal professional services to any person for reasons of race, color, religion, sex, handicap, familial status, or national origin. Realtors® shall not be parties to any plan or agreement to discriminate against a person or persons on the basis of race, color, religion, sex, handicap, familial, status or national origin."

X. CHAPTER SUMMARY

Economic decision making in real estate must involve a **market forecast**. The local and national economy, as well as the activities of local employers, government bodies, and competitors must be considered.

A **"break-even"** analysis shows at what rental and vacancy rate or sales price a property will break even regarding cash flow or recovery of investment. In development decisions, the developer must consider contingencies that could affect the break-even point. The developer's ready ability to reach a break-even status determines the developer's **risk exposure**. In economic decision making, explicit as well as implicit costs must be considered. **Explicit costs** are cash expenses, while **implicit costs** are non-cash expenses based on return from alternative investments. The risks of investment are many and must be weighed against returns and alternative investments.

Rent and sale prices should be established at the level that will result in the greatest net. Too high a price will result in property not being sold or rented, and too low a price will mean the owner has failed to maximize profits. **Economic predictions** should be made when estimating lease terms.

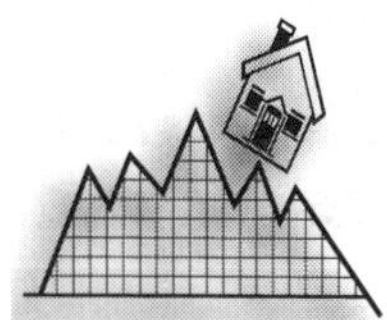

In an **inflationary market**, long-term leases could lock an owner into below-market rents. In a **deflationary period**, a long-term lease could lock in a tenant to above-market rents. Because of changing economic conditions, many leases are tied to an index such as the **Consumer Price Index (CPI)**.

Other economic decisions involve buying down interest, refinancing, evaluating the need for amenities and their effect, exchange decisions, leasing rather than purchasing, gift decisions, design decisions, types of loans, when to sell, and dealing with purchase offers. Whenever there are alternatives possible, decisions must be made.

While our real estate profession has a history of discrimination, we have embraced our **fair housing laws** and discovered fair housing is good business.

XI. GLOSSARY OF KEY TERMS

Americans with Disabilities Act – An act that requires places of public accommodation to make readily achievable modifications to accommodate the handicapped.

Annual Percentage Rate (APR) – The rate of interest charged expressed as simple interest.

Break Even Analysis – Analysis as to the point a property will show income sufficient to pay cash expenses.

Buying Down Interest – Paying an advance sum to a lender in order to obtain a below market interest rate.

Civil Rights Act of 1866 – Our first federal Civil Rights Act but it applied only to race.

Civil Rights Act of 1968 – A comprehensive act that applies to a broad range of groups.

Exchange – A trade of properties usually based on tax benefits.

Explicit Costs – Actual cash expenses.

Implicit Costs – Non-cash expenses of ownership and/or operations.

Imputed Interest – Interest taxed as if a market rate interest were received when a below-market interest rate is charged.

Internal Rate of Return – A method of measuring returns on investments that considers tax consequences and down payment.

Lessee's Market – A rental market with few prospective lessees and many vacancies.

Lessor's Market – A market with few vacancies and many prospective lessees.

Like-For-Like – An exchange of similar property that qualifies for a tax deferred exchange.

Opportunity Costs – The earnings that equity in a property could produce if it were invested.

Rent or Buy – Decision to own or to rent.

Short Sale – Lender agreement to accept sale proceeds in fall satisfaction of debt.

Upside Down Situation – Situation where loan balance exceeds property value.

Zero Interest Loans – A loan with no interest. The entire payment would apply to principal.

XII. CLASS DISCUSSION TOPICS

1. What economic factors will likely affect the economic health of your local company?

2. How would you regard the long-term economic prospects of your area?

3. What types of property in your area, if any, would you consider proper for a highly leveraged purchase?

4. Give examples of residential rental and commercial projects that have had recent owner improvements. Why?

5. Identify local structures where you would change the use. Explain what you would do and why.

6. Give local examples of what you would consider noneconomic decisions as to development.

7. Give examples of new subdivisions in your locale that you do not feel are improperly priced. Why?

8. Give examples, if any, of discrimination that you know of as to real estate practices that still exist in your community.

9. Give examples of building in your area with serious accessibility problems.

XIII. CHAPTER 15 QUIZ

1. A noneconomic benefit of real estate investment would be:

a. profit.
b. appreciation in value.
c. personal aggrandizement.
d. sheltering income from taxation.

2. An investor developing a new apartment building is conducting a break-even analysis. The break-even point will be when:

a. construction expenditure equals the construction loan.
b. income covers the total of fixed and variable costs.
c. the appraised value equals the investment.
d. investor's down payment has been returned by cash flow.

3. An investor who indicates she will hold the property forever if she does not get her price has failed to consider:

a. capital gains.
b. opportunity costs.
c. a tax deferred exchange.
d. appreciation.

4. Which of the following should be inversely related to risk?

a. Down payment
b. Total cost
c. Gross income
d. Profit

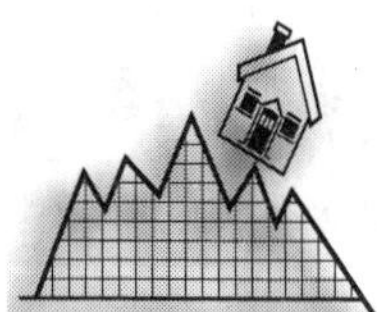

5. In an inflationary market, a speculator would consider:
   a. paying all cash to reduce risk.
   b. using the maximum possible leverage.
   c. reducing the contemplated holding period before sale.
   d. obtaining an adjustable rate mortgage.

6. An astute investor knowingly purchased a property with a negative cash flow. The investor expected:
   a. rents to remain stable.
   b. expenses to increase.
   c. values to decline.
   d. a future positive cash flow.

7. When properties placed on the market are bringing multiple offers, the sale price of a property should be set:
   a. based on past sales.
   b. based on very recent sales.
   c. slightly below recent comparable sales.
   d. above sales of recent comparable properties.

8. Even though a buyer expects interest rates to drop significantly from their present highs, an investor decides to buy a large income property with a 10 percent loan. The reason the investor went ahead with this investment was:
   a. the price.
   b. the fact that interest is deductible for tax purposes.
   c. the danger of recession.
   d. the possible greater depreciation benefits.

9. In setting the rent on a vacant commercial unit, an investor should give the greatest consideration to:
   a. rents being paid by tenants for similar property.
   b. rents being asked for similar vacant units.
   c. the investor's purchase cost.
   d. fixed and variable costs associated with ownership.

10. A commercial tenant is considering buying a property rather than continue renting. Advantages of renting over buying include all, except:
   a. liquidity.
   b. mobility.
   c. depreciation.
   d. deductibility of rent.

ANSWERS: 1. c; 2. b; 3. b; 4. a; 5. b; 6. d; 7. d; 8. b; 9. b; 10. c

Glossary

A

APR (Annual Percentage Rate): The rate of interest charged expressed as simple interest.

Abandonment: Owners walking away from property because continued ownership is not economically viable.

Abatement of Nuisance: Extinction or termination of a nuisance.

Acceleration Clause: Clause in trust deed or mortgage giving lender right to call all sums owing him to be immediately due and payable upon the happening of a certain event.

Accessory Dwelling Unit (ADU): An additional housing unit built on a lot already containing a single-family dwelling.

Accretion: An addition to land from natural causes as, for example, from gradual action of the ocean or river waters.

Accrued Depreciation: The difference between the cost of replacement new as of the date of the appraisal and the present appraised value.

Accrued Items of Expense: Those incurred expenses that are not yet payable. The seller's accrued expenses are credited to the purchaser in a closing statement.

Acquisition: The act or process by which a person procures property.

Acre: A measure of land equaling 160 square rods, or 4,840 square yards, or 43,560 square feet, or a tract about 208.71 feet square.

Adam Smith: The economist who founded the Classical School of Economics. Adam Smith believed in a capitalistic system, a system without government interference or direction. He also believed individual reactions to the economy would work to maintain an equilibrium.

Adjustable Rate Mortgage (ARM): A mortgage subject to future interest adjustment based on future changes in an interest rate index.

Adjustments: A means by which characteristics of a residential property are regulated by dollar amount or percentage to conform to similar characteristics of another residential property.

Affordability Index: An index prepared by the National Association of Realtors® which indicates the percentage of families who can afford the median priced house, based on the average sale price, financing, and current income.

Aesthetic Zoning: Zoning for appearance.

Agency: The relationship between principal and agent which arises out of a contract, either expressed or implied, written or oral, wherein the agent is employed by the principal to do certain acts dealing with a third party.

Agreement of Sale: A written agreement or contract between seller and purchaser in which they reach a meeting of minds on the terms and conditions of the sale.

Air Rights: The rights in real property to use the air space above the surface of the land.

Amenities: Satisfaction of enjoyable living to be derived from a home; conditions of agreeable living or a beneficial influence arising from the location or improvements.

Americans with Disabilities Act: Act that requires places of public accommodation to make readily achievable modifications for handicapped accessibility.

Amortization: The liquidation of a financial obligation on an installment basis; also, recovery, over a period, of cost or value.

Amortized Loan: A loan that is completely paid off, interest and principal, by a series of regular payments that are equal or nearly equal. Also called a Level Payments Loan.

Anchor Tenant: The major tenant for a shopping center, which creates traffic benefiting other tenants.

Annexation: Being joined to; generally refers to unincorporated land becoming part of a city.

Anticipation, Principle of: Affirms that value is created by anticipated benefits to be derived in the future.

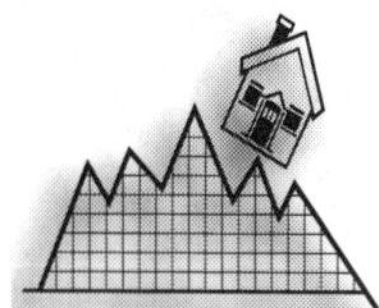

Appraisal: An opinion of value; a conclusion resulting from the analysis of facts.

Appraiser: One qualified by education, training and experience who is hired to estimate the value of real and personal property based on experience, judgment, facts, and use of formal appraisal processes.

Appurtenance: Something annexed to another thing, which may be transferred incident to it. That which belongs to another thing, as a barn, dwelling, garage, or orchard is incident to the land to which it is attached.

Arbitrage: Taking advantage of a price or interest differential. In real estate it has come to mean buying a property at one interest rate and selling it at a higher rate.

Architectural Style: Generally the appearance and character of a building's design and construction.

Assemblage (Plottage): The process of joining contiguous properties under common ownership so that the sum value is more than the values of the separate properties.

Assessed Value: Value placed on property as a basis for taxation.

Assessor: The official who has the responsibility of determining assessed values.

Assignment: A transfer or making over to another of the whole of any property, real or personal, in possession or in action, or of any estate or right therein.

Assisted Living Unit: Apartment unit offering available 24-hour assistance; meals may be included.

Assumption of Mortgage: The taking of title to property by a grantee, wherein he assumes liability for payment of an existing note secured by a mortgage or deed of trust against the property; becoming a co-guarantor for the payment of a mortgage or deed of trust note.

Attorney in Fact: One who is authorized to perform certain acts for another under a power of attorney; power of attorney may be limited to a specific act or acts, or be general.

Axial Growth: Growth outward from the city center following transportation routes.

B

Babcock, F.M.: The developer of the axial theory, which states that cities developed along axis routes based on the time/cost relationship of travel.

Balance of Trade: The difference between the value of exports and that of imports.

Bedroom Community: A suburban community whose residents commute primarily to and from work in a central city or other suburban community.

Benefit Principle of Taxation: The principle that people and property should be taxed based on public benefits received.

Bill of Sale: A written instrument given to pass title of personal property from vendor to the vendee.

Blanket Mortgage: A single mortgage, which covers more than one piece of real estate.

Blighted Area: A declining area in which real property values are seriously affected by destructive economic forces, such as encroaching inharmonious property usages, infiltration of lower social and economic classes of inhabitants, and/or rapidly depreciating buildings.

Boomburg: A suburb of over 100,000 people with a double-digit growth rate per decade.

Boot: Unlike property used to even out a trade: Boot is taxable as gain.

Break Even Analysis: Analysis as to the point a property will show income sufficient to pay cash expenses.

Broker: A person employed by another, to carry on any of the activities listed in the license law definition of a broker, for a fee.

Brownfields: Areas having contaminated soil.

Bubble: Investors driving up prices to the point where they exceed any possible explanation of value.

Buffer Zone: A transition or divider between land uses.

Building Codes: Codes setting construction standards with material or performance specifications.

Building Line: A line set by law a certain distance from a street line in front of which an owner cannot build on his lot. (A setback line.)

Building, Market Value of: The sum of money, which the presence of that structure adds to or subtracts from the value of the land it occupies. Land valued based on the highest and best use.

Building Moratorium: A cessation of construction, usually for a set time, in order to revise planning.

Bulk Zoning: Zoning for density, using setbacks, height limits, open space requirements, etc.

Burgess, Ernest: An urban economist who expanded upon Von Thunen's concentric circle idea regarding city growth.

Business Incubators: Space and services offered to aid new businesses and reduce the likelihood of failure.

Buying Down Interest: Paying an advance sum to a lender in order to obtain a below- market interest rate.

C

CC&Rs: Abbreviation for covenants, conditions, and restrictions.

Capital Assets: Assets of a permanent nature used in the production of an income, such as: land, buildings, machinery, equipment, etc. Under income tax law, it is usually distinguishable from "inventory," which comprises assets held for sale to customers in ordinary course of the taxpayers' trade or business.

Capital Gain: Income from a sale of an asset rather than from the general business activity. Capital gains are generally taxed at a lower rate than ordinary income.

Capitalism: An economic system where control over the means of production and distribution is under private control by individuals and firms working for profit.

Capitalization: In appraising, determining value of property by considering net income and percentage of reasonable return on the investment. Thus, the value of an income property is determined by dividing annual net income by the Capitalization Rate.

Capitalization Rate: The rate of interest, which is considered a reasonable return on the investment, and used in the process of determining value based upon net income. It may also be described as the yield rate that is necessary to attract the money of the average investor to a particular kind of investment. In the case of land improvements that depreciate to this yield rate, a factor is added to take into consideration the annual amortization factor necessary to recapture the initial investment in improvements. This amortization factor can be determined in various ways: (1) straight-line depreciation method, (2) Inwood Tables, and (3) Hoskold Tables. (To explore this subject in greater depth, the student should refer to current real estate appraisal texts.)

Cash Flow: Having cash available when needed to pay costs.

Cash on Cash Return: The ratio between cash invested and cash flow (cash received).

Caveat Emptor: "Let the buyer beware." The buyer must examine the goods or property and buy at his own risk.

Change, Principle of: Holds that it is the future, not the past, which is of prime importance in estimating value.

Christmas in April: A nonprofit organization that rehabilitates homes of low-income owners.

Civil Rights Act of 1866: The first federal civil rights act (applied to race discrimination).

Civil Rights Act of 1968: A comprehensive civil rights act that provides for fair housing.

Class "A" Office Buildings: Newer, most desirable office structures.

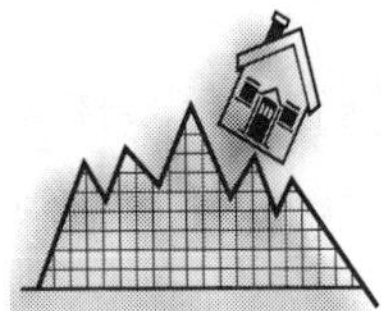

Class "B" Office Buildings: Older but well-maintained office structures.

Class "C" Office Buildings: The older, least desirable office structures.

Clean Industries: Industries that do not pollute water or air.

Co-Housing: A community-living project first designed by the Danish with a large community living area and separate small family buildings.

Command Economy: An economy where economic decisions are made by the government rather than by individuals reacting to the marketplace.

Commitment: A pledge or a promise or firm agreement.

Community Development Block Grants (CDBGs): This program gives large grants to "entitlement communities" for revitalization.

Community Reinvestment Act: Federal Act that requires federal regulatory agencies to consider a financial institution's community service when considering approval of mergers or new branch offices.

Community Shopping Center: A shopping center with one major department store as an anchor tenant.

Company Town: Town where all or most of the real estate is controlled by a single employer.

Comparable Sales: Sales that have similar characteristics as the subject property and are used for analysis in the appraisal process.

Compensating Balance: A minimum balance required to be kept on deposit by a borrower. The requirement raises the effective interest rate since borrower does not have use of all funds borrowed.

Competition, Principle of: Holds that profits tend to breed competition and excess profits tend to breed ruinous competition.

Composite Indexes: Groups of leading and lagging economic indicators compiled by the U.S. Commerce Department.

Concentric Circle Development: The growth of a city in a circular pattern of uses from the city center.

Condemnation: The act of taking private property for public use by a political subdivision; declaration that a structure is unfit for use.

Condominium: A system of individual fee ownership of units in a multifamily structure, combined with joint ownership of common areas of the structure and the land. (Sometimes referred to as a vertical subdivision.)

Condominium Conversion: Converting another use to condominiums.

Condotel: Hotel that has become a condominium with individual room ownership.

Conforming Loans: Loans that meet the purchase requirements of Freddie Mac and Fannie Mae.

Conformity, Principle of: Holds that the maximum of value is realized when a reasonable degree of homogeneity of improvements is present.

Conservation: The process of utilizing resources in such a manner that minimizes their depletion.

Consumer Price Index (CPI): An index of consumer prices used to measure the rate of inflation or deflation.

Contribution, Principle of: Holds that maximum real property values are achieved when the improvements on the site produce the highest (net) return commensurate with the investment.

Consumer Goods: These are goods used or bought for use primarily for personal, family, or household purposes.

Conurbation: An urban region encompassing a number of communities (sprawl).

Conventional Mortgage: A mortgage securing a loan made by investors without governmental underwriting, i.e., which is not F.H.A. insured or G.I. guaranteed.

Cooperative: Ownership by a corporation; individual stockholders have a right to occupy a unit with a lease.

Comer Influence Table: A statistical table that may be used to estimate the added value of a corner lot.

Corporate Mega Farms: Large farms operating under corporate ownership.

Corporation: A group or body of persons established and treated by law as an individual or unit with rights and liabilities or both, distinct and apart from those of the persons composing it. A corporation is a creature of law having certain powers and duties of a natural person. Being created by law it may continue for any length of time the law prescribes.

Cost: A historical record of past expenditures, or an amount, which would be given in exchange for other things.

Cost Approach: One of three methods in the appraisal process. An analysis in which a value estimate of a property is derived by estimating the replacement cost of the improvements, deducting them from the estimated accrued depreciation, then adding the market value of the land.

Cost-Push Inflation: An increase in sale prices caused by an increase in production and distribution costs.

Covenant: Agreements written into deeds and other instruments promising performance or nonperformance of certain acts or stipulating certain uses or nonuses of the property.

Creative Financing: Seller-carried financing.

Critical Rent Level: That rent level at which no new rental housing will be built.

Crowding Out: Government borrowing that raises interest rates and thus excludes some private borrowers from the marketplace.

Cumulative Zoning: Zoning that allows less restrictive uses as well as designated uses.

Curable Depreciation: Items of physical deterioration and functional obsolescence, which are customarily repaired or replaced by a prudent property owner.

Cycles: Recurring waves of economic activity.

D

Damages: The indemnity recoverable by a person who has sustained an injury, either in his person, property, or relative rights, through the act or default of another.

Dedication: An appropriation of land by its owner for some public use accepted for such use by authorized public officials on behalf of the public.

Deed Restrictions: This is a limitation in the deed to a property that dictates certain uses that may or may not be made of the property.

Default: Failure to fulfill a duty or promise or to discharge an obligation; omission or failure to perform any act.

Deferred Maintenance: Existing but unfulfilled requirements for repairs and rehabilitation.

Deflation: An economic period where the value of the dollar is increasing in purchasing power.

Demand Economy: An economy where demands of the marketplace, rather than governmental decisions, determine what and how much is produced.

Demand-Pull Inflation: An increase in prices caused by demand exceeding supply.

Demographics: A statistical study of a population with respect to age, sex, education, income, movement, etc.

Department of Housing and Urban Development (HUD): The federal agency that administers government housing programs.

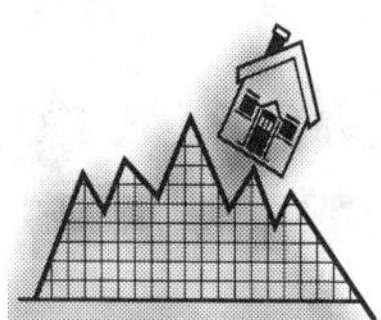

Depreciation: Loss of value in real property brought about by age, physical deterioration or functional or economic obsolescence. Broadly, a loss in value from any cause.

Depth Table: A statistical table that may be used to estimate the value of the added depth of a lot.

Deterioration (Impairment of Condition): One of the causes of depreciation and reflecting the loss in value brought about by wear and tear, disintegration, use in service, and the action of the elements.

Development Rights: Rights to develop property, which in some cases can be separately transferred from the property.

Development Subsidies: Requires developers to pay subsidies to offset the effect of their development project on the community.

Directional Growth: The location or direction toward which the residential sections of a city are destined or determined to grow.

Discount Rate: The interest rate charged by the Federal Reserve for loans to depository institutions.

Disequilibrium: A point in the marketplace where supply and demand are not equal, creating pressure for the price of goods to rise or fall.

Disintermediation: The relatively sudden withdrawal of substantial sums of money that savers have deposited with savings and loan associations, commercial banks, and mutual savings banks. This term can also be considered to include life insurance policy purchasers borrowing against the value of their policies. The essence of this phenomenon is financial intermediaries losing within a short period of time billions of dollars as owners of funds held by those institutional lenders exercise their prerogative of taking them out of the hands of these financial institutions.

Disposable Income: The after-tax income a household receives to spend on personal consumption.

Donut Cities: Central cities that have serious economic difficulties, but are surrounded by a ring of healthy suburbs.

Down Zoning: A change in zoning to a more restrictive use.

Due On Sale Clause: A clause in a trust deed or mortgage requiring that a loan be paid upon sale (non-assumable).

E

80-20 Loans: 100 percent financing with an 80 percent first mortgage and 20 percent second mortgage.

Easement: Created by grant or agreement for a specific purpose, an easement is the right, privilege, or interest which one party has in land of another. (Example: right-of-way.)

Echo Boom: A baby boom caused by children of a previous baby boom having children.

Economic Life: The period over which a property will yield a return on the investment, over and above the economic or ground rent due to land.

Economic Obsolescence: A loss in value due to factors away from the subject property, but adversely affecting the value of the subject property.

Economic Rent: The reasonable rental expectancy if the property were available for renting at the time of its valuation.

Economics: The science that studies how the market system prices and distributes goods and services.

Economy of Scale: A decrease in production costs per unit, resulting from efficiencies in production or procurement due to discounts when buying or producing large quantities.

Effective Age of Improvement: The number of years of age that is indicated by the condition of the structure.

Effective Interest Rate: The percentage of interest that is actually being paid by the borrower for the use of the money.

Effective Rent: Scheduled rent adjusted by concessions given.

Elasticity: The size or magnitutde of a reaction to a change in price.

Empowerment Zones: A HUD designation that allows business in the zone to take a quick write-off of investments and receive tax credits for a portion of the wages paid to new hires.

Environmental Impact Report (EIR): A state report as to the negative impact a development will have on an area's environment.

Equilibrium: The point or price in the marketplace where supply and demand are in balance.

Equity: The interest or value that an owner has in real estate over and above the liens against it; branch of remedial justice by and through which relief is afforded to suitors in courts of equity.

Escalator Clause: A clause in a contract providing for the upward or downward adjustment of certain items to cover specified contingencies.

Eviction: Dispossession by process of law. The act of depriving a person of the possession of lands, in pursuance of the judgment of a court.

Excess Land: Land that does not economically contribute to a project.

Exchange: A trade of properties usually based on tax benefits.

Exchange Rate: The exchange value of the dollar in relationship to other currencies.

Exclusionary Zoning: Zoning which prohibits a stated use.

Expenses: Certain items that may appear on a closing statement in connection with a real estate sale.

Explicit Costs: Actual cash expenses.

F

Fallow Land (Raw Land): Land lying barren, not in agricultural production.

Family Farm: Farm operated as a family business by family members.

Farm: According to the U.S. Department of Agriculture, any operation producing and selling at least $1,000 a year in agricultural products.

Farmers Home Administration: An agency of the Department of Agriculture. Primary responsibility is to provide financial assistance for farmers and others living in rural areas where financing is not available on reasonable terms from private sources.

Fair Market Value: This is the amount of money that would be paid for a property offered on the open market for a reasonable period of time, with both buyer and seller knowing all the uses to which the property could be put and with neither party being under pressure to buy or sell.

Feasibility Study: Economic study by a developer as to the desirability of a project.

Federal Deficit: The amount spent by the federal government exceeding what it receives in taxes and other revenues. Government bonds are issued to finance the deficit.

Federal Deposit Insurance Corporation (FDIC): Agency of the federal government, which insures deposits at commercial banks and savings banks.

Federal Home Loan Bank (FHLB): A district bank of the Federal Home Loan Bank system that lends only to member savings and loan associations.

Federal Home Loan Mortgage Corporation (FHLMC, "Freddie Mac"): A federal agency created to increase the availability of mortgage credit. It buys approved conventional residential loans and sells them to investors, in addition to selling mortgage participation certificates.

Federal Housing Administration (FHA): An agency of the federal government that insures mortgage loans.

Federal National Mortgage Association (FNMA, "Fannie Mae"): a quasi-public agency being converted into a private corporation whose primary function is to buy and sell FHA and VA mortgages in the secondary market.

Federal Reserve ("Fed"): Our nation's central bank that controls our money supply.

Federal Surplus: An excess of federal revenues over federal spending.

Filtering Down: The process of making housing available to successively lower income groups.

First Mortgage: A legal document pledging collateral for a loan (see "mortgage") that has first priority over all other claims against the property except taxes and bonded indebtedness.

Fiscal Controls: Federal tax revenue and expenditure policies used to control the level of economic activity.

Fiscal Policy: The government's policy of increasing or decreasing both spending and taxes to affect the disposable income of consumers.

Fisher, Irving: The economist who theorized that doubling a nation's money supply would merely double prices.

Fixed Costs: Costs such as taxes and insurance that would remain unchanged by property operations.

Fixer-Upper: Property in need of renovation or repair that can be purchased at an advantageous price.

Fixity of Location: The physical characteristic of real estate that subjects it to the influence of its surroundings.

Fixtures: Appurtenances attached to the land or improvements that usually cannot be removed without agreement, as they become real property; examples: plumbing fixtures, store fixtures built into the property, etc.

Flat Lease: A lease where the tenant pays a fixed monthly rental fee.

Flextime Workers: Workers who are allowed to set their own work schedules.

Flight Capital: Capital investment from areas of political and/or economic instability seeking safety.

Footloose Industries: Industries that are not dependent upon particular locations and can readily relocate.

Foreclosure: Procedure whereby property pledged as security for a debt is sold to pay the debt in event of default in payments or terms.

Friedman, Milton: An economist who believes the economy can expand 3-5 percent per year and that increasing the money supply at the rate of growth will allow prices to remain stable. Friedman's views are known as "Monetarism."

Front Foot: Property measurement for sale or valuation purposes; the property measures by the front foot on its street line—each front foot extending the depth of the lot.

Functional Obsolescence: A loss of value due to adverse factors from within the structure, which affect the utility of the structure.

Future Benefits: The anticipated benefits the present owner will receive from his property in the future.

G

General Plan: Comprehensive plan for community development.

Gentrification: A movement into an area of younger, more affluent residents.

Gottman, Jean: The French geographer who coined the word "megalopolis."

Government National Mortgage Association (GNMA, "Ginnie Mae"): A government corporation within the Department of Housing and Urban Development (HUD). It attracts financing for residential loans by selling mortgage-backed securities (MBS). It purchases mortgages for low income housing where loans are not otherwise available, and also disposes of federally owned mortgages.

Graduated Lease: Lease which provides for a varying rental rate, often based upon future determination or periodical appraisals; used largely in long-term leases.

Graduated Payment Mortgage: A loan where the payments increase at agreed times without a change in the interest rate.

Granny Flat: An accessory apartment free-standing or added on to a home.

Graying of the Suburbs: The increase of the average age of suburban dwellers.

Gridiron Plan: City plan based on rectangular blocks.

Gridlock: Traffic blockage on city streets, backing up from overcrowded freeway exits.

Gross Domestic Product (GDP): The market value of all final goods and services produced in an economy during a designated period, always one year. (Also see: **Real Gross Domestic Product**.)

Gross Income: Total income from property before any expenses are deducted.

Ground Lease: An agreement for the use of the land only, sometimes secured by improvements placed on the land by the user.

Ground Rent: Earnings of improved property credited to earnings of the ground itself after allowance is made for earnings of improvements; often termed economic rent.

Group Home: Supervised home for group of nonrelated persons with similar at-risk problems.

Growing Equity Mortgage (GEM): A graduated payment mortgage designed to materially shorten the payoff period.

H

Habitat for Humanity: A nonprofit organization that builds homes for lower income buyers using volunteer labor. They give no-interest loans.

Harris, Chauncy: With Edward Ullman, he developed the multiple nuclei theory of city growth.

Hawaiian Technique: A technique of financing and sale developed by William Zeckendorf that fractionalized loans and ownership.

Highest and Best Use: An appraisal phrase meaning that use, which at the time of an appraisal, is most likely to produce the greatest net return to the land and/or buildings over a given period of time; that use which will produce the greatest amount of amenities or profit.

Housing Opportunity Index: Index that shows the percentage of homes sold that a family with the median income could afford to buy.

Housing Trust Funds: Use of special taxes to establish funds to provide low-income housing or housing subsidies.

Housing Turnover: The number of times an inventory of housing is sold within a given period of time.

Hoyt, Home: Developer of sector theory of urban growth.

Hundred Percent Location: A city retail business location which is considered the best available for attracting business.

Hyperinflation: An inflation rate so great that money ceases to have value.

Hypothecate: To give an item as security without the necessity of giving up possession of it.

I

Image Structure (Trophy Building): A distinctive, usually expensive structure that contributes to the image of the tenant.

Implicit Costs: Non-cash expenses of ownership and/or operations.

Incentive Zoning: Zoning that offers a developer an incentive if something is included in the development.

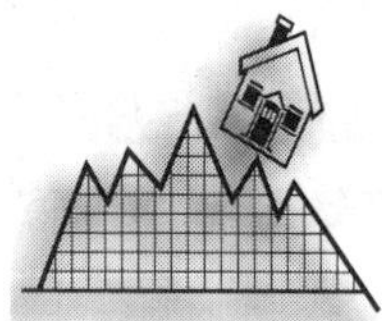

Imputed Interest: Interest that the IRS will tax, though not received, when an interest rate charged is too low.

Inclusionary Zoning: Zoning requiring the inclusion of a feature such as low-cost housing in future developments.

Inelastic: A supply or demand that will not materially change when the price is raised or lowered.

In-fill Development: Developing vacant property within a community.

Inflation: An economic period in which the value of the dollar is decreasing in purchasing power.

Interest: Money charged for the use of money or credit.

Interest Only Loan: Nonamortized loan with payment of interest only.

Intermediation: The deposit of savings into bank and savings bank accounts.

Internal Rate of Return: A method of measuring returns on investments that considers tax consequences.

Installment Reporting: A method of reporting capital gains by installments for successive tax years to minimize the impact of the totality of the capital gains tax in the year of the sale.

Interest: The charge in dollars for the use of money for a period of time. In a sense, the "rent" paid for the use of money.

Interest Rate: The percentage of a sum of money charged for its use.

Interim Loan: A short-term loan until long-term financing is available.

Investment Tax Credit: An investment whereby part of the cost is directly credited against tax owed by the investor.

J-L

Jumbo Loan: A loan that exceeds the maximum amount that will be purchased by Freddie Mac or Fannie Mae.

Keynes, John Maynard: An English economist who believed demand could be increased by increasing government spending or reducing taxes. He believed income and employment levels are directly related to private and public expenditures.

Kondratieff Long Wave: A 50-60 year economic cycle.

Lagging Indicators: Economic indicators that show what is happening in the economy after it has happened.

Laissez-Faire: The policy of government not interfering with business.

Land Bank: A land reserve to be kept free of development.

Landlord: One who rents his property to another.

Law of Diminishing Returns: The principle that, as additional units are added to production, a point will be reached where production will start to decrease with each additional unit added.

Leading Indicators: Economic indicators that point to what will probably happen in the economy in the future.

Leap-Frog Development: Developing beyond existing developments instead of contiguous developments.

Lease: A contract between owner and tenant, setting forth conditions upon which tenant may occupy and use the property, as well as the terms of the occupancy.

Leasehold Estate: A tenant's right to occupy real estate during the term of the lease. This is a personal property interest.

Lessee: One who contracts to rent property under a lease contract.

Lessee's Market: A rental market with few prospective lessees and many vacancies.

Lessor: An owner who enters into a lease with a tenant.

Lessor's Market: A market with few vacancies and many prospective lessees.

Letter of Intent: While not a contract, it is an indication that a firm intends to negotiate in good faith (generally to lease).

Level Payment Mortgage: A loan on real estate that is paid off by making a series of equal (or nearly equal) regular payments. Part of the payment is usually interest on the loan and part of it reduces the amount of the unpaid balance of the loan. Also sometimes called an "amortized mortgage."

Leverage: The use of other people's money (borrowed capital) for investment.

Lien: A form of encumbrance, which usually makes property security for the payment of a debt or discharge of an obligation. Example: judgments, taxes, mortgages, deeds of trust, etc.

Life Estate: An estate or interest in real property, which is held for the duration of the life of a certain person.

Life Care Facility: These are specialized developments for the care of dependent seniors. They are of two types: prepaid nursing care guaranteed for life and those excluding nursing care.

Light Rail Transportation: Railed trolley cars, usually electric.

Like For Like: An exchange of similar property that qualifies for a tax-deferred exchange.

Limited Partnership: A partnership composed of some partners whose contribution and liability are limited.

Linkage: Requires linking development of desirable property with the development of less desirable property or public property.

Listing: An employment contract between principal and agent authorizing the agent to perform services for the principal involving the latter's property; listing contracts are entered into for the purpose of securing persons to buy, lease, or rent property. Employment of an agent by a prospective purchaser or lessee to locate property for purchase or lease may be considered a listing.

Loan Application: The loan application is a source of information on which the lender bases his decision to make the loan; defines the terms of the loan contract; gives the name of the borrower, place of employment, salary, bank accounts, and credit references; and describes the real estate that is to be mortgaged. It also stipulates the amount of loan being applied for, and repayment terms.

Loan Closing: When all conditions have been met, the loan officer authorizes the recording of the trust deed or mortgage. The disbursal procedure of funds is similar to the closing of a real estate sales escrow. The borrower can expect to receive less than the amount of the loan, as title, recording, service, and other fees may be withheld, or he can expect to deposit the cost of these items into the loan escrow. This process is sometimes called "funding" the loan.

Loan Commitment: Lender's contractual commitment to a loan based on the appraisal and underwriting.

Loan-Value-Ratio: The percentage of a property's value that a lender can or may loan to a borrower. For example, if the ratio is 80% this means that a lender may loan 80% of the property's appraised value to a borrower.

Locational Analysis: Economic analysis of a site.

Loft: They are areas that were once factories or storage areas. Lofts are often referred to as artist's lofts. The landlord partitions the space into large, high-ceiling rooms with exposed plumbing and ducts. The simplest of bath and kitchen facilities are provided.

M

M_1: The nation's money supply in currency and coins, plus checking account balances and travelers checks.

M_2: The money supply of the nation, which includes checking accounts, savings accounts and money market account balances, in addition to currency and coins.

Macroeconomics: The study of the entire economic system as a unit rather than its individual elements.

Malthus, Thomas: An English economist who believed that in the absence of war or pestilence, the population would increase geometrically, while the food supply increased arithmetically, until it reached a misery level.

Manufactured Home: It is a factory built house constructed to the HUD Code.

Margin of Security: The difference between the amount of the mortgage loan(s) and the appraised value of the property.

Marginal Propensity to Consume: The ratio of consumption to increases in disposable income.

Marginal Propensity to Save: The ratio of savings to increases in disposable income.

Market Data Approach: One of the three methods in the appraisal process. A means of comparing recently sold similar residential properties to the subject property.

Market Price: The price paid regardless of pressures, motives, or intelligence.

Market Value: (1) The price at which a willing seller would sell and a willing buyer would buy, neither being under abnormal pressure; (2) as defined by the courts, is the highest price estimated in terms of money which a property will bring if exposed for sale in the open market allowing a reasonable time to find a purchaser with knowledge of property's use and capabilities for use.

Marx, Karl: The prophet of Socialism. Marx believed capitalism was an inefficient means of production that benefited only a few. He believed the means of production and distribution should be in the hands of the state. Marx believed socialism could be accomplished only through revolution.

Megalopolis: A vast urban sprawl of cities that have grown together.

Mega Mall: A huge mall-type shopping center.

Metropolis: A large urban center that can include more than one city.

Microeconomics: The study of the individual components, which together make up our economic system.

Mini-Mall Center: Small strip center anchored by a convenience store.

Misplaced Improvement: Improvements on land, which do not conform to the most profitable use of the site.

Modular Home: A building composed of modules constructed on an assembly line in a factory. Usually, the modules are self-contained and are delivered on trucks in either pre-assembled form or in units put together on-site.

Monetarism: The views expounded by Milton Friedman that the money supply could grow proportionately to the economy without causing prices to increase.

Monetary Controls: Federal Reserve tools for regulating the availability of money and credit to influence the level of economic activity.

Monetary Policy: The policy of the Federal Reserve in controlling the money supply.

Money: Our medium of exchange.

Monopoly: A market in which a single supplier controls the supply for an item.

Monopsony: A market where there is only one buyer for goods.

Moratorium: The temporary suspension, usually by statute, of the enforcement of liability for debt.

Moratorium on Construction: A prohibition of new construction for a stated period of time.

Mortgage: An instrument recognized by law by which property is hypothecated to secure the payment of a debt or obligation; procedure for foreclosure in event of default is established by statute.

Mortgage Guaranty Insurance: Private Mortgage Insurance (PMI) against financial loss available to mortgage lenders from Mortgage Guaranty Insurance Corporation, a private company organized in 1956.

Mortgagee: One to whom a mortgagor gives a mortgage to secure a loan or performance of an obligation, a lender. (See definition of Secured Party.)

Mortgagor: One who gives a mortgage on his property to secure a loan or assure performance of an obligation; a borrower. (See definition of Debtor.)

Multigenerational Housing: Housing for extended families.

Multiple Listing: A listing, usually an exclusive right to sell, taken by a member of an organization composed of real estate brokers, with the provisions that all members will have the opportunity to find an interested client; a cooperative listing.

Multiple Nuclei Development: A city that has developed from a number of separate centers.

Multiplier Effect: The relationship that the increase in one activity has on another. There is approximately a one-to-one relationship between new manufacturing positions and service positions. A dollar spent in a banking community will have the effect of being spent by those receiving it between four and five times before being removed from circulation by savings.

N

National Environmental Policy Act of 1969: Federal act requiring Environmental Impact Statement (EIS) for federal projects that will have an effect on the environment.

National Housing Act of 1934: The act that established the Federal Housing Administration (FHA).

National Historic Preservation Act of 1966: Federal act that provides for registry of historic buildings and historical districts.

Naturally Occurring Retirement Community (NORC): Community that has changed from family to retirement orientation.

Negative Amortization: A loan where the payments do not cover the interest causing the principal to increase.

Nehemiah Plan: A nonprofit program where buyers without much in savings can buy a home.

Neighborhood: An area of social conformity.

Neighborhood Shopping Center: A strip-type development anchored by a major food store.

Net Lease: Also known as a triple net lease, it is a lease where the tenant pays the lessor a flat rental fee or rate and also pays taxes, insurance, and maintenance expenses.

New Communities Act: Federal act that provided federal aid for planned suburban communities.

New Town: A planned community that was started from nothing, rather than from the growth of an existing community.

No Growth Legislation: Legislation that limits or excludes future development.

Nominal Interest Rates: The percentage of interest that is stated in loan documents.

Nonconforming Loans: Loans that fail to meet Freddie Mac and Fannie Mae purchase requirements.

Nonconforming Use: Use that existed prior to the zoning that excludes the use.

Noncumulative Zoning: Zoning that allows only the designated use.

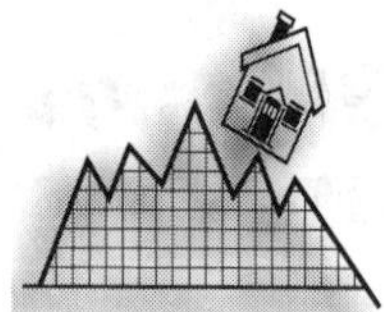

O

Obsolescence: Loss in value due to reduced desirability and usefulness of a structure because its design and construction become obsolete; loss because of becoming old-fashioned and not in keeping with modern needs, with consequent loss in income.

Officer Next Door: A HUD program where police officers can purchase HUD owned property in distressed areas for half price.

Oil Land: Land where value is primarily based on oil and/or gas deposits contained or believed to be contained under the land.

Oligopoly: A market in which there are limited suppliers so that the actions of one would affect the actions of others.

Oligopsony: A market where there are only a few buyers for goods.

One Hundred Percent Location: The best location in a community for a business.

Open-End Mortgage: A mortgage containing a clause that permits the mortgagor to borrow additional money after the loan has been reduced, without rewriting the mortgage.

Open Housing Law: Congress passed a law in April 1968 that prohibits discrimination in the sale of real estate because of race, color, or religion of buyers.

Open Market Operations: The Feds ability to buy and sell government securities to regulate the money supply.

Opportunity Costs: The savings that equity in a property could produce if it were invested.

Option ARM: An adjustable rate loan where the borrower has the option to make a minimum payment that results in negative amortization.

Orientation: Placing a house on its lot with regard to its exposure to the rays of the sun, prevailing winds, and privacy from the street, as well as protection from outside noises.

Other Urban Places: A Census Bureau classification for communities having populations from 2,500 to 50,000.

Overbuilding: Reaching a point in construction where the supply exceeds the demand at the price offered.

Over Improvement: An improvement that is not the highest and best use for the site on which it is placed by reason of excess size or cost.

P

Participation Loan: In addition to base interest on mortgage loans on income properties, a small percentage of gross income is required, sometimes predicated on certain conditions being fulfilled, such as minimum occupancy or a percentage of net income after expenses, debt service, and taxes.

PCBs: A carcinogenic used in electrical and hydraulic equipment.

Penalty: An extra payment or charge required of the borrower for deviating from the terms of the original loan agreement. Usually levied for being late in making regular payment or for paying off the loan before it is due.

Percentage Lease: Lease on the property, the rental for which is determined by amount of business done by the lessee; usually a percentage of gross receipts from the business with provision for a minimum rental.

Perchlorate: A soil and water contaminant used in propellants and explosives.

Physical Deterioration: Impairment of condition. Loss in value brought about by wear and tear, disintegration, use, and actions of the elements.

Planned Unit Development (PUD): A land-use design which provides intensive utilization of the land through a combination of private and common areas with prearranged sharing of responsibilities for the common areas.

Plottage Increment: The appreciation in unit value created by joining smaller ownerships into one large single ownership.

Points: Under FHA-insured or VA-guaranteed loans, discounts or points paid to lenders are, in effect, prepaid interest, and are used by lenders to adjust the effective interest rate so that it is equal to or nearly equal to the prevailing market rate (the rate charged on conventional loans). The sellers absorb the discounts and a point is one percent of the loan amount. On FHA-insured and VA-guaranteed loans, buyers may be charged only one percent "service charge." This restriction does not apply to conventional loans. Under conventional loans the charge for making a loan at most institutions is usually called a "loan fee," "service charge," "commitment fee," or may be referred to as "points to the buyer."

Police Power: The right of the State to enact laws and enforce them for the order, safety, health, morals, and general welfare of the public.

Precut Home: A kit that includes all materials and directions to build a house. The buyer assembles the home.

Prefabricated House: A house manufactured and sometimes partly assembled, before delivery to building site.

Premature Subdivision: The division and sale of parcels of land long before development would be economically feasible.

Prepayment Penalty: Penalty for the payment of a mortgage or trust deed note before it actually becomes due if the note does not provide for prepayment.

Present Value: The lump sum value today of an annuity. A $100 bill to be paid to someone in one year is worth less than if it were a $100 bill to be paid to someone today. This is due to several things, one of which is that the money has time value. How much the $100 bill to be paid in one year is worth today will depend on the interest rate that seems proper for the particular circumstances. For example, if 6% were the appropriate rate, the $100 to be paid one year from now would be worth $94.34 today.

Price: The amount paid for an item in the marketplace.

Prime Rate: The rate of interest offered by a commercial bank to its most favored customers.

Principal: This term is used to mean either the employer of an agent or the amount of money borrowed, or the amount of the loan.

Principle of Change: Values do not remain constant; they are always changing.

Principle of Competition: When extraordinary profits are being made, competition will enter the market and profits will decline.

Principle of Conformity: Maximum value will be obtained when a property is in an area of similar properties.

Principle of First Choice: A business that needs a particular type of location for a certain use will pay more for that location than would others.

Principle of Integration, Equilibrium, and Disintegration: Property goes through a development stage (integration), a period of maturity (equilibrium) and a decline in use and value (disintegration).

Principle of Substitution: A person will not pay more for a property than he or she would have to pay for another property having equal utility and desirability.

Private Mortgage Insurance (PMI): Mortgage insurance that protects lender against borrower default.

Profit: That portion of the return on an investment or business that exceeds the cost of the investment or operation.

Progression, Principle of: The worth of a lesser-valued residence tends to be enhanced by association with many higher-valued residences in the same area.

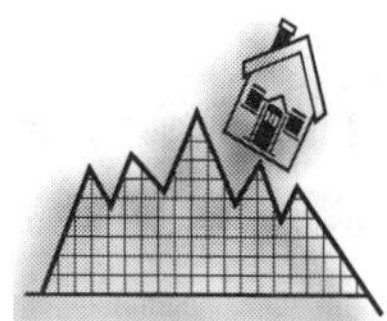

Property Tax: Tax on real and personal property.

Psychological Income: A non-cash benefit in the feeling of self-worth that comes with (hobby or retirement) farm ownership.

Public Housing: Low income, government-owned housing.

Purchase and Installment Sale-Back: Involves purchase of the property upon completion of construction and immediate sale-back on a long-term installment contract.

Purchase and Leaseback: Involves the purchase of property subject to an existing mortgage and immediate leaseback.

R

Real Estate Economics: The application of economic principles to real estate.

Real Estate Investment Trusts: A special arrangement under federal and state law whereby investors may pool funds for investments in real estate and mortgages and yet escape corporation taxes.

Real Gross Domestic Product: The gross national product adjusted for inflation.

Real Income: Income adjusted according to cost of living changes.

Realtor®: A real estate broker holding active membership in a real estate board affiliated with the National Association of Realtors®.

Recapture: The rate of interest necessary to provide for the return of an investment. Not to be confused with interest rate, which is a rate of interest on an investment.

Recession: That portion of an economic cycle in which growth in the Gross Domestic Product and employment are in a decline. (Two quarters of decline in GDP.)

Recovery: That portion of an economic cycle in which growth in the Gross Domestic Product and employment are increasing.

Recreational Land: Land sold primarily for recreational use.

Redevelopment: The clearance and development of an area. Generally, areas are redeveloped for uses other than previous uses.

Redlining: The unlawful refusal of lenders to make loans within particular areas.

Refinancing: The paying-off of an existing obligation and assuming a new obligation in its place.

Regional Shopping Center: A larger shopping center anchored by several major department stores.

Rehabilitation: The restoration of a property to satisfactory condition without drastically changing the plan, form, or style of architecture.

Reintermediation: The return of dollars to savings accounts after their previous withdrawal.

Rent Concession: Rent abatement or other concessions given to a tenant as an inducement to sign a lease.

Rent Control: Legislation that limits an owner's ability to increase rent.

Rent or Buy: Decision to own or to rent.

Rent Vouchers: A system whereby a voucher holder can apply a public voucher toward rent on the open market.

Replacement Cost: The cost to replace the structure with one having utility equivalent to that being appraised, but constructed with modern materials, and according to current standards, design, and layout.

Reproduction Costs: The cost of replacing the subject improvement with one that is the exact replica, having the same quality of workmanship, design, and layout.

Research and Development Facility: Industrial facility that develops tests and improves products.

Reserve Requirements: The requirement of the Federal Reserve as to the proportion of a bank's deposits that must be kept in reserve.

Restriction: The term as used relating to real property means the owner of real property is restricted or prohibited from doing certain things relating to the property, or using the property for certain purposes. Property restrictions fall into two general classifications—public and private. Zoning ordinances are examples of the former type. Private owners may create restrictions, typically by appropriate clauses in deeds, or in agreements, or in general plans of entire subdivisions. Usually they assume the form of a covenant or promise to do or not to do a certain thing.

Rezoning: A change in zoning.

Ripple Effect: The filtering down of commercial space.

Risk Analysis: A study made, usually by a lender, of the various factors that might affect the repayment of a loan.

Risk Rating: A process used by the lender to decide on the soundness (syn) of making a loan and to reduce all the various factors affecting the repayment of the loan to a qualified rating of some kind.

S

Sale-Leaseback: (1) A situation where the owner of a piece of property wishes to sell the property and retain occupancy by leasing it from the buyer. (2) A sale usually to an investor where the grantor becomes a lessee. The purpose is generally to free capital.

Sandwich Lease: A leasehold interest that lies between the primary lease and the operating lease.

Scatteration: Dispersed development.

Schwabe's Law: The rule that lower income people pay a higher percentage of their income for housing than upper income people.

Secondary Financing: A loan secured by a second mortgage or trust deed on real property. These can be third, fourth, fifth, sixth—on and on ad infinitum.

Section 8 Housing: Federally subsidized rentals.

Sector Growth: City growth outward from the city center, with uses expanding in pie-shaped areas.

Septic Tank: An underground tank in which sewage from the house is reduced to liquid by bacterial action and drained off.

Servicing: Supervising and administering a loan after it has been made. This involves such things as: collecting the payments, keeping accounting records, computing the interest and principal, foreclosure of defaulted loans, and so on.

Setback Ordinance: An ordinance prohibiting the erection of a building or structure between the curb and the setback line.

Shared Housing: Single people or families sharing living space, often based on economic need.

Shell Home: A home with the exterior generally completed (windows, siding, and roofing) and set on a foundation. The buyer completes the interior work (including plumbing, electrical, and heating).

Sherman Antitrust Act: Act prohibiting unfair trade tactics.

Shopping Center, Regional: A large shopping center with 250,000 to 1,000,000 square feet of store area, serving 200,000 or more people.

Short Sale: Lender agreement to accept sale proceeds as full satisfaction of debt.

Single Parcel Sales: Sales by suburban landowners, as a group, to developers for commercial redevelopment.

Single Room Occupancy: Often a room or apartment in or attached to a main home is rented out. There is very little of this type of housing available today.

Smart Buildings: Buildings that offer computer and other electronic services for tenants.

Smart Growth: Growth that increases density and minimizes sprawl.

Socialism: An economic system whereby the means of production and distribution are controlled by the state.

Special Assessment: Legal charge against real estate by a public authority to pay cost of public improvements such as: streetlights, sidewalks, street improvements, etc.

Specialized Buildings: Buildings that specialize in rentals to a particular type of business activity.

Speculators: Investors who are interested in a short-term investment. They buy for sale profit rather than income-generated earnings.

Spot Zoning: Zoning a parcel in an inconsistent manner from adjacent parcels.

Sprawl: Outward growth from the city center.

Stagflation: A period in which the economy is not growing as quickly as before (or is in a recession), but in which consumer prices are increasing.

Standard Metropolitan Statistical Area (SMSA): Population units used in economic study, which include a core metropolitan area plus economically dependent adjoining areas.

Starker Exchange: A tax-deferred delayed exchange.

Stick Built: Is a term that refers to housing fabricated primarily with on-site labor.

Straight Line Depreciation: Definite sum set aside annually from income to pay cost of replacing improvements, without reference to interest it earns.

Street People: Homeless people.

Strip Development: Development in a relatively narrow band along a major transportation route.

Sublease: A lease given by a lessee.

Submarginal Land: Land in which the income does not cover associated costs of production.

Subordination Clause: Clause in a junior or a second lien permitting retention of priority for prior liens. A subordination clause may also be used in a first deed of trust permitting it to be subordinated to subsequent liens as, for example, the liens of construction loans.

Subprime Loans: High interest loans to persons who would not otherwise qualify for loans.

Subsidies: Government grants or price supports to farmers.

Subsidized Housing: Private housing developed with government incentives such as special tax benefits or loans. The government then controls rents.

Substitution, Principle of: Affirms that the maximum value of a property tends to be set by the cost of acquiring an equally desirable and valuable substitute property, assuming no costly delay is encountered in making the substitution.

Suburb: A community outside the central city, which originally grew as a result of economic reliance on the city.

Super Liens: Priority liens against owners of toxic waste sites. The liens apply to all the property of the owner.

Supply and Demand, Principle of: Affirms that price or value varies directly, but not necessarily proportionally, with demand; and inversely, but not necessarily proportionately, with supply.

Supply and Demand (interaction of): The relationship between the amount of goods supplied and the demand by those consumers who are willing to pay for them. When elastic, supply and demand will react significantly to changes in price.

Surplus Productivity, Principle of: Affirms that the net income that remains after the proper costs of labor, organization, and capital have been paid, which surplus is imputable to the land and tends to fix the value thereof.

Sweat Equity: Homeowner equity resulting from improvement or repairs personally made by the homeowner.

Syndicate: A partnership organized for participation in a real estate venture. Partners may be limited or unlimited in their liability.

T

Takeout Loan: The loan arranged by the owner or builder-developer for a buyer. The construction loan made for construction of the improvements is usually paid from the proceeds of this loan.

Tax-Free Exchange: Income property exchanged on an even basis for other income property, the owner of which does not have to pay a capital gain tax at the time.

Tax Shelter: Using depreciation to shelter income from taxation.

Teacher Next Door: A HUD program where teachers can purchase HUD owned property in distressed areas for half price. (This program, as of 2002, is suspended.)

Tenant Partners: Making a tenant an equity partner in the structure as an inducement to sign a lease.

The Economic Person: A model person used for economic study, whose decisions are based solely on economic considerations.

Timeshare: Exclusive occupancy rights in a vacation property for a set period of time each year.

Topography: Nature of the surface of land; topography may be level, rolling, or mountainous.

Trading On Equity: Borrowing on property in order to invest in other property offering a greater return than is being paid in loan interest.

Trophy Property: Highly desirable landmark structure.

U

Ullman, Edward: A co-developer (with Chauncy Harris) of the multiple nuclei theory of city growth.

Under Improvement: An improvement, which, because of its deficiency in size or cost, is not the highest and best use of the site.

Underwriting: The technical analysis by a lender to determine the borrower's ability to repay a contemplated loan.

Unearned Increment: An increase in value of real estate due to no effort on the part of the owner; often due to increase in population.

Upside Down Situation: Situation where mortgage debt is greater than property value.

Upzoning: Rezoning for a more intensive use.

Urban: A classification by the U.S. Census Bureau of a community having 2,500 or more people.

Urban Area: A classification of the Census Bureau for communities having 50,000 or more population with a density of 1,000 or more per square mile.

Urban Blight: Deterioration caused by failure to maintain by landlords and/or tenants as well as by vandalism.

Urban Homesteading: The sale of city-owned housing to private owners for low cost with the requirement that the housing be rehabilitated.

Urban Property: City property; closely settled property.

Urban Village Concept: Urbanization of the suburbs characterized by concentrated commercial growth.

User Fees: Highway fees based directly on use.

Utilities: Refers to services rendered by public utility companies, such as: water, gas, electricity, and telephone.

Utility: The ability to give satisfaction and/or excite desire for possession.

V-Z

Vacancy Factor: Percentage of units or square feet that is vacant.

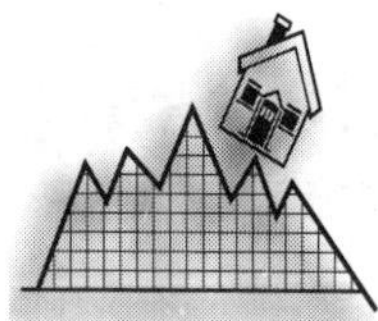

Valuation: Estimated worth or price. Estimation. The act of valuing by appraisal.

Value: The present worth of goods based on future benefits that can be derived from them.

Variable Costs: Costs relating to operation that can be deferred or changed.

Variance: An exception to the zoning.

Velocity of Money: The number of times money changes hands on average during a period of time throughout the entire economy.

Vulture Funds: Investment funds established to purchase buildings in financial difficulty.

Warehousing: A lender borrowing on its loan inventory until it can be sold.

White Flight: The exodus of Caucasians from an area. It is generally based on fear that minorities will dominate the area.

Wrap Around Mortgage: A second trust deed with a face value of both the new amount it secures and the balance due under the first trust deed. A wrap-around can take the form of a land contract or a deed of trust.

Yield: The interest earned by an investor on his investment (or bank on the money it has lent). Also called **Return**.

Yield Rate: The yield expressed as a percentage of the total investment. Also called **Rate of Return**.

Zero Interest Loans: A loan with no interest. The entire payment would apply to principal.

Zone: The area set off by the proper authorities for specific use; subject to certain restrictions or restraints.

Zoning: Act of city or county authorities specifying type of land use to which property may be put in specific areas.

Index

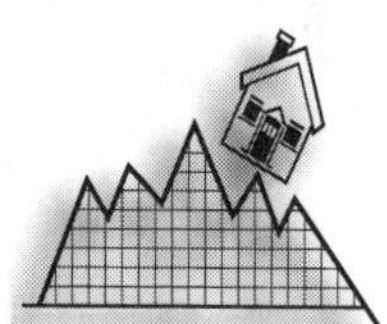

Index

D

E

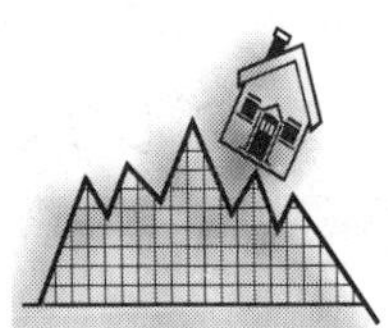

F

G

H

Index

I

J-K

L

M

N

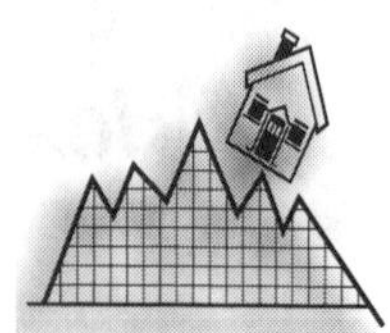

O

P

R

S

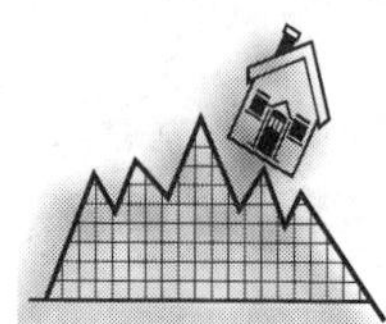

T

U